Triumph TR5, 250 & 6 Owners Workshop Manual

by J H Haynes

Member of the Guild of Motoring Writers

and B L Chalmers - Hunt

TEng (CEI), AMIMI, AMIRTE, AMVBRA

Models covered

UK	TR5 2498 cc. Fuel injection	
	TR6 2498 cc. Fuel injection	
USA	TR250	152 cu in. Twin carburettors
	TR6	152 cu in. Twin carburettors

ISBN 978 0 85733 647 7

(031-1N2)

THE BOOK

J H Haynes & Co. Ltd.
Haynes North America, Inc

www.haynes.com

Acknowledgements

Thanks are due to the Triumph Division of British Leyland for their permission to reproduce certain illustrations and the supply of technical information. Castrol Limited supplied the lubrication data and the Champion Sparking Plug Ltd supplied the illustrations showing the various spark plug conditions. The bodywork repair photographs used in this manual were provided by Lloyds Industries Limited who supply 'Turtle Wax', 'Duplicolor Holts', and other Holts range products. Lastly, thanks must go to all of those people at Sparkford who assisted in the production of this manual, particularly Stanley Rudolph, Bruce Gilmour, Ian Robson and John Rose.

About this manual

Its aim

The aim of this Manual is to help you get the best value from your car. It can do so in several ways. It can help you decide what work must be done (even should you chose to get it done by a garage), provide information on routine maintenance and servicing, and give a logical course of action and diagnosis when faults occur. However, it is hoped that you will make full use of the Manual by tackling the work yourself. On simpler jobs it may even be quicker than booking the car into a garage, and having to go there twice, to leave and collect it. Perhaps most important, a lot of money can be saved by avoiding the costs the garage must charge to cover its labour and overheads.

Its arrangement

The manual is divided into thirteen Chapters, each covering a logical sub-division of the vehicle. The Chapters are each divided into consecutively numbered Sections and the Sections into paragraphs (or sub-sections), with decimal numbers following on from the Section they are in, eg 5.1, 5.2, 5.3 etc.

It is freely illustrated, especially in those parts where there is a detailed sequence of operations to be carried out. There are two forms of illustration: figures and photographs. The figures are numbered in sequence with decimal numbers, according to their position in the Chapter: eg Fig. 6.4 is the 4th drawing/illustration in Chapter 6. Photographs are numbered (either individually or in related groups) the same as the Section or sub-section of the text where the operation they show is described.

There is an alphabetical index at the back of the manual as well as a contents list at the front.

References to the 'left' or 'right' of the vehicle are in the sense of a person facing forwards in the driver's seat.

Whilst every care is taken to ensure that the information in this manual is correct no liability can be accepted by the authors or publishers for loss, damage or injury caused by any errors in, or omissions from, the information given.

Introduction

The October 1967 Earls Court Motor Show heralded the Triumph TR5.

Its immediate claim to fame was the fitting of Lucas Petrol Injection to the 2000 six cylinder engine (enlarged to 2498 cc) installed in the familiar TR4A chassis. This was the first series produced with this form of fuel system. It was an exciting car, traditional in its style and handling, but fast and furious. In this form it was an appropriate continuation of the long line of successful Triumph sports cars starting with the TR2 in the early fifties.

A short time afterwards the American export version of the TR5 was announced for it had been in this market that the Triumph sports cars had been most successful. Their version was designated the TR250. Unfortunately it was only half the car the TR5 was for it did not feature petrol injection but was equipped with a twin carburettor version of the same engine. This gave it nearly 50% less power and a bearly adequate performance - the TR2 is probably faster! However there was good reasoning behind this for the fuel injected car would not pass the then current exhaust emission control regulations.

The TR6 was announced in January 1969 and is known by that designation in both the UK and USA. This featured a new body shell designed by Karmann Ghia, finally replacing the Michelotti designed body which had been used for the TR4, 4A and 5. The chassis and engine are very similar to those used for the TR5 and TR250. Once again fuel injection is used only on the UK and European cars and carburettors on the American version.

In 1973/1974 these cars can pretend to be nothing more than good solid sports cars in the 'traditional' way. They pander nothing to sophisticated chassis and engine design. However, at their present sales figures there would still seem to be a good demand for this type of car.

Contents

Safety first!

Professional motor mechanics are trained in safe working procedures. However enthusiastic you may be about getting on with the job in hand, do take the time to ensure that your safety is not put at risk. A moment's lack of attention can result in an accident, as can failure to observe certain elementary precautions.

There will always be new ways of having accidents, and the following points do not pretend to be a comprehensive list of all dangers; they are intended rather to make you aware of the risks and to encourage a safety-conscious approach to all work you carry out on your vehicle.

Essential DOs and DON'Ts

DON'T rely on a single jack when working underneath the vehicle. Always use reliable additional means of support, such as axle stands, securely placed under a part of the vehicle that you know will not give way.

DON'T attempt to loosen or tighten high-torque nuts (e.g. wheel hub nuts) while the vehicle is on a jack; it may be pulled off.

DON'T start the engine without first ascertaining that the transmission is in neutral (or 'Park' where applicable) and the parking brake applied.

DON'T suddenly remove the filler cap from a hot cooling system – cover it with a cloth and release the pressure gradually first, or you may get scalded by escaping coolant.

DON'T attempt to drain oil until you are sure it has cooled sufficiently to avoid scalding you.

DON'T grasp any part of the engine, exhaust or catalytic converter without first ascertaining that it is sufficiently cool to avoid burning you.

DON'T allow brake fluid or antifreeze to contact vehicle paintwork.

DON'T syphon toxic liquids such as fuel, brake fluid or antifreeze by mouth, or allow them to remain on your skin.

DON'T inhale dust – it may be injurious to health (see *Asbestos* below).

DON'T allow any spilt oil or grease to remain on the floor – wipe it up straight away, before someone slips on it.

DON'T use ill-fitting spanners or other tools which may slip and cause injury.

DON'T attempt to lift a heavy component which may be beyond your capability – get assistance.

DON'T rush to finish a job, or take unverified short cuts.

DON'T allow children or animals in or around an unattended vehicle.

DO wear eye protection when using power tools such as drill, sander, bench grinder etc, and when working under the vehicle.

DO use a barrier cream on your hands prior to undertaking dirty jobs – it will protect your skin from infection as well as making the dirt easier to remove afterwards; but make sure your hands aren't left slippery. Note that long-term contact with used engine oil can be a health hazard.

DO keep loose clothing (cuffs, tie etc) and long hair well out of the way of moving mechanical parts.

DO remove rings, wristwatch etc, before working on the vehicle – especially the electrical system.

DO ensure that any lifting tackle used has a safe working load rating adequate for the job.

DO keep your work area tidy – it is only too easy to fall over articles left lying around.

DO get someone to check periodically that all is well, when working alone on the vehicle.

DO carry out work in a logical sequence and check that everything is correctly assembled and tightened afterwards.

DO remember that your vehicle's safety affects that of yourself and others. If in doubt on any point, get specialist advice.

IF, in spite of following these precautions, you are unfortunate enough to injure yourself, seek medical attention as soon as possible.

Asbestos

Certain friction, insulating, sealing, and other products – such as brake linings, brake bands, clutch linings, torque converters, gaskets, etc – contain asbestos. *Extreme care must be taken to avoid inhalation of dust from such products since it is hazardous to health.* If in doubt, assume that they *do* contain asbestos.

Fire

Remember at all times that petrol (gasoline) is highly flammable. Never smoke, or have any kind of naked flame around, when working on the vehicle. But the risk does not end there – a spark caused by an electrical short-circuit, by two metal surfaces contacting each other, by careless use of tools, or even by static electricity built up in your body under certain conditions, can ignite petrol vapour, which in a confined space is highly explosive.

Always disconnect the battery earth (ground) terminal before working on any part of the fuel or electrical system, and never risk spilling fuel on to a hot engine or exhaust.

It is recommended that a fire extinguisher of a type suitable for fuel and electrical fires is kept handy in the garage or workplace at all times. Never try to extinguish a fuel or electrical fire with water.

Note: *Any reference to a 'torch' appearing in this manual should always be taken to mean a hand-held battery-operated electric lamp or flashlight. It does NOT mean a welding/gas torch or blowlamp.*

Fumes

Certain fumes are highly toxic and can quickly cause unconsciousness and even death if inhaled to any extent. Petrol (gasoline) vapour comes into this category, as do the vapours from certain solvents such as trichloroethylene. Any draining or pouring of such volatile fluids should be done in a well ventilated area.

When using cleaning fluids and solvents, read the instructions carefully. Never use materials from unmarked containers – they may give off poisonous vapours.

Never run the engine of a motor vehicle in an enclosed space such as a garage. Exhaust fumes contain carbon monoxide which is extremely poisonous; if you need to run the engine, always do so in the open air or at least have the rear of the vehicle outside the workplace.

If you are fortunate enough to have the use of an inspection pit, never drain or pour petrol, and never run the engine, while the vehicle is standing over it; the fumes, being heavier than air, will concentrate in the pit with possibly lethal results.

The battery

Never cause a spark, or allow a naked light, near the vehicle's battery. It will normally be giving off a certain amount of hydrogen gas, which is highly explosive.

Always disconnect the battery earth (ground) terminal before working on the fuel or electrical systems.

If possible, loosen the filler plugs or cover when charging the battery from an external source. Do not charge at an excessive rate or the battery may burst.

Take care when topping up and when carrying the battery. The acid electrolyte, even when diluted, is very corrosive and should not be allowed to contact the eyes or skin.

If you ever need to prepare electrolyte yourself, always add the acid slowly to the water, and never the other way round. Protect against splashes by wearing rubber gloves and goggles.

When jump starting a car using a booster battery, for negative earth (ground) vehicles, connect the jump leads in the following sequence: First connect one jump lead between the positive (+) terminals of the two batteries. Then connect the other jump lead first to the negative (–) terminal of the booster battery, and then to a good earthing (ground) point on the vehicle to be started, at least 18 in (45 cm) from the battery if possible. Ensure that hands and jump leads are clear of any moving parts, and that the two vehicles do not touch. Disconnect the leads in the reverse order.

Mains electricity and electrical equipment

When using an electric power tool, inspection light etc, always ensure that the appliance is correctly connected to its plug and that, where necessary, it is properly earthed (grounded). Do not use such appliances in damp conditions and, again, beware of creating a spark or applying excessive heat in the vicinity of fuel or fuel vapour. Also ensure that the appliances meet the relevant national safety standards.

Ignition HT voltage

A severe electric shock can result from touching certain parts of the ignition system, such as the HT leads, when the engine is running or being cranked, particularly if components are damp or the insulation is defective. Where an electronic ignition system is fitted, the HT voltage is much higher and could prove fatal.

1968 Triumph TR5

1968 Triumph TR250

1973 Triumph TR6 (UK model)

1973 Triumph TR6 (American specification)

Buying spare parts and vehicle identification numbers

Buying spare parts

Spare parts are available from many sources, for example: Leyland garages, other garages and accessory shops, and motor factors. Our advice regarding spare part sources is as follows:

Officially appointed Leyland garages - These are the best source of parts which are peculiar to your car and are otherwise not generally available (eg, complete cylinder heads, internal gearbox components, badges, interior trim, etc). It is also the only place at which you should buy parts if your car is still under warranty - non-Leyland components may invalidate the warranty. To be sure of obtaining the correct parts it will always be necessary to give the storeman your car's engine and chassis number, and if possible, to take the 'old' part along for positive identification. Remember that many parts are available on a factory exchange scheme - any parts returned should always be clean! It obviously makes good sense to go straight to the specialists on your car for this type of part for they are best equipped to supply you.

Other garages and accessory shops - These are often very good places to buy materials and components needed for the maintenance of your car (eg, oil filters, spark plugs, bulbs, fanbelts, oils and greases, touch-up paint, filler paste, etc). They also sell general accessories, usually have convenient opening hours, charge lower prices and can often be found not far from home.

Motor factors - Good factors will stock all of the more important components which wear out relatively quickly (eg, clutch components pistons, valves, exhaust systems, brake cylinders/pipes/hoses/seals/shoes and pads, etc). Motor factors will often provide new or reconditioned components on a part exchange basis - this can save a considerable amount of money.

Vehicle identification numbers

When ordering spare parts it is essential to give full details of your car to the storeman. He will want to know the commission, car, and engine numbers. When ordering parts for the transmission unit or body it is also necessary to quote the transmission casing and body numbers.

Location of commission and unit numbers (Left-hand and right-hand refer to left-hand and right-hand side of the car when viewed from the driving position).

The **Commission, Paint and Trim numbers** may be seen on the scuttle panel once the bonnet has been lifted.

The **Engine numbers** are located on the left-hand side of the cylinder block.

The **Gearbox** numbers are located on the left-hand side of the housing

The **Rear Axle numbers** are located on the hypoid housing flange.

Lubrication Chart

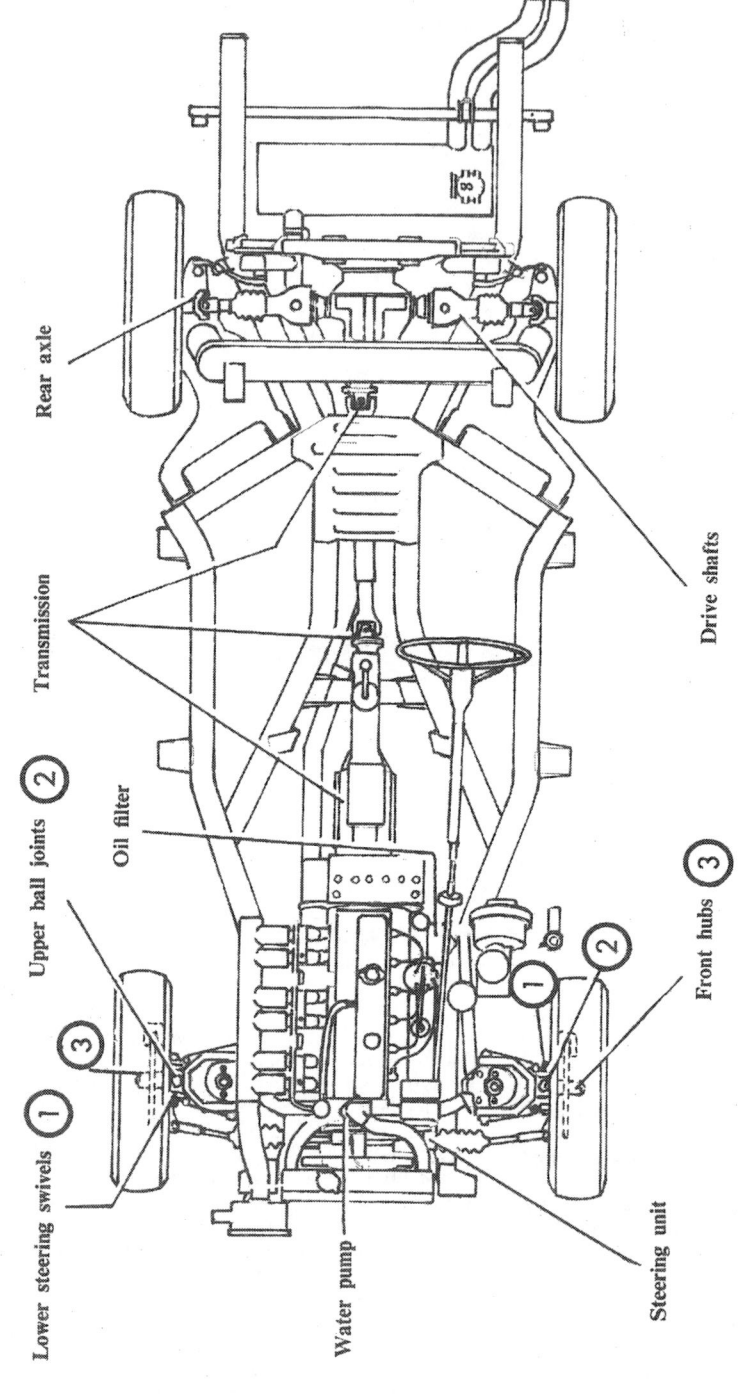

Lower steering swivels ①

Upper ball joints ②

Oil filter

Water pump

Steering unit

Front hubs ③

Drive shafts

Rear axle

Transmission

Recommended lubricants and fluids

COMPONENT	TYPE OF LUBRICANT OR FLUID	CORRECT CASTROL PRODUCTS
ENGINE	Multigrade. To API SE specification ...	Castrol GTX
GEARBOX	High quality EP90 gear oil to specification MIL-L-2105B and API service GL ...	Castrol Hypoy B
REAR AXLE	High quality EP90 gear oil	Castrol Hypoy B
GREASE POINTS	Multi-purpose high melting point lithium based grease	Castrol LM Grease
DISTRIBUTOR LUBRICATION ...	See text for details of application ...	Vaseline petroleum jelly and Castrol LM Grease
WINDSCREEN WIPER SPINDLES	Glycerine	
COOLING SYSTEM	Anti-freeze solution complying with BS 3151 or 3152	Castrol Anti-freeze
BRAKE AND CLUTCH HYDRAULIC SYSTEMS	Hydraulic brake fluid exceeding SAE specification J1703c	Castrol Girling Universal Brake and Clutch Fluid

Routine maintenance

The basic maintenance instructions listed are those recommended by the manufacturer. They are supplemented by additional maintenance tasks proven to be necessary.

The additional tasks are indicated by an asterisk and are primarily of a preventative nature in that they will assist in eliminating the unexpected failure of a component due to fair wear and tear.

When a new car is delivered the engine contains sufficient oil for the running in period. Providing the level is maintained between the low and high marks on the dipstick during this period topping up is unnecessary. At the first 'Free Service' the running in oil is drained and the sump replenished to the level of the high mark on the dip stick.

Where vehicles are being operated in areas controlled by U S Federal Regulations for exhaust emission it is very important to appreciate that any adjustments to the fuel and ignition system will probably result in the car failing to meet those legal requirements. Special test equipment is needed to check that any adjustment does not put the vehicle outside the legal requirement.

Information given in this Section, or Chapters 3 or 4 is aimed specifically at the owner who is able to have the various settings and adjustments checked at the time of adjustment or immediately afterwards.

The levels of the engine oil, radiator cooling water, windscreen washer water and battery electrolyte, also the tyre pressures, should be checked weekly, or more frequently if experience dictates this to be necessary. Similarly check the level of fluids in the clutch and brake master cylinder at monthly intervals.

6000 miles

Every 6,000 miles (10,000 Km) or six months if 6,000 miles are not exceeded.

1 Run the engine until it is hot and place a container of 8 pints (4.55 litres) capacity under the drain plug on the left hand side of the engine and allow the oil to drain for at least 10 minutes. Clean the plug and the surrounding area around the plug hole in the sump and replace the plug, tightening it firmly. Clean the oil filter with petrol, refill the sump with 8 pints (4.55 litres) of a recommended grade of oil and clean off any oil which may have been spilt over the engine or its components. the interval between oil changes should be reduced in very hot or dusty conditions or during cold weather with much slow stop/start driving.

2 Remove and thoroughly wash the filler cap in paraffin. Allow the cap to drain before refitting to the engine. DO NOT OIL.

3 The crankcase breather valve should be removed and washed in paraffin. Allow to dry and refit. See Chapter 3 Section 17.

4 Check the valve clearances and adjust, if necessary, as described in Chapter 1 Section 59.

5 Check, and adjust if necessary, the engine slow running. See Chapter 3 for full details.

6 Check and adjust the brakes if necessary, as described in Chapter 9, Section 5.

7 Examine and renew any defective hoses in the braking system. Ensure that there is adequate clearance between them and any chassis or other components to eliminate chafing. See Chapter 9 Section 4.

8 Examine the tyres and, should wear be apparent take the appropriate action to correct the cause, e.g. mis-alignment, poor wheel balancing, over or under inflation. If there is any doubt a Triumph garage should be consulted especially where alignment is suspect because complicated and expensive equipment is required to carry out the necessary check. Remove any flints or other road matter from the treads. Check the wheel nuts for tightness.

9 Apply grease to the handbrake cable guides and the compensator sector.

10 Lubricate with a recommended grade of oil, all hinges, locks, catches and controls to allow them to work freely and to prevent unnecessary wear.

11 Remove the spark plugs for cleaning and reset the gaps to 0.025 in (0.64 mm). Clean the ceramic insulators and examine them for cracks or other damage likely to cause 'tracking'.

12 Release the spring clips and remove the distributor cap and rotor arm. Apply a few drops of oil in the centre of the cam spindle and on the moving contact breaker pivot. Grease the cam surface very slightly. Apply a few drops of engine oil through the hole in the contact breaker base plate to lubricate the automatic timing control. Remove any excess oil or grease with a clean rag.

13 Clean and adjust the contact breaker points. See Chapter 4.

14 Clean air cleaner body and renew elements as described in Chapter 3.

15 Check the operation of all electrical equipment, particularly stop/tail lamps, number plate illumination and side lamps. Adjust, if necessary, the headlamp setting.

16 On engines fitted with Stromberg carburettors unscrew the plug from the top of each carburettor and withdraw the plug and damper assembly. Top up the damper chambers with engine oil. The oil level is correct when, using the damper as a dipstick, its threaded plug is 0.25 inch (6.35 mm) above the dashpots when resistance is felt. Refit the damper and hexagonal plug. On all carburettors apply thin oil to the throttle and choke control linkages.

17 Check, and if necessary tighten, the attachments securing the water pump, alternator and pulleys.

18 With the car standing on level ground, remove the oil level plug on the right hand side of the gearbox. Top up if necessary (with a can or dispenser having a flexible nozzle) the gearbox and overdrive with recommended oil until the oil starts to run out of the filler hole. Allow the surplus oil to drain away before cleaning the oil filler plug and surrounding area. Refit the plug tightening it firmly.

19 Apply the grease gun to the lower steering swivels and upper ball joints.

20 With the car standing on level ground remove the oil level plug on the left of the rear axle casing. If necessary, top up the rear axle with recommended oil (with a can or dispenser having a flexible nozzle) until the oil starts to run out of the filler hole. Alow the surplus oil to drain away before cleaning the oil filler plug and surrounding area. Refit the plug tightening it firmly.

21 Apply five strokes only of a grease gun to the inner drive shaft nipple (1 to each shaft) and propeller shaft universal joints.

22*Remove the carpets or mats and thoroughly vacuum clean the interior of the car. Beat out or vacuum clean the carpets. If the upholstery is soiled apply an upholstery cleaner with a damp sponge and wipe off with a clean dry cloth

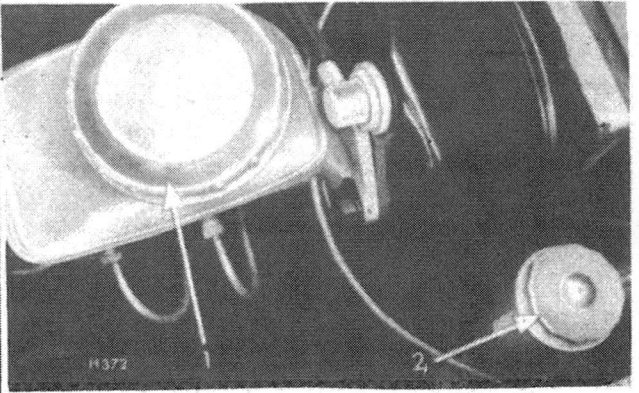 

3. Brake (1) and clutch (2) master cylinder

4. Engine sump drain plug (arrowed)

 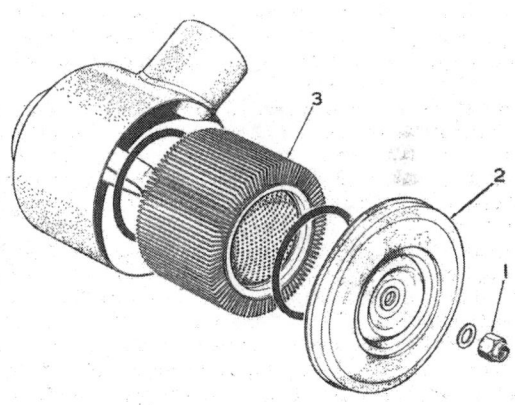

5. OIL FILTER REMOVAL

1	Centre bolt	3	Filter element
2	Filter casing	4	Sealing ring

6. AIR FILTER (P.I. MODELS)

1 Holding nut
2 Filter lid
3 Filter element

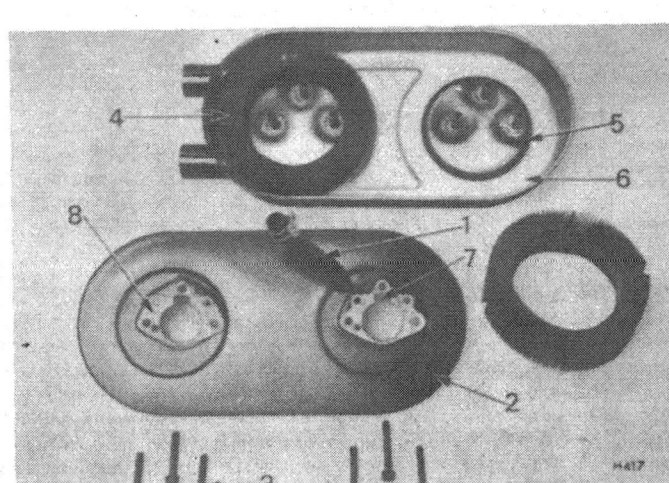

7. AIR FILTER (TR 250/6 CARBURETTORS)

1	Breather pipe	5	Locating ridge
2	Filter back plate	6	Outer casing
3	Fixing bolts	7	Locating cutout
4	Filter element	8	Gasket

8. Valve rocker adjustment

9. Pump cover (2) and securing bolt (1)
- TR250/6 carburettors

10. FUEL FILTER ASSEMBLY (PI MODELS)

1 Centre bolt
2 Seal
3 Element
4 Inner sealing ring

11. DISTRIBUTOR SERVICE POINTS

1 Points adjustment slot
2 Fixed point securing bolt
3 Points
4 Centre screw
5 Cam
6 Pivot

12. THROTTLE CABLE AND ALTERNATOR ADJUSTMENT
POINTS

1 Mounting points
2 Adjustment bolt
3 Free play

12,000 miles

Every 12,000 miles (20,000 Km) or twelve months if 12,000 miles are not exceeded.

1 Carry out the maintenance tasks listed for the 6,000 mile service.

2 Unscrew the securing bolt in the centre of the oil filter, on the left hand side of the engine, remove the container and take out and discard the element. Wash the container in petrol to remove matter trapped by the filter and take out the old rubber sealing ring. Renew and replace the element and sealing ring ensuring that the latter is correctly positioned in its groove in the cylinder block. Do not tighten the bolt more than is necessary to effect an oil tight joint. Before starting the engine ensure that the engine sump is filled to the correct level with clean oil.

3 Slacken the pipe clips from the crankcase breather valve and remove the pipes. Remove the nut and bolt retaining the unit to the mounting bracket and remove the valve. Disengage the clip from the valve body and lift out the diaphragm and spring. Clean the components by swilling them in methylated spirits. Ensure that the pipes are cleaned and serviceable. Reassembly is the reverse of the dismantling sequence. The oil filler cap should also be removed and renewed if unserviceable.

4 Examine, and if necessary tighten, the front and rear suspension attachments, steering connections, water pump, starter motor, alternator, oil filter and all universal couplings and bolts.

5 Examine the exhaust manifolds, pipes, silencer etc., for deterioration, leakage and damage.

6 Remove the fuel pump cover securing bolt and lift away the cover, sealing ring and wire gauge plate. Clean the filter and the sediment chamber. Refit the cover and sealing ring and secure with the bolt and fibre washer. Do not overtighten as it is easy to strip the threads [carburettor models only].

7 Renew the spark plugs, setting the gaps to 0.25 in (0.64mm). See Chapter 4.

8 P.I. models. Clean the fuel filter bowl and renew element as described in Chapter 3 Section 21.

9 Remove the plug on the top of the water pump and fit a screwed nipple. Apply a grease gun giving five strokes only. Remove the nipple and refit the plug. Over greasing can cause damage.

10 Remove the plug from the top of the steering unit and fit a screwed grease nipple. Apply the grease gun and give five strokes only. Remove the nipple and refit the plug. Over greasing can cause damage to the bellows.

11 Examine the front brakes for wear and deterioration. Renew the pads if they are insufficiently thick to ensure safe braking for a further 6,000 miles. Jack up the rear of the car and remove the road wheels and brake drums. Remove the dust from the drums and clean the backing plates. Examine the brake shoes and renew worn or contaminated shoes. Reassemble and adjust.

12 Check and if necessary adjust the front hubs as described in Chapter 11.

13*Visit your local main agent and have the underside of the body steam cleaned. This will take about 1½ hours. All traces of dirt and oil will be removed and the underside can then be inspected carefully for rust, damaged hydraulic pipes, frayed electrical wiring and similar maladies. The car should be greased on completion of this job.

14*At the same time the engine compartment should be cleaned. If steam cleaning facilities are not available then brush on 'Gunk' or a similar cleaner over the whole engine and engine compartment with a stiff paint brush working it well in where there is an accumulation of oil and dirt. Do not paint the ignition system but protect it with oily rags when the 'Gunk' is washed off; as the 'Gunk' is washed away it will take with it all traces of oil and dirt leaving the engine looking clean and bright.

13. Gearbox level and drain plug. Level plug arrowed

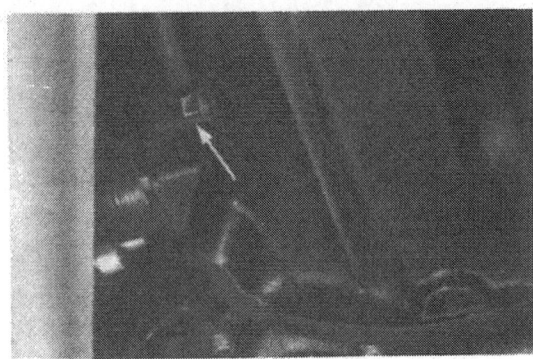
14. Final drive level plug

15. Water pump lubrication point

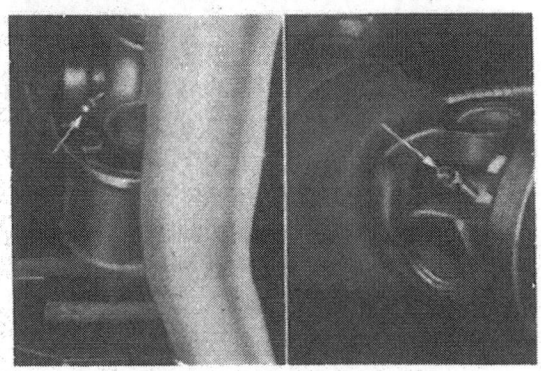
16. Propeller shaft lubrication points (arrowed)

17. CALIPER ATTACHMENT POINTS

1 Securing bolts
2 Caliper body

3 Dust shield bracket

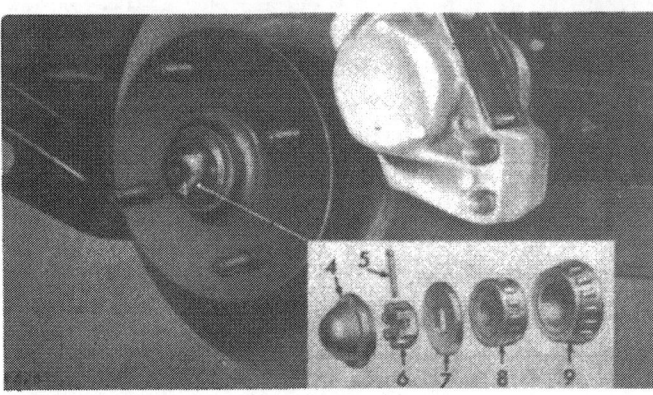

18. FRONT HUB COMPONENTS

4 Dust cap
5 Split pin
6 Castellated nut

7 Washer
8 Outer race
9 Inner race

19. PAD RETAINING PINS

1 Spring clips
2 Retaining pins

3 Pad
4 Anti-squeal shim

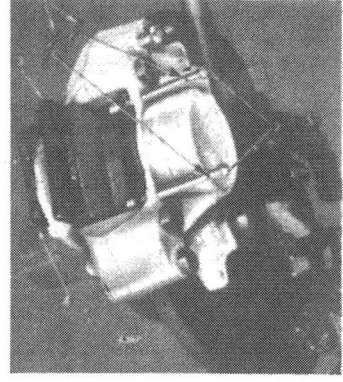

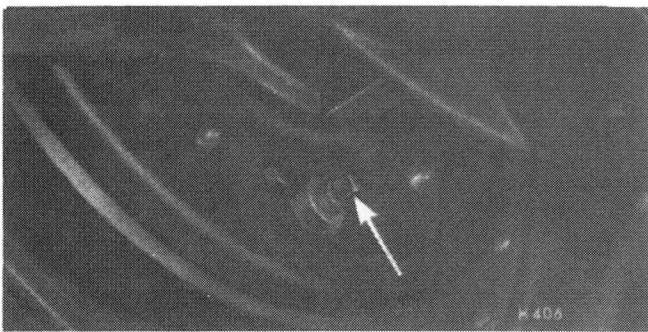

20. Rear brake adjuster (arrowed)

36,000 miles

Every 36,000 miles (60,000 Km) or three years if 36,000 miles are not exceeded.

1 Carry out the maintenance tasks listed for the 6,000 miles (10,000 Km) and 12,000 miles (20,000 Km) service.
2 All seals and flexible hoses throughout the braking system should be removed and renewed, the brake cylinders and pistons should be examined and replaced if wear is found, and brake pipes replaced if any damage is present. Further details are given in Chapter 9.
3 Drain and refill the manual gearbox and rear axle with the appropriate grades of oil. This is recommended so that any minute particles of metal are carried away in the old oil so helping to prevent further wear.
4 Renew servo unit air filter as described in Chapter 9, Section 18.

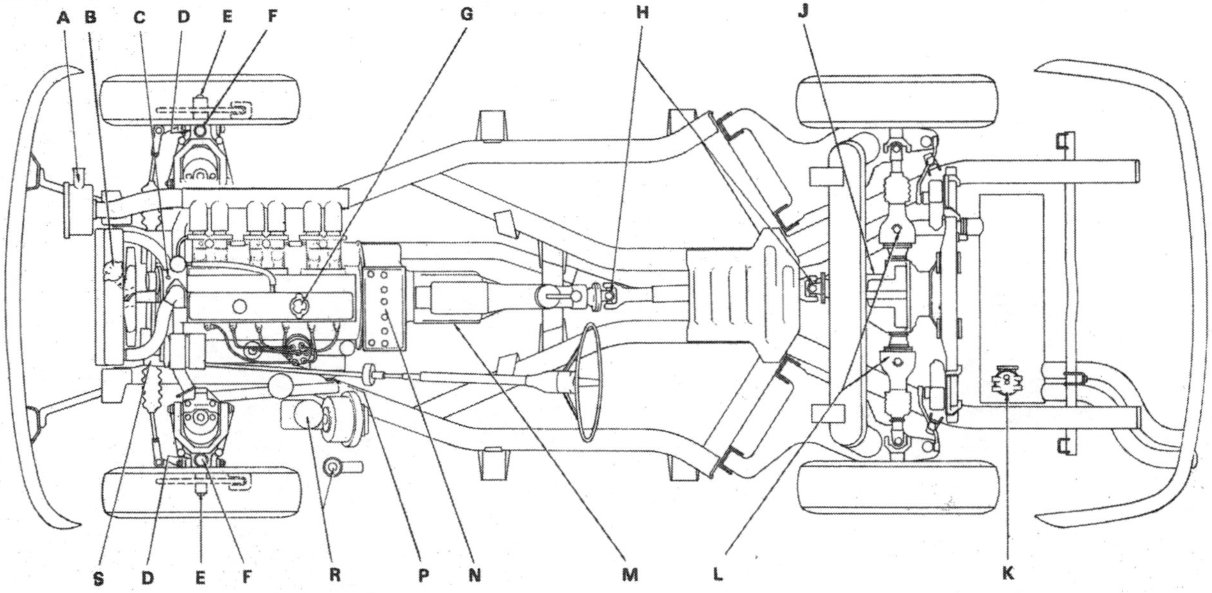

MAINTENANCE ITEMS TR5 AND TR6 PI

A Air cleaners
B Radiator
C Water pump
D Lower steering swivels
E Front hubs
F Upper balljoints
G Engine oil sump
H Propeller shaft
J Rear axle
K Fuel filter
L Drive shafts
M Transmission
N Battery
P Oil filter
R Clutch and brake master cylinders
S Steering unit

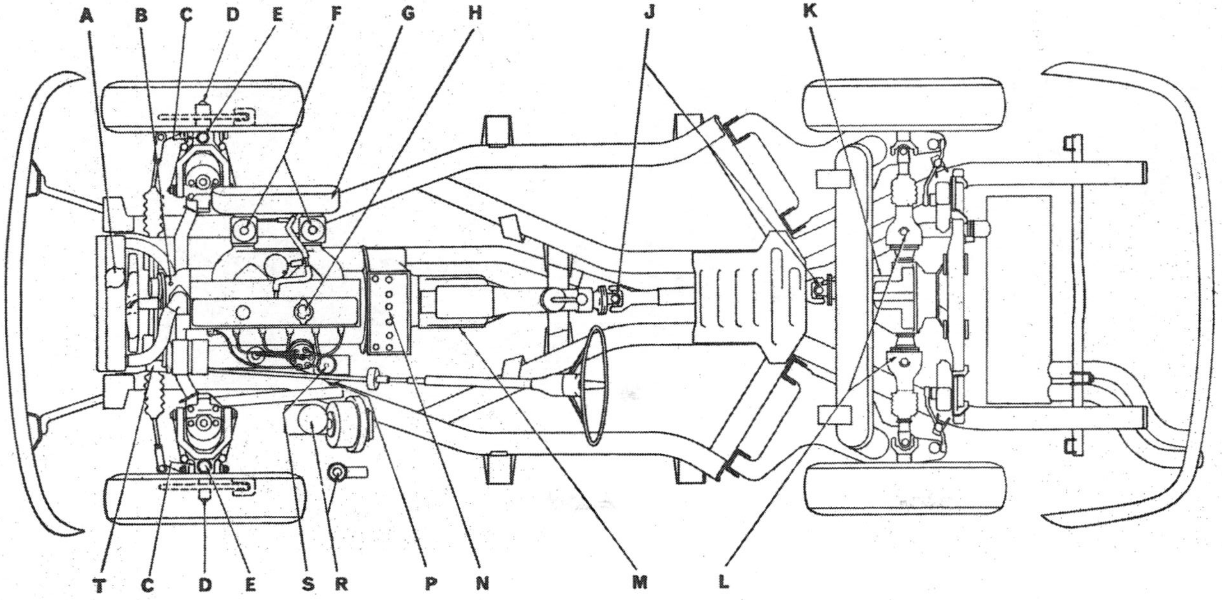

MAINTENANCE ITEMS TR250/6 CARBURETTORS

A Radiator
B Water pump
C Upper balljoints
D Front hubs
E Lower steering swivels
F Carburettor dampers
G Air cleaners
H Engine oil sump
J Propeller shaft
K Final drive
L Drive shafts
M Transmission
N Battery
P Oil filter
R Master cylinder - clutch and brake
S Fuel pump
T Steering unit

Fig. 1.1. Left hand view of engine - P.I. models

Fig. 1.2. Right hand view of engine - P.I. models

Chapter 1 Engine

Contents

Specifications

Type	ohv water cooled
Number of cylinders	6
Compression ratio	9.5 to 1 (TR250/6 carburettors 8.5:1)
Cubic capacity	2498cc (152 cu in)
Bore	2.94 in (74.7 mm)
Stroke	3.74 in (95 mm)
Firing order	1 5 3 6 2 4
Ignition timing	11° BTDC (10° BTDC — TR250)

Crankshaft and main bearings

Main journal diameter	2.311 - 2.3115 in (58.699 - 58.712 mm)
Crankpin diameter	1.875 - 1.8755 in (47.625 - 47.638 mm)
Crankshaft end thrust	Thrust washers on rear main bearing
End float	0.006 - 0.008 in (0.152 - 0.203 mm)
Main bearing internal diameter	2.002 - 2.0025 in (50.85 - 50.86 mm)
Main bearing housing internal diameter	2.146 - 2.1465 in (54.51 - 54.52 mm)
Rear journal width	1.360 - 1.362 in (34.54 - 34.59 mm)
Thickness of thrust washers	0.091 - 0.093 in (2.31 - 2.36 mm)
Undersize bearings available	0.010, 0.020, 0.030 in (0.254, 0.508, 0.762 mm)

Camshaft

Camshaft drive	Double roller chain

Camshaft journal diameter ... ...   1.8402 - 1.8407 in (46.741 - 46.745 mm)
Diametrical clearance   ...   .   0.0026 - 0.0046 in (0.066 - 0.116 mm)
End float   ...   .   0.004 - 0.008 in (0.102 - 0.203 mm)
End thrust   ...   .   Taken by end plate.

Connecting rods and big and little end bearings
Type ...   .   Angular split big end, fully floating small end
Big end bearings - type   ...   .   Shell
Big end bearings - internal diameter   ...   ...   1.877 - 1.8775 in (47.675 - 47.688 mm)
End float on crankpin   ...   .   0.0086 - 0.0125 in (0.218 - 0.317 mm)
Undersizes available ...   .   0.010, 0.020, 0.030 in (0.254, 0.508, 0.762 mm)

Cylinder block
Type ...   .   Cylinders cast integral with top half of crankcase
Water jacket ...   .   Full length
Oversize bores - first   ...   .   0.010 in (0.254 mm)
                 max.   ...   .   0.030 in (0.762 mm)

Cylinder head
Type ...   .   Cast iron with vertical valves
Port arrangement   ...   .   Inlet and exhaust on same side
Number of ports - exhaust ...   .   6 separate
                  inlet   ...   .   6 separate

Gudgeon pin
Type ...   .   Fully floating
Fit in piston ...   .   Light push fit at 68°F (20°C)
Outer diameter   ...   .   0.8123 - 0.8125 in (20.63 - 20.64 mm)

Lubrication system
Type ...   .   Pressure and splash. Wet sump
Oil filter   ...   .   Cartridge type full flow with by-pass valve
Sump capacity   ...   .   8 pints (9.64 US pints, 4.52 litres)
Oil pump type   ...   .   Eccentric rotor
Normal oil pressure at 2000 rpm ...   .   40 - 60 PSI (2.8 to 4.2 Kg m cm^2)

Pistons
Type ...   .   Aluminium alloy
No of rings ...   .   2 compression, 1 oil control
Clearance in cylinder - Top   ...   .   0.0035 - 0.0039 in (0.09 - 0.10mm)
                       Bottom   ...   .   0.0017 - 0.0021 in (0.045 - 0.055 mm)
Piston oversize available   ...   .   0.020 in (0.508 mm)

Piston rings
Compression rings ...   .   Parallel chrome plated
Compression ring width   ...   .   0.0615 - 0.0625 in (1.562 - 1.588 mm)
Gap ...   .   0.012 - 0.017 in (0.305 - 0.432 mm)
Oil control ring   ...   .   Slotted scraper
Oil control ring width   ...   .   0.1415 - 0.1515 in (3.594 - 3.838 mm)

Tappets
Type ...   .   Barrel with flat base
Outside diameter   ...   .   0.7996 - 0.8000 in (20.29 - 20.32 mm)

Rocker gear
Diameter of rocker shaft   ...   .   0.5607 - 0.5612 in (14.24 - 14.26 mm)
Bore of rockers   ...   .   0.563 - 0.564 in (14.3 - 14.33 mm)

Valves
Head diameter - inlet   ...   .   1.441 - 1.445 in (36.6 - 36.7 mm)
               exhaust   ...   .   1.256 - 1.26 in (31.9 - 32.0 mm)
Stem diameter - inlet   ...   .   0.3107 - 0.3112 in (7.891 - 7.904 mm)
                exhaust   ...   .   0.31 - 0.3105 in (7.87 - 7.89 mm)
Valve stem to rocker arm clearance (cold)   ...   ...   0.010 in (0.25 mm)

Valve guides
Length - inlet   ...   .   2.0625 in (52.386 mm)
         exhaust   ...   .   2.25 in (57.15 mm)
Outside diameter   ...   .   0.501 - 0.502 in (12.725 - 12.751 mm)
Height above cylinder head   ...   .   0.63 in (16.002 mm)

Valve timing
Inlet opens ...   .   35° BTDC

Inlet closes	65º ABDC
Exhaust opens	65º BBDC
Exhaust closes	35º ATDC

Valve springs

Type	Double, inner and outer spring
Free length - outer	1.57 in (39.878 mm)
inner	1.56 in (36.624 mm)
Fitted load - outer	150 lb in
inner	28.5 lb in

TORQUE WRENCH SETTINGS

	Description	Specified torque	
		lb ft	Kg m
Breather pipe attachment	5/16 in UNF x 1.16 in stud	12 - 14	1.659 - 1.936
Camshaft chainwheel attachment	5/16 in - 24 NF setscrew	24 - 26	3.318 - 3.595
Coil attachment	5/16 in UNF x ½ in setscrew	16 - 18	2.212 - 2.489
Distributor to pedestal	¼ in UNF x ½ in setscrew	8 - 10	1.106 - 1.383
Distributor clamp pinch bolt	¼ in BSF x 15/8 in bolt	3 - 4	0.415 - 0.553
Front engine plate and locating plate to cylinder block ...	5/16 in UNF x 7/8 in setscrew	18 - 20	2.489 - 2.765
Lifting eye attachment	5/16 in UNF x 5/8 in setscrew	16 - 18	2.212 - 2.489
Oil filter assembly ...		15 - 18	2.074 - 2.489
Oil gallery dryseal plug	¼ in NPSI plug	10 - 12	1.383 - 1.659
Oil gallery seals	7/16 in UNF x ½ in setscrew	25 - 30	3.456 - 4.148
Oil gallery seals	¾ in UNF x ½ in plug	25 - 30	3.456 - 4.148
Oil gallery seals	½ in NF x 0.38 in core plugs	25 - 30	3.456 - 4.148
Oil gallery seals	1/8 in NPSI plug	5 - 6	0.692 - 0.829
Oil pump to block	¼ in UNF x 3 in bolt	8 - 10	1.106 - 1.383
Petrol pump attachment	5/16 in UNF x 1.16 in	12 - 14	1.659 - 1.936
Rear engine plate to block	5/16 in UNF x ¾ in setscrew	18 - 20	2.489 - 2.765
Starter motor attachment	3/8 in UNF x 21/8 in bolt	28 - 30	3.871 - 4.148
Sump to block	5/16 in UNF x 5/8 in setscrew	16 - 18	2.212 - 2.489
Timing cover to front engine plate	5/16 in UNF x 3/8 in pan-head setscrew	8 - 10	1.106 - 1.383
Timing cover and front engine plate to cylinder block	5/16 in UNF x 7/8 in setscrew	16 - 18	2.212 - 2.489
Connecting rod bolts	3/8 in UNF x 1.69 in bolt	38 - 42	5.254 - 5.807
Clutch to flywheel	5/16 in UNC x ¾ in setscrew	20	2.765
Crankshaft pulley attachment	5/8 in UNF x 2½ in bolt	90 - 100	12.443 - 13.825
Fan to pulley	5/16 in UNF bolts	12 - 14	1.659 - 1.936
Flywheel to crankshaft	3/8 in x 24 TPI bolt	42 - 46	5.807 - 6.360
Front sealing block attachment	5/16 in UNF x 0.94 in Ch. head screw	12 - 14	1.659 - 1.936
Main bearing caps to block	7/16 in UNF x 3 in bolt	55 - 60	7.604 - 8.295
Rear main bearing oil seal attachment ...	5/16 in UNF x 11/8 in bolt	16 - 18	2.212 - 2.489
Accelerator support bracket to manifold	5/16 in UNF x ¾ in setscrew	18 - 20	2.489 - 2.765
Air cleaner attachment	5/16 in UNF x 21/8 in bolt	6 - 8	0.829 - 1.106
Carburettor attachment	5/16 in UNF x 1½ in stud	12 - 14	1.659 - 1.936
Manifolds - attachment	3/8 in UNF bolt	20 - 22	2.765 - 3.042
exhaust outlet	5/16 in UNF x 1.31 in stud	14 - 16	1.936 - 2.212
inlet to exhaust	3/8 in UNF x 1.56 in stud	20 - 22	2.765 - 3.042
Rocker cover to cylinder head	5/16 in UNF x 4.13 in stud	1.5	0.207
Rocker oil feed	5/16 in UNF x 3/8 in setscrew	16 - 18	2.212 - 2.489
Rocker pedestal to cylinder head	3/8 in UNF x 3.09 in stud	24 - 26	3.318 - 3.595
Water elbow attachment	5/16 in UNF bolt	18 - 20	2.489 - 2.765
Water pump pulley attachment	5/16 in UNF nyloc nut	14 - 16	1.936 - 2.212
Water pump to cylinder head	5/16 in UNF bolts	18 - 20	2.489 - 2.765
Alternator mounting bracket to cylinder block ...	5/16 in UNF x 1 in setscrew	18 - 20	2.490 - 2.770
Alternator to mounting bracket	5/16 in UNF x 47/8 in bolt	18 - 20	2.490 - 2.770
Alternator to adjusting link	5/16 in UNC x 7/8 in setscrew	18 - 20	2.490 - 2.770
Cylinder head attachment	7/16 in UNF x 4.84 in stud	65 - 70	8.987 - 9.678
Distributor and PI pump pedestal attachment ...	5/16 in UNF x 2½ in stud	12 - 14	1.660 - 1.940
Distributor and PI pump pedestal attachment ...	5/16 in UNF x 1.31 in stud	12 - 14	1.660 - 1.940
Distributor to pedestal	5/16 in UNF x 5/8 in setscrew	18 - 20	2.490 - 2.770
Distributor pedestal end plug	¼ in UNF x ½ in setscrew	8 - 10	1.110 - 1.380
Inlet manifold to stay	¼ in UNF x ¾ in setscrew	8 - 10	1.110 - 1.380
Petrol injection nozzle attachment	¼ in UNC x 3/8 in setscrew	6 - 8	0.830 - 1.110
Water pump plug	3/8 in UNF Dryseal plug	20 - 22	2.770 - 3.040
Water pump plug	5/8 in UNF plug	28 - 30	3.870 - 4.150

1 General description

The engine fitted to the TR5, 250 and 6 models are basically similar; therefore, throughout this chapter any deviations will be dealt with in there respective sections, whilst full specifications and data are given at the beginning of this chapter.

The engine is a six cylinder, overhead valve type. It is supported by rubber mountings in the interests of silence and lack of vibrations.

Two valves per cylinder are mounted vertically in the cast iron cylinder head and run in pressed-in valve guides. They are operated by rocker arms, push rods and tappets from the camshaft which is located at the base of the cylinder bores in the left hand side of the engine. The correct valve stem to rocker arm pad clearance can be obtained by the adjusting screws in the ends of the rocker arms.

The cylinder block and upper half of the crankcase are cast together. The bottom half of the crankcase consists of a pressed steel sump.

The pistons are made from anodised aluminium with split skirts. Two compression rings and a slotted oil control ring are fitted. The gudgeon pin is retained in the little end of the connecting rod by circlips.

Renewable shell type big end bearings are fitted. At the front of the engine a chain drives the camshaft via the camshaft and crankshaft chain wheels which are enclosed in a pressed steel cover.

The chain is tensioned automatically by a spring blade which presses against the non-driving side of the chain so avoiding any lash or rattle.

The camshaft is supported by bearings bored directly into the cylinder block. End float is controlled by a forked locating plate positioned on the front end plate.

The statically and dynamically balanced forged steel crankshaft is supported by four renewable thin wall shell main bearings, which are in turn supported by substantial webs which form part of the crankcase. Crankshaft end float is controlled by semi–circular thrust washers located on each side of the rear main bearing.

The centrifugal water pump and radiator cooling fan are driven, together with the alternator, from the crankshaft pulley wheel by a rubber/fabric belt. The distributor is mounted in the middle of the left hand side of the cylinder block and advances and retards the ignition timing by mechanical and vacuum means. The distributor is driven at half crankshaft speed by a short shaft and skew gear, from a skew gear on the camshaft located between the second and third journals.

The oil pump is located in the crankcase and is driven by a short shaft from the skew gear on the camshaft.

Attached to the end of the crankshaft by four bolts and one dowel is the flywheel to which is bolted the clutch. Attached to the engine end plate is the gearbox bell housing.

2 Routine maintenance

1 Once a week, or more frequently if necessary, remove the dipstick and check the engine oil level, which should be at the 'MAX' mark Top up the oil in the sump with the recommended grade (see page 9). On no account allow the oil to fall below the 'MIN' mark on the dipstick.

2 Every 6,000 miles (10,000 Km) run the engine till it is hot, place a container with a capacity of at least 8 pints (4.55 litres, 1.201 US pints) under the drain plug in the sump, undo and remove the drain plug and allow the oil to drain for at least ten minutes. While the oil is draining, wash the oil filter cap in petrol, shake dry and refit. DO NOT OIL.

3 Clean the drain plug, ensure the washer is in place, and return the plug to the sump, tightening the plug firmly. Refill the sump with 8 pints (4.55 litres, 1.201 US pints) of the recommended grade of oil (See page 9   for details). Every 12,000 miles (20,000 Km) the oil filter element should be renewed as described in the Routine Maintenance Section.

4 In very hot or dusty conditions, in cold weather with much slow stop/start driving, with much use of the choke, or when the engine has covered a very high mileage, it is beneficial to change the engine oil every 3,000 miles (5,000 Km) and the filter every 6,000 miles (10,000 Km).

3 Major operations with engine in place

The following major operations can be carried out to the engine with it in place in the body frame:-
1 Removal and replacement of the cylinder head.
2 Removal and replacement of the sump.
3 Removal and replacement of the big end bearings.

Fig. 1.3. Right hand view of engine in car

4 Removal and replacement of the pistons and connecting rods.
5 Removal and replacement of the timing chain and gears and the timing cover oil seal.*
6 Removal of the camshaft.
7 Removal and replacement of the oil pump.
8 It is possible to renew main bearing shells provided crankshaft journals are in a satisfactory condition.
*It is necessary to remove the steering rack U-bolts and move the assembly forward to clear the crankshaft pulley for this operation.

4 Major operations with the engine removed

The following major operations can be carried out with the engine out of the body frame and on the bench or floor:—
1 Removal and replacement of the main bearings.
2 Removal and replacement of the crankshaft.
3 Removal and replacement of the flywheel.

5 Methods of engine removal

There are two methods of engine removal. The engine can either be removed complete with gearbox, or the engine can be removed without the gearbox by separating it at the gearbox bell housing. Both methods are described. Irrespective of whether the engine is removed with or without the gearbox, it will be found to be one of the easiest units to take out and replace, apart from its size and weight. No pit or ramps are necessary as the jobs usually done underneath, such as propshaft/gearbox separation are all done from inside the car. As a further bonus engine accessibility is excellent.

6 Engine removal without gearbox

1 Practical experience has proved that the engine can be easily removed in about three hours (less with experience) by adhering to the following sequence of operations.
2 It must be pointed out that the basic procedure for removing the engine on all models covered by this manual is identical but there may be slight differences which will be apparent as work progresses.
3 Open the bonnet and prop it up to expose the engine and ancillary components. Turn on the drain taps to be found at the bottom of the radiator and on the side of the cylinder block. NOTE: Do not drain water in your garage or the place where you will remove the engine if receptacles are not at hand to catch the water.
4 Place a container with a capacity of 11 pints (13.2 US pints) under the drain plug in the sump, undo and remove the drain plug, and allow the oil to drain for at least ten minutes. Replace the drain plug.
5 A second person's assistance will be necessary to remove the bonnet. Using a pencil, mark the outline of the hinge on the bonnet lid to assist refitting.
6 Undo the three bolts on each hinge securing the hinge to the bonnet. Remove the bolts, spring and plain washers.
7 With the assistance of the second person lift away the bonnet.
8 Put the bonnet in one corner out of the way where it will not be scratched or damaged. It will assist working on the engine if any wing mirrors are removed.
9 Place some old blankets over the wings and the front of the car so paintwork is not damaged.
10 Disconnect the battery earth (negative) lead, followed by the live (positive) lead and then undo the battery clamp nuts and remove it from the car.
11 Remove the wiring connections from the alternator noting their correct positions for reassembly, undo and remove the alternator securing bolts and lift it from the car.
12 Disconnect the fuel feed pipe and spill pipe from the petrol injection fuel metering unit.
13 Disconnect the cold start cable from the metering unit.
14 Undo the air manifold air filter retaining clip at the manifold. Ease the filter unit from the manifold so as to allow access to the flexible air inlet hose, disconnect the hose from the air filter and lift away the filter.
15 Disconnect the two small bore rubber hoses from the air manifold and slacken the two outer air intake rubber hose clips.
16 Remove the two nuts and bolts which secure the air manifold to its mounting bracket. Lift away the air manifold and six air intake rubber hoses.
17 Undo the air manifold mounting bracket retaining nuts situated on studs on the side of the cylinder block. Lift away the bracket.
18 Disconnect the cold start cam return spring and also the cold start and accelerator cables at the butterfly control.
19 Undo the centre and rear rocker cover nuts and lift the pipes and cold start cable to the metering unit from the studs. Replace the nuts but do not tighten. Disconnect the injector pipes at the injectors.
20 In case of the TR 250 and TR6 where Stromberg carburettors are fitted, it is necessary to disconnect the throttle cable, choke cable and the fuel pipe where it enters the pump, remembering to clamp it or block it to prevent the loss of petrol, or dirt entering the system.
21 Remove the radiator as described in Chapter 2.
22 To give more room for removing the engine undo the three bolts at either end of the cross-tube in front of the engine.
23 Remove the 'U' clamps holding the steering gear to the chassis crossmember and draw the steering gear slightly forwards to clear the crankshaft pulley.
24 Undo the tachometer drive cable retainer from the side of the distributor pedestal and separate the drive cable. Tuck the cable out of harms way.
25 If carburettors are fitted undo the fuel line connection from the pump to the carburettors at the front carburettor.
26 In all cases undo the nut securing the inlet manifold to the cylinder head. Disconnect the exhaust manifold from the pipe, undo its retaining nuts and lift both manifolds from the cylinder head with the fuel injection gear or carburettors still attached (photo).
27 Pull off the oil pressure sender connector at the left rear of the crankcase.
28 Disconnect the wiring to the coil noting its positioning for reassembly.
29 Disconnect the wiring from the starter motor and remove the starter motor by undoing the retaining bolts.
30 Undo the engine earth strap where it is connected to the timing chain cover.
31 Undo the heater return hose pipe connection clip and disconnect the hose from the metal pipe at the rear of the engine.
32 Undo the heater feed pipe connection clip and disconnect the hose from the heater water valve connection.
33 Undo the heater water valve control outer cable connection from the bracket on the side of the water valve body.
34 Using a pair of pliers and an open ended spanner disconnect the water valve inner control cable from the lever.
35 Separate the inner control cable from the lever.
36 Undo the heater return pipe connection to be found at the rear of the water pump.
37 Undo the nut securing the heater return pipe bracket to the rear right hand side of the engine by the inlet manifold and lift away the pipe.
38 From inside the car lift away both seat cushions and also the carpeting from the boot wells.
39 Undo and remove the eight nuts securing the seats to their runners. Lift away the front seats to give better access to the floor centre section.
40 Make a note of the electrical cable connections at the rear of the switch and disconnect the electrical terminal. If a radio set is fitted this should be removed from its mounting.
41 Slacken the gear change lever knob locknut and unscrew the knob. Also unscrew the locknut.
42 Withdraw the gear change lever rubber from the gear change lever.
43 Disconnect the two dip switch cables from their snap connectors and remove the dip switch.

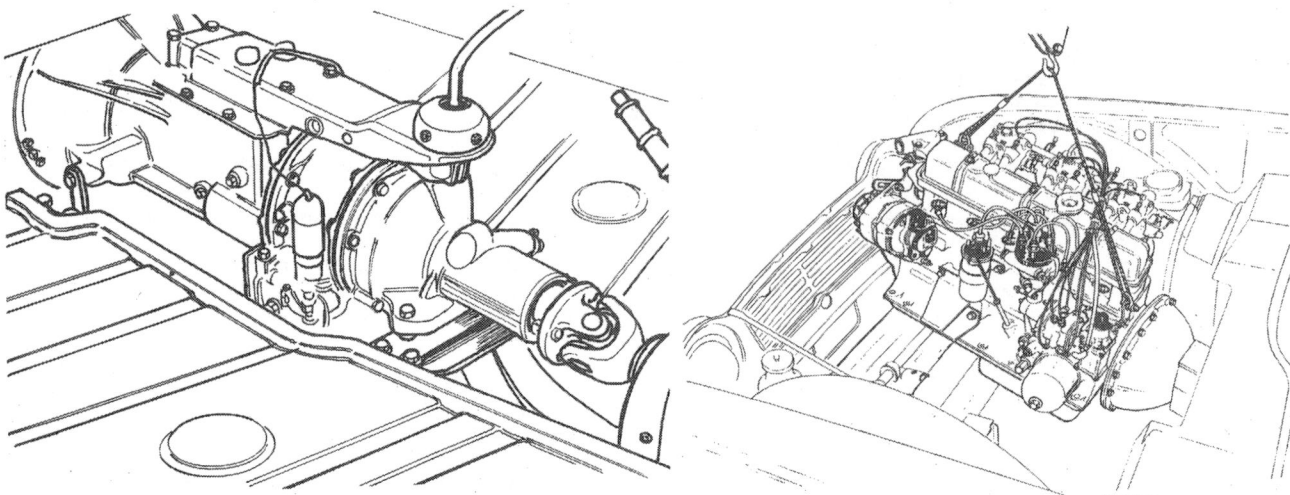

Fig. 1.4. Gearbox and overdrive unit in chassis with cover removed

Fig. 1.5. Lifting away engine and gearbox. Note location of sling pick up points

6.26 Removal of manifold securing bolts (TR250/6 carburettors)

9.5 Unscrewing oil pressure warning sender unit

44 Undo the two bolts holding the panel to the underside of the instrument panel switch console.

45 Undo the four bolts holding the facia support to the floor panels.

46 Disconnect the two heater control cables.

47 Withdraw the centre console from under the switch panel and lift away from the car.

48 Undo the sixteen bolts with plain washers holding the floor centre section to the floor panels and lift away the complete centre section.

49 Place a rope sling around the front and rear of the engine, or chains and hooks to the front and rear of the cylinder head, and take the weight of the engine from the mountings.

50 Using a garage hydraulic jack or other suitable means support the weight of the gearbox and overdrive unit if fitted.

51 Undo the two nuts which secure the engine front end plate mountings to the rubber mountings.

52 Undo the nuts and bolts which secure the clutch bell housing to the engine backplate. The top nuts and bolts are only accessible from inside the car.

53 Check that all electrical connections and pipes have been disconnected from the engine and that all vulnerable parts are protected or moved to one side parallel in movement until the gearbox first motion shaft (input) is free of the clutch.

54 Raise the engine and tilt the front end upwards.

55 Continue raising the engine making sure the front engine plate mounting feet clear the inside wing panels.

56 Finally lift the engine to clear the front panels and pull the engine away from the front of the car.

57 Carefully lower the engine to the ground.

58 To complete the job clear out any loose nuts and bolts and tools from the engine compartment a and put them where they will not be misplaced.

7 Engine removal with gearbox

1 Follow the instructions in Section 6 up to paragraph 51 inclusive then proceed as follows.

2 Disconnect the exhaust bracket from the gearbox mounting.

3 Disconnect the propeller shaft universal joint flange from the gearbox extension housing or overdrive unit flange by undoing the four nuts and bolts. Carefully lower the propeller shaft to the floor.

4 Using a pair of pliers undo the speedometer drive cable knurled collar from the gearbox extension housing (standard gearbox) or rear of the overdrive unit.

5 Undo and remove the right hand overdrive or gearbox silent block mounting bolt followed by the nut and spring washer. Then undo the bracket to chassis mounting nut and bolt.

6 Lift away the bracket noting that the nut is welded to the underside, to assist refitting.

7 Remove the bolt and washer securing the gearbox remote control support stay to the silentbloc mounting (standard gearbox) or silentbloc mounting flange on the side of the overdrive unit.

8 Lift away the little spacer from between the stay and overdrive unit mounting flange.

9 Disconnect the two wires from their terminals on the reverse light switch and also the two wires from the solenoid if the overdrive unit is fitted.

10 Turn the gearbox rear mounting through 90° and lift away from the underside of the unit.

11 Remove the gearbox support and allow the weight of the engine and gearbox unit to be taken by the sling.

12 Check that all electrical connections and pipes have been disconnected from the engine and gearbox and that all vulnerable parts are protected or moved to one side.

13 Carefully ease the complete power unit forwards and then raise the front of the engine so that the front engine plate feet clear the inside wing panels.

14 Continue to raise the front of the power unit as well as pulling forwards until it is over the engine compartment. Pull the unit over the front of the engine compartment and carefully lower to the ground.

15 To complete the job clear out any loose nuts, bolts or tools from the engine compartment and put them where they will not be misplaced.

8 Dismantling the engine - general

1 It is best to mount the engine on a dismantling stand, but if one is not available, then stand the engine on a strong bench so as to be at a comfortable working height. Failing this, the engine can be stripped down on the floor.

2 During the dismantling process the greatest care should be taken to keep the exposed parts free from dirt. As an aid to achieving this, it is a sound scheme to thoroughly clean down the outside of the engine, removing all traces of oil and congealed dirt.

3 Use paraffin or a good grease solvent such as 'Gunk'. The latter compound will make the job much easier, as, after the solvent has been applied and allowed to stand for a time, a vigorous jet of water will wash off all the solvent and the grease and filth. If the dirt is thick and deeply embedded, work the solvent into it with a stiff brush.

4 Finally wipe down the exterior of the engine with a rag and only then, when it is quite clean, should the dismantling process begin. As the engine is stripped, clean each part in a bath of paraffin or petrol.

5 Never immerse parts with oilways in paraffin, i.e. the crankshaft, but to clean, wipe down carefully with a petrol dampened rag. Oilways can be cleaned out with pipe cleaners. If an air line is present all parts can be blown dry and the oilways blown through as an added precaution.

6 Re-use of old engine gaskets is a false economy and can give rise to oil and water leaks, if nothing worse. To avoid the possibility of trouble after the engine has been reassembled always use new gaskets throughout.

7 Do not throw the old gaskets away as it sometimes happens that an immediate replacement cannot be found and the old gasket is then very useful as a template. Hang up the old gaskets, as they are removed, on a suitable hook or nail.

8 To strip the engine it is best to work from the top down. The sump provides a firm base on which the engine can be supported in an upright position. When the stage where the sump must be removed is reached, the engine can be turned on its side and all other work carried out with it in this position.

9 Wherever possible, replace nuts, bolts and washers finger tight from where they were removed. This helps avoid later loss and

muddle. If they cannot be replaced then lay them out in such a fashion that it is clear from where they came.

9 Removing ancillary engine components

1 Before basic engine dismantling begins the engine should be stripped of all its ancillary components. These items should also be removed if a factory exchange reconditioned unit is being purchased. The items comprise:-
   Water pump and thermostat housing;
   Distributor and spark plugs;
   Fuel pump and fuel pipes;
   Oil filter and dipstick:
   Oil filler cap;
   Clutch assembly;
   Breather pipe (where fitted);

2 Without exception all these items can be removed with the engine in the car if it is merely an individual item which requires attention. (it is necessary to remove the gearbox if the clutch is to be renewed with the engine in situ).

3 Take off the distributor and housing, after undoing the two nuts and washers which hold the bottom flange of the distributor housing to the cylinder block. Retain and note the shims between the housing and the block. Do not loosen the square nut on the clamp at the base of the distributor body or the timing will be lost. Undo the spark plugs.

4 The fuel pump on carburettor models is held in place by two nuts and studs. Undo the two nuts, remove together with spring washers and lift away the pump.

5 Undo and remove the low oil pressure warning sender unit (photo).

6 Remove the centre bolt from the oil filter and withdraw the complete unit.

7 Moving to the front of the engine undo the left hand thermostat housing cover bolt to free the clip which carries the fuel and vacuum advance/retard lines.

8 Remove all heater pipes from the engine.

9 Undo the bolts which hold the water pump in place on the front face of the block.

10 Remove the water pump from the block.

11 Where a breather pipe is fitted note that it is a press fit in the block and should be carefully twisted and pulled out.

12 Undo a quarter of a turn at a time the six bolts which hold the clutch pressure plate assembly to the flywheel.

13 Lift off the pressure plate together with the loose friction plate.

10 Cylinder head removal - engine away from the car

If the engine has been removed with the cylinder head still in position, or a separate engine requires attention, the cylinder head may be removed as follows:-

1 Unscrew the three rocker cover nuts and lift the rocker cover and gasket away.

2 Unscrew the rocker pedestal nuts (four) and lift off the rocker assembly.

3 Remove the three water pump retaining bolts. It will be noted that the top right bolt also acts as a mounting for the adjusting bracket for the alternator. Observe that all three bolts are of different lengths and it is important that they are replaced in their original positions.

4 Lift away the water pump from the front face of the cylinder head followed by the gasket.

5 Undo the fourteen cylinder head nuts half a turn at a time in the reverse order to that shown in Fig. 1.7. . When all the nuts are no longer under tension they may be screwed off the cylinder head one at a time.

6 Remove the pushrods, keeping them in the relative order in which they were removed. The easiest way to do this is to push them through a sheet of thick paper or thin card in the correct sequence.

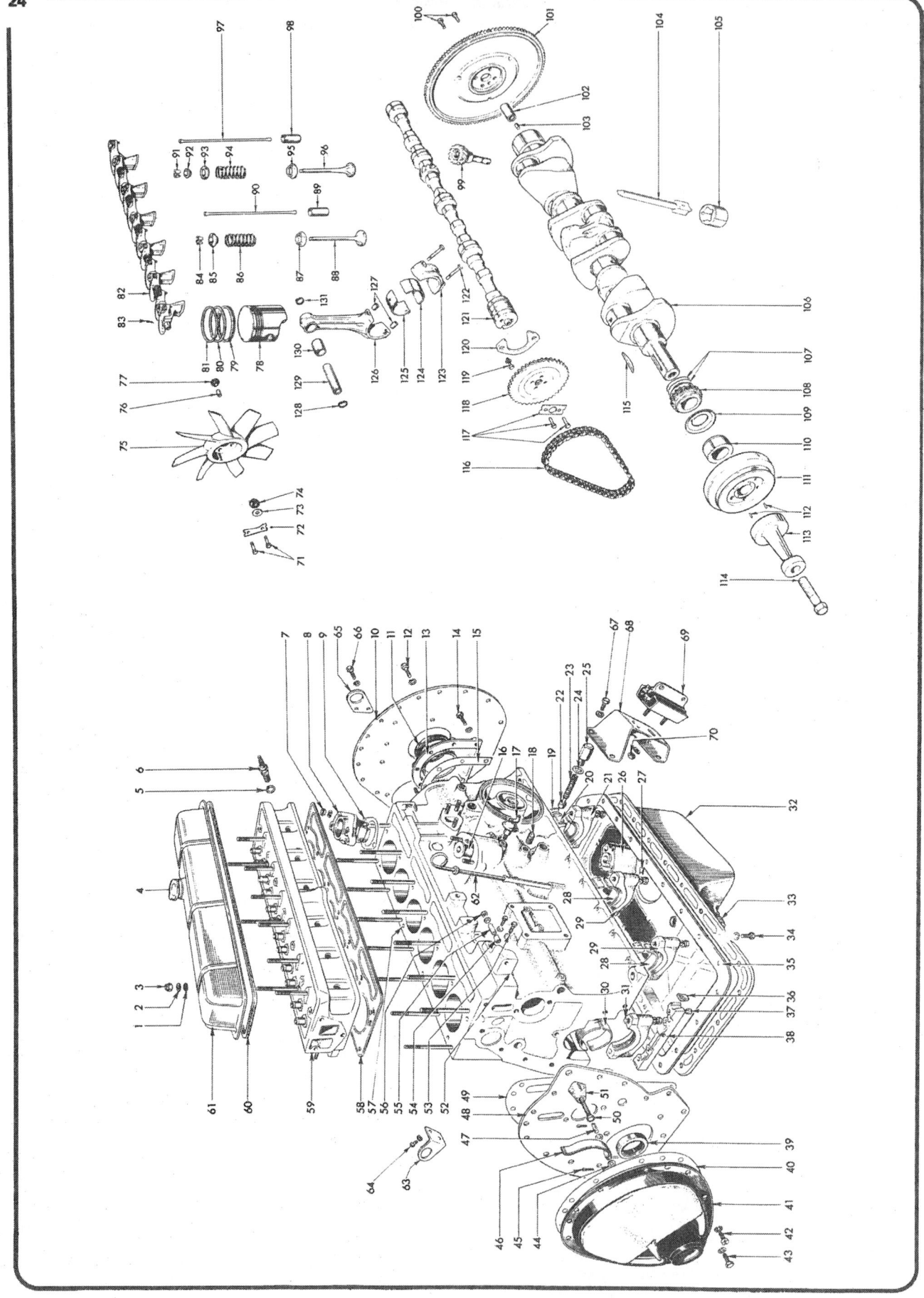

FIG. 1.6. ENGINE COMPONENTS

1 Fibre washer)
2 Plain washer) rocker cover
3 Nyloc nut) attachment
4 Filler cap
5 Sealing washer
6 Sparking plug
7 Nut
8 Distributor pedestal
9 Paper shim
10 Engine rear plate
11 Oil seal
12 Bolt - rear plate to block
13 Oil seal housing
14 Bolt - housing to bolt
15 Gasket - oil seal housing
16 Distributor drive gear bush
17 Oil pressure switch
18 Dry seal plug
19 Crankshaft thrust washer
20 Main bearing shell - rear
21 Main bearing cup - rear
22 Oil pressure relief valve
23 Valve spring
24 Copper washer
25 Cup nut
26 Oil pump body
27 Oil pump end plate
28 Main bearing shell - intermediate
29 Main bearing cup - intermediate
30 Main bearing shell - front
31 Main bearing cup - front
32 Oil sump
33 Drain plug
34 Bolt - sump attachment
35 Gasket
36 Filler piece - front sealing block
37 Cheese head screw - front sealing block
38 Front sealing block
39 Timing cover - front oil seal
40 Gasket
41 Timing cover
42 Cheese head) Timing
   screw) cover
43 Hexagon head) cover
44 Plain washer
45 Split pin
46 Chain tensioner
47 Pin
48 Front plate
49 Gasket
50 Bolt
51 Extension piece) Alternator
52 Bracket) attachment
53 Bolt)
54 Packing piece) Alternator
55 Distance tube) attachment
56 Nyloc nut)
57 Cylinder block
58 Gasket
59 Cylinder head
60 Gasket
61 Rocker cover
62 Dipstickl
63 Lifting eye - front
64 Bolt
65 Lifting eye - rear
66 Bolt
67 Bolt
68 Mounting bracket
69 Engine mounting rubber
70 Nut
71 Bolt
72 Lock-tab) Fan
73 Plain washer) attachment
74 Rubber bush)
75 Cooling fan
76 Steel bush) Fan
77 Rubber bush) attachment
78 Piston
79 Oil control ring (comprising two scraper rings and one expander)
80 Tapered compression ring
81 Plain compression ring
82 Rocker shaft assembly
83 Split pin - rocker shaft
84 Split collets
85 Collar
86 Spring
87 Lower collar
88 Inlet valve
89 Tappet
90 Push rod
91 Split collets
92 Inner collar (exhaust)
93 Outer collar (exhaust)
94 Spring
95 Lower collar
96 Exhaust valve
97 Push rod
98 Tappet
99 Distributor and oil pump drive gear
100 Bolt - flywheel attachment
101 Flywheel
102 Spigot bush
103 Locating dowel
104 Inner rotor and spindle - oil pump
105 Outer rotor - oil pump
106 Crankshaft
107 Shim
108 Sprocket
109 Flinger
110 Seal extension
111 Crankshaft pulley
112 Locating dowels
113 Crankshaft extension
114 Bolt
115 Woodruffe key
116 Timing chain
117 Bolts and lock-plate
118 Camshaft sprocket
119 Bolt
120 Keeper plate
121 Camshaft
122 Bolt
123 Con-rod cap
124 Con-rod bearing shell - lower
125 Con-rod bearing shell - upper
126 Con-rod
127 Dowels
128 Circlip
129 Gudgeon pin
130 Gudgeon pin bush
131 Circlip

7 The cylinder head can now be removed by lifting upwards. If the head is jammed, try to rock it to break the seal. Under no circumstances try to prise it apart from the block with a screwdriver or cold chisel as damage may be done to the faces of the head or block. If the head will not readily free, turn the engine over by the front pulley bolt and ring spanner or by the flywheel as the compression in the cylinders will often break the cylinder head joint. If this fails to work, strike the head sharply with a plastic headed hammer, or with a wooden hammer, or with a metal hammer with an interposed piece of wood to cushion the blows. Under no circumstances hit the head directly with a metal hammer as this may cause the casting to fracture. Several sharp taps with the hammer at the same time pulling upwards should free the head. Lift off the head and place onto one side (photo).

11 Cylinder head removal - engine in car

To remove the cylinder head with the engine still in the car the following procedure should be adhered to:-

1 Disconnect the battery by removing the lead from the negative terminal.

2 Drain the water from the cooling system by turning the taps at the base of the radiator, and at the bottom left hand corner of the cylinder block.

3 Slacken the alternator mounting bolts and push towards the engine. Lift the fan belt from the water pump pulley.

4 Release the electrical cable connection from the water temperature gauge transmitter located in the side of the water pump body.

5 Disconnect the top, by-pass and bottom hoses and if the car is fitted with a heater disconnect the return pipe at the rear of the pump body.

6 Remove the water pump retaining bolts. It will be noted that the top right bolt also acts as a mounting for the adjusting bracket for the alternator. Observe also that all three bolts are of different lengths and it is important that they are replaced in their original positions.

7 Lift away the water pump from the front face of the cylinder block followed by the gasket.

8 Disconnect the fuel feed pipe and spill pipe from the petrol injection fuel metering unit. The end of the fuel feed pipe should be plugged using a piece of tapered wood or a pencil to stop petrol running from the fuel tank.

9 Disconnect the cold start cable from the metering unit.

10 Undo the air manifold air filter retaining clip at the manifold. Ease the filter unit from the manifold so as to allow access to the flexible air inlet hose, disconnect the hose from the air filter and lift away the filter.

11 Disconnect the two small bore rubber hoses from the air manifold and slacken the two outer air intake rubber hose clips.

12 Remove the two nuts and bolts which secure the air manifold to its mounting bracket. Lift away the air manifold and six air intake rubber hoses.

13 Undo the air manifold mounting bracket retaining nuts situated on studs on the side of the cylinder block. Lift away the bracket.

14 Disconnect the cold start cam return spring and also the cold start and accelerator cables at the butterfly controls.

15 Undo the three rocker cover nuts and lift the pipes and cold start cable to the metering unit from the studs.

16 Disconnect the injector pipes from the injectors.

17 Undo the heater pipes from their respective connections at the rear of the cylinder head making a note of their locations for correct refitting.

18 Unscrew the three nuts securing the exhaust downpipe flange to the exhaust manifold. Separate the joint and lift away the old gasket.

19 Undo the terminal in the centre of the coil to free the H.T. lead to the distributor. Mark the spark plug leads to ensure correct refitting and remove the leads from the spark plugs.

20 Spring back the two clips holding the distributor cap and rotor arm.

Fig. 1.7. Cylinder head nut slackening and tightening sequence

10.7 Lifting cylinder head over studs

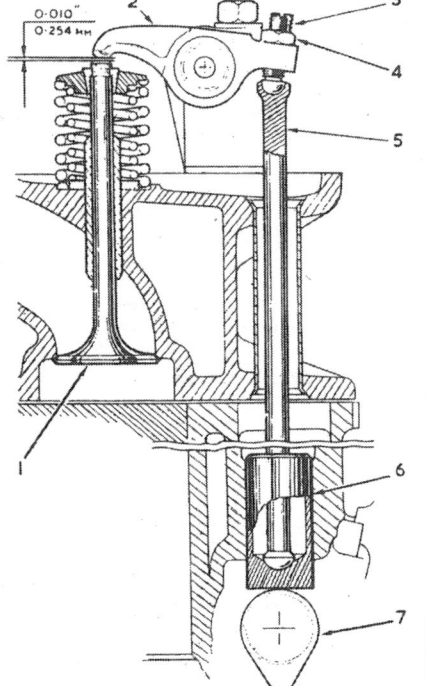

Fig. 1.9. Checking valve guide for wear

FIG. 1.8. COMPONENTS OF VALVE OPERATION SYSTEM

1 Valve	5 Push rod
2 Rocker	6 Cam follower
3 Adjuster	7 Camshaft
4 Locknut	

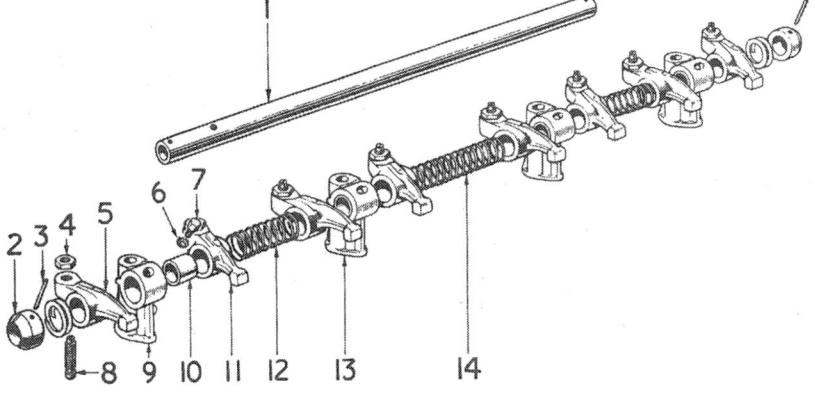

FIG. 1.10. ROCKER SHAFT PARTS

1 Rocker shaft	5 Rocker, R.H.	9 Rocker pedestal (rear)	12 Spring
2 End cap	6 Shakeproof washer	10 Rocker bush	13 Rocker pedestal
3 Pin	7 Screw	11 Rocker, L.H.	14 Spring
4 Locknut	8 Adjuster		

21 Unscrew the six bolts between the induction and exhaust manifold and lift away the bolts and special securing clamps. Undo the four remaining nuts and lift away the manifolds followed by the gaskets.

22 The procedure is now the same as for removing the cylinder head when the engine is away from the car. One tip worth noting is that should the cylinder head refuse to free easily the battery can be reconnected and the engine turned over using the sole-noid switch. Under no circumstances turn the ignition on and ensure the fuel inlet pipe is disconnected and plugged from the fuel pump.

12 Valve - removal

1 All engines covered by this manual have valves with double valve springs.

2 The valve spring retainers on all models are of the split collet type. These are removed as follows: Compress each pair of springs in turn with a valve spring compressor until the two halves of the collet can be removed. Release the compressor and remove the valve cap, upper spring seat (exhaust valve only), double valve springs and valve spring seats.

3 If, when the valve spring compressor is screwed down, the valve spring retaining cap refuses to free and expose the split collet, do not continue to screw down on the compressor as there is a likelihood of damaging it. Gently tap the top of the tool directly over the cap with a light hammer. This will free the cap. To avoid the compressor jumping off the valve spring retaining cap when it is tapped, hold the compressor firmly in position with one hand. Drop each valve out through the combustion chamber.

4 It is essential that the valves are kept in their correct sequence unless they are so badly worn that they are to be renewed. If they are going to be kept and used again, place them in a sheet of card having twelve holes numbered 1 to 12 corresponding with the relative positions the valves were in when fitted. Also keep the valve springs, washers, etc, in the correct order.

13 Valve guide - removal

To check a valve guide for wear lift insert on new valve until head is 0.5 in. (12.7 mm) above head surface and rock. If movement exceeds 0.020 in. (0.508 mm) the guide requires renewal. See also Section 42.

If it is wished to remove the valve guides they can be removed from the cylinder head in the following manner. Place the cylinder head with the gasket face on the bench and with a suitable hard steel punch drift the guides out of the cylinder head.

14 Rocker assembly - dismantling

1 To dismantle the rocker assembly, release the rocker shaft locating screw, remove the pins and caps, and spring washers from each end of the shaft and slide from the shaft the pedestals, rocker arms, and rocker spacing springs.

2 From the end of the shaft undo the plug which gives access to the inside of the rocker which can now be cleaned of sludge etc. Ensure the rocker arm lubrication holes are clear.

15 Timing cover, gears and chain - removal

The timing cover, gears and chain can be removed with the engine in the car providing the radiator and fan belt are first removed. The procedure for removing the timing cover, gears and chain is otherwise the same irrespective of whether the engine is in the car or on the bench, and is as follows:-

1 Remove the four bolts securing the fan and lift off the fan.

Remove the crankshaft end bolt and take off the fan extension, dowels and the crankshaft pulley and damper assembly.

2 The crankshaft pulley wheel may pull off quite easily. If not, place two large screwdrivers behind the pulley wheel at 180° to each other and carefully lever off the wheel. It is preferable to use a proper pulley extractor if this is available, but large screwdrivers or tyre levers are quite suitable, providing care is taken not to damage the pulley flange.

3 Remove the woodruff key from the crankshaft nose with a pair of pliers and note how the channel in the pulley is designed to fit over it. Place the woodruff key in a glass jam jar as it is a very small part and can easily become lost.

4 Unscrew the bolts holding the timing cover to the block. Note the special short screw adjacent to the crankshaft nose.

5 Pull off the timing cover and gasket. Check for chainwear by measuring how much the chain can be depressed away from a straight edge. More than 0.40 in. slack means that a new chain must be fitted on reassembly. It is always good policy, but not essential, to fit new chain wheels whenever a new chain is fitted as these are bound to be slightly worn as well.

6 With the timing cover off, take off the oil thrower. NOTE: The concave side faces the gearwheel.

7 With a drift or screwdriver tap back the tabs on the lock-washer under the two camshaft gearwheel retaining bolts and undo the bolts.

8 To remove the camshaft and crankshaft timing wheels complete with chain, ease each wheel forward a little at a time levering behind each gearwheel in turn with two large screwdrivers at 180° to each other. If the gearwheels are locked solid then it will be necessary to use a proper gearwheel and pulley extractor, and if one is available this should be used anyway in preference to a screwdriver. With both gearwheels safely off, remove the woodruff key from the crankshaft with a pair of pliers, and place them in the jam jar for safe keeping. Note the number of very thin packing washers behind the crankshaft gear-wheel and remove them very carefully.

16 Camshaft - removal

The camshaft can be removed with the engine in place in the car, or with the engine on the bench. If the camshaft is to be removed with the engine in the car, the radiator, and fan belt must be removed after the cooling system has been drained. The inlet exhaust manifolds, rocker gear, pushrods and tappets must also be removed. The timing cover, gears and chain, must be removed. It is necessary to remove the distributor drive gear. With the drive gear out of the way, proceed in the following manner:-

1 First measure the camshaft end float with a feeler gauge placed between the keeper plate and the flange. If end float exceeds 0.008in (0.2032 mm) it will be necessary to fit a new plate. Then remove the two bolts and spring washers which hold the camshaft locating plate to the block. The bolts are normally covered by the camshaft gearwheel.

2 Remove the plate. The camshaft can now be withdrawn. Take care to remove the camshaft gently, and in particular ensure that the cam peaks do not damage the camshaft bearing as the shaft is pulled forward.

17 Distributor drive - removal

1 To remove the distributor drive with the sump still in position first undo the two nuts which hold the distributor housing in place.

2 Lift off the distributor and distributor pedestal and then with a pair of pliers lift out the drive shaft. As the shaft is removed turn it slightly to allow the shaft skew gears to disengage with the camshaft skew gear.

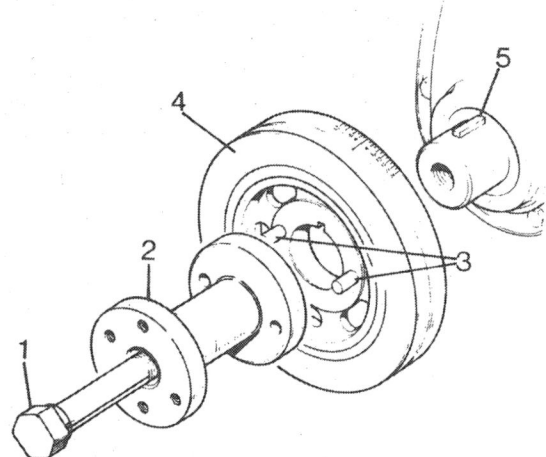

Fig. 1.11. View of engine compartment in preparation for removal of timing gear cover

Fig. 1.11a Removing the crankshaft pulley

1	Crankshaft end bolt	4	Crankshaft pulley and
2	Fan extension		damper assembly
3	Dowels	5	Key

18 Sump, piston, connecting rod and big end bearing - removal

1   The sump, pistons and connecting rods can be removed with the engine still in the car or with the engine on the bench. If in the car, proceed as for removing the cylinder head with the engine in the car. If on the bench proceed as for removing the cylinder head with the engine in this position. The pistons and connecting rods are drawn up out of the top of the cylinder bores.

2   Remove the bolts and washers holding the sump in position. Remove the sump and the sump gasket.

3   Remove the connecting rod big-end bearing cap retaining bolts.

4   Remove the big end caps one at a time, taking care to keep them in the right order and the correct way round. Also ensure that the shell bearings are kept with their correct connecting rods and caps unless they are to be renewed. Normally, the numbers 1 to 6 are stamped on adjacent sides of the big end caps and connecting rods, indicating which cap fits on which rod and which way round the cap fits. If no numbers or lines can be found then with a sharp screwdriver or file scratch mating marks across the joint from the rod to the cap. One line for connecting rod No.1, two for connecting rod No.2 and so on. This will

Fig. 1.12. Underside view of engine with sump removed

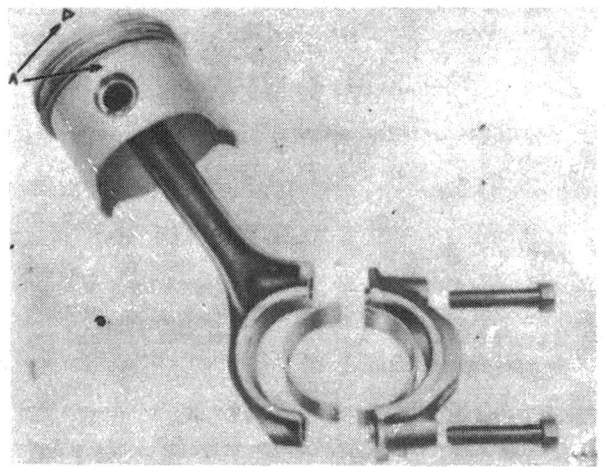

Fig. 1.13. Piston and connecting rod. Note mark 'A' which indicates front of piston

ensure there is no confusion later as it is most important that the caps go back in the correct position on the connecting rods from which they were removed.

5 If the big end caps are difficult to remove they may be gently tapped with a soft hammer.

6 To remove the shell bearings, press the bearings opposite the groove in both the connecting rod and the connecting rod caps and the bearings will slide out easily.

7 Withdraw the pistons and connecting rods upwards and ensure they are kept in the correct order for replacement in the same bore. Refit the connecting rod caps and bearings to the rods if the bearings do not require renewal, to minimise the risk of getting the caps and rods muddled.

19 Gudgeon pin - removal

1 To remove the gudgeon pin to free the piston from the connecting rod, remove one of the circlips from either end of the pin with a pair of circlip pliers.

2 Press out the pin from the rod and piston with your finger.

3 If the pin shows reluctance to move, then on no account force it out, as this could damage the piston. Immerse the piston in a pan of boiling water for three minutes. On removal the expansion of the aluminium should allow the gudgeon pin to slide out easily.

4 Make sure the pins are kept with the same piston for ease of refitting.

20 Piston ring - removal

1 To remove the piston rings, slide them carefully over the top of the piston, taking care not to scratch the aluminium alloy. Never slide them off the bottom of the piston skirt. It is very easy to break the iron piston rings if they are pulled off roughly so this operation should be done with extreme caution. It is helpful to make use of an old hacksaw blade, or better still, an old 0.020 in (0.508mm) feeler gauge.

2 Lift one end of the piston ring to be removed out of its groove and insert the end of the feeler gauge under it.

3 Turn the feeler gauge slowly round the piston and as the ring comes out of its groove apply slight upward pressure so that it rests on the land above. It can then be eased off the piston with the feeler gauge stopping it from slipping into any empty groove, if it is any but the top piston ring that is being removed.

21 Flywheel and engine end plate - removal

Having removed the clutch (see Chapter 5), the flywheel and engine end plate can be removed. It is possible for this operation to be carried out only with the engine out of the car.

1   Bend back the locking tabs from the four bolts which hold the flywheel to the flywheel flange on the rear of the crankshaft.

2   Unscrew the bolts and remove them, complete with the locking plates.

3   Lift the flywheel away from the crankshaft flange. NOTE: Some difficulty may be experienced in removing the bolts, by the rotation of the crankshaft every time pressure is put on the spanner. To lock the crankshaft in position while the bolts are removed, use a screwdriver as a wedge between a backplate stud and the ring gear. Alternatively a wooden wedge can be inserted between the crankshaft and the side of the block inside the crankcase.

4   The engine end plate is held in position by a number of bolts and spring washers of varying sizes. Release the bolts noting where different sizes fit and place them together to ensure none of them become lost. Lift away the end plate from the block complete with the paper gasket.

5   The front engine end plate is removed in identical fashion.

22 Crankshaft and main bearing - removal

With the engine out of the car, remove the timing gears, sump, oil pump and the big end bearings, pistons, flywheel and engine end plates. Removal of the crankshaft can be attempted only with the engine on the bench or floor. Take off the front sealing block and the packing pieces.

1   Undo by one turn the nuts which hold the four main bearing caps in place.

2   Unscrew the nuts and remove them together with the washers.

3   At the rear of the engine undo the seven bolts which hold the special oil retaining cover in place and remove the cover.

4   Remove the main bearing caps and the bottom half of each bearing shell, taking care to keep the bearing shells in the right caps.

5   When removing the rear bearing cap, NOTE the bottom semi-circular halves of the thrust washers, one half lying on either side of the main bearing. Lay them with the end bearing along the correct side.

6   Slightly rotate the crankshaft to free the upper halves of the bearing shells and thrust washers which should now be extracted and placed over the correct bearing cap.

7   Remove the crankshaft by lifting it away from the crankcase.

23 Lubrication and crankcase ventilation systems - description

A forced feed system of lubrication as shown in Fig. 1.15, is fitted with oil circulated round the engine from the sump below the block. The level of engine oil in the sump is indicated on the dipstick which is fitted on the left hand side of the engine. It is marked to indicate the optimum level which is the maximum mark.

The level of the oil in the sump, ideally, should not be above or below this line. Oil is replenished via the filler cap on the rocker cover.

The eccentric rotor type oil pump is bolted in the left hand side of the crankcase and is driven by a short shaft from the skew gear on the camshaft which also drives the distributor shaft.

The pump is the non-draining variety to allow rapid pressure build-up when starting from cold.

Oil is drawn into the pump from the sump via the pick-up pipe. From the oil pump the lubricant passes through a non-adjustable relief valve to the by-pass (early models only) or full flow filter. Filtered oil enters the main gallery which runs the length of the engine on the left hand side. Drillings from the main gallery carry the oil to the crankshaft journals.

The crankshaft is drilled so that oil under pressure reaches the crankpins from the crankshaft journals. The cylinder bores, pistons and gudgeon pins are all lubricated by splash and oil mist.

Oil is fed to the valve gear via the hollow rocker shaft at a

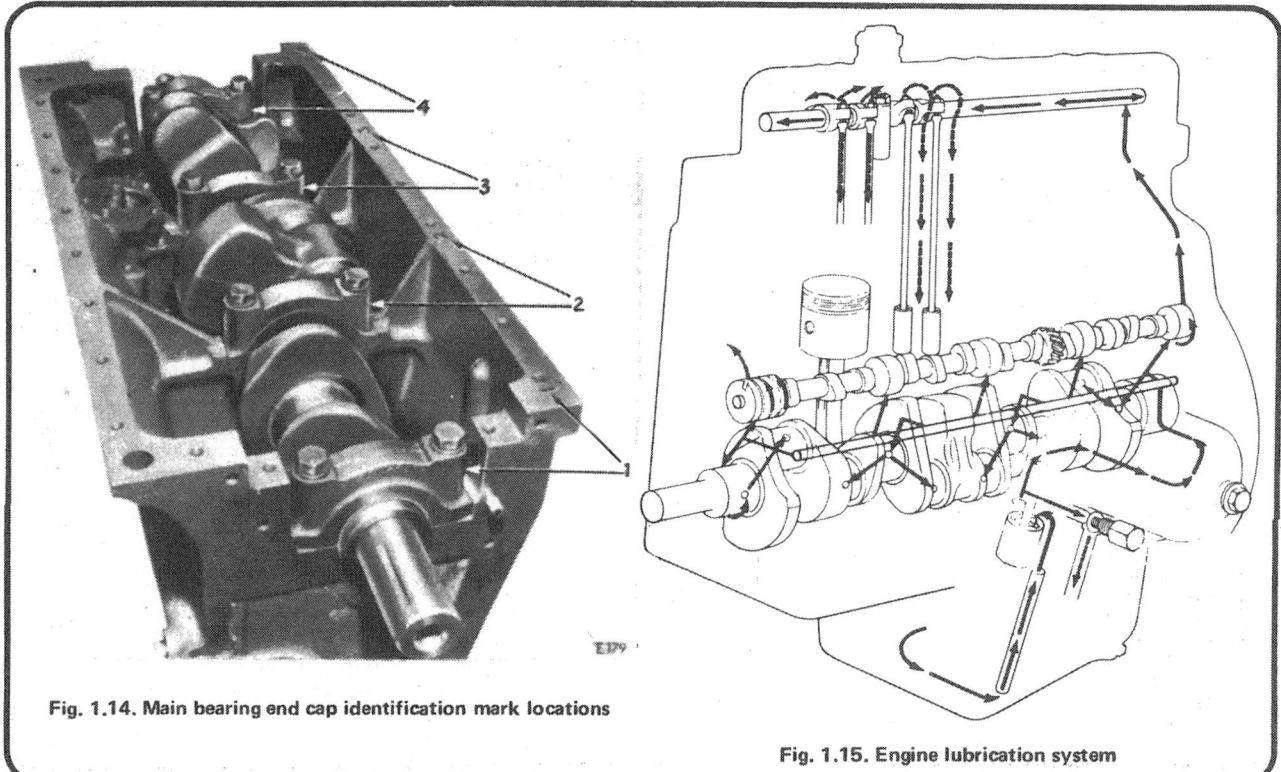

Fig. 1.14. Main bearing end cap identification mark locations

Fig. 1.15. Engine lubrication system

reduced pressure by means of a scroll and two flats on the camshaft rear journal.

Drillings and grooves in the camshaft front journal lubricate the camshaft thrust plate, and the timing chain and gearwheels. Oil returns to the sump by gravity, the pushrods and cam followers being lubricated by oil returning via the pushrod drillings in the block.

Any one of three types of crankcase ventilation system may be fitted depending on the model and its year of manufacture. The three systems are known as 'Open Ventilation', 'Closed Ventilation', and 'Emission Control'.

'Open Ventilation' is very straightforward and is fitted only to early models. It comprises an open angled tube fitted on the right hand side of the engine which relieves crankcase pressure directly into the air.

'Closed Ventilation' is a slightly more sophisticated system with crankcase pressure being relieved by means of a rubber pipe from the rocker cover to the air cleaner. The hole for the open road tube is blocked over and the possibility of crankcase fumes entering the car is considerably reduced.

'Emission Control' is similar to 'Closed Ventilation' but more efficient and complicated. An emission control valve is positioned on top of the inlet manifold to which it is connected. It is also connected to a tube from the rocker cover. The control valve works by manifold depression so that when the depression is greatest (i.e. on the overrun) crankcase gas flow is restricted. A special oil filler cap is also used and this contains a non-return valve which ensures that the crankcase and atmospheric pressures are kept in balance.

24 Oil filter - removal and replacement

1 It is easy to change the oil filter on all models.

2 It is located on the left hand side of the engine towards the rear. Unscrew the filter centre bolt and with a rag under the filter to catch spilled oil, withdraw the whole filter assembly.

3 Throw away the filter element and with a clean non-fluffy rag thoroughly clean the filter bowl.

4 Remove the rubber sealing ring that goes between the lip of the filter bowl and the crankcase and replace it with the new sealing ring that is always provided with a new filter element.

5 Place the new filter element in the bowl and reassemble the filter assembly to the crankcase.

6 Carefully check that the lip of the bowl is properly seated in the groove and that the rubber sealing ring is correctly in place before finally tightening down the centre bolt.

25 Oil pressure relief valve - removal and replacement

1 To prevent excessive oil pressure - for example when the engine is cold - an oil pressure relief valve is built into the left hand side of the engine immediately above the crankcase flange and in line vertically with the distributor.

2 The relief valve assembly is dismantled by undoing the large hexagonal headed bolt which holds the relief valve piston and spring in place.

3 Always renew the spring at a major overhaul. To replace the assembly, fit the valve piston into its orifice in the block, then the spring and then the bolt, ensuring that the sealing washer is in place on the latter.

26 Oil pump - removal

1 Undo the three bolts and spring washers which hold the pump to the block.

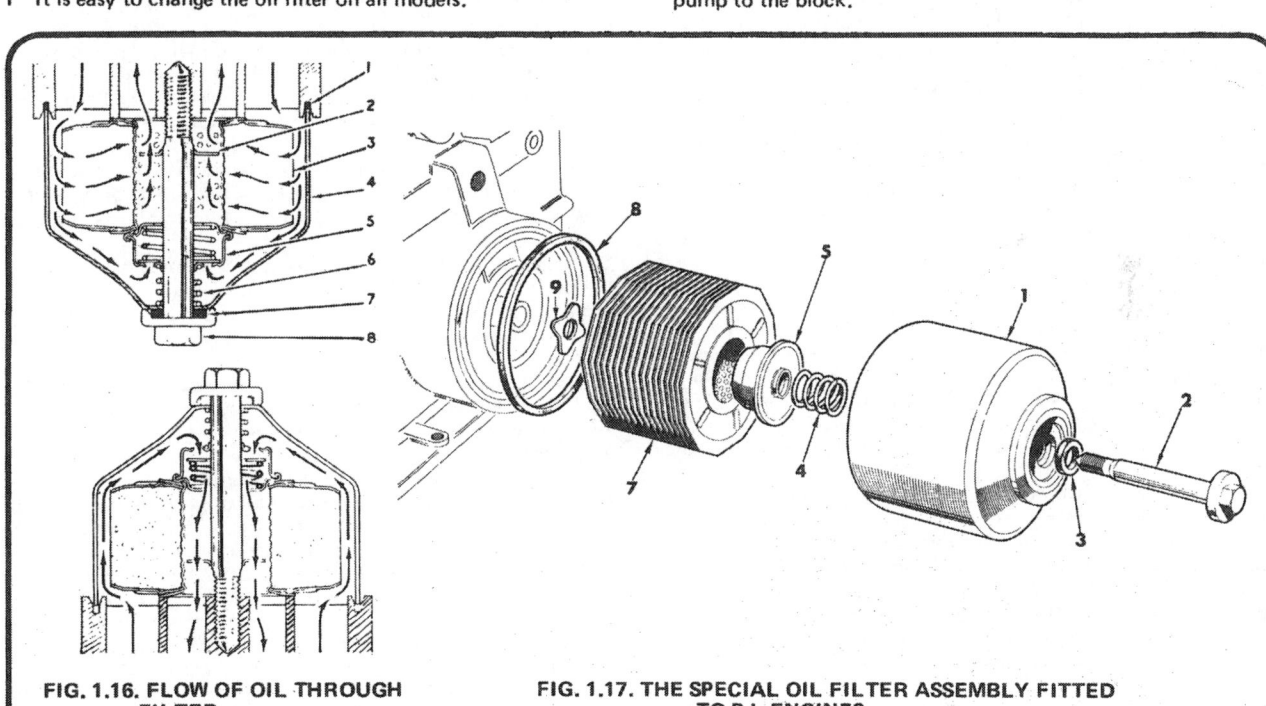

FIG. 1.16. FLOW OF OIL THROUGH FILTER

1 Rubber seal
2 Locating washer
3 Filter element
4 Container
5 Relief valve
6 Spring
7 Seal
8 Securing bolt

FIG. 1.17. THE SPECIAL OIL FILTER ASSEMBLY FITTED TO P.I. ENGINES

1 Shell assembly
2 Centre bolt
3 Seal
4 Spring
5 Valve
7 Filter element
8 Sealing ring
9 Centraliser

2 Removal of the bolts also releases the end cover so the pump can be taken from the engine and the outer and inner rotors pulled off together with the pump shaft.

27 Timing chain tensioner - removal and replacement

1 With time the spring blade timing chain tensioner will become worn and it should be renewed at the same time as the timing chain. Wear can be clearly seen as two grooves on the face of the tensioner where it presses against the chain.
2 To remove the tensioner bend it back and then pull out from its securing pins.
3 On replacement fit the open end of the tensioner over the pin and press the blade into place with the aid of a screwdriver until it snaps into place.

28 Examination and renovation-general

With the engine stripped down and all parts thoroughly cleaned, it is now time to examine everything for wear. The following items should be checked and where necessary renewed or renovated as described in the following sections:-

29 Crankshaft - examination and renovation

1 Examine the crankpin and main journal surfaces for signs of scoring or scratches. Check the ovality of the crankpins at different positions with a micrometer. If more than 0.001 in (0.0254mm) out of round, the crankpin will have to be reground. It will also have to be reground if there are any scores or scratches present. Also check the journals in the same fashion.
2 On highly tuned engines the centre main bearings have been known to break up. This is not always immediately apparent, but slight vibration in an otherwise normally smooth engine and a very slight drop in oil pressure under normal conditions are clues. If the centre main bearings are suspected of failure it should be immediately investigated by dropping the sump and removing the centre main bearing caps. Failure to do this will result in badly scored centre main journals. If it is necessary to regrind the crankshaft and fit new bearings, your local Triumph garage or engineering works will be able to decide how much metal to grind off and the correct undersize shells to fit.

30 Big end and main bearings - examination and renovation

1 Big end bearing failure is accompanied by a noisy knocking from the crankcase, and a slight drop in oil pressure. Main bearings failure is accompanied by vibration which can be quite severe as the engine speed rises and falls and a drop in oil pressure.
2 Bearings which have not broken up, but are badly worn will give rise to low oil pressure and some vibration. Inspect the big ends, main bearings, and thrust washers for signs of general wear, scoring, pitting and scratches. The bearings should be matt grey in colour. With lead-indium bearings, should a trace of copper colour be noticed, the bearings are badly worn as the lead bearing material has worn away to expose the indium underlay. Renew the bearings if they are in this condition or if there is any sign of scoring or pitting.
3 The undersizes available are designed to correspond with the regrind sizes, i.e. 0.010 in (0.0254mm) bearings are correct for a crankshaft reground -0.010 in (0.0254mm) undersize. The bearings are in fact, slightly more than the stated undersize as running clearances have been allowed for during their manufacture.
4 Very long engine life can be achieved by changing big end bearings at intervals of 30,000 miles (48,000Km) and main bearings at intervals of 50,000 miles (80,000Km) irrespective of bearing wear. Normally, crankshaft wear is infinitesimal and a

change of bearings will ensure mileages of between 100,000 to 120,000 miles (160,000 to 192,000Km) before crankshaft regrinding becomes necessary. Crankshafts normally have to be reground because of scoring due to bearing failure.

31 Cylinder bores - examination and renovation

1 The cylinder bores must be examined for taper, ovality, scoring and scratches. Start by carefully examining the top of the cylinder bores. If they are at all worn a very slight ridge will be found on the thrust side. This marks the top of the piston ring travel. The owner will have a good indication of the bore wear prior to dismantling the engine , or removing the cylinder head. Excessive oil consumption accompanied by blue smoke from the exhaust is a sure sign of worn cylinder bores and piston rings.
2 Measure the bore diameter just under the ridge with a micrometer and compare it with the diameter at the bottom of the bore, which is not subject to wear. If the difference between the two measurements is more than .006 inch then it will be necessary to fit special pistons and rings or to have the cylinders rebored and fit oversize pistons. If no micrometer is available remove the rings from a piston and place the piston in each bore in turn about 0.75 in (19.05 mm) below the top of the bore. If an 0.010 in (0.254 mm) feeler gauge can be slid between the piston and the cylinder wall on the thrust side of the bore then remedial action must be taken. Oversize pistons +0.020 in (.508 mm) are available and oversize rings in the following sizes:-
    +0.010 inch (0.254 mm)   +0.020 inch (0.508 mm)
    +0.030 inch (0.762 mm)
3 The oversize pistons are accurately machined to just below +.020 in (0.508mm) so as to provide correct running clearances in bores bored out to the exact oversize dimensions.
4 If the bores are slightly worn but not so badly worn as to justify reboring them, then special oil control rings and pistons can be fitted which will restore compression and stop the engine burning oil. Several different types are available and the manufacturers instructions concerning their fitting must be followed closely.
5 If the block is to be sent away for reboring it is essential to remove the cylinder head studs. Lock two nuts together on a stud and then wind the stud out by turning the bottom nut anti-clockwise.
6 If new pistons are being fitted and the bores have not been reground, it is essential to slightly roughen the hard glaze on the sides of the bores with fine glass paper so the new piston rings will have a chance to bed in properly.

32 Pistons and piston rings - examination and renovation

1 If the old pistons are to be refitted, carefully remove the piston rings and then thoroughly clean them. Take particular care to clean out the piston ring grooves. At the same time do not scratch the aluminium in any way. If new rings are to be fitted to the old pistons then the top ring should be stepped so as to clear the ridge left in the bore above the previous top ring. If a normal but oversize new ring is fitted, it will hit the ridge and break, because the new ring will not have worn in the same way as the old, which will have worn in unison with the ridge.
2 Before fitting the rings on the pistons each should be inserted approximately 3 in (76.2mm) down the cylinder bore and the gap measured with a feeler gauge. This should be between 0.015 in (0.381 mm) and 0.038 in (0.9652 mm). It is essential that the gap should be measured at the bottom of the ring travel, as if it is measured at the top of a worn bore and gives a perfect fit, it could easily seize at the bottom. If the ring gap is too small rub down the ends of the ring with a very fine file until the gap, when fitted, is correct. To keep the rings square in the bore for measurement line each up in turn by inserting an old piston in the bore upside down about 3 in (76.2mm). Remove the piston and measure the piston ring gap.

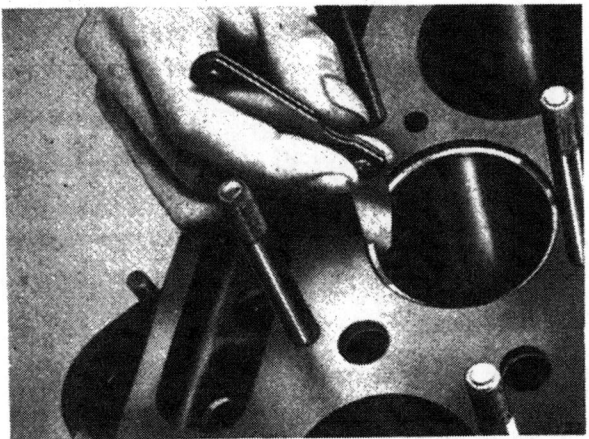

Fig. 1.18. Checking piston ring gap with feeler gauge

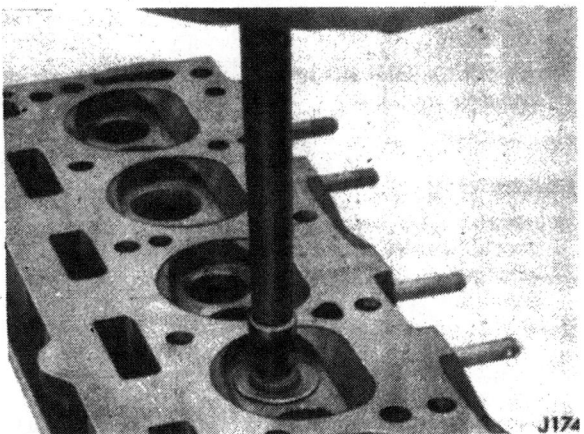

Fig. 1.19. Grinding valve seats using hand tool

3 When fitting new pistons and rings to a rebored engine the piston ring gap can be measured at the top of the bore as the bore will not now taper. It is unnecessary to measure the side clearance in the piston ring grooves with the rings fitted as the groove dimensions are accurately machined during manufacture. When fitting new oil control rings to old pistons it may be necessary to have the grooves widened by machining to accept the new wider rings. In this instance the manufacturers representative will make this quite clear and will supply the address to which the pistons must be sent for machining.

33 Camshaft and camshaft bearings - examination and renovation

1 On all engines the camshaft bearings are machined directly into the block and consequently are not replaceable.
2 The camshaft itself should show no signs of wear, but, if very slight scoring on the cams is noticed, the score marks can be removed by very gently rubbing with a very fine emery cloth. The greatest care should be taken to keep the cam profiles smooth.

34 Valves and valve seats - examination and renovation

1 Examine the heads of the valves for pitting and burning, especially the heads of the exhaust valves. The valve seating should be examined at the same time. If the pitting on valve and seat is very slight the marks can be removed by grinding the seats and valves together with coarse, and then fine, valve grinding paste. Where bad pitting has occured to the valve seats it will be necessary to recut them and fit new valves. If the valve seats are so worn that they cannot be recut, then it will be necessary to fit new valve seat inserts. These latter two jobs should be entrusted to the local Triumph agent or engineering works. In practice it is very seldom that the seats are so badly worn that they require renewal. Normally, it is the exhaust valve that is too badly worn for replacement, and the owner can easily purchase a new set of valves and match them to the seats by valve grinding.
2 Valve grinding is carried out as follows:-
   Smear a trace of coarse carborundum paste on the seat face and apply a suction grinder tool to the valve head. With a semi-rotary motion, grind the valve head to its seat, lifting the valve occasionally to re-distribute the grinding paste. When a dull matt even surface finish is produced on both the valve seat and the valve, wipe off the paste and repeat the process with fine carborundum paste, lifting and turning the valve to re-distribute the paste as before. A light spring placed under the valve head will greatly ease this operation. When a smooth, unbroken ring

of light grey matt finish is produced, on both valve and valve seat faces, the grinding operation is completed.
3 Scrape away all carbon from the valve head and the valve stem. Carefully clean away every trace of grinding compound, taking great care to leave none in the ports or in the valve guides. Clean the valves and valve seats with a paraffin soaked rag, then with a clean rag, and finally, if an air line is available, blow the valves, valve guides and valve ports clean.

35 Timing gears and chain - examination and renovation

1 Examine the teeth on both the crankshaft gearwheel and the camshaft gearwheel for wear. Each tooth forms an inverted 'V' with the gearwheel periphery, and if worn, the side of each tooth under tension will be slightly concave in shape, when compared with the other side of the tooth, i.e. one side of the inverted 'V' will be concave when compared with the other. If any sign of wear is present the gearwheels must be renewed.
2 Examine the links of the chain for side slackness and renew the chain if any slackness is noticeable when compared with a new chain. It is a sensible precaution to renew the chain at about 30,000 miles (48,000 Km) and at a lesser mileage if the engine is stripped down for a major overhaul. The actual rollers on a very badly worn chain may be slightly grooved.

36 Timing chain tensioner - examination and renovation

1 If the timing chain is badly worn it is more than likely that the tensioner will be too.
2 Examine the side of the tensioner which bears against the chain and renew if it is grooved or ridged. See Section 35 for details.

37 Rockers and rocker shaft - examination and renovation

1 Withdraw the cotter pins from the rocker shaft ends holding the end caps in place. Slide off the rockers, pedestals and springs from the front end of the shaft noting carefully the order in which they are removed. Remove the Phillips screw holding the rear pedestal to the shaft and withdraw the rear pedestal and rocker. Thoroughly clean out the shaft as its acts as the oil passage for the valve gear, also ensure that the oil holes in it are quite clean after having cleaned them out. Check the shaft for straightness by rolling it on the bench.
2 It is most unlikely that it will deviate from normal, but, if it does, then a judicious attempt must be made to straighten it. If this is not successful purchase a new shaft. The surface of the

shaft should be free from any worn ridges caused by the rocker arms. If any wear is present, renew the shaft. Wear is likely to have occured only if the rocker shaft oil holes have become blocked.

3   Check the rocker arms for wear of the rocker bushes; for wear at the rocker arm face which bears on the valve stem; and for wear of the adjusting ball ended screws. Wear in the rocker arm bush can be checked by gripping the rocker arm tip and holding the rocker arm in place on the shaft, noting if there is any lateral rocker arm shake. If shake is present, and the arm is very loose on the shaft, a new bush or rocker arm must be fitted.

4   Check the tip of the rocker arm where it bears on the valve head for cracking or serious wear on the case hardening. If none is present re-use the rocker arm. Check the lower half of the ball on the end of the rocker arm adjusting screw. On high performance engines wear on the ball and top of the pushrod is easily noted by the unworn 'pip' which fits in the small central oil hole on the ball. The larger this 'pip' the more wear has taken place to both the ball and the pushrod. Check the pushrods for straightness by rolling them on the bench. Renew any that are bent.

38 Tappets - examination and renovation

1   Examine the bearing surface of the tappets which lie on the camshaft. Any indentation in the surface or any cracks indicate serious wear and the tappets should be renewed.

2   Thoroughly clean them out, removing all traces of sludge. It is most unlikely that the sides of the tappets will prove worn, but, if they are a very loose fit in their bores and can readily be rocked, they should be exchanged for new units. It is very unusual to find any wear in the tappets, and any wear present is likely to occur only at very high mileages.

39 Flywheel starter ring - examination and renovation

1   If the teeth on the flywheel starter ring are badly worn, or if some are missing, then it will be necessary to remove the ring. This is achieved by splitting the ring with a cold chisel. The greatest care should be taken not to damage the flywheel during this process.

2   To fit a new ring heat it gently and evenly with an oxyacetylene flame until a temperature of approximately 350° C is reached. This is indicated by a light metallic blue surface colour. With the ring at this temperature, fit it to the flywheel with the front of the teeth facing the flywheel register. The ring should be tapped gently down onto its register and left to cool naturally when the shrinkage of the metal on cooling will ensure that it is a secure and permanent fit. Great care must be taken not to overheat the ring, as if this happens the temper of the ring will be lost.

40 Oil pump - examination and renovation

1   Thoroughly clean all the component parts in petrol and then check the rotor endfloat and lobe clearances in the following manner:-

2   Position the rotors in the pump and place the straight edge of a steel ruler across the joint face of the pump. Measure the gap between the bottom of the straight edge and the top of the rotors with a feeler gauge as in Fig. 1.21. If the measurement exceeds 0.004 in (0.102 mm) then check the lobe clearances as described in the following paragraphs. If the lobe clearances are correct then lap the joint face on a sheet of plate glass.

3   Measure with a feeler gauge the gap between the inner and outer rotors. It should not be more than 0.004 in (0.102 mm).

4   Then measure the gap between the outer rotor and the side of the pump body which should not exceed 0.010 in (0.254 mm). It is essential to renew the pump if the measurements are outside these figures. It can be safely assumed that any major

reconditioning indicates that the pump will need renewal.

41 Cylinder head - decarbonisation

1   This can be carried out with the engine either in or out of the car. With the cylinder head off, carefully remove with a wire brush and blunt scraper all traces of carbon deposits from the combustion spaces and the ports. The valve head stems and valve guides should also be freed from any carbon deposits. Wash the combustion spaces and ports down with petrol and scrape the cylinder head surface free of any foreign matter with the side of a steel rule, or a similar article.

2   Clean the pistons and top of the cylinder bores. If the pistons are still in the block it is essential that great care is taken to ensure that no carbon gets into the cylinder bores as this could scratch the cylinder walls or cause damage to the piston rings. To ensure that this does not happen, first turn the crankshaft so that two of the pistons are at the top of their bores. Stuff rag into the other two bores or seal them off with paper and masking tape. The waterways should also be covered with small pieces of masking tape to prevent particles of carbon entering the cooling system and damaging the water pump.

3   There are two schools of thought as to how much carbon should be removed from the piston crown. One school recommends that a ring of carbon should be left round the edge of the piston and on the cylinder bore wall as an aid to low oil consumption. Although this is probably true for early engines with worn bores, on later engines the thought of the second school can be applied, which is that for effective decarbonisation all traces of carbon should be removed.

4   If all traces of carbon are to be removed, press a little grease into the gap between the cylinder walls and the two pistons which are to be worked on. With a blunt scraper carefully scrape away the carbon from the piston crown, taking care not to scratch the aluminium. Also scrape away the carbon from the surrounding lip of the cylinder wall. When all carbon has been removed, scrape away the grease which will now be contaminated with carbon particles, taking care not to press any into the bores. To assist prevention of carbon build-up the piston crown can be polished with a metal polish so that the two pistons which were at the bottom are now at the top. Place rag or masking tape in the cylinders which have been decarbonised and proceed as just described.

5   If a ring of carbon is going to be left round the piston then this can be helped by inserting an old piston ring into the top of the bore to rest on the piston and ensure that carbon is not accidentally removed. Check that there are no particles of carbon in the cylinder bores. Decarbonising is now complete.

42 Valve guides - examination and renovation

Examine the valve guides internally for wear. If the valves are a very loose fit in the guides and there is the slightest suspicion of lateral rocking using a new valve, then new guides will have to be fitted. If the valve guides have been removed, compare them internally by visual inspection with a new guide as well as testing them for rocking with a new valve. See also Section 13.

43 Sump - examination and renovation

1   It is essential to thoroughly wash out the sump with petrol and this can be done properly only with the gauze removed.

2   With a screwdriver and a pair of pliers carefully pull back the tags which hold the gauze in place.

3   The gauze can then be lifted out and the inside cleaned out properly. Scrape all traces of the old sump gasket from the flange.

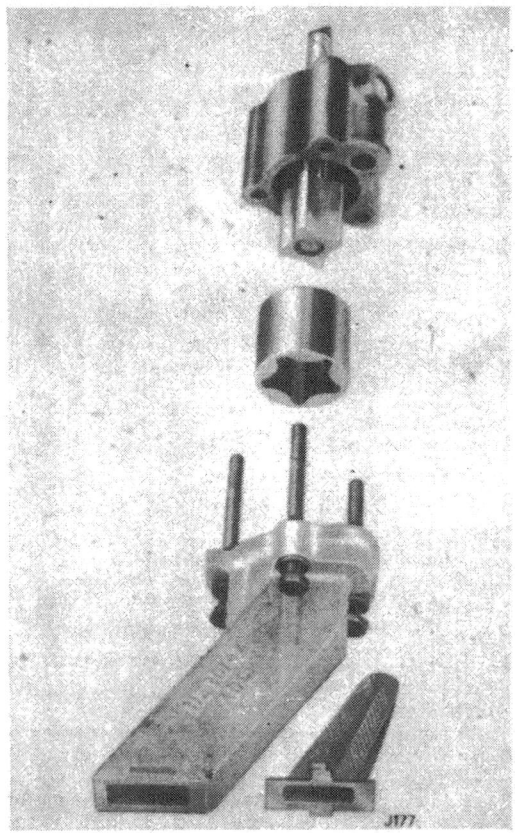

Fig. 1.20. Oil pump components

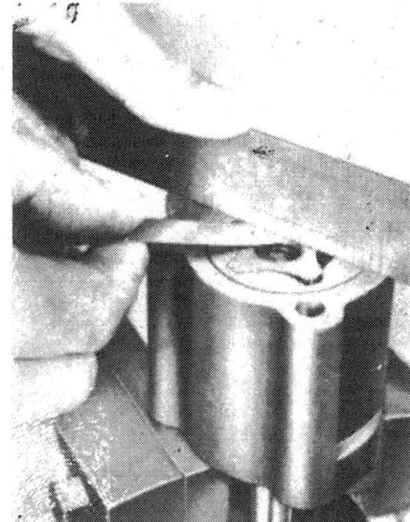

Fig. 1.21. Checking rotor end clearance which should not exceed 0.004 in (0.102 mm)

Fig. 1.22. Checking clearance between inner and outer rotors which should not exceed 0.004 in (0.102 mm)

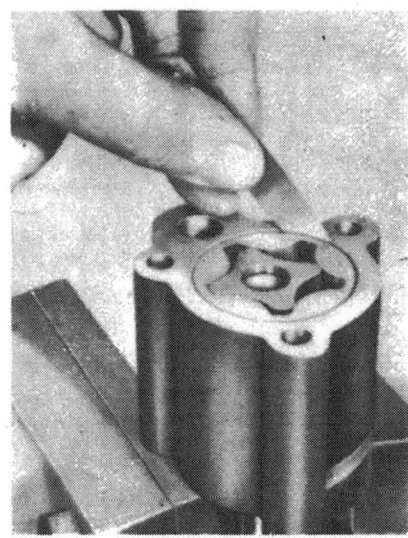

Fig. 1.23. Checking clearance between outer rotor and body. This should not exceed 0.010 in (0.254 mm)

44 Engine reassembly - general

1 To ensure maximum life with minimum trouble from a rebuilt engine, not only must everything be correctly assembled, but all the parts must be spotlessly clean; all the oilways must be clear; locking washers and spring washers must always be fitted where indicated; and all bearing and other working surfaces must be thoroughly lubricated during assembly. Before assembly begins renew any bolts or studs the threads of which are in any way damaged, and whenever possible use a new spring washer.

2 Check the core plugs for signs of weeping and always renew the plug at the front of the engine as it is normally covered by the engine endplate.

3 Drive a punch through the centre of the core plugs.

4 Using the punch as a lever lift out the old core plugs one at a time.

5 Thoroughly clean the core plug orifices and using a thin headed hammer as an expander firmly tap new core plugs into place, convex side facing out.

6 Apart from your normal tools, a supply of clean rag; an oil can filled with engine oil (an empty plastic detergent bottle thoroughly cleaned and washed out, will invariably do just as well); a new supply of assorted spring washers; a set of new gaskets; and preferably a torque spanner, should be collected together.

45 Crankshaft - replacement

Ensure that the crankcase is thoroughly clean and that all oilways are clean. A thin twist drill or a pipe cleaner is useful for cleaning them out. If possible blow them out with compressed air.

Treat the crankshaft in the same fashion, and then inject engine oil into the crankshaft oilways.

Commence work on rebuilding the engine by removing the crankshaft and main bearings:-

1 If the old main bearing shells are to be replaced, (not to do so is a false economy unless they are virtually new), fit the four upper halves of the main bearing shells to their location in the crankcase, after wiping the locations clean.

2 NOTE: At the back of each bearing is a tab which engages in locating grooves in either the crankcase or the main bearing cap housings.

3 If new bearings are being fitted, carefully clean away all traces of protective grease with which they are coated.

4 With the four upper bearing shells securely in place, wipe the lower bearing cap housings and fit the four lower shell bearings to their caps ensuring that the right shell goes into the right cap if the old bearings are to refitted.

5 Wipe the recesses either side of the main bearing which locate the thrust washers.

6 Generously lubricate the crankshaft journals and the upper and lower main bearing shells and carefully lower the crankshaft into place (photo).

7 Fit the upper halves of the thrust washers into their grooves either side of the rear main bearings, as shown in Fig. 1.24.

8 Rotate the crankshaft in the direction towards the main bearing tabs (so that the main bearing shells do not slide out). At the same time feed the thrust washers into their locations with their oil grooves outwards away from the bearing (photo).

9 Fit the main bearing caps in position ensuring they locate properly. The mating surfaces must be spotlessly clean or the caps will not seat correctly (photo). As the bearing caps are assembled to the cylinder block and the line bored during manufacture, it is essential that they are returned to the same positions from which they were removed.

10 Refit the main bearing cap bolts and locking tabs (if fitted) or spring washers (photo).

11 Tighten the bolts to a torque wrench setting of 55 lb ft (7 . 6 Kg Fm) (photo).

12 Test the crankshaft for freedom of rotation. Should it be

Fig.1.24   Fitting thrust washers to crankshaft.

very stiff to turn or possess high spots a most careful inspection must be made, preferably by a qualified mechanic with a micrometer to get to the cause of the trouble. It is very seldom that any trouble of this nature will be experienced when fitting the crankshaft.

13 Check the crankshaft end float with a feeler gauge measuring the longitudinal movement between the crankshaft and a thrust washer (photo). End float should be between 0.004 in and 0.008 in (0.1016 and 0.2032 mm). If end float is excessive, oversize thrust washers can be fitted.

14 Fit the gasket between the front main bearing cap and sealing block. Next smear the end faces of the sealing block with jointing compound and fit the block in place (photo A). Fit the securing screws but do not tighten fully. Fit new wedge seals at each end (photo B) and line up the front face of the block to the front of the cylinder block with a straight edge. Tighten the screws fully (photo C) and cut the wedge seals flush with the crankcase flange.

46 Piston and connecting rod - reassembly

1 If the same pistons are being used, then they must be mated to the same connecting rod with the same gudgeon pin. If new pistons are being fitted it does not matter which connecting rod they are used with, but, the gudgeon pins should be fitted on the basis of selective assembly.

2 All engines use fully floating gudgeon pins which in theory are a push fit at 68°F (20°C) but this is not always as simple as it seems.

3 Because aluminium alloy, when hot, expands more than steel, the gudgeon pin may be a very tight fit in the piston when they are cold. To avoid any damage to the piston it is best to heat it in boiling water when the pin will slide in easily.

4 Lay the correct piston adjacent to each connecting rod and remember that the same rod and piston must go back into the same bore. If new pistons are being used it is necessary to ensure only that the right connecting rod is placed in each bore.

5 Fit a gudgeon pin circlip in position at one end of the gudgeon pin hole in the piston.

6 Locate the connecting rod in the piston with the marking 'FRONT' on the piston crown towards the front of the engine, i.e. the timing cover end, and the connecting rod cap towards the camshaft side of the engine (see Fig. 1.13).

7 Slide the gudgeon pin in through the hole in the piston and through the connecting rod little end until it rests against the previously fitted circlip (photo). NOTE: The pin should be a push fit.

8 Fit the second circlip in position (photo). Repeat this procedure for all six pistons and connecting rods.

45.6 Lowering crankshaft into position

45.8 Fitting thrust washer to rear bearing

45.9 Fitting rear main bearing end cap

45.10 Main bearing cap bolts fitted

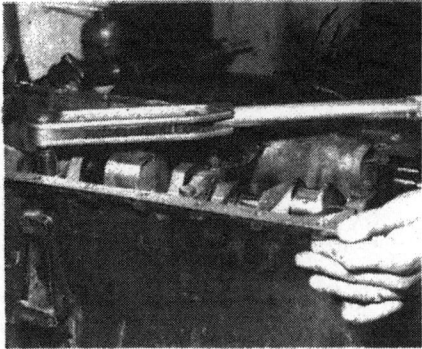
45.11 Tightening main bearing cap bolts with torque wrench

45.13 Checking crankshaft end float

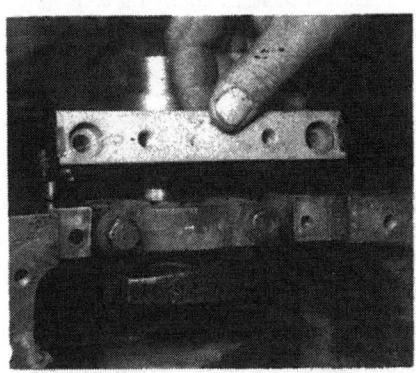
45.14a Fitting sealing block over front main bearing cap

45.14b Fitting new wedge seals

45.14c Tightening sealing block screws fully

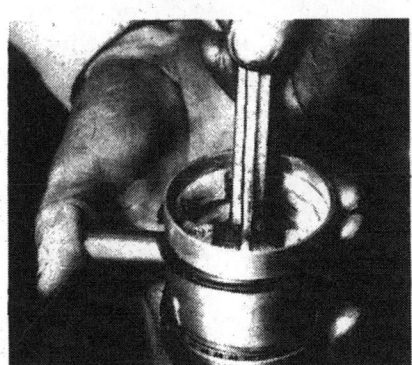
46.7 Refitting gudgeon pin

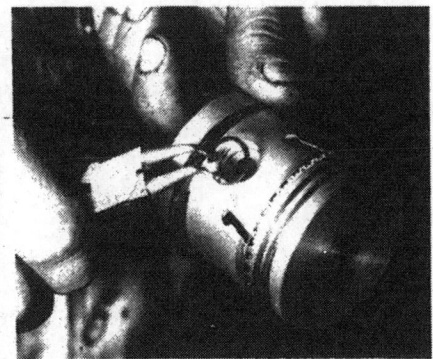
46.8 Securing gudgeon pin with second circlip

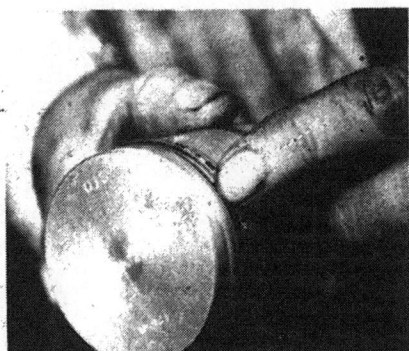
46.9 Checking fit of piston rings

9 Where special oil control piston rings are being fitted, should
position of the top ring be the same as the position of the
top ring on the old piston, ensure that a groove has been
machined on the top of the new ring so no fouling occurs
between the unworn portion at the top of the bore and the
piston ring when the latter is at the top of its stroke (photo).

47 Piston ring - replacement

1 Check that the piston ring grooves and oilways are thoroughly clean and unblocked. Piston rings must always be fitted
over the head of the piston and never from the bottom.
2 The easiest method to use when fitting rings is to wrap a
0.020 in (0.508 mm) feeler gauge round the top of the piston
and place the rings one at a time, starting with the bottom oil
control ring, over the feeler gauge.
3 The feeler gauge, complete with ring, can then be slid down
the piston over the other piston ring grooves until the correct
groove is reached. The piston ring is then slid gently off the
feeler gauge into the groove.
4 An alternative method is to fit the rings by holding them
slightly open with the thumbs and both of the index fingers.
This method requires a steady hand and great care as it is easy to
open the ring too much and break it.

48 Piston - replacement

The pistons, complete with connecting rods, can be fitted to
the cylinder bores in the following sequence:-
1 With a wad of clean rag wipe the cylinder bores clean.
2 The pistons, complete with connecting rods, are fitted to
their bores from the top of the block (photo). Note that in the
photographs special oil control pistons are being fitted.
3 As each piston is inserted into its bore ensure that it is the
correct piston/connecting rod assembly for that particular bore;
that the connecting rod is the right way round; and that the
front of the piston is towards the front of the bore, i.e. towards
the front of the engine.
4 The piston will slide into the bore only as far as the oil
control ring. It is then necessary to compress the piston rings
into a clamp (photo) and to gently tap the piston into the
cylinder bore with a wooden or plastic hammer. If a proper
piston ring clamp is not available then a suitable jubilee clip does
the job very well.

49 Connecting rod to crankshaft reassembly

1 Wipe clean the connecting rod, half of the big end bearing
cap and the underside of the shell bearing, and fit the shell
bearing in position with its locating tongue engaged with the
corresponding cut out in the rod (photo).
2 If the old bearings are nearly new and are being refitted then
ensure they are replaced in their correct locations on the correct
rods. Refit the end cap locating dowels (photo).
3 Generously lubricate the crankpin journals with engine oil
(photo), and turn the crankshaft so that the crankpin is in the
most advantageous position for the connecting rods to be drawn
onto it.
4 Wipe clean the connecting rod bearing cap and back of the
shell bearing, and fit the shell bearing in position ensuring that
the locating tongue at the back of the bearing engages with the
locating groove in the connecting rod cap.
5 Generously lubricate the shell bearing and offer up the
connecting rod bearing cap to the connecting rod (photo).
6 Fit the connecting rod big-end bearing cap retaining bolts
and tighten them to a torque wrench setting of 40 lbf ft
(5.5 kgf m).
7 When all the connecting rods have been fitted, rotate the
crankshaft to check that everything is free, and that there are no
high spots causing binding. The bottom half is now nearly built
up.

50 Front end plate - reassembly

1 Fit a new gasket in place over the front of the cylinder block
(photo).
2 Lower the front end plate into place noting the hole for the
dowel (arrowed) and then fit the securing bolt (where fitted)
immediately above the crankshaft nose (photo).

51 Camshaft - replacement

1 Wipe the camshaft bearing journals clean and lubricate them
generously with engine oil.
2 Insert the camshaft into the crankcase gently (photo), taking
care not to damage the camshaft bearings with the cams.

Fig. 1.25. Checking camshaft end float

Fig. 1.26. Checking timing gear alignment with a straight edge

48.2 Inserting piston and connecting rod into bore

48.4 Piston rings suitably clamped for final insertion into bore

49.1 Fitting shell bearing into end cap

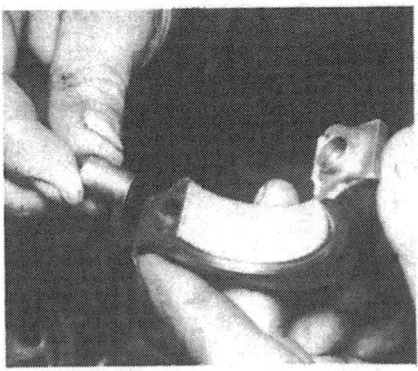

49.2 Refitting end cap locating dowels

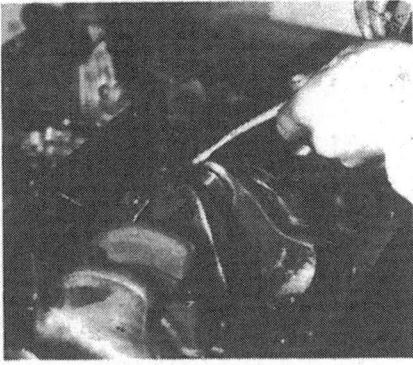

49.3 Lubrication of crankpin journal

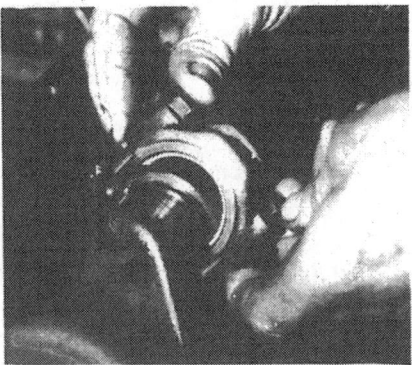

49.5 Fitting bearing cap to connecting rod

49.6 Tightening cap bolts with torque wrench

50.1 Fitting new gasket to front of cylinder block

50.2 Placing front end plate on cylinder block

51.2   Inserting camshaft into crankcase

51.3 Engaging locating plate in groove in camshaft

3 Replace the camshaft locating plate and tighten down the two retaining bolts and washers (photo).

52 Timing gears - chain tensioner - cover - replacement

1 Place the gearwheels in position without the timing chain and place the straight edge of a steel rule (Fig. 1.26) from the side of the camshaft gearteeth to the crankshaft gearwheel, and measure the gap (if any) between the steel rule and the crankshaft gearwheel. If a gap exists a suitable number of packing washers must be placed on the crankshaft nose to bring the crankshaft gearwheel onto the same plane as the camshaft gearwheel.
2 Fit the woodruff key to the slot in the crankshaft nose.
3 It is all too easy to fit the sproket wheel 180° out on the camshaft. The best way of ensuring that the wheel is fitted the right way round is to make certain that the two different slot marks on the back of the wheel correspond with the slots on the front of the camshaft (photo).
4 Lay the camshaft and crankshaft gearwheels on a clean surface so that the two timing marks are adjacent to each other. Slip the timing chain over them and pull the gearwheels back into mesh with the chain so that the timing marks, although further apart, are still adjacent to each other, as in the photo. A special point to note is that should the chain have a removable link (arrowed in photo), always position it so the spring clip faces forwards.
5 With the timing marks adjacent to each other hold the gearwheels above the crankshaft and camshaft. Turn the camshaft and crankshaft so that the woodruff key will enter the slot in the crankshaft gearwheel, and the camshaft gearwheel is in the correct position relative to the camshaft (see paragraph 3).
6 Fit the timing chain and gearwheel assembly onto the camshaft and crankshaft, keeping the timing marks adjacent (photo). Fit a new double tab washer in place on the camshaft gearwheel and fit the two retaining bolts.
7 Lever up the tabs on the lockwasher.
8 The oil seal in the front of the timing cover should be renewed. To remove it carefully drive it out with a screwdriver taking care not to damage the timing cover in the process (photo).
9 Evenly press a new seal into the cover using a vice (photo) ensuring that the seal lip is towards the crankshaft sprocket wheel.
10 Fit the oil thrower in place on the nose of the crankshaft making sure that the dished periphery is towards the cover (if dished type fitted).
11 Lubricate the front cover oil seal, fit a new gasket in place on the end plate, and fit the cover at an angle (photo), so as to catch the spring tensioner against the side of the chain. Swing the cover into its correct position and insert one or two bolts finger tight.
12 Note that the short screw headed bolt MUST be fitted to the hole indicated by the arrow in the photograph.
13 Now tighten down all the bolts and screws evenly (photo).
14 Drive the pulley onto the crankshaft. Check that the fan extension locating dowels are in position and fit the fan extension.
15 The next step is to replace the pulley wheel bolt.
16 Tighten the bolt and prevent the crankshaft from moving by temporarily refitting two bolts to the crankshaft rear flange and holding a strong screwdriver between them (photo).
17 It is not advisable to refit the fan at this stage as it may be damaged when the engine is replaced in the car.

53 Oil pump - replacement

1 Fit the pump and drive shaft to the crankcase (photo).
2 Prime the pump to preclude any possibility of oil starvation when the engine starts.
3 Refit the cover to the pump and tighten down the three securing bolts and washers (photo).

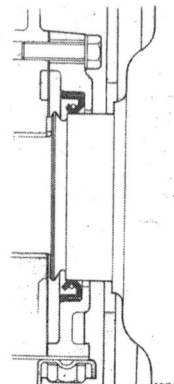

Fig. 1.27. Cross section through crankshaft rear oil seal

54 Crankshaft rear seal, housing, end plate and flywheel - replacement

1 A scroll type crankshaft rear oil seal was used on early models. Later models are fitted with a lip type seal.
2 To fit the scroll type seal coat a new gasket with jointing compound, position it on the seal housing (photo) and fit the housing to the crankcase, doing up the retaining bolts and spring washers finger tight.
3 Check with a feeler gauge that a gap of 0.003 in (0.076 mm), (aluminium housings only) exists all round the crankshaft journal, tapping the housing with a soft headed hammer until the seal is centralised (photo). Some later models make use of a cast iron housing. This is fitted in just the same way but the clearance should be 0.002 in (0.0508 mm).
4 To fit the lip type seal, first coat both sides of a new gasket with jointing compound and position the gasket on the crankcase joint face.
5 Press a new seal into the crankshaft housing with the lip of the seal facing the crankshaft. Oil the seal and carefully fit the housing making sure the lip of the seal is not turned over. Replace the housing bolts finger tight, turn the crankshaft over several times to centralise the seal, and tighten the bolts down firmly. Irrespective of what type of seal is used now fit the input shaft bush to the hole in the centre of the crankshaft rear journal (photo).
6 No gasket is fitted between the end plate and the block. Fit the end plate in place and tighten down the bolts and washers (photo).
7 Make certain that the flange on the crankshaft and the face of the flywheel are perfectly clean and offer up the flywheel to the end of the crankshaft. Ensure that the dowel engages into the special hole in the flywheel. Fit new tab washers, tighten down the four retaining bolts and turn up the lock tags.
8 Smear the crankshaft spigot bush with a small quantity of zinc oxide grease (photo).

55 Sump - replacement

1 After the sump has been thoroughly cleaned, fit the strainer gauge (photo) and turn over the tabs which hold it in place.
2 Scrape all traces of the oil sump gasket from the sump and crankcase flanges and fit a new gasket in place (photo).
3 Then refit the sump (photo).
4 Insert and tighten down the sump bolts and washers (photo).

56 Valve and valve spring - reassembly

To refit the valves and valve springs to the cylinder head, proceed as follows:-

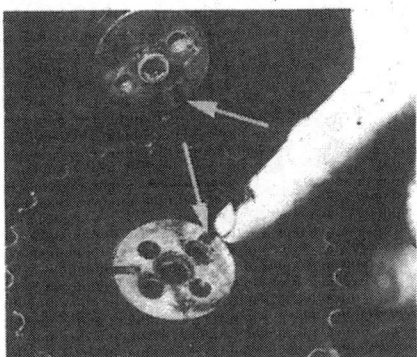

52.3 Sprocket engagement slots

52.4 Timing chain removable link

52.6 Timing marks to be kept correctly aligned

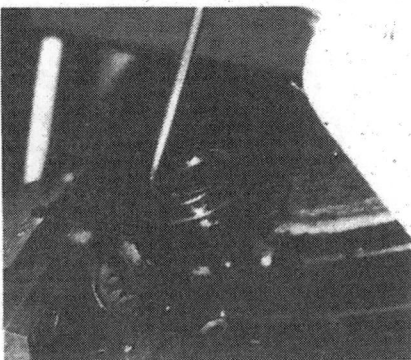

52.8 Removal of timing cover oil seal with screwdriver

52.9 Pressing new seal into timing cover

52.11 New timing cover gasket located and cover lowered onto front end plate

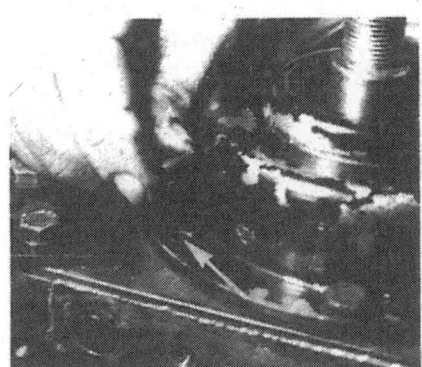

52.12 Correct location of short screw headed bolt

52.13 Tightening cover securing bolts

52.14 Refitting crankshaft pulley

52.16 Two bolts and screwdriver used to stop crankshaft rotating

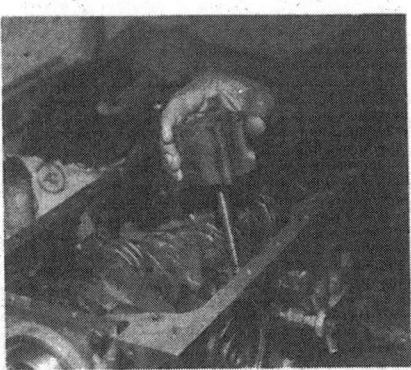

53.1 Fitting oil pump and shaft into crankcase

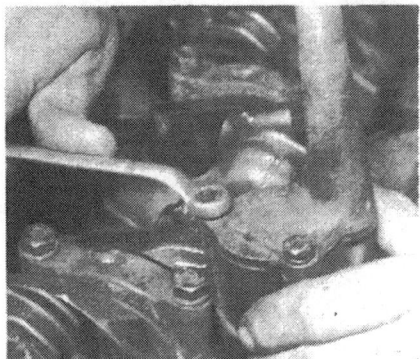
53.3 Tightening oil pump cover bolts

54.2 Seal housing with new gasket fitted ready for sliding over crankshaft

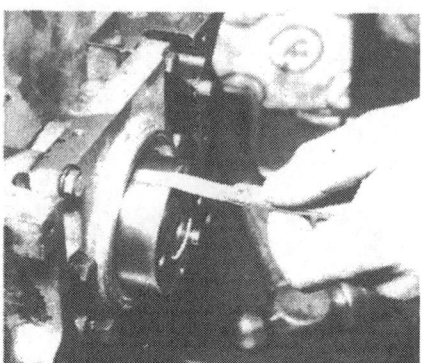
54.3 Checking seal centralisation

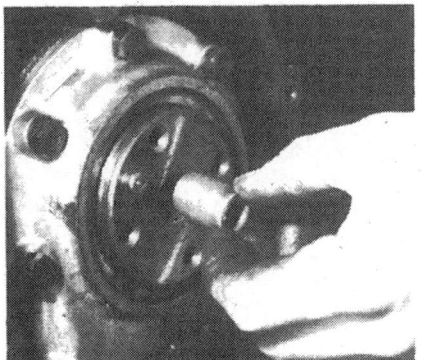
54.5 Refitting input shaft bush into crankshaft

54.6 Tightening end plate securing bolts

54.8 Crankshaft spigot bush lubricated with zinc oxide grease

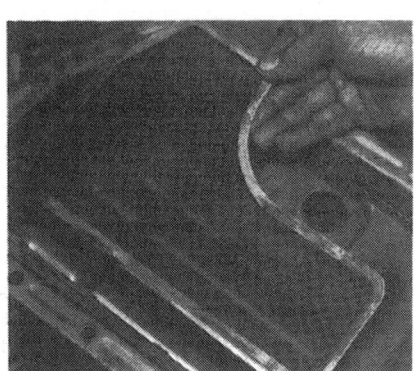
55.1 Fitting strainer gauze into sump

55.2 Fitting new sump gasket to underside of crankcase

55.3 Lowering sump onto gasket

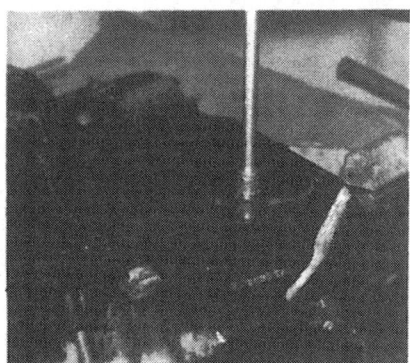
55.4 Tightening sump securing bolts

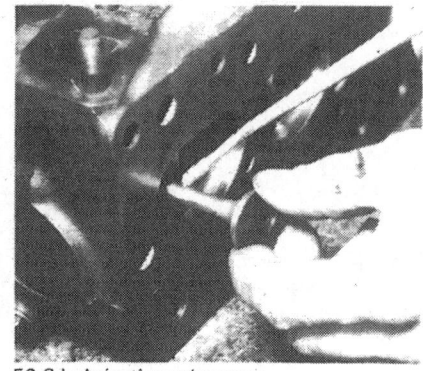
56.2 Lubricating valve stem

56.3 Sliding on lower collar

1 Rest the cylinder head on its side.

2 Fit each valve and valve spring in turn, wiping down and lubricating each valve stem as it is inserted into the same valve guide from which it was removed (photo).

3 Build up each valve assembly by first fitting the lower collar (photo).

4 Then fit the valve springs so that the closely coiled portion of each spring is adjacent to the cylinder head (photo).

5 Move the cylinder head towards the edge of the work bench if it is facing downwards and slide it over the edge of the bench so as to fit the bottom half of a valve spring compressor to the valve head. Slide the springs and collar over the valve stem.

6 With the base of the valve compressor on the valve head, compress the valve springs until the collars can be slipped into place in the cotter grooves. Gently release the compressor.

7 Repeat this procedure until all twelve valves and valve springs are fitted.

57 Rocker shaft and tappets - reassembly

1 Fit an end cap and pin to one end of the shaft and then slide on the springs, rockers, distance springs, and rocker pedestals in their correct order, as shown in Fig. 1.10.

2 Make sure that the Phillips screw on the rear rocker pedestal engages properly with the rocker shaft.

3 When all is correctly assembled fit the remaining end cap and oil the components thoroughly.

4 Generously lubricate the tappets internally and externally and insert them in the bores from which they were removed (photo).

58 Cylinder head - replacement

1 Thoroughly clean the cylinder block top face and then refit the cylinder head studs using the double nut method (photo).

2 Note that the two longer studs must be fitted to the last two holes towards the rear of the block on the right hand side (photo).

3 If it is wished to refit the head before replacing the engine in the car fit a new gasket in place (photo). If one side of the gasket is marked 'TOP' it must naturally be fitted with this side facing upwards.

4 Generously lubricate each cylinder with engine oil (photo).

5 Ensure that the cylinder head face is perfectly clean and then lower the cylinder head into place (photo), keeping it parallel to the block to avoid binding on any of the studs.

6 With the head now in place any attachments such as lifting eyes or accelerator cable attachments that were previously secured under the cylinder head nuts can be replaced.

7 Fit the cylinder head nuts and washers and tighten down the nuts half a turn at a time in the order shown in Fig. 1.7. to a torque of 65.70 lbf ft (9.0 - 9.68 Kg Fm).

8 Insert the pushrods into the block so the ball end rests in the tappet. Ensure the pushrods are replaced in the same order in which they were removed (photo)

9 Then refit the rocker shaft ensuring that the rocker arm ball joints seat in the pushrod cups (photo).

10 Replace the six rocker pedestal nuts and washers and tighten them down evenly (photo).

59 Rocker arm/valve - adjustments

1 The valve adjustments should be made with the engine cold. The importance of correct rocker arm/valve stem clearances cannot be over- stressed as they vitally affect the performance of the engine.

2 If the clearances are set too open, the efficiency of the engine is reduced as the valves open late and close earlier than was intended. If, on the other hand the clearances are set too close there is a danger that the stems will expand upon heating and

not allow the valves to close properly. This will cause burning of the valve head and seat, and possible warping.

3 If the engine is in the car, to get at the rockers it is merely necessary to remove the three holding down nuts from the rocker cover, and then to lift the rocker cover and gasket away.

4 It is important that the clearance is set when the tappet of the valve being adjusted is on the heel of the cam, (i.e. opposite the peak). This can be done by carrying out the adjustments in the following order, which also avoids turning the crankshaft more than necessary:-

Valves fully open	Check and adjust
Valve Nos. 1 and 3	Valve Nos. 10 and 12
" " 8 and 11	" " 2 and 5
" " 4 and 6	" " 7 and 9
" " 10 and 12	" " 1 and 3
" " 2 and 5	" " 8 and 11
" " 7 and 9	" " 4 and 6

5 The correct clearance of 0.010 in (0.254 mm) is obtained by slackening the hexagonal locknut with a spanner while holding the ball pin against rotation with the screwdriver (photo). Then, still pressing down with the screwdriver, insert a feeler gauge in the gap between the valve stem head and the rocker arm and adjust the ball pin until the feeler gauge will just move in and out without nipping, and, still holding the ball pin in the correct position, tighten the locknut.

6 An alternative method is to set the gaps with the engine running, and although this may be faster it is no more reliable.

60 Distributor and distributor drive - replacement

It is important to set the distributor drive correctly as otherwise the ignition timing will be totally incorrect. It is easy to set the distributor drive in apparently the right position, but in fact exactly 180° out, by omitting to select the correct cylinder which must not only be at T D C but must also be on its firing stroke with both valves closed. The distributor drive should therefore not be fitted until the cylinder head is in position and the valves can be observed. Alternatively, if the timing cover has not been replaced, the distributor drive can be replaced when the marks on the timing wheels are adjacent to each other. In addition, ensure that the leads in the distributor cap are positioned as they should be and that No 1 lead terminal is adjacent to the top of the rotor arm.

1 Rotate the crankshaft so that No 1 piston is at T D C and on its firing stroke.

2 If the timing gear cover has been replaced, this can be achieved by setting the pointer on the timing gear cover to the mark on the pulley wheel. Turn the oil pump drive shaft so the slot in the top of the shaft is at an angle of 45° with the side of the block (photo).

3 Insert the distributor drive into its housing so that when fully home the slot in the top of the drive is in the position shown in Fig. 1.29.

In each case the larger segment faces the rear of the engine. It may be necessary to turn the pump rotor shaft to allow the distributor drive to engage fully on P I models.

4 It is essential that between 0.003 and 0.007 in (0.0762 and 0.1778 mm) endfloat exists between the topside of the gear driven by the skew gear on the camshaft and the underside of the pedestal hose. If the same components are being used it will be safe to assume that the endfloat is correct but ensure the same number of packing washers are used (if any), and always fit a new gasket.

5 If the drive gears are assembled without end float, wear on the crankshaft gearwheels, chain and distributor drive gear will be very heavy. If new components are being fitted then cut a small notch in the outer edge of the distributor housing flange gasket and bolt the housing down firmly. Measure the thickness of the gasket with a feeler gauge placed in the notch. Then remove the distributor housing and gasket and replace the housing without the gasket. Measure the gap between the underside of the housing flange and the block, and subtract this latter figure from

56.4 Positioning valve springs

57.4 Lubricating tappets before insertion into bore

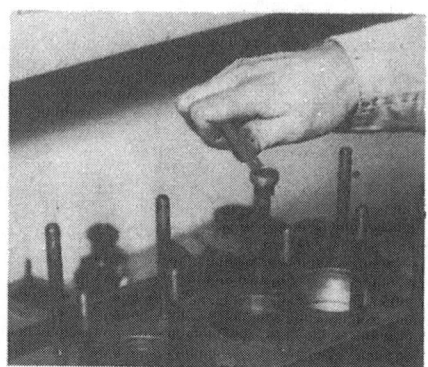
58.1 Refitting cylinder head studs

58.2 Correct location of two longer studs

58.3 Lowering gasket into position

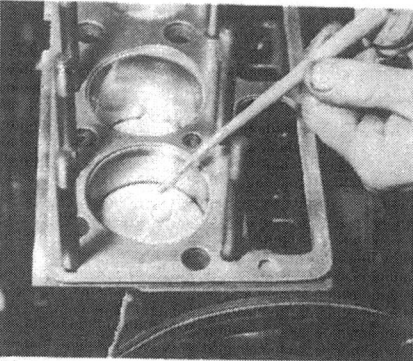
58.4 Lubrication of cylinders

58.5 Refitting cylinder head

58.8 Inserting push rods into cylinder head

58.9 Refitting rocker shaft

58.10 Tightening rocker pedestal securing nuts

59.5 Adjustment of valve/rocker arm clearance

60.2 Correct location of oil pump drive shaft slot ready to refit distributor

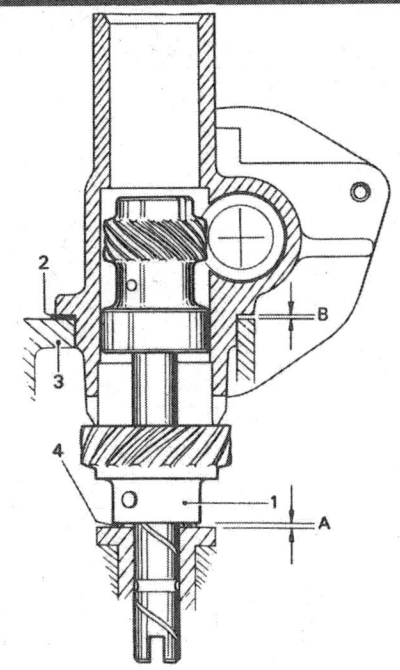

FIG. 1.28. DISTRIBUTOR DRIVE GEAR CLEARANCES

1 Drive gear   3 Cylinder block
2 Washer   4 Washer

Gaps A and B to be measured and washer thickness selected to give end float of 0.005 inch (0.127 mm)

Fig. 1.29. Distributor drive gear set position before refitting distributor

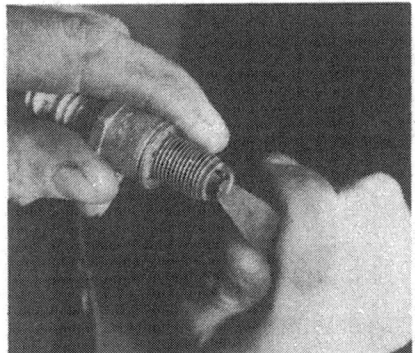

61.2(i) Checking spark plug gap before refitting

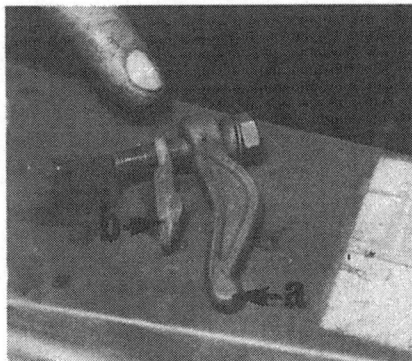

61.2(L(a)) Correct assembly order of clamp

61.2(L(b)) Location of clamp on manifold

61.2(L(c)) Manifold securing bolts replaced (TR250/6 carburettors)

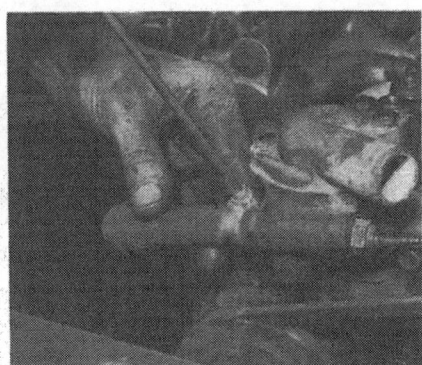

61.2(O) Tightening heater hose clip

61.2(Q(a)) Refitting vacuum advance pipe at distributor

the former to determine the end float with the standard gasket.

6 Turn the distributor so the rotor arm is pointing to the terminal in the cap which carries the lead to No. 1 cylinder, and fit the distributor to the distributor housing. The lip on the distributor should mate perfectly with the slot in the distributor drive shaft. Fit the bolt which holds the distributor clamp plate to the housing.

7 Tighten down the two nuts and washers which hold the distributor housing in place.

8 If the clamp bolt on the clamping plate was not previously loosened and the distributor body was not turned in the clamping plate , then the ignition timing will be as previously. If the clamping bolt has been loosened, then it will be necessary to re-time the ignition as described in Chapter 4.

61 Engine replacement

Although the engine or engine and gearbox can be replaced by one man and a suitable hoist, it is easier if two are present. Generally replacement is the reverse sequence to removal. In addition however:

1 Ensure all the loose leads, cables etc., are tucked out of the way. It is easy to trap one and cause much additional work after the engine is replaced.

2 Refit the following as applicable ;

a) Mounting nuts, bolts and washers.
b) Propeller shaft.
c) Reconnect the clutch pipe to the slave cylinder and bleed the system (chapter 5).
d) Speedometer cable.
e) Gearchange lever surround and console.
f) Floor panels and carpet.
g) Oil pressure gauge cable connection.
h) Water temperature indicator sender unit cable.
i) Wires to coil, distributor and alternator. Spark plugs (photo).
j) Carburettor controls and air cleaner.
k) Fuel injection equipment pipes and controls.

l) Exhaust manifold and downpipe (photos).
m) Clutch and starter motor cables.
n) Radiator and hoses.
o) Heater hoses (photo).
p) Engine closed circuit breather and servo unit hoses.
q) Vacuum advance and retard pipe (photos).
r) Battery.
s) Fuel line to carburettor/s and pump (photo).
t) Bonnet.

3 Finally check the drain taps are closed and refill the cooling system with water and the engine with Castrol GTX.

62 Engine - inital start up after overhaul and major repair

Make sure that the battery is fully charged and that all lubricants ,coolants and fuel are replenished.

If the fuel system has been dismantled, it will require several revolutions of the starter motor to pump petrol to the carburettors (TR 250/6 carburettor models). On P I models the system must be bled.

As soon as the engine fires and runs, keep it going at a fast tickover only (no faster) and bring it up to normal working temperatures.

As the engine warms up, there will be odd smells and some smoke from parts getting hot and burning off oil deposits. Look for water or oil which will be obvious if serious. Check also the clamp connection of the exhaust pipe to the manifold as these do not always 'find' their exact gas tight position until the warmth and vibration have acted on them, and it is almost certain that they will need tightening further. This should be done of course with the engine stationary.

When the engine running temperature has been reached adjust the idling speed as described in Chapter 3.

Road test the car to check that the timing is correct and giving the necessary smoothness and power. Do not race the engine. If new bearings and / or pistons and rings have been fitted, it should be treated as a new engine and run in at reduced speed for 500 miles (800 Km).

61.2(Qb) Refitting vacuum advance pipe at carburettor

61.2(S) Tightening fuel line unions at fuel pump (TR250/6 carburettors)

Symptom	Reason/s	Remedy
ENGINE FAILS TO TURN OVER WHEN STARTER BUTTON OPERATED		
No current at starter motor	Flat or defective battery	Charge or replace battery. Push-start car.
	Loose battery leads	Tighten both terminals and earth ends of earth lead.
	Defective starter solenoid or switch or broken wiring	Run a wire direct from the battery to the starter motor or by-pass the solenoid.
	Engine earth strap disconnected	Check and retighten strap.
Current at starter motor	Jammed starter motor drive pinion	Place car in gear and rock from side to side Alternatively, free exposed square end of shaft with spanner.
	Defective starter motor	Remove and recondition.
ENGINE TURNS OVER BUT WILL NOT START		
No spark at spark plug	Ignition damp or wet	Wipe dry the distributor cap and ignition leads.
	Ignition leads to spark plugs loose	Check and tighten at both spark plug and distributor cap ends.
	Shorted or disconnected low tension leads	Check the wiring on the CB and SW terminals of the coil and to the distributor.
	Dirty, incorrectly set, or pitted contact breaker points	Clean, file smooth, and adjust.
	Faulty condenser	Check contact breaker points for arcing, remove and fit new.
	Defective ignition switch	By-pass switch with wire.
	Ignition leads connected wrong way round	Remove and replace leads to spark plugs in correct order.
	Faulty coil	Remove and fit new coil.
	Contact breaker point spring earthed or broken	Check spring is not touching metal part of distributor. Check insulator washers are correctly placed. Renew points if the spring is broken.
No fuel at carburettor float chamber or at jets	No petrol in tank	Refill tank!
	Vapour lock in fuel line. (In hot conditions or at high altitude)	Blow into petrol tank, allow engine to cool, or apply a cold wet rag to the fuel line.
	Blocked float chamber needle valve	Remove, clean, and replace.
	Fuel pump filter blocked	Remove, clean and replace.
	Choked or blocked carburettor jets	Dismantle, and clean.
	Faulty fuel pump	Remove, overhaul, and replace. Check CB points on S.U. pumps.
Excess of petrol in cylinder or carburettor flooding	Too much choke allowing too rich a mixture to wet plugs	Remove and dry spark plugs or with wide open throttle, push-start the car.
	Float damaged or leaking or needle not seating	Remove, examine, clean and replace float and needle valve as necessary.
	Float lever incorrectly adjusted	Remove and adjust correctly.
ENGINE STALLS AND WILL NOT START		
No spark at spark plug	Ignition failure - Sudden	Check over low and high tension circuits for breaks in wiring.
	Ignition failure - Misfiring precludes total stoppage	Check contact breaker points, clean and adjust. Renew condenser if faulty.
	Ignition failure - In severe rain or after transversing water splash	Dry out ignition leads and distributor cap.
No fuel at jets	No petrol in petrol tank	Refill tank.
	Petrol tank breather choked	Remove petrol cap and clean out breather hole or pipe.
	Sudden obstruction in carburettor(s)	Check jets, filter, and needle valve in float chamber for blockage.
	Water in fuel system	Drain tank and blow out fuel lines.
ENGINE MISFIRES OR IDLES UNEVENLY		
Intermittent sparking at spark plug	Ignition leads loose	Check and tighten as necessary at spark plug and distributor cap ends.
ENGINE MISFIRES OR IDLES UNEVENLY		
Intermittent sparking at spark plug	Battery leads loose on terminals	Check and tighten terminal leads.
	Battery earth strap loose on body attachment point	Check and tighten earth lead to body attachment point.

	Engine earth lead loose	Tighten lead.
	Low tension leads to SW and CB terminals on coil loose	Check and tighten leads if found loose.
	Low tension lead from CB terminal side to distributor loose	Check and tighten if found loose.
	Dirty, or incorrectly gapped plugs	Remove, clean, and regap.
	Dirty, incorrectly set, or pitted contact breaker points	Clean, file smooth, and adjust.
	Tracking across inside of distributor cover	Remove and fit new cover.
	Ignition too retarded	Check and adjust ignition timing.
	Faulty coil	Remove and fit new coil.
Fuel shortage at engine	Mixture too weak	Check jets, float chamber needle valve, and filters for obstruction. Clean as necessary. Carburettor(s) incorrectly adjusted.
	Air leak in carburettor(s)	Remove and overhaul carburettor.
	Air leak at inlet manifold to cylinder	Test by pouring oil along joints. Bubbles, indicate leak. Renew manifold gasket as appropriate.
Mechanical wear	Incorrect valve clearances	Adjust rocker arms to take up wear.
	Burnt out exhaust valves	Remove cylinder head and renew defective valves.
	Sticking or leaking valves	Remove cylinder head, clean, check and renew valves as necessary.
	Weak or broken valve springs	Check and renew as necessary.
	Worn valve guides or stems	Renew valve guides and valves.
	Worn pistons and piston rings	Dismantle engine, renew pistons and rings.

LACK OF POWER AND POOR COMPRESSION

Fuel/air mixture leaking from cylinder	Burnt out exhaust valves	Remove cylinder head, renew defective valves
	Sticking or leaking valves	Remove cylinder head, clean, check, and renew valves as necessary.
	Worn valve guides and stems	Remove cylinder head and renew valves and valve guides.
	Weak or broken valves springs	Remove cylinder head, renew defective springs.
	Blown cylinder head gasket. (Accompanied by increase in noise)	Remove cylinder head and fit new gasket.
	Worn pistons and piston rings	Dismantle engine, renew pistons and rings.
	Worn or scored cylinder bores	Dismantle engine, rebore, renew pistons and rings.
Incorrect adjustments	Ignition timing wrongly set. Too advanced or retarded	Check and reset ignition timing.
	Contact breaker points incorrectly gapped	Check and reset contact breaker points.
	Incorrect valve clearances	Check and reset rocker arm to valve stem gap.
	Incorrect set spark plugs	Remove, clean and regap.
	Carburation too rich or too weak	Tune carburettor(s) for optimum performance.
Carburation and ignition faults	Dirty contact breaker points	Remove, clean, and replace.
	Fuel filters blocked causing top end fuel starvation	Dismantle, inspect, clean, and replace all fuel filters.
	Distributor automatic balance weights or vacuum advance and retard mechanisms not functioning correcty	Overhaul distributor.
	Faulty fuel pump giving top end fuel starvation	Remove, overhaul, or fit exchange reconditioned fuel pump.

EXCESSIVE OIL CONSUMPTION

Oil being burnt by engine	Badly worn, perished or missing valve stem oil seals	Remove, fit new oil seals to valve stems.
	Excessively worn valve stems and valve guides	Remove cylinder head and fit new valves and valve guides.
	Worn piston rings	Fit oil control rings to existing pistons or purchase new pistons.
	Worn pistons and cylinder bores	Fit new pistons and rings, rebore cylinders.
	Excessive piston ring gap allowing blow-by	Fit new piston rings and set gap correctly.
	Piston oil return holes choked	Decarbonise engine and pistons.
Oil being lost due to leaks	Leaking oil filter gasket	Inspect and fit new gasket as necessary.
	Leaking rocker cover gasket	Inspect and fit new gasket as necessary.
	Leaking tappet chest gasket	Inspect and fit new gasket as necessary.
	Leaking timing case gasket	Inspect and fit new gasket as necessary.
	Leaking sump gasket	Inspect and fit new gasket as necessary.
	Loose sump plug	Tighten, fit new gasket if necessary.

UNUSUAL NOISES FROM ENGINE
Excessive clearances due to mechanical wear

Worn valve gear. (Noisy tapping from rocker box)

Worn big end bearing. (Regular heavy knocking)

Worn timing chain and gears (Rattling from front of engine)

Worn main bearings. (Rumbling and vibration)

Worn crankshaft. (Knocking, rumbling and vibration)

Inspect and renew rocker shaft, rocker arms, and ball pins as necessary.

Drop sump, if bearings broken up clean out oil pump and oilways, fit new bearings. If bearings not broken but worn fit bearing shells.

Remove timing cover, fit new timing wheels and timing chain.

Drop sump, remove crankshaft, if bearings worn but not broken up, renew. If broken up strip oil pump and clean out.

Regrind crankshaft, fit new main and big end bearings.

Chapter 2 Cooling system

Contents

Specifications

Type of system	Pressurised, pump impeller and fan with translucent plastic overflow bottle
Normal temperature	Should not exceed 85°C (185°F)
Thermostat:	
Starts opening	70°C (158°F)
Fully open	90°C (197°F)
Maximum lift	0.281 - 0.407 in (7.137 - 10.337 mm)
Pressure cap release pressure	3.25 - 4.25 lb/sq in (0.228 - 0.298 Kg/sq cm)
Fan blades:	
Diameter	12.5 in (31.6 cm)
Number of blades	8
Tension of fan belt	0.75 in (19.05 mm) movement midway between the alternator and crankshaft pulley wheels
Type of water pump	Centrifugal
Water pump drive	Belt from crankshaft pulley
Capacity (including heater and water bottle)	11 pints (6.2 litres (13.2 U.S. pints)

TORQUE WRENCH SETTINGS	lb ft	Kg m
Water pump pulley	14 - 16	1.94 - 2.21
Water pump stud nut	12 - 14	1.66 - 1.94
Water pump securing bolts	18 - 20	2.49 - 2.77
Water elbow attachment	18 - 20	2.49 - 2.77

1 General description

The engine cooling water is circulated by a thermo-syphon, water pump assisted system and the coolant is pressurised. This is to prevent premature boiling of the coolant in adverse conditions.

The radiator cap is of the pressurised type and increases the boiling point to 267.7°C (225°F). If the water temperature exceeds this figure and the water boils, the pressure in the system forces the internal part of the cap off its seat, thus exposing the overflow pipe down which the steam from the boiling water escapes and is condensed in the translucent plastic bottle. The pressure is thus relieved.

It is, therefore, important to check that the radiator cap is in good condition and that the spring behind the sealing washer has not weakened.

The cooling system comprises the radiator translucent plastic overflow bottle, top and bottom water hoses, heater hoses, and the impeller water pump (mounted on the front of the engine and driven by the fan belt), the thermostat and two drain taps located as shown in Fig. 2.1.

The system functions in the following manner. Cold water in the bottom of the radiator circulates up the lower radiator hose to the water pump where it is pushed round the water passages in the cylinder block, helping to keep the cylinder bores and pistons cool.

The water then travels up into the cylinder head and circulates round the combustion spaces and valve seats absorbing more heat, and then, when the engine is at its correct operating temperature, travels out of the cylinder head, past the open thermostat into the upper radiator hose and so into the radiator header tank.

The water travels down the radiator where it is rapidly cooled by the in-rush of cold air through the radiator core which is created by both the fan and the motion of the car. The water, now cold, reaches the bottom of the radiator when the cycle is repeated.

When the engine is cold the thermostat (which is a valve which opens and closes according to the temperature of the

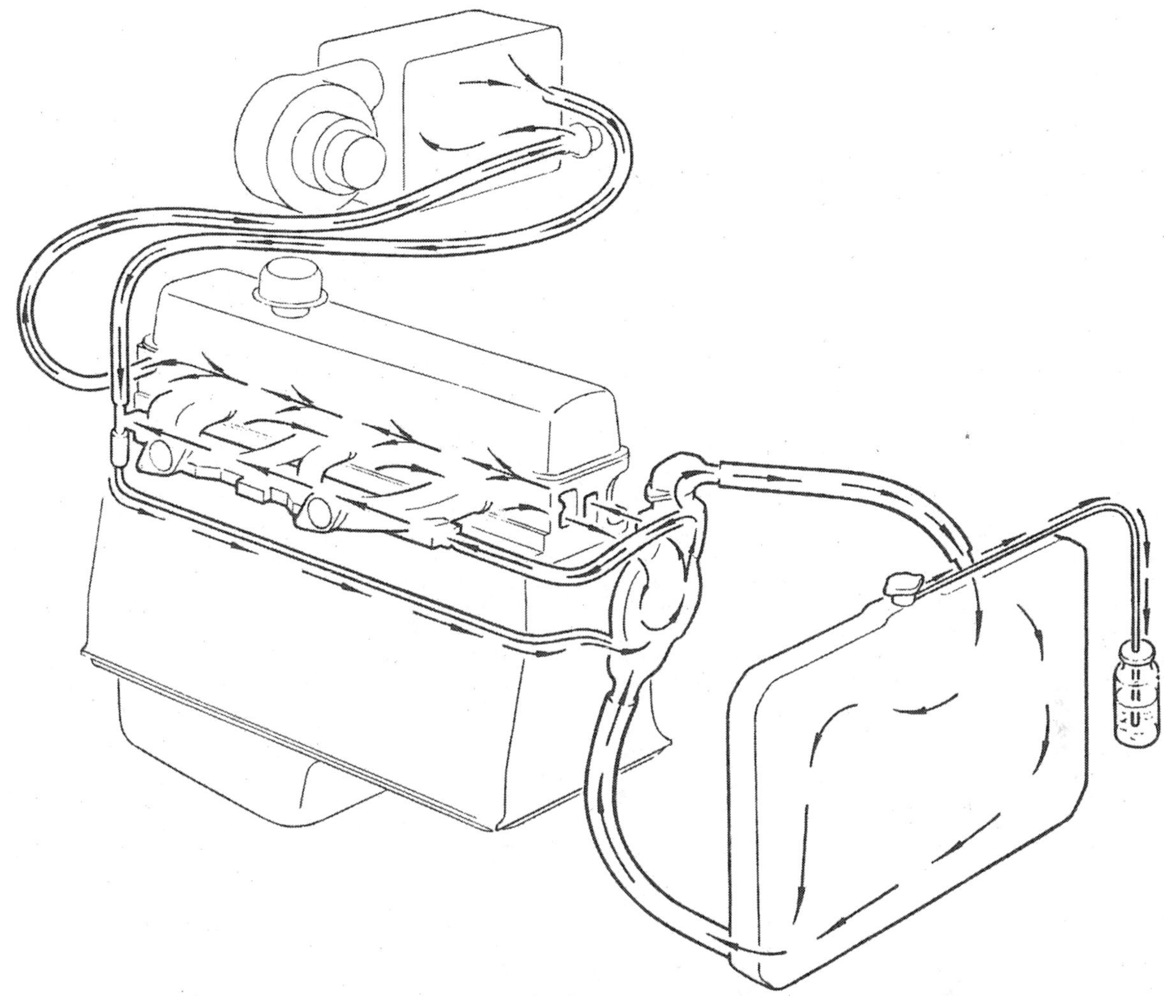

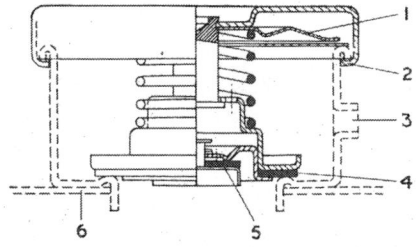

Fig. 2.1. Cooling system water flow

water) maintains the circulation of the same water in the engine.

Only when the correct minimum operating temperature has been reached, as shown in the specification, does the thermostat begin to open, allowing water to return to the radiator.

An overflow pipe is connected to an expansion bottle so that as the coolant temperature drops a partial vacuum exists in the radiator and the overflow is drawn back from the expansion bottle, through a little vacuum relief valve in the filler cap back into the radiator top tank.

2 Cooling system - draining

1 With the car on level ground drain the system as follows.
2 If the engine is cold remove the filler cap from the radiator by turning the cap anti-clockwise. If the engine is hot, having just been run, then turn the filler cap very slightly until the pressure in the system has had time to disperse. Use a rag over the cap to protect your hand from escaping steam. If, with the engine very hot, the cap is released suddenly, the drop in pressure can result in the water boiling. With the pressure released the cap can be removed.
3 If anti-freeze is in the radiator drain it into a clean bucket or bowl for re-use.
4 Open the two drain taps and ensure the heater control is in the hot position. On later models drain plugs may be fitted instead of taps. Remove the plugs with a spanner. The drain taps are located at the bottom of the radiator and at the rear on the

Fig. 2.2. Radiator cap component parts

right hand side of the block.
5 When the water has finished running, probe the drain tap orifices with a short piece of wire to dislodge any particles of rust or sediment which may be blocking the taps and preventing all the water draining out.

3 Cooling system - flushing

1 With time, the cooling system will gradually lose its efficiency as the radiator becomes choked with rust, scales, deposits from the water and other sediment. To clear the system out, remove the radiator cap and the drain taps and leave a hose running in the radiator cap orifice for ten to fifteen minutes.

2 Then close the drain taps and refill with water and a proprietary cleaning compound. Run the engine for 10 to 15 minutes and then drain it and flush out thoroughly for a further ten minutes. All sediment and sludge should now have been removed.

3 In very bad cases the radiator should be reverse flushed. This can be done with the radiator in position. The cylinder block tap is closed and a hose placed over the open radiator drain tap. Water, under pressure, is then forced up through the radiator and out of the header tank filler orifice.

4 The hose is then removed and placed in the filler orifice and the radiator washed out in the usual fashion.

4 Cooling system - filling

1 Close the two drain taps.

2 Fill the system ensuring that no air locks develop. If heater is fitted, check that the valve to the heater unit is open, otherwise an air lock may form in the heater. The best type of water to use in the cooling system is rain water, so use this whenever possible.

3 Do not fill the system higher than within 0.5 in (12.7 mm) of the filler orifice. Overfilling will merely result in wastage, which is especially to be avoided when anti-freeze is in use.

4 Only use anti-freeze mixture with a glycerine or ethylene base.

5 Replace the filler cap and turn it firmly clockwise to lock it in position.

5 Radiator – removal, inspection, cleaning and replacement

1 To remove the radiator first drain the cooling system as described in Section 2.

2 Where air deflectors are fitted, undo and remove the seven screws which secure the air deflector to the front panel. Lift away the air deflector.

3 Undo the jubilee clips which hold the radiator top hose to the radiator followed by the jubilee clip which holds the bottom radiator hose to the radiator. Disconnect the overflow pipe from the neck of the radiator filler cap. (Fig. 2.3.).

4 Undo the nuts and bolts that secure the two reinforcement stays to the top corner of the radiator.

5 Slacken and remove the radiator stay retaining nuts from the crossmember bracket and lift the two stays away.

6 Undo and remove the two radiator mounting nuts and bolts and lift the radiator from the engine compartment taking great care not to damage the radiator matrix on the fan blades.

7 Lift away the radiator packing pieces fitted between the lower radiator mounting and chassis brackets.

8 With the radiator away from the car any leaks can be soldered up or repaired with a substance such as 'Cataloy'. Clean out the inside of the radiator by flushing as detailed in Section 3. When the radiator is away from the car it is advantageous to invert it for reverse flushing. Clean the exterior of the radiator by hosing down the radiator matrix with a strong jet of water to clear away any road dirt, dead flies etc.

9 Inspect the radiator hoses for cracks, internal or external perishing, and damage caused by overtightening of the securing clips. Replace the hoses as necessary. Examine the radiator hose securing clips and renew them if they are rusted or distorted. The drain taps should be renewed if leaking. Note - ensure that the leak is not a faulty washer behind the tap. If the tap is suspected try a new washer to see if this clears the trouble first.

10 Refitting the radiator is the reverse sequence to removal.

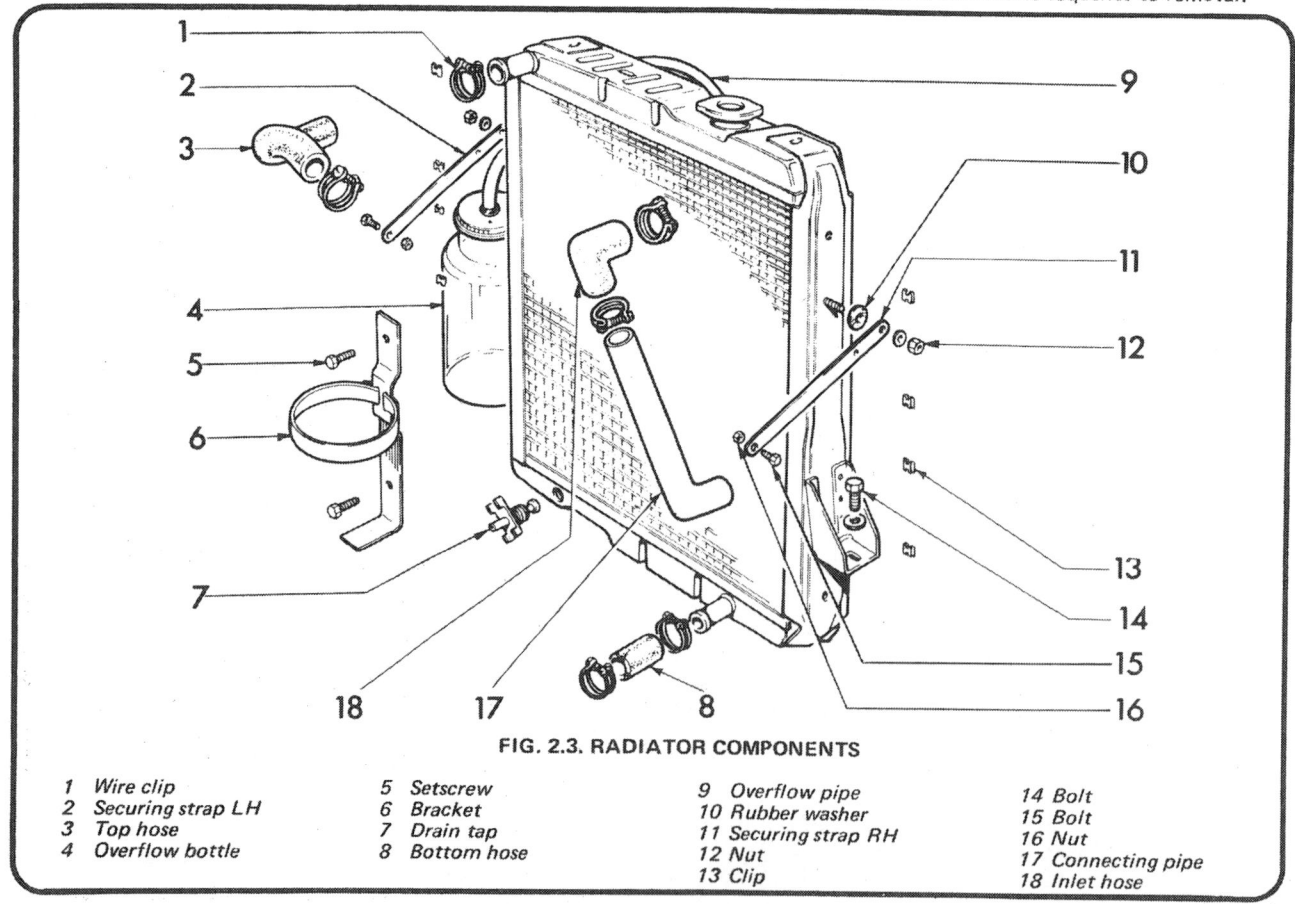

FIG. 2.3. RADIATOR COMPONENTS

1 Wire clip	5 Setscrew	9 Overflow pipe	14 Bolt
2 Securing strap LH	6 Bracket	10 Rubber washer	15 Bolt
3 Top hose	7 Drain tap	11 Securing strap RH	16 Nut
4 Overflow bottle	8 Bottom hose	12 Nut	17 Connecting pipe
		13 Clip	18 Inlet hose

11 Position the packing pieces fitted between the lower radiator mounting and chassis brackets before replacing the radiator.

12 Fill the cooling system as detailed in Section 4 and run the engine until it reaches normal operating temperature. Check for leaks.

6 Thermostat - removal, testing and replacement

1 To remove the thermostat partially drain the cooling system (4 pints, 2.27 litres, 4.804 US pints) is enough, loosen the upper radiator hose jubilee clips.

2 Undo and remove the two long bolts and spring washers that secure the thermostat housing elbow to the top of the water pump body.

3 Lift away the thermostat housing elbow and gasket. Take care not to damage it if a new one is not available.

4 Test the thermostat for correct functioning by dangling it by a length of wire or string in a saucepan of cold water together with a thermometer.

5 Heat the water and note when the thermostat begins to open. This temperature is stamped on the flange of the thermostat and is also given in the specifications on page 50.

6 Discard the thermostat if it opens too early. Continue heating the water until the thermostat is fully open. Then let it cool down naturally. If the thermostat will not open fully in boiling water, or does not close down as the water cools then a new one must be fitted.

7 If the thermostat is stuck open when cold this will have been apparent when removing it from the housing.

8 Replacing the thermostat is a reversal of the removal procedure. If at all possible always use a new paper gasket between the thermostat housing front cover and the body. Renew the complete housing if it badly corroded.

7 Water pump - removal and replacement

1 If the water pump is badly worn normal practice is to fit an exchange reconditioned unit. Drain the complete cooling system as described in Section 2.

2 Slacken the alternator adjustment bolts and the two pivot bolts and push the alternator towards the engine. Lift off the fan belt from the water pump pulley.

3 Undo the jubilee clips holding the radiator top hose to the thermostat housing elbow and the bottom radiator hose to the water pump body. Carefully detach the two hoses.

4 Detach the Lucar connector at the temperature transmitter.

5 Undo and remove the three bolts and spring washers that secure the water pump to the front of the engine. Note the difference in lengths.

6 Lift the water pump away from the engine followed by the gasket.

7 It is possible to remove the bearing housing assembly leaving the body still attached to the engine. Drain the cooling system and lift away the fan belt as previously described. Undo and remove the three nuts and spring washers that secure the bearing housing to the water pump body. Lift away the bearing housing and gasket.

8 Refitting is a straightforward reversal of the removal sequence. Always use a new gasket. Note that the fan belt tension must be correct when all is reassembled. If the fan belt is too tight undue strain will be placed on the water pump and alternator bearings, and if the belt is too loose it will slip and wear rapidly as well as giving rise to low electrical output from the alternator.

8 Water pump - dismantling and reassembly

1 If it is wished to repair the pump first ascertain that spare parts are available because less and less firms stock spare parts as opposed to rebuilt pump unit.

2 The component parts are shown in Fig. 2.6. Undo and remove the nyloc nut and plain washer that secures the pulley to the spindle. Using a universal pulley carefully draw off the pulley.

3 Undo and remove the three nuts and spring washers that secure the bearing housing assembly to the pump body. Lift away the bearing housing assembly and gasket.

4 Carefully remove the circlip located at the forward end of the spindle and then, using a suitable diameter drift and hammer tap the spindle through the impeller towards the pulley side of the bearing housing. If it is very tight it will be necessary to use either a large vice or press.

5 Remove the following parts from the spindle: woodruff key,

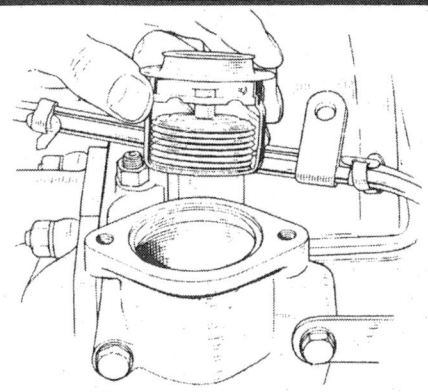

Fig. 2.4. Thermostat removal

FIG. 2.5. PARTS REQUIRING ATTENTION FOR WATER PUMP REMOVAL

1 Manifold water jacket hose clip
2 Thermostat housing water elbow clip
3 Top hose clip
4 Alternator adjustment bracket bolt
5 Lower water pump mounting bolt
6 Fuel line clip retained by water pump mounting bolt
7 Heater return pipe union at rear of water pump
8 Bottom hose clip

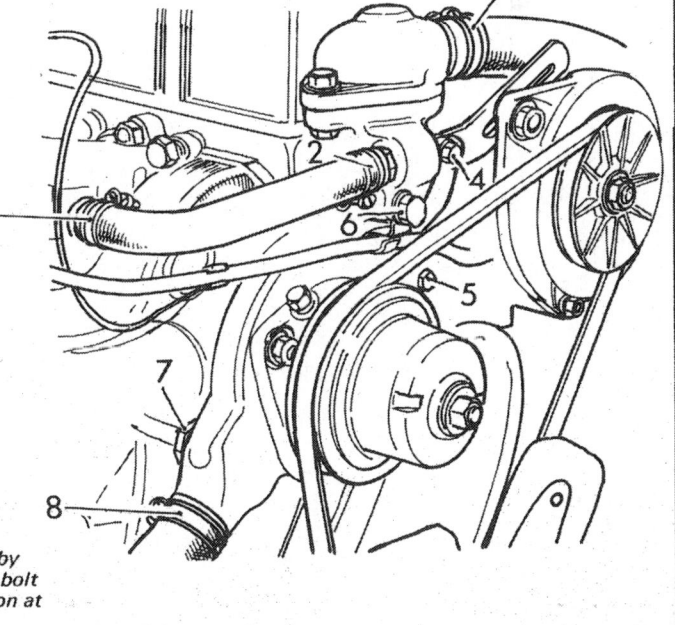

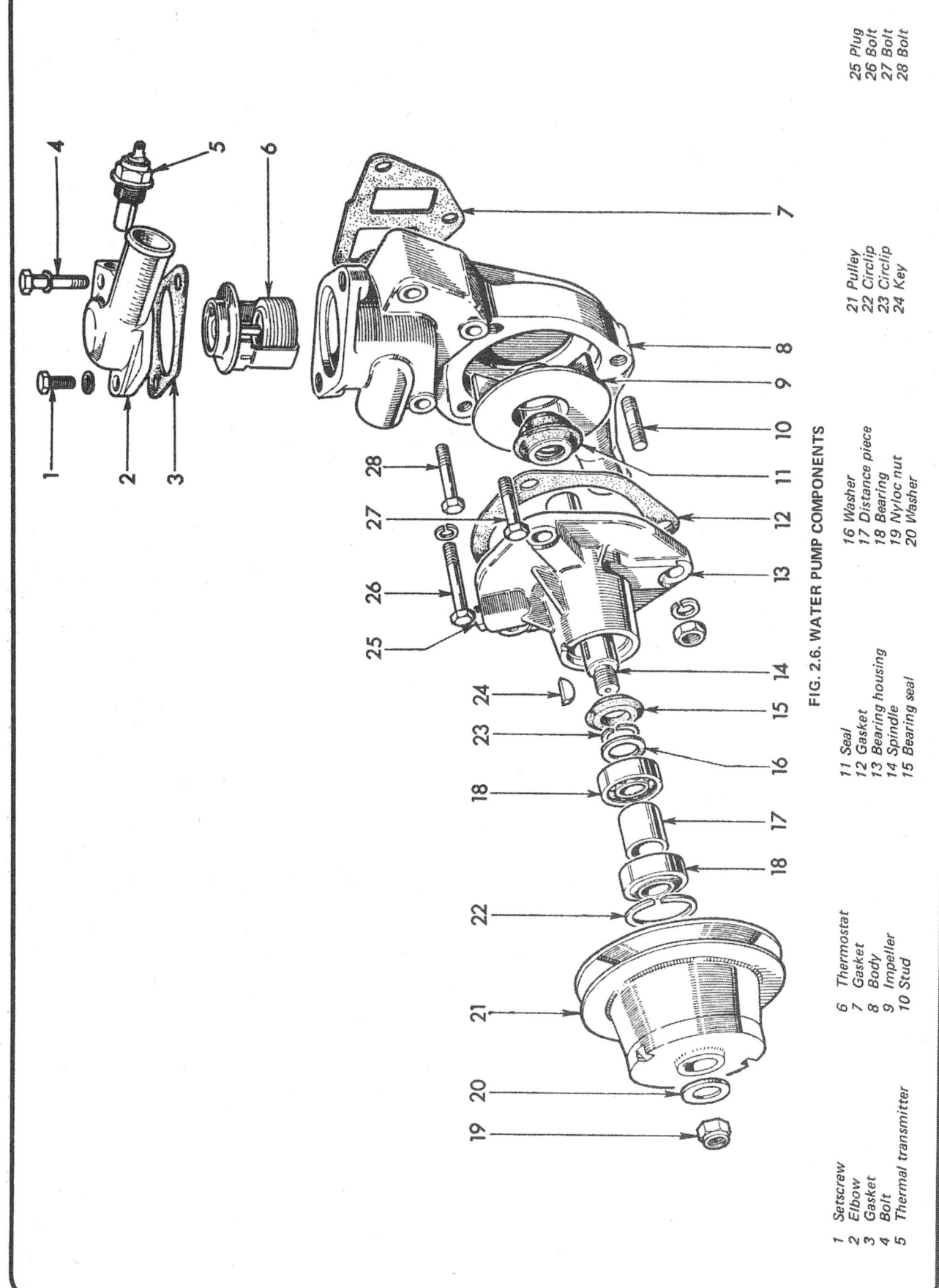

FIG. 2.6. WATER PUMP COMPONENTS

1 Setscrew
2 Elbow
3 Gasket
4 Bolt
5 Thermal transmitter

6 Thermostat
7 Gasket
8 Body
9 Impeller
10 Stud

11 Seal
12 Gasket
13 Bearing housing
14 Spindle
15 Bearing seal

16 Washer
17 Distance piece
18 Bearing
19 Nyloc nut
20 Washer

21 Pulley
22 Circlip
23 Circlip
24 Key

25 Plug
26 Bolt
27 Bolt
28 Bolt

bearing, spacer, washer, circlip and spinner.

6 The sealing gland may now be removed from the centre of the impeller.

7 To reassemble the bearing housing assembly first fit the spinner circlip and washer to the spindle. Carefully pack the bearings with a waterproof grease and then press them onto the spindle. The sealed faces must face outwards and do not forget the spacer. Refit the circlip.

8 Using a 0.030 in (0.762 mm) spacer press the impeller onto the shaft until the spacer is just nipped.

9 Lift away the spacer and fit the woodruff key and pulley to the shaft. Secure with a new Nyloc nut and plain washer.

10 Make sure the mating faces of the bearing housing assembly and water pump body are clean and fit a new gasket over the three studs on the body. Refit the bearing housing assembly and secure with three nuts and spring washers.

9 Anti-freeze mixture

1 In circumstances where it is likely that the temperature will drop to below freezing it is essential that some of the water is drained and an adequate amount of ethylene glycol anti-freeze such as Bluecol is added to the cooling system.

2 If Bluecol is not available any anti-freeze which conforms with specification B.S.3151 or B.S. 3152 can be used. Never use an anti-freeze with an alcohol base as evaporation is too high.

3 Bluecol anti-freeze with an anti corrosion additive can be left in the cooling system for up to two years, but after six months it is advisable to have the specific gravity of the coolant checked at your local garage, and thereafter once every three months.

4 Listed below are the amounts of Bluecol which should be added to ensure adequate protection down to the temperature given:

Amount of Anti-freeze	Protection to
1.7 pints (1 litre) (2.102 US pints)	- 17.8°C (0°F)
2.0 pints (1.3 litres) (2.402 US pints)	-28.9°C (-20°F)
2.3 pints (1.43 litres) (2.777 US pints)	-34.5°C (-30°F)
3 pints (1.70 litres) (3.603 US pints)	-40°C (-40°F)

10 Temperature gauge - fault finding

1 If the temperature gauge fails to work, either the gauge, the sender unit, the wiring or the connections are at fault.

2 It is not possible to repair the gauge or the sender unit and they must be replaced by new units if at fault.

3 First check the wiring connections and if sound check the wiring for breaks using an ohmmeter. The sender unit and gauge should be tested by substitution.

11 Temperature gauge and sender unit - removal and replacement

1 For details of how to remove and replace the temperature gauge see Chapter 10.

2 To remove the sender unit disconnect the battery, pull off the wire at the snap connector on the unit located on the side of the thermostat housing. Undo the unit with a spanner.

3 On replacement renew the fibre washer to prevent the possibility of leaks developing.

12 Fan belt - adjustment

1 It is important to keep the fan belt correctly adjusted and although not listed by the manufacturer, it is considered that this should be a regular maintenance task performed every 6,000 miles (10,000 km).

2 If the belt is too loose it will slip, wear rapidly and cause the alternator and water pump to malfunction. If the belt is too tight the alternator and water pump bearings will wear rapidly causing premature failure of these components.

3 The fan belt tension is correct when there is 0.75 inch (19.05 mm) of lateral movement at the midpoint position of the belt between the pulley wheel and the crankshaft pulley wheel.

4 To adjust the fan belt slacken the alternator securing bolts (Fig. 2.5).) and move the alternator either in or out until the correct tension is obtained. It is easier if the alternator bolts are only slackened a little so it requires some force to move the alternator. In this way the tension of the belt can be arrived at more quickly than by making frequent adjustments.

5 With the alternator bolts only slightly loosened, difficulty may be experienced in moving the alternator away from the engine. A long spanner placed behind the alternator and resting against the block serves as a very good lever and can be held in this position while the bolts are tightened. On no account overtighten the fan belt. It is better for the belt to be too loose than too tight.

13 Fan belt - removal and replacement

1 If the fan belt is worn or has stretched unduly it should be replaced. The most usual reason for replacement is that the belt has broken in service. It is therefore recommended that a belt is always carried as a spare and is fitted as detailed below.

2 Loosen the two alternator pivot bolts and the nut on the adjusting link and push the alternator towards the engine.

3 Undo and remove the three bolts each side of the cross tube positioned directly by the crankshaft pulley. Move the cross tube to one side. The reason for moving the cross tube is that it is very near to the pulley and it is not possible to fit a new fan belt to the pulley with the cross tube in position.

4 Slip the belt over the crankshaft, alternator and water pump pulleys.

5 Adjust the belt as described in Section 12 and tighten the alternator mounting nuts. NOTE. After fitting a new belt it will require adjustment 250 miles later.

6 Before refitting the cross member obtain a spare fan belt and bind it tightly to the cross member in such a position that it may be slipped onto the crankshaft pulley at some future date. It will save the trouble of removing the cross member if the belt breaks some time in the future.

See next page for 'Fault Finding'.

14 Fault finding

Symptom	Reason/s	Remedy
OVERHEATING Heat generated in cylinder not being successfully disposed of by radiator	Insufficient water in cooling system Fan belt slipping (accompanied by a shrieking noise on rapid engine acceleration Radiator core blocked or radiator grille restricted Bottom water hose collapsed, impeding flow Thermostat not opening properly Ignition advance and retard incorrectly set (accompanied by loss of power, and perhaps, misfiring) Fuel injection system or carburettors incorrectly adjusted (mixture too weak) Exhaust system partially blocked Oil level in sump too low Blown cylinder head gasket (Water/steam being forced down the radiator overflow pipe under pressure) Engine not yet run-in Brakes binding	Top up radiator. Tighten fan belt to recommended tension or replace if worn. Reverse flush radiator, remove obstruction. Remove and fit new hose. Remove and fit new thermostat. Check and reset ignition timing. Reset fuel injection system or tune carburrettors. Check exhaust pipes for constrictive dents and blockage. Top up sump to full mark on dipstick Remove cylinder head, fit new gasket. Run-in slowly and carefully. Check and adjust brakes if necessary.
UNDERHEATING Too much heat being dispersed by radiator	Thermostat jammed open Incorrect grade of thermostat fitted allowing premature opening of valve Thermostat missing	Remove and renew thermostat. Remove and replace with new thermostat which opens at a higher temperature. Check and fit correct thermostat.
LOSS OF COOLING WATER Leaks in system	Loose clips on water hoses Top, bottom, or by-pass water hoses perished and leaking. Radiator core leaking Thermostat gasket leaking Radiator pressure cap spring worn or seal ineffective Blown cylinder head gasket (pressure in system forcing water/steam down overflow pipe). Cylinder wall or head cracked	Check and tighten clips if necessary. Check and replace any faulty hoses. Remove radiator and repair. Inspect and renew gasket. Renew radiator pressure cap. Remove cylinder head and fit new gasket. Dismantle engine, dispatch to engineering works for repair.

Chapter 3 Fuel systems

Contents

Specifications

Carburation
Carburettor installation - (TR250/6 carburettors, emission control)

Fuel pump
Type	AC mechanically operated
Pump pressure	1.5 to 2.5 lb/sq in (0.1 to 0.18 Kg m^2)
Fitted length of diaphragm spring	0.468 in (11.9062 mm)
Fitted load	4.125 to 4.375 lb
Free length	1.125 in (38.575 mm)

Carburettors
Type	Twin sidedraft Stromberg 175 CDSE
Idle speed	800 - 850
Idle CO level - engine warm	2.5% - 3.5%
Equivalent air/fuel ratio at idle	13.5:1 approx.
Accelerator control adjustment	0.09375 in (2.3812 mm) [use drill shank]
Float adjustment	16.0 - 17.0 mm

Petrol injection system TR5 and 6
Type	Lucas Mk II
Metering	Vacuum controlled shuttle type
Fuel line pressure	106 - 110 lb/sq in (7.452 - 7.733 Kg/cm^2)
Injector opening pressure	40 - 50 lb/sq in (2.812 - 3.515 Kg/cm^2)
Fuel filter	Replaceable paper element

General
Air cleaner	
Type	Combined air cleaner and silencer with replaceable paper element
Tank capacity	11.25 gallons (51 litres, 13.5 US gallons)

TORQUE WRENCH SETTINGS

	lb ft	Kg m
Emission control models		
Carburettor attachment	12 - 14	1.659 - 1.936
Fuel pump studs	12 - 14	1.659 - 1.936
PI models		
Flexible pipe to metering unit	18 - 20	2.49 - 2.77
Flexible pipe main feed	16 - 18	2.21 - 2.49
Main feed pipe to double end union	16 - 18	2.21 - 2.49

Intermediate delivery pipe to double end union		...	...				16 - 18	2.21 - 2.49
Intermediate delivery pipe to relief valve ...		...	...				16 - 18	2.21 - 2.49
Flexible pipe to relief valve	...	...	...	...			18 - 20	2.49 - 2.77
Flexible pipe to motor pump	...	...	...	...			18 - 20	2.49 - 2.77
Flexible pipe to relief valve	...	...	...	...			16 - 18	2 21 - 2.49
Flexible pipe to filter	...	...	...	...	...		6 - 8	0.83 - 1.11
Vent pipe to tank	...	...	...	...	...		4 - 6	0.55 - 0.83
Pipe to motor pump	...	...	...	...	...		16 - 18	2.21 - 2.49
Pipe to filter ...	...	...	...	...	...	...	6 - 8	0.83 - 1.11

General

Exhaust pipe to manifold	...	...	...	...			24 - 26	3.32 - 3.60
Exhaust tail pipe to rubber strap	...	...	...				2 - 3	0.28 - 0.42
Exhaust front pipe attachment	...	...	...	...			6 - 8	0.83 - 1.11
Exhaust intermediate pipe attachment	...	...	...				6 - 8	0.83 - 1.11
Exhaust front pipe attachment clip to bracket	...	...					6 - 8	0.83 - 1.11
Exhaust pipe to silencer	...	...	...	...	...		6 - 8	0.83 - 1.11

1 General description

Two types of fuel system have been fitted: TR5 and 6 with Petrol Injection (PI) and TR250 and 6 for the United States with carburettors. The carburettor system is described first.

The fuel system fitted to models produced to comply with the U.S. Federal regulations comprises two Zenith - Stromberg carburettors type 175 CDSE, a fuel tank at the rear and an A C mechanical fuel pump mounted on the left hand side of the engine. Other slight modifications were made to the engines produced for fitment, commencing with 1968 model cars. These modifications include :

a) Stellite faced exhaust valves to ensure effective valve seating between major service intervals.
b) Modified cylinder head giving a compression ratio of 8.5:1.
c) Modified crankshaft to match cylinder head. This gives a 10 - 50 - 50 - 10 timing which enables better control of emission during idling and low speed motoring.
d) Special distributor with double acting advance system. See Chapter 4.
e) Air cleaners have additional holes for matching with those provided in the emission carburettor flanges.
f) Special choke control assembly is used for bringing two separate and independently adjustable choke cables to a single controlling cable.
g) Modified accelerator linkage to provide a positive idle stop and incorporates 'lost motion' for operating a vacuum control valve when the throttles are closed.
h) A vacuum control valve mechanically connected to and operated by the accelerator linkage, to permit normal vacuum ignition advance under part throttle conditions.
i) A crankcase emission control valve fitted to the crankcase to remove blow by gases.
j) Metal pipes are used in the fuel system to ensure no fuel leaks.

Information on the petrol injection system fitted to PI models will be found in later Sections.

2 U.S Federal Regulations and servicing

It is very important to appreciate that any adjustments made to the fuel system as well as the ignition system (see Chapter 4) will probably result in the car failing to meet the legal requirements in respect of air pollution unless special test equipment is used at the same time as making the adjustments.

Information given in this chapter is aimed specifically at the owner who is able to have the various settings and adjustments checked at the earliest possible opportunity.

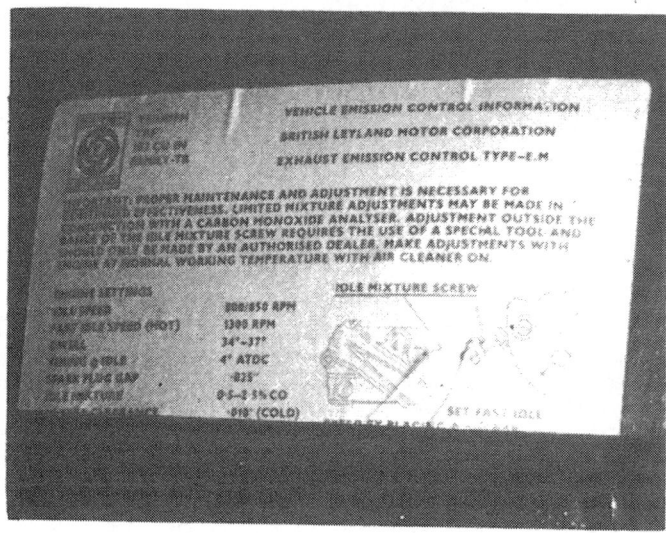

Typical vehicle emission control information plate

3 Air cleaner - removal, servicing and replacement

1 All emission controlled models use paper element air cleaners which should be checked for cleaniness every 6,000 miles (10,000 Km) and changed every 12,000 miles (20,000 Km). In dusty conditions it may be necessary to renew the elements more frequently.

2 To remove the paper filter elements release the flexible intake pipes from the front of the box, undo the four bolts which hold the container box to the carburettors and withdraw the complete box together with the gaskets.

3 Undo the centre bolt and separate the two halves of the container box. This exposes the filter elements which can now be cleaned with air from a foot pump or replaced as necessary.

4 Before reassembly carefully examine all gaskets and replace any that are damaged.

5 Reassembly is a direct reversal of the above procedure but care should be taken to align the slots in the centre holes of the filter elements and the carburettor flange gaskets with the corresponding slots on the flanges of the Stromberg carburettors.

4 A C fuel pump - description

1 The mechanically operated AC fuel pump is actuated through a spring loaded rocker arm. One arm of the rocker bears against an eccentric in front of the camshaft gear and the other arm operates a diaphragm pull rod.

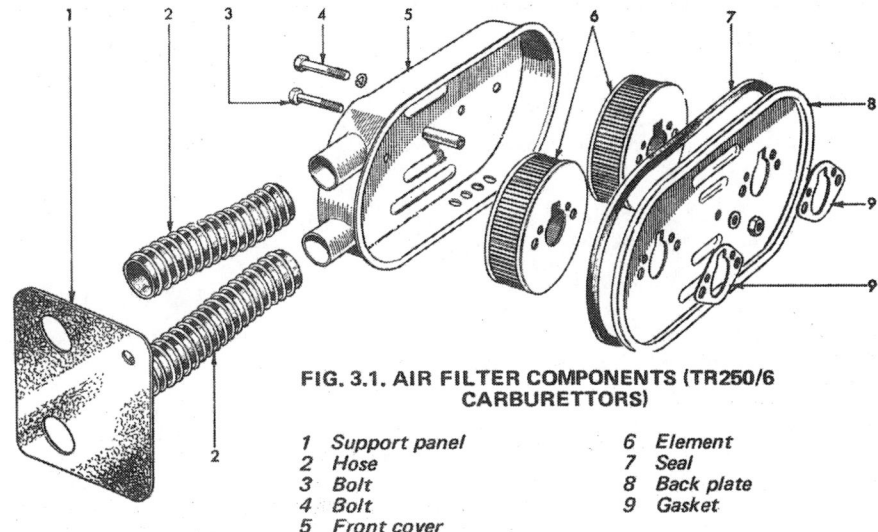

FIG. 3.1. AIR FILTER COMPONENTS (TR250/6 CARBURETTORS)

1 Support panel
2 Hose
3 Bolt
4 Bolt
5 Front cover
6 Element
7 Seal
8 Back plate
9 Gasket

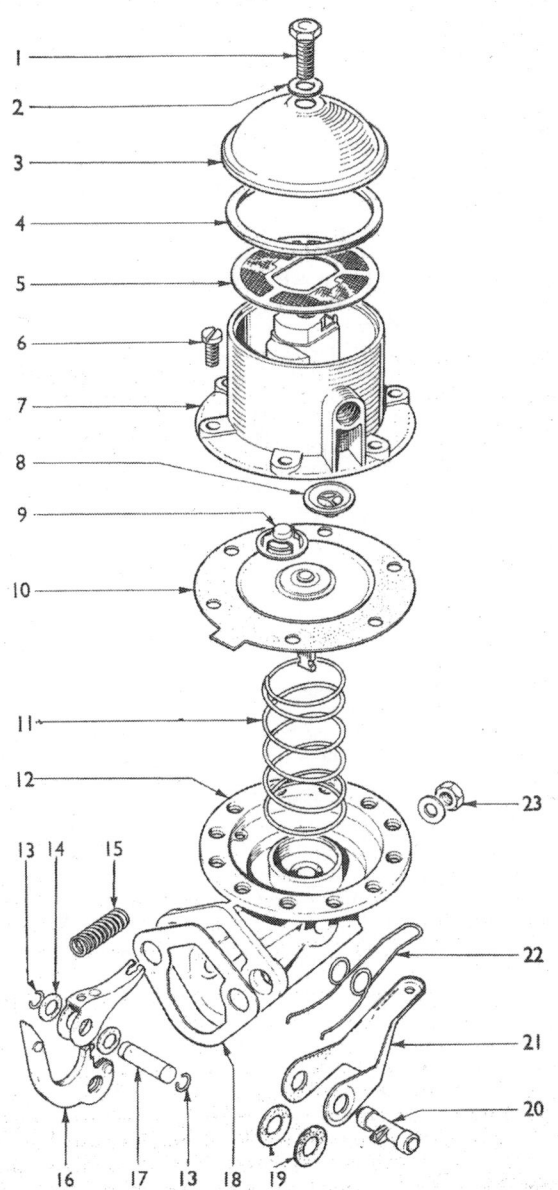

FIG. 3.2. FUEL PUMP COMPONENT PARTS

1 Retaining screw
2 Washer
3 Cover
4 Joint
5 Gauze
6 Screw
7 Body
8 Inlet valve
9 Outlet valve
10 Diaphragm assembly
11 Diaphragm spring
12 Lower body
13 Circlip
14 Distance washer
15 Return spring
16 Rocker arm
17 Rocker arm pin
18 Gasket
19 Cork seals
20 Primer lever shaft
21 Primer lever
22 Primer lever spring
23 Pump retainer nut

2 As the engine camshaft rotates, the eccentric moves the pivoted rocker arm outwards which in turn pulls the diaphragm pull rod and the diaphragm down against the pressure of the diaphragm spring.

3 This creates sufficient vacuum in the pump chamber to draw in fuel from the tank through the fuel filter gauze and non return valve.

4 The rocker arm is held in constant contact with the eccentric by an anti-rattle spring, and as the engine camshaft continues to rotate the eccentric allows the rocker arm to move inwards. The diaphragm spring is thus free to push the diaphragm upwards forcing the fuel in the pump chamber out to the carburettor through the non return outlet valve.

5 When the float chamber in the carburettor is full the float chamber needle valve will close so preventing further flow from the fuel pump.

6 The pressure in the delivery line will hold the diaphragm downwards against the pressure of the diaphragm spring, and it will remain in this position until the needle valve in the float chamber opens to admit more petrol.

5 A C fuel pump - removal and replacement

1 Remove the fuel inlet and outlet pipes by unscrewing the union nuts. Plug the end of the fuel inlet pipe with a bolt, or piece of tapered wood such as a pencil to stop petrol syphoning from the tank.

2 Undo the two nuts and spring washers which hold the pump to the crankcase.

3 Lift the pump together with the gasket away from the crankcase.

4 Replacement of the pump is a reversal of the above process. Remember to use a new crankcase to fuel pump gasket to ensure no oil leaks, ensure that both faces of the flange are perfectly clean, and check that the rocker arm lies on top of the camshaft eccentric and not underneath it.

6 A C fuel pump - testing

Presuming that the fuel lines and unions are in good condition and that there are no leaks anywhere, check the performance of the fuel pump in the following manner: Disconnect the fuel pipe at the carburettor inlet union, and the high tension lead to the coil, and with a suitable container or a large rag in position to catch the ejected fuel, turn the engine over on the starter motor solenoid. A good spurt of petrol should emerge from the end of the pipe every second revolution.

7 A C fuel pump - dismantling

1 Undo the bolt and lift away the bolt, fibre washer, dome, joint and gauze filter.

2 If the condition of the diaphragm is suspect or for any other reason it is wished to dismantle the pump fully, proceed as follows: Mark the upper and lower flanges that are adjacent to each other. Undo the screws and spring washers which hold the two halves of the pump together. Separate the two halves of the pump with great care, ensuring that the diaphragm does not stick to either of the two flanges.

3 If it is necessary to remove the two valves, first note that the inlet valve points towards the diaphragm and the outlet valve points away from the diaphragm. Using a fine chisel knock back the peened over metal and carefully remove the valves.

4 Note the position of the diaphragm tag for correct refitting and rotate the diaphragm 90° in either direction to release the pull rod from the operating lever and lift away the diaphragm and pull rod (which is securely fixed to the diaphragm and cannot be removed from it). Remove the diaphragm spring.

5 If it is necessary to dismantle the rocker arm assembly remove the retaining circlips and washers from the rocker

arm pivot rod and slide out the rod which will then free the rocker arm and lever and anti-rattle spring.

8 A C pump - examination and reassembly

1 Check the conditions of the cork cover sealing washer, and if it is hardened or broken it must be replaced. The diaphragm should be checked similarly and replaced if faulty. Clean the pump thoroughly and agitate the valves in paraffin to clean them out. This will also improve the contact between the valve seat and the valve. It is unlikely that the pump body will be damaged, but check for fractures and cracks. Renew the cover if distorted by over tightening.

2 To reassemble the pump proceed as follows: Replace the rocker arm assembly comprising the operating lever, rocker arm, anti-rattle spring and washers in their relative position in the pump lower body. Align the holes in the operating lever, rocker arm and washers with the holes in the body and insert the pivot pin.

3 Refit the circlips to the grooves in each end of the pivot pin.

4 If the valves have been removed, refit them so that they are correctly positioned as previously noted during dismantling. Peen over the surrounding body metal to ensure a tight fit. Check with a suitable piece of wire, that the valves are working properly.

5 Refit the diaphragm return spring to the lower body.

6 Replace the diaphragm and pull rod assembly with the pull rod downwards and the small tab on the diaphragm at 90° to the centre of the flange and rocker arm as previously noted during dismantling.

7 With the body of the pump held so that the rocker arm is facing away from one, press down the diaphragm turning it a quarter of a turn to the left at the same time. This engages the slot on the pull rod with the operating lever. The small tab on the diaphragm should now be adjacent to the flange and rocker arm and the diaphragm should be firmly located.

8 Move the rocker arm until the diaphragm is level with the body flanges and hold the arm in this position. Reassemble the two halves of the pump ensuring that the previously made marks on the flanges are adjacent to each other.

9 Insert the screws and lockwashers and tighten them down finger tight.

10 Move the rocker arm up and down several times to centralise the diaphragm, and then with the arm held down, tighten the screws securely in a diagonal manner.

11 Replace the gauze filter in position. Fit the cork cover sealing washer, fit the cover, securing bolt and fibre washer and tighten the bolt just sufficiently to ensure a petrol tight seal.

9 Stromberg 175 CDSE carburettor - description

The principle of operation is basically indentical to that of the 150 CD series carburettor but with modifications as described at the end of this section.

When starting from cold pulling the choke out rotates the lever and bar , which lifts the piston type air valve and needle. On no account should the accelerator be pressed before the engine fires. The metering needle tapers slightly and fits into the jet orifice. The higher the needle is raised the richer the mixture becomes, because of the increased discharge area available at the mouth of the jet.

At the same time as the choke is pulled out a cam on the lever opens the throttle beyond its normal idling position, the extent to which the throttle is opened, depending on the setting of the fast idle screw.

As soon as the engine starts, increased vacuum in the inlet manifold lifts the piston, so weakening the mixture to prevent the engine stalling because of over richness. As the engine warms up the choke is pushed in gradually until the lever is back in its normal position.

When the throttle is opened the decrease in pressure in the

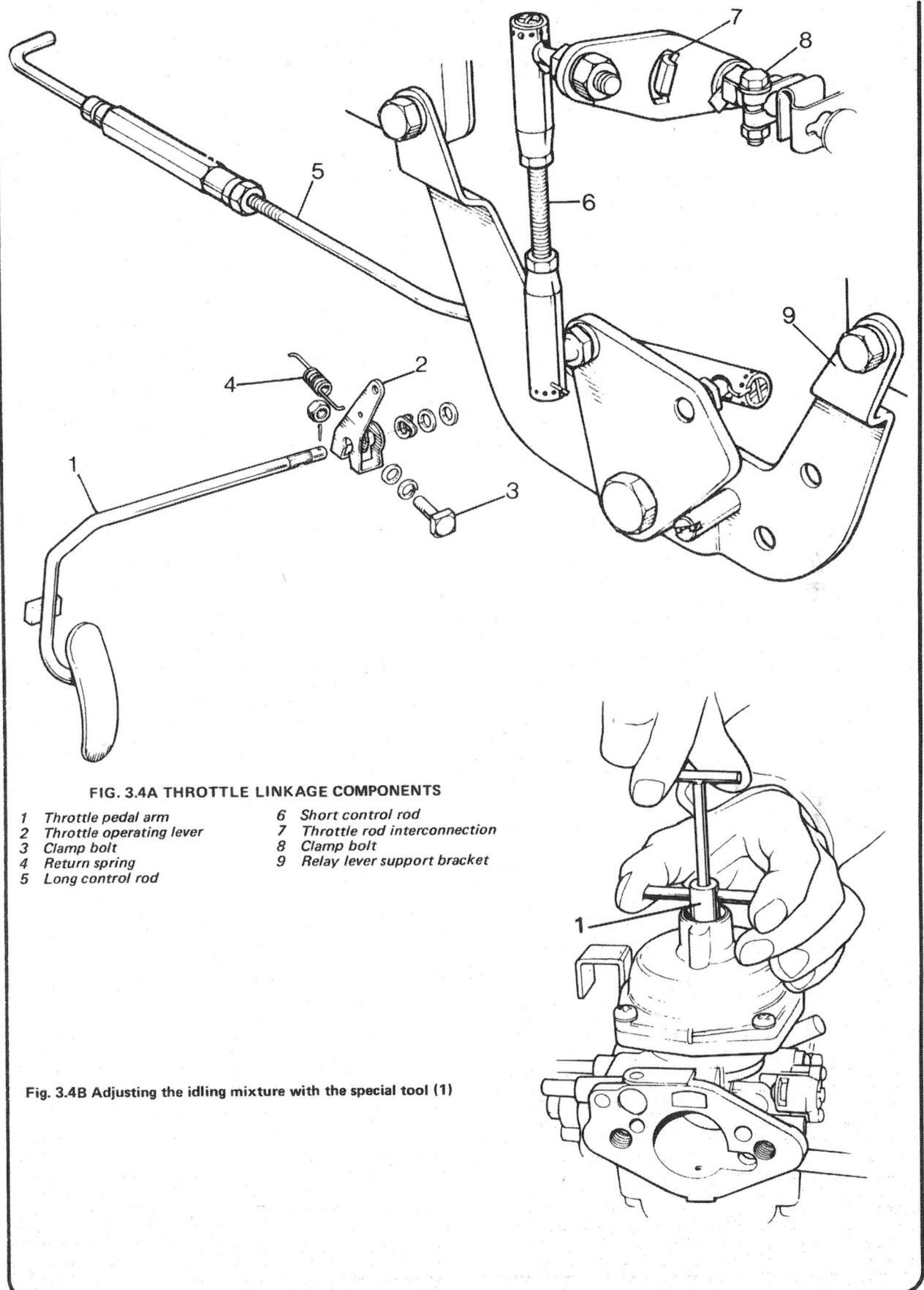

FIG. 3.4A THROTTLE LINKAGE COMPONENTS

1   *Throttle pedal arm*
2   *Throttle operating lever*
3   *Clamp bolt*
4   *Return spring*
5   *Long control rod*

6   *Short control rod*
7   *Throttle rod interconnection*
8   *Clamp bolt*
9   *Relay lever support bracket*

Fig. 3.4B Adjusting the idling mixture with the special tool (1)

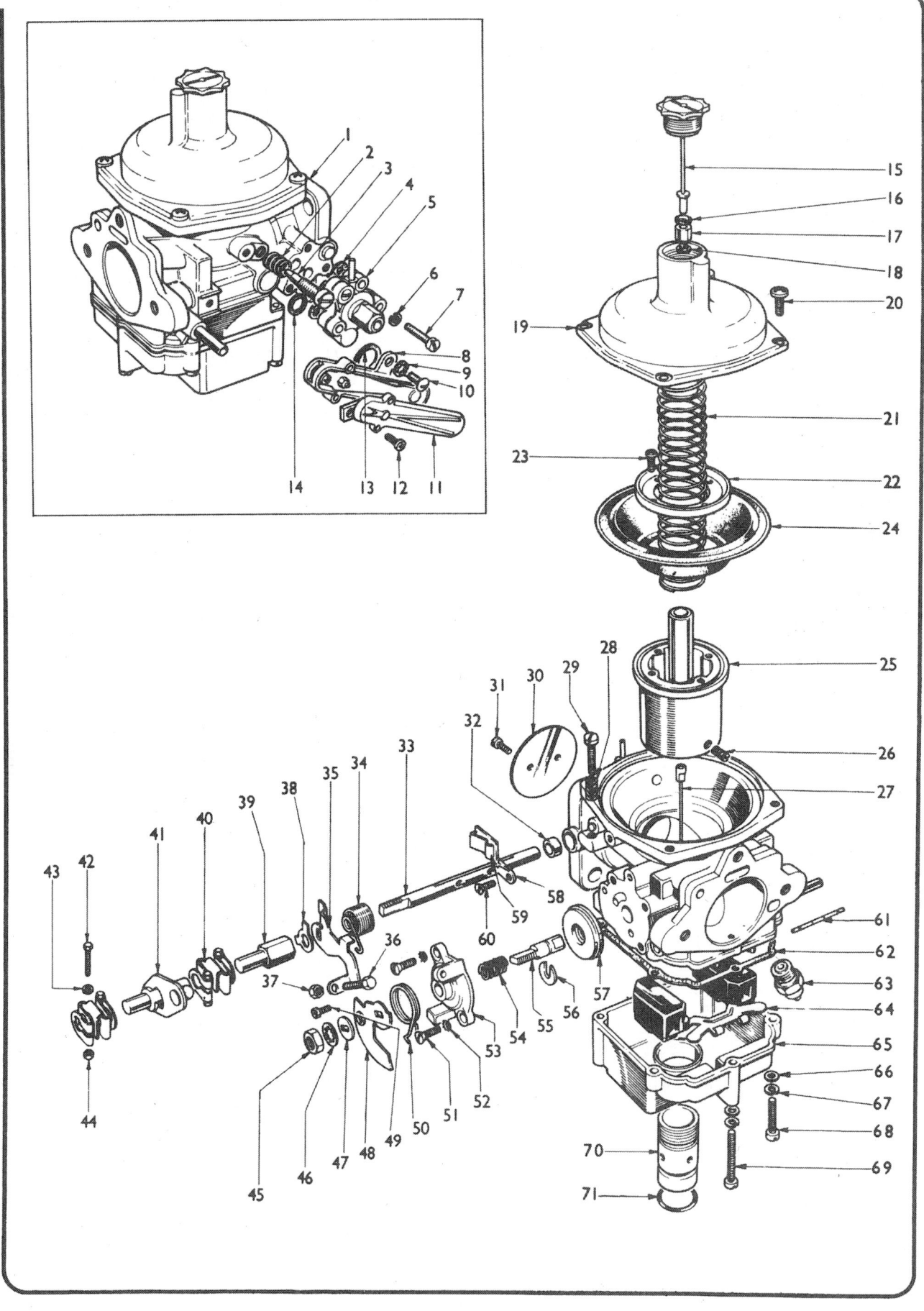

FIG. 3.4C. EXPLODED VIEW OF STROMBERG 175 CDSE CARBURETTOR

1 Carburettor
2 Spring - idle trimming screw
3 Idle trimming screw
4 Gasket - by-pass valve
5 By-pass valve
6 Lockwasher under (7)
7 Screw - securing (5)
8 Temperature compensator unit
9 Lockwasher under (10)
10 Securing screw (8)
11 Cover - temperature compensator
12 Securing screw (11)
13 Seal - on compensator body
14 Seal - inside carburettor
15 Damper rod) damper
16 Washer) assembly
17 Distance sleeve)
18 Circlip)
19 Cover - air valve
20 Securing screws (19)
21 Air valve return spring
22 Ring - diaphragm attachment
23 Screw - securing
24 Diaphragm
25 Air valve
26 Securing screw (27)
27 Needle assembly
28 Idle adjusting screw spring
29 Idle adjusting screw
30 Throttle disc
31 Securing screw (30)
32 Throttle spindle seal
33 Throttle spindle
34 Throttle return spring
35 Throttle lever
36 Fast idle screw
37 Locknut - securing (36)
38 Lockwasher - retaining (39)
39 Nut - throttle spindle
40 Coupling - throttle spindles
41 Connecting lever assembly
42 Clamping bolt
43 Washer (42)
44 Nut - securing (42)
45 Nut)
46 Shakeproof washer)
47 Washer)
48 Lever)
49 Cable attachment screw)
50 Return spring) Starter box
51 Screw) assembly
52 Shakeproof washer)
53 Starter box cover)
54 Spring)
55 Spindle)
56 Retainer)
57 Valve plate)
58 Cable abutment bracket
59 Spring clip
60 Securing screw (58)
61 Float pivot pin
62 Gasket - float chamber
63 Needle valve
64 Float assembly
65 Float chamber cover
66 Washer
67 Spring washer
68 Screw
69 Screw
70 Plug
71 Rubber 'O' ring

induction manifold is also felt in the suction chamber above the piston because of the drilling in the piston base. Because the suction chamber is sealed from the main body by means of a diaphragm, pressure above the piston is decreased and the piston lifts. As this happens, the choke area is increased and the depression above the piston is reduced. In this way the pressure drop across the jet orifice and air velocity remains virtually constant at all speeds irrespective of throttle opening. Thus the piston rises and falls, and the choke area varies as the engine's demands alter. The tapered needle protruding from the base of the piston moves up and down in the jet, and the space between the needle and the jet increases and decreases as the piston rises and falls.

This, of course, varies the mixture strength, and accounts for the influence of needle shape on engine performance.

Snap acceleration requires a richer mixture. The Stromberg is now faced with an additional difficulty. Sudden throttle opening could increase suction over the piston to such an extent that the piston would rise very rapidly to the top of the chamber. This would lower the depression in the jet and cause a weakening of the mixture just when it should be enriched. In fact, this difficulty is avoided by the inclusion of a piston damper in the design. The oil well in the middle of the piston rod has a spindle in it which is attached to the screw cap. On the end of the spindle is a sleeve which provides opposition to the oil flow as the piston rises, but not when it falls. This obstruction decreases the speed of the piston's rise and thus increases mixture strength when the throttle is opened suddenly. The level of this oil should be up to ¼ in of the end of the well.

To control exhaust emission the following modifications have been made to the standard carburettor:

a) The jet assembly and biased needle are now fixed to ensure a consistent air/fuel ratio.
b) There is a leak balancing screw for setting the carburettors to a common datum during production and once set the screw is sealed to prevent tampering.
c) A temperature compensator assembly is fitted and this progressively opens at high engine temperatures to correct the air/fuel mixture and restore even running.
d) There is a throttle by-pass valve which is set to open at a pre-determined manifold depression thereby admitting air during deceleration conditions.
e) The carburettors' cover is wire locked and sealed to discourage tampering.

10 Carburettor servicing

Because of the Federal Regulations as described in Section 2 all major work on the carburettor is discouraged. At high mileages it may be considered advisable to fit a replacement carburettor. However there are four service operations which must be completed every 24,000 miles (40,000 Km) and these are described in the following sections. Before commencing work obtain a service kit - Red Emission Pack 'B' which contains the following items:
   2 float - chambers gaskets (Red).
   2 'O' rings.
   2 needle valves.
   2 diaphragms.
   4 throttle spindle seals.
   4 temperature compensator seals.
   2 by-pass valve body gaskets.
Because the carburettors are manufactured to very fine tolerances it is very important that parts are not interchanged. Always complete one carburettor before beginning on the second one.

11 Carburettor installation - removal and refitting

1   Refer to Section 3 and remove the air cleaner assembly.

2 Detach the mixture control cables from each carburettor after loosening the retaining screws.

3 Carefully pull the emission control hoses from each carburettor and, where fitted, detach the vacuum pipe from the thermostatic switch on the rear carburettor.

4 Disconnect the rear throttle linkage at the countershaft.

5 Pull the main fuel supply rubber pipes from each carburettor, then disconnect and remove the fuel pipe and place it to one side.

6 Unscrew and remove the four nuts and spring washers securing each carburettor to the inlet manifold, and carefully withdraw both carburettors together with the interconnecting throttle linkage.

7 Remove the gaskets from the inlet manifold, noting that the tabs are uppermost and that the wide section segment is sandwiched between the two thin segments.

8 Refitting the carburettors is a reversal of the removal procedure but it will be necessary to fit new gaskets; make sure that the inlet manifold and carburettor joint faces are clean. After refitting the carburettors it will be necessary to adjust the idling and mixture settings.

12 Carburettor - dismantling, inspection, and reassembly

1 Remove the carburettor as described in Section 11.

2 Unscrew and remove the damper from the top cover.

3 Prise the plug from the float chamber then drain the oil and fuel from the carburettor into a suitable container.

4 Carefully prise the rubber O-ring from the bottom plug using a small screwdriver.

5 Unscrew and remove the retaining screws from the float chamber and detach the float chamber from the body.

6 Using a small screwdriver, prise the float assembly spindle from the retaining clips and withdraw the float assembly.

7 Unscrew and remove the needle valve and washer from the carburettor body.

8 Mark the top cover in relation to the main body to facilitate refitting, then unscrew and remove the four retaining screws in diagonal sequence and withdraw the top cover.

9 Remove the spring from the air valve, noting which way round it is fitted, then carefully lift the air valve assembly from the main body.

10 Unscrew and remove the four screws retaining the rubber diaphragm to the air valve, and remove the retaining ring and diaphragm, noting the location of the inner tag. It is important not to damage the metering needle during this operation.

11 Hold the air valve firmly in one hand and loosen the needle retaining grub screw with a small screwdriver.

12 Using the special needle height adjusting tool (BLMC part number S 353) inserted into the air valve stem, turn the adjustment anti-clockwise approximately two turns and extract the needle and housing from the air valve.

13 Unscrew and remove the two screws securing the starter assembly to the main body and withdraw the starter assembly.

14 Unscrew and remove the two screws securing the temperature compensator to the main body and withdraw the temperature compensator, noting that the two sealing rubbers are of different diameters.

15 Unscrew and remove the three slotted screws securing the bypass valve to the main body and remove the bypass valve and joint.

16 With the throttle butterfly held closed, unscrew and remove the two retaining screws, and then fully open the butterfly to remove it from the spindle.

17 Unhook the spindle return spring and carefully withdraw the spindle and spring assembly from the main body.

18 Using a small screwdriver prise the two spindle seals from the main body.

19 The carburettor is now completely dismantled and all the components should be thoroughly cleaned in fuel and allowed to dry.

20 Place the components on a clean piece of paper and carefully

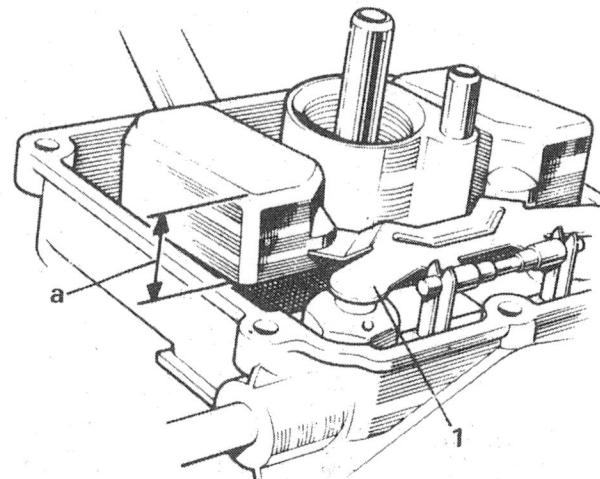

FIG. 3.5. FLOAT LEVEL ADJUSTMENT - THE FLOAT LEVEL IS CORRECT WHEN THE DISTANCE BETWEEN THE BOTTOM OF THE FLOAT AND THE FLANGE IS 16 - 17 MM (DIMENSION A)

1 Adjusting tab

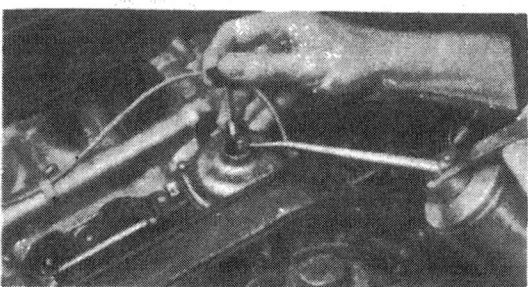

Fig. 3.6. Topping up dampers

examine them individually for excessive wear and deterioration; in particular check the diaphragm for splitting, and the metering needle, needle valve and air valve for wear.

21 Use a tyre pump to blow through the internal drillings of the main body and starter box.

22 Start reassembly of the carburettor by fitting two new spindle seals to the main body, tapping them in carefully until their metal casings are flush with the main body.

23 Insert the throttle spindle into the main body and locate the return spring.

24 Carefully refit the butterfly to the spindle (fully open) so that the two raised locating spots enter first, then close the throttle and insert the two retaining screws; the locating spots should be visible when viewed from the manifold end of the carburettor. Tighten the two screws and check that the throttle operates correctly.

25 Fit the starter box and tighten the retaining screws evenly.

26 Fit the bypass valve, at the same time locating a new gasket, then tighten the retaining screws evenly.

27 Fit the temperature compensator and tighten the retaining screws evenly.

28 Carefully locate the metering needle and housing assembly into the bottom of the air valve, then insert the special tool (BLMC part number S 353) into the air valve stem, turning it clockwise until the slot in the needle housing is aligned with the grub screw hole.

29 Tighten the grub screw into the slot; this ensures that the metering needle is biased towards the air cleaner at all times, regardless of the adjustment position.

30 Locate the rubber diaphragm onto the top of the air valve making sure that the inner tag engages with the special cut-out.

31 Place the retaining ring over the diaphragm and tighten the four screws in diagonal sequence.

32 Carefully fit the air valve assembly to the carburettor body making sure that the outer tag engages with the recess; ensure that the diaphragm is fully seated in the main body.

33 Place the return spring over the air valve stem in the correct position as previously noted.

34 Fit the top cover of the main body, with the previously made marks aligned, then insert the retaining screws and tighten them evenly in diagonal sequence; the extension on the cover should face the air intake side of the carburettor.

35 Locate the sealing washers onto the needle valve, then screw it into the main body and tighten evenly.

36 Locate the float assembly to the main body and lever the pivot pin into the retaining clips with a screwdriver.

37 The float height must now be checked. Invert the carburettor and check the distance between the highest point of each float and the adjacent face of the main carburettor body (without the gasket); the distance should be within the limits given in the Specifications and must be the same for both floats. To adjust the floats, carefully bend the tab which operates the needle valve until the dimension is correct, but make sure that the tab remains at right-angles to the needle to prevent the needle sticking. Alternatively a thin fibre washer can be inserted beneath the needle valve housing.

38 Place a new gasket onto the main body and carefully fit the float chamber; insert the six retaining screws and tighten them evenly in diagonal sequence.

39 Using the fingers only, manipulate the rubber O-ring onto the bottom plug then carefully press the plug into the base of the float chamber.

40 Fill the damper dashpot with engine oil until, with the damper inserted, resistance can be felt when the damper threaded cover is 0.25 in (6.0 mm) from the dashpot cover.

41 When the oil level is correct, tighten the damper cover.

13 Carburettor diaphragm - removal and refitting

1 Follow the instructions given in Section 12, paragraphs 8 to 10 inclusive, 30 to 34 inclusive, 40 and 41.

2 Adjust the mixture and idle settings as described in Sections 14 and 15.

14 Carburettor - mixture adjustment

1 Before starting this procedure it will be necessary to obtain a special adjusting tool (BLMC part number S 353).

2 Start and run the engine until normal operating temperature is reached.

3 Stop the engine and remove the air cleaner assembly as described in Section 3 of this chapter.

4 Loosen the throttle interconnecting coupling nuts and unscrew the slow running screw on both carburettors.

5 Push the choke control knob fully home into the dash panel and check that a clearance exists between the fast idle cam and adjustment screw on both carburettors.

6 Screw in each idle adjustment screw until it just touches the throttle lever, then turn each screw a further 1½ turns.

7 Start the engine and, using a screwdriver, lift each carburettor air valve in turn approximately 0.25 in (6.0 mm). The engine response to this action should be noted; if the engine speed increases immediately, the mixture is too rich, if it decreases or stalls, the mixture is too weak. The correct response is a slight increase in engine speed followed by a return to the original speed.

8 To adjust the carburettors, first stop the engine, then unscrew and remove the damper from the dash pot.

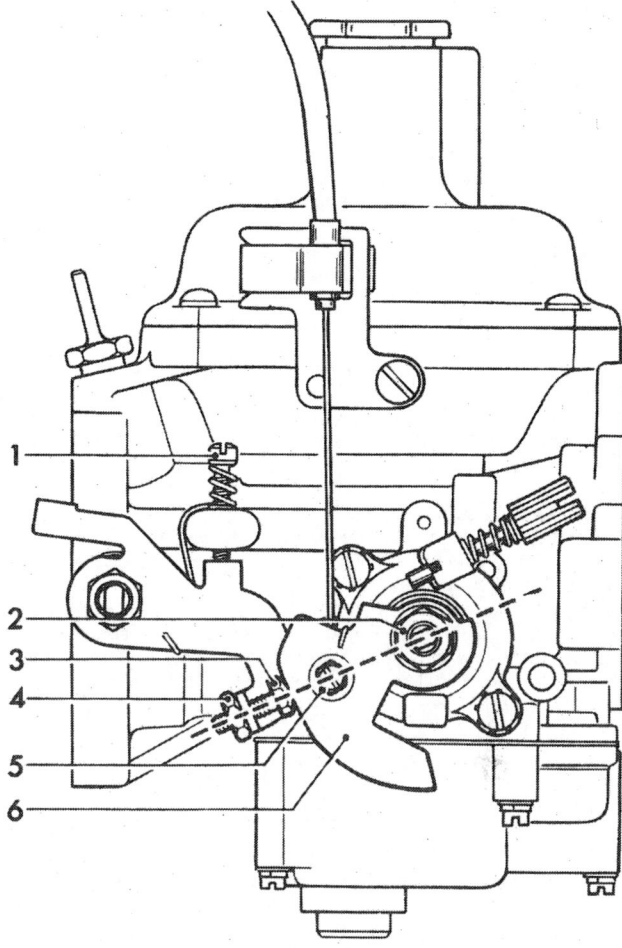

FIG. 3.7. CORRECT POSITION OF CHOKE CAM LEVER WHEN MAKING FAST IDLE ADJUSTMENT

1	Idling screw	4	Locknut
2	Starter box	5	Cable trunnion
3	Fast idle screw	6	Choke cam-lever

9 Insert the special tool mentioned in paragraph 1, ensuring that the outer member is fully engaged. Hold the outer member stationary and screw the inner member clockwise to enrich, or anti-clockwise to weaken the mixture. Make only minor adjustments at a time, and check the mixture setting again as described in paragraph 7; the damper must be installed when checking the adjustment.

10 When the adjustment is correct, top-up the dashpot with engine oil as described in Section 12.

11 In certain territories it is recommended that the exhaust CO level is checked in accordance with the local requirements.

15 Carburettor - idle and choke fast idle adjustment

Idle adjustment

1 Start and run the engine until normal operating temperature is reached.

2 Stop the engine and remove the air cleaner assembly as described in Section 3 of this Chapter.

3 Start the engine and use a length of rubber or plastic tube to synchronise the carburettors using the following procedure.

4 Hold one end of the tube to the ear and the other end to the centre of the carburettor flange. Listen to the amount of 'hiss' emanating from the intake, then transfer the tube to the other carburettor and compare the 'hiss' with the original carburettor;

unequal amounts indicate that the carburettors are not synchronised.

5 Carry out the instructions given in Section 14, paragraphs 4, 5 and 6.

6 Stop the engine and connect a tachometer in accordance with the maker's instructions.

7 Start the engine and turn the idle adjustment screws on each carburettor until the 'hiss' is equal, then turn the screws by equal amounts until the idle speed is correct (see Specifications).

8 Stop the engine and, with the relay lever against its stop, insert a 3/32 in (2.4 mm) drill between the tongue and the slot on the interconnecting lever. Tighten the interconnecting spring coupling nuts and bolts, and remove the drill shank.

9 Start the engine and increase the speed to 1500 rpm using the throttle pedal. Hold the engine at this speed and check the synchronisation of the carburettors using the length of tube.

10 With the engine at idling speed, recheck the synchronisation and rpm, making any minor adjustment on the adjusting screws as necessary.

Choke fast idle adjustment

11 With the engine stopped, check that the choke cable operates smoothly and that the mixture control cams on the carburettors return to their stops correctly.

12 Pull the choke control knob out from the dash panel and then insert a 5/16 in (7.9 mm) diameter bar between the fast idle cam and its stop on each carburettor in turn.

13 Loosen the fast idle adjustment screw locknut and adjust the screw until it just touches the fast idle cam. Repeat the adjustment on the remaining carburettor.

14 With the bar removed, push the choke control knob fully into the dash panel, then start the engine from cold and pull the control fully out.

15 Check that the fast idle speed is between 1100 and 1300 rpm; if not, adjust the adjustment screws on each carburettor by equal amounts until correct.

16 Return the choke control knob into the dash panel, stop the engine, and refit the air cleaner assembly as described in Section 3.

17 Disconnect the tachometer from the engine.

16 Throttle linkage - removal and refitting

1 Detach the horizontal control rod from the throttle pedal operating lever.

2 Unscrew and remove the two retaining screws and detach the relay lever support bracket from the carburettors.

3 Disconnect the control rod from the intermediate lever.

4 Withdraw the throttle linkage.

5 To refit the throttle linkage, first adjust the length of the long control rod to 11.94 in (303.3 mm) between pivot centres, and the short control rod to 3.18 in (80.8 mm) between pivot centres.

6 Refit the throttle linkage using the reverse order to removal, then adjust the carburettors as described in Section 14 and 15.

18 Fault finding diagnosis - emission control models

Symptom	Reason/s	Remedy
FUEL CONSUMPTION EXCESSIVE		
Carburation and ignition faults	Air cleaner choked giving rich mixture	Remove, clean and replace air cleaner.
	Fuel leaking from carburettors, fuel pumps, or fuel lines	Check for and eliminate all fuel leaks. Tighten fuel line union nuts.
	Float chamber flooding	Check and adjust float level.
	Generally worn carburettors	Remove, overhaul and replace.
	Distributor condenser faulty	Remove, and fit new unit.
	Balance weights or vacuum advance mechanism in distributor faulty	Remove, and overhaul distributor.
Incorrect adjustment	Carburettors incorrectly adjusted, (mixture too rich) or worn	Tune and adjust carburettors. Overhaul carburettors.
	Idling speed too high	Adjust idling speed.
	Contact breaker gap incorrect	Check and reset gap.
	Valve clearances incorrect	Check valve clearances.
	Incorrectly set spark plugs	Remove, clean and regap.
	Tyres under-inflated	Check tyre pressures and inflate as necessary.
	Wrong spark plugs fitted	Remove and replace with correct units.
	Brakes dragging	Check and adjust brakes.
INSUFFICIENT FUEL DELIVERY OR WEAK MIXTURE DUE TO AIR LEAKS		
Dirt in system	Petrol tank air vent restricted	Remove petrol cap and clean out air vent.
	Partially clogged filters in pump and carburettors	Remove and clean filters.
	Dirt lodged in float chamber needle housing	Remove and clean out float chamber and needle valve assembly.
	Incorrectly seating valves in fuel pump	Remove, dismantle, and clean out fuel pump.
Fuel pump faults	Fuel pump diaphragm leaking or damaged	Remove and overhaul fuel pump.
	Gasket in fuel pump damaged	Remove, and overhaul fuel pump.
	Fuel pump valves sticking due to petrol gumming	Remove and thoroughly clean fuel pump.
Air leaks	Too little fuel in fuel tank (prevalent when climbing steep hills)	Refill fuel tank.
	Union joints on pipe connections loose	Tighten joints and check for air leaks.
	Split in fuel pipe on suction side of fuel pump	Examine, locate, and repair.
	Inlet manifold to block or inlet manifold to carburettors gasket leaking	Test by pouring oil along joints-bubbles indicate leak. Renew gasket as appropriate.

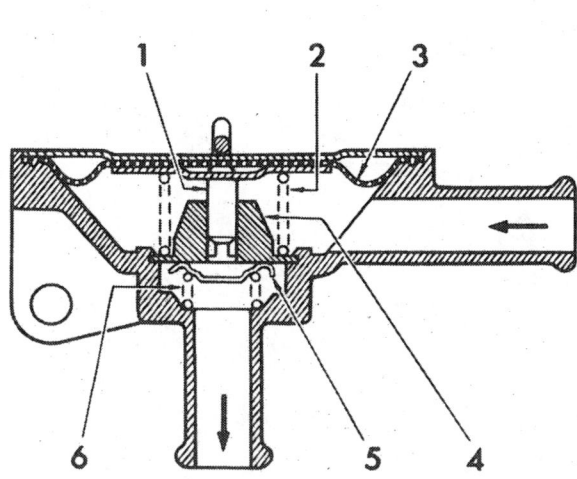

FIG. 3.8. CRANKCASE EMISSION CONTROL VALVE COMPONENTS (TR250/6)

1 Valve pin   4 Orifice plate
2 Spring   5 Plate valve
3 Diaphragm   6 Spring

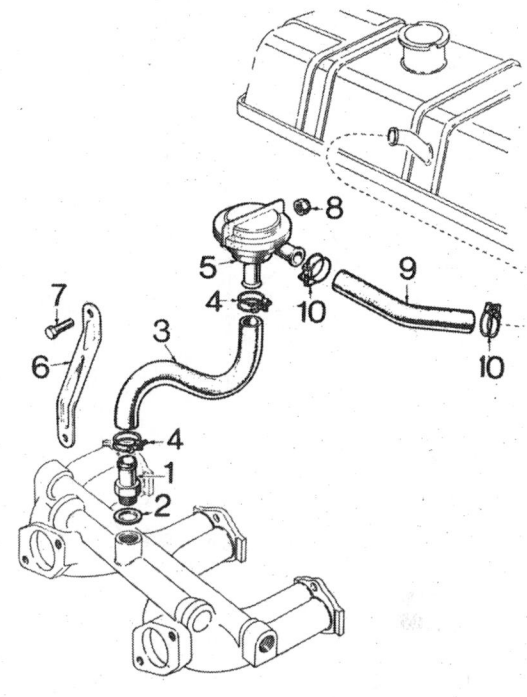

FIG. 3.9. EXPLODED VIEW OF CLOSED CIRCUIT BREATHER LAYOUT (TR250/6 CARBURETTOR)

1 Adaptor   6 Bracket
2 Fibre washer   7 Screw
3 Hose   8 Nyloc
4 Clip   9 Hose
5 Emission control valve   10 Clip
  assembly

19 Petrol injection - general description

All PI models are fitted with the Lucas Mk II petrol injection system whereby instead of carburettors special injectors squirt a fine spray of petrol into the air intakes at an accurately pre-determined time. The amount of petrol sprayed depending on engine and throttle conditions. The charge is then drawn into the combustion chamber, compressed and ignited in the usual manner.

The system is shown in diagrammatic form in Fig. 3.14. and operates as follows: Petrol from the tank passes under the influence of gravity. When required, petrol passes through the main fuel line to an electrically driven pump. Petrol under pressure passes from the pump to the metering unit which pre-determines the amount of petrol to be injected into the air intake and at what time in sequence through the pipes to the injectors.

The petrol pump maintains a line pressure of between 106 - 110 psi and by using a pressure relief valve any excess petrol is returned to the tank.

As petrol is used to lubricate the metering unit a continuous flow system is used whereby petrol is in circulation at all times during engine operation and it is returned to the tank via a pipe connecting the metering unit to the tank. The metering unit is driven in conjuction with the ignition distributor drive.

The petrol filter is also designed to act as an anti-surge device so preventing loss of petrol during high speed cornering, the negotiation of steep hills, or excessive braking conditions.

The electric pump, fuel filter and pressure relief valve are located behind the trim panel in the luggage compartment.

There is an inertia switch fitted into the electrical circuit of the fuel pump motor so that in the event of an accident the circuit will be broken.

Any service work, other than mentioned in this manual, must be entrusted to the agent or petrol injection specialist as special equipment is required to diagnose faults and set the various components of the petrol injection equipment.

20 Service precautions - PI Models

Engines fitted with petrol injection equipment are serviced in the normal way on all common items but in addition there are

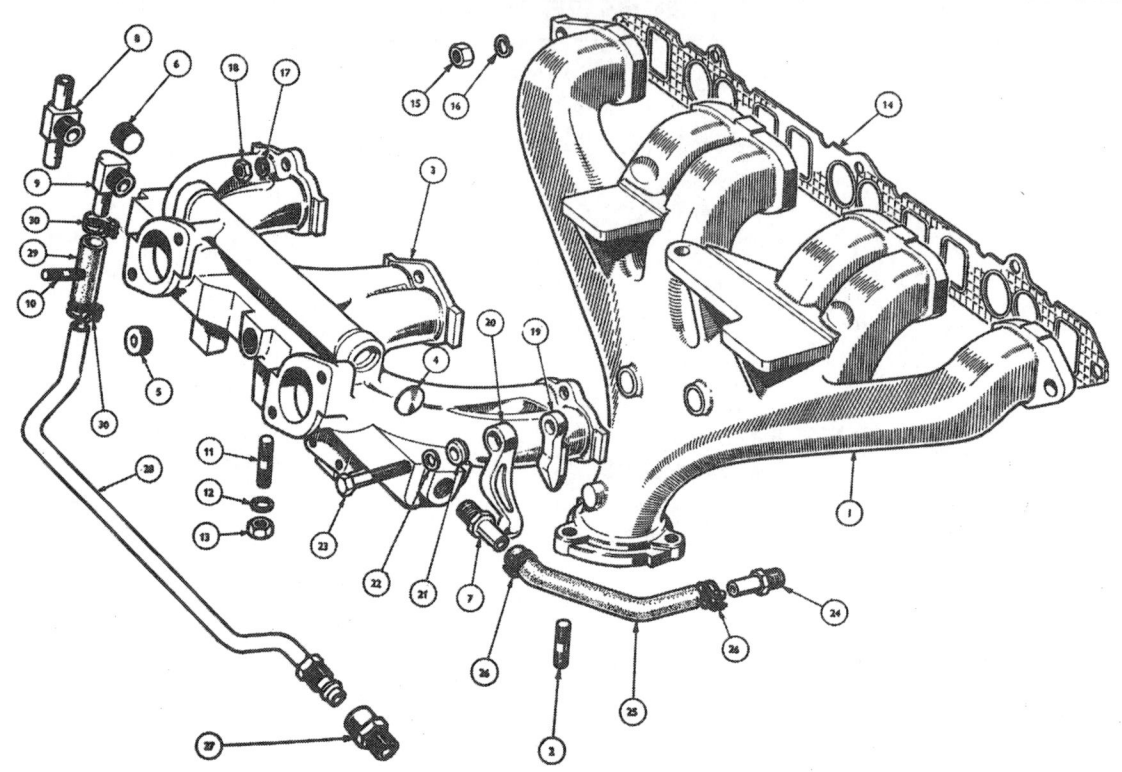

FIG. 3.10. EXPLODED VIEW OF INLET AND EXHAUST MANIFOLD (TR250/6 CARBURETTORS)
NOTE: THE INLET MANIFOLD IS FITTED TO EARLY PRODUCED MODELS ONLY.
LATER TYPE SHOWN IN FIG. 3.11.

1 Exhaust manifold	heater is fitted)	16 Washer	24 Adaptor
2 Stud	9 Elbow	17 Washer	25 Hose
3 Inlet manifold	10 Stud	18 Nut	26 Hose clip
4 Core plug	11 Stud	19 Clamp plate	27 Adaptor
5 Dryseal plug	12 Washer	20 Clamp	28 Pipe
6 Inlet manifold plug	13 Nut	21 Washer	29 Hose
7 Adapter	14 Washer	22 Plain washer	30 Clip
8 'T' piece (required only when	15 Nut	23 Bolt	

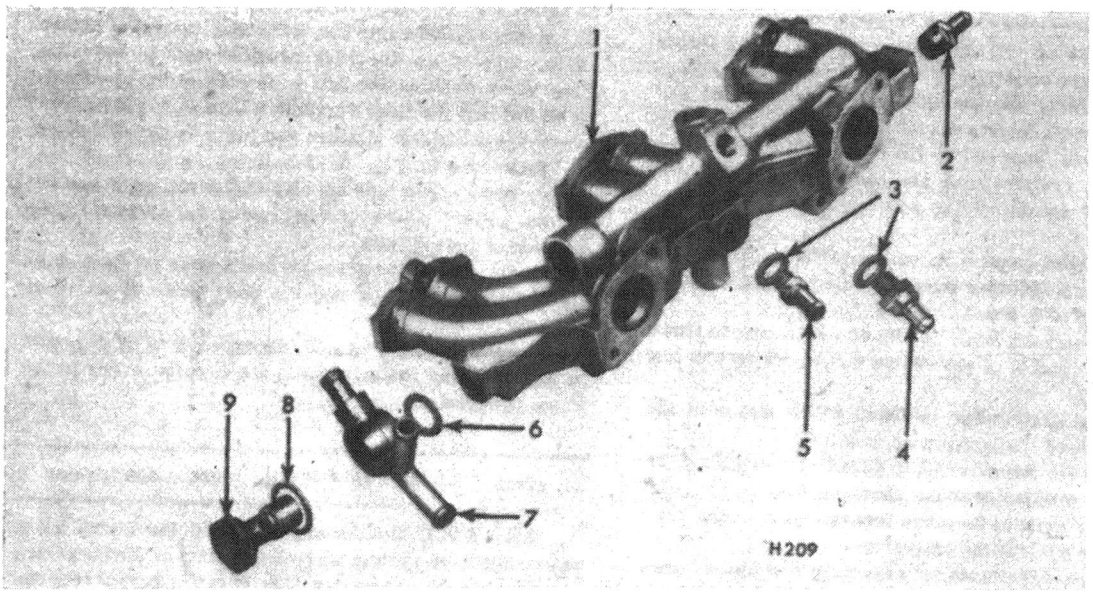

FIG. 3.11. LATER TYPE INLET MANIFOLD

1 Inlet manifold	3 Fibre washer	5 Adaptor	8 Washer (large hole)
2 Adaptor (front water feed to manifold)	4 Non-return valve (Brake Servo Unit)	6 Washer (small hole)	9 Banjo bolt
		7 Adaptor assembly	

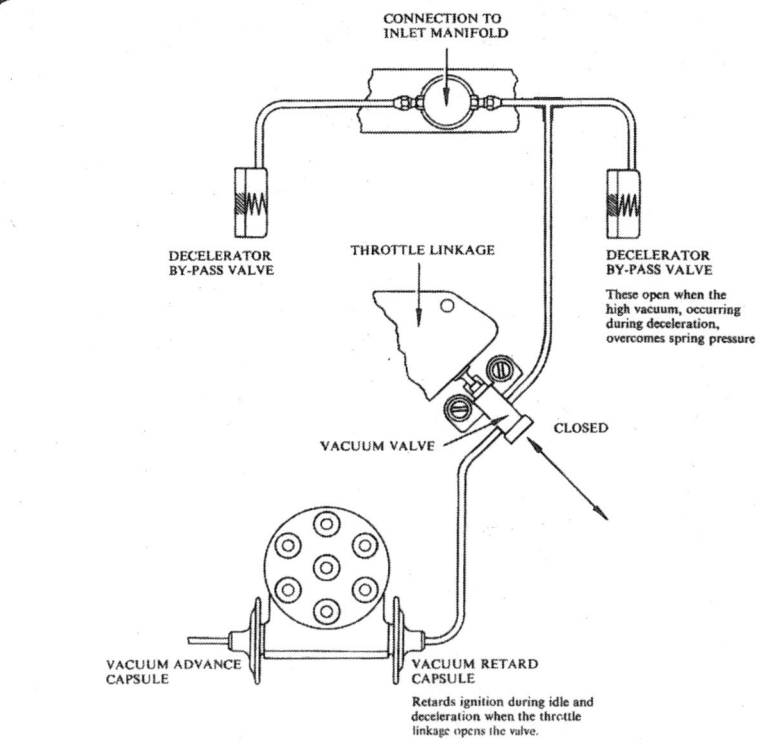

Fig. 3.12. Vacuum circuit for deceleration control (TR250/6 carburettors) - see also Chapter 4

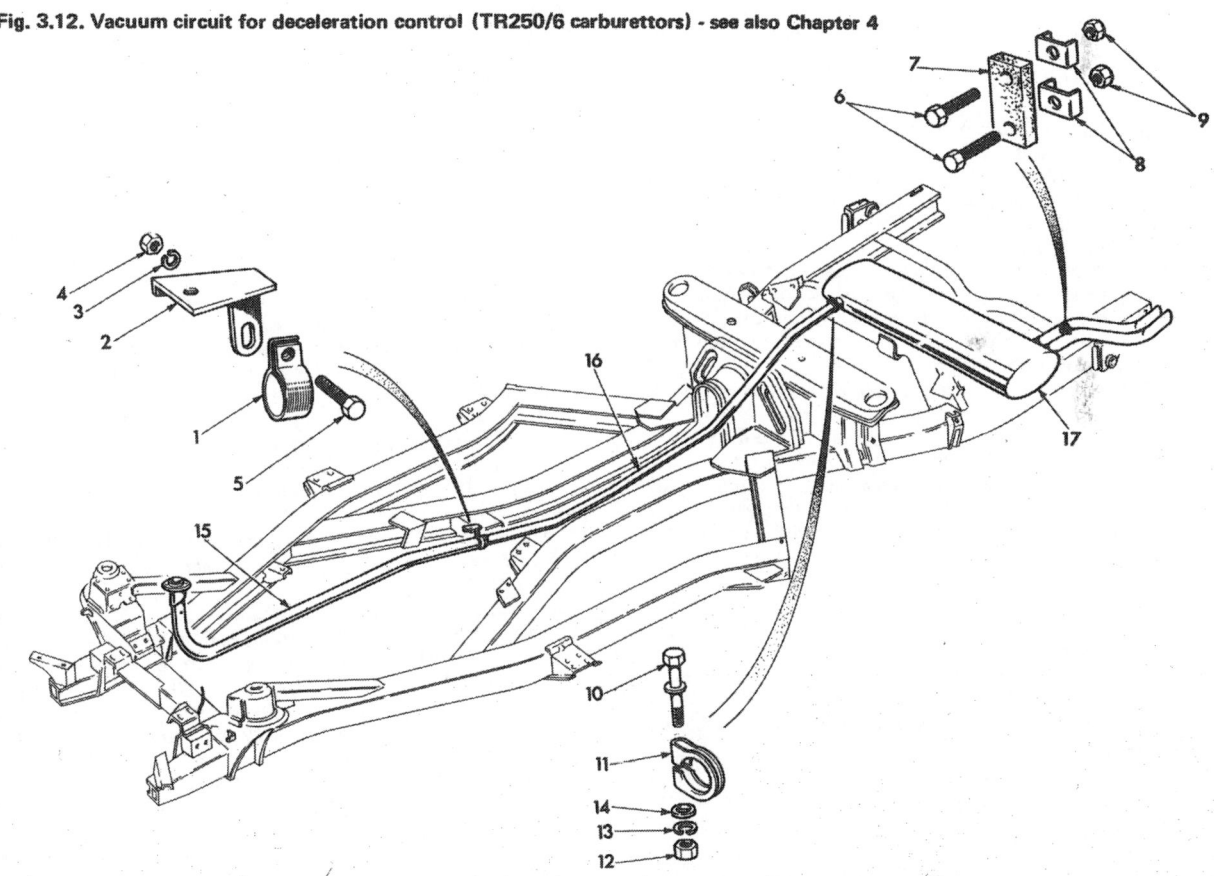

FIG. 3.13. LAYOUT OF EXHAUST SYSTEM (TR250/6 CARBURETTORS)

1	Clip	5	Bolt	9	Nut	13	Spring washer
2	Bracket	6	Bolt	10	Bolt	14	Plain washer
3	Spring washer	7	Flexible mounting	11	Clamp	15	Front pipe
4	Nut	8	Reinforcing bracket	12	Nut	16	Intermediate pipe
						17	Silencer

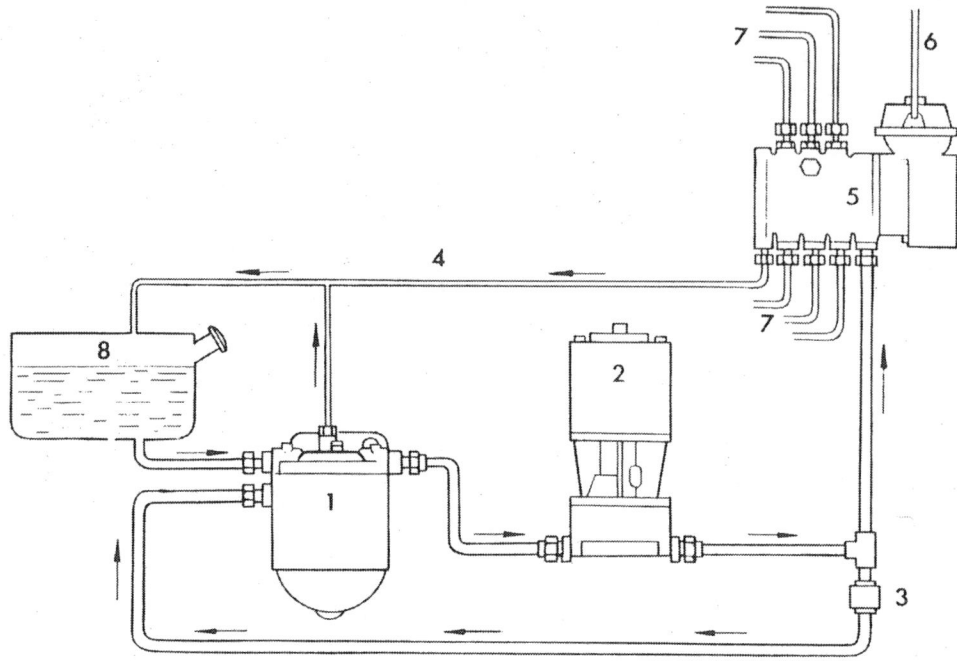

FIG. 3.14. DIAGRAMMATIC VIEW OF P.I. SYSTEM

1 *Filter*	3 *Pressure relief valve*	5 *Metering distributor control unit*	6 *Connection to manifold*
2 *Motor driven pump*	4 *Leakage fuel*		7 *To injectors*
			8 *Fuel tank*

◄■■ Direction of fuel flow

five additional points which must be strictly adhered to otherwise expensive damage can result:-

1 If the car is to be off the road for a while due to overhaul or other reasons, a petrol sludge inhibitor should be added to the petrol and the engine run for a short while to ensure complete circulation through the system.

2 It is important that the petrol pump is not switched on whilst any part of the high pressure circuit has been disconnected.

3 The petrol pump must not remain on for long periods with the engine not running. If this condition is necessary disconnect the petrol pump electrical terminals.

4 Any seals or gaskets displaced during maintenance must be renewed.

5 After overhaul or removal of a major part of the system it will be necessary to re-prime the system. Pull out the choke control fully and with the battery in a high state of charge rotate the engine until it starts. Do not try to re-prime the system if the battery is discharged as it probably will not be able to cope with the starter motor need.

21 Routine maintenance (PI)

The routine maintenance of the petrol injection system is limited to that of fitting a new fuel filter element every 12,000 miles (20,000 Km).

1 Remove the spare wheel and place a shallow container beneath the filter. To prevent petrol draining from the tank use a mole type wrench to clamp the hose or alternatively plug the filter inlet pipe.

2 Unscrew the centre retaining bolt and lift away the filter element and lower casing.

3 Remove the sealing rings in the upper and lower casings and the bolt sealing washer.

4 Fit a new element, sealing rings and washer taking care to ensure that all seals are correctly fitted. It is important that the correct filter element is used and for petrol filtration as the action of petrol on an element designed for diesel oil causes it to

break down.

22 Air cleaner (PI)

1 All PI models use a paper element air cleaner which should be checked for cleanliness every 6,000 miles (10,000 Km) or more often in dusty conditions. Fit a new element every 12,000 miles (20,000 Km) or whenever necessary.

2 Release the air cleaner by slackening the clips and detaching the two convoluted hoses. Gently ease it from the air intake manifold.

3 Undo the centre retaining wing nut Fig. 3.15 and lift off the cover followed by the element and sealing rings.

4 Clean between the folds of the element using a soft brush or air from a foot pump or fit a new element as required. DO NOT wash in petrol or paraffin.

5 Reassembling is the reverse procedure to removal. Take care to ensure that the sealing rings are correctly located.

23 Injector (PI) - removal, servicing and replacement

1 Should it be absolutely necessary to remove an injector from the air inlet manifold first clean the area of all dirt and dust.

2 Disconnect the injector pipe by holding the hexagon on the injector with an open ended spanner and with a second open ended spanner undo the pipe union (Fig. 3.23).

3 Undo the bolt securing the injector retaining plate to the inlet manifold. Lift away the plate followed by the injector.

4 The nylon holder and 'O' ring can be removed using open ended spanners.

5 To clean out the injector go to your local garage and using a compressed air jet suitably filtered to exclude moisture and set to a pressure of 80 psi blow through the injector from the fuel inlet side. Apart from this cleaning operation no other servicing may be carried out except with specialist equipment.

6 Refitting is the reverse sequence to removal. Strict cleanliness must be observed at all times.

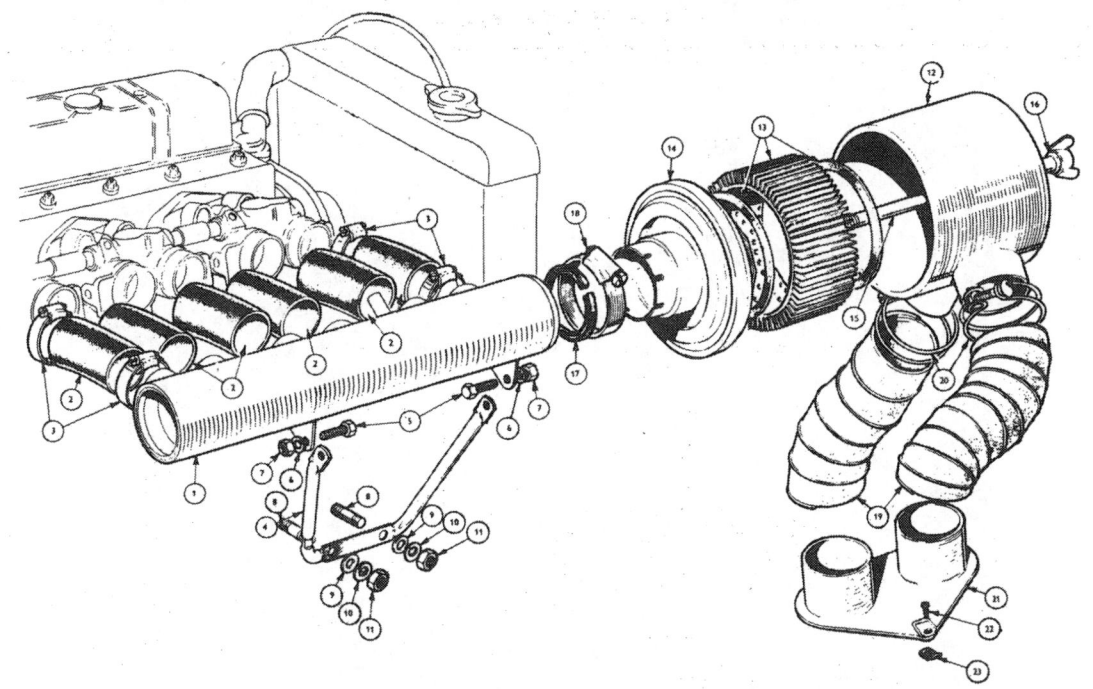

FIG. 3.15. EXPLODED VIEW OF THE AIR MANIFOLD AND AIR CLEANER

1 Air manifold assembly	7 Nut	13 Air cleaner element	19 Air intake hose
2 Hose	8 Stud	14 Bottom plate assembly	20 Clip
3 Hose clip	9 Plain washer	15 Centre bolt	21 Adaptor
4 Stay	10 Lock washer	16 Wing nut	22 Setscrew
5 Setscrew	11 Nut	17 Flange finisher	23 Nut
6 Lock washer	12 Air cleaner assembly cover	18 Clip	

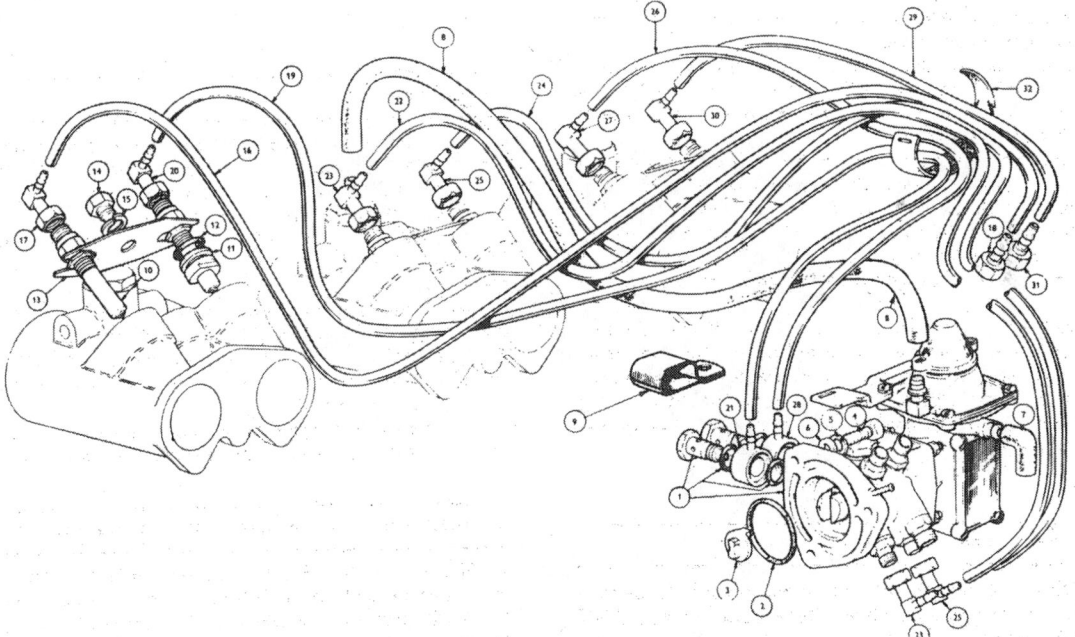

FIG. 3.16. EXPLODED VIEW OF THE FUEL INJECTION METERING PUMP UNIT, INJECTION NOZZLES AND PIPES

1 Metering pump unit	9 Clip	17 Elbow	25 Elbow - No 4 injector pipe
2 'O' ring	10 Injector nozzle assembly	18 Nipple & nut	26 Tube - No 5 injector pipe
3 Pump coupling	11 Block	19 Tube - No 2 injector pipe	27 Elbow "
4 Setscrew	12 'O' ring	20 Elbow "	28 Banjo "
5 Lock washer	13 Plate	21 Banjo "	29 Tube - No 6 injector pipe
6 Plain washer	14 Setscrew	22 Tube - No 3 injector pipe	30 Elbow "
7 Rubber elbow	15 Plain washer	23 Elbow	31 Nipple & nut - No 6 injector pipe
8 Metering hose	16 Tube - No 1 injector pipe	24 Tube - No 4 injector pipe	32 Firtree clip

FIG. 3.17. LUGGAGE COMPARTMENT VIEW OF P.I. EQUIPMENT

1 Pressure relief valve	3 Filter outlet	5 Pump leak drain	6 Fuel pump motor
2 Fuel filter	4 Pump inlet	pipe	

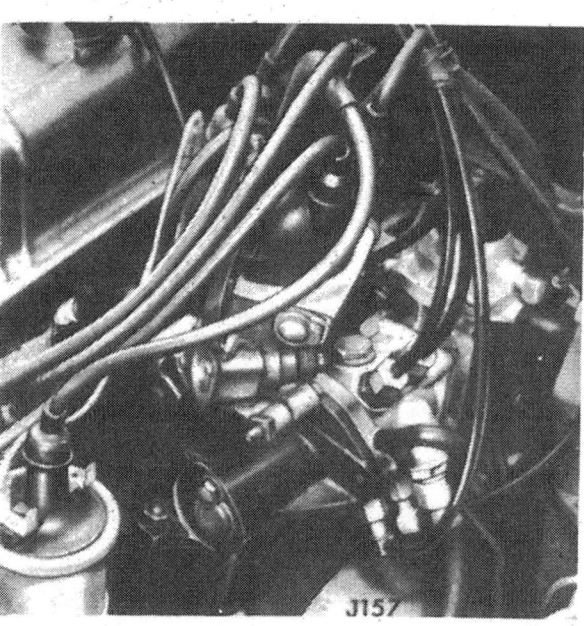

Fig. 3.18. Metering unit location on engine

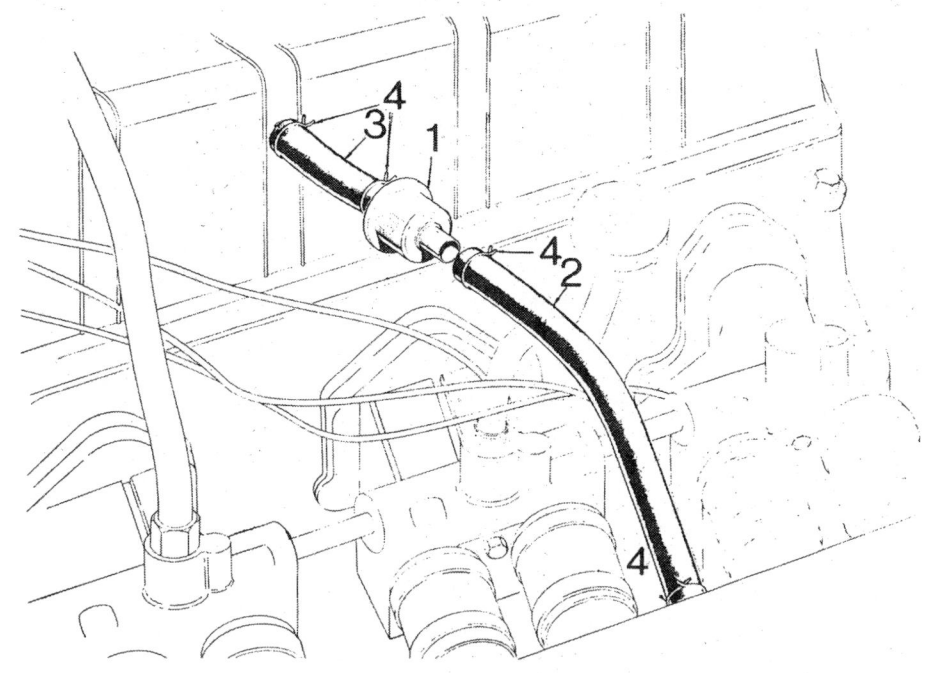

FIG. 3.19. CLOSED CIRCUIT BREATHER (P.I.)

| 1 Breather assembly | 2 Hose, breather to air mani-fold | 3 Hose, breather to rocker cover | 4 Hose clip |

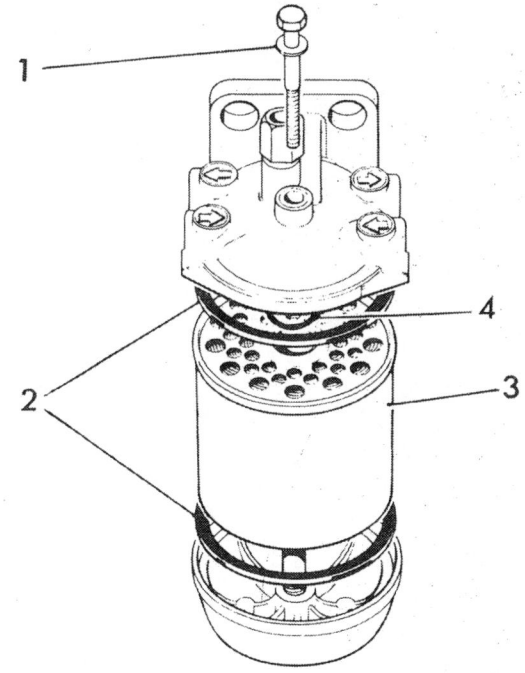

FIG. 3.20 FUEL FILTER COMPONENTS (P.I.)

1 Centre bolt
2 Element sealing rings
3 Element
4 Inner sealing ring

FIG. 3.21. INJECTION LOCATION ON MANIFOLD

1 Retaining bolt
2 Retaining plate
3 Injector
4 Injector pipe union

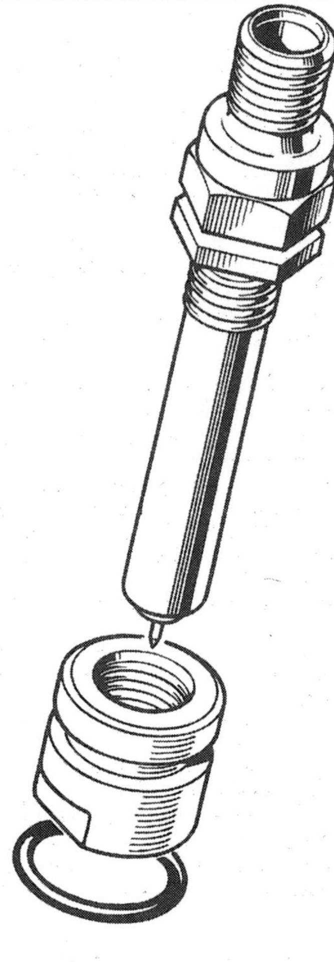

Fig. 3.22. Injector, holder and 'O' ring

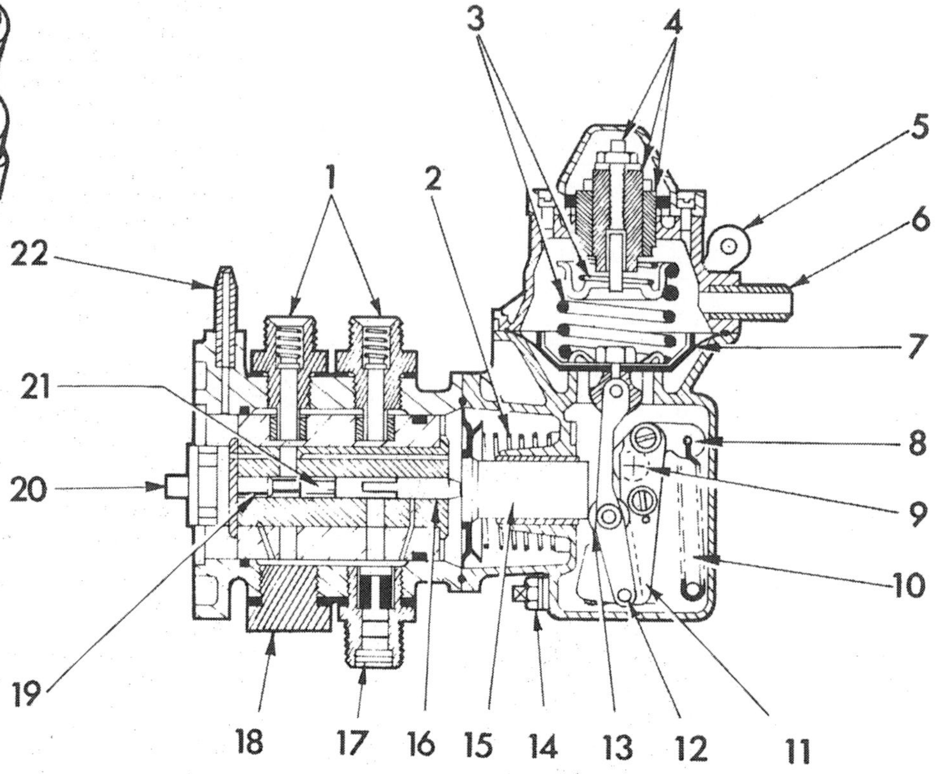

FIG. 3.23. METERING DISTRIBUTOR CROSS SECTION

1 Outlet valves	12 Control links
2 Balance spring	13 Rollers
3 Calibration springs	14 Full load setting screw
4 Calibration screws	15 Follower
5 Excess fuel lever	16 Control stop
6 Connection to manifold	17 Fuel inlet
7 Diaphragm	18 Blanking plug
8 Fuel cam carrier	19 Fixed stop
9 Pivot 'X'	20 Rotor drive
10 Return spring	21 Shuttle
11 Fuel cam	22 Leakage fuel

24 Metering distributor unit (PI) - removal and refitting

Removal:-

1 Disconnect the negative terminal from the battery .

2 Refer to the previous section and disconnect the injector pipes at the injectors. Mark the pipes to ensure correct refitting.

3 Remove No 1 spark plug and turn the engine until No 1 cylinder is at T D C on the firing stroke. (Reference to the timing marks will assist here).

4 Disconnect the vacuum pipe from the metering unit.

5 Partially drain the petrol tank until it is under ¼ full, to stop syphoning from the tank. Disconnect the fuel inlet pipe at the metering unit and blank off the end using a piece of tapered wood or a pencil.

6 Disconnect the lubricating fuel return pipe from the metering unit.

7 Disconnect the cold start cable from the metering unit.

8 Undo the three bolts that hold the metering unit to the drive pedestal.

9 Very carefully lift away the metering unit and injector pipes from the drive pedestal. Lift out the little plastic drive dog.

10 Undo the bolt that holds the sealing plug in position at the forward end of the pedestal and using the fingers only push out the drive gear and plug.

11 It is possible to remove the distributor, pedestal and metering unit as one complete assembly but it will be necessary to separate them before refitting to the engine. Further details of this may be found in Chapter 1.

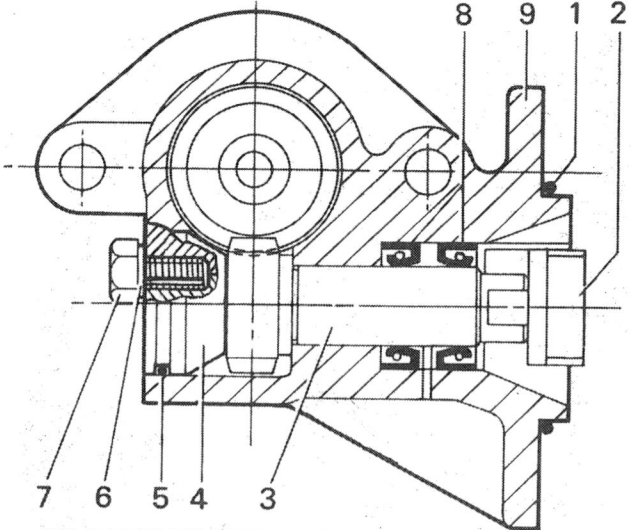

FIG. 3.24 CROSS SECTION OF PEDESTAL AND DRIVE PINION

1 'O' ring	6 Washer
2 Drive dog	7 Retaining bolt
3 Pinion	8 Lip seals
4 Plug	9 Pedestal
5 Plug 'O' ring	

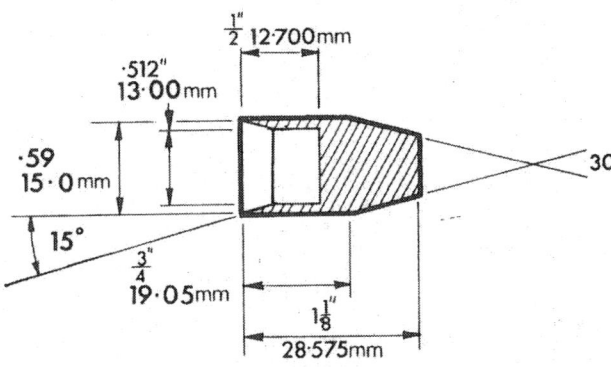

Fig. 3.25. Pinion protective cover dimensions

Fig. 3.26. Drive pinion in alignment

Fig. 3.27. Metering unit in alignment

Refitting:-

1 With No 1 spark plug removed rotate the engine until No 1 cylinder is at T D C on the compression stroke (reference to the timing marks will assist here).

2 So that the delicate seals are not damaged fit the protective cover to the end of the drive gear pinion. If workshop facilities are available the cover may be made to the dimensions given in Fig. 3.26. or as a last resort the drive gear should be very well lubricated with a heavy grade oil.

3 Very carefully insert the gear through the pedestal aperture so that when fitted the slot milled in the end of the pinion is vertical.

4 Fit a new 'O' ring to the plug and insert the plug into the aperture. Lock this in position by refitting the bolt and its washer.

5 Smear the plastic drive dog with a little thick grease and fit to the pinion. The grease should hold the dog in place.

6 Refit a new pedestal 'O' ring seal around the pedestal boss making sure that it is positioned correctly.

7 Rotate the slotted drive on the metering unit to the horizontal position with the scribed lines on the drive and body correctly aligned. If the number 6 cylinder outlet adaptor is removed the rotator hole should be seen to be at the start of its injection period.

8 Refit the metering unit to the pedestal and replace the three retaining bolts.

9 Wipe the ends of the pipes and the injectors with a clean non-fluffy rag and reconnect the fuel injection pipes in the previously noted correct order.

10 Reconnect the vacuum pipe to the metering unit.

11 Refit the fuel inlet pipe to the metering unit.

12 Reconnect the cold start cable to the metering unit.

13 Reconnect the battery negative terminal.

14 The system will have to be re-primed. Pull out the choke control fully and with the battery in a high state of charge , rotate the engine until it starts. Do not try to re-prime the system if the battery is discharged as it probably will not be able to cope with the starter motor's needs.

25 Pipes and unions (PI)

As the petrol injection is dependant on fuel tight joints and pipes in perfect condition, care must always be taken to ensure utmost cleanliness at all unions during dismantling or re-assembly. Regular inspections must be carried out for loose connections, fretting pipes, kinking, leaks or joints seeping and if there are any signs of these, immediate remedial action must be taken. All replacement pipes should be obtained complete with unions from the Triumph agents.

26 Setting throttle butterflies (PI)

1 This is an adjustment that can be carried out by the owner providing each step is taken with care and is completed satisfactorily before the next step is taken. The only item of special equipment necessary is an air flow meter which you may be able to borrow from the local garage - most garages have them.

2 Before commencing work and carrying out the various adjustments it is imperative that ignition timing as well as the metering distributor timing is correct. Full details of timing the ignition are given in Chapter 4.

3 To check the metering distributor timing turn the engine until No 1 cylinder is at TDC on the compression stroke. Removal of the No 6 injection pipe outlet adaptor will show the rotor hole as an elliptical hole at the start of its injection position. Once conditions so far are satisfactory continue as follows:

4 Disconnect the air intake manifold and lift away from the

Fig. 3.28 Adjusting the air valve

FIG. 3.29. THROTTLE ADJUSTMENT POINTS

1 Cold start screw   3 Slow running screw
2 Cable adjuster   4 Adjusting rod locknuts

Fig. 3.30. Adjustment of butterfly clearances

Fig. 3.31. Adjustment of centre butterflies to fully open
position

Fig. 3.32. Cold start control adjustment

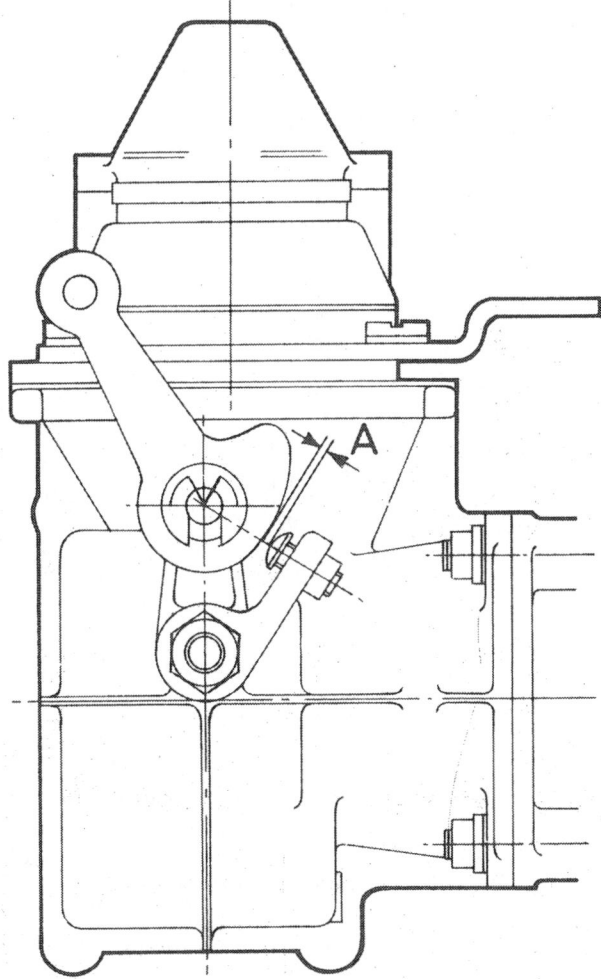

Fig. 3.33. Setting for excess fuel lever
A = 0.006 - 0.008 inch (0.15 - 0.2 mm)

engine compartment.

5 Run the engine until it has reached its normal operating temperature. Check that the cold start knob is pushed in fully.

6 Slacken off the cold start cam adjusting screw.

7 Slacken off the accelerator cable adjustment.

8 Turn the butterfly adjusting screws so that one thread is just protruding below each bracket.

9 Release the locknuts on the vertical adjusting rods.

10 Place a 0.1 in (2.54 mm) thick spacer between the cross shaft stop and bracket so that the butterflies can be checked for closure without interference from the cross shaft mechanism stop. Inspect the position of all butterflies to ensure that they are completely closed.

11 Adjust the three vertical rods using a screwdriver so that all play has been eliminated from the linkage yet without any movement of the butterflies. When completed re-tighten the locknuts.

12 With a screwdriver adjust the cold start cam adjustment screw so that a clearance of 0.002 in (0.0508 mm) exists between the screw head and the cam. When correctly set re-tighten the locknut.

13 Eliminate the free play from the cold start cable by adjustment of the outer cable.

14 Eliminate the free play from the accelerator cable by adjustment of the outer cable.

15 Start the engine and again allow to come up to normal operating temperature. Turn the air valve screw until the slow running speed is set to between 750 - 800 rpm.

16 Inspect the butterfly closure by shutting off the air valve pipe with the thumb, this should stop the engine when all butterflies are closed correctly. Should the engine continue to run check the air flow at all ports with an air flow meter. The butterflies allowing air to pass should be reset by adjustment of the vertical rod. However, should only one of a pair of butterflies show a difference in air flow reading the butterfly should be inspected for distortion or the spindle twisting. Fit new parts as necessary

17 Screw in the three butterfly stop screws to the position where they are taking the weight of the butterfly return springs but not altering the closed position of the butterflies. The reason for fitting stop screws is to prevent the butterflies digging into the inlet manifolds. They should not be used to alter the slow running speed.

18 Recheck the slow running speed and place the thumb over the air valve pipe to check for full closure of the butterflies.

19 Test the fast idle by pulling on the cold start cable to the fully open position and this should give an increase of engine speed to 2,500 rpm with the engine at normal operating temperature.

20 Allow the engine to cool down and test for starting from cold. Pull out the cold start knob and it should give an initial idle speed of between 1,700 to 2,000 rpm for several seconds. Thereafter the speed should drop because of an over rich mixture. Push in the knob to its midway position and the engine idle speed should settle to between 1,500 to 1,700 rpm.

21 Replace the air intake manifold system.

27 Pressure relief valve (PI)

If operation of the pressure relief valve is suspect it should be checked using a pressure gauge and adaptor. This is a job best left to the local Triumph garage.

To remove the valve proceed as follows:

1 Detach the return to filter pipe from the pressure relief valve. Also detach the second return pipe from the valve and plug the ends to prevent dirt entering the fuel system.

2 Undo and remove the two securing nuts and bolts and lift away the valve.

3 To gain access to the strainer place the body in a vice, remove the relief valve from the body, and lift away the strainer. Clean and refit the strainer.

4 Refitting the valve is the reverse sequence to removal.

28 Fuel pump (PI) - general

An exploded view of the motorised pump is shown in Fig 3. 34. Normally the unit requires no service attention but if the unit should fail it should be taken to the local Triumph garage. The unit may be considered as a motor and pump and it should be possible to obtain one of these two parts. The local Triumph garage will be able to advise definitely upon the inspection of the unit.

If the pump becomes noisy but otherwise operation is satisfactory the armature end float may be adjusted. With the unit held vertically with the adjuster uppermost slacken the locknut. Screw in the adjuster until slight resistance is felt and then back off the adjuster one quarter of a turn. Retighten the locknut.

A fuel strainer is located behind the inlet connection so if it is suspected that it is blocked detach the inlet connection and withdraw the strainer. Wash the strainer in petrol, shake dry and refit.

29 Fault diagnosis - Petrol injection

Most faults such as excessive fuel consumption, poor engine performance, and erratic running may be blamed on the petrol injection system but after correct diagnosis the cause may be found to be in one of the other systems including ignition, electrical, cooling or that there is insufficient clean petrol in the tank. If none of these systems is the cause of the trouble it is recommended that the car be taken to the agents for further diagnosis. As a guide to fault diagnosis the details below should give an indication as to the cause.

FAULT FINDING
Effects of a fault in the petrol injection system.
A fault will usually be revealed in one of four ways:
a) the engine cannot be started or can be started only with difficulty;
b) the engine starts but runs erratically over the whole or part of the speed range;
c) fuel consumption is excessive;
d) the engine starts but does not respond to movement of the throttle.

Overfuel control lever check
Faults (a), (b) and (c) may be due to incorrect operations of the overfuel control lever. Check that it is fully responsive to manual control over its full range and that when in the OFF position there is a clearance of 0.004 - 0.008 in between the lever and the adjustment screw upon which it bears.
a) Engine fails to start or can be started only with difficulty.
1 Switch on the ignition and check (audibly or by touch) that the fuel pump motor is running.
2 If the pump motor is running, disconnect one of the low tension cable connections at the coil but leave the ignition switch on.
3 Grip each injector feed line in turn lightly with the hand and crank the engine. A distinct pulsation should be felt with each line as fuel is injected.
NOTE: The feed lines are cleated together and must be separated to avoid the misleading effect of reflected pulsations.

If obvious pulsations are felt in each line the petrol injection system is unlikely to be the cause of failure to start and some other cause must be found.

If pulsations cannot be felt in any line although the pump motor is working apparently normally, check fuel pressure. If pressure and relief valve settings are satisfactory, switch off the ignition and remove the metering control unit for examination of the drive coupling, which may have broken.

Finally, remember to restore the coil low tension connection.
b) Engine starts but runs erratically over the whole or part of the speed range.

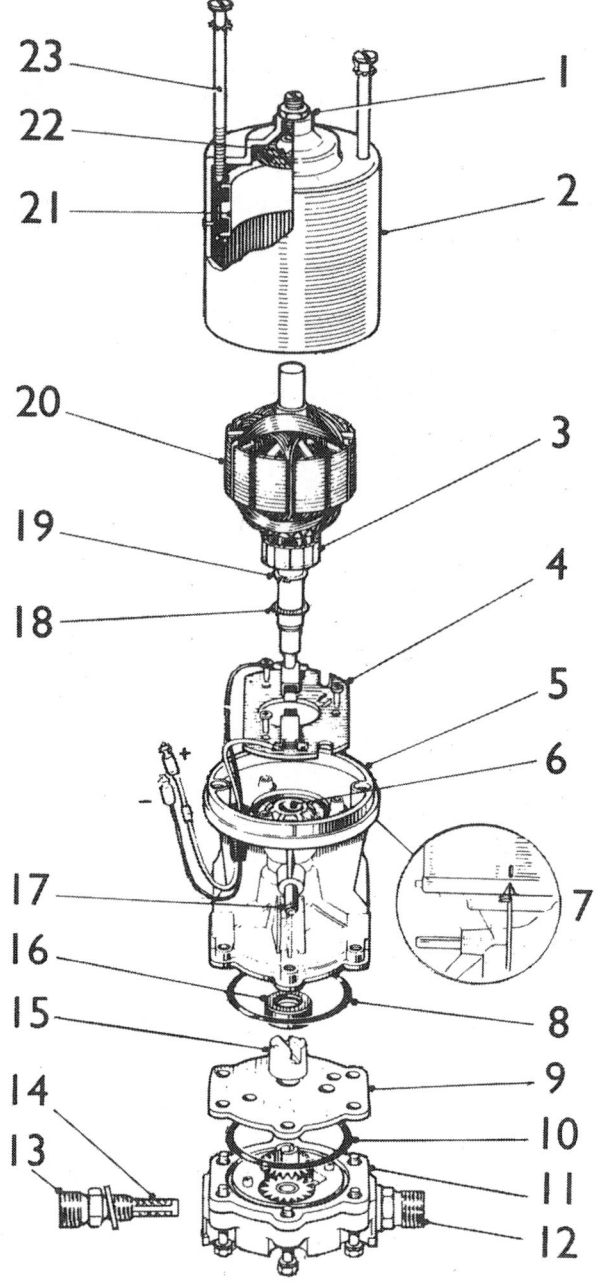

FIG. 3.34. EXPLODED VIEW OF FUEL PUMP (P.I.)

1 Armature end float adjuster	12 Outlet connection
2 Cover	13 Inlet connection
3 Commutator	14 Strainer
4 Brushplate assembly	15 Drive coupling
5 Base casting	16 Shaft seal
6 Bearing	17 'Tell tail' pipe
7 Aligning marks	18 Thrust washer
8 Rubber 'O' ring	19 Circlip
9 Top plate	20 Armature
10 Rubber 'O' ring	21 Permanent magnet
11 Gear pump	22 Bearing
	23 Through bolt

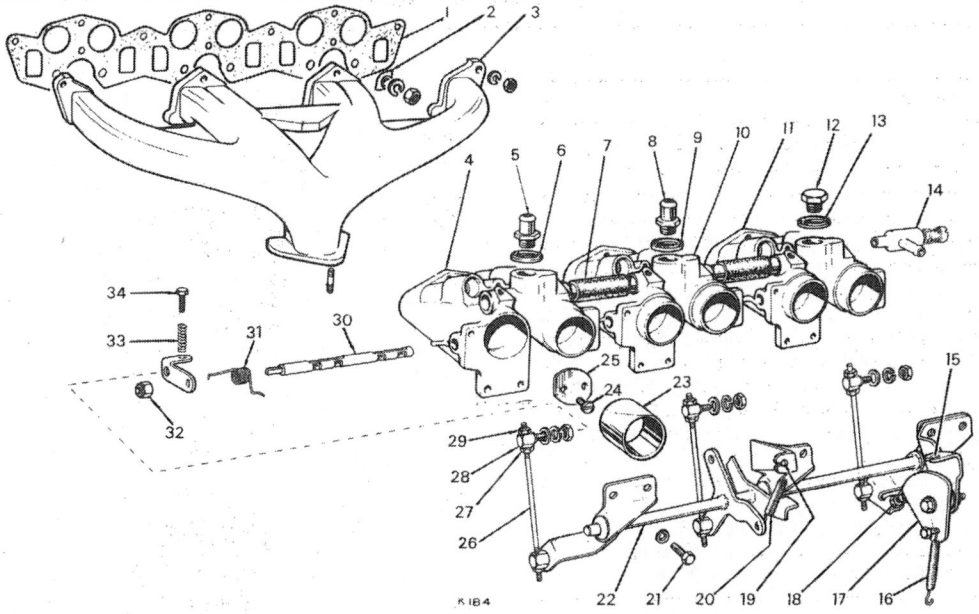

FIG. 3.35. THROTTLE LINKAGE AND MANIFOLDS

1 Manifold gasket
2 Clamp
3 Exhaust manifold
4 Inlet manifold - rear
5 Servo adaptor
6 Sealing washer
7 Balance plug
8 Metering unit vacuum adaptor
9 Sealing washer

10 Inlet manifold - centre
11 Inlet manifold - front
12 Plug
13 Sealing washer
14 Air valve assembly
15 Cold start abutment
16 Return spring
17 Cold start cam
18 Adjusting screw
19 Accelerator abutment

20 Accelerator return spring
21 Linkage securing bolt
22 Accelerator cross rod
23 Air inlet tube
24 Butterfly securing screw
25 Butterfly valve
26 Vertical adjusting rod
27 Locknut

28 Trunion
29 Locknut
30 Butterfly spindle
31 Return spring
32 Spindle nut
33 Adjusting screw spring
34 Adjusting screw

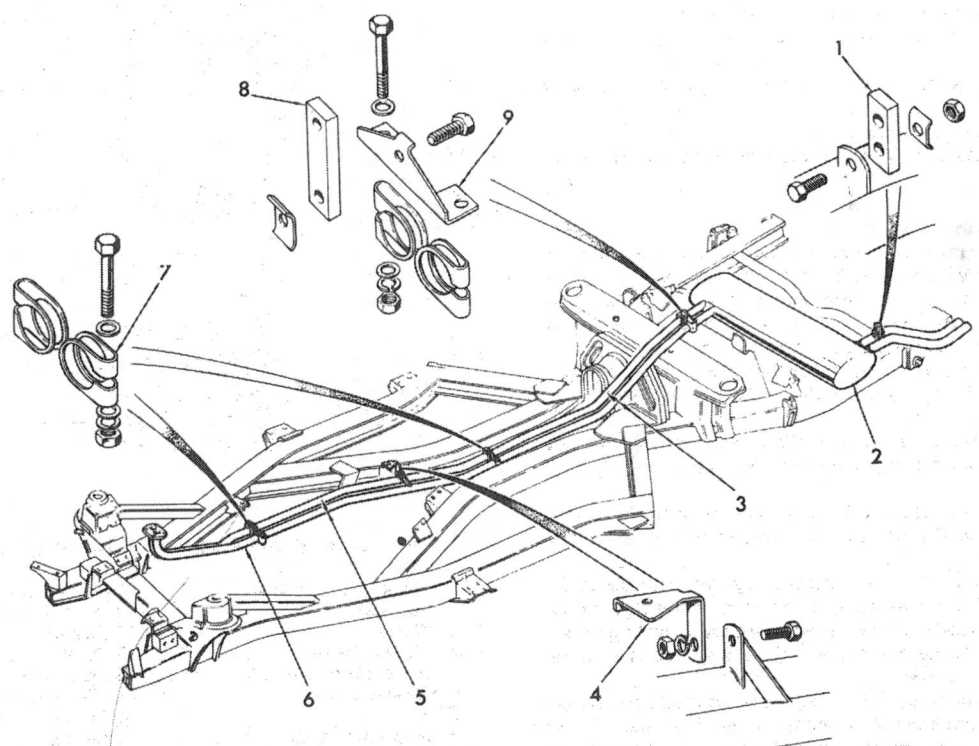

FIG. 3.36. EXHAUST SYSTEM LAYOUT (P.I. MODELS)

1 Flexible mounting (tail pipes)
2 Silencer and tail pipes
3 Rear intermediate pipes
4 Front mounting assembly
5 Front intermediate pipes
6 Front pipes and flange assembly
7 Pipe clamp assembly
8 Intermediate flexible mounting
9 Intermediate mounting bracket

1   Check the setting of the overfuel control lever. Erratic running may otherwise be caused by:-

An irregularity in the fuel supply to one cylinder only or some failing which is affecting all cylinders. In the former case, the fault is most likely to be a stuck open injector and fouling of the associated spark plug will almost certainly have occurred.

2   Short circuit each plug to earth in turn and if one does not affect the engine running note when shorted out, remove, clean and refit this plug.

3   Withdraw the associated injector from the engine and detach from its feed line.

4   Connect the injector to a dry, filtered air supply at a pressure of 80 psi in the forward (injection) direction. This will almost invariably cure a faulty injector (sticking open due to a foreign particle becoming trapped) and if it does so the injector can be refitted to the engine. If it does not, a new injector must be fitted.

NOTE: Plastic feed pipes must not be heat treated to enable fitment, but must be put on cold.

5   Where the failure affects all cylinders but is more pronounced with higher speed, check pressure and relief valve setting. If the metering distributor/control unit has recently been removed, check that it has not been fitted 180° out as regards timing.

6   Provided that the timing is correct; the overfuel control lever working correctly; the injectors are in good order; and fuel pressure is satisfactory; then a faulty control unit is indicated. In this instance fit a new complete metering distributor /control unit. NO ATTEMPT SHOULD BE MADE TO ALTER THE CONTROL UNIT SETTING.

c) Fuel consumption excessive.

This may not necessarily arise from a defect in the petrol injection system and the fault must be correctly traced before taking remedial action. The following checks are therefore given on the assumption that other likely causes have been checked first:—

1   Check for correct operation of the overfuel control lever.

2   Check the relief valve setting.

3   If the above 1 and 2 are satisfactory then the control unit is suspect and a replacement metering unit must be fitted. This latter step should be taken only when other likely causes such as plugs, points, leaking pipes, etc., have been eliminated.

d) Engine starts but does not respond to movement of the throttle:-

1   Ensure the movement of the accelerator pedal is being relayed to the throttle butterflies.

2   Remove and check that the pipe connecting the manifold to the control unit is air tight.

3   Check the relief valve setting.

4   If both the above 1 and 2 are satisfactory, it will be necessary to fit a replacement metering distributor/control unit.

30 Fuel tank - removal and replacement

1   If it is known beforehand that the fuel tank is to be removed, it is advisable to allow the level of fuel to drop so that the minimum has to be drained from the tank.

2   For safety reasons disconnect the battery earth terminal and remove the filler cap.

3   Place a container under the fuel tank of a suitable capacity to collect fuel from the tank and remove the drain plug situated in the centre of the tank.

4   Undo and remove the centre capping of the rear elbow rail retaining screws and slide the capping to one side until its other end is clear of the side capping. Withdraw the centre section.

5   Empty the luggage compartment of tools, etc., and undo the carpet fixing screws and lift away the carpet . Undo and remove the fuel tank cover board fixing screws. Ease the board from the side capping and upper retaining clips and lift away the cover board.

6   Slacken the filler hose clips on the filler pipe assembly. Gently ease the short hose from the tank filler neck.

7   Undo and remove the banjo bolt securing the vent pipe to the tank.

8   Disconnect the electric cable from the fuel gauge tank sender unit.

9   Undo the petrol feed pipe from the underside of the tank taking care not to kink the metal pipe.

10 Undo and remove the tank securing bolts and lock washers.

11 The fuel tank may now be lifted away from the car.

12 Refitting is the reverse sequence to removal.

31 Fuel tank sender unit - removal and replacement

1   Refer to section 29 and remove the fuel tank.

2   Undo and remove the six screws and spring washers that secure the fuel tank sender unit to the tank. Note the relative position of the sender unit.

3   Lift away the sender unit taking care not to bend the float wire as it is being drawn through the hole. Recover the sealing washer.

4   Refitting the sender unit is the reverse sequence to removal. Whenever possible always use a new gasket to prevent subsequent oil leaks.

Chapter 4 Ignition system

Contents

Specifications

Spark plugs:

Type (all models except TR 250)	Champion N - 9Y
TR 250	Champion UN - 12Y
Gap	0.025 in (0.63 mm)
Firing order	1 5 3 6 2 4
Ignition coil	Lucas HA 12
Primary winding resistance	1.43 - 1.58 ohms

Distributor

Type	Lucas 22 D 6
Direction of rotation	Anti clockwise viewed on rotor
Contact breaker gap	0.014 - 0.016 in (0.35 - 0.41 mm)
Dwell angle	35 ± 3°
Moving contact spring tension	18 - 24 oz
Condenser capacity	0.20 m fd

Centrifugal advance data
To be checked at decelerating speeds

Distributor rpm	Degrees distributor advance		Crankshaft rpm	Degrees crankshaft advance	
	minimum	maximum		minimum	maximum
A) TR 5 PI — Early distributor					
Below 250	no advance		Below 500	no advance	
400	0	2	800	0	4
850	2	4	1700	4	8
1300	4	6	2600	8	12
2000	4	6	4000	8	12
B) TR 5 PI — Later distributor with 'B' suffix to Lucas part number					
Below 175	no advance		Below 350	no advance	
450	0	2.0	900	0	4
800	2.5	4.5	1600	5	9
1300	6.0	8.0	2600	12	16
2000	6.0	8.0	4000	12	16
C) TR 6 PI					
See B					
D) TR 250 — Early distributor					
Below 350	no advance		Below 700	no advance	
450	0	1	900	0	2
900	5	7	1800	10	14
1850	10	12	3700	20	24
2300	12	14	4600	24	28
2800	12	14	5600	24	28

E) TR 250 – Later distributor

Below 375		no advance		Below 750		no advance	
450	0		1	900	0		2
850	4		6	1700	8		12
1500	6		8	3000	12		16
2500	9		11	5000	18		22
3000	9		11	6000	18		22

Ignition timing (Static)

TR 5 PI	...	...	...	...	...	...	...	11º BTDC
TR 6 PI	...	...	...	...	...	...	...	11º BTDC
TR 250	0.57 in (14.48 mm)	Pulley/pointer measurement						10º BTDC

TORQUE WRENCH SETTING

						lb ft	Kg m
Distributor to pedestal	...	...	...	...	...	8 - 10	1.11 - 1.38

1 General description

In order that the engine can run correctly it is necessary for an electrical spark to ignite the fuel/air mixture in the combustion chamber at exactly the right moment in relation to engine speed and load. The ignition system is based on feeding low tension voltage from the battery to the coil where it is converted to high tension voltage. The high tension voltage is powerful enough to jump the spark plug gap in the cylinder many times a second under high compression pressures, providing that the system is in good condition and that all adjustments are correct.

The ignition system is divided into two circuits, the low tension circuit and the high tension circuit.

The low tension circuit (sometimes known as the primary circuit) consists of the battery, lead to the control box, lead to the ignition switch, lead from the ignition switch to the low tension or primary coil windings (terminal SW) and the lead from the low tension coil windings (coil terminal CB) to the contact breaker points and condenser to the distributor.

The high tension circuit consists of the high tension or secondary coil windings, the heavy ignition lead from the centre of the coil to the centre of the distributor cap, the rotor arm, and the spark plug leads and spark plugs. The system functions in the following manner.

Low tension voltage is changed in the coil into high tension voltage by the opening and closing of the contact breaker points in the low tension circuit. High tension voltage is then fed via the carbon brush in the centre of the distributor cap to the rotor arm of the distributor. The rotor arm revolves inside the distributor cap and each time it comes in line with one of the four metal segments in the cap, which are connected to the spark plug leads, the opening and closing of the contact breaker points causes the high tension voltage to build up, jump the gap from the rotor arm to the appropriate metal segment and so via the spark plug lead to the spark plug where it finally jumps the spark plug gap before going to earth.

The ignition is advanced and retarded automatically, to ensure the spark occurs at just the right instant for the particular load at the prevailing engine speed.

The ignition advance is controlled by a mechanically operated system which comprises two lead weights which move out from the distributor shaft as the engine speed rises due to centrifugal force. As they move outwards they rotate the cam relative to the distributor shaft, and so advance the spark. The weights are held in position by two light springs and it is the tension of the springs which is largely responsible for correct spark advancement.

On some models a vacuum advance and retard unit may be fitted but this is not used and is blanked off. A micrometer adjustment is provided to enable slight alterations to the ignition point to be made by hand. This is to compensate for changes in engine condition or for the use of different grades of petrol.

A special rotor arm is fitted to some models so that when an engine speed of between 5,700 - 5,900 rpm is reached it will cause erratic running and misfiring. This prevents over revving of the engine. The drive gear for the tachometer is incorporated in the lower half of the distributor body.

2 Contact breaker - adjustment

1 To adjust the contact breaker points to the correct gap, first pull off the two clips securing the distributor cap to the distributor body, and lift away the cap. Clean the cap inside and out with a dry cloth. It is unlikely that the six segments will be badly burned or scored, but if they are the cap will have to be renewed.

2 Push in the carbon brush located in the top of the cap once or twice to make sure that it moves freely.

3 Gently prise the contact breaker points open to examine the condition of their faces. If they are rough, pitted or dirty, it will be necessary to remove them for resurfacing, or for replacement points to be fitted.

4 Presuming the points are satisfactory, or that they have been cleaned and replaced, measure the gap between the points by turning the engine over until the contact breaker arm is on the peak of one of the six cam lobes.

5 A 0.015 inch (0.481 mm) feeler gauge should now just fit between the points.

6 If the gap varies slacken the contact plate securing screw.

7 Adjust the contact gap by inserting a screwdriver in the notched hole at the end of the plate, turningg clockwise to decrease and anti clockwise to increase the gap. Tighten the securing screw and check the gap again.

8 Replace the rotor arm and distributor cap and clip the spring blade retainers into position.

3 Removing and replacing contact breaker points

1 If the contact breaker points are burned, pitted or badly worn, they must be removed and either replaced, or their faces must be filed smooth.

2 To remove the points unscrew the terminal nut and remove it together with the steel washer under its head. Remove the flanged nylon bush and then the condenser lead and the low tension lead from the terminal pin. Lift off the contact breaker arm and then remove the large fibre washer from the terminal pin.

3 The adjustable contact breaker plate is removed by unscrewing the one holding down screw and removing it, complete with spring and flat washer.

4 To reface the points rub their faces on a fine carborundum stone or on fine emery paper. It is important that the faces are rubbed flat and parallel to each other so that there will be complete face to face contact when the points are closed. One of the points will be pitted and the other will have deposits on it.

5 It is necessary to completely remove the built up deposits but not necessary to rub the pitted point right down to the stage where all the pitting has disappeared, though obviously if this is done it will prolong the time before the operation of refacing the points has to be repeated.

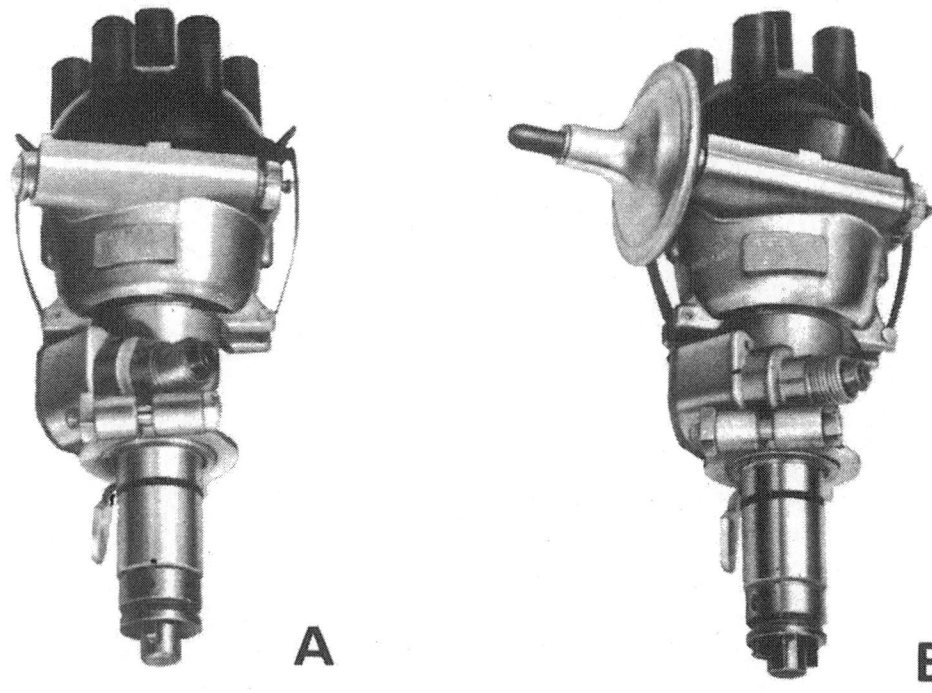

FIG. 4.1. DISTRIBUTOR IDENTIFICATION

A Ignition distributor Lucas part number 41219B
B Ignition distributor Lucas part number 41219D

FIG. 4.2. CONTACT BREAKER TABLE COMPONENTS

1 Notch for point adjustment
2 Six lobe cam
3 Cam spindle screw
4 Pivot
5 Knurled adjustment screw
6 Vacuum unit connection
   to contact breaker table
7 Contact breaker points
8 Adjustment screw
9 Vacuum unit

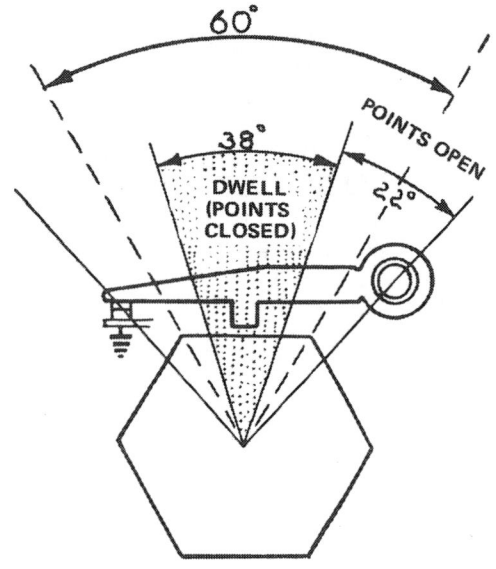

Fig. 4.3. Diagrammatic representation of the term "Dwell Angle". It is the period during which the contact breaker points remain closed for each ignition cycle when the primary current is building up in the ignition coil magnetic field in preparation for the next ignition cycle.

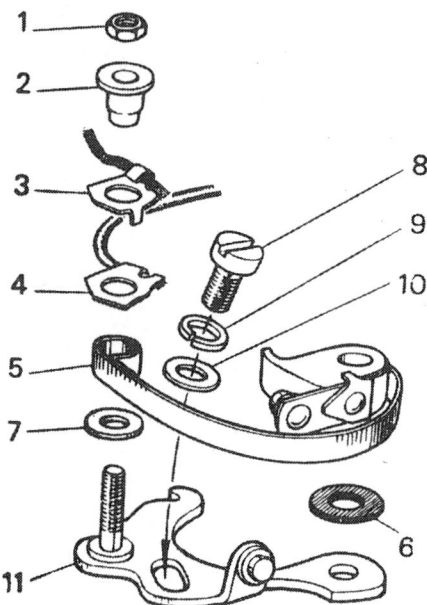

FIG. 4.4. CONTACT BREAKER POINTS COMPONENT PARTS

1 Nut	6 Insulating washer
2 Insulating sleeve	7 Insulating washer
3 Condenser terminal	8 Adjustment screw
4 LT terminal	9 Spring washer
5 Spring contact	10 Plain washer
	11 Fixed contact

6 To replace the points first position the adjustable contact breaker plate over the terminal pin.

7 Secure the contact plate by screwing in the screw which should have a spring and a flat washer under its head.

8 Then fit the fibre washer over the terminal pin.

9 Next fit the contact breaker arm complete with spring over the terminal pin.

10 Drop the fibre washer over the terminal bolt.

11 Then bend back the spring of the contact breaker arm and fit it over the terminal bolt.

12 Place the terminals of the low tension lead and the condenser over the terminal bolt.

13 Then fit the flanged nylon bush over the terminal bolt with the two leads immediately under its flange as shown.

14 Next fit a steel washer and then a 'star' washer over the nylon bush.

15 Then fit the nut over the terminal bolt and tighten it down as shown.

16 The points are now reassembled and the gap should be set as described in the previous section.

17 Finally replace the rotor arm and then the distributor cap.

4 Condenser - removal, testing and replacement

1 The purpose of the condenser (sometimes known as a capacitor) is to ensure that when the contact breaker points open there is no sparking across them which would waste voltage and cause wear.

2 The condenser is fitted in parallel with the contact breaker points. If it develops a short circuit, it will cause ignition failure as the points will be prevented from interrupting the low tension circuit.

3 If the engine becomes very difficult to start or begins to miss after several miles running and the breaker points show signs of excessive burning, then the condition of the condenser must be

suspect. A further test can be made by separating the points by hand with the ignition switched on. If this is accompanied by a flash it is indicative that the condenser has failed.

4 Without special test equipment the only sure way to diagnose condenser trouble is to replace a suspected unit with a new one and note if there is any improvement.

5 To remove the condenser from the distributor, remove the distributor cap and the rotor arm.

6 Loosen the outer nut from the contact stud and pull off the condenser lead.

7 Undo the mounting bracket screw and remove the condenser.

8 Replacement is simply a reversal of the removal process. Take particular care that the condenser lead does not short circuit against any portion of the breaker plate.

5 Distributor - lubrication

1 It is important that the distributor cam is lubricated with petroleum jelly at the specified mileages and that the breaker arm, governor weights, and cam spindles are lubricated with engine oil once every 1,000 miles (1,600 km). In practice it will be found that lubrication every 3,000 miles (5,000 km) is adequate, though once every 1,000 miles (1,600 km) is best.

2 Great care should be taken not to use too much lubricant as any excess that finds its way into the contact breaker points could cause burning and misfiring.

3 To gain access to the cam spindles lift away the rotor arm. Drop no more than two drops of engine oil onto the screw head. This will run down the spindle when the engine is hot and lubricate the bearings.

4 To lubricate the automatic timing control allow a few drops of oil to pass through the hole in the contact breaker base plate through which the four sided cam emerges. Apply not more than one drop of oil to the pivot post and remove any excess.

6 Distributor - removal

1 To remove the distributor from the engine, start by pulling the terminals off each of the spark plugs. Release the Lucar connector or small nut which holds the low tension lead to the terminal on the side of the distributor and unscrew the high tension lead retaining cap from the coil and remove the lead.

2 Detach the tachometer drive cable from the distributor body by unscrewing the knurled nut and drawing away the cable.

3 Remove the distributor body clamp bolt and two washers which holds the distributor clamp plate to the side of the drive pedestal.

4 Lift the distributor upwards and away from the pedestal. It may be necessary to pull upwards sharply to free it.

5 NOTE. If it is not wished to disturb the timing then under no circumstances should the clamp pinch bolt, which secures the distributor in its relative position in the clamp, be loosened. Providing the distributor is removed without the clamp being loosened from the distributor body, the timing will not be lost.

6 Replacement is a reversal of the above process, providing that the engine has not been turned in the meantime. If the engine has been turned it will be best to retime the ignition. This will also be necessary if the clamp pinch bolt has been loosened.

7 Distributor - dismantling

1 With the distributor removed from the car and on the bench, remove the distributor cap and lift off the rotor arm. If very tight lever it off gently with a screwdriver.

2 Remove the points from the distributor as described in Section 3.

3 Remove the condenser from the contact breaker plate by releasing its securing screw.

4 Unscrew the two screws and lock washers and lift away. Note that the moving plate earth lead is retained by one of the two screws.

5 Slide out the terminal block from the side of the distributor body.

6 Detach the link carrier spring from the moving plate and then lift out the contact breaker base plate.

7 To remove the link carrier spring off the small circlip which secures the advance adjustment nut which should then be unscrewed. With the micrometer adjusting nut removed, release the spring and the micrometer adjusting nut lock spring clip. This is the clip that is responsible for the 'clicks' when the micrometer adjuster is turned and it is small and easily lost as is the circlip, so put them in a safe place. Do not forget to replace the lock spring clip on reassembly.

8 Before dismantling further undo and remove the two screws and spring washers that secure the tachometer drive end cover to the distributor body. Lift away the end cover and its gasket.

9 Carefully withdraw the tachometer drive gear.

10 Note the position of the slot in the rotor arm drive in relation to the offset drive dog at the opposite end of the distributor. It is essential that this is reassembled correctly as otherwise the timing may be 180° out. (Fig. 4.5).

11 Using a suitable diameter parallel pin punch, tap out the driving dog pin. Lift away the driving dog and thrust washer.

12 The cam spindle, shaft and action plate may now be drawn upwards through the distributor body.

13 Unscrew the cam spindle retaining screw which is located in the centre of the rotor arm drive and remove the cam spindle.

14 Finally lift away the centrifugal weights. The distributor is now completely dismantled.

8 Distributor - inspection and repair

1 Check the points as described in Section 3. Check the distributor cap for signs of tracking, indicated by a thin black line between the segments. Replace the cap if any signs of tracking

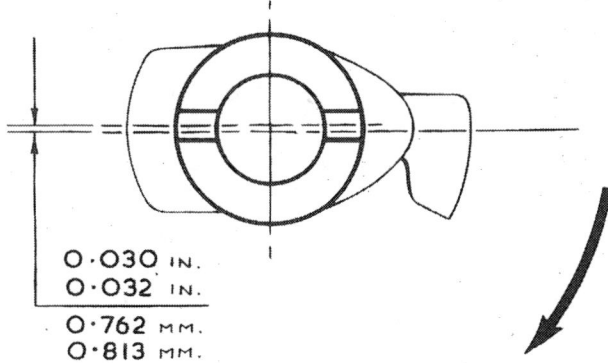

O·030 IN.
O·032 IN.
O·762 MM.
O·813 MM.

Fig. 4.5. The relationship of driving dog offset Tongue to rotor - view on driving dog

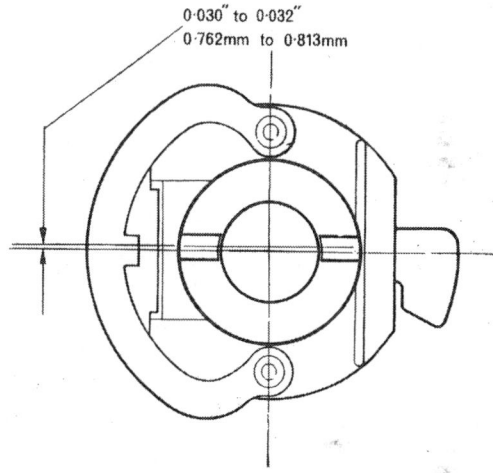

0·030" to 0·032"
0·762mm to 0·813mm

Fig. 4.6. Rotor arm with centrifugally operated cut-out. Also shown is driving dog Tongue offset

are found.

2 If the metal portion of the rotor arm is badly burned or loose, renew the arm. If slightly burnt clean the arm with a fine file.

3 Check that the carbon brush moves freely in the centre of the distributor cover.

4 Examine the fit of the breaker plate on the bearing plate and also check the breaker arm pivot for looseness or wear and renew as necessary.

5 Examine the balance weights and pivot pins for wear and renew the weights or cam assembly if a degree of wear is found.

6 Examine the shaft and the fit of the cam assembly on the shaft. If the clearance is excessive compare the items with new units and renew either, or both, if they show excessive wear.

7 If the shaft is a loose fit in the distributor bush and can be seen to be worn, it will be necessary to fit a new shaft and bush. The single bush is simply pressed out. NOTE that before inserting a new bush it should be stood in engine oil for at least 24 hours.

8 Examine the length of the balance weight springs and compare them with new springs. If they have stretched they must be renewed.

9 Inspect the tachometer drive gear for signs of wear, and, if evident obtain a new gear.

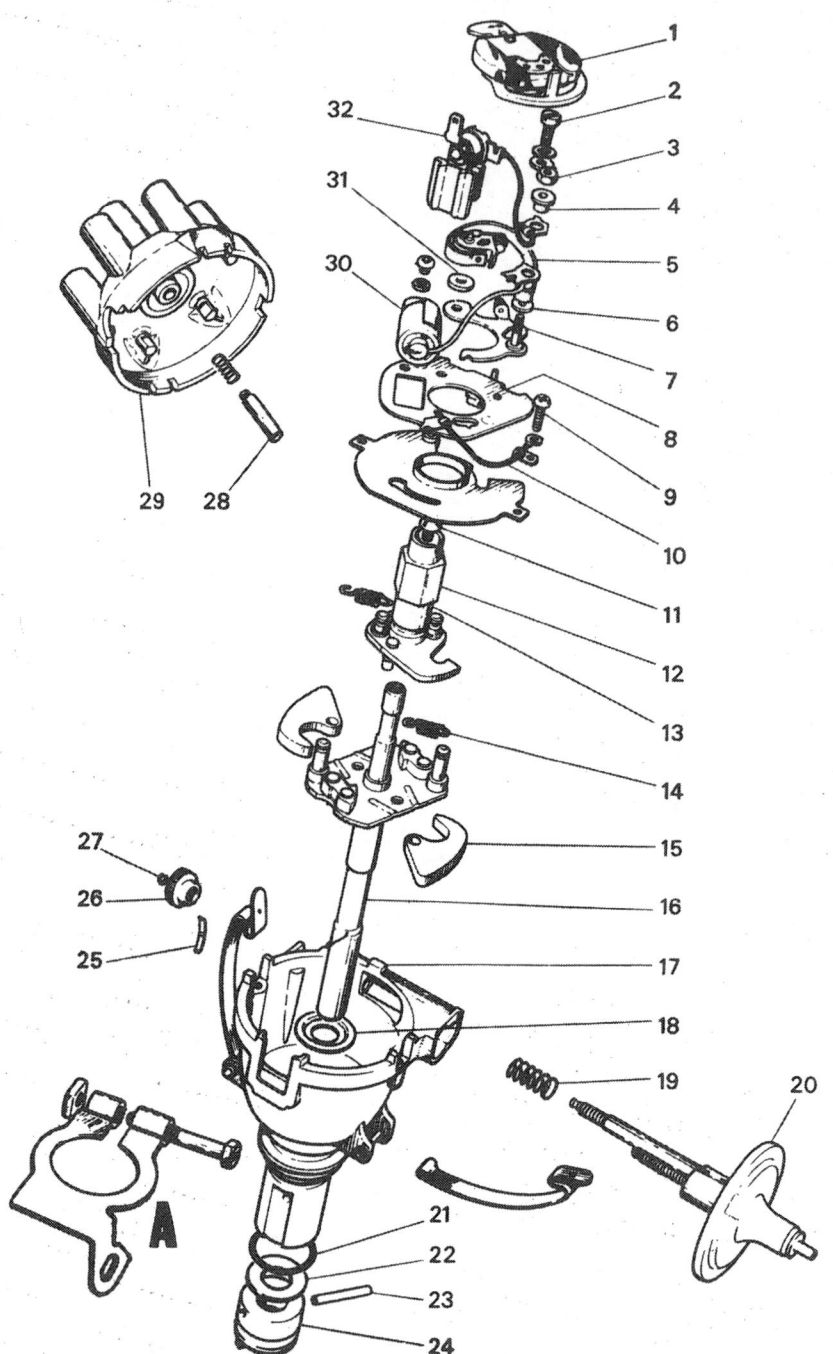

FIG. 4.7. DISTRIBUTOR TYPE 41219D COMPONENTS

1 Rotor incorporating igni-tion cut out	8 Moving plate	17 Body	25 Ratchet spring
2 Lock screw	9 Side screw	18 Distance collar	26 Micrometer adjustment nut
3 Nut	10 Moving plate earth lead	19 Spring	27 Circlip
4 Insulation piece	11 Cam spindle screw	20 Vacuum timing control	28 High tension carbon brush
5 Moving contact	12 Cam	21 Rubber 'O' ring	29 Cover
6 Small insulation washer	13 Cam spindle	22 Thrust washer	30 Capacitor
7 Fixed contact	14 Control spring	23 Driving dog pin	31 Large insulation washer
	15 Weight	24 Driving dog	32 Terminal block
	16 Shaft and action plate		

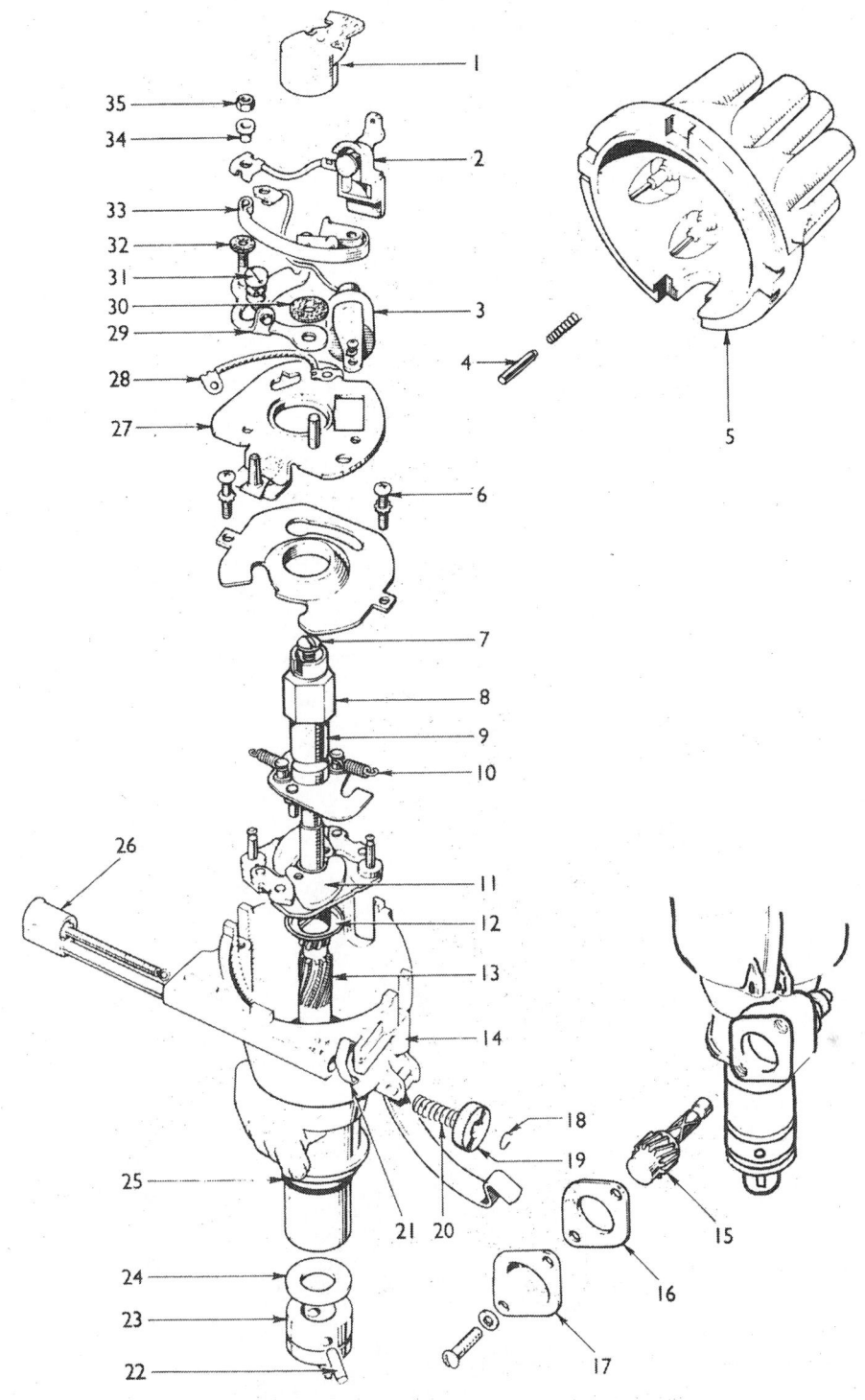

FIG. 4.8. DISTRIBUTOR TYPE 41219B COMPONENTS

1 Rotor
2 Terminal block
3 Capacitor
4 High tension carbon brush
5 Cover
6 Side screw
7 Cam spindle screw
8 Cam
9 Cam spindle

10 Control spring
11 Weight
12 Distance collar
13 Shaft and action plate
14 Body
15 Tachometer drive gear
16 Gasket
17 Cover
18 Circlip
19 Micrometer adjustment nut

20 Spring
21 Ratchet spring
22 Driving dog pin
23 Driving dog
24 Thrust washer
25 Rubber 'O' ring
26 Link carrier
27 Moving plate
28 Moving plate earth lead
29 Fixed contact

30 Large insulation washer
31 Lock screw
32 Small insulation washer
33 Moving contact
34 Insulation piece
35 Nut

9 Distributor - reassembly

1 Reassembly is a straightforward reversal of the dismantling process but there are several points which should be noted in addition to those already given in the section on dismantling.

2 Lubricate with engine oil the centrifugal weights and other parts of the mechanical advance mechanism, the cam and also the shaft and action plate.

3 Always use a new upper and lower thrust washer if they show signs of wear or the end float exceeds 0.002 - 0.005 inch (0.0508 - 0.1270 mm).

4 Always well lubricate the tachometer drive gear and its shaft.

5 On reassembling the cam driving pins with the centrifugal weights check that they are in the correct position so that when viewed from above, the rotor arm should be at the 6 o'clock position and the small offset on the driving dog must be on the right.

6 Check the action of the weights in the fully advanced and fully retarded positions and ensure they are not binding.

7 Tighten the micrometer adjusting nut to the middle position of the timing scale.

8 Finally, set the contact breaker gap to the correct clearance of 0.015 inch (0.481 mm).

10 Ignition timing

1 If the clamp plate pinch bolt on the distributor has been loosened, or if a reconditioned distributor is being fitted it is necessary to set the ignition timing.

2 Turn the engine over so that No. 1 piston is coming up to TDC on the compression stroke. (This can be checked by removing No. 1 spark plug and feeling the pressure being developed in the cylinder). If this check is not made it is all too easy to set the timing 180° out, as both No. 1 and 6 cylinders come up to TDC at the same time, but only one is on the firing stroke. Continue to rotate the crankshaft until the scale on the crankshaft pulley lines up with the pointer on the timing cover.

The exact position of the scale depends on the engine specification which will be found at the beginning of this Chapter.

3 Remove the distributor cover, slacken off the distributor body clamp bolt, and with the rotor arm pointing towards the No. 1 terminal (check this position with the distributor cap and lead to No. 1 spark plug) insert the distributor into the distributor pedestal. The dog on the drive shaft should match up with the slot in the distributor driving spindle. Insert the one bolt holding the distributor in position.

4 Slowly and carefully turn the distributor body anti clockwise until with the heel of the fibre rocker arm in the cam the points just begin to open. Check that with the heel on the peak of the cam the points gap does not exceed 0.015 in (0.481 mm).

5 Tighten the distributor clamp bolt, with the distributor in this position. Check that the rotor arm is still pointing to the segment in the distributor cap which leads to No. 1 lead and plugs.

6 Difficulty is sometimes experienced in determining exactly when the contact breaker points open. This can be ascertained most accurately by connection of a 12 volt bulb in parallel with the contact breaker points (one lead to earth and the other from the distributor low tension terminal as shown in photos). Switch on the ignition and turn the advance and retard adjuster until the bulb lights up indicating that the points have just opened.

7 It must be noted that to get the very best setting the final adjustment should be made on the road. The distributor can be moved about ¼ of a division at a time until the best setting is obtained. The amount of wear in the engine, quality of petrol used, and amount of carbon in the combustion chambers, all contribute to make the recommended settings no more than nominal ones. To obtain the best setting under running conditions first start the engine and allow to warm up to normal temperature, and then accelerate in top gear from 30 to 50 mph, listening for heavy pinking. If this occurs, the ignition needs to be retarded slightly until just the faintest trace of pinking can be heard under these operating conditions.

8 Since the ignition advance adjustment enables the firing point to be related correctly in relation to the grade of fuel used, the fullest advantage of any change of fuel will be obtained only by re-adjustment of the ignition settings.

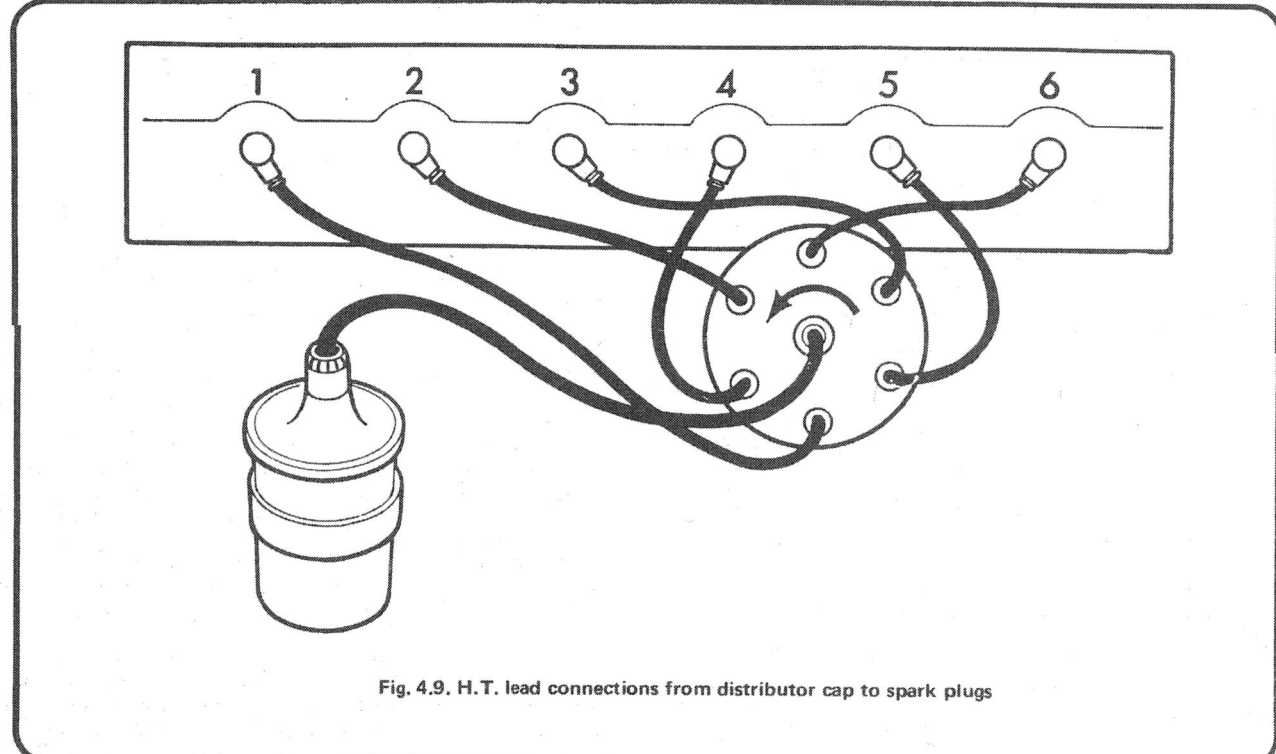

Fig. 4.9. H.T. lead connections from distributor cap to spark plugs

10.6a One test lamp lead attached to battery earth cable

10.6b The other lead attached to the low tension terminal on side of distributor

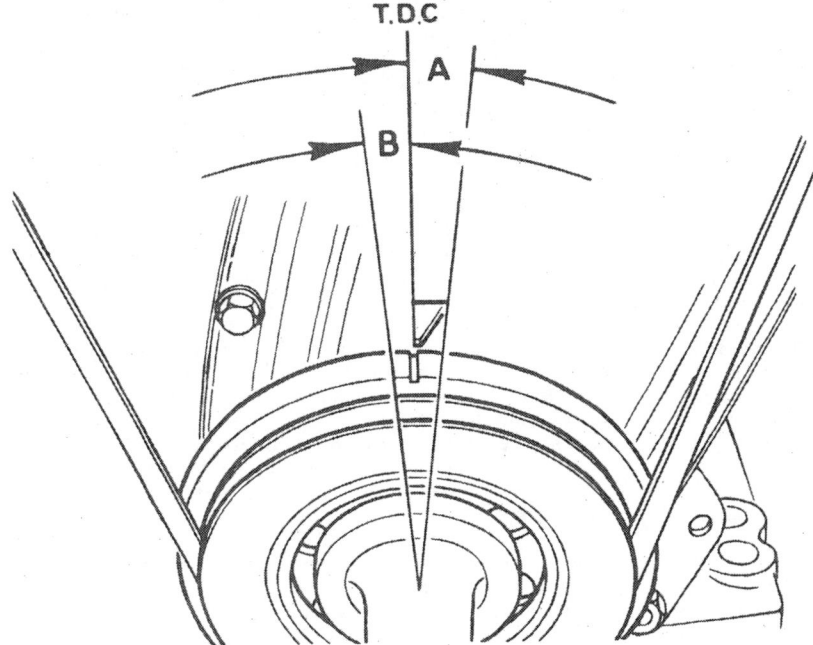

FIG. 4.10. ENGINE TIMING MARKS
Pointer and mark on crankshaft pulley at TDC position.
For exhaust emission control models, dimension:

A = 0.57 inch (14.478 mm) which is equivalent to 10° BTDC - STATIC

B = 0.23 inch (5.842 mm) which is equivalent to 4° ATDC with engine at idle speed of 800 - 850 rpm - STROBE

11 Spark plugs and leads

1 The correct functioning of the spark plugs is vital for the correct running and efficiency of the engine.

2 At intervals of 6,000 miles (10,000 km) the plugs should be removed, examined, cleaned, and if worn excessively, replaced. The condition of the spark plug will also tell much about the overall condition of the engine.

3 If the insulator nose of the spark plug is clean and white, with no deposits, this is indicative of a weak mixture, or too hot a plug. (A hot plug transfers heat away from the electrode slowly - a cold plug transfers it away quickly).

4 The plugs fitted as standard are manufactured by Champion (see specifications). If the top and insulator nose is covered with hard black looking deposits, then this is indicative that the mixture is too rich. Should the plug be black and oily, then it is likely that the engine is fairly worn, as well as the mixture being too rich.

5 If the insulator nose is covered with light tan to greyish brown deposits, the mixture is correct and it is likely that the engine is in good condition.

6 If there are any traces of long brown tapering stains on the outside of the white portion of the plug, then the plug will have to be renewed, as this shows that there is a faulty joint between the plug body and the insulator, and compression is being allowed to leak away.

7 Plugs should be cleaned by a sand blasting machine, which will free them from carbon more thoroughly than cleaning by hand. The machine will also test the condition of the plugs under compression. Any plug that fails to spark at the recommended pressure should be renewed.

8 The spark plug gap is of considerable importance, as, if it is too large or too small the size of the spark and its efficiency will be seriously impaired. The spark plug gap should be set to 0.025 inch (0.63 mm) for the best results.

9 To set it, measure the gap with a feeler gauge, and then bend open, or close, the outer plug electrode until the correct gap is achieved. The centre electrode should never be bent as this may crack the insulation and cause plug failure if nothing worse.

10 When replacing the plugs, remember to use a new plug washer, and replace the leads from the distributor in the correct firing order, (see specifications).

11 The plug leads require no routine attention other than being kept clean and wiped over regularly. At intervals of 12,000 miles (20,000 km), however, pull each lead off the plug in turn and remove them from the distributor by unscrewing the knurled moulded terminal knobs. Water can seep down into these joints giving rise to a white corrosive deposit which must be carefully removed from the brass washer at the end of each cable through which the ignition wires pass.

12 Distributor - modifications

The earlier produced models were fitted with a Lucas 22D 6 distributor and this has slightly different advance curve characteristics from those fitted to later produced models. Later produced models were fitted with a Lucas 22D 6B and latest TR6 models this was changed to type 22D 6D. This latter type has a vacuum controlled advance unit fitted but is blanked off. Otherwise the distributor is similar to type 22D 6B.

13 Ignition system - fault finding

By far the majority of breakdown and running troubles are caused by faults in the ignition system either in the low tension or high tension circuits.

14 Ignition system - fault symptoms

There are two main symptoms indicating ignition faults, either the engine will not start or fire, or the engine is difficult to start and misfires. If it is a regular misfire, i.e. the engine is running on only two or three cylinders the fault is almost sure to be in the secondary, or high tension circuit. If the misfiring is intermittent, the fault could be in either the high or low tension circuits. If the car stops suddenly or will not start at all it is likely that the fault is in the low tension circuit. Loss of power and overheating, apart from faulty carburation or fuel injection settings, are normally due to faults in the distributor or incorrect ignition timing.

15 Fault diagnosis - engine fails to start

1 If the engine fails to start and the car was running normally when it was last used, first check there is fuel in the petrol tank. If the engine turns over normally on the starter motor and the battery is evidently well charged, then the fault may be in either the high or low tension circuits. First check the HT circuit. NOTE, if the battery is known to be fully charged, the ignition light comes on, and the starter motor fails to turn the engine. CHECK THE TIGHTNESS OF THE LEADS OF THE BATTERY TERMINALS and also the secureness of the earth lead to its CONNECTION TO THE BODY. It is quite common for the leads to have worked loose, even if they look and feel secure. If one of the battery terminal posts gets very hot when trying to work the starter motor this is a sure indication of a faulty connection to that terminal.

2 One of the commonest reasons for bad starting is wet or damp spark plugs, leads and distributor. Remove the distributor cap. If condensation is visible internally, dry the cap with a rag and also wipe over the leads. Replace the cap.

3 If the engine still fails to start, check that current is reaching the plugs, by disconnecting each plug lead in turn at the spark plug end, and holding the end of the cable about 0.188 inch (4.76 mm) away from the cylinder block. Spin the engine on the starter motor by pressing the rubber button on the starter motor solenoid switch (under the bonnet).

4 Sparking between the end of the cable and the block should be fairly strong with a regular blue spark. (Hold the lead with rubber to avoid electric shocks). If current is reaching the plugs, then remove them and clean and regap them to 0.025 inch (0.63 mm). The engine should now start.

5 Spin the engine as before, when a rapid succession of blue sparks between the end of the lead and the block indicates that the coil is in order, and that either the distributor cap is cracked, the carbon brush is stuck or worn, the rotor arm is faulty, or the contact points are burnt, pitted or dirty. If the points are in bad shape, clean and reset them as described in Section 3.

6 If there are no sparks from the end of the lead from the coil, then check the connections of the lead to the coil and distributor head, and if they are in order, check out the low tension circuit starting with the battery.

7 Switch on the ignition and turn the crankshaft so the contact breaker points have fully opened. Then with either a 12 volt voltmeter or bulb and length of wire, check that current from the battery is reaching the starter solenoid switch. No reading indicates that there is a fault in the cable to the switch, or in the connections at the switch or at the battery terminals. Alternatively the battery earth lead may not be properly earthed to the body.

8 If in order check that current is reaching terminal '3' of the starter switch (the one connected to the cable coloured white with a red tracer), by connecting the voltmeter between '3' and earth. If there is no reading this indicates a faulty cable or loose connections between the solenoid switch and the '3' terminal. Remedy and the car will start.

9 Check with the voltmeter between ignition switch terminal '2' and earth, (the one connected to the cable coloured white). No reading means a fault in the switch. Fit a new switch, and start the car.

10 If current is reaching the ignition switch output terminal, then check the connection at the fuse box, (the one with the white cables grouped together). No reading indicates loose connections or broken wire from the ignition switch. If this proves to be the fault remedy and start the car.

11 If current is reaching the fuse box connection then check the SW terminal on the ignition coil (it is marked 'SW' or +) - cable colour white. No reading indicates loose connections or broken wire from the ignition switch. If this proves to be the fault, remedy and start the car.

12 Check the CB terminal on the coil (it is marked 'CB' or -) and if no reading is recorded on the voltmeter then the coil is broken and must be renewed. The car should start when a new coil has been fitted.

13 If a reading is obtained at the CB terminal then check the low tension terminal on the side of the distributor (cable colour white with black tracer). If no reading then check the wire for loose connections etc. If a reading is obtained then the final check on the low tension is across the breaker points. No reading means a broken condenser which when replaced will enable the car to finally start.

16 Fault diagnosis - engine misfires

1 If the engine misfires regularly, run it at a fast idling speed, and short out each of the plugs in turn by placing a short screwdriver across from the plug terminal to the cylinder. Ensure that the screwdriver has a WOODEN or PLASTIC INSULATED HANDLE.

2 No difference in engine running will be noticed when the plug in the defective cylinder is short circuited. Short circuiting the working plugs will accentuate the misfire.

3 Remove the plug lead from the end of the defective plug and hold it about 0.188 inch (4.76 mm) from the block. Restart the engine. If the sparking is fairly strong and regular the fault must lie in the spark plug.

4 The plug may be loose, the insulation may be cracked, or the points may have burnt away giving too wide a gap for the spark to jump. Worse still, one of the points may have broken off. Either renew the plug, or clean it, reset the gap, and then test it.

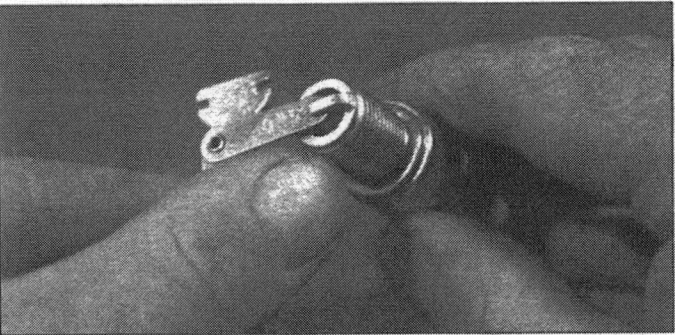

Measuring plug gap. A feeler gauge of the correct size (see ignition system specifications) should have a slight "drag" when slid between the electrodes. Adjust gap if necessary

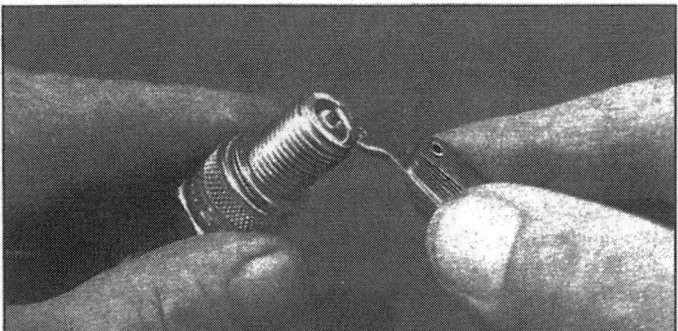

Adjusting plug gap. The plug gap is adjusted by bending the earth electrode inwards, or outwards, as necessary until the correct clearance is obtained. Note the use of the correct tool

Normal. Grey-brown deposits, lightly coated core nose. Gap increasing by around 0.001 in (0.025 mm) per 1000 miles (1600 km). Plugs ideally suited to engine, and engine in good condition

Carbon fouling. Dry, black, sooty deposits. Will cause weak spark and eventually misfire. Fault: over-rich fuel mixture. Check:carburettor mixture settings, float level and jet sizes; choke operation and cleanliness of air filter. Plugs can be re-used after cleaning

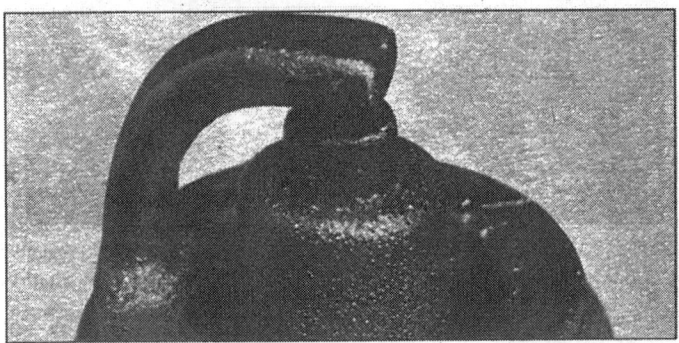

Oil fouling. Wet, oily deposits. Will cause weak spark and eventually misfire. Fault: worn bores/piston rings or valve guides; sometimes occurs (temporarily) during running-in period. Plugs can be re-used after thorough cleaning

Overheating. Electrodes have glazed appearance, core nose very white - few deposits. Fault: plug overheating. Check: plug value, ignition timing, fuel octane rating (too low) and fuel mixture (too weak). Discard plugs and cure fault immediately

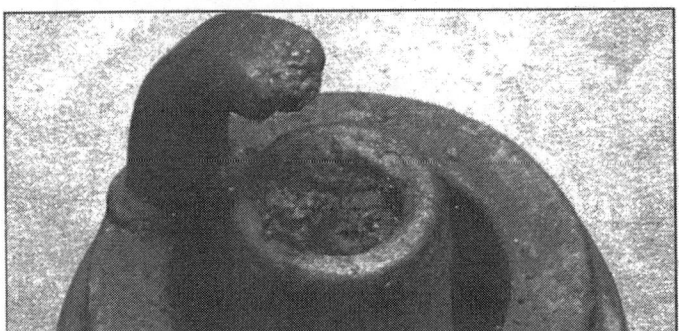

Electrode damage. Electrodes burned away; core nose has burned, glazed appearance. Fault: pre-ignition. Check: as for "Overheating" but may be more severe. Discard plugs and remedy fault before piston or valve damage occurs

Split core nose (may appear initially as a crack). Damage is self-evident, but cracks will only show after cleaning. Fault: pre-ignition or wrong gap-setting technique. Check: ignition timing, cooling system, fuel octane rating (too low) and fuel mixture (too weak). Discard plugs, rectify fault immediately

92

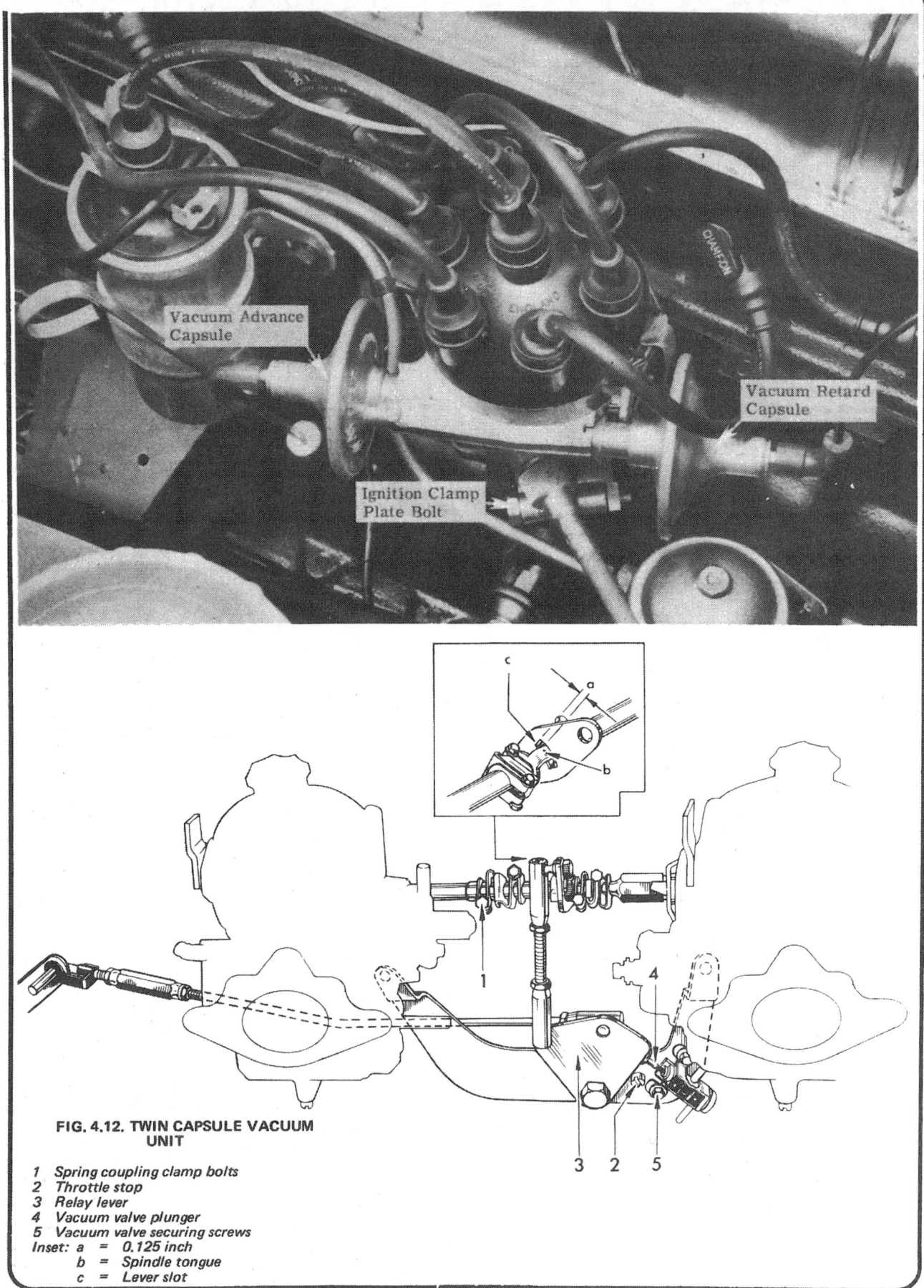

FIG. 4.12. TWIN CAPSULE VACUUM UNIT

1 Spring coupling clamp bolts
2 Throttle stop
3 Relay lever
4 Vacuum valve plunger
5 Vacuum valve securing screws
Inset: a = 0.125 inch
b = Spindle tongue
c = Lever slot

5 If there is no spark at the end of the plug lead or if it is weak and intermittent, check the ignition lead from the distributor to the plug. If the insulation is cracked or perished, renew the lead. Check connections at the distributor cap.

6 If there is still no spark, examine the distributor cap carefully for tracking. This can be recognised by a very thin black line running between two or more electrodes, or between an electrode and some other part of the distributor. These lines are paths which now conduct electricity across the cap thus letting it run to earth. The only answer is a new distributor cap.

7 Apart from the ignition timing being incorrect, other causes of misfiring have already been dealt with under the section dealing with the failure of the engine to start (section 15).

8 If the ignition timing is too far retarded, it should be noted that the engine will tend to overheat and there will be quite noticeable drop in power. If the engine is overheating and the power is down, and the ignition timing is correct, then the carburettors or fuel injection system should be checked, as it is likely that this is where the fault lies. See Chapter 3 for details of this.

---

17 US Federal standards - control of air pollution

It is important that when cars are being operated in territories which come under the control of US Federal regulations, there is no unauthorised interference with, or adjustments made to the ignition distributor or ignition timing. If these are made without using special test equipment, the results obtained will probably result in the car failing to meet the legal requirements in respect of air pollution.

The ignition system fitted to cars modified to meet the legal requirements is identical to that described in this Chapter with the exception that a vacuum timing control is attached to the distributor so that fuel economy is improved by timing the spark earlier under part throttle conditions. It therefore provides additional retard at idle and during deceleration to reduce exhaust emission. No micrometer adjustments nut is fitted to the distributor body.

Fig. 4.12. shows the twin capsules of the vacuum circuit.

Further information will be found in Chapter 3.

When setting the ignition timing the static timing may only be used to start the engine. Thereafter the timing must be set accurately to a figure of 4° ATDC at 800-850 rpm using a strobe light and electronic tachometer. This assumes that the carburation/fuel injection system is correctly adjusted first. Normally it is necessary to check and reset the two systems in conjunction with each other.

Chapter 5 Clutch and actuating mechanism

Contents

Specifications

Make	Laycock
Type	Diaphragm spring
Diameter	8½ in (215 mm)
Adjustment	Self adjusting
Clutch release bearing	Single row ball bearing
Lining material	Ferodo RYZ or Mintex HIB
Travel release	0.315 in (8.001 mm)
Flywheel to spring tips	1.465 ± 0.050 in (37.21 ± 1.27 mm)
Clutch slave cylinder bore	1 in (25.4 mm)

TORQUE WRENCH SETTINGS

	lb ft	Kg m
Clutch to flywheel	20	2.77
Clutch slave cylinder	18 - 20	2.49 - 2.77

1 General description

All Triumph models covered by this manual are fitted with an 8.5 inch (215 mm) diameter Laycock diaphragm spring clutch operated hydraulically by a master cylinder and slave cylinder.

The clutch comprises a steel cover which is bolted and dowelled to rear face of the flywheel and contains a pressure plate and clutch disc or driven plate.

The pressure plate, diaphragm spring, and release plate are all attached to the clutch assembly cover.

The clutch disc is free to slide along the splined first motion shaft and is held in position between the flywheel and the pressure plate by the pressure of the diaphragm spring.

Friction lining material is riveted to the clutch disc which has a spring cushioned hub to absorb transmission shocks and to help ensure a smooth take off.

The clutch is actuated hydraulically. The pedant clutch pedal is connected to the clutch master cylinder and hydraulic fluid reservoir by a short pushrod. The master cylinder and hydraulic reservoir are mounted on the engine side of the bulkhead in front of the driver.

Depressing the clutch pedal moves the piston in the master cylinder forwards, so forcing hydraulic fluid through the clutch hydraulic pipe to the slave cylinder.

The piston in the slave cylinder moves forward on the entry of the fluid and actuates the clutch release arm by means of a short pushrod. The opposite end of the release arm is forked and is located behind the release bearing.

As this pivoted clutch release arm moves backwards it bears against the release bearing pushing it forwards to bear against the release plate, so moving the centre of the diaphragm spring

inwards. The spring is sandwiched between two annular rings which act as a fulcrum point. As the centre of the spring is pushed in, the outside of the spring is pushed out, so moving the pressure plate backwards and disengaging the pressure plate from the clutch disc.

When the clutch pedal is released, the diaphragm spring forces the pressure plate into contact with the high friction linings on the clutch disc and at the same time pushes the clutch disc a fraction of an inch forwards on its splines so engaging the clutch disc with the flywheel. The clutch disc is now firmly sandwiched between the pressure plate and the flywheel so the drive is taken up.

As the friction linings on the clutch disc wear, the pressure plate automatically moves closer to the disc to compensate for this. There is therefore no need to periodically adjust the clutch.

2 Clutch system - bleeding

1 Gather together a clean jam jar, a 9 inch length of rubber tubing which fits tightly over the bleed nipple in the slave cylinder, a tin of hydraulic brake fluid, and someone to help.
2 Check that the master cylinder is full. If it is not, fill it and cover the bottom 2 inches (50.8 mm) of the jar with hydraulic fluid.
3 Remove the rubber dust cap from the bleed nipple on the slave cylinder and with a suitable spanner open the bleed nipple one turn.
4 Place one end of the tube securely over the nipple and insert the other end in the jam jar so that the tube orifice is below the level of the fluid.
5 An assistant should now pump the clutch pedal up and down

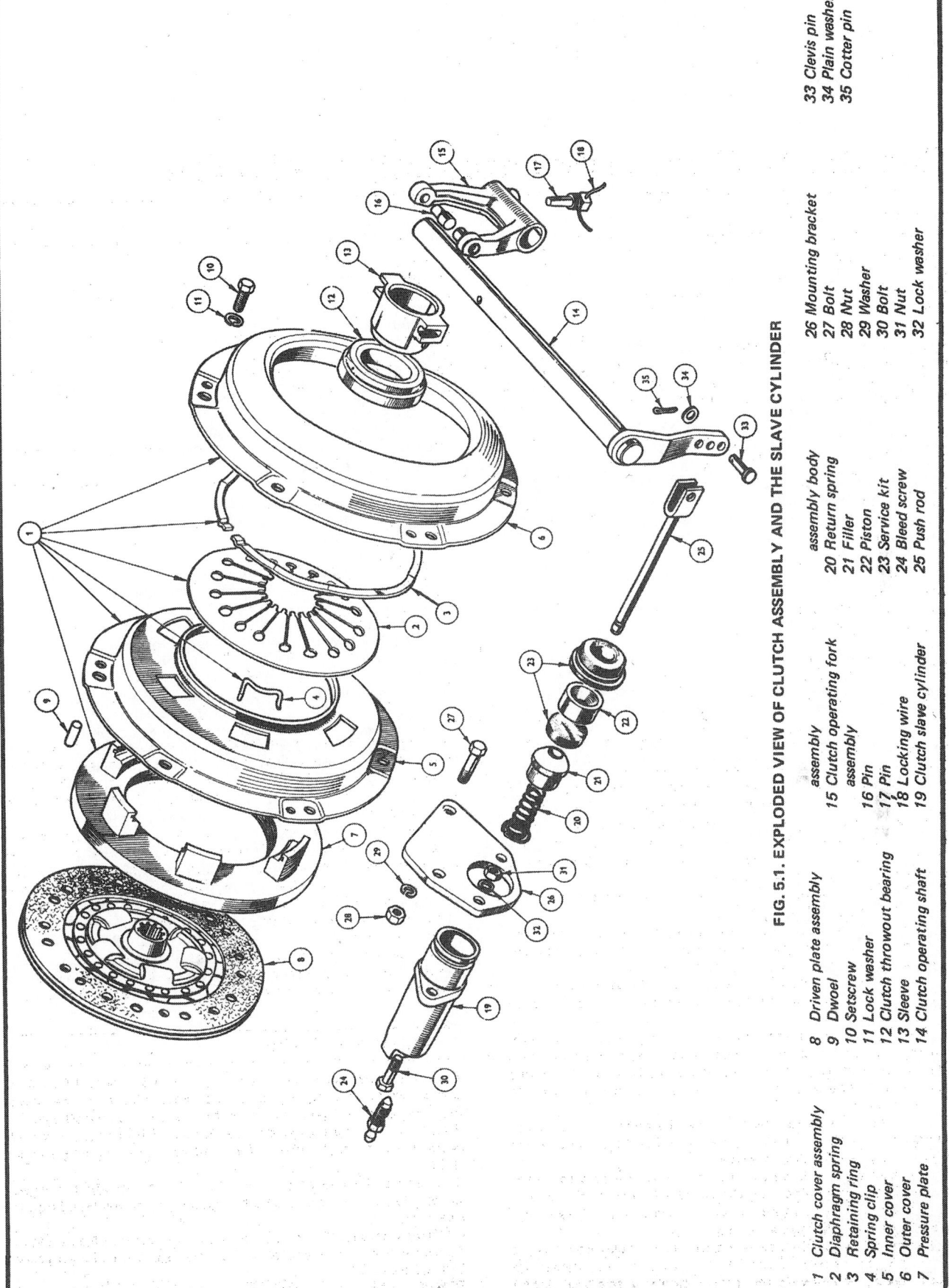

FIG. 5.1. EXPLODED VIEW OF CLUTCH ASSEMBLY AND THE SLAVE CYLINDER

1 Clutch cover assembly
2 Diaphragm spring
3 Retaining ring
4 Spring clip
5 Inner cover
6 Outer cover
7 Pressure plate

8 Driven plate assembly
9 Dwoel
10 Setscrew
11 Lock washer
12 Clutch throwout bearing
13 Sleeve
14 Clutch operating shaft

15 Clutch operating fork assembly
16 Pin
17 Pin
18 Locking wire
19 Clutch slave cylinder assembly body
20 Return spring
21 Filler
22 Piston
23 Service kit
24 Bleed screw
25 Push rod

26 Mounting bracket
27 Bolt
28 Nut
29 Washer
30 Bolt
31 Nut
32 Lock washer
33 Clevis pin
34 Plain washer
35 Cotter pin

slowly until air bubbles cease to emerge from the end of the tubing. He should also check the reservoir frequently to ensure that the hydraulic fluid level does not drop too far so letting air back into the system.

6   When no more air bubbles appear, tighten the bleed nipple on the down stroke of the clutch pedal. Replace the rubber dust cap over the bleed nipple.

3 Clutch pedal - removal and replacement

1   The clutch pedal is removed and replaced exactly the same way as the brake pedal.
2   A full description of how to remove and replace the brake pedal can be found in Chapter 10.

4 Clutch - removal

1   Remove the gearbox as described in Chapter 6, Section 2.
2   Remove the clutch assembly by unscrewing the 6 bolts holding the cover to the rear face of the flywheel. Unscrew the bolts diagonally half a turn at a time to prevent distortion of the cover flange.
3   With the bolts and spring washers removed, lift the clutch assembly off the locating dowels. The driven plate or clutch disc will fall out at this stage as it is not attached to either the clutch cover assembly or the flywheel. Note which way round the disc is fitted.

5 Clutch - replacement

1   It is important that no oil or grease gets on the clutch disc friction linings, or the pressure plate and flywheel faces. It is advisable to replace the clutch with clean hands and to wipe down the pressure plate and the flywheel faces with a clean dry rag before assembly begins.
2   Place the clutch disc against the flywheel with the longer end of the hub facing outwards away from the flywheel. On no account should the clutch disc be replaced with the longer end of the centre hub facing in †owards the flywheel as on reassembly is will be found quite impossible to operate the clutch with the friction disc in this position.
3   Replace the clutch cover assembly loosely on the dowels. Replace the six bolts and spring washers and tighten them finger tight so that the clutch disc is gripped but can still be moved.
4   The clutch disc must now be centralised so that when the engine and gearbox are mated, the gearbox input shaft splines will pass through the splines in the centre of the driven plate hub.
5   Centralisation can be carried out quite easily by inserting a round bar or long screwdriver in the centre of the clutch so that the end of the bar rests in the small hole in the end of the crankshaft containing the input shaft bearing bush. Moving the bar sideways or up and down will move the clutch disc in whichever direction is necessary to achieve centralisation.
6   Centralisation is easily judged by moving the bar and viewing the driven plate hub in relation to the whole of the end of the crankshaft. When the hub appears exactly in the centre all is correct. Alternatively, if an old Triumph input shaft can be borrowed this will eliminate all the guesswork as it will fit the bush and centre of the clutch hub exactly, obviating the need for visual alignment.
7   Tighten the clutch bolts firmly in a diagonal sequence to ensure that the cover plate is pulled down evenly and without distortion of the flange.
8   Mate the engine and gearbox, bleed the slave cylinder if the pipe was disconnected and check the clutch for correct operation.

6 Clutch - dismantling and reassembly

1   In the normal course of events clutch dismantling and reassembly is the term used for simply fitting a new clutch pressure plate and friction disc. Under no circumstances must the diaphragm clutch unit be dismantled. If a fault develops in the pressure plate assembly an exchange replacement unit must be fitted.
2   If a new clutch disc is being fitted it is false economy not to renew the release bearing at the same time. This will preclude having to replace it at a later date when wear on the clutch linings is still very small.

7 Clutch - inspection

1   Examine the of the clutch disc friction linings for wear or loose rivets and the disc for rim distortion, cracks and worn splines.
2   It is always best to renew the clutch driven plate as an assembly to preclude further trouble.
3   Check the machined faces of the flywheel and the pressure plate; if either is badly grooved it should be machined until smooth, or replaced with a new item. If the pressure plate is cracked or split it must be renewed.

8 Clutch release bearing and cross shaft - removal and reassembly

1   With the gearbox and engine separated to provide access to the clutch, attention can be given to the release bearing and cross shaft located in the gearbox bell housing, as shown in Fig. 5.5.
2   Refer to Fig. 5.5. and undo the cross shaft to fork taper bolt, having first removed the soft iron wire threaded through the bolt head.
3   Carefully slide the cross shaft from the bell housing.
4   Lift away the fork followed by the sleeve and bearing. Note that there are two little end caps fitted to the fork fingers.
5   As the sleeve is pressed into the bearing the two parts may be separated by placing the bearing on the top of the open jaws of a firm bench vice and using a drift of suitable diameter tapping out the sleeve.
6   Inspect the cross shaft, the fork, the end caps and sleeve for signs of excessive wear and fit new parts as necessary. Hold the outer track of the release bearing and rotate the inner track. If it feels rough during rotation fit a new bearing.
7   Reassembly is the reverse sequence to removal. Smear a little high melting point grease on the inside of the sleeve and also on the outer surface of the end caps and cross shaft before refitting. Do not forget to lock the taper bolt with soft iron wire.

9 Clutch slave cylinder - removal, dismantling, examination and reassembly

1   The clutch slave cylinder is positioned on the left hand side of the bell housing as shown in Fig. 5.3.
2   Before removing the slave cylinder take off the clutch master cylinder reservoir cap and place a piece of thin polythene over the top of the reservoir, screw the cap down tightly over the polythene. This will stop syphoning during subsequent operations.
3   Extract the split pin, washer and clevis pin from the clutch push pin yoke and withdraw the pushrod from the slave cylinder.
4   Undo the two bolts holding the slave cylinder to the bracket on the engine end plate.
5   Wipe the area clean of dust and dirt where the hydraulic pipe is connected to the slave cylinder and disconnect the hydraulic pipe from the slave cylinder by releasing the unit with an open ended spanner and rotating the slave cylinder. Take care not to kink or twist the flexible hose.

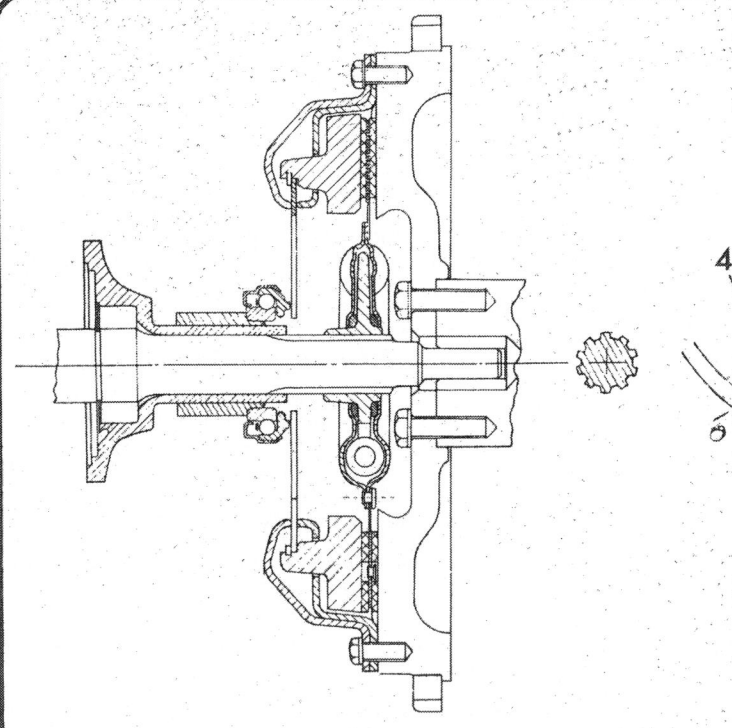

Fig. 5.2. Cross section of clutch when mounted onto flywheel

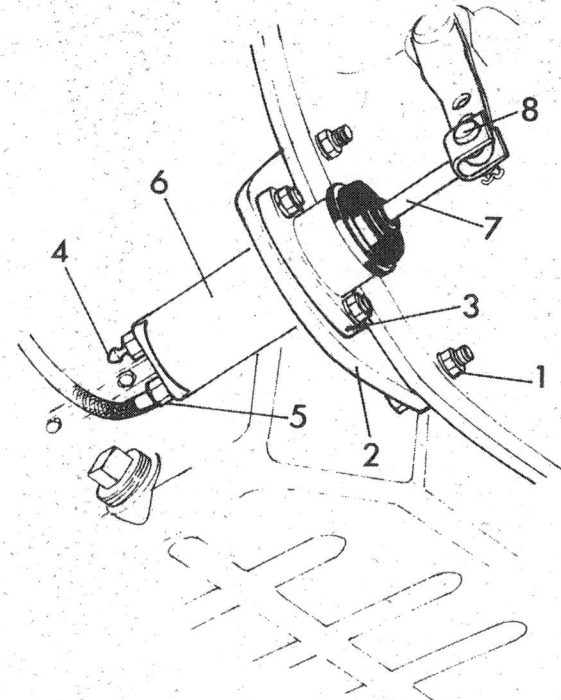

FIG. 5.3. CLUTCH SLAVE CYLINDER
MOUNTED TO ENGINE BACKPLATE

1 Bracket retaining nut
  and bolt
2 Bracket
3 Slave cylinder mounting
  nut and bolt
4 Bleed nipple

5 Hydraulic flexible hose
  connection
6 Slave cylinder
7 Push rod
8 Clevis pin

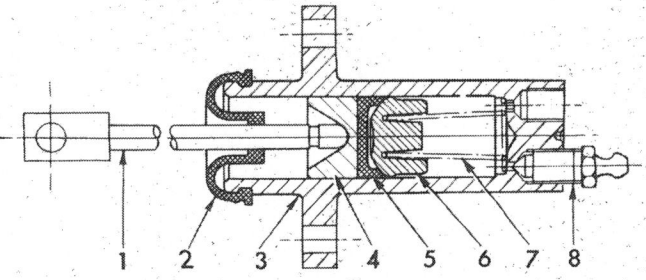

Fig. 5.4. Clutch slave cylinder component parts

1 Push rod
2 Dust cover
3 Body
4 Piston

5 Seal
6 Filler block
7 Spring
8 Bleed nipple

Fig. 5.5 Clutch release mechanism component parts

1 Release bearing
2 Bearing sleeve
3 Input shaft
4 Front cover
5 Fork
6 Grease nipple
7 Fibre washer

8 Cross-shaft
9 Anti-rattle spring
10 Tapered locking bolt
11 Fibre washer
12 Grease nipple
13 Locating bolt
14 Lockwasher

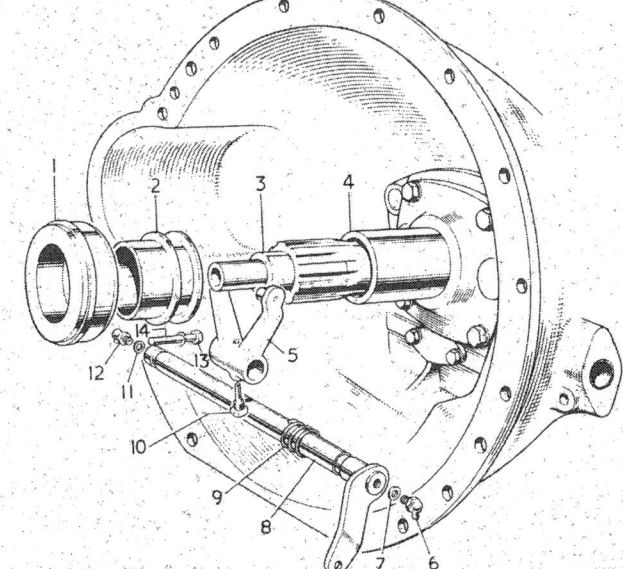

6 Clean the outside of the cylinder before dismantling.

7 Refer to Fig. 5.4. and pull off the rubber dust cover. By shaking hard the piston, seal, filler block and spring should come out of the cylinder bore.

8 If they prove stubborn carefully use a foot pump air jet on the hydraulic hose connection and this should remove the internal parts; do take care as they will fly out. It is recommended that a pad is placed over the dust cover end to catch the parts.

9 Wash all the internal parts with either brake fluid or methylated spirits and dry using a clean non-fluffy rag.

10 Inspect the bore and piston for signs of deep scoring, which, if evident, means a new cylinder should be fitted.

11 Carefully examine the rubber components for signs of swelling, distortion, splitting, hardening or other wear although it is recommended new rubber parts are always fitted after dismantling.

12 Reassembly is a straight reversal of the dismantling procedure but NOTE the following points:-

a) As the component parts are refitted to the slave cylinder bore, smear them with clean hydraulic fluid.

b) When refitting the piston seal ensure that it is positioned the correct way round as shown in Fig. 5.4.

c) On completion of the fitting to its mounting bracket, top up the reservoir with the correct grade hydraulic fluid and bleed the system. Do not forget to replace the rubber dust cap on the bleed nipple and remove the polythene from the top of the clutch master cylinder.

10 Clutch master cylinder - removal, dismantling, examination and reassembly

1 Drain the fluid from the clutch master cylinder reservoir by attaching a rubber tube to the slave cylinder bleed nipple. Undo the screw at the base of the nipple one turn, and then pump the fluid out into a suitable container by means of operating the clutch pedal. Note that the pedal must be held against the floor at the completion of each stroke and the bleed nipple tightened before the pedal is allowed to return. When the pedal has returned to its normal position loosen the bleed nipple and repeat the process, until the clutch master cylinder is empty.

2 Place a rag under the master cylinder to catch any hydraulic fluid that may be spilt. Unscrew the union nut from the end of the hydraulic pipe where it enters the clutch master cylinder and gently pull the pipe clear.

3 From inside the car extract the split pin from the pushrod yoke to pedal clevis pin and lift away the washer and clevis noting which way round the clevis is fitted.

4 Unscrew the two nuts holding the clutch master cylinder to the support bracket, lift away the two nuts, bolts and spring washers.

5 Remove the master cylinder and reservoir taking care not to allow any hydraulic fluid to come into contact with the paintwork as it acts as a solvent. Unscrew the filler cap and drain any hydraulic fluid into a clean container.

6 Referring to Fig. 5.6., pull off the rubber boot to expose the circlip which must next be removed so that the pushrod complete with the metal pushrod stop can be pulled out from the master cylinder bore.

7 By shaking hard, the piston with the seal, dished washer and seal should come out of the cylinder bore. Also the spring and rod retainer may be removed.

8 If they prove stubborn carefully use a foot pump air jet on the hydraulic pipe connection and this should remove the internal parts, but do take care as they will fly out. It is recommended that a pad is placed over the pushrod end to catch the parts.

9 Separate the spring retainer and secondary seal from the piston.

10 Thoroughly clean the parts in brake fluid or methylated spirits. After drying them inspect the seals for signs of distortion, swelling, splitting or hardening although it is recommended new

rubber parts are always fitted after dismantling as a matter of course.

11 Inspect the bore and piston for signs of deep scoring which, if evident, means a new cylinder should be fitted. Make sure that the by-pass ports are clear by poking gently with a piece of thin wire.

12 As the parts are refitted to the cylinder bore make sure that they are thoroughly wetted with hydraulic fluid.

13 Fit the secondary seal to the piston and the spring retainer to the spring.

14 Insert the large end of the spring into the cylinder bore followed by the primary seal ensuring that the lip is inserted first. Great care must be taken not to turn back the lip on the seal.

15 Replace the dished washer, concave side adjacent to the rubber seal, and the piston into the cylinder bore.

16 Insert the pushrod and guide into the rubber bush cover and fit the pushrod complete with stop plate into position in the master cylinder. Replace the circlip holding the components into the cylinder bore and finally replace the dust cover.

17 Replacement of the unit in the car is a straightforward reversal of the removal sequence. Bleed the system as described in Section 2 of this Chapter.

11 Clutch - faults

There are four main faults to which the clutch and release mechanism are prone. They may occur by themselves or in conjunction with any of the other faults. They are clutch squeal, slip, spin and judder.

12 Clutch squeal - diagnosis and cure

1 If on taking up the drive or when changing gear, the clutch squeals, this is a sure indication of a badly worn clutch release bearing.

2 As well as regular wear due to normal use, wear on the clutch release bearing is much accentuated if the clutch is ridden or held down for long periods with a gear selected and the engine running. To minimise wear of this component the car should always be taken out of gear at traffic lights and for similar hold ups.

3 The clutch release bearing is not an expensive item but difficult to get at.

13 Clutch slip - diagnosis and cure

1 Clutch slip is a self evident condition which occurs when the clutch friction plate is badly worn, oil or grease having got onto the flywheel or pressure plate faces, or the pressure plate itself is faulty.

2 The reason for clutch slip is that due to one of the faults above, there is insufficient pressure from the pressure plate, or insufficient friction from the friction plate to ensure solid drive.

3 If small amounts of oil get onto the clutch, they will be burnt off by the heat of the clutch engagement, and in the process gradually darken the linings. Excessive oil on the clutch will burn off leaving a carbon deposit which can cause quite bad slip, or fierceness, spin and judder.

4 If clutch slip is suspected, and confirmation of this condition is required, there are several tests which can be made.

5 With the engine in second or third gear and pulling lightly up a moderate incline, sudden depression of the accelerator pedal may cause the engine to increase its speed without any increase in road speed. Easing off on the accelerator pedal will then give a definite drop in engine speed without the car showing signs of slowing.

6 In extreme cases of clutch slip the engine will race under normal acceleration conditions.

7 If slip is due to oil or grease on the linings a temporary cure

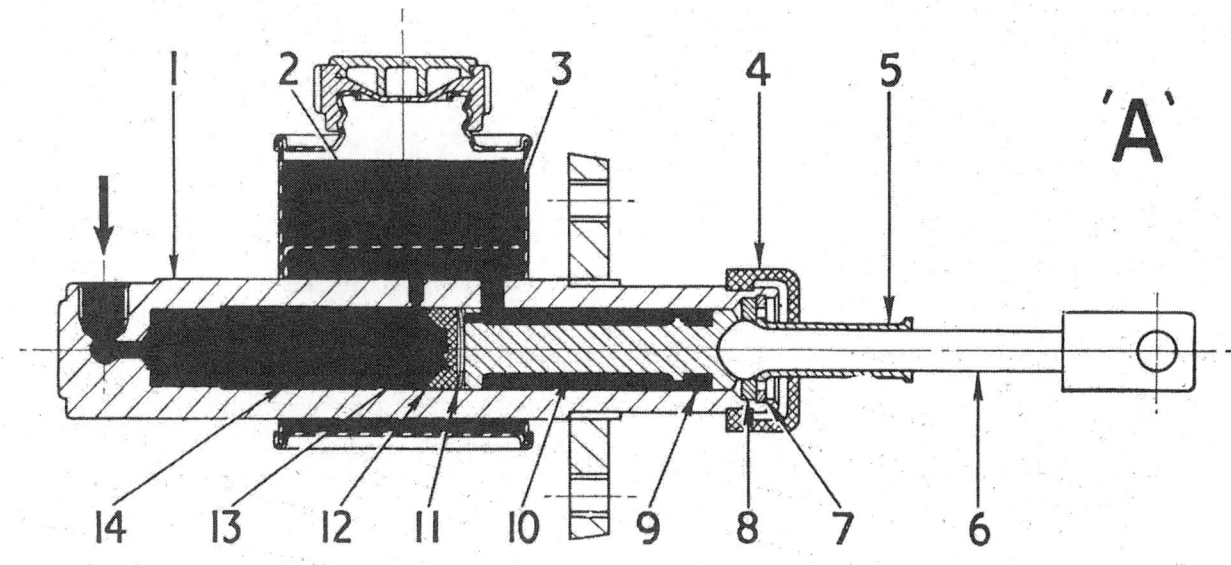

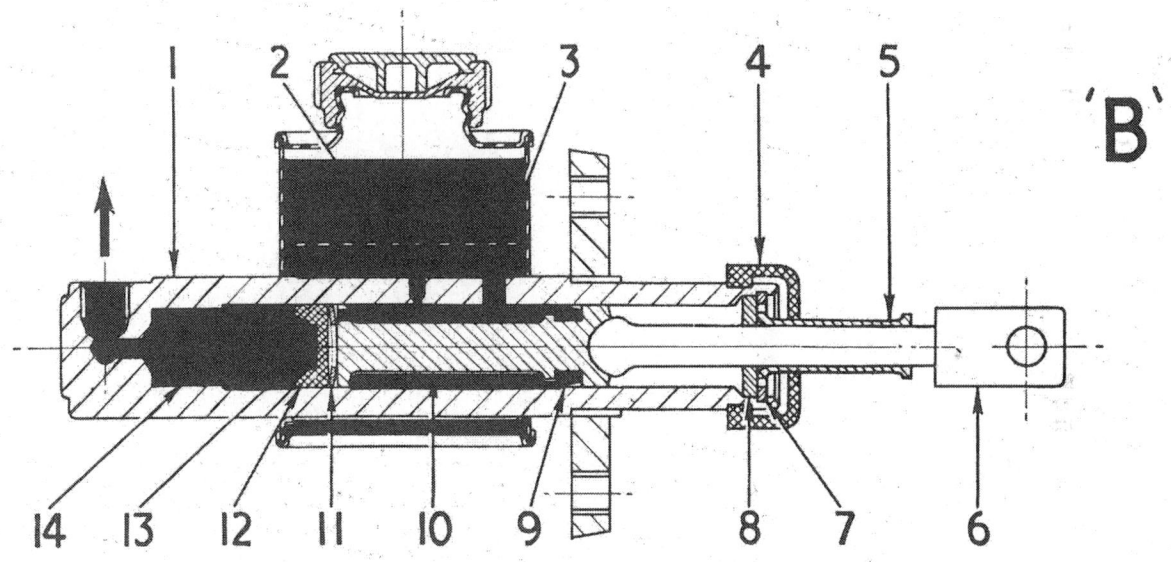

FIG. 5.6. THE CLUTCH MASTER CYLINDER

1	Body	4	Dust cover	7	Circlip	11 Dished washer
2	By-pass hole	5	Push rod guide	8	Push rod stop	12 Primary seal
3	Feed hole	6	Push rod	9	Seal	13 Spring retainer
				10	Piston	14 Spring

'A'   Clutch pedal 'up' - clutch engaged

'B'   Clutch pedal 'down' - clutch disengaged

can sometimes be effected by squirting carbon tetrachloride into the clutch. The permanent cure is, of course, to renew the clutch driven plate and trace and rectify the oil leak.

14 Clutch spin - diagnosis and cure

1 Clutch spin is a condition which occurs when there is a leak in the clutch hydraulic actuating mechanism; there is an obstruction in the clutch either on the input shaft splines or in the operating lever itself; or the oil may have partially burnt off the clutch linings and has left a resinous deposit which is causing the clutch disc to stick to the pressure plate or flywheel.

2 The reason for clutch spin is that due to any, or a combination of, the faults just listed, the clutch pressure plate is not completely freeing from the centre plate even with the clutch pedal fully depressed.

3 If clutch spin is suspected, the condition can be confirmed by extreme difficulty in engaging first or reverse gear from rest, difficulty in changing gear, and very sudden take up of the clutch drive at the fully depressed end of the clutch pedal travel as the clutch is released.

4 Check the clutch master cylinder and slave cylinder and the connecting hydraulic pipe for leaks. Fluid in one of the rubber boots fitted over the end of either the master cylinder or slave cylinder is a sure sign of a leaking piston seal.

5 If these points are checked and found to be in order then the fault lies internally in the clutch, and it will be necessary to remove the clutch for examination.

15 Clutch judder - diagnosis and cure

1 Clutch judder is a self evident condition which occurs when the gearbox or engine mountings are loose or too flexible; when there is oil on the face of the clutch friction plate; or when the clutch pressure plate has been incorrectly adjusted.

2 The reason for clutch judder is that due to one of the faults just listed, the clutch pressure plate is not freeing smoothly from the friction disc and is snatching.

3 Clutch judder normally occurs when the clutch pedal is released in first or reverse gears and the whole of the car shudders when it moves backwards or forwards.

Chapter 6 Gearbox and overdrive

Contents

Specifications

Gearbox

Number of forward speeds	4
Synchromesh	forward gears

Overall gearbox ratios

Top	1.00:1
Third	1.33:1
Second	2.01:1
First	3.14:1
Reverse	3.22:1

Dimensions and tolerances

Mainshaft journal diameter	1.2500 to 1.2505 in	(31.75 to 31.7627 mm)
Overall end float of second and third gear bushes and thrust washers	0.003 to 0.009 in	(0.0762 to 0.2286 mm)
Overall end float of first gear bushes and thrust washers	0.003 to 0.009 in	(0.0762 to 0.2286 mm)
Inside diameter of first, second and third gear bushes ...	1.251 to 1.252 in	(31.7754 to 31.8008 mm)
Outside diameter of first and third gear bushes	1.4983 to 1.4978 in	(38.057 to 38.044 mm)
End float of first, second and third gear on bushes ...	0.004 to 0.008 in	(0.1016 to 0.2032 mm)

Thrust washers

Part number 129941 Self finish	0.120 to 0.118 in	(3.048 to 2.997 mm)
Part number 129942 Green	0.123 to 0.121 in	(3.124 to 3.0734 mm)
Part number 129943 Blue	0.126 to 0.124 in	(3.200 to 3.1496 mm)
Part number 129944 Orange	0.129 to 0.127 in	(3.2766 to 3.2258 mm)
Part number 134670 Yellow	0.134 to 0.132 in	(3.4036 to 3.3528 mm)

Gear bores

First	1.4995 to 1.5005 in	(38.087 to 38.1127 mm)
Second	1.5672 to 1.5680 in	(39.807 to 39.827 mm)
Third	1.4995 to 1.5005 in	(38.087 to 38.1127 mm)

Layshaft

Diameter	0.8120 to 0.8125 in	(20.625 to 20.637 mm)
Thickness of front thrust washer	0.066 to 0.068 in	(1.6764 to 1.7272 mm)
Thickness of rear thrust washer	0.105 to 0.107 in	(2.667 to 2.718 mm)
Layshaft end float	0.007 to 0.012 in	(0.1778 to 0.3048 mm)

Synchromesh release loads

First and second gear synchro unit	25 lb to 27 lb	(11.34 to 12.247 Kg)
Third and top gear synchro unit	19 lb to 21 lb	(8.618 to 9.525 Kg)

Selector shaft release loads

First, second	32 lb to 34 lb	(14.515 to 15.422 Kg)
Third, top	26 lb to 28 lb	(11.793 to 12.701 Kg)
Reverse	26 lb to 28 lb	(11.793 to 12.701 Kg)

Overdrive unit - early fitment

Type	Laycock de Normanville	

Pump

Plunger diameter	0.3742 to 0.3746 in	(9.504 to 9.514 mm)
Pump body bore	0.3748 to 0.3758 in	(9.52 - 9.545 mm)
Pin for roller diameter	0.2497 to 0.2502 in	(6.342 to 6.355 mm)
Roller bore diameter	0.2510 to 0.2520 in	(6.375 to 6.4 mm)

Pump roller bush

Outside diameter of bush	0.3736 to 0.3745 in	(9.49 - 9.512 mm)
Inside diameter of roller	0.3750 to 0.3759 in	(9.525 to 9.548 mm)
Inside diameter of bush	0.2510 to 0.2518 in	(6.375 to 6.396 mm)
Outside diameter pin	0.2497 to 0.2502 in	(6.342 to 6.355 mm)

Accumulators

1 1/8 in piston diameter	1.1232 to 1.1241 in	(28.524 to 28.547 mm)
1 1/8 in housing bore diameter	1.1245 to 1.1255 in	(28.600 to 28.626 mm)

Operating valve

Valve diameter	0.2494 to 0.2497 in	(6.335 to 6.342 mm)
Bore diameter	0.2500 to 0.2506 in	(6.35 to 6.365 mm)

Gear train

Planet pin diameter	0.4372 to 0.4375 in	(11.105 to 11.112 mm)
Planet gear bore (caged bearing)	0.6245 to 0.6250 in	(28.557 to 28.570 mm)
End float of sunwheel	0.0800 to 0.0140 in	(0.2032 to 0.3556 mm)

Overdrive mainshaft

Diameter of steady bushes	1.1544 to 1.1553 in	(29.312 to 29.335 mm)
Inside diameter of bushes	1.1582 to 1.1592 in	(29.413 to 29.439 mm)
Diameter at sunwheel	1.1544 to 1.1553 in	(29.312 to 29.335 mm)
Inside diameter of sunwheel bush	1.1582 to 1.1592 in	(29.413 to 29.439 mm)
Diameter of spigot bearing	0.6235 to 0.6242 in	(15.837 to 15.855 mm)
Inside diameter of spigot bearing	0.6250 to 0.6260 in	(16.058 to 16.082 mm)

Miscellaneous

Clutch movement from direct to overdrive	0.0800 to 0.1200 in	(2.032 to 3.048 mm)
Hydraulic operating pressure	330 to 350 lb per sq in	(23.201 to 24.6074 Kg per sq cm)

Overdrive

Later fitment

Type	Laycock-de Normanville, model J	
Cam:		
Outside diameter of cam	1.4590 to 1.4600 in	(37.059 to 37.084 mm)
Inside diameter of pump strap	1.4610 to 1.4620 in	(37.11 to 37.135 mm)

Gearbox mainshaft

Diameter of oil transfer	0.9840 to 0.9650 in	(24.485 to 24.511 mm)
Inside diameter of main case at oil transfer ...	0.9660 to 0.9670 in	(24.536 to 24.561 mm)
Diameter at sunwheel	0.9410 to 0.9430 in	(23.901 to 23.951 mm)
Inside diameter of sunwheel bush (where fitted) ...	0.9470 to 0.9490 in	(24.052 to 24.103 mm)
Diameter at mainshaft spigot	0.5620 to 0.5625 in	(14.274 to 14.2875 mm)
Inside diameter at spigot bearing	0.5628 to 0.5638 in	(14.294 to 14.320 mm)

Operating pistons

Operating piston diameter	1.2492 to 1.2497 in	(31.3297 to 31.7424 mm)
Operating piston bore diameter	1.2500 to 1.2512 in	(31.75 to 32.0091 mm)

Pump

Pump plunger diameter	0.4996 to 0.500 in	(12.6868 to 12.700 mm)
Pump body bore	0.5003 to 0.5009 in	(12.7076 to 12.7228 mm)

Relief valve

Outside diameter of relief valve piston	0.2496 to 0.2498 in	(6.3398 to 6.3449 mm)
Inside diameter of relief valve body	0.2500 to 0.2505 in	(6.35 to 6.3627 mm)
Outside diameter of dashpot piston	0.9370 to 0.9373 in	(23.799 to 23.8066 mm)
Inside diameter of dashpot sleeve	0.9375 to 0.9385 in	(23.8125 to 23.8377 mm)

Speedometer pinion

Outside diameter of speedometer pinion	0.3105 to 0.3110 in (7.8867 to 7.9004 mm)
Inside diameter of speedometer bearing	0.3120 to 0.3135 in (7.924 to 7.9629 mm)

Sliding member travel from direct drive to overdrive

(Measured at bridge pieces)	0.0510 to 0.1000 in (1.2954 to 2.54 mm)

Minimum engagement/disengagement speed ... ...   30 mph (48 Kph) (Top gear)

Hydraulic system residual pressure ... ...   20 psi (1.41 Kph)

Capacities

Gearbox (dry)	2 pints (2.4 US pints, 1.13 litres)
Gearbox and overdrive	3.5 pints (4.2 US pints, 2.0 litres)

TORQUE WRENCH SETTINGS

	lb ft	Kg fm
Gearbox and early type overdrive		
Clutch slave cylinder	16 - 20	2.21 - 2.77
Countershaft to gearbox	11 - 14	1.50 - 1.94
Cap to gearbox top cover	7 - 9	0.97 - 1.24
Flange to mainshaft	90 - 100	12.4 - 15.2
Gearbox lever to top cover	7 - 9	0.97 - 1.24
Reverse operating lever fulcrum pin to gearbox	20 - 24	2.77 - 3.32
Front end cover to gearbox	16 - 20	2.21 - 2.77
Gearbox to rear engine plate	16 - 20	2.21 - 2.77
Gear lever knob	7 - 9	0.97 - 1.24
Gearbox extension to housing	16 - 20	2.21 - 2.77
Speedo drive attachment	7 - 9	0.97 - 1.24
Selector shaftsealing ring cover	7 - 9	0.97 - 1.24
Top cover to gearbox	16 - 20	2.21 - 2.77
Drain plug and oil filter plug	20 - 24	2.77 - 3.32
Overdrive adaptor plate	16 - 20	2.21 - 2.77
Selector fork taper setscrew	7 - 9	0.97 - 1.24
Overdrive to gearbox	16 - 20	2.21 - 2.77
Cap to top cover and overdrive switch bracket	7 - 9	0.97 - 1.24
Overdrive unit - later type		
Pump non return valve to main casing	16	2.2
Pressure filter base plug	16	2.2
Speedometer drive gear retaining nut	50 to 60	6.910 to 8.28
Coupling flange securing nut	80 to 130	11.0 to 17.9

1 General description

The gearbox fitted has four forward speeds and reverse with synchromesh action on all forward speeds. Gears are selected by means of a remote control assembly mounted on the top of the gearbox. A Laycock de Normanville overdrive unit operating on second, third and top gear is fitted to certain cars as an option. Later produced TR6 overdrive operates on third and top only.

Fig. 6.1. shows the layout of the various moving parts whilst Fig. 6.2. shows the various fixed components and the gear selection system. The clutch driven plate slides on the splines of the first motion shaft (input shaft), which is in constant mesh with the layshaft gear. This constant mesh layshaft gear is splined to the layshaft hub which is able to revolve at all times including when no gears have been selected. The laygear hub assembly is supported at either end in needle roller bearings. Thrust washers are fitted at either end of the layshaft to take up excessive end float of the laygear.

The mainshaft carries the four forward gears and their respective synchromesh assemblies. The front of the shaft is supported in a needle roller bearing located in an annulus in the rear of the first motion shaft. The rear end of the mainshaft is splined to the flange to which is connected the propeller shaft universal joint coupling flange. Various thickness thrust washers are fitted onto the main shaft to control the end float of the bushes and gear assemblies on the mainshaft.

Two types of overdrive unit are fitted as optional equipment and both these are described in detail because of differences in operation and construction.

2 Gearbox - removal and refitting

1 The best method of removing the gearbox is to separate the gearbox bell housing from the engine end plate and to lift the gearbox away from the inside of the car. It is recommended that during the final stages of removal the assistance of a second person is obtained especially if an overdrive unit is fitted.

2 Disconnect the battery earth terminal, raise the car and put on axle stands if a ramp is not available. The higher the car is off the ground the easier it will be to work underneath.

3 Lift away both seat cushions and the carpeting from the front foot wells.

4 Undo the gearbox drain plug and drain the oil into a clean container. When all the oil has drained out replace the drain plug.

5 Undo and remove the eight nuts securing the seats to their seat runners. Lift away the front seats to give better access to the floor centre section.

6 Make a note of the electrical cable connections at the rear of the switches and disconnect the electrical terminals. If a radio is fitted this should be removed from its mountings (photo).

7 Slacken the gear change lever knob locknut and unscrew the knob. Also unscrew the locknut (photo).

8 Withdraw the gear change lever rubber boot from the gear change lever (photo).

9 Disconnect the two dip switch cables from their snap connections and remove the dip switch (photo).

10 Undo the two bolts holding the panel to the underside of the instrument panel switch console (photo).

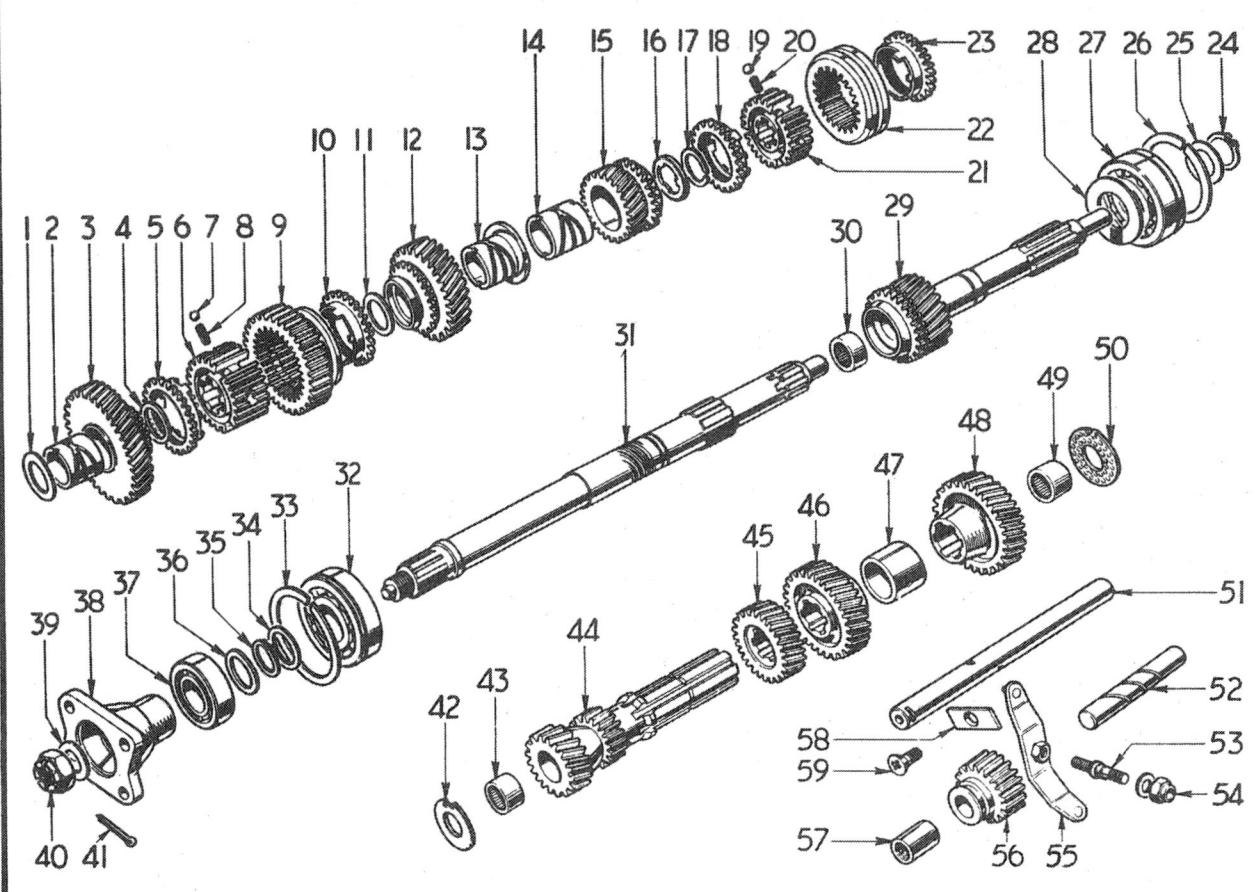

FIG. 6.1. GEARBOX INTERNAL MOVING PARTS

1 Thrust washer	15 3rd speed gear	30 Needle roller bearing	45 2nd speed layshaft gear
2 Bush - 1st speed gear	16 Thrust washer	31 Mainshaft	46 3rd speed layshaft gear
3 1st speed gear	17 Circlip	32 Ball race	47 Distance piece
4 Thrust washer	18 3rd speed synchro cup	33 Circlip	48 Layshaft gear
5 1st speed synchro cup	19 Synchro ball	34 Distance washer	49 Needle roller bearing
6 1st/2nd speed synchro hub	20 Spring	35 Circlip	50 Front thrust washer
7 Synchro ball	21 3rd/top synchro hub	36 Distance washer	51 Layshaft
8 Spring	22 Synchro sleeve	37 Rear ball race	52 Reverse gear shaft
9 Reverse mainshaft gear and	23 Top gear synchro cup	38 Flange	53 Pivot stud
synchro outer sleeve	24 Circlip	39 Plain washer	54 Nyloc nut and washer
10 2nd speed synchro cup	25 Distance washer	40 Slotted nut	55 Reverse gear operating lever
11 Thrust washer	26 Circlip	41 Split pin	56 Reverse gear
12 2nd speed gear	27 Ball race	42 Rear thrust washer	57 Reverse gear bush
13 Bush - 2nd speed gear	28 Oil deflector plate	43 Needle roller bearing	58 Locating plate
14 Bush - 3rd speed gear	29 Input shaft	44 Layshaft hub	59 Screw

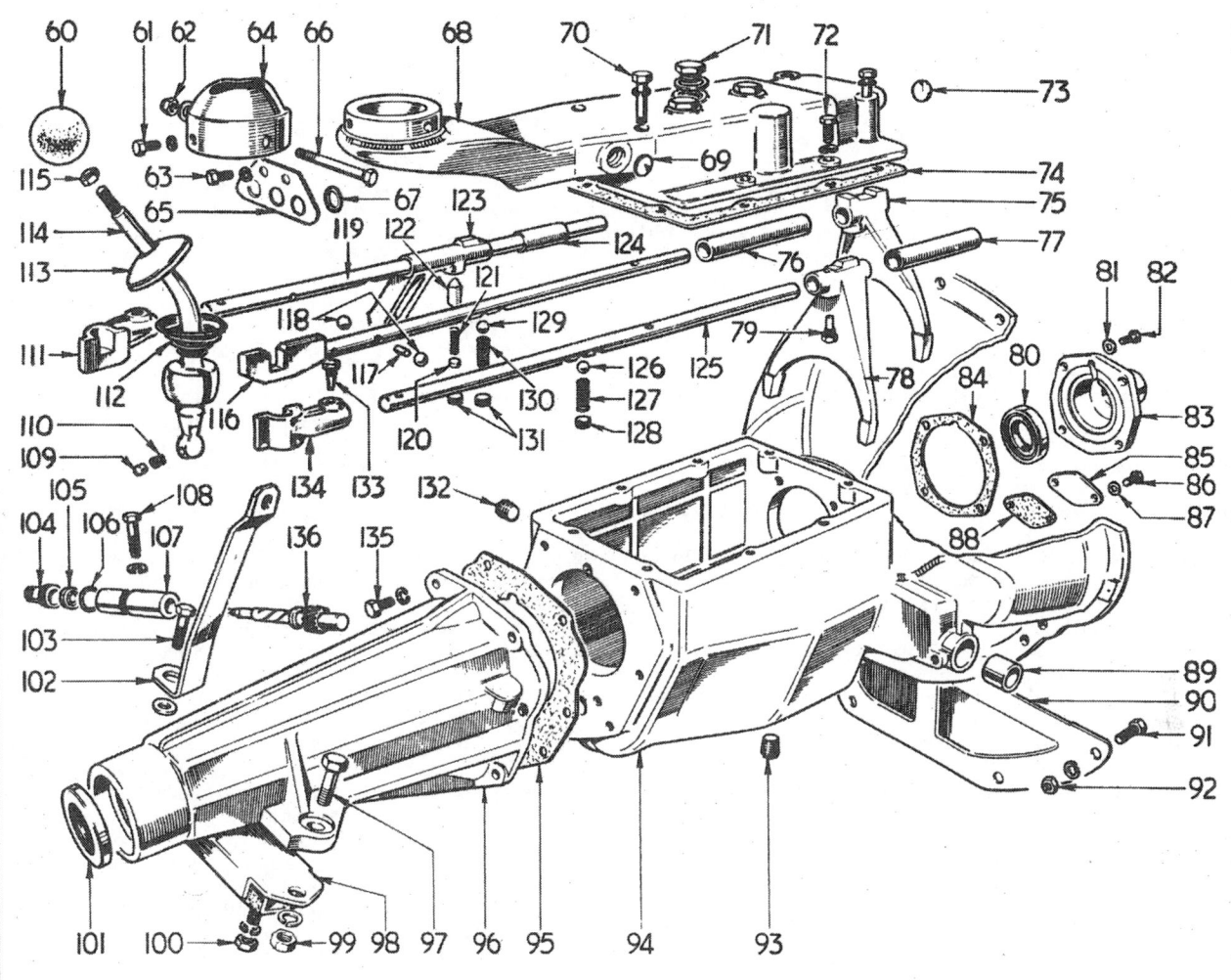

FIG.6.2. GEARBOX CASING AND EXTENSION HOUSING WITH TOP COVER AND SELECTOR SYSTEM COMPONENTS

60 Knob
61 Setscrew
62 Nyloc nut
63 Setscrew
64 Cap
65 End plate
66 Cross bolt
67 Rubber 'O' ring
68 Top cover
69 Welch plug
70 Bolt
71 Plug
72 Bolt
73 Welch plug
74 Gasket
75 Top/3rd selector fork
76 Distance tube
77 Distance tube
78 2nd/1st selector fork
79 Peg bolt

80 Oil seal
81 Copper washer
82 Bolt
83 Front cover
84 Gasket
85 Countershaft end plate
86 Setscrew
87 Copper washer
88 Gasket
89 Bush
90 Cover plate
91 Setscrew
92 Nut
93 Drain plug
94 Casing
95 Gasket
96 Extension housing
97 Bolt
98 Silentbloc mounting
99 Nut

100 Nut
101 Oil seal
102 Stay
103 Bolt
104 Speedometer cable adaptor
105 Seal
106 Rubber 'O' ring
107 Housing
108 Peg bolt
109 Plunger - anti-rattle
110 Spring
111 Selector - reverse
112 Spring
113 Cap disc
114 Lever
115 Nut
116 Top/3rd selector shaft
117 Interlock plunger
118 Balls - interlock
119 Reverse selector shaft

120 Shim
121 Spring
122 Plunger
123 Reverse actuator
124 Distance piece
125 2nd/1st selector shaft
126 Ball - detent
127 Spring
128 Plug
129 Ball - detent
130 Spring
131 Plug
132 Level/filler plug
133 Peg bolt
134 Selector 1st/2nd
135 Bolt
136 Speedo drive gear

11 Undo the four bolts holding the facia support to the floor panels (photo).

12 Disconnect the two heater control cables (photo).

13 Withdraw the centre console from under the switch panel and lift away from the car (photo).

14 Undo the sixteen bolts with plain washers holding the floor centre section to the floor panels and lift away the complete centre section.

15 Undo the propeller shaft universal joint flange retaining nyloc nuts and bolts and washers from the flange at the rear of the gearbox extension housing (standard gearbox) or rear of the overdrive unit. Scribe a mark across the two flanges to ensure replacement in the same relative position (photo).

16 Using a pair of pliers undo the speedometer drive cable knurled retainer from the gearbox extension housing (standard gearbox) or rear of the overdrive unit (photo).

17 Support the weight of the rear of the engine by placing a jack with a piece of wood on the saddle at the rear of the engine (photo).

18 Undo and remove the right hand overdrive or gearbox silent-bloc bolt followed by the nut and spring washer. Then undo the bracket to the chassis mounting nut and bolt (photo).

19 Lift away the bracket noting that the nut is welded to the underside to assist refitting (photo).

20 Remove the bolt and washer securing the gearbox remote control support stay to the silentbloc mounting (standard gearbox), or silentbloc mounting flange on the side of the overdrive unit (photo).

21 Lift away the little spacer from between the stay and overdrive unit mounting flange (photo).

22 Disconnect the clutch pedal returns spring from the slave cylinder pushrod (photo).

23 Extract the clutch slave cylinder pushrod clevis split pin and withdraw the clevis to separate the linkage (photo).

24 Disconnect the heavy duty cable from the rear of the starter motor.

25 Undo the two starter motor retaining bolts and push the starter motor forwards so as to clear the clutch bellhousing.

26 Disconnect the two wires from their terminals of the reverse light switch and also the two wires from the solenoid if the overdrive is fitted.

27 Undo and remove the four bolts and nuts securing the clutch bellhousing cover plate to the bellhousing cover plate to the bellhousing (photo).

28 Note the spring washers which are fitted between the nut and bellhousing flange.

29 Lift away the bellhousing cover plate (photo).

30 The clutch slave cylinder must next be removed from its location. The mounting nuts will have already been undone to remove the cover. Extract the pushrod from the end of the slave cylinder and put in a safe place. Tie the slave cylinder out of the way. It will not be necessary to disconnect the hydraulic hose from the rear of the slave cylinder (photo).

31 Turn the gearbox rear mounting through 90° and lift away the underside of the unit (photo).

32 Undo the nuts and bolts holding the gearbox clutch bell-housing to the engine backplate.

33 The next operations must be done with care and the assistance of a second person is necessary. Pass a rope sling around the rear of the gearbox extension housing or overdrive unit so that one person can lift up the rear of the unit (photo).

34 With the weight of the rear of the gearbox being taken by the rope sling held by a person standing at the rear of the front seat area carefully withdraw the gearbox taking care not to allow any weight to be taken by the gearbox input shaft otherwise it may bend.

35 When the input shaft is clear of the clutch swing the rear of the gearbox round to the left and withdraw through the front n/s door aperture (photo).

36 Before any work is to be carried out on the gearbox or over-drive unit it should be thoroughly washed in paraffin or gunk and dried using a non-fluffy rag (photo).

37 Replacement is the reverse sequence to removal. Do not forget to refill the gearbox with 2 pints (2.4 U.S. pints 1.13 litres) or 3.5 pints (4.2 U S pints 2.0 litres) if overdrive is fitted of recommended grade oil. It will be easier to do this before the centre floor is refitted.

3 Gearbox - dismantling

NOTE: When dismantling or reassembling the gearbox carefully follow the photographs as well as the exploded diagrams.

1 Undo the eight ½ A F bolts that hold the remote control and top cover onto the top of the gearbox (photo). Lift away the bolts and spring washers noting that the four longer bolts are to the front and rear of the top cover.

2 Lift away the remote control and top cover from the top of the gearbox noting the gasket placed between the two parts (photo).

3 Refer to Figs. 6.1 and 6.2.BB and remove the speedometer drive from the side of the extension housing.

4 Extract the split pin from the slotted nut and undo the nut from the end of the mainshaft. Lift away the nut followed by the plain washer.

5 Carefully tap the flange using a soft faced hammer, from the rear of the gearbox extension.

6 Using a pair of circlip pliers or a small screwdriver remove the circlip from the end of the mainshaft.

7 Undo the bolts holding the extension housing to the rear of the gearbox and remove the bolts and spring washers.

8 Carefully tap the extension housing with a soft faced hammer to break the joint, and withdraw the extension housing and gasket.

9 If an overdrive unit is fitted to the gearbox undo the ½ A F nuts which hold the overdrive unit to the end of the gearbox casing. This should be done in a diagonal manner as there are strong springs which will automatically separate the two parts and if the pressure is not even the mating flanges could be strained. Remove the nuts and spring washers (photo).

10 Under the action of the strong springs in the front of the overdrive unit the overdrive unit will automatically separate, this being controlled by the two long studs situated on either side of the unit (photo).

11 Note that there are eight springs in the front of the overdrive unit and that the upper and lowermost rows have springs of slightly longer length than the remaining (photo). Although the four inner springs look as if they are longer they are merely further forward.

12 Cut the locking wire securing the square headed bolt which locates the clutch release fork to the cross shaft (photo).

13 Undo the square headed bolt and completely remove (photo).

14 Pull the release bearing forwards so disengaging it from the clutch release fork and completely remove it (photo).

15 To release the cross shaft undo the bolt which locks it in position, situated on the right hand side of the clutch housing on the cross shaft bush housing.

16 Pull the shaft from the side of the bellhousing and at the same time pull the release fork from the shaft. The release fork can be a tight fit on the shaft but with care can be removed (photo).

17 Undo the four bolts that hold the front cover to the front of the gearbox casing (photo). Lift away the bolts and spring washers.

18 Remove the front cover and its gasket making a note that there is a small cut out on the gasket and front cover which matches an oil hole in the gearbox casing by the ball race (photos).

19 Undo the two bolts that hold the layshaft coverplate to the front of the gearbox (photo). Lift away the bolts, spring washer, cover plate and gasket.

20 On gearboxes fitted with overdrive unit an adaptor plate is fitted to the rear end. Undo the six adaptor plate retaining bolts (photo).

21 Gently tap the end of the adaptor plate to release it from the

2.6 If radio set is fitted this must be removed

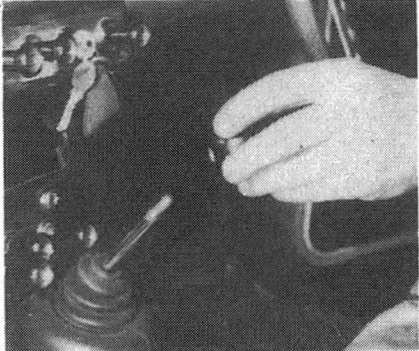

2.7 Removal of gear change lever knob

2.8 Withdrawing rubber boot

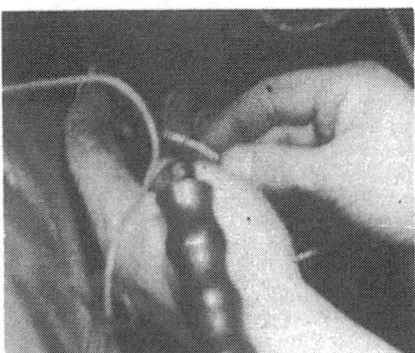

2.9 Dipswitch cable detachment

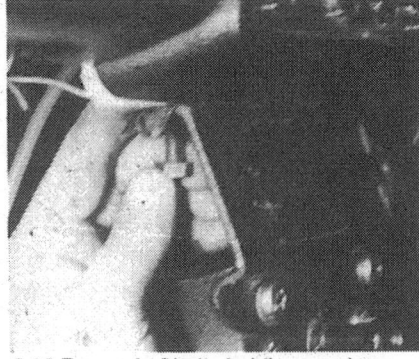

2.10 Removal of bolts holding panel to switch console

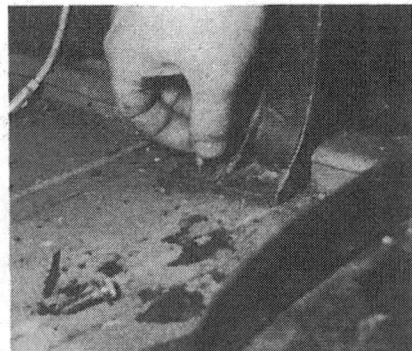

2.11 Facia support securing bolt removal

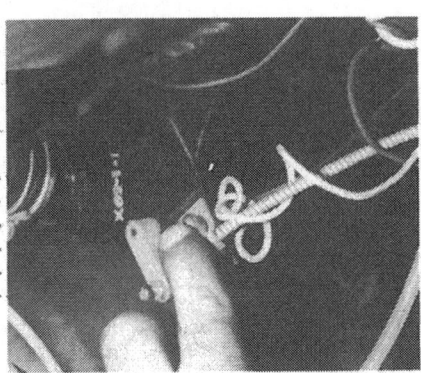

2.12 Heater control cable detachment

2.13 Removal of console

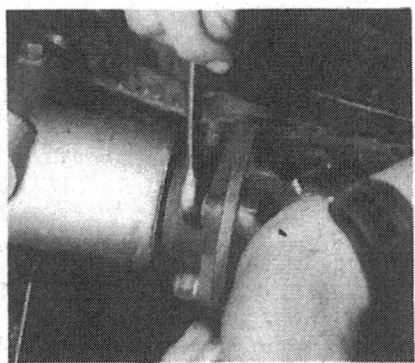

2.15 Propeller shaft universal joint flange detachment

2.16 Speedometer cable retainer removal

2.17 Supporting weight of engine

2.18 Undoing bracket to chassis mounting nut and bolt

2.19 Lifting away bracket

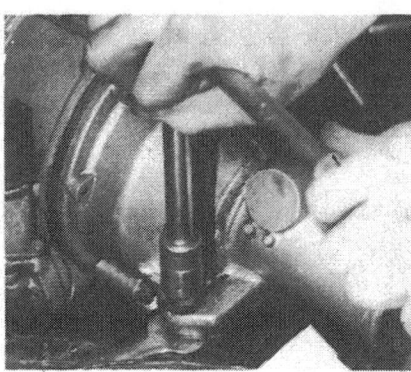
2.20 Overdrive silentbloc mounting bolt removal

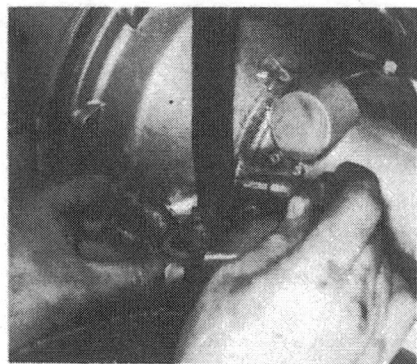
2.21 Lifting away spacer from between stay and overdrive unit mounting flange

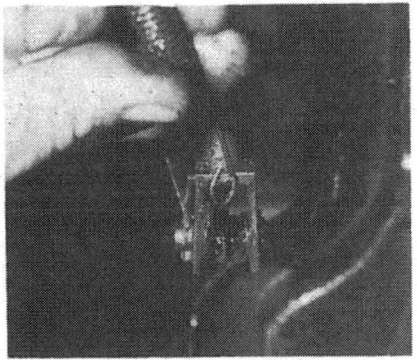
2.22 Detaching clutch pedal return spring

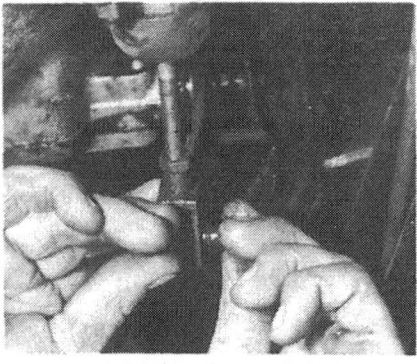
2.23 Removal of clutch slave cylinder pushrod clevis pin

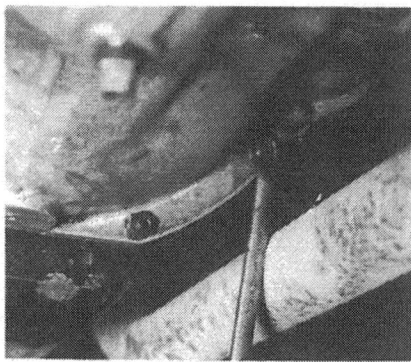
2.27 Clutch bell housing cover plate securing nut and bolt removal

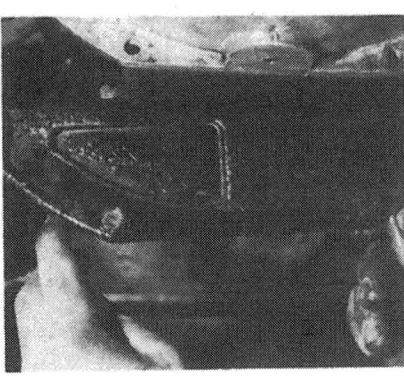
2.29 Lifting away cover plate

2.30 Withdrawing clutch slave cylinder.

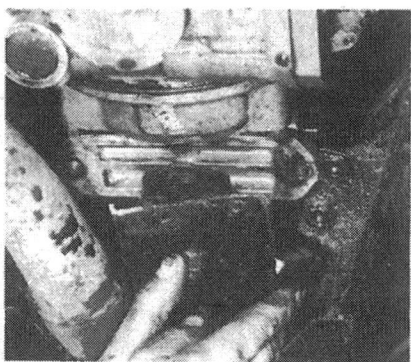
2.31 Gearbox rear mounting removal

2.35 Lifting away gearbox assembly

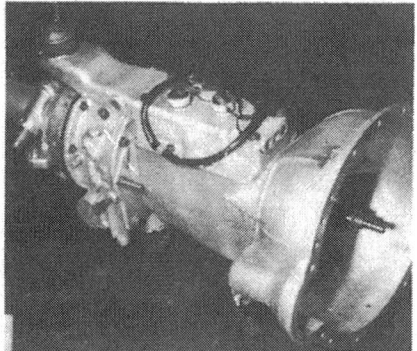
2.36 The gearbox and overdrive unit

3.1 Removing remote control and top cover securing bolts and sliding off gear change lever cap

3.2 Lifting away remote control and top cover

3.9 Removal of overdrive unit securing nuts

3.10 Location of long stud on side of overdrive unit

3.11 Layout of springs in front of over-drive unit

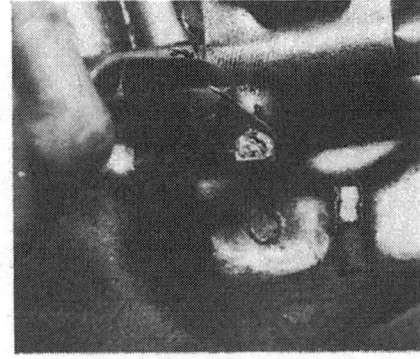

3.12 Cutting locking wire securing square headed bolt

3.13 Removal of square headed bolt

3.14 Pulling release bearing forwards

3.16 Pulling out release fork shaft

3.17 Front cover securing bolt removal

3.18a Removal of front cover

3.18b Small cut out in gasket to match oil hole (arrowed)

3.19 Layshaft cover securing bolt re-moval

3.20 Removal of overdrive adaptor plate securing bolts

3.21 Lifting away adaptor plate

3.22 Keeper plate Phillips head screw

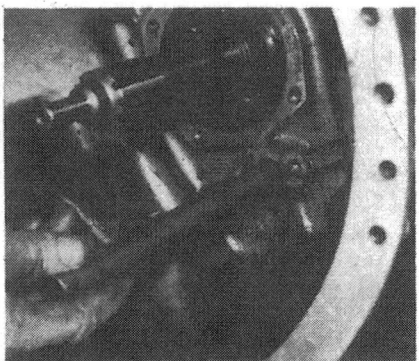

3.23 Inserting metal rod to remove layshaft

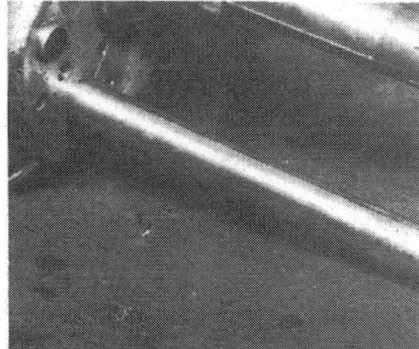

3.24 Layshaft spindle removal

3.26 Tapping out first motion shaft

3.27 Lifting away first motion shaft

3.28 Removal of overdrive unit pump cam

3.29 Removal of circlip from mainshaft

3.30 Easing circ lip along mainshaft

3.31 Removal of distance washer

3.32 Tapping mainshaft with soft faced hammer

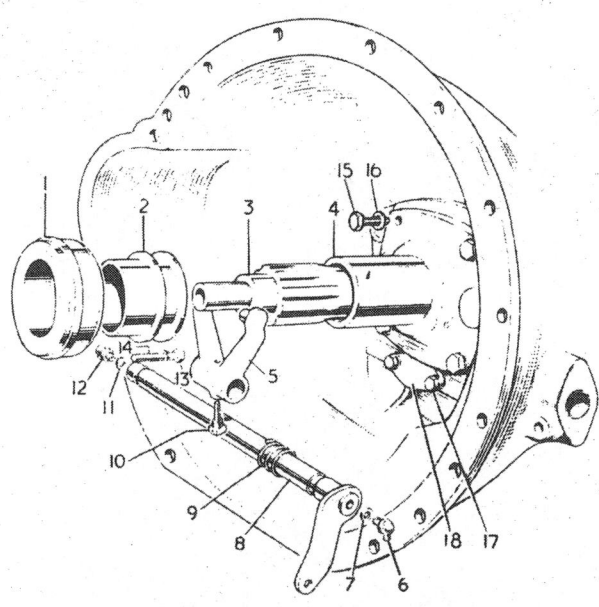

**FIG.6.3. CLUTCH RELEASE SYSTEM IN
GEARBOX BELLHOUSING**

1	*Release bearing*	10	*Screwed taper pin*
2	*Sleeve*	11	*Fibre washer*
3	*Input shaft*	12	*Grease nipple*
4	*Front cover*	13	*Cross-shaft locating bolt*
5	*Fork*	14	*Spring washer*
6	*Grease nipple*	15	*Wedglok bolts*
7	*Fibre washer*	16	*Washers*
8	*Cross-shaft*	17	*Bolts*
9	*Anti-rattle spring*	18	*Plate*

gearbox (photo).

22 Undo the large Phillips head screw which holds the keeper plate in position. The keeper plate locks the layshaft spindle and reverse pinion shaft to the gearbox. Lift away the Phillips screw and slide out the keeper plate (photo).

23 Obtain a piece of metal rod of approximately the same diameter as the layshaft but longer, insert the rod in the layshaft hole in the bellhousing and push out the layshaft so it emerges from the rear of the gearbox (photo).

24 Note that there is a milled slot in the layshaft spindle which must be to the rear during reassembly so that the keeper plate, which was previously removed, may engage in the slot (photo).

25 Withdraw the metal rod that was used to remove the layshaft spindle and allow the layshaft assembly to drop to the bottom of the gearbox.

26 The first motion shaft should next be removed. Using a metal drift gently tap the first motion shaft bearing outwards, through the front of the gearbox casing (photo).

27 Lift the first motion shaft complete with bearing from the front of the gearbox (photo).

28 Turning to the rear of the gearbox slide off the cam that drives the pump in the overdrive unit (if fitted) (photo).

29 Using a pair of circlip pliers extract the circlip from its groove in the mainshaft (photo).

30 With a screwdriver ease the circlip over the mainshaft splines (photo).

31 Slide the distance washer from the face of the bearing inner track and remove from the mainshaft (photo).

32 To remove the rear mainshaft bearing use a soft faced hammer and drive the mainshaft into the gearbox as shown in the photo, until the bearing is at the rear of the mainshaft splines. Note the bearing circlip on the outer race periphery is still in position.

33 Carefully ease the bearing rearwards using two open ended spanners and tapping the mainshaft into the gearbox. Continue this operation until the bearing is completely free of the splines and lift away the bearing (photo).

34 If difficulty is experienced in levering the bearing along the mainshaft place the gearbox on its end with the mainshaft vertical (photo).

35 The mainshaft assembly may now be lifted through the gearbox as shown in the photograph.

36 Withdraw the reverse idler shaft from the rear of the gearbox. Note the slot in the rear of the shaft into which engages the keeper plate (photo).

37 Lift away the reverse idler gear having made a note of which way round it fits.

38 Lift out the laygear rear thrust washer (photo).

39 Lift out the laygear front thrust washer (photo) and finally remove the complete laygear assembly.

40 The laygear may be dismantled by sliding off the gears and bushing from the splined layshaft hub (photos).

4 Gearbox - examination and renovation

1 Carefully clean and then examine all the component parts for general wear, distortion, slackness of fit, and damage to machined faces and threads.

2 Examine the gearwheels for excessive wear and chipping of the teeth. Renew them as necessary. If the laygear endfloat is above the permitted tolerance of 0.012 in the thrust washers must be renewed. New thrust washers will almost certainly be required on any car that has completed more than 50,000 miles.

3 Examine the layshaft for signs of wear, where the laygear needle roller bearing bears, and check the laygear on a new shaft for worn bearings. These are simply drifted out if new ones are to be fitted.

4 The four synchroniser rings are bound to be badly worn and it is false economy not to renew them. New rings will improve the smoothness and speed of the gearchange considerably.

5 The needle roller bearing and cage located between the nose of the mainshaft and the annulus in the rear of the shaft is also liable to wear, and should be renewed as a matter of course.

6 Examine the condition of the three ball bearing assemblies, one on the first motion shaft, one on the mainshaft and the other in the tail of the gearbox extension. Check them for noisy operation, looseness between the inner and outer races, and for general wear. Normally they should be renewed on a gearbox that is being rebuilt.

7 Examine the mainshaft bushes and fit them on the mainshaft to check for overall endfloat.

8 Fit the inner thrust washer, bushes, second thrust washer and finally the circlip. With a feeler gauge measure the endfloat between the inner thrust washer and the adjacent bush. This should be between 0.003 and 0.009 in . If outside these figures experiment with alternative thrust washers until the end float is correct.

9 To dismantle the synchromesh units, first wrap a length of clean rag completely round a unit and then pull off the outer synchro sleeve. The cloth will catch the spring loaded balls and springs which are bound to fly out. Compare the length of the old springs with new and replace any that are worn. Note that an interlock plunger and ball is fitted to the second speed synchromesh hub.

10 Parts of the remote control gearchange are bound to be worn on any high mileage model and this is dealt with in Section 9.

11 NOTE: Later type gearboxes have a laygear with roller bearings in each end which are retained by circlips. On early models the roller bearings are a press fit and are positioned with a special tool. If you have to get an exchange laygear ensure that it is of the second type and that you not only get the roller bearings to fit it but also the circlips.

12 If the gearbox is to be left for any time it is a good idea to wire the respective components of the laygear together, in their respective order, so as to avoid confusion later on.

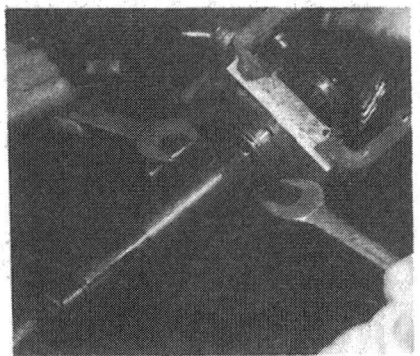

3.33 Easing mainshaft bearing rearwards

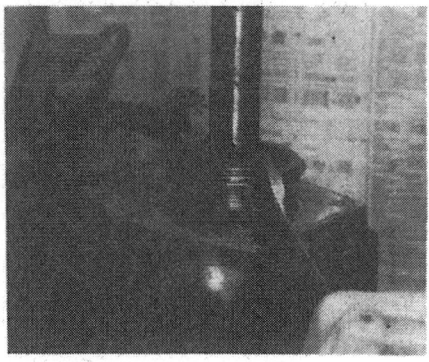

3.34 Gearbox placed in vertical position

3.35 Lifting mainshaft from gearbox

3.36 Reverse idler shaft removal

3.38 Rear thrust washer removal

3.39 Layshaft front thrust washer removal

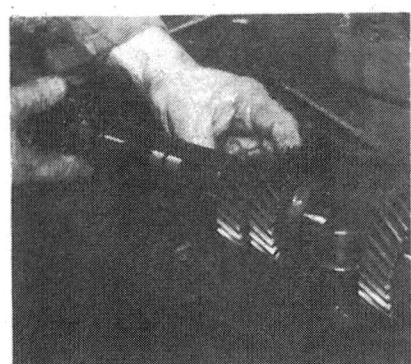

3.40a Dismantling layshaft

3.40b Keep gears in order

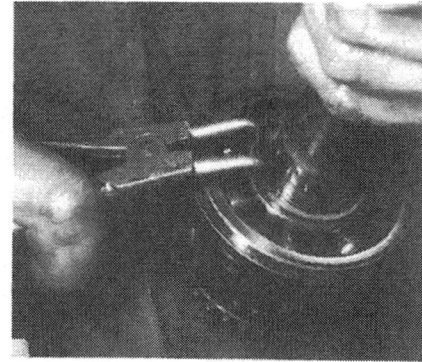

5.1 Removal of circlip from first motion shaft

5.2 Sliding off spacer washer

5.3 Drifting first motion shaft through bearing

5.5 Component parts of first motion shaft

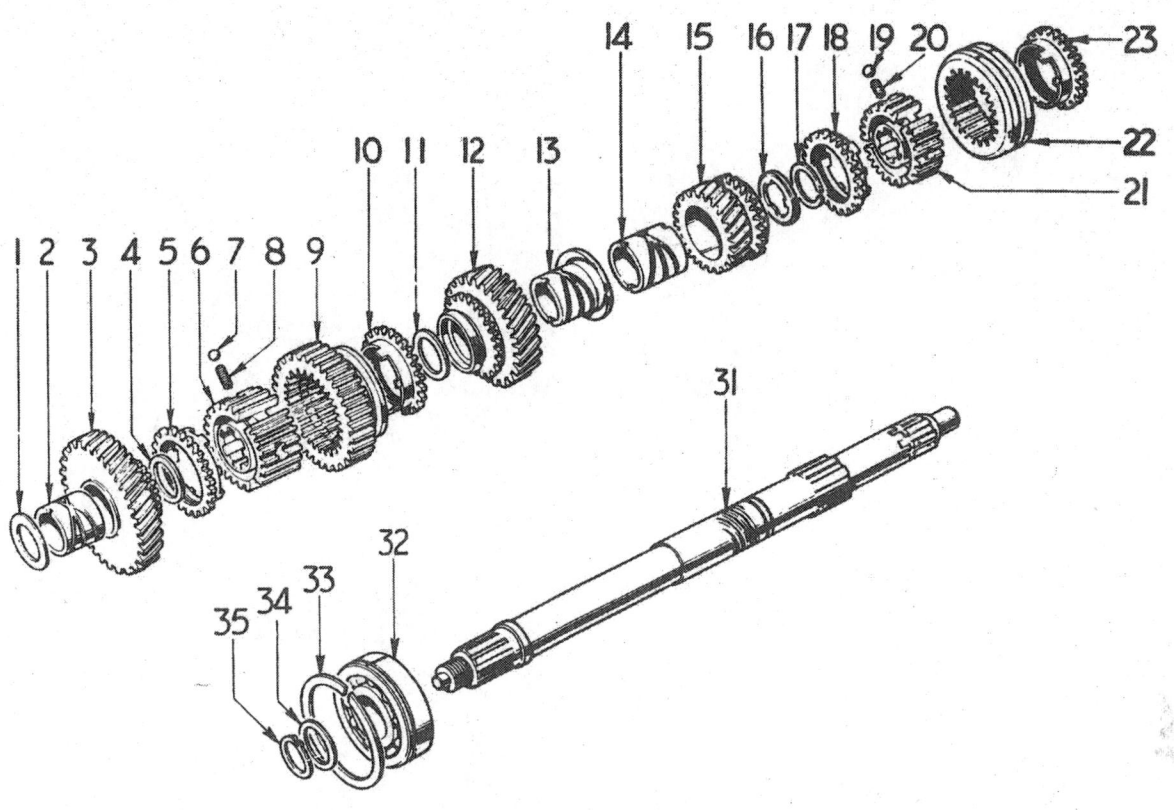

FIG.6.4. COMPONENT PARTS OF MAINSHAFT

1 Thrust washer	8 Spring	15 3rd speed gear	22 Synchro sleeve
2 Bush 1st speed	9 Reverse mainshaft gear	16 Thrust washer	23 Top gear synchro cup
3 1st speed gear	10 2nd speed synchro cup	17 Circlip	31 Mainshaft
4 Thrust washer	11 Thrust washer	18 3rd speed synchro cup	32 Ball race
5 1st speed synchro cup	12 2nd speed gear	19 Synchro ball	33 Circlip
6 1st/2nd speed synchro hub	13 Bush 2nd speed	20 Spring	34 Distance washer
7 Synchro ball	14 Bush 3rd speed	21 3rd/top synchro hub	35 Circlip

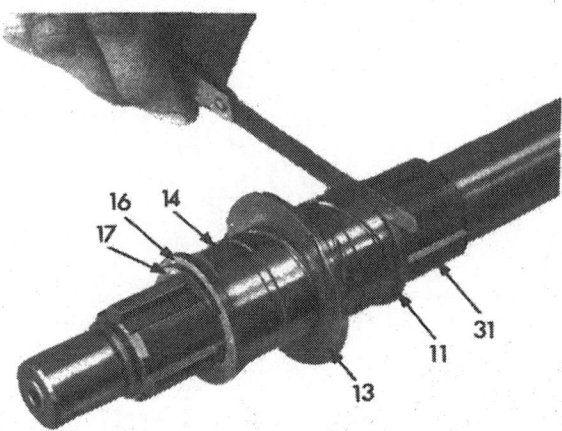

FIG.6.5. USING FEELER GAUGE TO MEASURE BUSH END-FLOAT

11 Thrust washer	16 Thrust washer
13 Bush-second speed gear	17 Circlip
14 Bush-third speed gear	31 Mainshaft

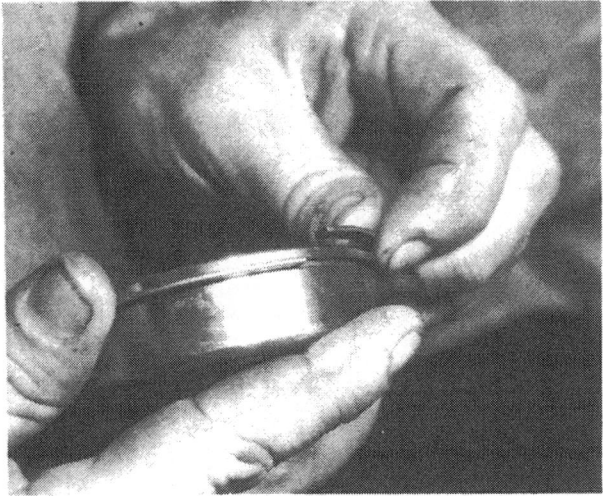

5.6 Fitting circlip to bearing outer track

5.8 Drifting first motion shaft onto bearing

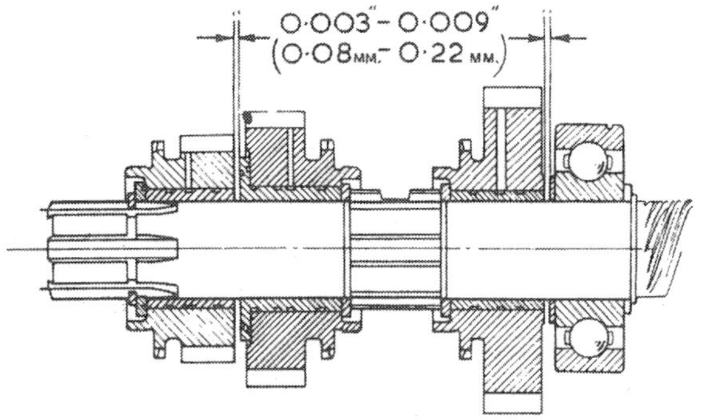

0·003″ - 0·009″
(0·08 mm. - 0·22 mm.)

Fig.6.6. Cross sectional view through mainshaft assembly. The arrows denote end-float of mainshaft bushes

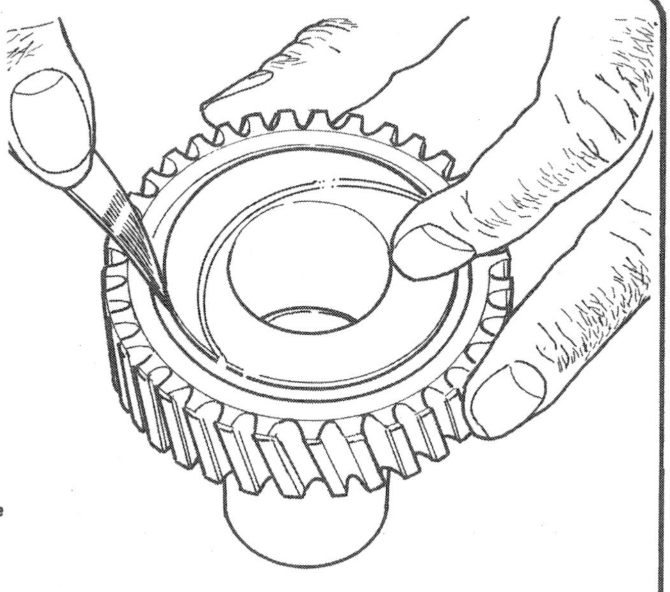

Fig.6.7. Using feeler gauges to check second gear end-float

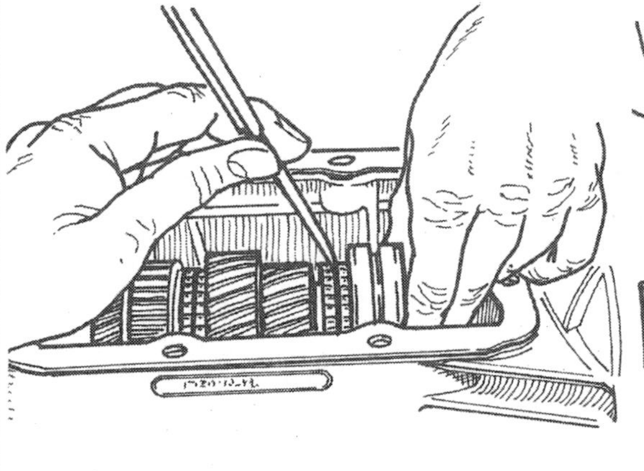

Fig.6.8. The measurement to gap between baulk ring teeth and cone

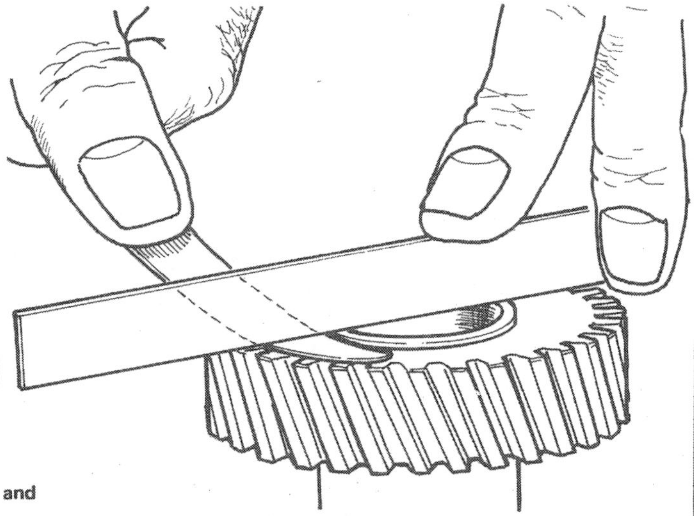

Fig.6.9. Using a straight edge and feeler gauges to check the end-float between the mainshaft 3rd gear and its bush

5 First motion shaft - dismantling and reassembly

1 The first motion shaft may be dismantled by first removing the circlip from its groove in the shaft (photo).

2 Slide off the spacer washer from the face of the race inner track and place the first motion shaft on the top of the vice with the outer track of the race resting on soft faces (photo).

3 Using a soft faced hammer drift the first motion shaft through the race inner track (photo). The strain placed on the bearing does not matter, as the bearing would not be removed unless it was being renewed.

4 Lift away the race from the first motion shaft followed by the oil deflector plate.

5 The component parts of the first motion shaft are shown in the photo.

6 To assemble the first motion shaft first fit the circlip to the bearing race outer track (photo).

7 Slide the oil deflector plate onto the first motion shaft and then the ball race with the circlip away from the constant mesh gears.

8 Place the race against soft metal on the top of the jaws of a vice and using a drift located in the spigot bearing hole, drive the shaft into the bearing (photo).

9 Replace the spacer washer and finally the circlip. Ensure that the circlip seats correctly in its groove.

6 Mainshaft - dismantling and reassembly

1 Place two pieces of soft metal in the jaws of a firm bench vice ready for holding the mainshaft.

2 Place the end of the mainshaft between the soft faces of the vice so that it is parallel with the bench top.

3 Commence dismantling the mainshaft by sliding off the third and fourth gear synchromesh hub and the conical synchromesh ring (photo). Note which way round it fits on the mainshaft.

4 Using a pair of circlip pliers remove the circlip that holds the third gear in position (photo).

5 This can be a little difficult to remove so an assistant working with two screwdrivers will probably make this operation easier. With one end of the circlip released from the groove gradually work the way round until it is free of the groove and then ease it along the splines of the mainshaft (photo).

6 Remove the third gear thrust washer from the mainshaft. Note which way round it fits as there is a flange on the inside (photo).

7 Slide the third gear and bush from the mainshaft (photo). Note that in the recess of the third gear is a spline.

8 Remove the second speed gear and second speed bush (photo). Note that there is a thrust washer inside the cone portion of the second speed gear.

9 Remove the first and second gear synchromesh hub which also incorporates the reverse gear machined on its periphery. Also remove the two grooved synchromesh rings (photo).

10 Remove the mainshaft from the vice and slide off the first gear and bush from the longer end of the mainshaft. Note that there is a thrust washer between the mainshaft larger diameter splines and the first gear bush (photo).

11 Dismantling the mainshaft is now complete.

12 Before reassembling the components to the mainshaft it will be necessary to determine the overall end float of the bushes. To do this refer to Fig. 6.5 and assemble the thrust washer bush, and thrust washer onto the mainshaft and hold the components in place with an old circlip. Using feeler gauges determine the total endfloat of both bushes. It should be between 0.004 - 0.009 in (0.0762 - 0.2286 mm). If necessary adjust the endfloat by selecting thrust washers of various thicknessess.

13 Assemble to the longer end of the mainshaft the thrust washer, followed by the first gear bush, the first gear with the conical end towards the first thrust washer and then the second thrust washer (photo).

14 Next mount the longer end (tail end) of the mainshaft

between soft jaws of a vice and fit from the shorter end the synchromesh ring followed by the first and second gear selector hub which incorporates on its forward periphery (part nearest the first gear) the reverse gear teeth (photo).

15 Continue building the front end of the mainshaft by fitting the synchromesh cone followed by a spacer, then second gear followed by the second gear bush which should be positioned with the raised lip on the end nearest to the front of the shaft (photo).

16 Ensure that when refitting the synchromesh rings the tonque on the ring mates with the recess in the synchromesh hub as shown in the photo.

17 Refit the third gear, the third gear bush and the thrust washer so that the end of the spacer abuts inside the recess in the forward end of the gear.

18 Fit the spring circlip into position on the front of the mainshaft. Difficulty may be experienced in seating the circlip into its groove in the mainshaft but with care it can be done (photo).

19 This photo shows how the mainshaft looks when the front end is fully assembled with the two remaining synchromesh rings and the third and fourth gear synchromesh hub being placed in position. The protruding end of the hub must face the front of the mainshaft. Do not fit these parts yet but leave until the mainshaft has been inserted into the gearbox casing.

7 Gearbox - reassembly

1 To reassemble the layshaft gear first grease the two needle roller bearings, and insert them into the ends of the hub (photo). Note that on later produced gearboxes circlips are used to retain the needle bearings in the layshaft gear. Refit the circlips as applicable.

2 Lubricate the hub splines and slide the second gear, third gear, distance tube and countershaft gear onto the splines. The photo shows the gears positioned the correct way round for refitting. They have been previously wired together to ensure they are not separated.

3 Fit the front thrust washer for the countershaft gear in place in the gearbox casing having first coated the gearbox casing with grease to retain the thrust washer (photo). Do not fit the rear thrust washer at this stage.

4 Carefully insert the layshaft into the bottom of the gearbox ensuring that the thrust washer does not slip out. The largest gearwheel on the layshaft goes towards the bellhousing end of the gearbox casing (photo).

5 Grease the smaller thrust washer to the end of the gearbox casing ensuring that the tongue in the washer seats in the groove, at the same time it will be necessary to lift the countershaft up slightly (photo).

6 Temporarily fit the layshaft and using feeler gauges check the endfloat of the countershaft which should be 0.007 - 0.012 in (0.1778 - 0.3048 mm) measured between the rear thrust washer and the gear. Any excessive endfloat may be reduced by selective assembly of thrust washers. Remove the layshaft spindle again.

7 Insert the reverse idler gear into the casing locating the end of the actuating lever into its location groove on the rear of the gear. Slide the reverse gear shaft into position so that the milled notch is at the rear of the gearbox (photo).

8 Insert the tail end of the mainshaft through the large cut out for the bearing in the rear of the gearbox casing (photo).

9 Position the third and top synchromesh unit onto the front of the mainshaft before the front end finally passes into the gearbox (photo). Do not forget the syncho ring.

10 Push the rear bearing onto the mainshaft as far as it will go. The circlip should be towards the rear of the bearing as shown in the photo.

11 It is not possible to tap home the rear bearing of the tail end of the mainshaft without a support on the front end of the mainshaft, because otherwise this gearwheel hits the third gear on the countershaft which could mean chipped gear teeth. Invert the gearbox so that the flange of the clutch bellhousing is on the bench and position wood blocks under the end of the mainshaft

6.3 Sliding off third and fourth gear synchromesh hub

6.4 Removal of third gear retaining circlip

6.5 Using two screwdrivers to slide circlip along mainshaft

6.6 Third gear thrust washer removal

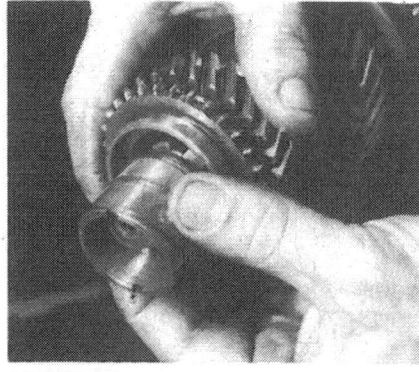

6.7 Sliding third speed gear and bush off mainshaft

6.8 Removal of second speed gear and bush

6.9 Removal of first and second speed gear synchronizer hub

6.10 Sliding off first speed gear and bush

6.13 Thrust washers assembled to mainshaft

6.14 Refitting first and second speed gear selector hub

6.15 Second speed gear and bush location on mainshaft

6.16 Refitting synchromesh ring to hub

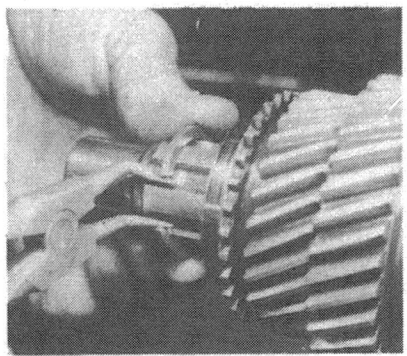

6.18 Easing circlip into position

6.19 Third and fourth speed gear synchro mesh assembly on mainshaft

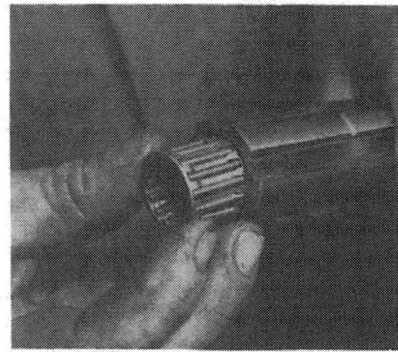

7.1 Fitting layshaft needle roller bearings

7.2 Fitting gears onto layshaft

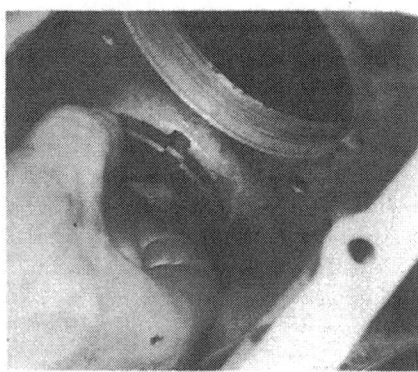

7.3 Fitting front end thrust washer

7.4 Fitting layshaft in bottom of gearbox casing

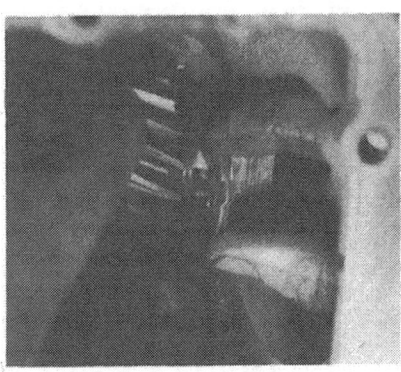

7.5 Fitting thrust washer between gearbox casing and layshaft

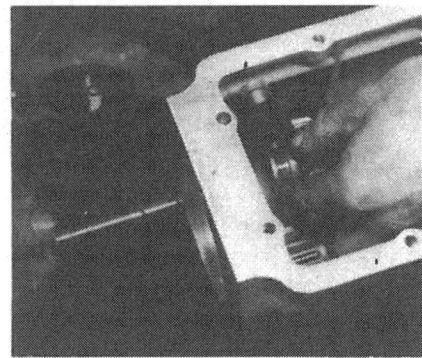

7.7 Fitting reverse gear shaft

7.8 Fitting mainshaft into gearbox casing

7.9 Third and top synchromesh unit fitted to mainshaft

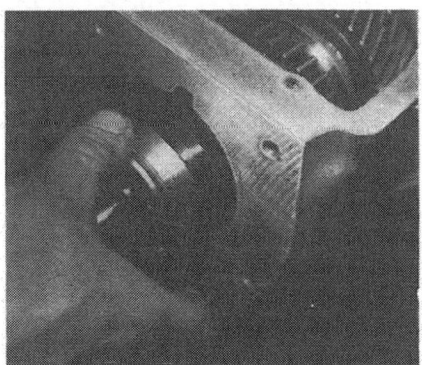

7.10 Fitting bearing onto mainshaft

7.12 Tapping bearing into position

so that it is well supported.

12 Using a soft metal drift tap the rear main bearing down on the mainshaft by alternatively tapping the inner and outer tracks (photo).

13 Continue tapping the bearing tracks until the bearing is fully positioned onto the mainshaft so that there is approximately 0.1875 in (4.764 mm) between the inner race of the bearing on the tail end of the mainshaft and the groove which holds the circlip (photo).

14 Once the bearing is fully on in this position, the supports inside the bellhousing which are supporting the front or the nose of the mainshaft can be removed, and the bellhousing allowed to rest flange downwards on the bench. It is now necessary to drive the outer race of the bearing fully into the rear of the gearbox casing until the circlip on the outer race track is adjacent to the face of the casing (photo).

15 With the gearbox still in the inverted position fit the spacer and lock in position with the circlip (photo).

16 Well lubricate the needle roller bearings in the annulus of the first motion shaft. Fit the top gear baulk ring onto the end of the first motion shaft and insert it into the casing (photo).

17 Using a soft faced hammer carefully drive the first motion shaft into position with the circlip hard up against the gearbox face (photo).

18 Position the gearbox casing on the bench as shown in the photo with a wood block under the rear end of the gear casing. The countershaft gears should now drop into mesh with mainshaft and first motion shaft gears. Insert the layshaft (photo) until the milled slot is flush with the machined face at the rear of the casing. Turn it until the slot faces the slot in the reverse idler shaft.

19 Locate the keeper plate in the milled slots of the layshaft and reverse idler spindle (photo) and refit the phillip head screw. This should be done as tight as possible.

20 Fit the countershaft plate and new gasket to the front of the gearbox and secure with two bolts and copper washers (photo). To assist the gasket to seal coat with gasket cement and also apply a little to the bolt threads.

21 The front cover should be fitted next. Refer to the photo and note that there is a cut out which should be positioned to the left when looking at the first motion shaft. Fit a new gasket to the end cover.

22 Tighten the end cover bolts fitted with spring washers (photo).

23 Now fit the gasket to the rear end of the gearbox using hermatite to ensure an oil tight joint. On overdrive models fit the overdrive adaptor plate (photo), whilst on ordinary models fit the gearbox extension.

24 Fit the six ½ in A F bolts and flat washers and tighten

securely.

(The information in this paragraph down to and including paragraph 30 applies to overdrive models only).

25 Fit a new gasket to the rear end of the gearbox casing adaptor plate suitable coated with gasket cement.

26 The splines on the mainshaft have to go through sets of splines inside the overdrive. It is therefore essential to line up these splines in relation to one another. A torch will assist here.

27 Secure the overdrive unit in the critical position and insert the eight springs. It is important that these are correctly positioned whereby the four inner springs although they are higher than the outer springs are in fact shorter. The photo shows a finger pointing to one of the shorter springs.

28 Now slide the cam, which operates the hydraulic pump in the overdrive unit, into place on the tail end of the mainshaft. The lowest part of the cam (pointed at in photo) must abutt the spring loaded plunger. In this latter photo the cam has been removed from the mainshaft and placed against the plunger to show how they fit together. Place a piece of wire around the head of the plunger rod so that the spring can be compressed whilst the two units are being assembled. The reason for this is that the plunger rod for the hydraulic pump is spring loaded and may cause the overdrive unit and gearbox to join when being fitted together.

29 With an assistant to help gradually lower the gearbox to the overdrive unit. Pull on the wire so as to compress the spring and when the gearbox adaptor plate is nearly in position withdraw the wire.

30 Refit the ½ in A F nuts and spring washers to the overdrive to adaptor plate studs and tighten in a diagonal manner so as to compress the eight springs.

31 For a conventional gearbox refit the circlip (Fig. 6.1.), to the end of the mainshaft.

32 Carefully tap the flange using a soft faced hammer until it is in position on the mainshaft.

33 Replace the plain washer and the castellated nut and tighten the nut securely. Lock the nut with a new split pin.

34 Replace the speedometer drive (Fig. 6.2.) on the side of the gearbox extension housing.

35 Ensure that all gears are in their neutral position and using an oil can well lubricate all moving parts of the selector mechanism and synchromesh units (photo).

36 Carefully lower the remote control and top cover with a new gasket fitted onto the top of the gearbox housing. Take care that all the selector forks are locating correctly in their grooves especially the reverse selector fork (photo).

37 Refit the eight ½ in A F bolts with spring washers noting that the four longer bolts fit the front and rear of the top cover only. Tighten securely in a diagonal manner (photo).

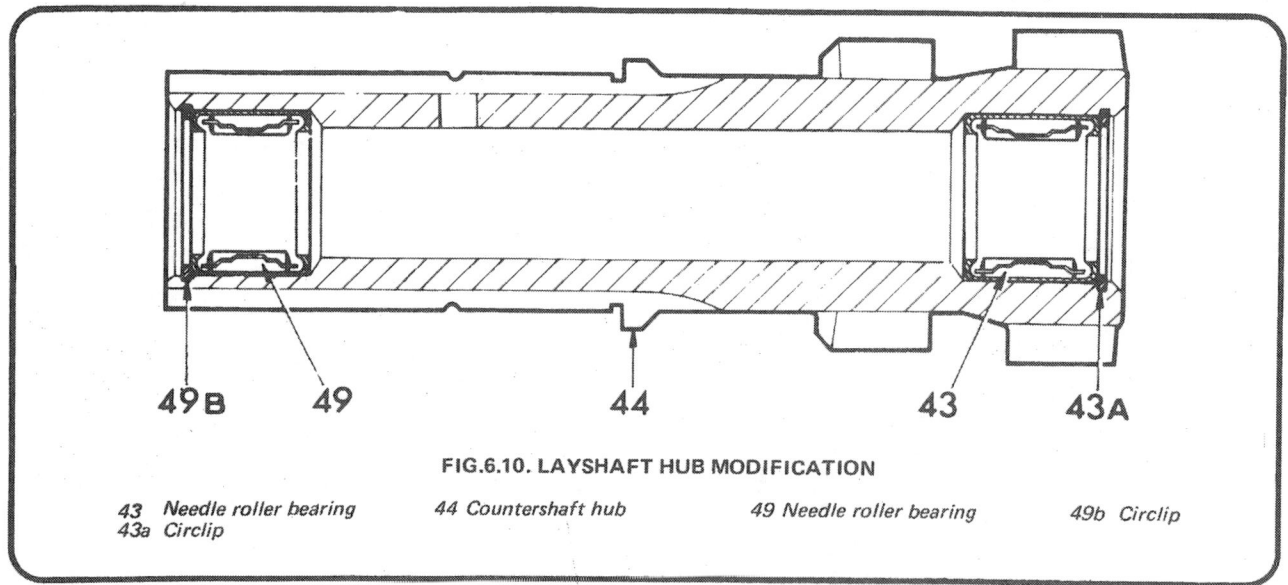

FIG.6.10. LAYSHAFT HUB MODIFICATION

43 *Needle roller bearing*   *44 Countershaft hub*   *49 Needle roller bearing*   *49b Circlip*
43a *Circlip*

7.13 Bearing fitted on mainshaft

7.14 Final fitted position of bearing

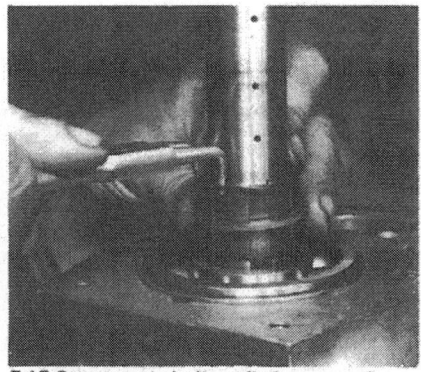

7.15 Spacer and circlip refitting on mainshaft

7.16 Refitting first motion shaft

7.17 Tapping first motion shaft into final position

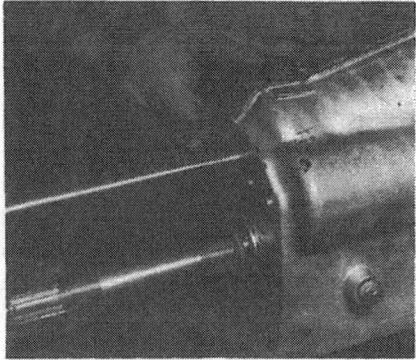

7.18 Layshaft spindle refitting

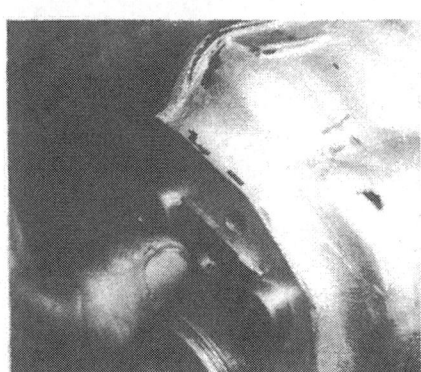

7.19 Keeper plate replacement

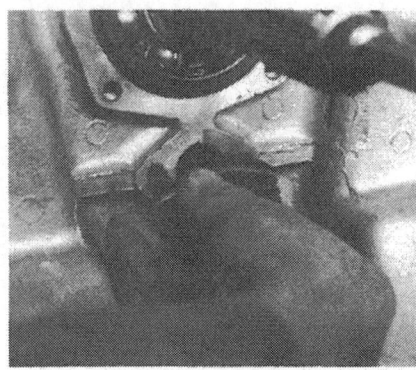

7.20 Countershaft cover plate refitting

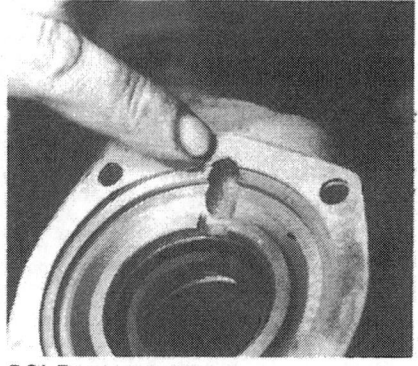

7.21 Front cover cut-out

7.22 Front cover replacement

7.23 Adaptor plate replacement

7.27 Correct location of overdrive springs

7.28 Refitting pump cam

7.35 Lubrication of gears

7.36 Lowering remote control and top cover into position

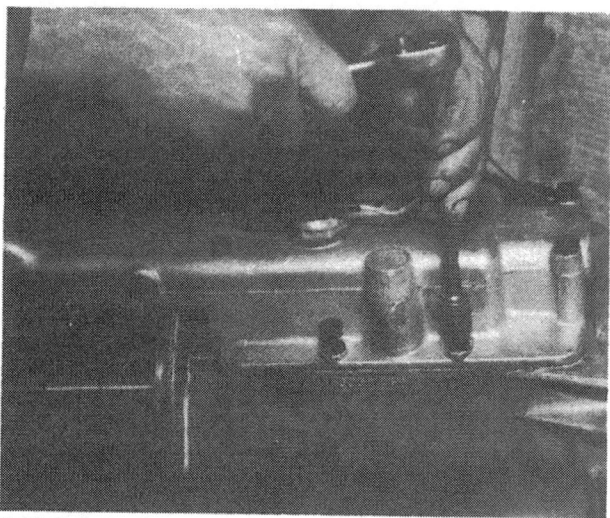

7.37 Securing remote control and top cover with bolts and spring washers

8 Top cover and remote control assembly - overhaul

1 The components of the top cover and remote control assembly are shown in Fig. 6.11.

2 To remove the assembly undo the eight ½ in A F bolts that hold the remote control and top cover onto the top of the gearbox. Lift away the bolts and spring washers noting that the four longer bolts are to the front and rear of the top cover.

3 Lift away the remote control and top cover from the top of the gearbox noting the gasket placed between the two parts.

4 Turn the cover and unscrew the plugs and lift away the distance piece springs, plungers and ball bearing.

5 Undo the peg bolts holding the selector forks to the selector rods.

6 Check that the selectors are in the neutral position and withdraw the third/top gear selector shaft. As the shaft is being removed collect the interlock plunger and ball bearings as they are released.

7 Lift away the third/top selector fork and distance tube from the top cover.

8 Repeat operations in paragraphs 6 and 7 for the first/second and also reverse gear selector shafts.

9 Undo the two setscrews and remove together with spring washers and lift away the retaining plate.

10 Lift away the three sealing rings from their recess in the casing.

11 The selectors may be removed from their respective shafts by undoing the peg bolts.

12 Inspect all parts for signs of wear and, if evident, new parts should be fitted. The seals should be renewed every time the assembly is dismantled.

13 To reassemble first fit the selectors to their respective shafts secure with peg bolts.

14 Replace new 'O' ring seals into their recesses in the rear cover and fit the retaining plate. Replace the two bolts and spring washers.

15 Place the interlock plunger in the third/top selector shaft and insert the shaft into the top cover. Engage the selector fork, distance tube and secure the fork with a peg bolt.

16 Replace the interlock ball bearing between the reverse and third/top selector shaft bores retaining the ball with grease.

17 Insert the reverse selector shaft into the top cover, engaging it with the reverse actuator and distance tube. Fit the peg bolt to the selector fork.

18 Check that the reverse and third/top selector shafts are in neutral and fit the second interlock ball, retaining the ball with grease.

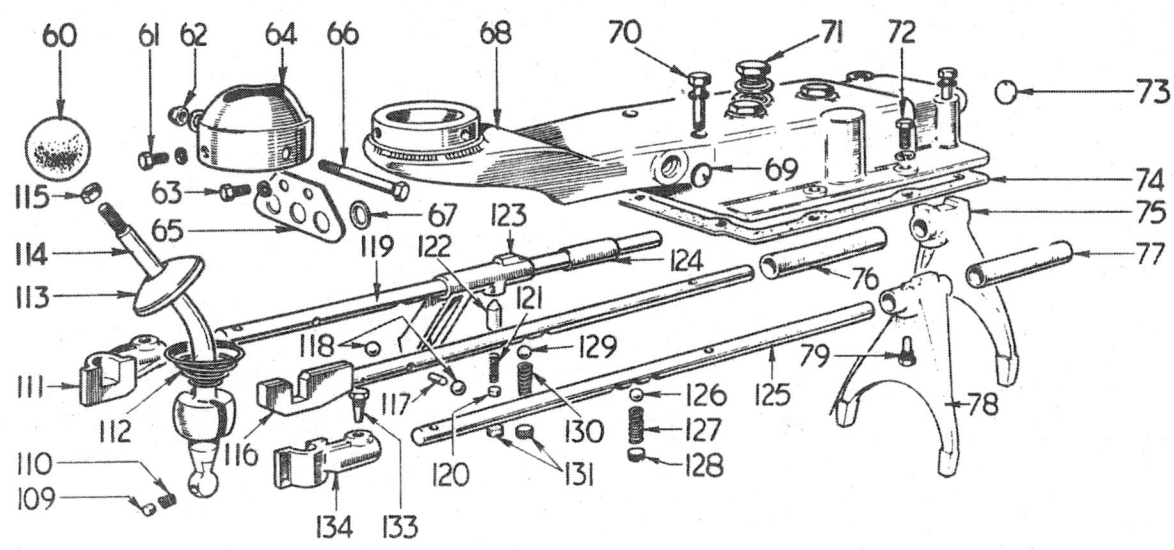

FIG.6.11. GEARBOX TOP COVER AND SELECTOR COMPONENTS

63 Setscrew	111 Selector (reverse)	123 Reverse actuator	130 Spring
65 Endplate	116 Top/3rd selector shaft	124 Distance piece	131 Plug
67 Rubber 'O' ring	118 Balls - interlock	125 2nd/1st selector shaft	133 Peg bolt
75 Top/3rd selector fork	119 Reverse selector shaft	126 Ball - detent	134 Selector 1st/2nd
76 Distance tube	120 Shim	127 Spring	
77 Distance tube	121 Spring	128 Plug	
78 2nd/1st selector fork	122 Plunger	129 Ball - detent	

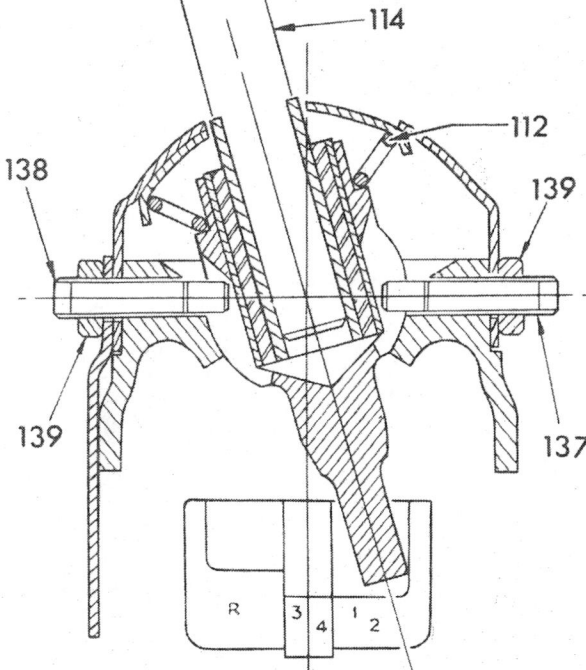

**FIG.6.12. GEAR CHANGE LEVER
MODIFICATION**

112 Spring	138 Locating pins
114 Gear lever assembly	139 Locknuts
137 Locating pins	

19 Insert the first/second selector shaft into the top cover, passing the shaft through the first/second selector fork and distance tube.

20 Lubricate all moving parts and refit to the top of the gearbox, preferably using a new gasket.

21 It should be noted that on later produced gearboxes the gear change lever has been modified and a rubber bush fitted as shown in Fig. 6.12. so preventing transference of noise to the car interior through the gearbox lever. The spring has been deleted. Adjustable locating pins are now used instead.

22 To adjust the later type gear lever movement, move the lever into the first/second gate position and screw the locating pin in a clockwise direction until slight movement of the gear lever is noted. Screw the locating pin a further ½ turn and secure with the locknut.

23 Now move the gear lever to the reverse gate position and adjust the second pin in a similar manner to the first pin.

9 Overdrive - early fitment - general description

The overdrive unit is attached to the extension on the rear of the gearbox by eight studs and nuts, and takes the form of a hydraulically operated epicyclic gear. Overdrive operates on third and fourth speeds to provide fast cruising at lower engine revolutions. The overdrive 'in out' switch on the right hand of the steering wheel actuates a solenoid attached to the side of the overdrive unit. In turn the solenoid operates a valve which opens the hydraulic circuit which pushes the cone clutch into contact with the annulus when overdrive is engaged.

During high speed motoring, the engine speed is decreased with the engagement of overdrive so that with continual use of the unit there should be an increase in petrol economy and slight decrease in engine wear.

A special switch called an inhibitor switch is incorporated in the electrical circuit and prevents the engagement of overdrive in reverse and first gears. The switch is located on the top of the gearbox top cover.

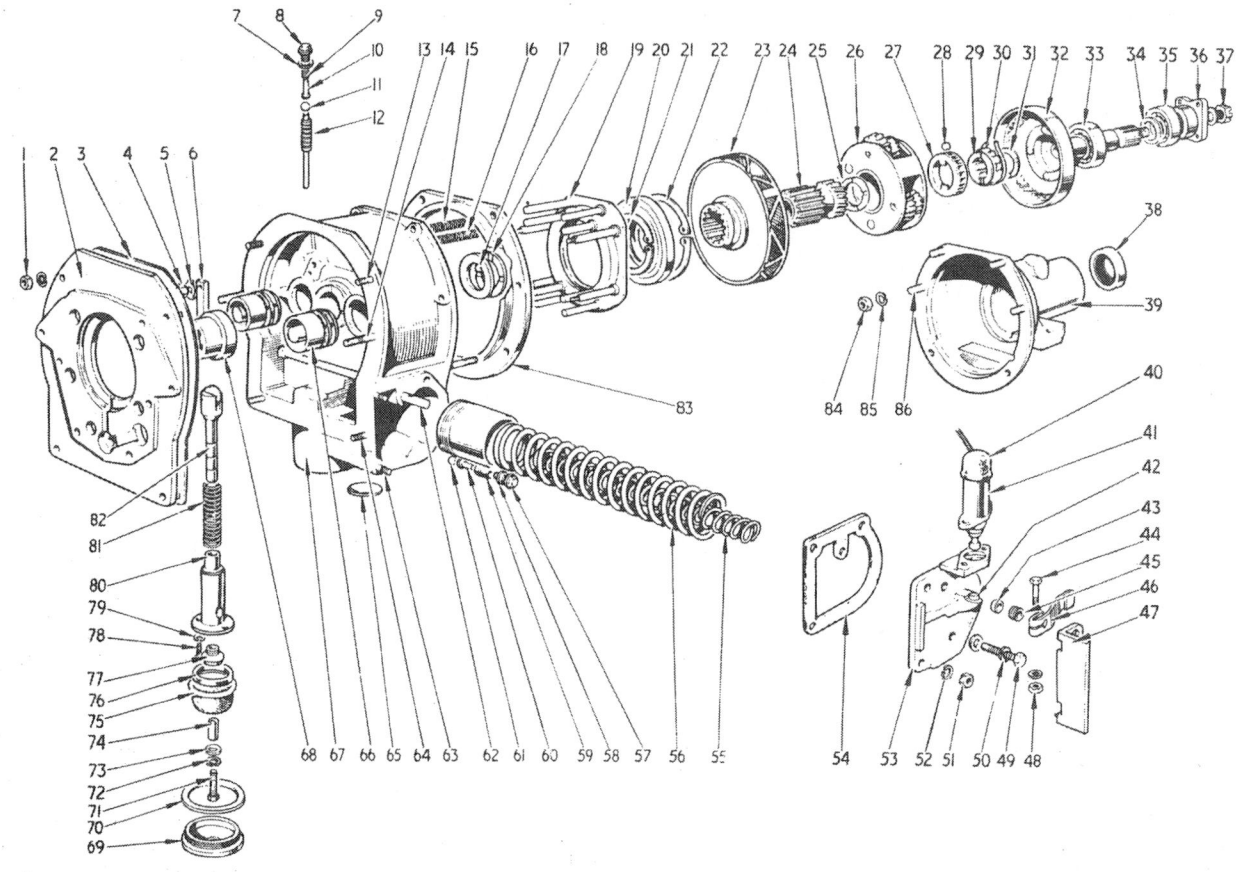

FIG. 6.13. OVERDRIVE UNIT COMPONENTS (EARLY TYPE)

1 Nut
2 Adaptor plate
3 Gasket
4 Nut
5 Tab washer
6 Bridge piece
7 Washer
8 Plug
9 Spring
10 Plunger
11 Ball
12 Valve
13 Stud (short)
14 Stud (long)
15 Stud (long)
16 Spring (short)
17 Thrust washer (steel)
18 Thrust washer (bronze)
19 Thrust ring assembly
20 Thrust race
21 Circlip
22 Circlip

23 Clutch sliding member
24 Sun wheel
25 Thrust washer
26 Planet carrier assembly
27 Roller cage
28 Clutch roller
29 Uni-directional clutch
     inner member
30 Spring - inner member to
     cage
31 Thrust washer
32 Annulus and output shaft
33 Ball race (front)
34 Distance washer
35 Ball race (rear)
36 Driving flange
37 Slotted nut
38 Oil seal
39 Rear housing
40 Rubber cover
41 Solenoid
42 Rubber stop button

43 Seal
44 Pinch bolt
45 Collar
46 Operating lever
47 Dust shield
48 Nut
49 Setscrew
50 Spring washer
51 Nut
52 Spring washer
53 Cover plate
54 Gasket
55 Inner accumulator spring
56 Outer accumulator spring
57 Plug
58 Sealing washer
59 Spring
60 Plunger
61 Ball
62 Operating valve cross shaft
63 Stud
64 Stud

65 Welch plug
66 Piston
67 Body
68 Pump eccentric
69 Drain plug
70 Sealing washer
71 Setscrew
72 Spring washer
73 Plain washer
74 Distance tube
75 Filter gauze
76 Seal
77 Pump end plug
78 Screw
79 Spring washer
80 Pump body
81 Pump return spring
82 Pump plunger
83 Brake ring
84 Nut
85 Spring washer
86 Stud

The normal minimum engagement speeds are top gear 40 mph and third gear 30 mph, whilst the minimum disengagement speed in top is under the control of the driver who must take care not to over rev the engine at high speeds. For third speed the disengagement should occur at a maximum of 70 mph.

The overdrive unit operates in the following manner:

The operating gears in the overdrive are of epicyclic design and comprises a sunwheel which meshes with three plate gears carried in a circular metal carrier.

These planet gears mesh with an annulus which has internal teeth. The planet carrier is attached to the input shaft which is the output shaft of the gearbox. The annulus is an integral part of the output shaft. When the driver selects overdrive, hydraulic pressure is built up by a plunger type pump which operates from a cam splined to the input shaft, i.e., the output shaft from the gearbox. The hydraulic pressure built up by the pump forces the two pistons against bridge pieces which are themselves attached to the thrust ring. The thrust ring is pushed forwards by the pistons so engaging the clutch with the brake ring with sufficient force to hold the sunwheel firmly at rest.

The planet carrier is now able to rotate with the input shaft allowing the planet wheels in the planet carrier assembly to rotate about their own axes so driving the annulus at a faster speed than the input shaft is rotating.

Oil is drawn by the pump through a wire mesh filter and delivers it to the operating valve through an hydraulic accumulator the amount of pressure being controlled by a pressure relief valve built into the accumulator. The oil is free to pass between the gearbox and overdrive unit and there is one common level for both units. The oil level is indicated by a 'level' plug on the side of the gearbox.

Whenever the oil is drained the two drain plugs, one on the underside of the gearbox and the other on the underside of the overdrive unit, must be removed but it is usual practice not to change the oil during normal servicing but to top up. Only recommended grades of oil must be used and it is important that under no circumstances must oil antifriction additives be used otherwise the overdrive unit will not operate correctly.

Cleanliness is very important so do not remove the drain plug without first wiping it and the surrounding area. Whenever the oil is drained for service/repair work on either the gearbox or the overdrive always clean the mesh filter.

The overdrive is normally a very reliable unit and trouble is usually due to either the solenoid sticking, a fault in the hydraulic system due to dirt ingress, insufficient oil, or incorrect solenoid operating lever adjustment.

10 Overdrive - removal and replacement

1 It is unnecessary to remove the overdrive from the car in order to attend to the following: The hydraulic lever setting: the relief valve; the non-return valve; the solenoid; and the operating valve.

2 If the unit as a whole requires overhaul it must be removed from the car together with the gearbox as described in Chapter 6, Section 2.

3 To separate the overdrive from the gearbox undo the eight nuts from the ¼ in (6.35 mm) diameter studs (noting the extra length of two of the studs) to separate the main overdrive casing from the gearbox rear extension. Carefully pull the overdrive off the end of the mainshaft.

4 To mate the overdrive and gearbox, start by placing the overdrive in an upright position and then line up the splines of the clutch and planet carrier by eye, turning them anti-clockwise only, with the aid of a long thick screwdriver. Make certain that the spring clip is correctly positioned in the groove in the main shaft and that it does not protrude above the mainshaft splines.

5 Under normal circumstances if everything is in line the gearbox mainshaft should enter the overdrive easily. If trouble is experienced do not try and force the components. Place the gearbox in top gear while refitting.

6 As the mainshaft is fed into the overdrive, gently rotate the input shaft to and fro to help in mating the mainshaft into the splines. At the same time make certain that the lowest portion of the cam on the mainshaft will rest against the pump and that as the gearbox extension and overdrive come together, the end of the mainshaft enters into the needle roller bearing in the tailshaft.

7 The remainder of the replacement procedure is a straightforward reversal of the removal sequence.

11 Overdrive - dismantling, overhaul and reassembly

1 To enable a satisfactory overhaul to be completed there are several special tools that will be required. Full details of these are given as and where they are needed, and they should be obtained before work commences. It may however be more economic to exchange the unit if the fault is serious - rebuilding an overdrive is no light task.

2 It is recommended that, before the unit is dismantled, the exterior is thoroughly cleaned and dried as it is important that

FIG. 6.14. LOCATION OF THRUST SPRINGS

1 Long springs   *2 Short springs*

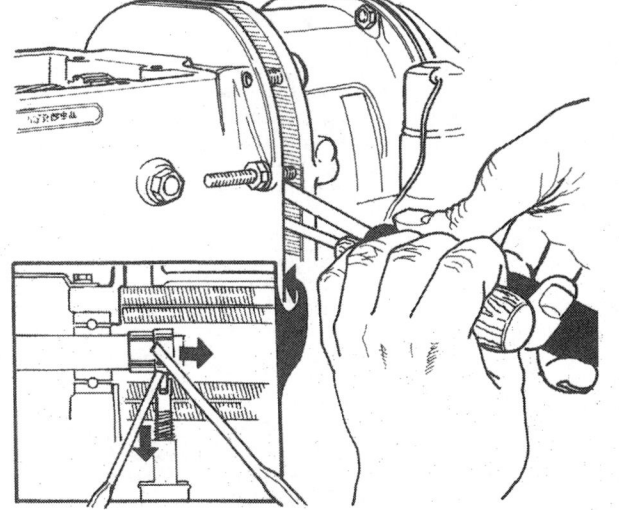

Fig. 6.15. Method of attaching gearbox to overdrive unit

no dirt gets into any of the internal parts of the unit.

3 Place the unit on a clean bench and lift away the clutch return springs and place in a clean jam jar for safe keeping.

4 Bend back the tab washers and unscrew the four nuts. Lift away the nuts, tab washers and bridge pieces.

5 Undo the six nuts and lift away the nuts and spring washers from the studs.

6 The two casings may now be separated. Lift away the brake ring.

7 Working from the forward end of the sunwheel, first remove the steel thrust washer followed by the phosphor bronze thrust washer. Lift out the clutch sliding member complete with the thrust ring and bearing.

8 Withdraw the sunwheel and the planet carrier assembly.

9 Unscrew and remove the operating valve plug and copper washer. Lift out the spring, plunger and ball bearing followed by the valve.

10 Using a pair of pliers carefully grip the operating pistons on the centre bosses and rotate whilst pulling the pistons out of the front casing.

11 Undo the three cover plate retaining screws and lift away the screw spring washers, cover plate and its joint washer.

12 Remove the two screws and spring washers that secure the solenoid to the solenoid bracket assembly. Lift away the solenoid, carefully easing the plunger from the yoke of the valve operating lever.

13 Slacken the clamp bolt and retaining nut on the valve operating lever and withdraw the lever and distance collar from the shaft.

14 Remove the nuts and spring washers from the two short studs that secure the solenoid bracket assembly to the main casing. Also undo the two set-screws (painted red), so as to release the accumulator spring tension. Do not remove the two set-screws first. Lift away the solenoid bracket followed by the spring and the spacer tube assembly.

15 If it is necessary to remove the accumulator sleeve and piston assembly a special tool is required. Insert tool number L 182 into the accumulator sleeve and tighten the lower wing nut. Withdraw the accumulator sleeve and piston assembly by applying a rotary pull to the upper wing bolt of the tool. There is no other way of removing these parts without causing damage to their very fine surface finish.

16 The next part to be removed is the pump return valve which is positioned in the cavity of the main body casing once the solenoid bracket assembly is removed. Undo and lift out the hexagonal plug and washer, followed by the spring, plunger and ball bearing. It is important that these parts are removed before the pump is removed from the main casing.

17 Undo and remove the drain plug. Lift away the filter. It will be seen that there are three magnetic rings positioned in the recess of the drain plug.

18 To remove the pump another special tool is required having a part number L 183A/1. Undo and remove the two retaining screws and the base plug. Screw the short threaded portion of the spindle of the tool into the pump body. Locate the adaptor in position against the casing and tighten the wing nut which will cause the body to be withdrawn from the main casing. Lift out the plunger and spring.

19 Using a pair of circlip pliers remove the circlip from its groove in the forward end of the clutch hub and taking great care not to damage the clutch member or friction lining, drive the clutch member from the thrust ring and bearing using a soft metal drift and hammer.

20 With a pair of circlip pliers remove the large diameter circlip and using a vice and piece of suitable diameter tube, press the bearing from the thrust ring.

21 Should it be necessary to remove the uni-directional clutch, special assembly ring tool number L 178 is necessary. Position the assembly ring over the front face of the annulus and lift the inner member of the uni-directional clutch up into it.

22 Then remove the assembly ring and allow the rollers to come out followed by the hub so exposing the spring.

23 Lift away the phospher bronze thrust washer that is fitted between the uni-directional clutch and the annulus.

24 Undo and remove the speedometer dowel screw and spring washer. Using special tool L 214 so as to prevent damage to the thread of the bearing assembly withdraw the speedometer drive bearing and pinion. Note the 'O' ring on the bearing centre outer circumference.

25 Extract the split pin securing the castellated nut to the annulus. Undo the castellated nut and remove followed by the thick plain washer. Slide the coupling flange from the splines on the annulus.

26 Using a press or a hammer and block of wood on the end of the annulus with the castellated nut replaced to protect the threads, remove the annulus from the rear casing.

27 The front bearing should remain in position on the annulus but if it must be removed a suitable two leg puller or a press should be used. Note the position of the spring washer which should be located on a shoulder in front of the annulus splines.

28 If the oil seal has shown signs of leaking or the bearing is to be renewed, prise the oil seal from the rear casing making a note of which way round it fits. The bearing may be drifted from the rear casing using a long soft metal drift.

29 Thoroughly clean all the component parts and then examine them carefully. Check that the oil pump plunger and body are not worn and that the spring has not contracted (free length should not be less than 2 inches). Examine the 'O' rings from the operating pistons and renew them if worn or if they are becoming hard, and check that the cylinder bores are free from score marks and wear. Check all the ball bearings for roughness when turned and for looseness between the inner and outer races. Examine the splines for burrs and wear, and the rollers of the uni-directional clutch for chips and flat spots.

30 Renew the clutch linings if they are burnt or worn and carefully examine the main and rear casings for cracks or other damage. Renew the steady bush if it is worn and examine the gear teeth for cracks, chips, and general wear. Examine the sealing balls for ridges which will prevent them seating properly and check the free length of the springs, the measurements being given in the specifications.

31 Assembly of the unit can commence after any damaged or worn parts have been exchanged and new gaskets and seals obtained.

32 The first part to be refitted is the pump assembly for which tool number L 184 is required to ensure accurate refitting. Screw the two guide pegs of the tool into the two holes in the bottom pump face.

33 Refit the spring to the pump plunger and insert this into the pump body. Insert the pump assembly into the casing positioning the flange of the body over both guide pegs of the tool L 184, and locating the flat of the pump plunger against the guide peg in the front casing adjacent guide bushes.

34 Drift the pump body home fully using the drift, this being part of tool L 184. Undo and remove the two guide pegs and fit the two retaining screws and spring washers.

35 Refit the base plug. Reassemble the three magnetic rings and fibre sealing washer onto the drain plug. Locate the filter onto the central boss of the drain plug and screw onto the body. Tighten fully to prevent subsequent oil leaks.

36 Insert the non return valve ball bearing into its drilling. Note that this ball bearing has a diameter of ¼ in. Using a soft metal drift of diameter slightly less than ¼ in, tap the ball bearing lightly so as to seat it in its drilling. Insert the plunger, spring and plug with a new copper washer fitted under its head. Check that the copper washer seats on its location correctly to ensure no oil leaks.

37 Refit the piston into the sleeve taking care that the piston rings are not damaged. With the sleeve upright push the piston down until the rings are resting on the top of the bore. Using two thumbs compress each ring whilst a second person pushes the piston down.

38 Insert the accumulator spring into the tube and fit the accumulator tube into the recess in the accumulator sleeve and then carefully push into the casing, easing the sealing rings into the bore.

39 Fit a new 'O' ring over the operating shaft if one was originally fitted and using a new joint washer refit the solenoid bracket ensuring that the accumulator spring locates over a dowel in the brackets.

40 Tighten the two screws with spring washers evenly and then the nuts with spring washers onto the two short studs.

41 Fit new 'O' rings to the pistons and lubricate with oil. Insert the pistons into their respective bores carefully easing the rubber 'O' rings into the bores in the casing. Note that the centre bosses of the pistons face outwards to the front of the casing.

42 Insert the operating valve into its bore in the casing ensuring that it is the correct way up with the hemispherical end engaging on the flat of the small cam on the operating shaft.

43 Drop in the ball bearing (0.313 in, 7.7938 mm) diameter followed by the plunger with the larger diameter innermost, and the spring. Fit a new copper washer onto the operating valve plug and refit the plug. Ensure the copper washer is sealing correctly on its location on the plug and tighten securely.

44 If any new parts are to be refitted to the rear casing or annulus a special tailshaft end float setting gauge will be necessary. This is numbered L 190A and will enable the thickness of the spacing washer to be determined so that the bearings will not have excessive end float or pre-load. The gauge comprises an inner member which rests against the end of the annulus output shaft. The outer part rests on the rear bearing abutment in the rear casing.

45 Using a drift of suitable diameter to locate on the outer track of the front bearing insert the bearing into the rear casing until the outer track abuts against a shoulder in the casing. Next using a press or a drift of suitable dimater insert the annulus into the front bearing which has been inserted into the casing.

46 Fit the gauge over the output shaft of the annulus until the outer member contacts the rear bearing shoulder in the rear casing. Gently press down the inner member and using feeler gauges determine dimension A (Fig.6.16). Select a spacing washer of the same thickness as the measurement just made using the feeler gauges. A range of washers is available in the following sizes 0.146, 0.151, 0.156, 0.161, 0.166 in. Remove the setting gauge.

47 Fit the previously selected washer onto the annulus output shaft and using a drift of suitable diameter drive the rear bearing into position in the rear casing. Also use the drift to refit the oil seal ensuring that the lip is facing inwards. Lubricate the oil seal inner face.

48 Refit the rear coupling flange into the splines of the annulus output shaft followed by the plain washer and castellated nut. Tighten the nut and secure with a new split pin.

49 Fit a new 'O' ring to the bearing and insert the speedometer pinion gear into the bearing. Insert the bearing and gear assembly into the casing and to ensure correct meshing rotate the annulus. Align the holes in the casing and the bush and fit the dowel screw with a new copper washer under its head. Tighten the dowel screw securely.

50 Refit the spring into the roller cage of the uni-direction clutch. Insert the inner member into the cage and engage it into the other end of the spring. Also engage the slots of the inner member with the tongues on the roller cage ensuring that the spring is able to rotate the cage, so moving the rollers when they are refitted up the inclined faces of the inner member. The cage should be spring loaded in an anti-clockwise direction when looking at it from the front.

51 Insert this assembly into the special assembly ring, tool number L 178 with its front end facing downwards and insert the rollers through the milled slot in the tool. It will be necessary to turn the uni-directional clutch in a clockwise direction until all collets are in place.

52 Refit the uni-directional clutch assembly to the annulus having first inserted the thrust washer. The assembly tool will allow the rollers to enter into the annulus without falling out or jamming. If the tool is not available a strong elastic band should be wrapped around the cage and then lifted to allow each roller to be inserted.

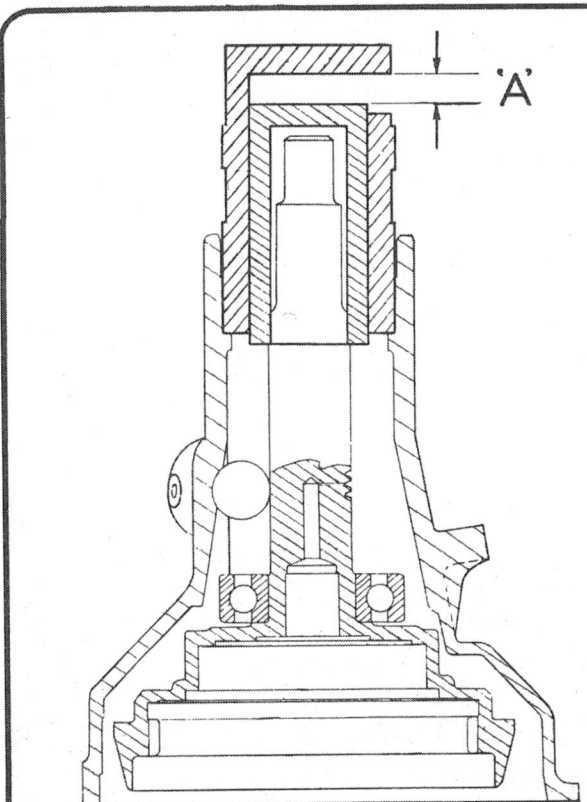

Fig. 6.16. Tool L190A being used to determine thickness of spacing washer

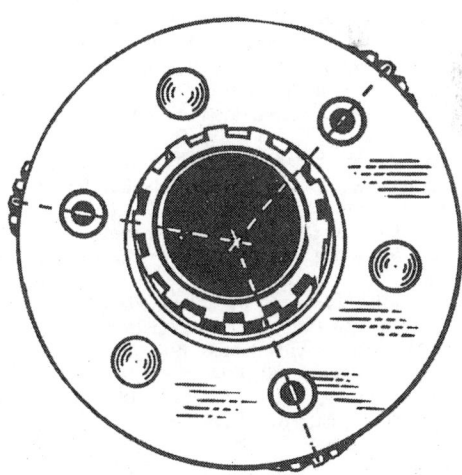

Fig. 6.17. The position of the markings on the planet wheels when correctly fitted to the sun wheel

53 Before the planet carrier is refitted the gears must be specially set. Turn each planet gear in turn until a dot mark on one of the teeth of the large gear is positioned radially outwards. Locate the phosher bronze washer in its recess in the planet carrier and insert the sunwheel.

54 Ensure that the sunwheel meshes correctly with the planet gears at the same time keeping the dot marks in their originally set position.

55 Insert the planet carrier and sunwheel assembly into the annulus.

56 Obtain a piece of metal bar the same diameter as the output shaft of the gearbox and insert it into the sunwheel until the rod engages the planet carrier and uni-directional clutch splines.

57 The end float of the sunwheel must be checked to ensure that it is within the limits of between 0.008 and 0.014 in. To do this slide an additional thrust washer of known thickness over the previously inserted metal rod until it rests on the top of the sunwheel followed by the original phospher bronze thrust washer and the steel thrust washer.

58 Fit the brake ring into the front casing and using a soft faced hammer tap it firmly in position. Carefully slide the front casing over the metal rod and position it up to the rear casing assembly.

59 As an additional thrust washer has been fitted a gap between the two casings should now be evident. Using feeler gauges measure this gap. The thickness of the extra thrust washer MINUS the end float of the sunwheel is the required dimension.

60 If this indicated end float is outside the limit specified in paragraph 57 it must be adjusted by replacing the STEEL thrust washer at the front of the sunwheel with a new one of greater or less thickness.

61 Remove the front casing and thrust washers previously positioned as necessary.

62 Using a vice press the thrust bearing into the thrust ring and refit the large diameter circlip into its groove in the thrust ring.

63 Next press the thrust ring assembly into the hub of the clutch sliding member and lock in position using the smaller diameter circlip.

64 Carefully fit the clutch sliding member over the sunwheel splines and engage the inner linings on the annulus assembly. Fit the phospher bronze washer on the top of the sunwheel and the steel washer of suitable thickness as previously determined.

65 Lightly smear a little jointing compound onto both sides of the brake ring flange and tap this home on the main casing.

66 Fit the main casing and brake ring to the rear casing taking care that the thrust ring pins are positioned through the four corresponding holes in the main casing. Fit spring washers into the six studs followed by the retaining nuts and tighten securely in a diagonal manner.

67 Replace the two operating piston bridge pieces and secure on the studs using a new tab washer and nuts. Bend over the locking tabs.

68 Slide the distance collar onto the lever shaft.

69 Refit the operating lever shaft and lightly tighten the locknut.

70 Fit a new joint washer to the solenoid bracket and insert the solenoid plunger into the yoke in the operating lever. Secure the solenoid to the bracket with the two bolts and spring washer.

71 It will now be necessary to set the solenoid operating lever and full details of this are given in Section 13 of this Chapter.

72 Fit a new cover plate gasket and then the cover plate. Secure with three bolts and spring washers.

73 Reassembly is now complete. Do not forget to refill with oil the gearbox and overdrive once the unit has been refitted.

12 Overdrive - operating lever adjustment

1 If the overdrive does not engage, or will not release when it is switched out, providing the solenoid is not at fault the trouble is likely to be that the operating lever is out of adjustment. Adjustment can be made without removing the overdrive.

2 To one end of a shaft passing through the overdrive casing is attached a setting lever having a 0.188 in (4.763 mm) hole in its

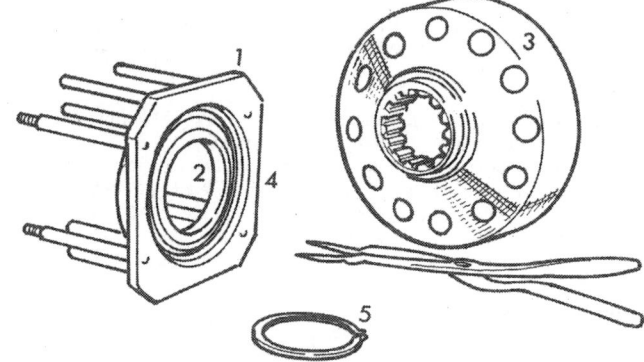

FIG. 6.18. CLUTCH SLIDING MEMBER

1	Thrust ring	4	Circlip
2	Ball bearing	5	Circlip
3	Cone clutch		

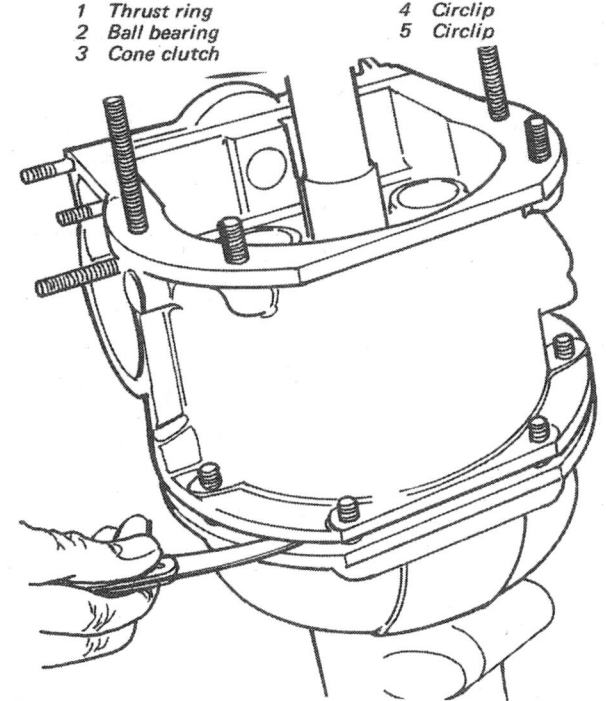

Fig. 6.19. Use of feeler gauges to determine sun wheel end float

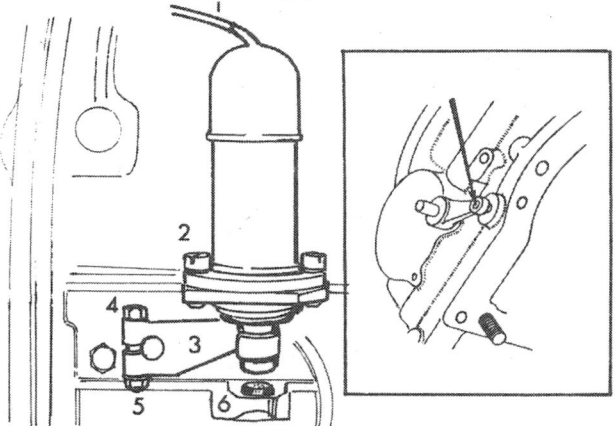

FIG. 6.20. THE OVERDRIVE SOLENOID AND OPERATING LEVER

1	Cable	4	Bolt
2	Solenoid mounting bolt	5	Nut
3	Operating lever	6	Rubber stop

(Inset shows 3/16 inch diameter rod in setting lever)

outer end as shown in Fig. 6.20. The other end of the shaft is attached to a solenoid lever as shown in Fig. 6.20.

3 Switch on the ignition and set the overdrive switch to energise the solenoid. The hole in the setting lever should align with a similar hole in the casing which will indicate that the operating valve is fully open. To check this try and insert a 0.188 in (4.763 mm) diameter rod, through both holes. If it is not possible adjustment is necessary. Switch off the ignition.

4 Undo the three solenoid housing cover retaining bolts and lift away the cover.

5 Slacken the clamp bolt on the operating lever and rotate the shaft until the 0.188 in (4.763 mm) diameter rod is able to pass into the hole in the casing.

6 Approximately 0.008 in (0.2032 mm) end float should be allowed for on the shaft. Push the solenoid plunger fully home at the same time holding the fork of the lever against the collar in the plunger.

7 Tighten the clamp bolt so securing the lever to the shaft.

8 Still continuing to push the plunger hard home in the solenoid set the adjustable stop until there is a gap of 0.150 to 0.155 in (3.81 - 3.937 mm) between the end of the plunger and the stop.

9 Remove the 0.188 inch diameter rod and energize the solenoid. Check the alignment of the two setting holes with feeler gauges to the value of 0.150 to 0.155 in (3.81 to 3.937) between the stop and the plunger.

10 Operate the switch several times checking with the test rod to ensure that the adjustment remains correct.

11 Measure the current consumed by the solenoid switch which, with the operating arm correctly set should be about 2 amps. If a reading 15 - 20 amp is obtained it is an indication that the solenoid plunger is not moving sufficiently to switch to the holding coil from the operating coil. If very fine adjustment will not remedy this condition, fit a new solenoid and plunger.

12 Replace the solenoid housing cover and tighten the three retaining bolts.

13 Overdrive - operating valve

Should the overdrive unit not function correctly and the fault be diagnosed from the fault diagnosis chart as with the operating valve, it may be removed and checked as follows:

1 It will be seen from referring to Fig. 6.13. that the operating valve components are located in the top of the main casing. To gain access to the valve with the unit in the car the console tray must be removed as detailed in Section 2 paragraphs 4 - 7 inclusive.

2 Switch on the ignition but do not start the engine. Activate the overdrive control switch several times so as to operate the solenoid, thus releasing any residual oil pressure. Wipe the area around the valve plug free of dust.

3 Unscrew and remove the operating valve plug and copper washer. Using a paper clip which has been straightened and the end bent to a small hook withdraw the spring. The plunger may be removed using a small magnet or magnetized screwdriver. Also remove the ball bearing.

4 Using the other end of the paper clip with a slight kink in it carefully insert it into the centre of the valve and withdraw the valve.

5 Clean the removed parts in petrol and allow to dry. Locate the small drilling near to the base of the valve and check that it is free of dirt.

6 Inspect the ball bearing for signs of pitting which, if evident, indicate that a new ball bearing should be obtained. It has a diameter of 0.3125 in (7.9375 mm).

7 If the ball bearing is satisfactory re-seat it by placing the ball bearing on a block of soft wood. Invert the valve and place on top of the ball bearing and lightly tap the end. If it is tapped too hard the drilling in the side of the valve or in the end may be closed.

8 Reassembling the valve is the reverse sequence to removal.

14 Non-return valve - removal and replacement

1 Access to the relief and non-return valve located in the bottom of the overdrive is simply gained. First drain the oil from the gearbox and overdrive.

2 Cut through the locking wire, unscrew the plugs and remove and clean components. Note that the valve cap and non-return valve body are unscrewed from the pump, and that the relief valve body is removed with circlip pliers.

3 Examine the seatings for pits or chips, and the ball for wear, and ridges. The steel ball in the non-return valve is very hard and if the ball is undamaged and the seating is suspect tap the ball firmly into its seat with a soft metal drift.

4 Reassembly is a straightforward reversal of the removal sequence. Do not omit to fit the copper washer on the relief valve between the cap and main casing, and hold the non-return valve ball to its spring with petroleum jelly during refitment.

5 Access to the operating valve can be gained only after removing the remote control assembly from inside the car. Undo the plug and check that the ball is lifted 1/32 inch when the solenoid is actuated. Failure to move, points to a fault in the solenoid or operating arm.

6 The ball can be removed with a magnet, and the valve with a piece of   0.125 in (3.175 mm) wire. Check the ball and seat and clean out the small hole in the side of the valve tube. Check if the oil pump is working by jacking the rear of the car off the ground, placing the car in top gear, engaging overdrive and with the engine running watching if oil is being pumped into the valve chamber. Replacement is a reversal of the removal procedure.

15 Overdrive - pump non-return valve

If the overdrive unit does not function correctly, and the fault is diagnosed from the fault diagnosis chart that the pump non-return valve is not operating properly it may be removed and checked as follows:

1 It will be seen that by referring to Fig. 6.13. the pump non-return valve components are situated in the solenoid side of the main casing. To gain access to the valve first drain the oil from the unit by undoing and removing the drain plug.

2 It is recommended that whenever the drain plug is removed the filter and three magnetic rings be cleaned before refitting.

3 Undo the three bolts, spring washers, cover plate and gasket.

4 Undo the solenoid retaining bolts and lift away the bolts, spring washers and the solenoid by disconnecting the solenoid plunger from the yoke of the operating valve lever.

5 Slacken the clamp bolt nut and withdraw the operating lever from the end of the valve operating shaft followed by the distance collar.

6 Remove the nuts and spring washers from the two short studs that secure the solenoid bracket assembly to the main casing. Also undo the two setscrews (painted red) so as to release the accumulator spring tension. Do not remove the two setscrews first. Lift away the solenoid bracket followed by the spring and spacer tube assembly.

7 The pump return valve is positioned in the cavity of the main body casing once the solenoid bracket assembly is removed. Undo and lift out the hexagonal plug and washer followed by the spring, plunger and ball bearing.

8 Wash all valve parts in petrol and allow to dry. Ensure that the valve is clear of any foreign matter. Inspect the ball bearing for signs of pitting   and, if evident   a new bearing should be obtained. It has a diameter of 0.25 in (6.35 mm).

9 Insert the ball bearing and tap, using a soft metal drift and a hammer, to re-set it. Insert the plunger, spring and plug with a new copper washer, fitted under its head. Check that the copper washer seats on its location correctly to ensure no oil leaks.

10 Insert the accumulator spring into the tube and fit the accumulator tube into the recess in the accumulator sleeve still in the main casing.

11 Fit a new 'O' ring over the operating shaft if one was originally fitted and using a new joint washer refit the solenoid bracket ensuring that the accumulator spring locates over a dowel in the bracket.

12 Tighten the two screws with spring washers evenly and then the nuts with spring washers onto the two short studs.

13 Slide the distance collar onto the lever shaft.

14 Refit the operating lever to the lever shaft and lightly tighten the locknut.

15 Fit a new joint washer to the solenoid bracket and insert the solenoid plunger into the yoke in the operating lever.

16 Secure the solenoid to the bracket with the two bolts and spring washers.

17 It will now be necessary to set the solenoid operating lever and full details of this are given in Section 13 of this Chapter.

18 Fit a new cover plate gasket and then the cover plate. Secure with three bolts and spring washers.

19 Top up the level of oil in the gearbox and overdrive unit.

16 Overdrive - later fitment - general description

This overdrive unit is offered as a factory fitted option to TR6 models produced after February 1973. It is attached to the rear of the gearbox and takes the form of an hydraulically operated epicyclic gear. Overdrive operates on third and top gears to provide fast cruising at lower engine revolutions. The overdrive is engaged or disengaged by a driver controlled switch which controls an electric solenoid mounted on the overdrive unit. A further switch called an inhibitor switch is included in the electrical circuit to prevent accidental engagement of overdrive in reverse, first or second gears.

The overdrive unit is designed to be engaged or disengaged when engine power is being transmitted through the power line and also without the use of the clutch pedal at any throttle opening or road speed. It is important that the overdrive is not disengaged at high road speeds as this will cause excessive high engine speeds.

The overdrive gears are epicyclic and comprise a central sunwheel which is in mesh with three planet wheels. These three gears are also in mesh with an internally toothed annulus. The planet carrier is splined to the input shaft which is, in fact, the mainshaft of the manual gearbox. The annulus is an integral part of the output shaft.

When the overdrive is disengaged the engine torque is transmitted from the input shaft to the inner member of an uni-directional clutch and then onto the outer member of the clutch via rollers which are driven up inclined faces, and wedge or lock the inner and outer members. The outer member of the clutch forms part of the combined annulus and the output shaft. Thus, as the gear train is not operative the drive is direct through the overdrive unit.

Mounted on the externally splined extension shaft of the sun gear is a cone clutch and this is pressed onto the annulus by a number of springs which press against the overdrive unit casing. The spring pressure is transmitted to the clutch member by a thrust ring and ball bearing, so causing the inner friction lining of the cone clutch to be in contact with the outer cone of the annulus and rotate with the annulus whilst the springs and thrust ring remain stationary.

As the sunwheel is splined to the clutch member, the whole gear train is locked together so permitting over run and engine torque in reverse gear to be transmitted through the overdrive unit. Also an additional load is imparted to the clutch during over run and reverse conditions by the sun wheel, which, due to the special helix angle of the gear teeth, thrust are rearwards and has for its reaction member the cone clutch.

When the overdrive unit is engaged, the cone clutch takes up a new position, whereby it is no longer in contact with the annulus, but has now moved forward, so that its outer friction lining, is in contact with the brake ring which is part of the overdrive unit casing. The sunwheel to which the clutch is attached is now held still. The planet carrier rotates with the

input shaft and the three planet wheels are caused to rotate about their own axes and drive the annulus at a greater speed and the input shaft. This is made possible because the uni-directional clutch outer member can over run the inner member. Hydraulic pressure generated by a pump in the overdrive unit acts on two pistons when a little valve is opened and moves the cone clutch in a forward direction. The little valve is controlled by the solenoid which is operated by the driver using an electric switch. This hydraulic pressure is sufficiently light to overcome the spring pressure that holds the clutch member onto the annulus and causes the clutch to engage with the brake ring and hold the sunwheel at rest. As the overdrive unit is attached to the rear of the gearbox, it is able to share the oil in the gearbox. The cam operated plunger pump draws the oil from the overdrive oil sump and via drillings, passes it to the two operating piston chambers, the ball type operating valve and the pressure relief valve. Oil is also passed to the various other parts of the overdrive unit for lubrication purposes.

When the driver moves the overdrive switch to the 'engaged' position current passes to the solenoid and causes the operating valve to close. Pressure built up in the hydraulic system causes the two pistons to move against the action of the springs which hold the sliding member onto the annulus. Therefore the sliding member is moved into contact with the brake ring.

Oil is then continued to be pumped into the hydraulic operating system so compressing the modulator springs that are inside the pistons resulting in a cushioning effect by the progressive application of the load, between the sliding member and the brake ring. As the sunwheel is now in a locked condition and the planet gears are free to revolve, the overdrive condition is in existence. Any further delivery of oil will open the pressure relief valve which will allow oil to pass to the various components for lubrication purposes and then return to the overdrive oil sump.

When the driver moves the overdrive switch to the 'disengaged' position, current will cease to flow to the solenoid and the operating valve ball will be unseated by hydraulic pressure so uncovering the exhaust port. The spring load on the sliding member will force oil to pass from the piston chambers whilst, at the same time, oil will continue to be pumped into the circuit and with the two circuits connected allowing mixing of the two oil flows, causing action against each other, and will control the movement of the sliding member. The sliding member is, therefore, disengaged from the brake ring and this time engaged with the annulus at a controlled rate. The oil flow will then pass through the exhaust port and provide lubrication for the various internal parts.

17 Overdrive - removal and replacement

1 It should not be necessary to remove the overdrive unit from the vehicle in order to attend to the following :- Solenoid and operating valve, relief and low pressure valve, pump and non-return valve.

2 If the unit as a whole requires overhaul it must be removed from the vehicle together with the gearbox, details of which will be found in Section 2 of this Chapter. It should however be pointed out that several special tools are required to correctly dismantle and reassemble the overdrive unit, so before work commences make sure that these are available.

3 Before beginning the sequence to remove the gearbox and overdrive unit it is necessary to drive the vehicle and engage overdrive and then disengage with the clutch depressed. This will release the spline loading between the planet carrier and uni-directional clutch which could make removal difficult.

18 Overdrive - dismantling, overhaul and reassembly

1 Using a screwdriver or small chisel, bend back the tab washers that lock the four nuts that secure the operating piston bridge pieces and undo the four nuts. Lift away the four nuts and tab

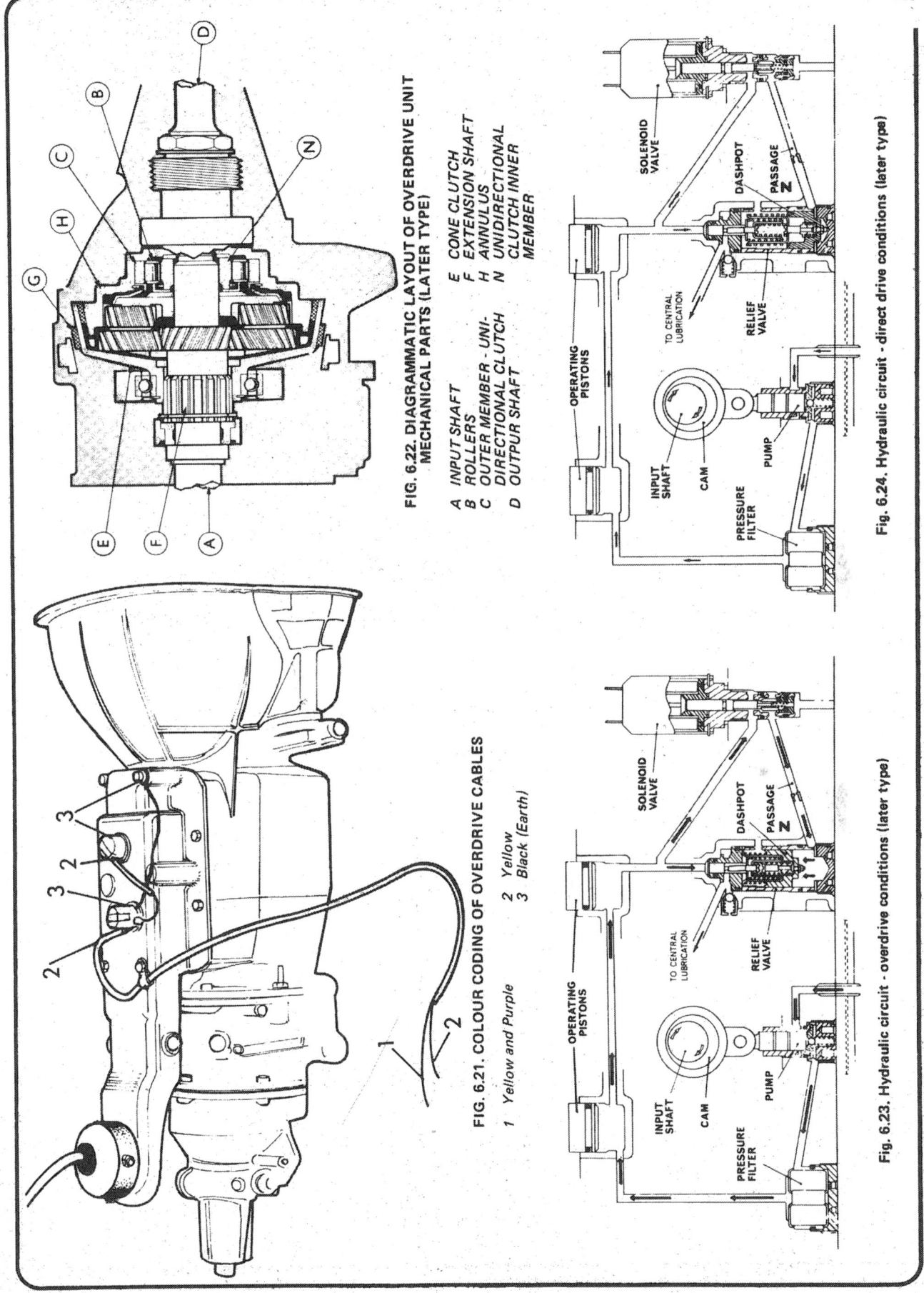

FIG. 6.22. DIAGRAMMATIC LAYOUT OF OVERDRIVE UNIT MECHANICAL PARTS (LATER TYPE)

A INPUT SHAFT
B ROLLERS
C OUTER MEMBER - UNI-DIRECTIONAL CLUTCH
D OUTPUR SHAFT
E CONE CLUTCH
F EXTENSION SHAFT
H ANNULUS
N UNIDIRECTIONAL CLUTCH INNER MEMBER

FIG. 6.21. COLOUR CODING OF OVERDRIVE CABLES

1 Yellow and Purple
2 Yellow
3 Black (Earth)

Fig. 6.24. Hydraulic circuit - direct drive conditions (later type)

SOLENOID VALVE
DASHPOT
PASSAGE Z
TO CENTRAL LUBRICATION
RELIEF VALVE
OPERATING PISTONS
INPUT SHAFT
CAM
PUMP
PRESSURE FILTER

Fig. 6.23. Hydraulic circuit - overdrive conditions (later type)

SOLENOID VALVE
DASHPOT
PASSAGE Z
TO CENTRAL LUBRICATION
RELIEF VALVE
OPERATING PISTONS
INPUT SHAFT
CAM
PUMP
PRESSURE FILTER

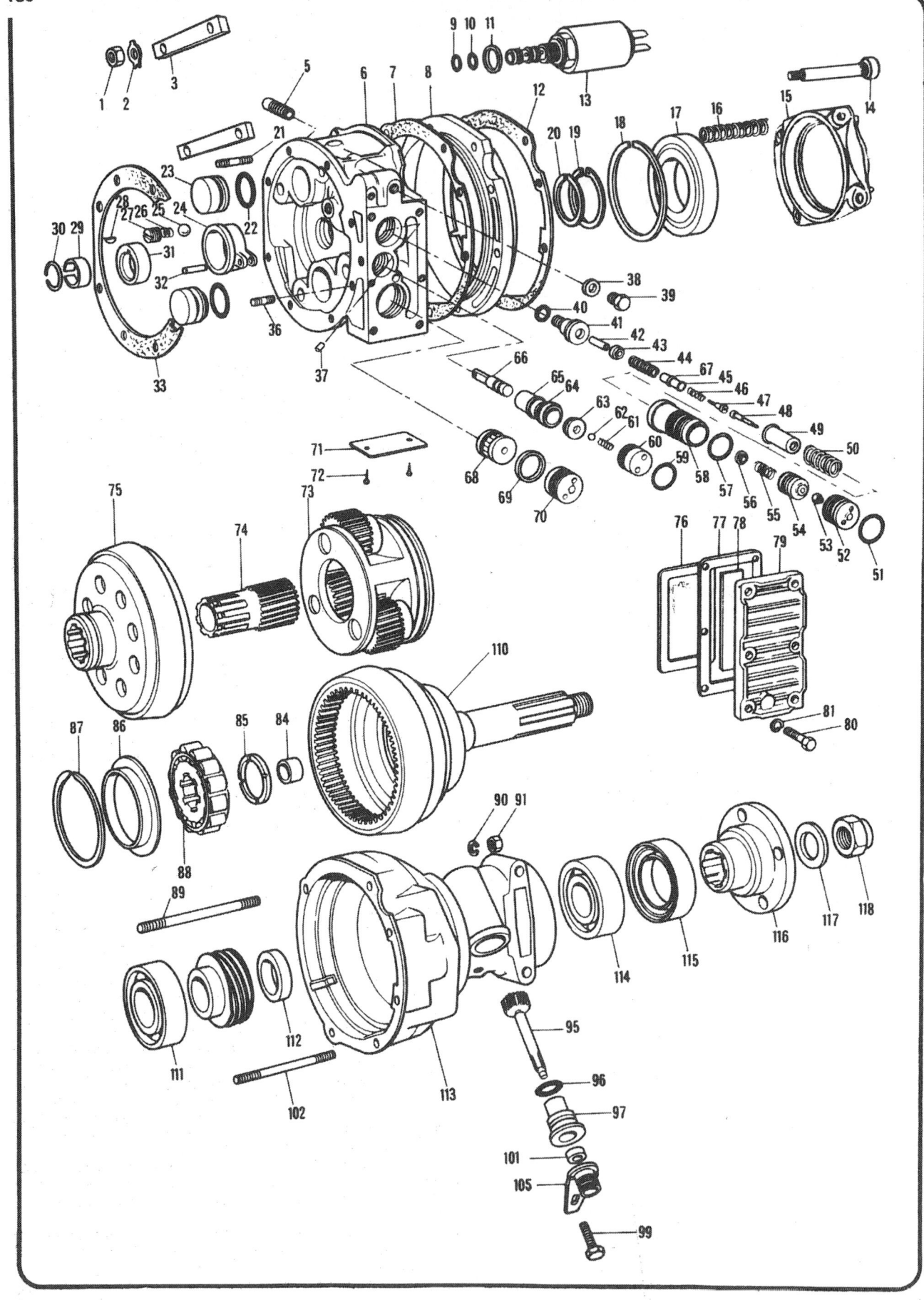

FIG. 6.25. COMPONENTS OF OVERDRIVE UNIT (LATER TYPE)

1 Nut	55 Double dashpot spring
2 Tabwasher	56 Spring retainer
3 Bridge piece	57 'O' ring
5 Breather	58 Dashpot sleeve
6 Main case	59 'O' ring
7 Gasket	60 Pump plug
8 Brake ring	61 Non return valve spring
9 'O' ring	62 Steel ball
10 'O' ring	63 Non return valve seat
11 Washer	64 'O' ring
12 Gasket	65 Pump body
13 Solenoid	66 Pump plunger
14 Thrust pin	67 Packing washer
15 Thrust ring	68 Pressure filter
16 Clutch return springs	69 Pressure filter washer
17 Thrust ball race	70 Pressure filter plug
18 Retaining circlip	71 Name plate
19 Circlip for sliding member	72 Securing screws
20 Circlip for sunwheel	73 Planet carrier assembly
21 Stud	74 Sunwheel
22 'O' ring	75 Clutch sliding member
23 Operating piston	76 Sump filter
24 Pump strap	77 Sump gasket
25 Steel ball	78 Sump magnet
26 Lubrication relief valve spring	79 Sump
27 Lubrication relief valve plug	80 Sump setscrews
28 Woodruff key	81 Shakeproof washer
29 Spring ring for mainshaft	84 Mainshaft support bush
30 Circlip	85 Thrust washer
31 Cam	86 Oil thrower
32 Pump pin	87 Circlip
33 Gasket	88 Free wheel assembly
36 Stud	89 Stud
37 Restrictor plug	90 Shakeproof washer
38 Washer	91 Nut
39 Pressure tapping plug	95 Speedo driven gear
40 'O' ring	96 'O' ring
41 Relief valve body	97 Speedo bearing
42 Relief valve spindle	99 Setscrew
43 Relief valve spring plate	101 Oil seal
44 Relief valve spring	102 Stud
45 Relief valve spring cup	105 Speedo tabwasher
46 Residual spring	110 Annulus
47 Relief valve spindle	111 Annulus front ball race
48 Dashpot spindle	112 Annulus front ball race
49 Dashpot spring cup	113 Rear case
50 Dashpot spring	114 Annulus rear ball race
51 'O' ring	115 Oil seal
52 Dashpot plug	116 Coupling flange
53 Dashpot piston locknut	117 Washer
54 Dashpot piston	118 Locknut

washers followed by the two bridge pieces.

2 Undo and remove the six nuts that secure the main casing to the rear casing in a progressive manner as these two parts will be under the influence of the clutch return spring pressure. Note the position of the copper washers which fit on the two studs at the top of the casing.

3 The main casing complete with brake ring can now be separated from the rear casing.

4 Lift out the sliding member assembly complete with the sunwheel followed by the planet carrier assembly. This should be done with care as it is easy to accidentally damage the oil catcher which is located under the planet carrier assembly.

5 To dismantle the main casing and brake ring first tap the brake ring from its spigot in the main casing using a suitable drift.

6 Using a pair of pliers carefully remove the two operating pistons.

7 Undo and remove the six bolts and spring washers securing the sump to the main casing. Lift away the sump gasket and suction filter.

8 To remove the relief valve and dashpot assembly a special tool is now necessary. It has a part number of L 354 A. Remove the relief valve and then withdraw the dashpot piston complete with its component springs and cap, followed by the residual pressure spring. It should be noted that this spring is the only loose spring in the assembly.

9 The relief valve piston can now be withdrawn by pulling down carefully using a pair of pliers.

10 A further special tool is required to remove the relief valve. Using tool number L 40 1A inserted into the now exposed relief bore, withdraw the relief valve together with the dashpot sleeve. Take great care not to damage these parts during removal.

11 Using tool number L 354 A undo and remove the pump plug taking care not to lose the non-return valve spring and ball bearing.

12 The pump valve seat can now be withdrawn. The pump body will be held in position by its 'O' ring so to remove this hook a piece of wire into the inlet port and draw the assembly downwards.

13 To remove the pressure filter use tool number L 401 and unscrew the pressure filter base plug. The filter element will be released with the plug. Note the aluminium washer which locates on the shoulder in the filter bore.

14 Using a 1 inch (25 mm) A.F. open ended spanner unscrew the solenoid control valve. Do not use a wrench on the cylindrical body as it will be irrepairably damaged.

15 With a screwdriver carefully remove the circlip from the sunwheel extension and lift out the sunwheel.

16 Again using a screwdriver remove the circlip from its groove on the cone clutch hub and tap the clutch from the thrust ring bearing with a soft faced hammer.

17 If necessary the bearing may be removed from its housing using a vice and suitable packing. It will be necessary to remove the larger circlip which retains it before removal commences.

18 Reverse spline type overdrive. For fixed flange type proceed to paragraph 25. Using a screwdriver remove the circlip which retains the uni-directional clutch. Lift away the oil thrower.

19 Place tool number L 178 A over the now exposed uni-directional clutch and lift the inner member complete with rollers into the special tool. Lift away the bronze thrust washer.

20 Withdraw the speedometer driven gear and bearing.

21 To remove the annulus first drive a centre punch into the welch plug located at the top of the rear casing and lever it out.

22 Using a pair of circlip pliers expand the circlip which secures the annulus bearing.

23 Place the rear casing vertically over supports and with a light blow from a soft faced hammer on the end of the annulus, drive the annulus complete with bearing downwards from the rear casing.

24 Undo and remove the nut that secures the speedometer driving gear and with the aid of a universal puller withdraw the ball race.

25 If the fixed flange type overdrive is fitted first remove the

uni-directional clutch as described in paragraphs 18 and 19.

26 Remove the speedometer driven gear.

27 Undo and remove the coupling flange nut and washers and withdraw the flange using a universal puller.

28 Remove the annulus as described in paragraph 23. The front bearing speedometer driving gear and spacer will also be withdrawn with the annulus. The rear bearing and oil seal will remain in position in the rear casing and these may be drifted out using a suitable soft metal drift.

29 The overdrive unit is now fully dismantled and may be inspected for wear.

30 Inspect the teeth and cone surface of the annulus for wear. Check that the uni-directional clutch rollers are not chipped and that the inner and outer members are free from damage.

31 Examine the spring and cage for distortion. Check that the lubrication part at the rear of the annulus is clear.

32 Inspect the rear casing bush and oil seal for wear or damage.

33 Examine the clutch linings on the sliding member for signs of excessive wear or overheating. Should there be signs of these conditions the whole sliding member assembly must be renewed. It is not possible to fit new linings as these are precision machined after bonding.

34 Make sure that the ball race rotates smoothly as this can be a source of noise when the car is running in direct gear.

35 Inspect the clutch return spring for any signs of distortion, damage or loss of springiness.

36 Check the sunwheel teeth for signs of wear or damage.

37 Inspect the main casing for cracks or damage. Examine the operating cylinder bores for scores or wear. Check the operating pistons for wear and replace the sealing if there is any sign of damage.

38 Check the pump plunger assembly and ensure that the strap is a good fit on the mainshaft cam and that there is no excess play between the plunger and strap.

39 Should the pump plunger assembly be worn or damaged this must be replaced as a complete assembly.

40 With the non-return valve assembly clean, inspect the ball and valve seat and also the 'O' rings for signs of damage.

41 Check the relief valve and dashpot assembly for wear. The pistons must move freely in their respective housings. Ensure that the rings are in good order.

42 Do not dismantle the dashpot and relief valve piston assemblies otherwise the pre-determined spring pressures will be disturbed.

43 Finally examine the 'O' rings on the solenoid valve for damage and, if evident they should be renewed together with sealing washers.

44 Clean the sump filter in petrol and if any particles are stuck in the gauze rub with an old toothbrush. Wipe the magnetic plug free of any metallic particles.

45 Reassembly of the unit can commence after any damaged or worn parts have been exchanged and new gasket and seals obtained. Do not use jointing compound during assembly.

46 Reverse spline type overdrive: For fixed flange type proceed to paragraph 54. Fit a new annulus ball race and then position the speedometer driving gear so that the plain portion is facing the ball race. Secure with the nut and a new locking washer. Tighten the nut to a torque wrench setting of 50 to 60 lb ft (6.910 to 8.28 Kgm).

47 Place the ball race circlip in the rear casing and expand using a pair of circlip pliers.

48 Press the annulus through the circlip and into the casing until the bearing is fully home and the circlip is located in its groove. This must be done carefully so that the rear bush and oil seal are not damaged.

49 Fit a new welch plug and secure by striking lightly in the centre with a suitable size flat faced punch.

50 Next position the spring and inner member of the uni-directional clutch into the cage, locating the spring so that the cage is spring loaded in an anti-clockwise direction when viewed from the front.

51 Place this assembly onto tool L 178 A with the open side of the cage uppermost and feed the clutch in a clockwise direction

until all the rollers are in place. Refit the bronze thrust washer in the recess in the annulus.

52 Transfer the uni-directional clutch assembly from the special assembly tool into its outer member in the annulus.

53 Re-fit the oil thrower and secure with the circlip. Check that the clutch rotates in an anti-clockwise direction only.

54 Fixed flange type: Place the speedometer driving gear in the rear casing with its plain boss facing the front bearing. Note that the speedometer driving gear cannot be fitted from the rear of the casing.

55 Press the front bearing into the rear casing making sure that its outer track abuts against the shoulder in the casing.

56 Place the annulus with the inner face resting on a suitable packing piece. Using a piece of tube of suitable diameter press the front bearing together with the rear casing and speedometer driving gear onto the annulus until the bearing abuts on the locating shoulder. Fit the spacer onto the annulus.

57 Using the same piece of tube press the rear bearing onto the annulus and into the rear casing simultaneously. Finally press on the coupling flange and secure with the washer and self locking nut. Tighten to a torque wrench setting of 80 to 130 lb ft (11.00 to 17.12 Kgm).

58 Both models. To assemble the clutch sliding member assembly fit the ball into its housing and secure with the large circlip.

59 Place this assembly onto the hub of the cone clutch and fit the circlip into its groove.

60 Insert the sunwheel into the hub and refit the circlip onto the sunwheel extension.

61 Lightly smear the operating pistons with oil and refit to the main casing.

62 Place a new gasket into the main casing and fit the brake ring ensuring it is fully home on its spigot location.

63 Before refitting the relief valve and dashpot assembly ensure that all component parts are clean and lightly oiled. Insert the relief body in the bore, and using the relief valve outer sleeve push it fully home. Note the end with the 'O' ring is nearest to the outside of the casing.

64 Next place the relief valve spring and piston assembly into the dashpot cup taking care that the ends of the residual pressure spring are correctly located.

65 Place these parts in the relief valve outer sleeve whilst at the same time engaging the relief valve piston in its housing.

66 Finally fit the base plug and tighten flush with the housing to a torque wrench setting of 16 lb ft (2.2 Kgm).

67 Place the pump non-return valve spring in the non-return valve plug and then place the ball on the spring.

68 The non-return seat can now be located on the ball and the complete assembly screwed into the main casing using tool L 354. Tighten to a torque wrench setting of 16 lb ft (2.2 Kgm).

69 Refit the pressure filter and new aluminium washer. Tighten the plug to a torque wrench setting of 16 lb ft (2.2 Kgm).

70 Refit the overdrive sump, suction filter and gasket and secure with the six bolts and spring washers.

71 Refit the solenoid control valve and tighten firmly using an open ended spanner.

72 Mount the rear casing assembly vertically in a bench vice and insert the planet carrier assembly. The gears may be meshed in any position.

73 Place the sliding member assembly complete with clutch non-return springs onto the cone of the annulus, at the same time engaging the sunwheel with the planet gears. Fit the brake ring into its spigot in the tail casing using a new joint washer on both sides.

74 Position the main casing assembly onto the thrust housing pins, at the same time entering the studs in the brake ring.

75 Fit the two operating piston bridge pieces and secure with the four nuts and new tab washers.

76 Fit the six nuts which secure the rear and main casing assemblies ensuring that the two copper washers are correctly located on the two top studs. It will be observed that as the nuts are tightened the clutch return spring pressure will be felt.

77 The unit is now ready for refitting to the gearbox as described in section 8, paragraphs 33 to 39 inclusive.

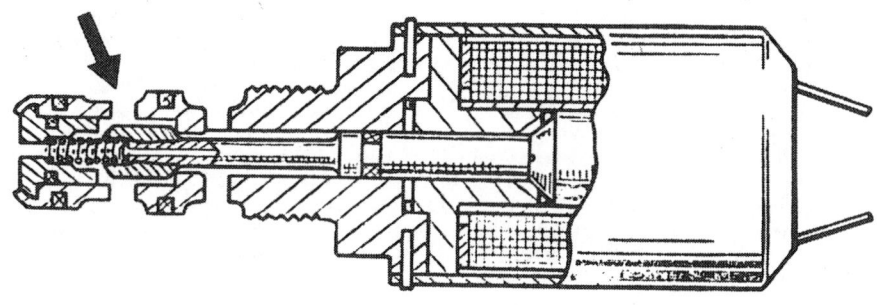

Fig. 6.26. Solenoid control valve. Arrow shows valve assembly

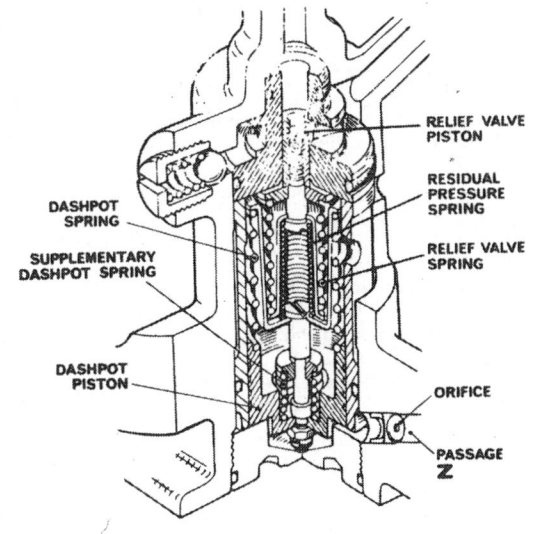

RELIEF VALVE PISTON

RESIDUAL PRESSURE SPRING

RELIEF VALVE SPRING

DASHPOT SPRING

SUPPLEMENTARY DASHPOT SPRING

DASHPOT PISTON

ORIFICE

PASSAGE Z

Fig. 6.27. Relief valve and dashpot assembly

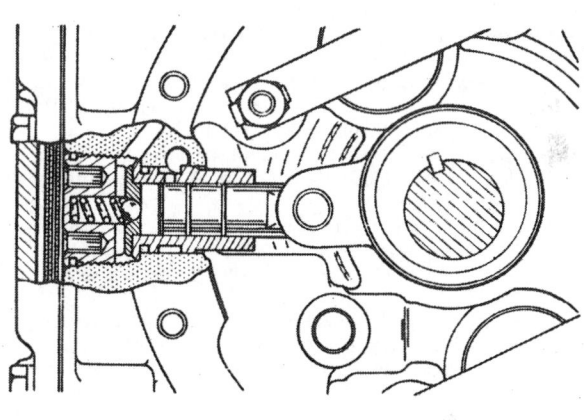

Fig. 6.28. Pump assembly

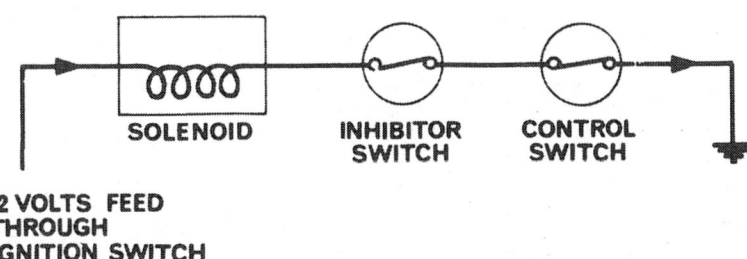

SOLENOID

INHIBITOR SWITCH

CONTROL SWITCH

12 VOLTS FEED THROUGH IGNITION SWITCH

Fig. 6.29. Overdrive solenoid control valve theretical circuit diagram

19 Solenoid control valve- removal and refitting

1 The solenoid and operating valve are a self contained factory sealed unit.

2 Disconnect the two terminals at the rear of the solenoid noting which way round the cables are fitted.

3 Using a 1 in (25 mm) A F open ended spanner unscrew the assembly. Do not use a wrench around the cylindrical body of the solenoid valve otherwise it will be severely damaged.

4 To test the solenoid connect up to a 12 volt battery and ammeter. The solenoid should require approximately 2 amps.

5 Check that the plunger in the valve moves forwards when the solenoid is energised and is returned to its direct drive position by spring pressure when de-energised.

6 It should be noted that this type of solenoid does not operate with a 'click' as observed in other types of overdrive.

7 Inspect the 'O' rings on the solenoid valve for damage and if necessary renew them together with a sealing washer.

8 If it is necessary to clean the operating valve, immerse this part of the solenoid valve only in paraffin until the valve is clean.

9 If the solenoid proves to be faulty it should be renewed as a complete unit.

10 Refitting is the reverse sequence to removal

20 Relief valve and dashpot assembly - removal and refitting

1 For this a special tool L 354 is necessary to remove the relief valve plug. If the vehicle has been recently used take care to avoid burns from hot oil which will be released.

2 Undo and remove the six bolts and spring washers securing the overdrive sump oil gauze filter. Lift away the sump joint washer and gauze filter.

3 Lift out the dashpot piston complete with its component springs and cup followed by the residual pressure spring.

4 The relief valve piston assembly may now be withdrawn by carefully pulling down with a pair of pliers.

5 Another special tool is required, part number L 401 which should be inserted into the now exposed relief valve bore. Withdraw the relief valve together with the dashpot sleeve taking

extreme care not to damage the valve bore.

6 Do not attempt to dismantle the dashpot and relief valve piston assemblies otherwise the pre-determined spring pressures will be disturbed.

7 Inspect the pistons and ensure that they move freely in their respective housings. Make sure the 'O' rings are not damaged.

8 Before assembly make sure all components are clean and lightly oiled.

9 Insert the relief body in the bore and using the relief valve outer sleeve push fully home.

10 It should be noted that the end with the 'O' ring is nearest the outside of the main casing.

11 Next position the relief valve spring and piston into the dashpot cup taking care that both ends of the residual pressure spring are correctly located. Carefully position these components in the relief valve outer sleeve at the same time engaging the relief valve piston in its housing. Fit the base plug and tighten flush with the main housing to a torque wrench setting of 16 lb ft (2.2 Kgm).

12 Refit the filter, gasket and sump and secure with the six bolts and spring washers.

21 Pump non-return valve - removal and refitting

1 For removal a special tool L 354 is necessary to remove the pump plug. If the vehicle has been recently used take care to avoid burns from hot oil which will be released.

2 Undo and remove the six bolts and spring washers securing the overdrive sump and gauze filter. Lift away the sump, joint washer and gauze filter.

3 Using tool L 354 remove the pressure filter base plug.

4 The filter element will come away with the plug. Note the aluminium washer which locates on the shoulder in the filter bore.

5 Remove any dirt and thoroughly wash the element in petrol or paraffin.

6 Refitting is the reverse sequence to removal. Always fit a new aluminium washer. Tighten the plug to a torque wrench setting of 16 lb ft (2.2 Kgm).

23 Fault finding - Gearbox

Symptom	Reason/s	Remedy
WEAK OR INEFFECTIVE SYNCHROMESH		
General wear	Synchronising cones worn, split or damaged	Dismantle and overhaul gearbox. Fit new gear wheels and synchronising cones.
	Baulk ring synchromesh dogs worn, or damaged	Dismantle and overhaul gearbox. Fit new baulk ring synchromesh.
JUMPS OUT OF GEAR		
General wear or damage	Broken gearchange fork rod spring	Dismantle and replace spring.
	Gearbox coupling dogs badly worn	Dismantle gearbox. Fit new coupling dogs.
	Selector fork rod groove badly worn	Fit new selector fork rod.
	Selector fork rod securing screw and locknut loose	Remove side cover, tighten securing screw and locknut.
EXCESSIVE NOISE		
Lack of maintenance	Incorrect grade of oil in gearbox or oil level too low	Drain, refill, to top up gearbox with correct grade of oil.
General wear	Bush or needle roller bearings worn or damaged	Dismantle and overhaul gearbox. Renew bearings.
	Gearteeth excessively worn or damaged	Dismantle, overhaul gearbox. Renew gearwheels.
	Laygear thrust washers worn allowing excessive end play	Dismantle and overhaul gearbox. Renew thrust washers.
EXCESSIVE DIFFICULTY IN ENGAGING GEAR		
Clutch not fully disengaging	Clutch pedal adjustment incorrect	Adjust clutch pedal correctly.

Overdrive

1 Overdrive does not engage

a   Insufficient oil in gearbox.
b   Failure of switches or wiring (visually check solenoid operation)
c   Control mechanism out of adjustment.
d   Check hydraulic pressure.
e   If insufficient pressure, clean and re-seat oil pump non-return valve.
f   Damaged parts within the unit requiring removal and inspection of the assembly.

2 Overdrive does not release

a   Control mechanism out of adjustment.
b   Solenoid sticking.
c   Blocked restrictor jet in operating valve.
d   Electrical circuit earthed.
e   Sticking clutch (can sometimes be freed by tapping casing with soft mallet).

f   Damaged parts within the unit necessitating removal and inspection of the assembly.

3 Clutch slip in overdrive

a   Insufficient oil in gearbox.
b   Solenoid lever out of adjustment.
c   Insufficient hydraulic pressure due to pump non-return valve incorrectly seating.
d   Insufficient hydraulic pressure due to worn accumulator piston.
e   Operating valve incorrectly seating.
f   Worn or glazed clutch lining.

4 Clutch slip in reverse or free-wheel condition of overdrive

a   Check solenoid setting.
b   Partially blocked restrictor jet in operating valve.
c   Worn clutch lining.

Chapter 7 Propeller shaft and universal joints

Contents

Specifications

Make	Hardy specer series 1300
Type	Tubular steel
Diameter	2 in (50.8 mm)
Overall length ... ... '	28.563 in (725.5 mm)
Type of universal joints	Needle rolier

1 General description

Drive is transmitted from the gearbox to the final drive by means of a finely balanced Hardy Spicer tubular propeller shaft.

Fitted at each end of the shaft is a universal joint which allows for vertical movement at the rear of the gearbox. Each universal joint comprises a four legged centre spider, four needle roller bearings and two yokes.

Slight for and aft movement of the final drive or power unit is absorbed by a sliding spline in the front of the propeller shaft, which is splined and mates with a sleeve and yoke assembly. When assembled a dust cap, steel washer, and cork washer seal the end of the sleeve and sliding joint.

The yoke flange of the front universal joint is fitted to the gearbox mainshaft flange with four bolts, spring washers and nuts, and the yoke flange of the rear universal joint is secured to the pinion flange on the rear axle in the same way.

The propeller shaft is a relatively simple component and is fairly easy to overhaul or repair providing that spare parts are available.

2 Propeller shaft - removal and replacement

1 Jack up the rear of the car, or position the rear of the car over a pit or a ramp.

2 If the rear of the car is jacked up supplement the jack with support blocks so that danger is minimised should the jack collapse.

3 If the rear wheels are off the ground place the car in gear or put the handbrake on to ensure that the propeller shaft does not turn when an attempt is made to loosen the four nuts on each flange.

4 The propeller shaft is carefully balanced to fine limits and it is important that it is replaced in exactly the same position as it was in prior to its removal. Scratch a mark on the propeller shaft and final drive flanges and the gearbox flanges to ensure accurate mating when the time comes for reassembly.

5 Unscrew and remove the four self locking nuts, bolts, and securing washers which hold the flange on the propeller shaft to the flange on the final drive, and then unscrew and remove the four self locking nuts, bolts, and washers which hold the front flange of the propeller shaft to the flange on the rear of the gearbox or overdrive unit. Lower the propeller shaft to the

ground.

6 Replacement of the propeller shaft is a reversal of the above procedure. Ensure that the mating marks scratched on the side of the propeller shaft flanges line up with those on the gearbox and final drive flanges.

3 Universal joints - inspection and repair

1 Wear in the needle roller bearings is characterised by the vibration in the transmission, 'clonks' on taking up drive, and in extreme cases of lack of lubrication, metallic squeaking, and ultimately grating and shrieking sounds as the needle roller bearings start to break up.

2 It is easy to check if the needle roller bearings are worn with the propeller shaft in position, by trying to turn the shaft with one hand, the other hand holding the final drive flange when the rear universal joint is being checked, and the front gearbox coupling when the front universal joint is being checked. Any movement between the propeller shaft and the front and the rear half couplings is indicative of considerable wear.

3 If worn, the old bearings and spiders will have to be discarded and a repair kit comprising new universal joints, spider, bearings, oil seals, and retainers purchased. Check also by trying to lift the shaft and noticing any movement in the joints.

4 Examine the propeller shaft spline for wear, to do this unscrew the dust cap from the sleeve, and then slide the sleeve from the shaft. Take off the steel washer and the cork washer. With the sleeve separated from the shaft assembly the splines can be inspected. If worn it will be necessary to purchase a new front sleeve assembly, or if the yokes are badly worn an exchange propeller shaft. It is not possible to fit oversize bearings and journals to the trunnion bearing holes.

4 Universal joints - dismantling

1 Before commencing the dismantling of the propeller shaft always ascertain that spare parts are immediately available.

2 Clean away all traces of dirt and grease from the circlips located on the ends of the spiders, and remove the clips by pressing their open ends together with a pair of pliers and levering them out with a screwdriver. NOTE: If they are difficult to remove tap the bearing face resting on top of the spider with a mallet which will ease the pressure on the circlip. (photo)

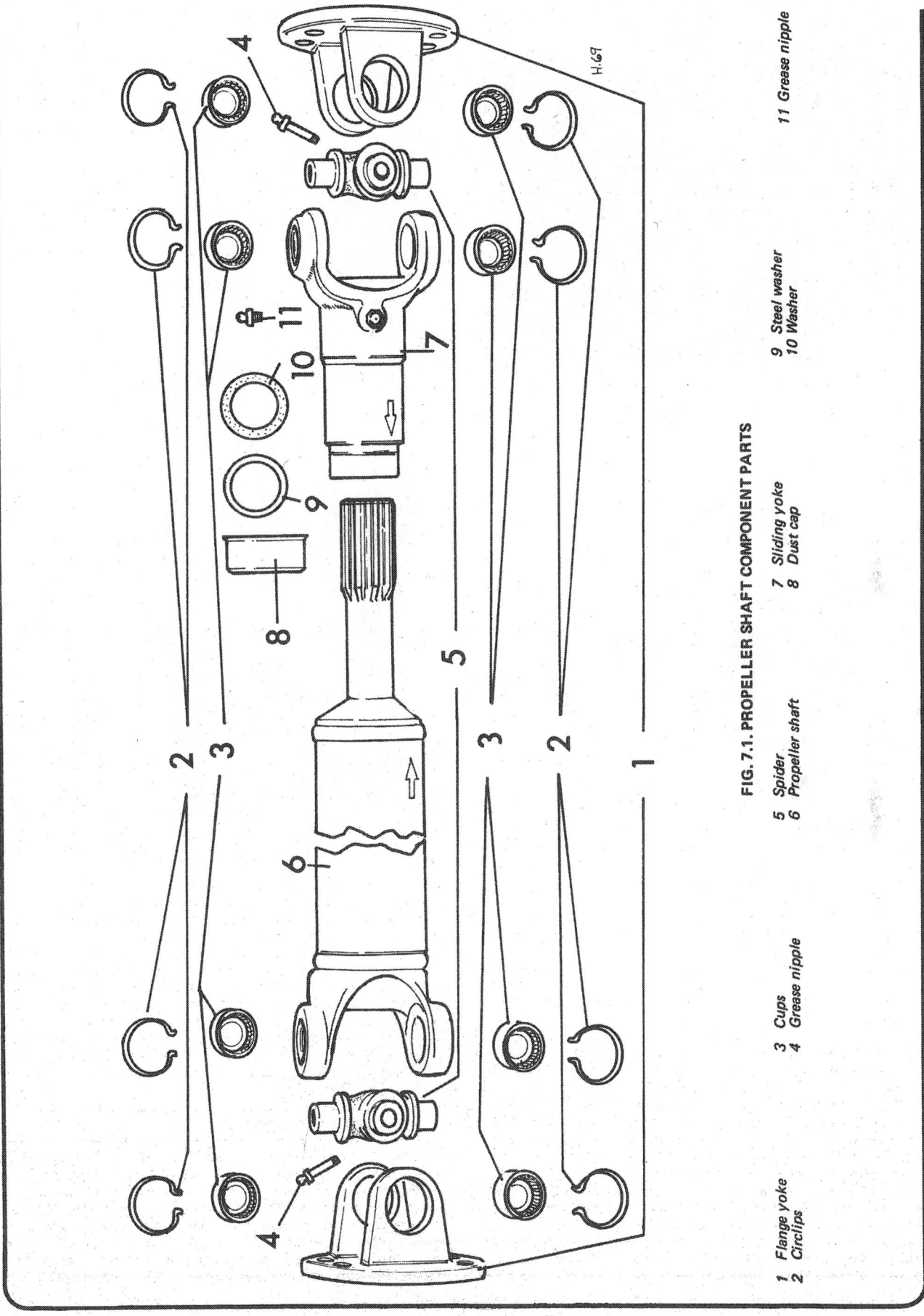

H.69

FIG. 7.1. PROPELLER SHAFT COMPONENT PARTS

1 Flange yoke
2 Circlips

3 Cups
4 Grease nipple

5 Spider
6 Propeller shaft

7 Sliding yoke
8 Dust cap

9 Steel washer
10 Washer

11 Grease nipple

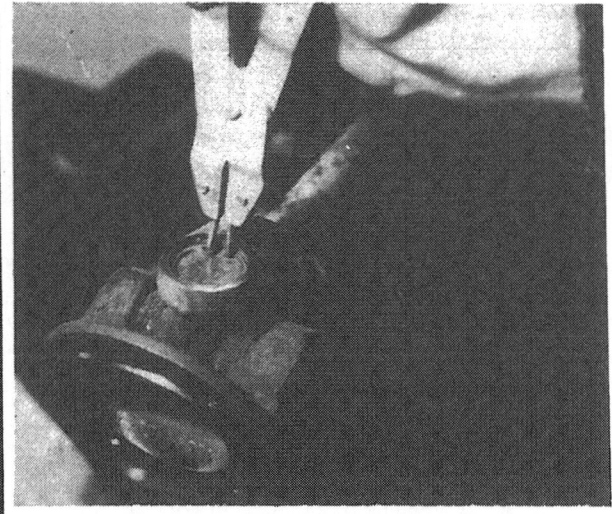

4.2 Removal of bearing cap retaining circlip

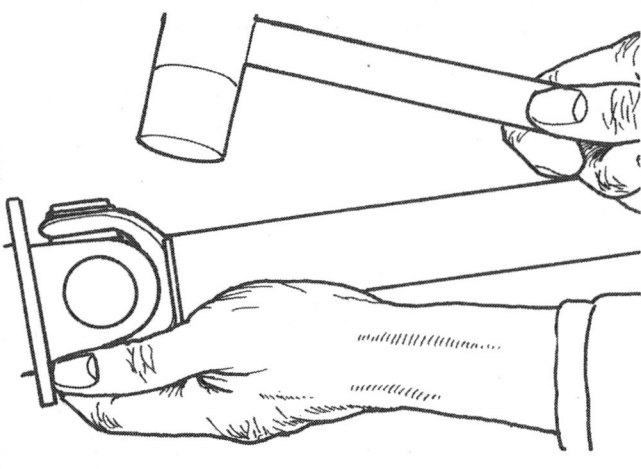

Fig. 7.2. Using a soft hammer to tap bearing cap from yoke

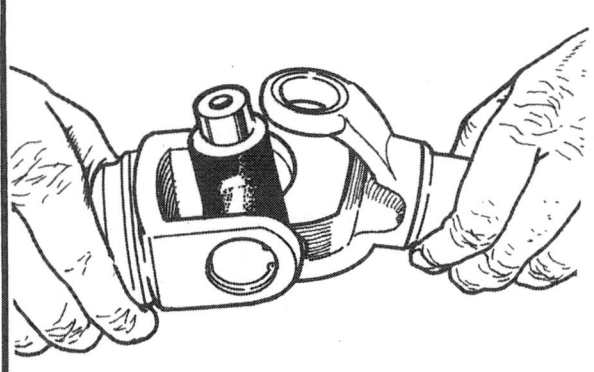

Fig. 7.3. Removal of spider from yoke

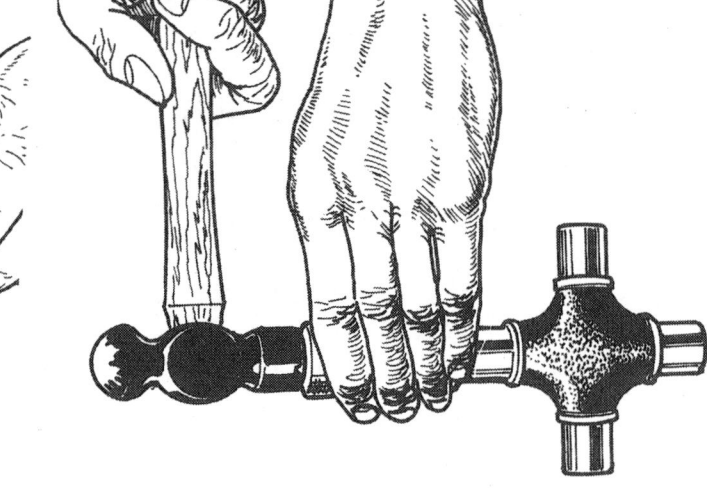

Fig. 7.4. Using a hammer and tubular drift to refit spider journal seal retainer

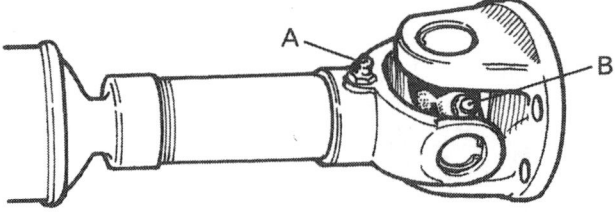

Fig. 7.5. Correct alignment of sliding yoke

3 Hold the shaft in one hand, as shown in Fig. 7.2. and remove the bearing cups and needle rollers by tapping the yoke at each bearing with a copper hide faced hammer. As soon as the bearings start to emerge they can be drawn out using the fingers. If the bearing cup refuses to move then place a thin bar against the inside of the bearing and tap it gently until the cup starts to emerge.

4 With the bearings removed it is relatively easy to extract the spiders from their yokes (Fig. 7.3). If the bearings and spider journals are thought to be badly worn this can easily be ascertained visually with the universal joint dismantled.

5 Universal joints - reassembly

1 Thoroughly clean out the yokes and journals. Make certain that the grease passages are quite clear.

2 Place the spider on the propeller shaft yoke and assemble the needle rollers in the bearing races with the assistance of some thin grease. NOTE: It is essential to fit the spiders in the yoke flanges so that the lubrication nipples are facing the propeller shaft and not the yoke flanges. If fitted the wrong way round it will be impossible to lubricate the universal joints. This is of course only applicable where grease nipples are fitted.

3 Refit the bearing cups on the spider and tap the bearings home so that they lie squarely in position.

4 Replace the circlips and lubricate the bearings well with lithium based grease.

5 Fit the dust cap, steel washer, and a new cork gasket over the splined part of the propeller shaft.

6 Grease the splines and then line up the arrow on the sleeve assembly with the arrow on the splined portion of the propeller shaft and then push the sleeve over the splines. Fit the washers to the sleeve and screw up the dust cap. The final assembly is shown in Fig. 7.5.

7 If correctly assembled the forked yokes on both shafts will have their axes parallel to each other. This is essential if vibration is to be eliminated.

Chapter 8 Rear axle

Contents

Specifications

Type	Independant rear suspenion with semi-floating axle shafts
Differential	Hypoid bevel gears
Ratio: TR5 and TR6	3.45:1
Ratio: TR250	3.70:1
Capacity	2.5 pints (1.421 litres) (3.0 US pints)

Differential unit
Sun Gears

Number of teeth	16
Journal diameter	1.4993 - 1.4985 in (38.08 - 38.06 mm)
Clearance in cage	0.002 - 0.004 in (0.05 - 0.10 mm)
Number of splines	24
Internal diameter	0.979 - 0.975 in (24.87 - 24.77 mm)
Thrust washer thickness	0.0495 - 0.0465 in (1.26 - 1.18 mm)

Planet gears

Number of gears	2
Number of teeth	10
Internal diameter	0.6265 - 0.6250 in (15.91 - 15.88 mm)
Clearance on cross shaft	0.0028 - 0.0008 in (0.07 - 0.02 mm)
Thrust washer thickness	0.0495 - 0.0465 in (1.26 - 1.18 mm)

Cross shaft

Diameter	0.6242 - 0.6237 in (15.85 - 15.84 mm)
Length	4.20 - 4.18 in (106.68 - 106.17 mm)

Differential cage

Location diameter for crownwheel	4.374 - 4.373 in (111.10 - 111.07 mm)
Trunnion diameter	1.5018 - 1.5012 in (38.15 - 38.13 mm)
Bearing press fit - interference	0.0006 - 0.0018 in (0.015 - 0.046 mm)
Internal diameter for sun gears	1.5025 - 1.5013 in (38.16 - 38.13 mm)
Clearance on gears	0.002 - 0.004 in (0.05 - 0.10 mm)
Width between trunnion bearing abutment	5.317 - 5.312 in (135.05 - 134.92 mm)
Bearing abutment to crownwheel mounting face ...	1.568 - 1.562 in (39.83 - 39.67 mm)
Width between sun wheel thrust faces	2.366 - 2.362 in (60.10 - 60.00 mm)
Diameter of cross shaft bores	0.6257 - 0.6254 in (15.89 - 15.86 mm)
Clearance on shaft	0.0003 - 0.002 in (0.007 - 0.05 mm)
Differential bearing pre load	0.004 - 0.002 in (0.10 - 0.05 mm)

TORQUE WRENCH SETTINGS	lb ft	Kg m
Cover and rear mounting plate	26 - 28	3.60 - 3.87
Inner driving flange to inner axle	100 - 110	13.83 - 15.21
Nose plate to axle	35	4.84
Oil seal housing to hypoid housing	16 - 18	2.21 - 2.49
Propeller shaft flange to pinion	90 - 100	12.44 - 13.83
Rear mounting plate to frame	26 - 28	3.60 - 3.87
Crown wheel bolts	22 - 24	3.04 - 3.3
Differential bearing caps	34 - 36	4.7 - 4.8

1 General description

The main rear axle component is the hypoid differential unit which is fixed to the chassis at the rear of the unit by a bracket using two part rubber mountings. The front of the differential unit is mounted on a second bracket also using two part rubber mountings. Splined swing axle drive shafts, pivoting at their inner ends on universal joints attached to the differential drive flanges, carry the drive to the hub via needle roller and ball bearings mounted in independent suspension arms.

The crownwheel and pinion each run on opposed taper roller bearings, the bearing pre-load and meshing of the crownwheel and pinion being controlled by shims. Spring loaded lip contact type oil seals are used at the differential nose piece and also in the two bearing retainers, one on each side of the main casing.

2 Differential unit - removal and refitting

1 Chock the front wheels at the front and rear, raise the rear of the car as high as possible and place on axle stands under the chassis members.

2 Disconnect the two silencer and tail pipe sections at the clips located in front of the silencers. Also release the two tail pipe straps and lift away the rear part of the twin pipe exhaust system.

3 Undo the four nyloc nuts securing the propeller shaft rear universal joint coupling to the differential unit companion flange (18). Fig. 8.1. Lift away the nuts and bolts and lower the propeller shaft.

4 Undo and remove the four nyloc nuts (30) securing the axle shaft yoke (30a) to the differential unit flange (28). Lift away the nuts, plain washers (29) and the bolts (32). Repeat this operation for the second shaft.

5 Undo the two nyloc nuts (61) securing the rear mounting (65) to the chassis frame. Lift away the backing plate (62) and lower buffer (63).

6 Support the weight of the rear axle using a hydraulic jack or other suitable means and undo the two nyloc nuts (22) securing the front mounting (19) to the chassis. Lift away the backing plate (21) and lower the rubber buffer (20).

7 Carefully lower the differential unit axle casing and withdraw from under the car.

8 Recover the rear mounting upper rubber buffers (64) and front mounting upper rubber buffers (17).

9 Refitting is the reverse sequence to removal. If the unit has been dismantled do not forget to refill with 2.5 pints (1.42 litres) (3.0 U.S. pints) of the recommended oil.

3 Differential unit - dismantling, inspection, reassembly and adjustment

Most garages will prefer to fit a complete set of gears, bearings, spacers and thrust washers rather than renew parts which may have worn. To do the job properly requires the use of special and expensive tools which the majority of garages do not have.

The primary object of these special tools is to enable the mesh of the crownwheel to the pinion to be very accurately set and thus ensure that noise is kept to a minimum. If any increase in noise cannot be tolerated then it is best to allow a Triumph garage to carry out the repairs.

Differential units have been rebuilt without the use of special tools so if the possibility of a slight increase in noise can be tolerated then it is quite possible for any do-it-yourself mechanic to successfully recondition this unit. It is necessary to use one special tool which has a part number S101 to enable the differential unit to be removed from the housing. See paragraph 13 for further information.

1 If the exterior is dirty wash in paraffin or Gunk and dry using an absorbant cloth.

2 Undo the four nyloc nuts (67) (Fig. 8.1).) from the studs (68) on the back of the rear cover (70). Lift away the nuts and the rear mounting. Note which way round the rear mounting is fitted marking it if necessary to ensure correct refitting.

3 Unscrew and remove the eight bolts (69) with spring washers that secure the rear cover (70) to the axle casing (11) and lift away the rear cover. Note which way round the rear cover fits for correct refitting.

4 Carefully remove the joint (75) from the axle casing.

5 Undo and remove the four bolts and spring washers which secure the inner axle shaft (34), bearing retainer (26) to the axle casing. Mark the bearing retainer to ensure that it is refitted in its original position.

6 Carefully withdraw the inner axle shaft assembly from the axle casing (11) and keep separate so that the parts are not interchanged at any stage.

7 Undo and remove the nyloc nut (30) from the end of the inner axle shaft followed by the plain washer (29).

8 Using a two leg puller separate the flange (28) from the inner axle shaft. An alternative method is to place the flange (28) on top of the jaws of a firm vice and with the shaft in a vertical position tap the end of the inner axle shaft with nyloc nut refitted to ensure the thread is not damaged.

9 Lift away the rectangular key (33) and put in a safe place so that it is not lost.

10 Remove the bearing retainer (26) with the oil seal (27) in position.

11 Using an internal bearing puller or a soft metal drift remove the bearing (57) from the bearing retainer making a note of which way round the bearing is fitted.

12 Undo the four bearing cap bolts (8) and lift away the bolts and spring washers. Mark the bearing caps (9) to ensure correct refitting in their original positions and lift away the bearing caps.

13 A special tool having a part number S101 together with adaptors will now be required to spread the axle casing. Fit the axle spread adaptor plates to the axle casing using four 3/8 inch UNF bolts 2.25 inches long. Next mount the spreader onto the adaptor plate ensuring that the pegs in the arms of the spreader fit into the large holes in the adaptor plate. Rotate the jacking screw until it is hand tight and then rotate a further half a turn using an open ended spanner. It should now just be possible to lift out the differential unit.

14 Remove the differential unit and place on the bench. Make sure it does not roll onto the floor. It is important that the bearing outer races are not interchanged so suitably mark them for correct refitting in their original positions unless, of course they are to be renewed.

15 Mark the relative position of the crownwheel (7) to the differential casing (71) to ensure correct refitting in its original position and undo the crownwheel retaining bolts (72). Lift away the retaining bolts and spring washers. (Fig. 8.5). .

16 Extract the split pin (15) locking the castellated nut (23) to the pinion shaft (7) and undo the castellated nut. Lift away the nut followed by the plain washer (16). Withdraw the pinion driving flange (18) from the pinion shaft splines. If it is tight, tap with a soft faced hammer.

17 Undo the four bolts (25) securing the front mounting (19) to the axle casing (11) and lift away the bolts and spring washers (24). The front mounting may now be removed.

18 The pinion may next be removed from the axle casing by temporarily refitting the castellated nut, and with a soft faced hammer, tapping the pinion assembly rearwards.

19 Carefully recover the shims (10) that are placed between the race (12) and the spacer (58) for possible reuse during reassembly.

20 Remove the pinion head bearing inner cone. Using a soft metal drift carefully drive out the pinion outer track. It should be noted that when the outer track of the tail bearing is removed the oil seal and tail bearing inner cone will also be released.

21 Upon removal of the pinion head bearing outer track, shims (59) will be released from between the outer track and the casing. Place these to one side for possible reuse during reassembly.

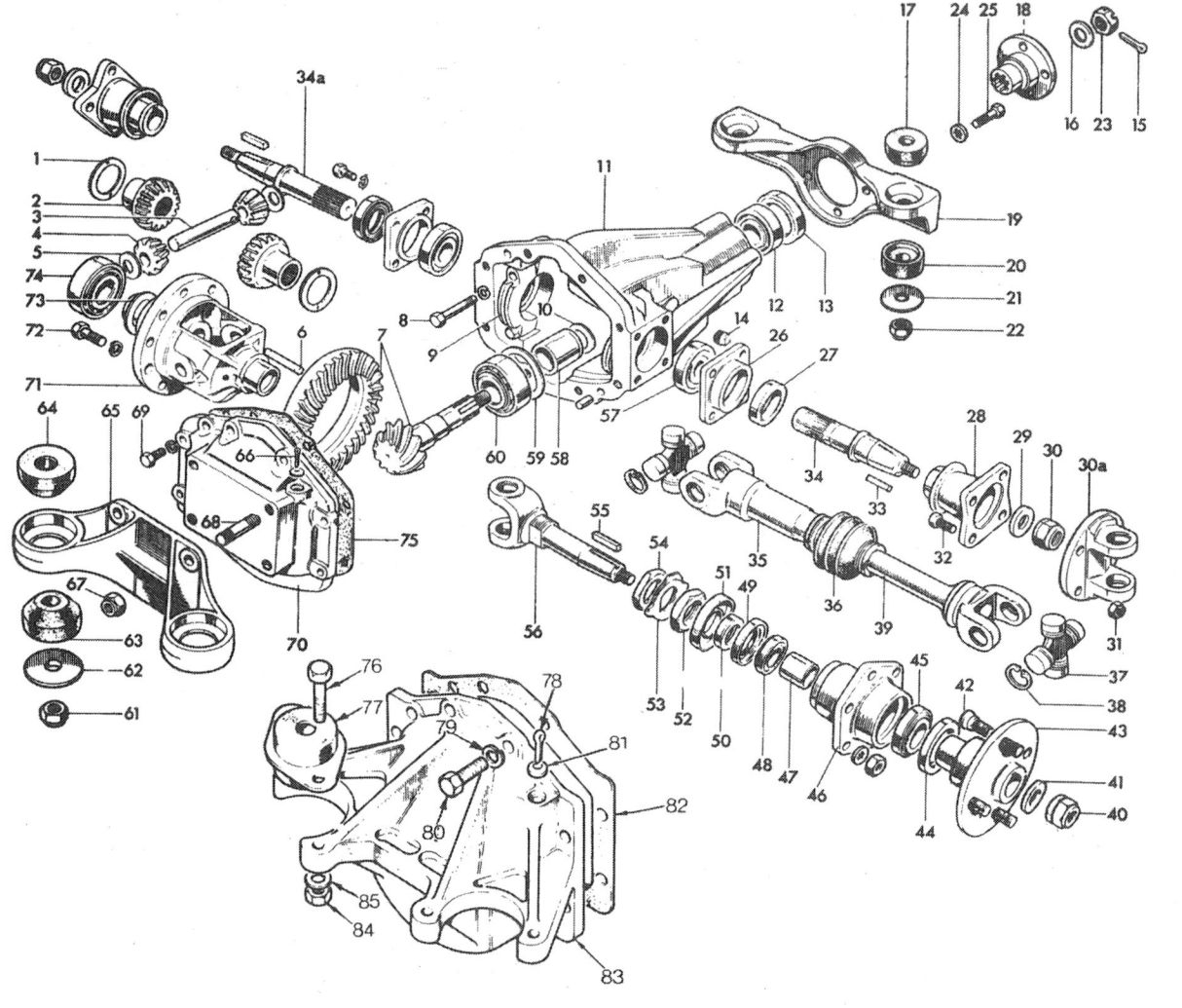

FIG. 8.1. FINAL DRIVE COMPONENT PARTS

1 Thrust washer - sun wheel	30 Nut	57 Bearing, inner axle shaft
2 Sun wheel	30a Yoke	58 Spacer, pinion bearing
3 Cross shaft	31 Nut, nyloc	59 Shim, pinion locating
4 Planet wheel	32 Bolt	60 Head bearing, pinion
5 Thrust washer - planet wheel	33 Key	61 Nut, nyloc
6 Locking pin - cross shaft	34 Axle shaft, inner, short	62 Backing plate
7 Crownwheel and pinion	34a Axle shaft, inner, long	63 Buffer, lower
8 Bolt, bearing cap	35 Axle shaft, fixed, outer	64 Buffer, upper
9 Bearing cap	36 Gaiter	65 Mounting, rear
10 Shim, pinion pre-loading	37 Universal spider	66 Split pin - breather
11 Axle casing	38 Circlip	67 Nut, nyloc
12 Tail bearing, pinion	39 Axle shaft, sliding, outer	68 Stud
13 Oil seal, pinion	40 Nut	69 Bolt
14 Filler plug - oil level	41 Washer	70 Rear cover
15 Split pin	42 Wheel stud	71 Differential cage
16 Washer	43 Hub	72 Bolt
17 Rubber buffer, upper	44 Oil seal	73 Shim, crownwheel pre-load
18 Companion flange	45 Hub bearing	74 Bearing, differential cage
19 Mounting, front	46 Bearing housing	75 Gasket, rear cover
20 Rubber buffer, lower	47 Bearing spacer, collapsible	76 Bolt (later models)
21 Backing plate	48 Hub bearing, inner	77 Rubber mounting (later models)
22 Nyloc nut	49 Oil seal	78 Split pin (later models)
23 Castellated nut	50 Bearing spacer	79 Lockwasher (later models)
24 Lockwasher	51 Stone guard	80 Setscrew (later models)
25 Bolt	52 Adjusting nut	81 Plug (later models)
26 Bearing retainer	53 Tab washer	82 Gasket (later models)
27 Oil seal	54 Locknut	83 Rear cover (later models)
28 Flange	55 Key	84 Nut (later models)
29 Washer	56 Stub shaft	85 Washer (later models)

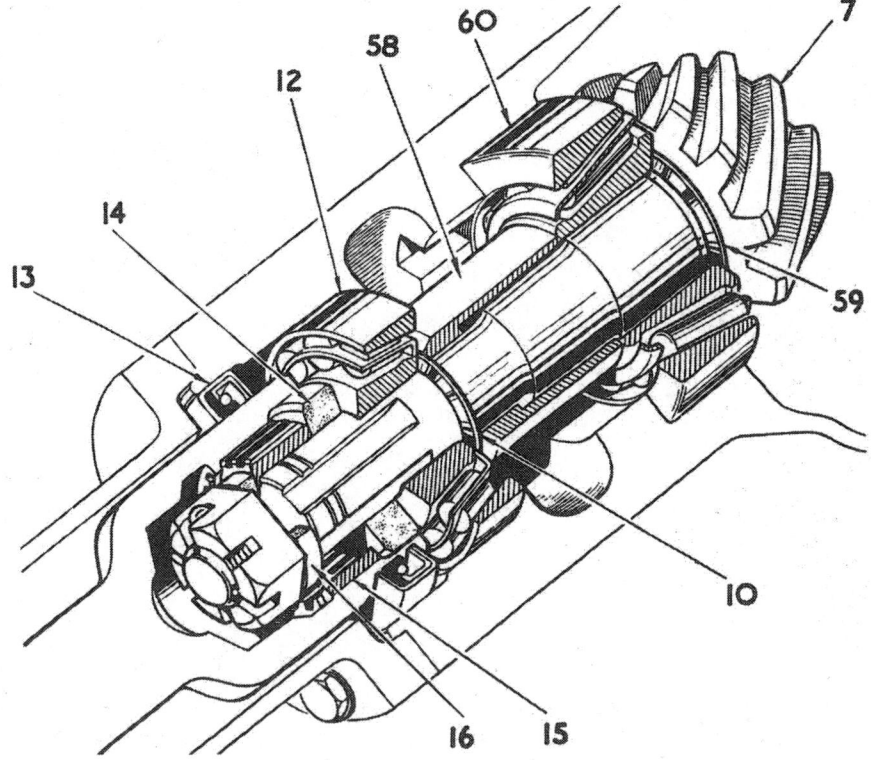

FIG. 8.2. MODIFIED PINION ASSEMBLY

7   Pinion
10 Shims - pre-load
12 Tail-bearing

13 Oil seal
14 Centralising collar
15 Coupling muff

16 Washer
58 Spacer, pinion bearings
59 Selective spacer

60 Headbearing,
    pinion

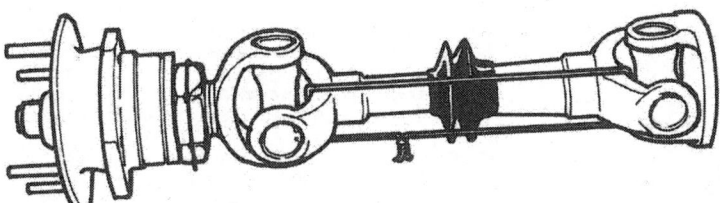

Fig. 8.3. Wiring together both universal joint couplings to stop separation

Fig. 8.4. Bearing retainer oil seal remover

Fig. 8.5. Removing crownwheel mounting bolts

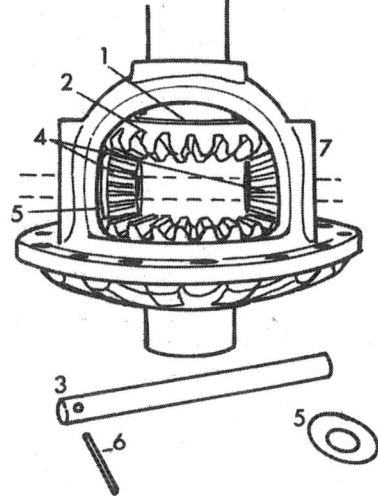

FIG. 8.6. GEARWHEELS ASSEMBLED INTO DIFFEREN—TIAL HOUSING

1	Thrust washer	5	Thrust washer
2	Sunwheel	6	Lockpin
3	Shaft	7	Differential case
4	Planet wheel		

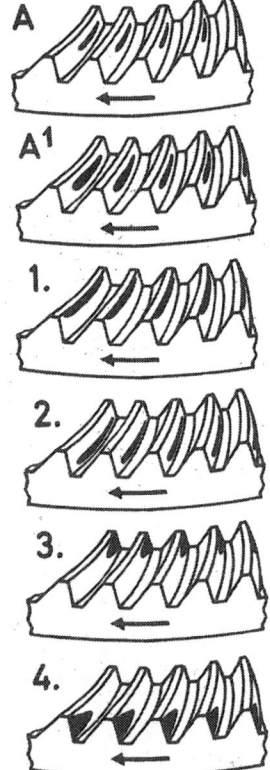

FIG. 8.7. CONTACT MARKING ON CROWNWHEEL

A Correct contact marking picture without load.
A1 When subjected to load the contact picture is displaced somewhat towards the outside.

Displacement of the crownwheel changes primarily the backlash, in addition the contact picture is displaced in the axial direction of the teeth.

Displacement of the pinion primarily moves the contact marking in the direction of the tooth height, while the backlash changes only marginally.

In addition the four fundamentally **false** contact markings, which usually occur in conjunction with each other, but knowledge of which simplifies the actual adjustment work.

1 High, narrow contact marking (tip contact) on crownwheel. **Correction: displace the pinion toward the crownwheel axis** and, if necessary, correct backlash by moving the crownwheel away from the pinion.

2 Deep, narrow contact marking (roof contact) on crownwheel. **Correction: move the pinion away from the crownwheel axis** and, if necessary, correct backlash by pushing the crownwheel toward the pinion.

3 Short contact marking on smallest tooth end (toe contact) of the crownwheel. **Correction: move the crownwheel away from the pinion** and, if necessary, move the pinion closer toward the crownwheel axis.

4 Short contact marking on large tooth end (heel contact) of the crownwheel. **Correction: move the crownwheel toward the pinion** and, if necessary, move the pinion away from the crownwheel axis.

22 At this point refit the differential unit to the axle casing and release the tension of the axle case spreader.

23 Mount a dial indicator gauge onto the axle casing and place the probe onto the crownwheel mounting face. Rotate the differential unit and check that the runout does not exceed 0.003 inch (0.0762 mm).

24 Tension the spreader and remove the differential unit. Release the tension again on the spreader.

25 Using a parallel pin punch very carefully drive out the cross shaft lock pin (6). Also remove the cross shaft (3) using a soft metal drift.

26 Rotate the sun wheels (2) which will in turn rotate the planet wheels (4) until the planet wheels with their respective thrust washer (5) are opposite the cut away portions of the differential casing (71) from which they can be lifted out.

27 Lift away the sun wheels (2) and the thrust washers (1).

28 The bearings (74) may be removed from the differential casing (71) by using a two leg puller and suitable thrust block. Note the shims (73) placed between the bearing track and the differential casing. Keep these for possible reuse during reassembly if new bearings are being used. If the original bearings are satisfactory there should be no reason to disturb these.

29 Check the rollers and races for general wear, score marks and pitting and renew these components as necessary.

30 Examine the teeth of the crownwheel and pinion for pitting, score marks, chipping and general wear. If a new crownwheel and pinion are required, a mated crownwheel and pinion must be fitted. It is asking for trouble to renew one without the other.

31 Examine the thrust washers, sun and planet gears and cross shaft for signs of wear and, if evident, obtain new parts.

32 To reassemble first fit the two outer tracks of the two pinion bearings using a soft metal drift. Make sure that they are fitted squarely and they are the correct way round.

33 Position the shims on the pinion head bearing outer track abutment face and refit the pinion bearing outer tracks using a soft metal drift or a piece of suitable diameter tube.

34 Refit the pinion head bearing inner cone into the pinion shaft using a piece of suitable diameter tube.

35 The bearing spacer should be placed on the pinion shaft with the chamfer outwards (splined end of pinion shaft). The shims previously removed during dismantling of the unit should next be fitted to the pinion, and the pinion assembly placed into the axle casing. The actual thickness of the last set of shims may have to be altered to correct the bearing pre-load.

36 Using a soft metal drift carefully tap the inner cone of the pinion tail bearing into position on the pinion and ensure that it is fitted against the shims (10) in front of the distance spacer (58).

37 Refit the flange (18) to the pinion shaft end followed by the plain washer (16) and the castellated nut (23). Tighten the nut using a torque wrench set to between 90 - 100 lb ft (12.44 - 13.83 kg m). Use a large wrench to hold the pinion driving flange to stop the pinion rotating. NOTE: The oil seal is not fitted at this stage.

38 Using a torque wrench check that the bearing pre-load is between 15 - 18 lb in. If the pre-load is above this figure extra shims must be fitted to the shim pack (10), and conversely if the pre-load is not sufficient, some shims must be removed.

39 Once the correct bearing pre-load is obtained, undo the castellated nut (23) and remove it followed by the plain washer (16) and driving flange (18). Carefully fit the oil seal (13)

ensuring that it is fitted with the lips inwards using a piece of suitable diameter tube. Lubricate the oil seal.

40 Refit the front mounting (19) and secure in position with the four bolts (25) and spring washers (24).

41 Refit the flange (18), plain washer (16) and castellated nut (23). Tighten the nut to a torque wrench setting of between 85 and 100 lb ft (11.7 - 13.8 kg m) and lock using a new split pin.

42 Refit the thrust washers (1) to the sun gears (2). Insert the sun gears (2) and thrust washers (1) into the differential carrier followed by the two planet gears (4) and thrust washers (5). Rotate the sun gears and the planet gears will automatically position themselves ready for the cross shaft (3) to be inserted. Note that the cross pin has a hole drilled at one end for the lock pin (6) to pass through.

43 Insert the lock pin (6) into the differential casing and secure in position with a centre punch.

44 Wipe clean the mating faces of the crownwheel and the differential casing and refit the crownwheel in its original position by aligning the previously made marks.

45 Fit the retaining bolts (72) and spring washers to the crownwheel and tighten the bolts in a diagonal manner using a torque wrench set to read between 22 and 24 lb ft (3.04 - 3.3 kg m).

46 Using a suitable diameter tube fit the bearings and shims to the differential casing.

47 Refit the differential unit to the axle casing and replace the cap, retaining bolts and spring washers. Tighten down the bolts using a torque wrench set to read between 34 - 36 lb ft (4.7 - 4.8 kg m).

48 Using a dial indicator gauge check the crownwheel and pinion backlash which should be between 0.004 - 0.006 inch (0.1016 - 0.1524 mm) to be taken on several teeth throughout the circumference of the crownwheel.

49 Check the meshing of the crownwheel and pinion by smearing engineers blue on the crownwheel and then turning the pinion. The contact mark on the teeth should appear as shown in Fig. 8.7., where it will be seen it is in the middle of the crownwheel teeth. If the mark appears on the toe or on the heel of the crownwheel teeth then shims must be removed from one side of the differential bearings to the other side until the marks are in the correct position.

50 When all is correct, fit a new axle cover joint (75) and replace the axle cover (70) ensuring that it is the correct way up. Refit the cover retaining bolts (69) and spring washers and tighten in a diagonal manner.

51 Refit the rear mounting (65) to the studs on the axle cover and secure in place with the four nyloc nuts (67).

52 Replace the bearing (57) in the bearing retainer (26) making sure it is the correct way round. Using a piece of suitable diameter tube refit the oil seal (27), making sure that the lips are facing inwards. Lubricate the oil seal.

53 Refit the inner axle shaft to the bearing in the bearing retainer. Check that the correct inner axle shaft has been selected as they are of different lengths.

54 Locate the rectangular key in its slot in the inner axle shaft and fit the flange onto the shaft. Replace the plain washer (29), and secure the flange in place with the nyloc nut (30). Repeat this sequence for the second shaft.

55 Reassembly is now complete. Do not forget to fill the unit with 2.5 pints (1.42 litres, 3.0 U.S. pints) of the correct grade oil.

Chapter 9 Braking system

Contents

Specifications

Brake system
Type	Hydraulic, servo assisted on all four wheels
Front	Dual line disc self adjusting
Rear	Dual line, drum
Handbrake	Mechanical, on rear wheels only
Manufacturer	Girling

Front
Disc diameter	10.875 in (27.62 cm)
Lining area	20.7 in^2 (174.2 cm^2)
Swept area	233 in^2 (1483.8 cm^2)
Max. disc runout	0.002 in (0.05 mm)
Min. pad thickness	0.06 - 0.12 in (1.5 - 3 mm)

Rear
Drum diameter	9 in (22.9 cm)
Drum width	1.75 in (4.45 cm)
Lining area	60.5 in^2 (419.3 cm^2)
Swept area	99 in^2 (638.7 cm^2)
Minimum lining thickness	0.06 in (1.52 mm)

General
Total lining area	81.2 in^2 (522.8 cm^2)
Total swept area	332 in^2 (2130 cm^2)
Max. retardation	0.98 G.

Master cylinder
Type	Dual hydraulic tandem
LHD models only	Pressure differential warning actuator (PDWA)
Handbrake	Centrally mounted, mechanically coupled to rear wheels only by twin cables.

Servo unit
Type	Super Vac

TORQUE WRENCH SETTINGS
	lb ft	Kg m
Brake servo attachment	12 - 14	1.66 - 1.94
Brake limiting valve to body	8 - 10	1.11 - 1.38
Brake master cylinder to servo	20 - 22	2.77 - 3.04
Brake and clutch pedal box and clutch master cylinder bracket attachment	6 - 8	0.38 - 1.11
Brake and clutch pedal shaft cover attachment	16 - 18	2.21 - 2.49

1 General description

Disc brakes are fitted to the front wheels and drum brakes to the rear. All are operated under servo assistance from the brake pedal, this being connected to the master cylinder and servo assembly mounted on the bulkhead.

The hydraulic system is of the dual line principle whereby the front disc brake calipers have a separate hydraulic system to the rear drum brake wheel cylinders so that if failure of the hydraulic pipes to the front or rear brakes occurs half the braking system is still operative. Servo assistance in this condition is still available.

The front brake disc is secured to the hub flange and the caliper mounted on the front suspension vertical link, so that the disc is able to rotate in between the two halves of the caliper. Inside each half of the caliper is a hydraulic cylinder this being interconnected by a drilling which allows hydraulic fluid pressure to be transmitted to both halves. A piston operates in each cylinder, and is in contact with the outer face of the pad. By depressing the brake pedal, hydraulic fluid pressure is increased by the servo unit and transmitted to the caliper by a system of metal pipes and flexible hoses wherefore the pistons are moved outwards so pushing the pads onto the face of the disc so slowing down the rotational speed of the disc.

The rear brakes have one cylinder operating two shoes. When the brake pedal is depressed hydraulic fluid pressure, increased by the servo unit, is transmitted to the rear brake wheel cylinders by a system of metal and flexible pipes. The pressure moves the pistons outwards so pushing the shoe linings into contact with the inside circumference of the brake drum and slowing the rotational speed of the drum.

The handbrake provides an independent means of rear brake application.

On left hand drive models both systems are corrected to opposing sides of a Pressure Differential Warning Actuator which operates an electrical switch when a pressure drop on one side of the valve causes a shuttle to move from its mid position. The P.D.W.A. switch operates a warning light on the facia which is connected in series/parallel with the oil warning light. When the brakes are operating correctly, the brake warning light and the oil warning light are both extinguished as the engine speed is increased from idle. In the event of a partial failure the brake warning system is earthed directly, causing the warning light to glow brightly.

2 Bleeding the hydraulic system

1 Removal of all the air from the hydraulic system is essential to the correct operation of the braking system, and before undertaking this, examine the fluid reservoir cap to ensure that the vent hole is clear. Check the level of fluid in the reservoir and top up if required.
2 Check all brake line unions and connections for possible seepage, and at the same time check the condition of the rubber hoses which could be perished.
3 If the condition of the caliper or wheel cylinders is in doubt, check for possible signs of fluid leakage.
4 If there is any possibility that incorrect fluid has been used in the system, drain all the fluid out and flush through with methylated spirits. Renew all piston seals and cups since they will be affected and could possibly fail under pressure.
5 Gather together a clean glass jar, a 12 in length of tubing which fits tightly over the bleed screws and a tin of the correct brake fluid.
6 To bleed the system, clean the area around the bleed valves and remove the rubber cup from one of the bleed screws.
7 Place the end of the tube in the clean jar which should contain sufficient fluid to keep the end of the tube underneath during the operation.
8 Open the bleed screw ¼ turn with a spanner and depress the brake pedal. After slowly releasing the pedal, pause for a

moment to allow the fluid to recoup in the master cylinder and then depress again. This will force air from the system. Continue until no more air bubbles can be seen coming from the tube. At intervals make certain that the reservoir is kept topped up, otherwise air will enter at this point again.
9 Finally press the pedal down fully and hold it there whilst the bleed screw is tightened. To ensure correct seating it should be tightened to a torque wrench setting of 5 - 7 lb f ft (0.70 - 1.0 Kg Fm).
10 Repeat this operation for the remaining three bleed screws. Do not operate the brake pedal between bleed sessions otherwise the P D W A valve (if fitted) will require resetting.
11 When completed check the level of the fluid in the reservoir and then check the feed of the brake pedal, which should be firm and free from any 'spongy' action, which is normally associated with air in the system.
12 It will be noticed that during the bleeding operation the effort required to press the pedal the full stroke will increase because of the loss of vacuum assistance as it is destroyed by repeated operation of the servo unit. Although the servo will be inoperative as far as assistance is concerned it does not affect the brake bleed operation.
13 If one caliper or wheel cylinder only has been detached and providing the reservoir level has been kept topped up it should only be necessary to bleed either the front half or rear half of the hydraulic system.

3 P D W A piston re-centralisation

Should it be necessary to centralise the shuttle in the P D W A proceed as follows:
1 Fit the bleed tube to a brake bleed screw at the opposite end of the car to that which has just been bled.
2 Open the bleed screw. Switch on the ignition but do not start the engine. - The brake warning light will glow but the oil warning light will remain off.
3 Depress the brake pedal slowly but evenly until the brake light dims and the oil light glows. At this condition a click should be felt on the pedal as the shuttle returns to its mid position. Retighten the bleed screw.
4 Should the brake pedal be pushed too hard the shuttle will move to the other side of the valve, thus requiring the procedure to be repeated on a brake at the opposite end of the car.

4 Flexible hose - inspection, removal and replacement

1 Inspect the condition of the flexible hydraulic hoses leading from the chassis mounted metal pipes to the brake backplates. If any are swollen, damaged, cut or chafed they must be renewed.
2 Unscrew the metal pipe union nut from its connection to the hose and then holding the hexagon on the hose with a spanner, unscrew the attachment nut and washer.
3 The chassis end of the hose can now be pulled from the chassis mounting bracket and will be quite free.
4 Disconnect the flexible hydraulic hose at the backplate by unscrewing it from the brake cylinder. NOTE when releasing the hose from the backplate the chassis end must always be freed first.
5 Replacement is a straightforward reversal of the above procedure.

5 Rear brakes - adjustment

1 Place chocks on the front wheels, jack up the rear of the car and place on firm axle stands.
2 Release the handbrake and firmly depress the brake pedal several times so that the shoes and wheel cylinder are centralised relative to the brake drum.
3 It is not necessary to remove the rear wheels as the small headed adjuster will be found on the rear of each backplate.

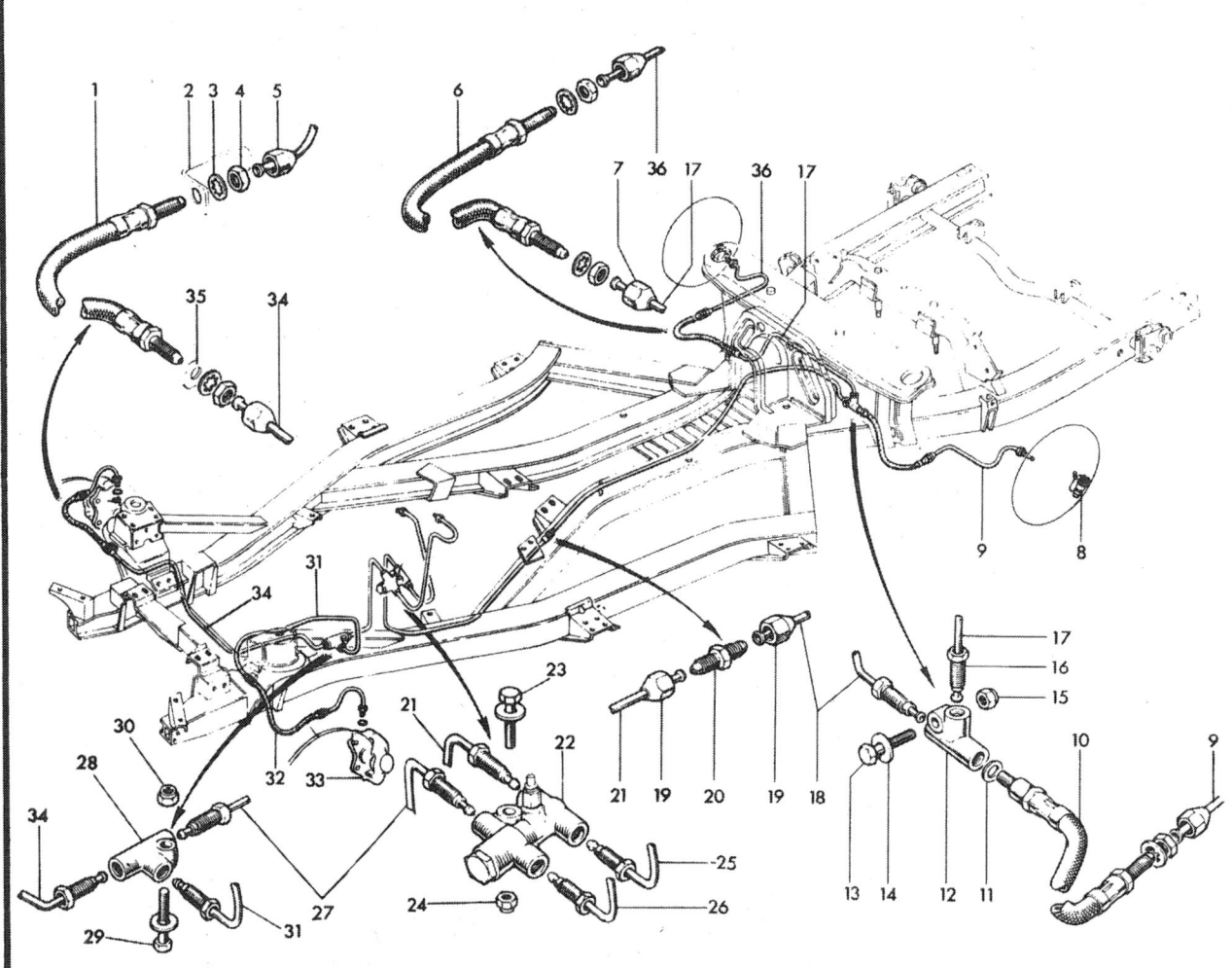

FIG. 9.1. BRAKE HYDRAULIC PIPE LAYOUT

1 Flexible hose - R.H. front	19 Tube nut - female
2 Support bracket - hose to caliper	20 Pipe connector
3 Shakeproof washer	21 Pipe - P.D.W.A. to connector)
4 Nut	22 Pressure differential warning actuator)
5 Tube nut - female	23 Bolt) LHD
6 Flexible hose - R.H. rear	24 Nyloc nut) vehicles
7 Tube nut - female	25 Pipe - P.D.W.A. to master cylinder) only
8 Wheel cylinder	26 Pipe - P.D.W.A. to master cylinder)
9 Pipe - hose to rear cylinder	27 Pipe - P.D.W.A. front three-way)
10 Flexible hose - L. H. rear	28 Three-way connector - front
11 Copper washer	29 Bolt
12 Three-way union	30 Nyloc nut
13 Bolt	31 Pipe - three way to L.H. front hose
14 Washer	32 Flexible hose - L.H. front
15 Nut	33 Disc brake caliper - L.H. front
16 Tube nut - male	34 Pipe - three-way to R.H. front hose
17 Pipe - three way to R.H. rear hose	35 Bracket - flexible hose support
18 Pipe - connector to three way	36 Pipe - hose to R.H. rear cylinder

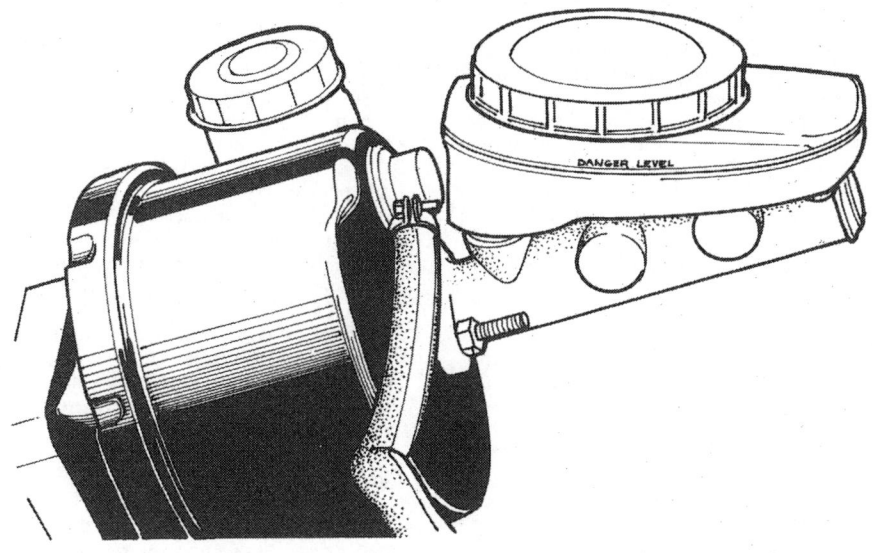

Fig. 9.2. Brake master cylinder minimum fluid level

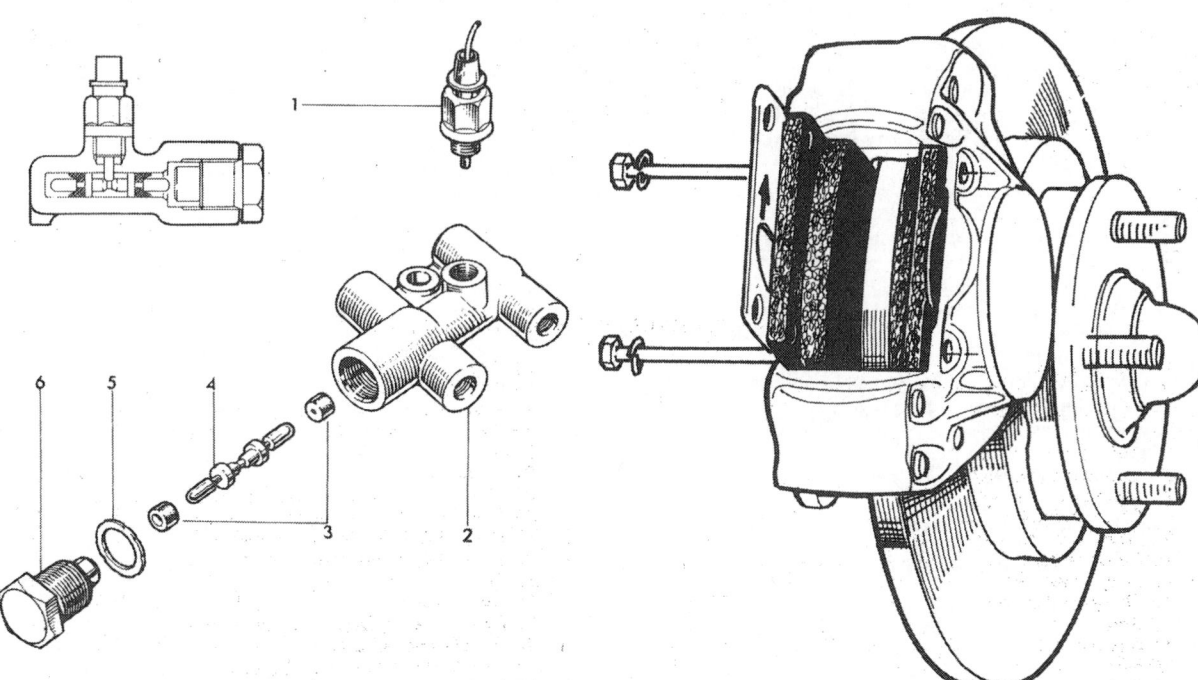

FIG. 9.3. PRESSURE DIFFERENTIAL WARNING ACTUATION COMPONENTS

1	Switch	4	Shuttle valve
2	Body	5	Washer
3	Seal	6	End plug

FIG. 9.4. REMOVAL OF BRAKE PAD

Note: The arrow on the anti squeal shims is pointing in the direction of forward rotation of the road wheel.

4 Soak the adjusters in penetrating oil before adjustment is attempted as the adjusters are very prone to rust.

5 As the edges of the adjusters are easily burred do not use an ordinary spanner, adjustable spanner, wrench or pliers but only use a square headed brake adjusting spanner.

6 Turn the adjuster clockwise a notch at a time until the wheel is locked. Then turn back the adjuster one notch or more so the wheel will rotate without binding.

7 Spin the wheel and apply the brakes hard to centralise the shoe and wheel cylinder or alternatively depress the brake pedal firmly several times.

8 Recheck that it is not possible to turn the adjuster further without locking the shoe.

9 NOTE: A rubbing noise when the wheel is spun is usually due to dust in the brake drum. If there is no obvious slowing of the wheel due to brake binding there is no need to slacken off the adjusters until the noise disappears. Better to remove the drum and blow out the dust.

6 Front brake pad - inspection, removal and refitting

1 Remove the front wheels and inspect the amount of friction material left on the friction pads. The pads must be renewed when the thickness of the material has worn down to 0.06 - 0.12 in (1.5 - 3 mm).

2 Pull out the wire clips which secure the pad retaining pins in place and remove the pins.

3 The friction pads and anti-squeal shims can now be lifted from the caliper.

4 Carefully clean the recesses in the calliper in which the friction pad assemblies lie and the exposed face of each piston from all traces of dirt and rust.

5 Remove the cap from the hydraulic fluid reservoir and place a large rag underneath the unit. Press the pistons in half of the calliper right in; this will cause the fluid level in the reservoir to rise and possibly to spill over the brim onto the protective rag.

6 Fit new pads and refit the anti-squeal shims with the arrow towards the direction of rotation as shown in Fig. 9.4.   Insert the pad retainer pins and secure them with the retainer clips.

7 Front brake caliper - removal, overhaul and refitting

1 Jack up the car, remove the road wheel and disconnect the flexible hydraulic pipe as previously detailed in Section 4.

2 Remove the disc brake friction pads and anti-squeal shims as previously described.

3 Unscrew the two calliper mounting bolts and lockwashers and remove the calliper assembly from the disc.

4 Pull off the dust covers and remove the pistons from the calliper body.

5 Very carefully remove the rubber piston sealing rings from their recesses in the calliper. The pistons, cylinders, and rubbers should be cleaned only with brake fluid.

6 Examine the components carefully, renew the rubbers as a matter of course and replace the pistons if slightly grooved or otherwise worn.

7 Reassembly commences by carefully fitting new piston sealing rings into the recesses in the calliper cylinders.

8 Fit the larger diameter lip of the rubber dust cover to the groove on the outside of the top of the cylinder.

9 Slide the pistons closed end first into the cylinders, with great care, and then fit the outer lip of the dust excluder into the groove in the outer end of the piston.

10 Fit the calliper over the disc, insert the two securing bolts, replace the anti-squeal shims and the pads. Reconnect the flexible brake hose and bleed the system as described in Section 2.

8 Disc and hub - removal and replacement

1 Jack up the front of the car and place on axle stands. Chock the rear wheels and apply the handbrake firmly.

2 Remove the road wheel on whichever side the disc and hub are to be serviced.

3 The grease cap, or sometimes called the dust cover, is a very tight fit and is removed by levering with a screwdriver or tapping the flange with a hammer.

4 Extract the split pin from the castellated nut. Undo the castellated nut and remove the nut followed by the washer. If a grease nipple is fitted to the end of the stub axle this should next be removed.

5 Undo the two calliper retaining bolts securing the calliper to the vertical swivel link of the front suspension and carefully lift away from the disc. Hang the calliper out of the way using a piece of wire or string. Remember not to depress the brake pedal as otherwise the pistons could be ejected.

6 Withdraw the hub and disc assembly from the stub axle. If this is difficult to remove use a 2 or 3 leg universal puller as sometimes it can be a tight fit.

7 Before separating the disc and hub, make an alignment mark so an indentical position can be regained upon reassembly.

8 To free the brake disc from the hub undo the four bolts and spring washers and separate the two parts.

9 Inspect the discs for signs of excessive scoring and, if evident, the discs may be reground but no more than a maximum total of 0.060 in (1.524 mm) may be removed from the disc. The desirable finish should be 32 micro in. maximum when measured circumferentially and 50 micro in. when measured radially.

10 Refitting is the reverse sequence to removal. The hub will require adjusting as detailed in Chapter 11.

11 Measure the run out at the outer periphery of the disc by means of a feeler gauge positioned between the inside of the calliper and the disc. If the run out on the friction faces of the disc exceeds 0.002 in (0.0508 mm) remove the disc and reposition it on the hub casing. If the run out is really bad the disc is probably distorted due to overheating and a new one should be fitted.

9 Drum brake shoe - inspection, removal and replacement

1 After high mileages it will be necessary to fit replacement brake shoes with new linings. Refitting new brake linings to old shoes is not always satisfactory but if the services of a local garage or workshop with brake lining equipment are available, then there is no reason why your own shoes should not be successfully relined.

2 Remove the hub cap, loosen off the wheel nuts, then securely jack up the car and remove the road wheel. Ensure the handbrake is off. Where wire wheels are fitted, knock off the hub nut and remove the wheel.

3 Completely slacken off the brake adjustment and take out the two setscrews which hold the drum in place.

4 Remove the brake drum. If it proves obstinate tap the rim gently with a soft headed hammer. The shoes are now exposed for inspection.

5 The brake linings should be renewed if they are so worn that the rivet heads are flush with the surface of the lining. If bonded linings are fitted they must be removed when the material has worn down to 0.06 in (1.52 mm) at its thinnest point. If the shoes are being removed to give access to the wheel cylinders then cover the linings with masking tape to prevent any possibility of their becoming contaminated with grease.

6 Press in each brake shoe steady pin securing washer against the pressure of its spring.

7 Turn the head of the washer 90° so the slot will clear the securing bar on the steady pin and remove the spring and washer. On later models withdraw the pin spring clip.

8 Detach the shoes and return springs by pulling one end of the shoes away from the slot in the closed end of one of the brake

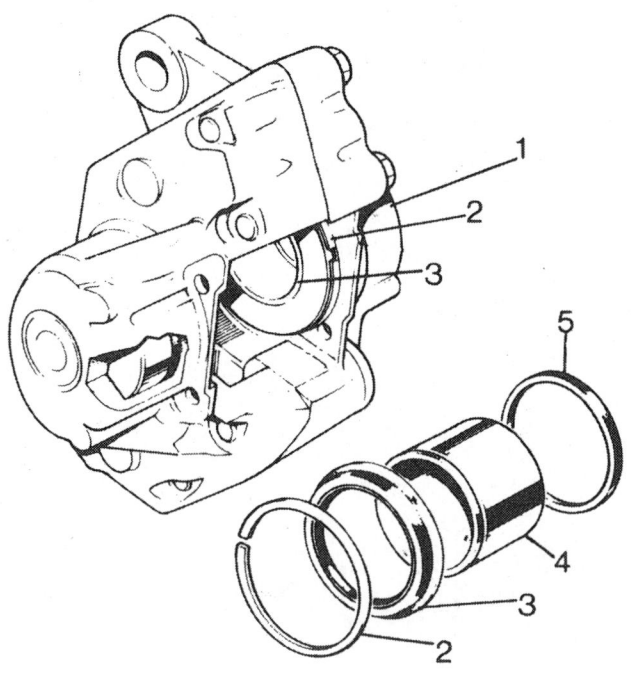

FIG. 9.5. FRONT DISC BRAKE CALIPER PISTON ASSEMBLY

1 Caliper
2 Circlip
3 Dust cover

4 Piston
5 Sealing ring

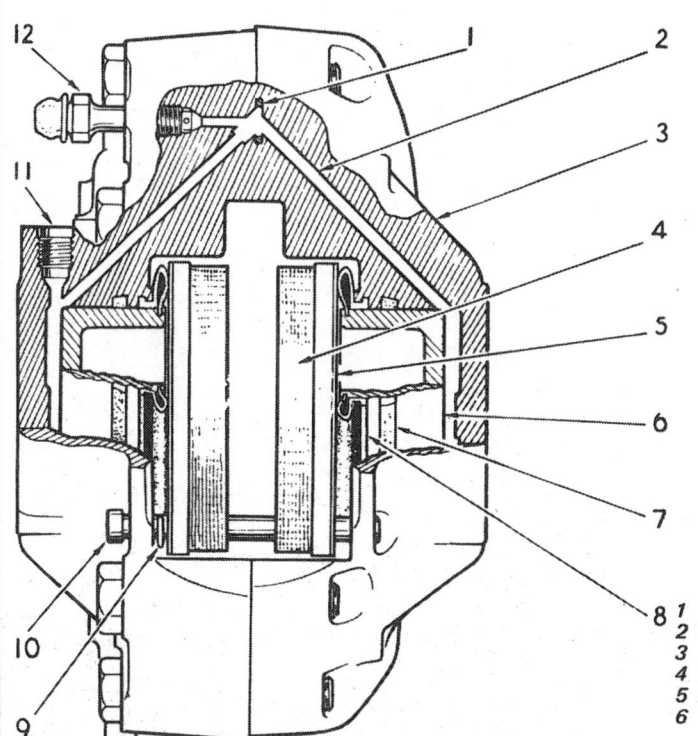

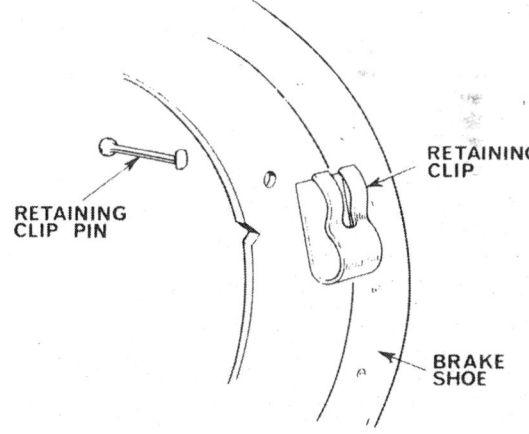

Fig. 9.7. Modified brake shoe retaining pin and clip

RETAINING CLIP PIN

RETAINING CLIP

BRAKE SHOE

FIG. 9.6. DISC BRAKE CALIPER CROSS SECTION

1 Rubber 'O' ring
2 Fluid transfer channels
3 Caliper body
4 Friction pad
5 Anti-squeal shim
6 Piston

7 Piston sealing ring
8 Dust cover
9 Retaining clip
10 Retaining pin
11 Flexible hose connection
12 Bleed nipple

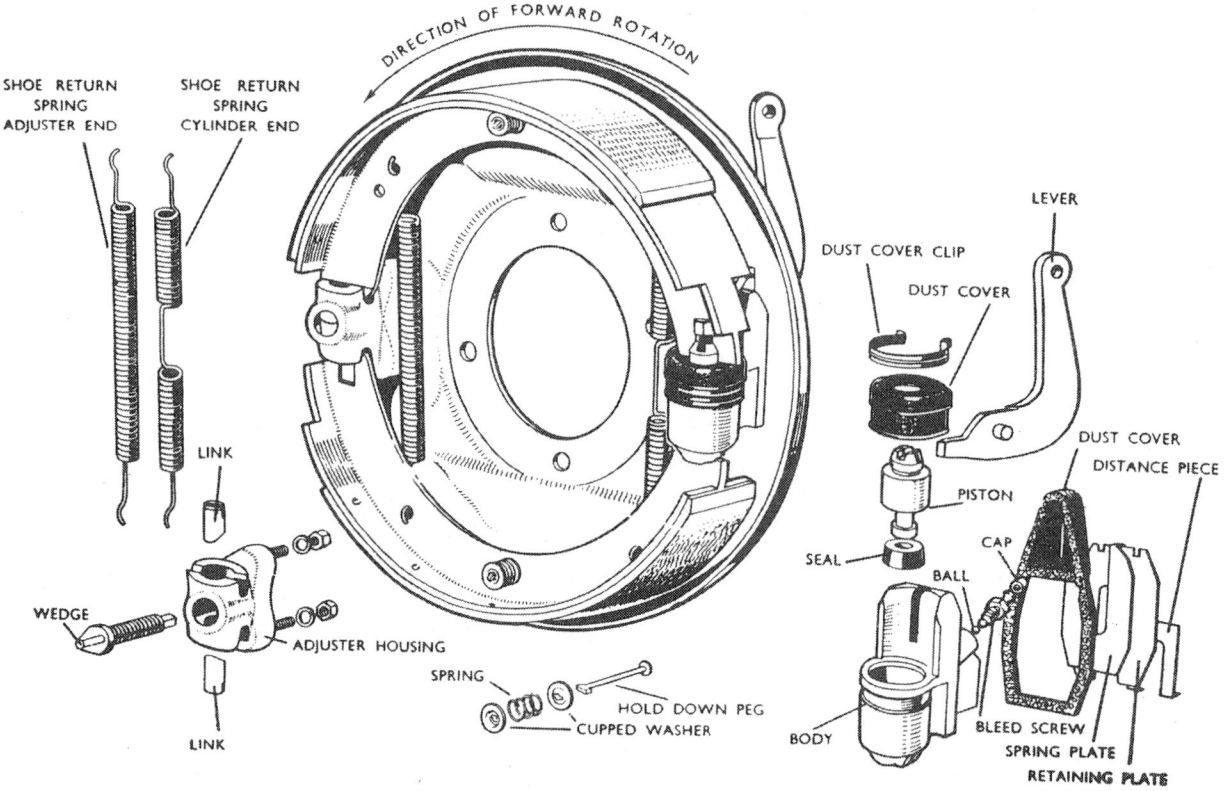

Fig. 9.8. Rear drum brake components

cylinders.

9 Disengage the brake shoe from the return spring carefully noting the holes into which the spring fits and then remove the remaining shoes in similar fashion. Place rubber bands over the wheel cylinders to prevent any possibility of the pistons dropping out.

10 Thoroughly clean all traces of dust from the shoes, backplates and brake drums with a dry paint brush and compressed air, if available. Brake dust can cause squeal and judder and it is therefore important to clean out the brakes thoroughly.

11 Check that the pistons are free in their cylinders and that the rubber dust covers are undamaged and in position and that there are no hydraulic fluid leaks.

12 Prior to reassembly smear a trace of white brake grease to all sliding surfaces. The shoes should be quite free to slide on the closed end of the cylinder and the piston anchorage point. It is vital that no grease or oil come into contact with the brake drums or the brake linings.

13 Replacement is a straightforward reversal of the removal procedure but note the following points:-

a) Check that when the adjusters are replaced they are backed right off.

b) Do not omit to fit the steady pins and inner and outer washers if they were removed (early models).

c) Ensure that the return springs are in their correct holes in the shoes and lie between them and the backplate.

10 Drum brake wheel cylinder seals - inspection and overhaul

1 If hydraulic fluid is leaking from one of the brake cylinders it will be necessary to dismantle the cylinder and replace the dust cover and piston sealing rubber. If brake fluid is found running down the side of the wheel, or it is noticed that a pool of liquid forms alongside one wheel and the level in the master cylinder has dropped, and the hoses are all in good order, proceed as follows.

2 Remove the brake drums and shoes as described earlier in this Chapter in Section 9.

3 Ensure that all the other wheels and the other brake drum is in place. Remove the dust cover clip and lift away the cover from the wheel cylinder. Disconnect the handbrake lever.

4 Using a screwdriver carefully prise apart the wheel cylinder retaining plate and the spring plate. Gently tap the retaining plate out from beneath the neck of the cylinder. Lift away the dust cover from the rear of the wheel cylinder and pull the wheel cylinder through the backplate towards the front.

5 Slowly depress the brake pedal so as to eject the piston with the seal attached.

6 Place a quantity of rag under the backplate or a tray to catch the hydraulic fluid as it pours out of the cylinder.

7 Inspect the inside of the cylinder for score marks caused by impurities in the hydraulic fluid. If any are found the cylinder and piston will require renewal together as an exchange assembly.

8 If the cylinder is sound thoroughly clean it out with fresh hydraulic fluid.

9 The old rubber seal will probably be swollen and visibly torn. Smear the new rubber seal with hydraulic fluid and reassemble the seal to the piston with the cup towards the closed end of the wheel cylinder. Insert the piston and seal assembly into the wheel cylinder and then the rubber dust cover and its clip.

10 Refit the wheel cylinder to the backplate in the reverse sequence to removal.

11 Replenish the brake fluid, replace the brake shoes and brake drum and bleed the hydraulic system as previously described.

11 Brake master cylinder - removal and replacement

The tandem master cylinder comprises two independent cylinders, one known as the primary is connected to the front

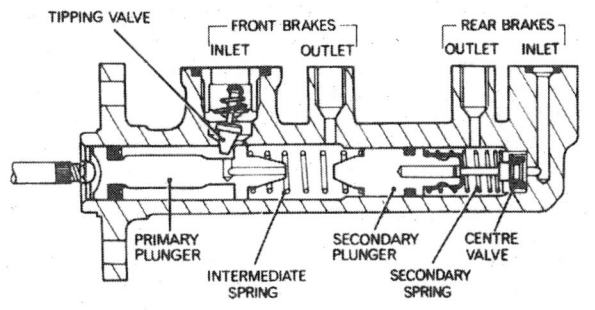

Fig. 9.9. Brake master cylinder operation

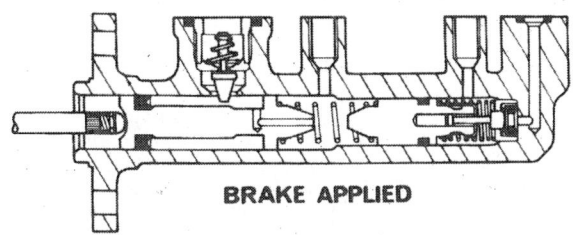

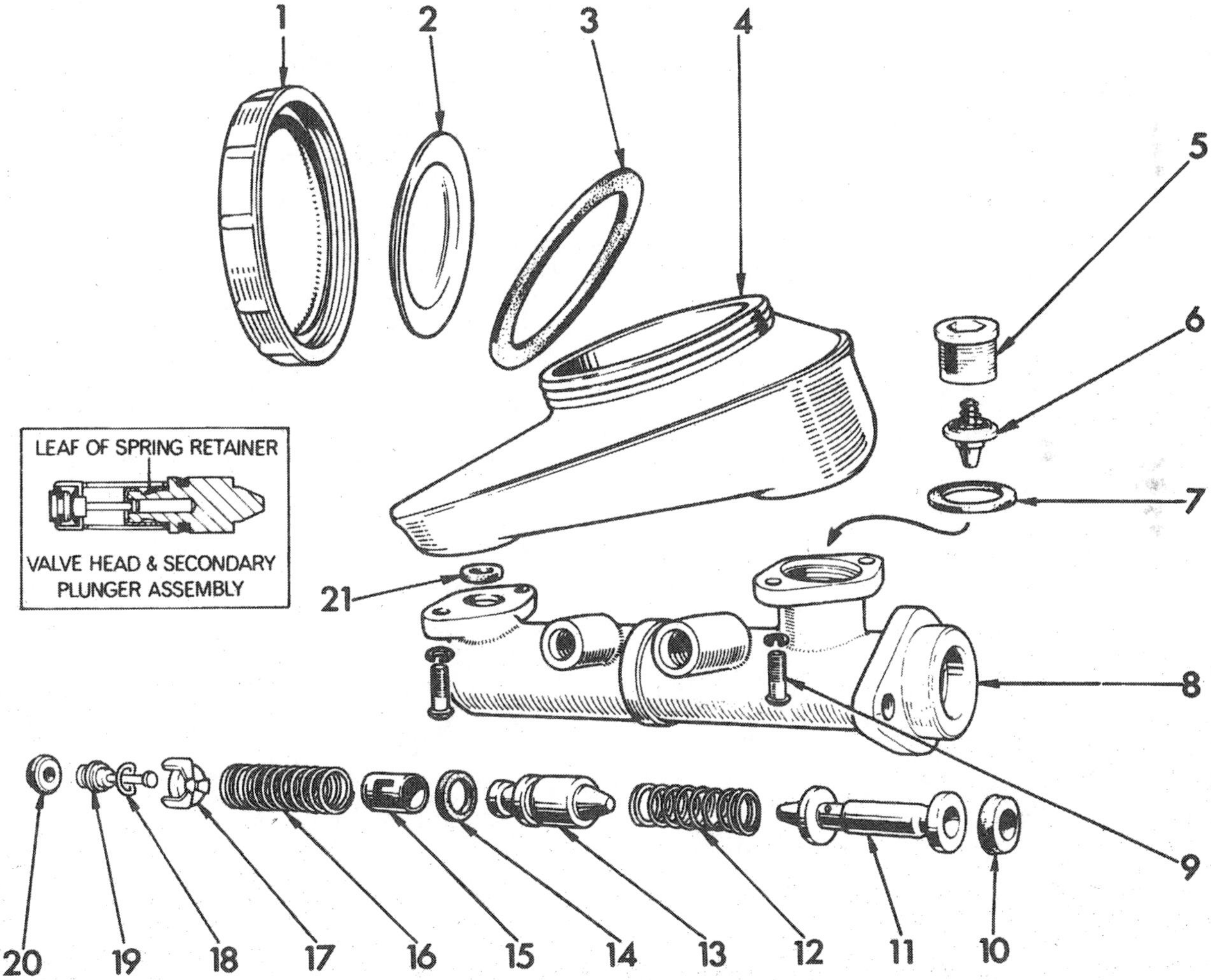

FIG. 9.10. MASTER CYLINDER COMPONENTS

1 Cap	6 Tipping valve	11 Primary plunger	16 Secondary spring
2 Baffle plate	7 Seal - reservoir to body	12 Intermediate spring	17 Valve spacer
3 Seal	8 Body	13 Secondary plunger	18 Spring washer
4 Reservoir	9 Screw - reservoir to body	14 Seal	19 Valve
5 Tipping valve securing nut	10 Seal	15 Spring retainer	20 Seal
			21 Seal - reservoir to body

disc brakes, and the other known as secondary is connected to the rear drum brakes. By having this arrangement, should one system fail the second system will usually be operative.

The combined operation comes into effect when the brake pedal is depressed and the servo pushrod moves the primary plunger up its bore and the tipping valve closes the primary supply port. Once closed any further movement of the servo pushrod applies pressure to the front brakes. Simultaneously this pressure, together with the increasing pressure of the intermediate spring, overcomes the secondary spring and the secondary plunger moves down the bore. As with the primary plunger, first movement closes the secondary supply port and hydraulic pressure is transmitted to the rear drum brakes via the hydraulic pipes.

To remove the master cylinder proceed as follows:

1 Apply the handbrake and chock the front wheels. Slacken the bleed screw on one of the rear wheel cylinder bleed screws and drain the hydraulic master cylinder secondary bore and reservoir fluid. Slacken the front wheel caliper bleed screw and drain hydraulic fluid from the master cylinder primary bore.

2 Wipe the master cylinder hydraulic pipe connections with a clean non-fluffy rag and disconnect the unions. Wrap the end in a piece of clean rag around the unions to stop dirt ingress or fluid dripping onto the paintwork. Plug the master cylinder union connections to stop accidental dirt entering into the master cylinders.

3 Remove the two master cylinder to servo unit mounting nuts, lift away the spring washers and withdraw the master cylinder.

4 The master cylinder refitting procedure is the reverse to removal. Bleed the complete hydraulic system and road test the car to check for satisfactory operation.

12 Brake master cylinder - dismantling and reassembly

Before dismantling make sure that the correct overhaul kit has been obtained by quoting the car commission number. Master cylinders have been fitted with different volume ratio and the parts are not interchangeable

1 Remove the two screws holding the reservoir to the cylinder body. Lift away the reservoir. Using a suitable size Allen key or wrench unscrew tipping valve nut and lift away the seal. Using a suitable diameter rod push the primary plunger down the bore., this operation enabling the tipping valve to be withdrawn.

2 Using a compressed air jet very carefully applied to the rear outlet pipe connection blow out all the master cylinder internal components. Alternatively shake out all the parts. Take care that adequate precautions are taken to ensure all parts are caught as they emerge.

3 Separate the primary and secondary plungers from the intermediate spring. Use the fingers to remove the gland seal from the primary plunger.

4 The secondary plunger assembly should be separated by lifting the thimble leaf over the shouldered end of the plunger. Using the fingers remove the seal from the secondary plunger.

5 Depress the secondary spring allowing the valve stem to slide through the keyhole in the thimble thus releasing the tension on the spring.

6 Detach the valve spacer taking care of the spring washer which will be found located under the valve head.

7 Examine the bore of the cylinder carefully for any signs of scores or ridges, and if this is found to be smooth all over, new seals can be fitted. If there is any doubt of the condition of bore, then a new cylinder must be fitted.

8 If examination of the seals shows them to be apparently oversize or swollen, or very loose on the plungers, suspect oil contamination in the system. Oil will swell these rubber seals, and if one is found to be swollen, it is reasonable to assume that all seals in the braking system will need attention.

9 Thoroughly clean all parts in either Girling Cleansing Fluid or Industrial methylated spirits. Ensure that the by-pass ports are clear.

10 All components should be assembled wet by dipping in clean brake fluid. Using fingers only, fit new seals to the primary and secondary plungers ensuring that they are the correct way round. Place the dished washer with the dome against the underside of the valve seat. Hold it in position with the valve spacer ensuring that the legs face towards the valve seal.

11 Replace the plunger return spring centrally on the spacer, insert the thimble into the spring and depress until the valve stem engages in the keyhole of the thimble.

12 Insert the reduced end of the plunger into the thimble until the thimble engages under the shoulder of the plunger and press home the thimble leaf. Replace the intermediate spring between the primary and secondary plungers.

13 Check that the master cylinder bore is clean and smear with clean brake fluid. With the complete assembly suitably wetted with brake fluid carefully insert the assembly into the bore. Ease the lips of the plunger seals carefully into the bore. Push the assembly fully home.

14 Refit the tipping valve assembly and seal to the cylinder bore and tighten the securing nut to a torque wrench setting of 35 - 45 lb f ft.(4.8 - 6.22 Kg Fm). Replace the hydraulic fluid reservoir and tighten the two retaining screws.

15 The master cylinder is now ready for refitting to the servo unit. Bleed the complete hydraulic system and road test the car.

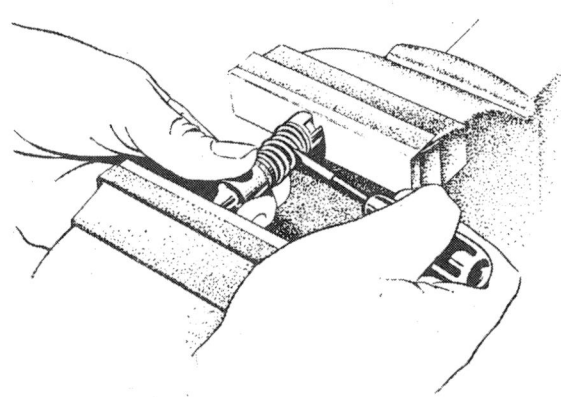

Fig. 9.11. Using screwdriver to press the spring retainer back against the secondary plunger

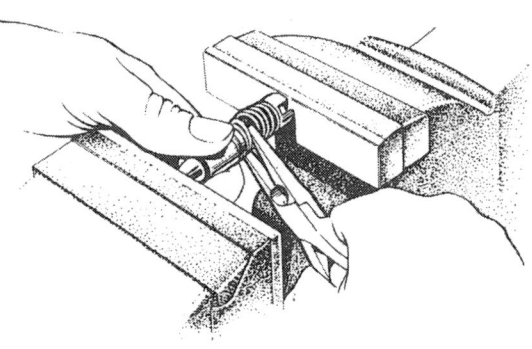

Fig. 9.12. Using pointed pliers to depress the leaf of the spring retainer behind the head of the plunger

13 Handbrake cables - removal, refitting and adjustment

Removal

1 The handbrake cable system is shown in Fig. 9 MM and it will be observed that there are two individual cables which can be separately removed if required.

2 Chock the front wheels, raise the rear of the car and place on firmly based stands.

3 Remove the rear wheels.

4 Undo the eight self tapping screws securing the cardboard cover to the floor panel. Lift away the cover easing it over the handbrake lever assembly.

5 Release the handbrake and pull the outer cable towards the rear and disconnect it from the tunnel mounting by pivoting it forwards and vertically.

6 Lift the ball on the end of the inner cable from its location hole in the top of the compensator.

7 Extract the split pin from the fork end clevis pins, lift away the washer followed by the clevis pin.

8 Undo the nut securing the outer cable holder from its mounting. Lift away the nut followed by the spring washer. Remove the holder and the rubber cover.

9 Withdraw the cable from the underside of the car.

10 Repeat operations 5,6,7,8 and 9 to remove the second cable.

Refitting

1 Refitting is the reverse sequence to removal.

2 Thoroughly grease all cables and pivot points during refitting. Always use new clevis pins if they show signs of wear and also never use a split pin twice.

Adjustment

1 Chock the front wheels, raise the rear of the car and place on firmly based axle stands.

2 Remove the rear wheels and adjust the rear brakes.

3 Undo the eight self tapping screws securing the cardboard cover to the floor panel. Lift away the cover easing it over the handbrake lever assembly.

4 Extract the split pins securing the fork end clevis pin at the handbrake lever on the backplate. Lift away the plain washer followed by the clevis pin. Note that the head of the clevis pin is on top of the fork end.

5 Undo the locknut and screw each fork end along the inner cable so as to bring the compensator lever and the handbrake lever tight when pulled onto the fifth notch of the rachet.

6 When this adjustment is obtained tighten the locknuts. Refit the clevis pin with the head uppermost followed by the plain

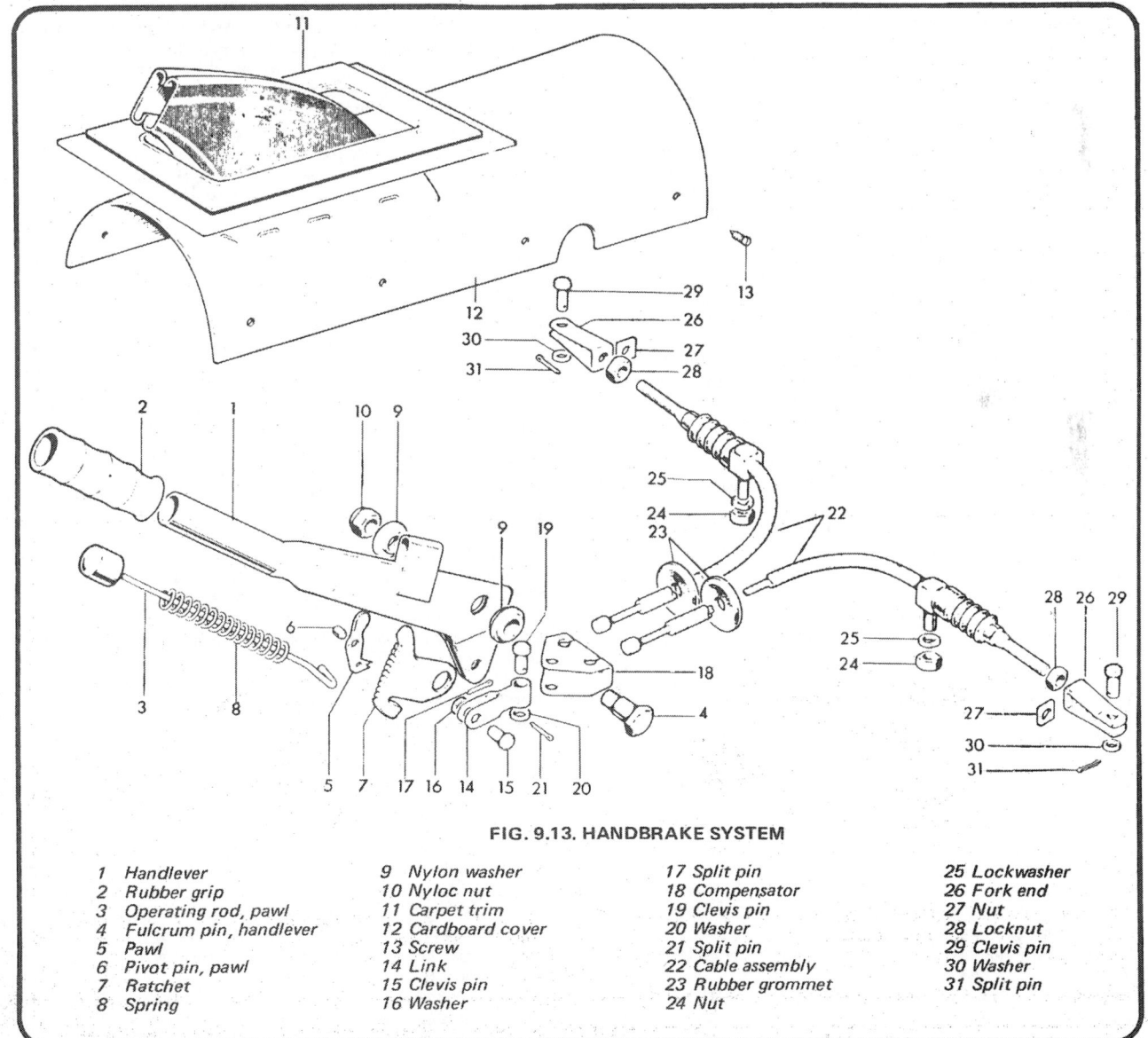

FIG. 9.13. HANDBRAKE SYSTEM

1 Handlever	9 Nylon washer	17 Split pin	25 Lockwasher
2 Rubber grip	10 Nyloc nut	18 Compensator	26 Fork end
3 Operating rod, pawl	11 Carpet trim	19 Clevis pin	27 Nut
4 Fulcrum pin, handlever	12 Cardboard cover	20 Washer	28 Locknut
5 Pawl	13 Screw	21 Split pin	29 Clevis pin
6 Pivot pin, pawl	14 Link	22 Cable assembly	30 Washer
7 Ratchet	15 Clevis pin	23 Rubber grommet	31 Split pin
8 Spring	16 Washer	24 Nut	

washer and a new split pin.

7 Refit the handbrake lever cover assembly and secure with the eight self tapping screws.

8 Replace the road wheel and thoroughly road test.

14 Pressure differential warning actuator - removal, overhaul and refitting

1 Detach the electrical cable connection from the actuator.

2 Wipe the area around the actuator and then disconnect the two inlet and two outlet pipe unions. Plug the open ports to prevent syphoning out of the fluid or dirt ingress.

3 Undo and remove the bolt that secures the actuator to the bulkhead and lift away the unit.

4 Should it be necessary to overhaul the unit it is recommended that due to possible difficulties in obtaining indivdual parts it is far better to obtain a factory reconditioned unit. An exploded view of the components is shown in Fig. 9.3.

5 Refitting the acuator is the reverse sequence to removal. It will be necessary to bleed the brake hydraulic system as described in Section 2 and centralise the P D W A piston as described in Section 3.

15 Vacuum servo unit - general description

The brake vacuum servo unit is fitted into the braking system of a car to make braking easier by reducing the physical effort required by the driver to depress the brake pedal and so bring the car to a halt or slow down from high speed.

The servo unit and hydraulic master cylinder are connected together so that the servo unit piston rod acts as the master cylinder pushrod. The driver's braking effort is transmitted through another pushrod to the servo unit piston and its built in control system. The servo unit piston does not fit tightly into the cylinder but has a strong diaphragm to keep its edges in constant contact with the cylinder walls so assuring an air tight seal between the two pads. The forward chamber is held under vacuum conditions created in the inlet manifold of the engine and, during periods when the brake pedal is not in use, the controls open a passage to the rear chamber so placing it under vacuum conditions as well. When the brake pedal is depressed the vacuum passage to the rear chamber is cut off and the chamber opened to atmospheric pressure. The consequent rush of air pushes the servo piston forward in the vacuum chamber and operates the main pushrod to the master cylinder.

The controls are designed so that assistance is given under all conditions and when the brakes are not required vacuum in the rear chamber is established when the brake pedal is released. All air from the atmosphere entering the rear chamber is passed through a small air filter.

It must be emphasised that if a servo unit requires overhaul it is far better to obtain a service exchange unit rather than to try to repair the original unit if at all possible.

16 Vacuum servo unit - removal and refitting

1 First remove the master cylinder as described in Section 11 of this chapter.

2 Disconnect the vacuum hose from the vacuum servo unit cylinder.

3 Working inside the car extract the split pin from the clevis pin connecting the pushrod fork to the brake pedal. Lift away the washer and clevis pin.

4 Undo the four nuts securing the servo unit to the pedal box, and remove together with their spring and plain washers.

5 Lift away the servo unit and spacer.

6 Refitting is the reverse sequence to removal. Do not forget to reconnect the vacuum pipe.

7 Bleed the hydraulic system as described in Section 2 of this Chapter.

17 Vacuum servo unit - dismantling, inspection and reassembly

Thoroughly clean the outside of the unit using a stiff brush and wipe with a non-fluffy rag. It cannot be too strongly emphasised that cleanliness is important when working on the unit. Before any attempt is made to dismantle refer to Fig. 9.15. where it will be seen two items of equipment are required. Firstly, a base plate must be made similar to the form shown. Without this, and the second item, a lever, it is impossible to dismantle satisfactorily.

To dismantle the unit proceed as follows:-

1 Refer to Fig. 9.15. and using a file or scriber mark a line across the two halves of the unit to act as a datum for alignment.

2 Fit the previously made base plate into a firm vice and attach the unit to the plate using the master cylinder studs as shown in Fig. 9.15.

3 Fit the lever to the four studs on the rear of the servo unit.

4 Use a piece of long rubber hose and connect one end to the adaptor on the engine inlet manifold and the other end to the non-return valve. Start the engine and this will create a vacuum in the unit so drawing the two halves together.

5 Rotate the lever in an anti- clockwise direction until the front shell indentations are in line with the recesses in the rim of the rear shell. Then press the lever assembly down firmly whilst an assistant stops the car engine and quickly removes the vacuum pipe from the inlet manifold connector. Depress the operating rod so as to release the vacuum, whereupon the front and rear halves should part. If necessary use a soft faced hammer and lightly tap the front half to break the bond.

6 Lift away the rear shell followed by the diaphragm return spring, the dust cover, end cap and the filter. Also withdraw the diaphragm. Press down the valve rod and shake out the valve retaining plate, then separate the valve rod assembly from the diaphragm plate.

7 Gently ease the spring washer from the diaphragm plate and withdraw the pushrod and reaction disc.

8 The seal and plate assembly in the end of the front wheel are a press fit. It is recommended that unless the seal is to be renewed they be left in situ.

9 Thoroughly clean all parts in Girling Cleaning Fluid and wipe dry using a non-fluffy rag. Inspect all parts for signs of damage, stripped threads etc., and fit new parts as necessary. All seals should be renewed and for this a 'major' repair kit should be purchased. This kit will also contain two separate greases which must be used as directed and not interchanged.

10 To reassemble first smear the seal and bearing with grease numbered 64949008 and refit the rear shell, positioning it such that the flat face of the seal is towards the bearing. Press into position and refit the retainers.

11 Lightly smear the disc and hydraulic pushrod with grease numbered 64949008. Refit the reaction disc and pushrod to the diaphragm plate and press in the large washer. The small sprag washer supplied in the 'major repair kit' is not required. It is important that the length of the pushrod is not in any way altered and any attempt to move the adjustment bolt will strip the threads. If a new hydraulic pushrod has been required the length will have to be set. Details of this operation are given at the end of this Section.

12 Lightly smear the outer diameter of the diaphragm plateneck and the bearing surfaces of the valve plunger with grease numbered 64949008. Carefully fit the valve rod assembly into the neck of the diaphragm and fix with the retaining plate.

13 Fit the diaphragm into position and also the non-return valve to the front shell. Next smear the seal and plate assembly with grease numbered 64949008 and press into the front shell with the plate facing inwards.

14 Fit the shell to the base plate and the lever to the rear shell. Reconnect the vacuum hose to the non-return valve and the adaptor to the engine's induction manifold. Position the diaphragm return spring in the front shell. Lightly smear the outer bead of the diaphragm with grease numbered 64949009 and locate the diaphragm assembly into the rear shell. Position the

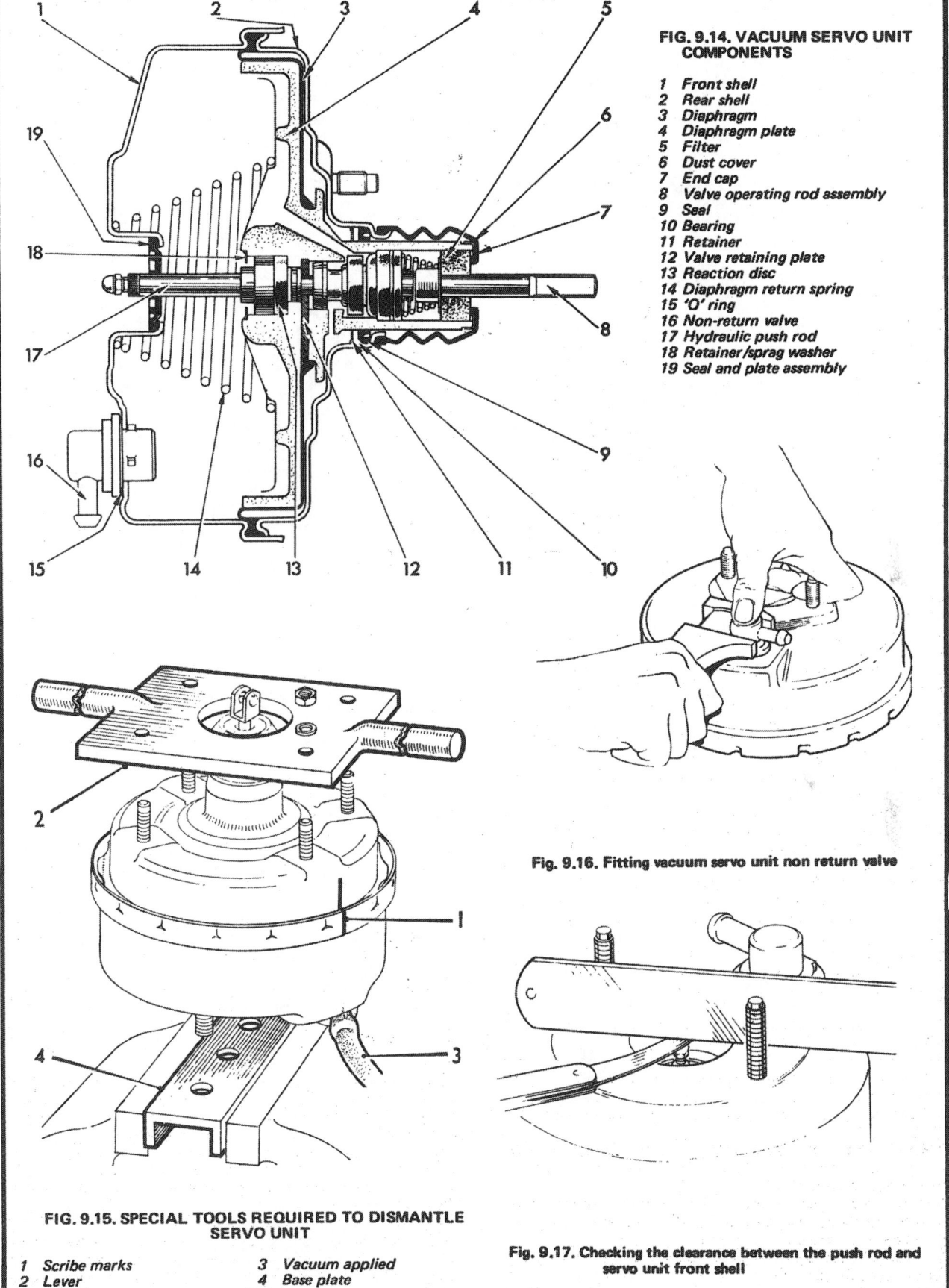

FIG. 9.14. VACUUM SERVO UNIT COMPONENTS

1 Front shell
2 Rear shell
3 Diaphragm
4 Diaphragm plate
5 Filter
6 Dust cover
7 End cap
8 Valve operating rod assembly
9 Seal
10 Bearing
11 Retainer
12 Valve retaining plate
13 Reaction disc
14 Diaphragm return spring
15 'O' ring
16 Non-return valve
17 Hydraulic push rod
18 Retainer/sprag washer
19 Seal and plate assembly

Fig. 9.16. Fitting vacuum servo unit non return valve

FIG. 9.15. SPECIAL TOOLS REQUIRED TO DISMANTLE SERVO UNIT

1 Scribe marks
2 Lever
3 Vacuum applied
4 Base plate

Fig. 9.17. Checking the clearance between the push rod and servo unit front shell

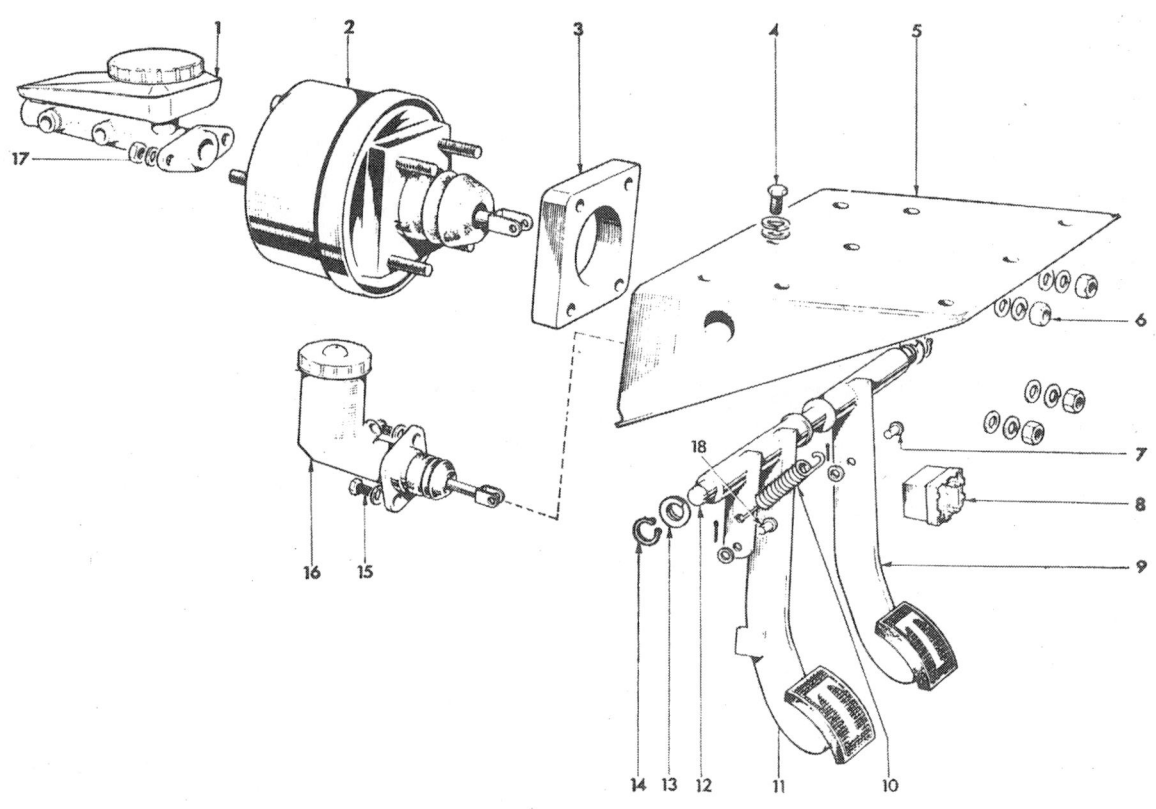

FIG. 9.18. BRAKE PEDAL AND MASTER CYLINDERS LAYOUT

1 Brake master cylinder	5 Pedal box	9 Brake pedal	14 Circlip
2 Servo unit	6 Nut	10 Clutch pedal pull-off spring	15 Bolt
3 Spacer	7 Clevis pin - brake	11 Clutch pedal	16 Clutch master cylinder
4 Bolt	8 Stop light switch	12 Pedal fulcrum shaft	17 Nut
		13 Spring washer	18 Clevis pin - clutch

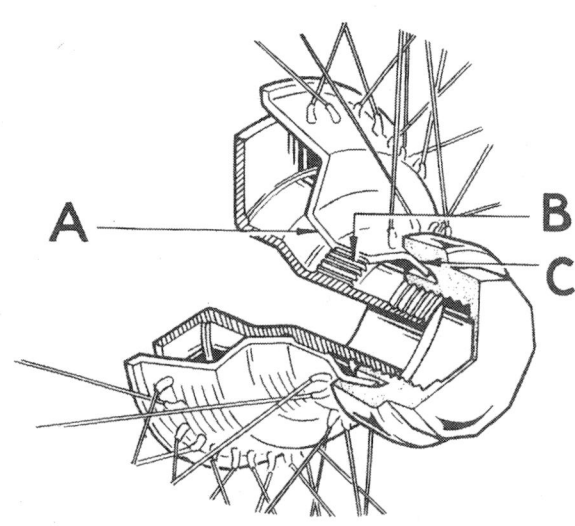

FIG. 9.19. WIRE WHEEL HUB

A Wheel centre pressing   B Spline engagement   C Mating tapers

rear shell assembly on the return spring and line up the previously made scribe marks.

15 The assistant should start the engine. Watching one's fingers very carefully, press the two halves of the unit together and using the lever tool turn clockwise to lock the two halves together. Stop the engine and disconnect the hose.

16 Press a new filter into the neck of the diaphragm plate, refit the end cap and position the dust cover onto the special lugs of the rear shell.

17 Hydraulic pushrod adjustment.

This applies only if a new pushrod has been fitted. It will be seen by referring to Fig. 9.14. hat there is a bolt screwed into the end of the pushrod. The amount of protrusion has to be adjusted in the following manner:-

Remove the bolt and coat the threaded portion with Loctite Grade B. Reconnect the vacuum hose to the adaptor on the inlet valve and non-return valve. Start the engine and screw the prepared bolt into the end of the pushrod. Adjust the position of the bolt head so that it is 0.001 to 0.016 in (0.0254 to 0.4064 mm) below the face of the front shell. Leave the unit for a minimum of twenty four hours to allow the Loctite to set hard.

18 Refit the servo unit to the car as described in the previous section. To test the servo unit for correct operation after overhaul, start the engine and run for a minimum period of two minutes and then switch off. Wait ten minutes and apply the footbrake, very carefully listening to hear the rush of air into the servo unit. This will indicate that vacuum was retained and, therefore, operating correctly.

18 Vacuum servo unit air filter - renewal

To remove the air filter carefully pull back the rubber dust cover and prise off the end cap. Withdraw the new filter diagonally from the outer edge to the centre hole. Push the new filter into the diaphragm plate and retain with the end cap. Replace the rubber dust cover.

19 Brake pedal box - removal and refitting

1   Refer to Section 11 and remove the brake master cylinder.
2   Refer to Section 16 and remove the vacuum servo unit.
3   Refer to Chapter 5 and remove the clutch master cylinder.
4   Disconnect the stop light switch electrical connections.
5   Undo and remove the nine bolts, spring and plain washers located on the top of the bulkhead panel. Lift away the pedal box assembly.
6   To dismantle the assembly first detach the clutch pedal return spring. Next remove the stop light switch.
7   Release the circlip from one end of the fulcrum shaft and withdraw the fulcrum shaft.
8   Reassembly and refitting of the brake pedal box is the reverse sequence to removal.

20 Fault finding - Braking system

Symptom	Reason/s	Remedy
PEDAL TRAVELS ALMOST TO FLOOR BEFORE BRAKES OPERATE		
Leaks and air bubbles in hydraulic system	Brake fluid level too low	Top up master cylinder reservoir. Check for leaks.
	Wheel cylinder or caliper leaking	Dismantle wheel cylinder or caliper, clean, fit new rubbers and bleed brakes.
	Master cylinder leaking (bubbles in master cylinder fluid)	Dismantle master cylinder, clean and fit new rubbers. Bleed brakes.
	Brake flexible hose leaking	Examine and fit new hose if old hose leaking. Bleed brakes.
	Brake line fractured	Replace with new brake pipe. Bleed brakes.
	Brake system unions loose	Check all unions in brake system and tighten as necessary. Bleed brakes.
Normal wear	Linings over 75% worn	Fit replacement shoes and brake linings.
	Brakes badly out of adjustment	Jack up car and adjust brakes.
BRAKE PEDAL FEELS SPRINGY		
Brake lining renewal	New linings not yet bedded-in	Use brakes gently until springy pedal feeling leaves.
Excessive wear or damage	Brake drums badly worn and weak or cracked	Fit new brake drums.
Lack of maintenance	Master cylinder securing nuts loose	Tighten master cylinder securing nuts. Ensure spring washers are fitted.
BRAKE PEDAL FEELS SPONGY AND SOGGY		
Leaks or bubbles in hydraulic system	Wheel cylinder or caliper leaking	Dismantle wheel cylinder or caliper, clean, fit new rubbers and bleed brakes.
	Master cylinder leaking (bubbles in master cylinder reservoir)	Dismantle master cylinder, clean, and fit new rubbers and bleed brakes. Replace cylinder if internal walls scored.
	Brake pipe line or flexible hose leaking	Fit new pipeline or hose.
	Unions in brake system loose	Examine for leaks, tighten as necessary.
EXCESSIVE EFFORT REQUIRED TO BRAKE CAR		
Lining type or condition	Linings badly worn	Fit replacement brake shoes and linings.
	New linings recently fitted - not yet bedded-in	Use brakes gently until braking effort normal.
	Harder linings fitted than standard causing increase in pedal pressure.	Remove linings and replace with normal units.

Oil or grease leaks	Linings and brake drums or discs contaminated with oil, grease, or hydraulic fluid	Rectify source of leak, clean brake drums, fit new linings.

BRAKES UNEVEN AND PULLING TO ONE SIDE

Oil or grease leaks	Linings and brake drums or discs contaminated with oil, grease or hydraulic fluid	Ascertain and rectify source of leak, clean brake drums or discs, fit new linings.
Lack of maintenance	Tyre pressures unequal	Check and inflate as necessary.
	Radial ply tyres fitted at one end of car only.	Fit radial ply tyres of the same make to all four wheels.
	Brake backplate loose	Tighten backplate securing nuts and bolts.
	Brake shoes fitted incorrectly	Remove and fit shoes correct way round.
	Different type of linings fitted at each wheel	Fit the linings specified by the manufacturers all round.
	Anchorages for front or rear suspension loose	Tighten front and rear suspension pick-up points.
	Brake drums or discs badly worn, cracked or distorted	Fit new brake drums or discs.

BRAKES TEND TO BIND, DRAG, OR LOCK-ON

Incorrect adjustment	Brake shoes adjusted too tightly	Slacken off brake shoe adjusters two clicks.
	Handbrake cable over-tightened	Slacken off handbrake cable adjustment.
Wear or dirt in hydraulic system or incorrect fluid.	Reservoir vent hole in cap blocked with dirt	Clean and blow through hole.
	Master cylinder by-pass port restricted - brakes seize in 'on' operation	Dismantle, clean and overhaul master cylinder. Bleed brakes.
	Wheel cylinder or caliper seizes in 'on' position	Dismantle, clean and overhaul wheel cylinder or caliper. Bleed brakes.
Mechanical wear	Brake shoe pull off springs broken, stretched or loose	Examine springs and replace if worn or loose.
Incorrect brake assembly	Brake shoe pull off springs fitted wrong way round, omitted, or wrong type used	Examine and rectify as appropriate.
Neglect	Handbrake system rusted or seized in the 'on' position	Apply 'Plus Gas' to free, clean and lubricate.

Chapter 10 Electrical system

Contents

Specifications

Battery

Type	Lucas lead acid 12 volt
Model ... ..., ...	BT9A
Earthed terminal	Negative
Capacity at 20 hour rate (ampere hours)	57
Plates per cell	9
Normal charge rate	5 amps
Electrolyte to fill one cell	0.75 pint (0.426 litre, 0.901 US pints)

Alternator

Type ... ..., ...	Lucas 15AC
Nominal output	28 amperes
Control unit ... ..., ...	Lucas 4TR

Starter motor (inertia type)

Type	M35G
Construction	Four pole, four brush, series wound
Brush spring tension	34.0 ounces
Minimum brush length	0.406 in (10.319 mm)

Starter motor (pre-engaged type)

Type	Lucas M418G
Brush spring tension	36 ounces
Minimum brush length	0.3125 in (7.9375 mm)

Windscreen washer pump

Type	Lucas screenjet 5SJ
Maximum running current	2 amps
Brush length (minimum)	0.0625 in (1.587 mm)
Container capacity	1 litre (1.76 pint)

Windscreen wiper motor

Type	Lucas 14W
Armature end float	0.002 - 0.008 in (0.508 - 0.2032 mm)
Brush length (minimum)	0.1875 in (4.7625 mm)
Brush tension	5 - 7 ounces (141.747 - 198.446 mm)

Flasher unit

Type	Lucas 8FL
Rating	4.1 amp
Flasher per minute	60 - 120

Hazard warning system

Manufacturer	Signal - stat (made in Brooklyn, New York, USA. available through Lucas dealers).
Flashes per minute	60 - 120
Total bulb load	94.2 watts

Hazard relay

Manufacturer	Lucas 6RA

Brake pressure differential warning actuator assembly

Manufacturer	Lockheed
Operating pressure	150 - 200 lb/sq in (10.5 - 14.1 Kg/ sq. cm)

Oil pressure switch

Manufacturer	AC or Smiths
Operating pressure	3 - 5 lb/sq in (0.21 - 0.35 Kg/ sq. cm)

Fuse unit

Type	Lucas
Rating	35 amp
Fuse rating	35 amp
Number of fuses	4

Overdrive relay

Type	Lucas 6RA

Bulbs

Description	Rating
Headlights	
LH Dip	60/45
RH Dip (normal)	45/40
USA	50/40
Front direction indicator	21
Front side lights	6
Direction indicator repeater	5
Stop/tail	6/21
Rear direction indicator	21
Reverse lights	21
Number plate lights	6
Instrument illumination	2.2
Warning lights	2.2
Rear marker light	5

1 General description

The electrical system is of the 12 volt negative earth type and the major components comprise a 12 volt battery of which the negative terminal is earthed, an alternator which is driven from the crankshaft pulley and a starter motor.

The battery supplies a steady amount of current for the ignition, lighting and other electrical circuits and provides a reserve of electricity when the current consumed by the electrical equipment exceeds that being produced by the alternator.

The alternator has its own integral regulator which ensures a high output if the battery is in a low state of charge or the demand from the electrical equipment is high, and a low output if the battery is fully charged and there is little demand for the electrical equipment.

When fitting electrical accessories to cars with a negative earth system it is important, if they contain silicone diodes or transistors, that they are connected correctly, otherwise serious damage may result to the components concerned. Items such as radios, tape recoders, electronic ignition systems, automatic headlight dipping etc., should all be checked for correct polarity.

It is important that the battery positive lead is always disconnected if the battery is to be boost charged. Also if body repairs are to be carried out using electric arc welding equipment, the alternator must be disconnected otherwise serious damage can be caused to the more delicate instruments. Whenever the battery has to be disconnected it must always be reconnected with the negative terminal earthed.

2 Battery - removal and replacement

1 The battery is on a carrier fitted to the rear of the engine compartment. It should be removed once every three months for cleaning and testing. Disconnect the negative and the positive leads from the battery terminals by slackening the clamp bolts and lifting away the clamps.
2 Undo the clamp bar securing nuts and lift the clamp bar from the top edge of the battery. Carefully lift the battery from its carrier and hold it vertically to ensure that none of the electrolyte is spilled.
3 Replacement is a direct reversal of the removal procedure. Smear the terminals and clamps with vaseline to prevent corrosion. NEVER use an ordinary grease.

3 Battery - maintenance and inspection

1 Normal weekly battery maintenance consists of checking the electrolyte level of each cell to ensure that the separators are covered by ¼ inch of electrolyte. If the level has fallen top up the battery using distilled water only. Do not overfill. If a battery is overfilled or any electrolyte spilled, immediately wipe away the excess as electrolyte attacks and corrodes any metal it comes into contact with very rapidly.
2 As well as keeping the terminals clean and covered with petroleum jelly, the top of the battery, and especially the top of the cells, should be kept clean and dry. This helps to prevent corrosion and ensures that the battery does not become partially discharged by leakage through dampness and dirt.
3 Once every three months remove the battery and inspect the battery securing bolts, the battery clamp plate, tray, and battery leads for corrosion (white fluffy deposits on the metal which are brittle to touch). If any corrosion is found, clean off the deposits with ammonia and paint over the clean metal with an anti-rust/anti-acid paint.
4 At the same time inspect the battery case for cracks. If a crack is found, clean and plug it with one of the proprietary compounds marketed by firms such as Holts for this purpose. If leakage through the crack has been excessive it will be necessary to refill the appropriate cell with fresh electrolyte as detailed later. Cracks are frequently caused to the top of a battery case by pouring in distilled water in the middle of winter after, instead of before, a run. This gives the water no chance to mix with the electrolyte and so the former freezes and splits the battery case.
5 If topping up the battery becomes excessive and the case has been inspected for cracks that could cause leakage, but none are found, the battery is being overcharged and the voltage regulator will have to be checked and reset.
6 With the battery on the bench, at the three monthly interval check, measure its specific gravity with a hydrometer to determine the state of the charge and condition of the electrolyte. There should be very little variation between the different cells and, if variation in excess of 0.025 is present, it will be due to either:-
a) Loss of electrolyte from the battery at some time caused by spillage or a leak resulting in a drop in the specific gravity of the electrolyte, when the deficiency was replaced with distilled water instead of fresh electrolyte.
b) An internal short circuit caused by a buckled plate or a similar malady pointing to the likelihood of total battery failure in the near future.
7 The specific gravity of the electrolyte for fully charged conditions at the electrolyte temperature indicated is listed in Table A. The specific gravity of a fully discharged battery at different temperatures of the electrolyte is given in Table B.
8 Specific gravity is measured by drawing up into the body of a hydrometer sufficient electrolyte to allow the indicator to float

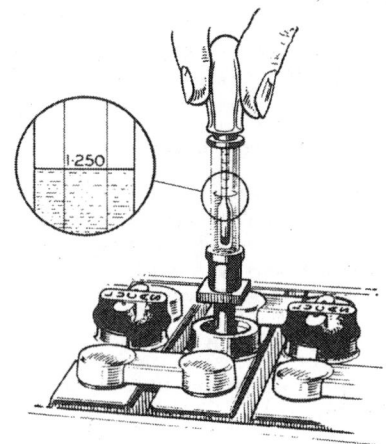

Fig. 10.1. Measuring battery specific gravity

freely (see Fig 10.1). The level at which the indicator floats indicates the specific gravity.

Table A

Specific Gravity - Battery Fully Charged

1.268 at 100°F or 38°C electrolyte temperature
1.272 at 90°F or 32°C electrolyte temperature
1.276 at 80°F or 27°C electrolyte temperature
1.280 at 70°F or 21°C electrolyte temperature
1.284 at 60°F or 16°C electrolyte temperature
1.288 at 50°F or 10°C electrolyte temperature
1.292 at 40°F or 4°C electrolyte temperature
1.296 at 30°F or -1.5°C electrolyte temperature

Table B

Specific Gravity - Battery Fully Discharged

1.098 at 100°F or 38°C electrolyte temperature
1.102 at 90°F or 32°C electrolyte temperature
1.106 at 80°F or 27°C electrolyte temperature
1.110 at 70°F or 21°C electrolyte temperature
1.114 at 60°F or 16°C electrolyte temperature
1.118 at 50°F or 10°C electrolyte temperature
1.122 at 40°F or 4°C electrolyte temperature
1.126 at 30°F or -1.5°C electrolyte temperature

4 Electrolyte replenishment

1 if the battery is in a fully charged state and one of the cells maintains a specific gravity reading which is 0.025 or more lower than the others, and a check of each cell has been made with a voltage meter to check for short circuits (a four to seven second test should give a steady reading of between 1.2 to 1.8 volts), then it is likely that electrolyte has been lost from the cell with the low reading at some time.
2 Top the cell up with a solution of 1 part sulphuric acid to 2.5 parts of water. If the cell is already fully topped up draw some electrolyte out of it with a pipette. The total capacity of each cell is ¾ pint.
3 When mixing the sulphuric acid and water NEVER ADD WATER TO SULPHURIC ACID - always pour the acid slowly onto the water in a glass container. IF WATER IS ADDED TO SULPHURIC ACID IT WILL EXPLODE.
4 Continue to top up the cell with the freshly made electrolyte and then recharge the battery and check the hydrometer readings.

5 Battery - charging

1 In winter time when heavy demand is placed upon the battery, such as when starting from cold, and much electrical equipment is continually in use, it is a good idea to occasionally have the battery fully charged from an external source at the rate of 3.5 to 4 amps.

2 Continue to charge the battery at this rate until no further rise in specific gravity is noted over a four hour period.

3 Alternatively, a trickle charger charging at the rate of 1.5 amps can be safely used overnight.

4 Specially rapid 'boost' charges, which are claimed to restore the power of the battery in 1 to 2 hours, are most dangerous as they can cause serious damage to the battery plates through over-heating.

5 While charging the battery note that the temperature should never exceed 100°F.

6 Lucas 15 ACR alternator - general description

The main advantage of the alternator over a dynamo lies in its ability to provide a high charge at low revolutions.

An important feature of the alternator system is its output control, this being based on thick film hybrid integrated micro circuit techniques.

The alternator is of rotating field, ventilated design. It comprises principally, a laminated stator on which is wound a star connected 3 phase output; an 8 pole rotor carrying the field windings. The front end of the rotor shaft runs in a ball race bearing and the rear in a needle roller race each of which are lubricated for lift, and nature finish aluminium die cast end brackets incorporating the mounting lugs.

The rotor is belt driven from the engine through a pulley keyed to the rotor shaft and a pressed steel fan adjacent to the pulley draws cooling air through the machine. This fan forms an integral part of the alternator specification. It has been designed to provide adequate air flow with a minimum of noise and to withstand the high stresses associated with maximum speed.

The brush gear for the field system is mounted on the slip ring end brackets. Two carbon brushes bear against a pair of concentric brass slip rings carried on a moulded disc attached to the end of the rotor. Also attached to the slip ring end bracket are six silicone diodes connected in a three phase bridge to rectify the generated alternating current to direct current for use in charging the battery and supplying power to the electrical system.

The alternator output is controlled by an electric voltage regulator unit and a warning light control unit to indicate to the driver when all is not well.

7 Alternator - routine maintenance

1 The equipment has been designed for the minimum amount of maintenance in service, the only items subject to wear being the brushes and bearings.

2 Brushes should be examined after about 75,000 miles (120,000 Km), and renewed if necessary. The bearings are pre-packed with grease for life and should not require further attention.

3 Check the 'V' belt drive every 6,000 miles (10,000 Km) for correct adjustment which should be 0.5 in (12.7 mm) total movement at the centre of the longest run.

8 Alternator - special procedures

Whenever the electrical system of the car is being attended to or external means of starting the engine there are certain precautions that must be taken otherwise serious and expensive damage can result.

1 Always make sure that the negative terminal of the battery is earthed. If the terminal connections are accidentally reversed or if the battery has been reverse charged the alternator will burn out.

2 The output terminal on the alternator marked 'BAT' must never be earthed but should always be connected directly to the positive terminal of the battery.

3 Whenever the alternator is to be removed, or disconnecting the terminals of the alternator circuit always disconnect the battery earth terminal first.

4 The alternator must never be operated without the battery to alternator cable connected.

5 If the battery is to be charged by external means always disconnect both battery cables before the external charger is connected.

6 Should it be necessary to use a booster charger or booster battery to start the engine always double check that the negative cables are connected to negative terminals and positive cables to positive terminals.

9 Alternator - removal and refitting

1 Disconnect both battery leads.

2 Note the terminal connections at the rear of the alternator and disconnect the cables.

3 Undo and remove the alternator adjustment arm bolt, slacken the alternator mounting bolts and remove the 'V' drive belt from the pulley.

4 Remove the remaining two mounting bolts and carefully lift the alternator away from the car.

5 Take care not to knock or drop the alternator otherwise this can cause irreparable damage.

6 Refitting the alternator is the reverse sequence to removal. Adjust the 'V' drive belt so that it has 0.5 in (12.7 mm) maximum deflection at the centre of its longest run.

10 Alternator - fault finding and repair

Due to the specialist knowledge and equipment required to test or service an alternator it is recommended that if the performance is suspect, the car be taken to an automobile electrician who will have the facilities for such work. Because of this recommendation no further detailed service information is given other than the exploded view of the unit.

11 Warning light control - general description

With an alternator, a warning light is fitted and its indication is for similar reasons to the ignition warning light, fitted with dynamo charging systems. The warning light is illuminated when the alternator is stationery or is being driven slowly. The light is extinguished when the output voltage begins to rise.

The light control unit is a thermally operated relay for controlling the switching on and off of a facia panel warning light. It is connected through the alternator terminal A L to the centre point of one pair of the six alternator control diodes and to earth.

Should the warning light indicate lack of charge check this unit before the alternator. If it is suspect it must be replaced with a similar new unit. Although similar in design to the direction indicator flasher it is not interchangeable.

12 Starter motor (inertia type) - general description

The starter motor is mounted on the left hand side of the engine end plate, and is held in position by two bolts which also clamp the bellhousing flange. The motor is of the four field coil, four pole piece type, and utilises four spring loaded commutator brushes. Two of these brushes are earthed, and the other two are

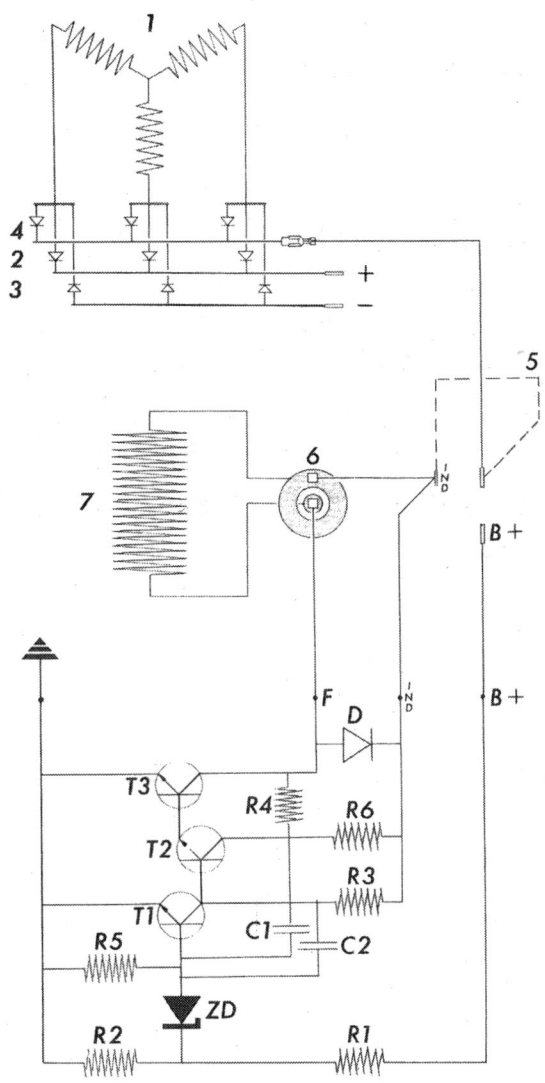

FIG. 10.2. ALTERNATOR AND CONTROL UNIT INTERNAL WIRING CIRCUIT

1	Stator windings	
2	Live side output diodes	
3	Earth side output diodes	
4	Field winding supply diodes	
5	Harness loop	Circuit is made when multi-socket connector is fitted and broken when connector is removed
6	Brushes and slip rings	
7	Field winding	
R3	Resistor	Restricts T2 base current supplied from 'field winding supply' diodes
T2	Intermediate transistor	Controls T3 base current direct
R6	Resistor	Restricts T3 base current supplied from 'field winding supply' diodes
T3	Output transistor	Controls field winding earth return circuit
R1 and R2	Potential divider	Senses battery reference voltage
ZD	Zener diode	Voltage sensitive component. Opposes passage of current until breakdown voltage - approximately 8 volts - is reached
		Controls T1 base current direct
T1	Input transistor	Controls T2 base current by diverting current passing through R3 to earth when ZD is conducting
C1 and R4	Capacitor and Resistor	Prevents transistor overheating by providing positive feed back circuit to ensure quick switching of transistors from 'fully on' to 'fully off'.
R5	Resistor	Path for small leakage current which may pass through ZD at high temperatures
D	Surge quench diode	Connected across field winding. Protects T3 from field winding high induced voltage surge and smooths field winding current
C2	Condenser	Radio interference suppression

Fig. 10.3. Alternator mounted on left hand side of engine

Fig. 10.4. Location of alternator control unit

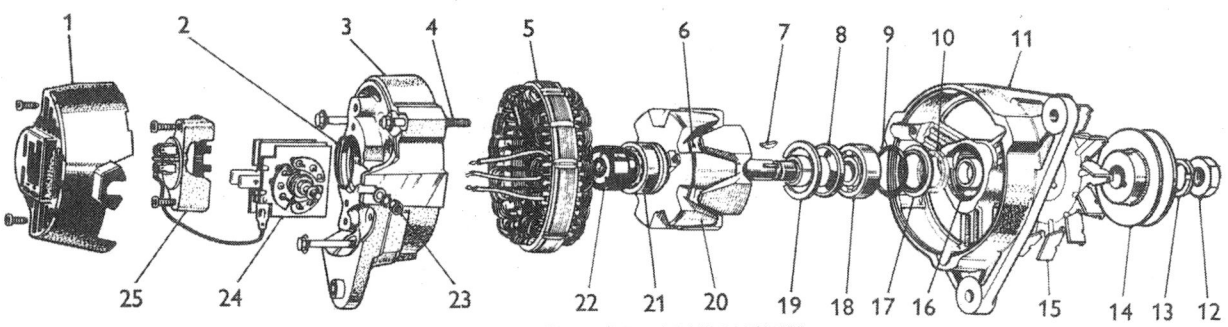

FIG. 10.5. ALTERNATOR COMPONENTS

1	Moulded cover	14	Pulley
2	Rubber 'O' ring	15	Fan
3	Slip ring end bracket	16	Spacer
4	Through bolt	17	Pressure ring and felt
5	Stator windings		ring retaining plate
6	Field winding	18	Drive end bearing
7	Key	19	Circlip
8	Bearing retaining plate	20	Rotor
9	Pressure ring	21	Slip ring end bearing
10	Felt ring	22	Slip ring moulding
11	Drive end bracket	23	Nut
12	Nut	24	Rectifier pack
13	Spring washer	25	Brushbox assembly

insulated and attached to the field coil ends.

13 Starter motor (inertia type) - testing on engine

1 If the starter motor fails to operate then check the condition of the battery by turning on the headlamps. If they glow brightly for several seconds and then gradually dim, the battery is in an uncharged condition.

2 If the headlamps continue to glow brightly and it is obvious that the battery is in good condition then check the tightness of the earth lead from the battery terminal to its connection on the bodyframe particularly, and other battery wiring. Check the tightness of the connections at the relay switch and at the starter motor. Check the wiring with a voltmeter for breaks or shorts.

3 If the wiring is in order then check that the starter motor switch is operating. To do this press the rubber covered button in the centre of the relay switch under the bonnet. If it is working the starter motor will be heard to 'click' as it tries to rotate. Alternatively check it with a voltmeter.

4 If the battery is fully charged, the wiring in order, and the switch working and the starter motor fails to operate then it will

have to be removed from the car for examination. Before this is done, however, ensure that the starter pinion has not jammed in mesh with the flywheel. Check by turning the square end of the armature shaft with a spanner. This will free the pinion if it is stuck in engagement with the flywheel teeth (Fig. 10.8).

14 Starter motor (inertia type) - removal and replacement

1 Disconnect the battery earth lead from the terminal.

2 Disconnect the heavy lead to the starter motor at the solenoid terminal. (This end is much more accessible than the end fitted to the starter motor).

3 Undo and remove the two bolts which hold the starter motor in place and withdraw it upwards together with the distance piece.

4 Generally replacement is a straightforward reversal of the removal sequence. Check that the electrical cable is firmly attached to the starter motor terminal before fitting the starter motor in place. Also ensure that any packing washers originally fitted are replaced so as to give the correct out of mesh clearance between that stationery starter pinion and the flywheel ring gear of 0.09375 - 0.1563 in (2.3812 - 3.969 mm).

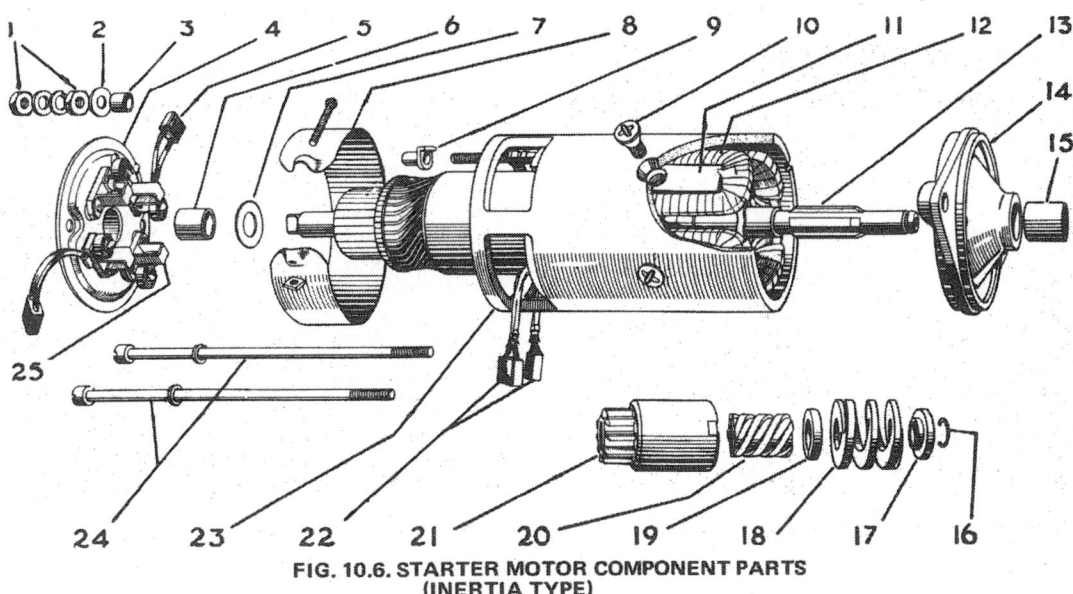

FIG. 10.6. STARTER MOTOR COMPONENT PARTS (INERTIA TYPE)

1	Terminal nuts and washers	14 End bracket
2	Insulating washer	15 Bush
3	Insulating bush	16 Jump ring
4	End plate	17 Retainer
5	Brush	18 Main spring
6	Bush	19 Thrust washer
7	Thrust washer	20 Sleeve
8	Cover band	21 Pinion and barrel assembly
9	Insulating bush	22 Brushes
10	Pole securing screw	23 Yoke
11	Pole piece	24 Through bolts
12	Field coil	25 Brush box
13	Shaft	

Fig. 10.7. Starter motor relay (Inertia type). Arrow shows relay over-ride button

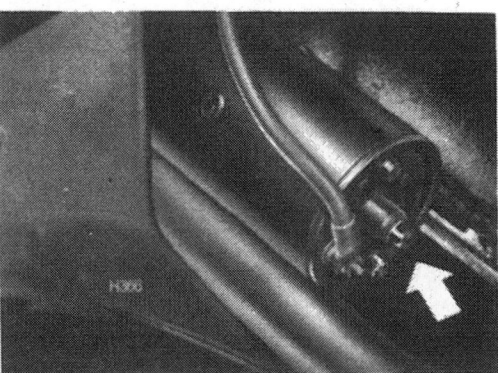

Fig. 10.8. Starter motor squared end - to be used with spanner when drive sticks in mesh with flywheel

15 Starter motor (inertia type) - dismantling and reassembly

1 With the starter motor on the bench, loosen the screw on the cover band and slip the cover band off. With a piece of wire bent into the shape of a hook, lift back each of the brush springs in turn and check the movement of the brushes in their holders by pulling on the flexible connectors. If the brushes are so worn that their faces do not rest against the commutator, or if the ends of the brush leads are exposed on their working face, they must be renewed.

2 If any of the brushes tend to stick in their holders then wash them with a petrol moistened cloth and, if necessary, lightly polish the sides of the brush with a very fine file, until the brushes move quite freely in their holders.

3 If the surface of the commutator is dirty or blackened,

clean it with a petrol moistened rag. Secure the starter motor in a vice and check it by connecting a heavy gauge cable between the starter motor terminal and a 12 volt battery.

4 Connect the cable from the other battery terminal to earth in the starter motor body. If the motor turns at high speed it is in good order.

5 If the starter motor still fails to function or if it is wished to renew the brushes, then it is necessary to further dismantle the motor.

6 Lift the brush springs with the hook and lift all four brushes out of their holders one at a time.

7 Remove the terminal nuts and washers from the terminal post on the commutator end bracket.

8 Unscrew the two through bolts which hold the end plates together and pull off the commutator end bracket. Also remove the driving end bracket which will come away complete with the

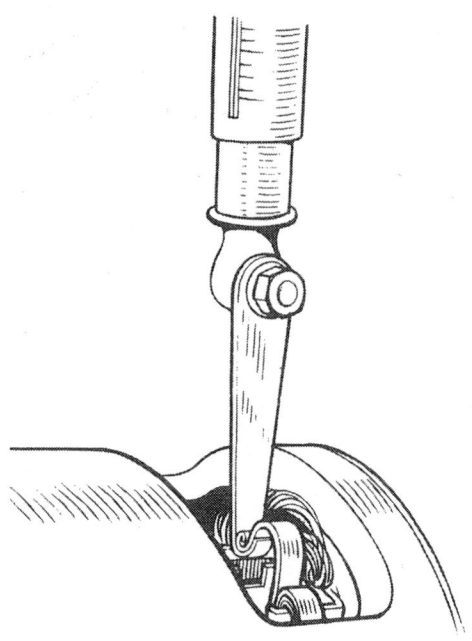

Fig. 10.9. Use of spring scale to test brush spring tension

armature.

9   At this stage if the brushes are renewed, their flexible connectors must be unsoldered and the connectors of new brushes soldered in their place. Check that the new brushes move freely in their holders as detailed above. If cleaning the commutator with petrol fails to remove all the burnt area and spots, then wrap a piece of glass paper round the commutator and rotate the armature.

10 If the commutator is very badly worn, remove the drive gear as detailed in the following section. Then mount the armature in a lathe and with the lathe turning at high speed, take a very fine cut-out of the commutator and finish the surface by polishing with glass paper. DO NOT UNDERCUT THE MICA INSULATORS BETWEEN THE COMMUTATOR SEGMENTS.

11 With the starter motor dismantled, test the four field coils for an open circuit. Connect a 12 volt battery with a 12 volt bulb in one of the leads between the field terminal post and the tapping point of the field coils to which the brushes are connected. An open circuit is proved by the bulb not lighting.

12 If the bulb lights, it does not necessarily mean that the field coils are in order, as there is a possibility that one of the coils will be earthed to the starter yoke or pole shoes. To check this, remove the lead from the brush connector and place it against a clean portion of the starter yoke. If the bulb lights the field coils are earthing. Replacement   of the field coil calls for the use of a wheel operated screwdriver, a soldering iron, caulking and riveting operations, and is beyond the scope of the majority of owners. The starter yoke should be taken to a reputable electrical engineering works for new field coils to be fitted. Alternatively, purchase an exchange Lucas starter motor.

13 If the armature is damaged this will be evident after visual inspection. Look for signs of burning, discolouration, and for conductors that have lifted away from the commutator. Reassembly is a straightforward reversal of the dismantling procedure.

16 Starter motor drive (inertia type) - general description

1   The starter motor drive is of the outboard type. When the starter motor is operated the pinion moves into contact with the flywheel gear ring by moving in towards the starter motor.

2   If the engine kicks back, or the pinion fails to engage with the flywheel gear ring when the starter motor is actuated no undue strain is placed on the armature shaft, as the pinion sleeve disengages from the pinion and turns independently.

17 Starter motor drive (inertia type) - removal and replacement

1   To dismantle the drive first use a press to push the retainer clear of the circlip which can then be removed. Lift away the retainer (Fig.10.6), and main spring.

2   Slide the remaining parts with a rotary action of the armature shaft.

3   It is most important that the drive gear is completely free from oil, grease and dirt. With the drive gear removed, clean all parts thoroughly in paraffin. UNDER NO CIRCUMSTANCES OIL THE DRIVE COMPONENTS   Lubrication of the drive components could easily cause the pinion to stick.

4   Reassembly is the reverse sequence to removal. Use a press to compress the spring and retainer sufficiently to allow a new circlip to be fitted to its groove on the shaft. Remove the press.

18 Starter motor bushes (inertia type) - inspection, removal and replacement

1   With the starter motor stripped down check the condition of the bushes. They should be renewed when they are sufficiently worn to allow visible side movement of the armature shaft.

2   The old bushes are simply driven out with a suitable drift and the new bushes inserted by the same method. As the bearings are of the phospher bronze type it is essential that they are allowed to stand in S.A.E. 30 engine oil for a least 24 hours before fitment.

19 Starter motor (pre-engaged type) - general description

This type of motor is fitted to P.I. models and differs in construction from that fitted to the normal carburettor, emission control models in the method of engagement of the pinion. The motor consists of a solenoid, a lever, starter drive gear and the motor. By referring to Fig.10.12 it will be seen that the solenoid is fitted to the top of the motor. The plunger inside the solenoid is connected to a centre pivoting lever the other end of which is in contact with the drive sleeve and drive gear.

When the starter motor switch is operated the solenoid is energized causing the plunger to move into the solenoid and the pinion to move into mesh with the starter ring gear on the flywheel. Upon the pinion being in full mesh with the ring gear heavy duty contacts in the rear of the solenoid are closed and current is supplied to the motor so rotating the pinion and ring gear.

Once the engine has started the starter switch is released and under spring action the plunger is moved from the centre of the solenoid and by means of the pivoting lever the pinion is moved out of mesh of the ring gear.

20 Starter motor (pre-engaged type) - testing on engine

1   If the starter motor fails to operate then check the condition of the battery by turning on the headlamps. If they glow brightly for several seconds and then gradually dim, the battery is in an uncharged condition.

2   If the headlamps continue to glow brightly and it is obvious that the battery is in good condition, then check the tightness of the earth lead from the battery terminal to its connection on the body frame particularly, and other battery wiring. Check the tightness of the connections at the rear of the solenoid. Check the wiring with a voltmeter for breaks or short circuits.

3   If the wiring is in order check the starter motor for continuity using a voltmeter.

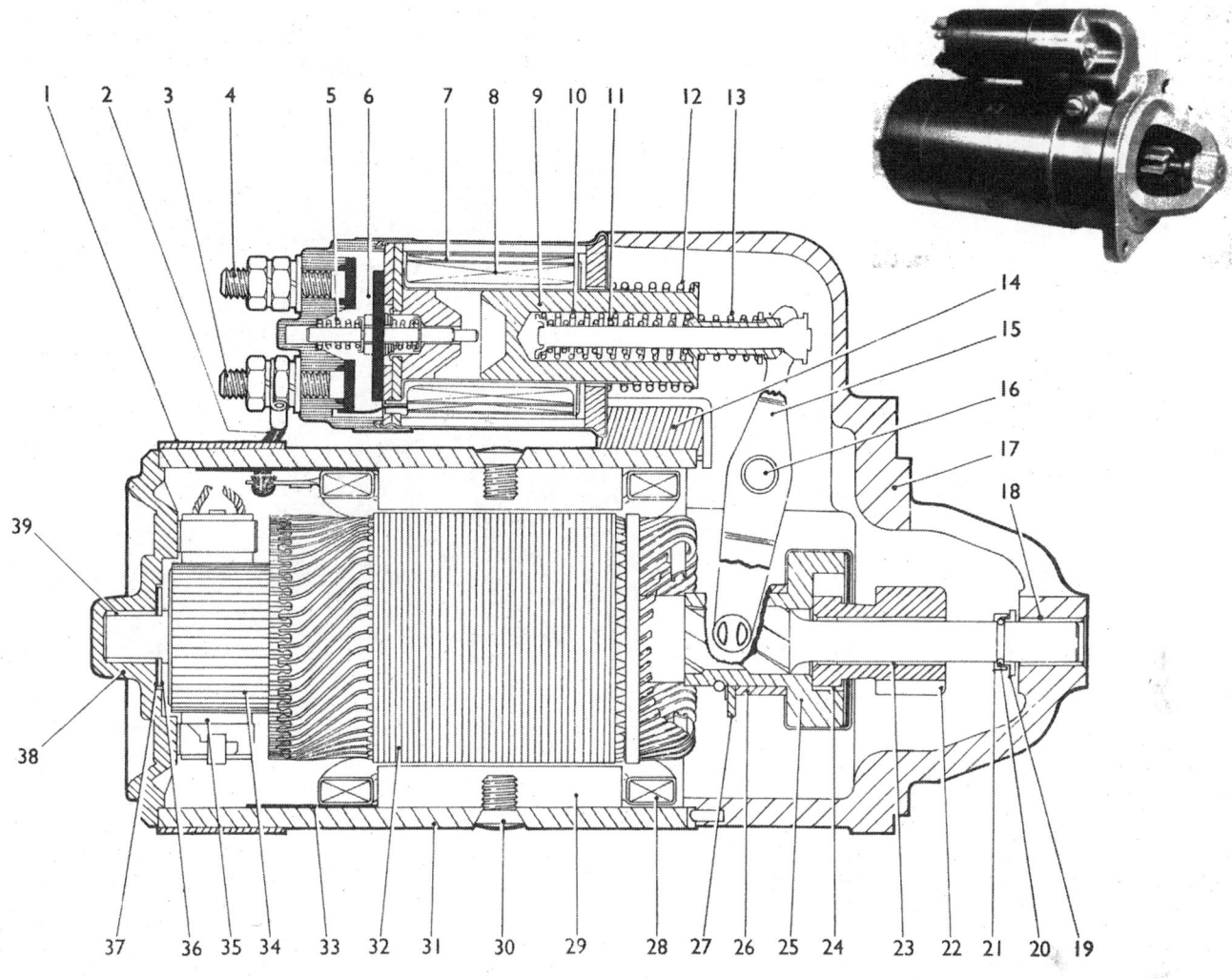

**FIG. 10.10. STARTER MOTOR COMPONENT PARTS
(PRE-ENGAGED TYPE)**

1 Cover band	11 Inner engaging spring	21 Thrust collar	30 Pole shoe screw
2 Motor lead	12 Return spring	Starter drive—	31 Yoke
3 'STA' terminal	13 Lost motion spring	22 Pinion	32 Armature
4 Solenoid battery terminal	14 Rubber moulding	23 Pinion bearing	33 Insulation strip
5 Contact assembly spring	15 Engaging lever	24 Roller clutch action	34 Commutator
6 Contact assembly	16 Eccentric pin	25 Drive sleeve	35 Brush
7 Hold in winding	17 Fixing bracket	26 Distance piece	36 Steel thrust washer
8 Pull in winding	18 Fixing bracjet bearing bush	27 Drive operating plate	37 Fabric thrust washer
9 Plunger	19 Thrust washer	28 Field winding	38 Commutator end bracket
10 Outer engaging spring	20 Jump ring	29 Pole shoe	39 Commutator end bracket bearing bush

4 If the battery is fully charged, the wiring in order and the motor electrical circuit checked for continuity and it still fails to operate then it will have to be removed from the car for examination. Before this is done, however, ensure that the pinion gear has not jammed in mesh with the flywheel due either to a broken solenoid spring or dirty pinion gear splines. To release the pinion, engage a low gear and with the ignition switched off, rock the car backwards and forwards which should release the pinion from mesh with the ring gear. If the pinion still remains jammed the starter motor must be removed for further examination.

21 Starter motor (pre-engaged type) - removal and replacement

1 Disconnect the negative terminal from the battery.

2 Make a note of the electrical connections at the rear of the solenoid and disconnect the top heavy duty cable. Also release the two Lucas terminals situated below the heavy duty cable. There is no need to undo the lower heavy duty cable at the rear of the solenoid.

3 Undo and remove the two bolts which hold the starter motor in place and lift away upwards through the engine compartment.

4 Generally replacement is a straightforward reversal of the removal sequence. Check that the electrical cable connections are clean and firmly attached to their respective terminals.

22 Starter motor (pre-engaged type) - dismantling and overhaul

1 With the starter motor on the bench, loosen the screw on the cover band and slip the cover band off with a piece of wire bent

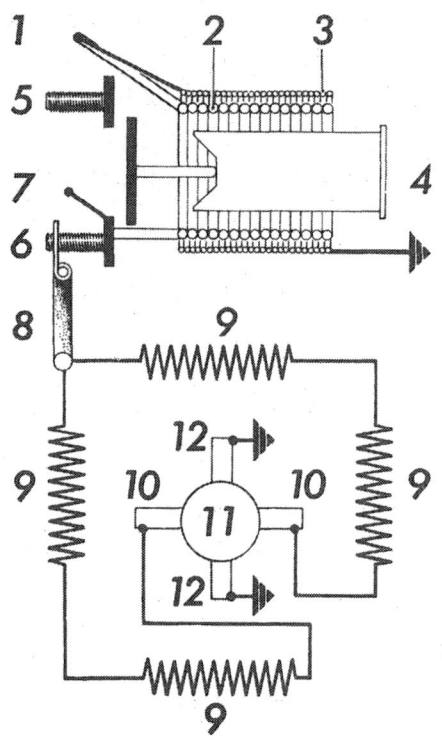

FIG. 10.11. PRE-ENGAGED STARTER MOTOR INTER—
NAL CIRCUIT

1 Unmarked 'WR wire' connector
2 Pull in winding
3 Hold in winding
4 Plunger
5 Solenoid battery terminal
6 'STA' terminal
7 'IGN' connector - not used on Triumph T2.5 P.I. This connector is only used on a vehicle fitted with a 'ballast
   ignition system'. Full system voltage is available at the
   connector when the solenoid is energised
8 Motor lead
9 Field windings
10 Field winding brushes
11 Commutator
12 Earth brushes

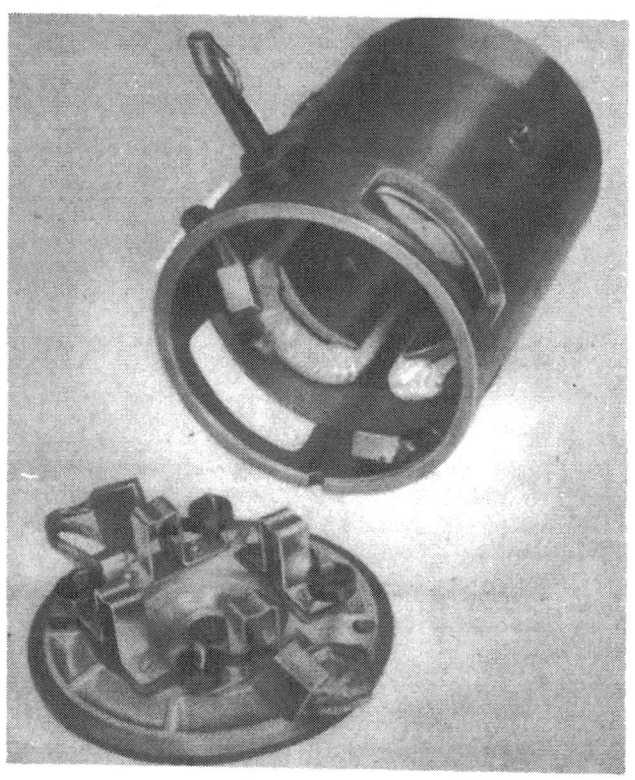

Fig. 10.13. Starter motor - pre-engaged type. The commutator
end bracket removed

FIG. 10.12. STARTER MOTOR PRE-ENGAGED TYPE
SOLENOID CONNECTIONS

1 Small Lucar connector
5 Heavy duty cable connection to solenoid
6 Heavy duty cable connection to motor
7 Large Lucar connector (Ign)
8 Heavy duty cable to motor

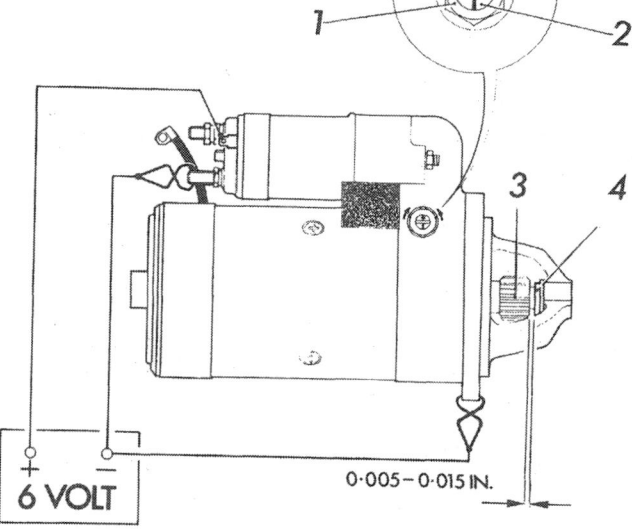

FIG. 10.14. PINION MOVEMENT ADJUSTMENT (PRE-
ENGAGED TYPE)

1 Locknut   3 Pinion
2 Eccentric pin   4 Thrust collar

into the shape of a hook. Lift back each of the brush springs in turn and check the movement of the brushes in their holders by pulling on the flexible connectors. If the brushes are so worn that their faces do not rest against the commutator or if the ends of the brush leads are exposed on their working faces they must be renewed.

2 If any of the brushes tend to stick in their holders then wash them with a petrol moistened cloth and, if necessary, lightly polish the sides of the brushes with a very fine file, until the brushes move quite freely in their holders.

3 Undo the large nut holding the heavy duty cable to the lower solenoid terminal (marked STA). Remove the nut, spring washer and cable connector.

4 Undo the two nuts securing the solenoid to the front fixing bracket. Remove the nuts and spring washers and carefully withdraw the solenoid from its mounting. It will be observed that the plunger will be left attached to the engagement lever.

5 Lift the plunger return spring away from the plunger and put in a safe place. Disengage the end of the plunger from the top of the engagement lever.

6 Undo the locknut securing the eccentric pin to the starter motor body. This will be found at the front towards the top of the motor on the right hand side. Unscrew the eccentric pin.

7 Unscrew the two through bolts from the rear of the starter motor body which will release the yoke from the fixing bracket. To separate the two parts using a soft faced hammer, tap the fixing bracket mounting lugs whilst holding the yoke. This will release the locating dowels in the end of the fixing bracket.

8 Pull the commutator end bracket off the rear of the yoke. Lift off the steel thrust washer and fibre thrust washer from the spigot on the end of the commutator. Also lift away the rubber moulding located at the top of the yoke and the fixing bracket.

9 Carefully withdraw the armature with the drive pinion assembly and engagement lever from the fixing bracket. It should be noted that there is a small thrust washer at the pinion end of the armature shaft which is next removed.

10 If it is necessary to dismantle the starter pinion drive obtain a 0.625 in (15.875 mm) internal diameter tube, position the tube over the end of the shaft and force the thrust collar from the jump ring towards the starter driver. Using a screwdriver carefully prise the ring from the shaft groove.

11 Lift away the thrust collar and slide off the starter pinion drive assembly.

12 At this stage if the brushes are to be renewed, their flexible connectors must be unsoldered and the connectors of new brushes soldered in their place. Check that the new brushes move freely in their holders as detailed above. If cleaning the commutator with petrol fails to remove all the burnt areas and spots, then wrap a piece of glass paper round the commutator and rotate the armature.

13 If the commutator is very badly worn, remove the drive gear as detailed in the following section. Then mount the armature in a lathe and with the lathe turning at high speed, take a very fine cut out of the commutator and finish the surface by polishing with glass paper. DO NOT UNDERCUT THE MICA INSULATORS BETWEEN THE COMMUTATOR SEGMENTS.

14 With the starter motor dismantled, test the four field coils for an open circuit. Connect a 12 volt battery with a 12 volt bulb in one of the leads between the field terminal post and the tapping points of the field coils to which the brushes are connected. An open circuit is proved by the bulb not lighting.

15 If the bulb lights, it does not necessarily mean that the field coils are in order, as there is a possibility that one of the coils will be earthed to the starter yoke or pole shoes. To check this, remove the lead from the brush connector and place it against a clean portion of the starter yoke. If the bulb lights the field coils are earthing. Replacement of the field coil calls for the use of a wheel operated screwdriver, a soldering iron, caulking and riveting operations and is beyond the scope of the majority of owners. The starter yoke should be taken to a reputable electrical engineering works for new field coils to be fitted. Alternatively purchase an exchange Lucas starter motor.

16 If the armature is damaged this will be evident after visual

inspection. Look for signs of burning, discolouration, and for conductors that have lifted away from the commutator.

17 Reassembly is the reverse sequence to dismantling but it will be necessary to adjust the pinion movement.

18 Once the starter motor has been completely reassembled, test for correct operation by securing it in a vice and connecting a heavy gauge cable between the starter motor solenoid lower terminal and a 12 volt battery. Connect the cable from the other battery terminal to earth on the starter motor body. If the motor turns at high speed it is in good order

19 Disconnect the heavy duty cable from the lower terminal marked 'STA' and by referring to Fig. 10.11.connect a 6 volt battery to the starter motor as shown. Do not make the final battery connection yet.

20 Undo but do not remove the eccentric pin locknut on the side of the fixing bracket. Then screw the eccentric pin in fully.

21 Connect the final battery connection so energizing the solenoid, pull in winding and hold in working which will, via the engaging lever, move the pinion to its engagement position.

22 Refer to Fig. 10.13. and locate a feeler gauge between the pinion and thrust washer. With the fingers gently press the pinion towards the motor so that any lost motion in the linkage may be taken up.

23 Using a screwdriver rotate the eccentric pin until the gap is between 0.005 - 0.015 in (0.127 - 0.381 mm). Finally tighten the eccentric pin locknuts.

23 Starter motor bushes (pre-engaged type) - inspection, removal and replacement

1 With the starter motor stripped down check the condition of the bushes. They should be renewed when they are sufficiently worn to allow visible side movement of the armature shaft.

2 The old bushes are simply driven out with a suitable drift and the new bushes inserted by the same method. As the bearings are of the phosphor bronze type it is essential that they are allowed to stand in S.A.E. 30 engine oil for at least 24 hours before fitment.

24 Flasher unit

The flasher unit comprises a moulded base which carries a snap action metal vane held in tension by a metal ribbon. A pair of normally closed contacts are positioned on the base and ribbon. A pressed aluminium cover is crimped to the base.

Current is supplied to terminal B and flows immediately across the contacts, though the ribbon and vane to terminal L. From terminal L current flows to the selected lights giving immediate indication of the driver's selection. This current heats the ribbon and causes expansion which finally allows the vane to release and the contacts open. At this point the current flow ceases the lights extinguish and the ribbon cools and contracts. The vane is re-tensioned until the contacts close and a second cycle commences.

If the unit is suspect first check all the bulbs and terminal connectors and if satisfactory the unit should be removed and checked by substitution.

It is located on the bulkhead end panel adjacent to the passenger's feet and retained by a clip. To remove the unit pull from the clip and detach the Lucar connectors. Refitting is the reverse sequence to removal.

25 Windscreen wiper arms - removal and replacement

1 Before removing a wiper arm, turn the windscreen switch on and off to ensure the arms are in their normal parked position parallel with the bottom of the windscreen.

2 To remove the arm, pivot the arm back and pull the wiper arm head off the splined drive.

3 When replacing an arm, place it so it is in the correct relative parked position and then press the arm head onto the splined

Fig. 10.15. Location of direction indicator flasher unit

FIG. 10.16. DIRECTION INDICATOR INTERNAL WIRING

B Supply
L Output terminal to lamps

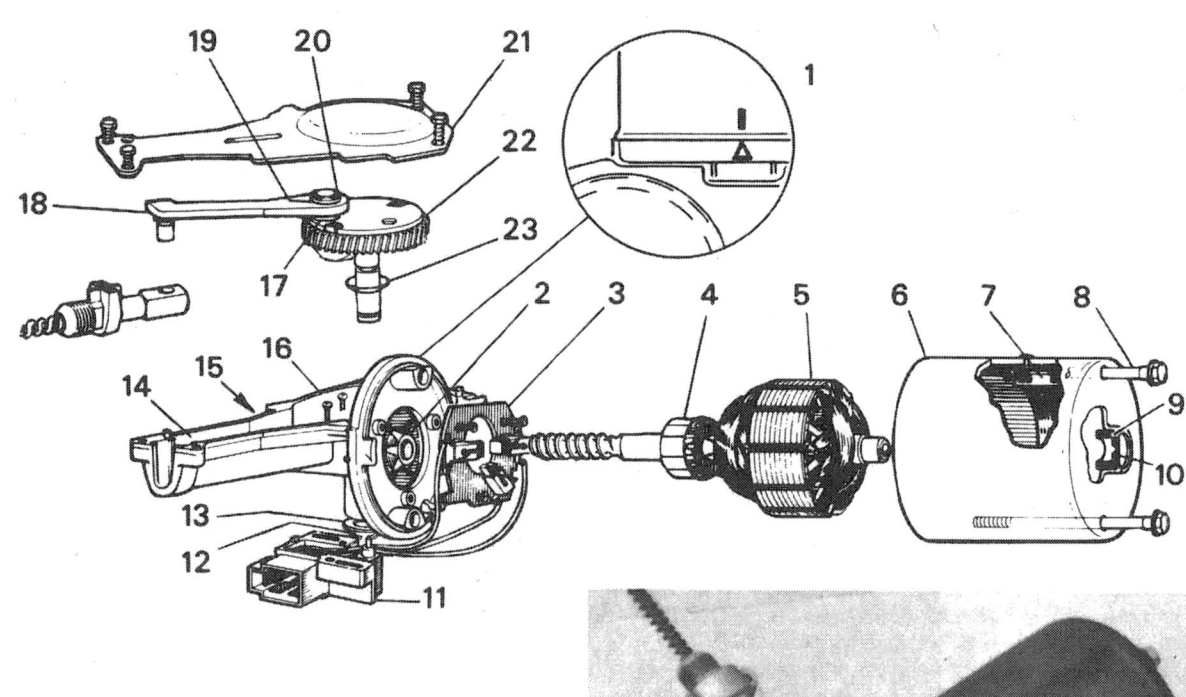

FIG. 10.17. WINDSCREEN WIPER MOTOR COMPONENT PARTS

1 Aligning marks
2 Self aligning bearing
3 Brush assembly
4 Commutator
5 Armature
6 Cover
7 Permanent magnet
8 Through bolt
9 Cover bearing
10 Felt washer
11 Limit switch unit
12 Final gear shaft spring clip
13 Washer
14 Crosshead guide channel
15 Thrust screw (non adjustable) or thrust screw and lock nut (adjustable)
16 Gearbox
17 Washer
18 Connecting rod
19 Washer
20 Crankpin spring clip
21 Gearbox cover
22 Final gear
23 Dished washer

drive till the retaining clip clicks into place.

26 Windscreen wiper mechanism - fault diagnosis and rectification

Should the windscreen wipers fail, or work very slowly, then check the terminals for loose connections, and make sure the insulation of the external wiring is not broken or cracked. If this is in order then check the current the motor is taking by connecting up a 1-20 volt voltmeter in the circuit and turning on the wiper switch. Consumption should be between 2.3 to 3.1 amps.

If no current is passing through check the 1 - 2 fuse. If the fuse has blown replace it after having checked the wiring of the motor and other electrical circuits serviced by this fuse for short circuits. If the fuse is in good condition check the wiper switch.

If the wiper takes a very high current check the wiper blades for freedom of movement. If this is satisfactory check the gearbox cover and gear assembly for damage and measure the armature end float which should be between 0.002 - 0.008 in (0.0508 - 0.2032 mm). The end float is set by the adjusting screw. Check that excessive friction in the cable connecting tubes caused by too small a curvature is not the cause of the high current consumption.

If the motor takes a very low current ensure that the battery is fully charged. Check the brush gear after removing the commutator end bracket and ensure that the brushes are free to move and, if necessary, renew the tension spring. If the brushes are very worn they should be replaced with new ones. The brush levers should be quite free on their pivots. If stiff, loosen them by moving them backwards and forwards by hand and by applying a little thin machine oil. Check the armature by substitution if this unit is suspected.

27 Windscreen wiper blades - changing wiping arc

If it is wished to change the area through which the wiper blades move, this is simply done by removing each blade in turn from each splined drive, and then replacing it on the drive in a slightly different position.

28 Windscreen wiper mechanism - removal and replacement

1 Remove the windscreen wiper arms by lifting the blades carefully raising the retaining clip with a screwdriver, and then pulling the arms off the splined driveshaft.
2 Disconnect the electrical cables from the wiper motor and release the outer cable from the gearbox housing.
3 Undo the large nut that secures the outer tubing.
4 Undo and remove the three bolts that hold the wiper motor mounting bracket. It should be noted that two of these bolts can be reached from the inside of the car. The third bolt is accessible through the engine compartment.
5 Remove the motor complete with its mounting bracket, at the same time withdrawing the cable rack.
6 Disconnect the battery earth terminal and working under the facia panel disconnect the two demister hoses from the nozzles and undo the two nozzle securing nuts and spring washers. Remove the two nuts and washers and remove the demister nozzles.
7 Undo and remove the cover plates which are positioned underneath the wiper system wheelboxes. Each cover plate is held in position with two screws.
8 Undo and remove the nut from each wheelbox and lift up the jet and bush assembly for about 2.0 in (50.8 mm).
9 Disconnect the washer water pipes at the jets. If it recommended that a piece of electrical cable is placed around the right hand rigid tubing so as to keep it in place.
10 Remove the wheelbox backplate by undoing the two screws and lifting away the backplate. Ease out the rigid tubing so

disengaging it from the wheelbox body.
11 Use a pair of long nosed pliers to grip the rear of the wheelbox and lift it out of the aperture.
12 Reassembly of the wheel boxes, motor and cable is the reverse sequence to removal. It may be necessary to rotate the rack cable so as to engage it with the gear in the wheelboxes.

29 Windscreen wiper motor - dismantling, inspection and reassembly

1 Refer to Fig.10.17 and remove the four gearbox cover retaining screws and lift away the cover. Release the circlip and flat washer securing the connecting rod to the crankpin on the shaft and gear. Lift away the connecting rod followed by the second flat washer.
2 Release the circlip and washer securing the shaft and gear to the gearbox body.
3 De-burr the gear shaft and lift away the gear making a careful note of the location of the dished washer.
4 Scribe a mark on the yoke assembly and gearbox to ensure correct reassembly and unscrew the two yoke bolts from the motor yoke assembly. Part the yoke assembly including armature from the gearbox body. As the yoke assembly has residual magnetism ensure that the yoke is kept well away from metallic dust.
5 Unscrew the two screws securing the brush gear and the terminal and switch assembly and remove both the assemblies.
6 Inspect the brushes for signs of excessive wear. If the main brushes are worn to a limit of 0.1875 in (4.7625 mm) or the narrow section of the third brush is worn to the full width of the brush fit a new brush gear assembly. Ensure that the three brushes move freely in their boxes. If a push type spring gauge is available check the spring rate which should be between 5 - 7 ounces (141.747 - 198.446 gms) when the bottom of the brush is level with the bottom of the slot in the brush box. Again if the spring rate is incorrect fit a new brush gear assembly.
7 If the armature is suspect take it to an automobile electrician to test for open or short circuiting.
8 Inspect the gear wheel for signs of excessive wear or damage and fit a new one if necessary.
9 Reassembly is the reverse procedure to dismantling but there are several points that require special attention.
10 Use only Ragosine Listate grease to lubricate the gear wheel teeth and cam, the armature shaft worm gear, connecting rod and its connecting pin, the cross head slide and cable rack and wheelbox gear wheels.
11 Use only Shell Turbo 41 oil to lubricate the bearing bushes, the armature shaft bearing journals (sparingly), the gear wheel shaft and crankpin, the felt washer in the yoke bearing (thoroughly soak) and the wheelbox spindles.
12 The yoke assembly fixing bolts should be tightened using a torque wrench set to 14 lbs in.
13 When a replacement armature is to be fitted, slacken the thrust screw so as to provide end float for fitting the yoke.
14 The thrust disc inside the yoke bearing should be fitted with

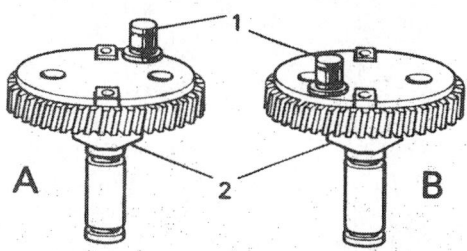

FIG. 10.18. RELATIONSHIP OF CRANKPIN TO CAM FOR CORRECT PARK POSITION

A Park position - cable rack retracted   1 Crankpin
B Park position - cable rack extended   2 Cam

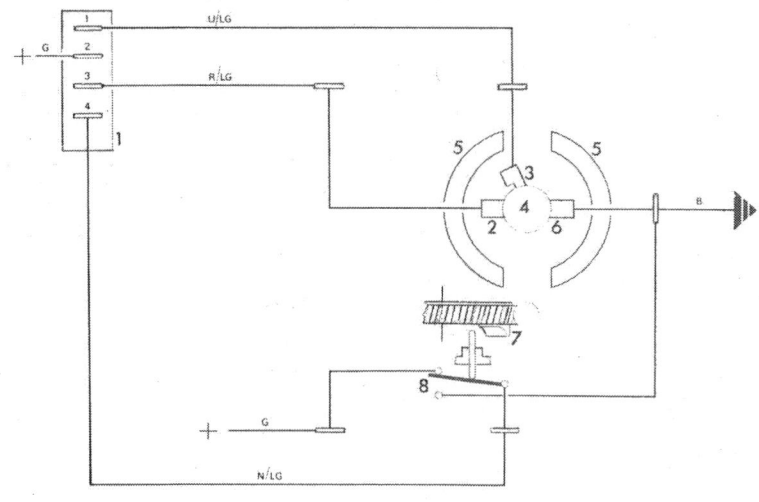

**FIG. 10.19. WINDSCREEN WIPER MOTOR AND SWITCH
WIRING DIAGRAM**

+	Supply		3	High speed brush
1	Facia switch		4	Commutator
	OFF	3 connected to 4	5	Permanent magnet
			6	Earth brush
	NORMAL	2 connected to 3	7	Final gear cam
	HIGH	2 connected to 1	8	Limit switch unit
2	Normal speed brush			

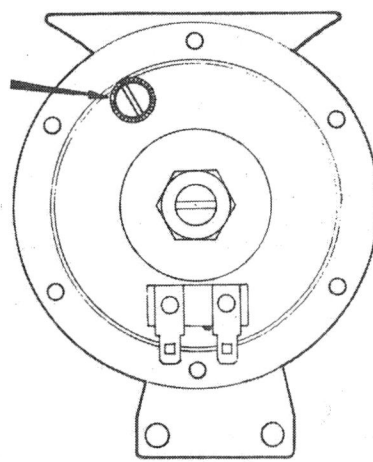

Fig. 10.20. Location of horn adjustment screw (arrowed)

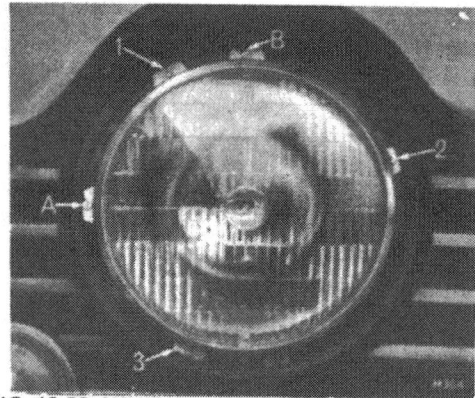

**FIG. 10.22. HEADLIGHT UNIT RETAINING SCREW
IDENTIFICATION**

1, 2, 3	Inner rim retaining screws
A	Vertical beam adjustment
B	Horizontal beam adjustment

Fig. 10.21. Using screwdriver to release chrome rim

Fig. 10.23. Detachment of socket connector from light unit

the concave side towards the end face of the bearing. The dished washer fitted beneath the gear wheel should have its concave side towards the gear wheel as shown in Fig. 10.17.

15 The larger of the two flat washers is fitted underneath the connecting rod and the smaller one on top, under the retaining circlip.

16 To adjust the armature end float, tighten the thrust screw and then turn back one quarter of a turn so giving an end float of between 0.002 - 0.008 in (0.0508 - 0.2032 mm). The gap should be measured under the head of the thrust screw. Fit a shim of suitable size beneath the head and tighten the screw.

30 Horns - fault tracing and rectifcation

1 If a horn works badly or fails completely first check the wiring leading to it for short circuits, blown fuse or loose connections. Also check that the horn is firmly secured and that there is nothing lying on the horn body.

2 Twin horns are fitted and are of two different notes. The high note horn has a letter H on the inside of the trumpet and the low note horn has a letter L similarly positioned on the trumpet.

3 If a horn loses its adjustment it will not alter the pitch as the tone of a horn depends on the vibration of an air column. It will however give a softer and more harsh sound. Also excessive current will be required which is one cause for fuses to blow.

4 Further information on servicing is given in Section 31.

31 Horns - servicing and adjustment

1 The horn should never be dismantled but it is possible to adjust it. This adjustment is to compensate for wear only and will not affect the tone. At the rear of the horn is a small adjustment screw on the broad rim, nearly opposite the two terminals. Do not confuse this with the large screw in the centre.

2 Turn the adjustment screw anti-clockwise until the horn just fails to sound. Then turn the screw a quarter of a turn clockwise, which is the optimum setting.

32 Headlights

1 To remove a headlight sealed beam unit first insert a wide blade screwdriver behind the rim at the lower edge and twist the screwdriver so as to release the rim from the clip. Lift the rim from the upper retainers (Fig. 10.22).

2 Undo and remove the three small crosshead screws and lift away the retaining rim (Fig. 10.22).

3 The light unit may now be drawn forwards and detached from the connector (Fig. 10.23).

4 Do not disturb the two beam diming screws located at the top end side of the light unit housing.

5 Refitting the light unit is the reverse sequence to removal. Make sure that the clip projection on the rim is not bent otherwise it will be difficult to secure the rim.

33 Headlight alignment

1 It is always advisable to have the headlights aligned using special optical beam setting equipment but if this is not available the following procedure may be used.

2 Position the car on level ground 10 ft (3 m) in front of a dark wall or board. The wall or board must be at right angles to the centre line of the car.

3 Draw a vertical line on the board in line with the centre line of the car.

4 Bounce the car on its suspension to ensure correct settlement and then measure the height between the ground and the centre of the headlights.

5 Draw a horizontal line across the board at this measured height. On this horizontal line mark a cross either side of the

vertical line equal to half the distance between the centres of the two headlights. Switch the headlights onto main beam.

6 By careful adjustment of the two beam adjustment screws set the centre of each beam onto the crosses which have been previously marked on the board or wall.

7 Bounce the car once more and recheck the sitting. Now lower the beams by about 1.5 in (38.1 mm) so as not to dazzle other road users and to compensate for those occasions when there is weight in the back of the car.

34 Side light and direction bulbs - removal and refitting
TR 5/250 Side light

1 Carefully push in and turn the rim and lens in an anti-clockwise direction. Lift away the lens assembly.

2 To detach the bulb press in and turn in an anti-clockwise direction to release the bayonet fixing and lift away the bulb.

3 Refitting the bulb and lens is the reverse sequence to removal. Make sure that the wide flange and slot are correctly aligned.

TR5/250 Direction indicator

1 Use a small screwdriver and turn back the lip retaining the rim. Carefully ease out the rim.

2 Remove the lens in a similar manner as for the rim.

3 Push the bulb in and turn in an anti-clockwise direction so as to release the bayonet fitting.

4 Refitting the bulb, lens and rim is the reverse sequence to removal. It is best to locate the lens and rim using a screwdriver to ease the rubber lip over the lens and rim flanges.

TR6

The side lights, and flashers are located together in a cluster on the front lower panel. To gain access to the bulb undo and remove the two screws that secure the lens to the body. Lift away the lens.

To detach the bulb press in and turn in an anti-clockwise direction to release the bayonet fixing and lift away the bulb.

Refitting is the reverse sequence to removal. Make sure that the seal is correctly fitted before replacing the lens.

35 Front direction indicator repeater light bulb (TR5) removal and refitting

1 Undo and remove the small screw that retains the lens onto the light body.

2 Slide the lens rearwards so as to allow the forward lug to release. The bulb may now be pulled from its retainer - a capless bulb is used.

3 Refitting the bulb is the reverse sequence to removal.

36 Rear direction indicator, stop and tail light, and side marker bulbs - removal and replacement

1 Undo and remove the three screws that secure the one piece lens to the light body. Carefully lift away the lens.

2 Remove the applicable bulb by pressing and turning in an anti-clockwise direction.

3 Refitting the bulb and lens is the reverse sequence to removal. Take care to ensure the stop/tail bulb is located the correct way round and also that lens sealing washer is correctly fitted to prevent dirt and water ingress.

Rear marker light (TR5 and early TR250)

To gain access to the bulb, undo and remove the single screw that retains the lens. Draw the lens forwards to allow the rear clip to release and lift away the lens. The bulb, which is of the capless type may now be pulled out. Refitting the bulb and lens is the reverse sequence to removal. Make sure that the sealing

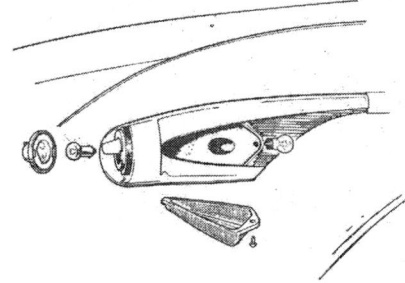

Fig. 10.24. Front side light and marker light assembly (TR5, early TR250)

Fig. 10.25. Direction indicator light assembly (TR5, early TR250)

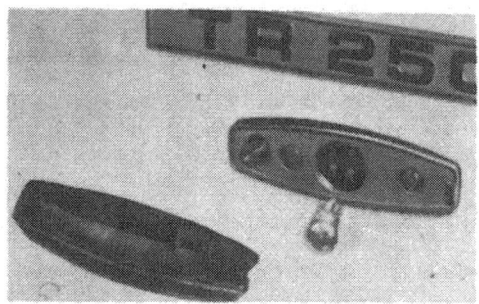

Fig. 10.26. Rear marker light assembly (TR5, early TR250)

Fig. 10.27. Rear number plate light assembly (TR5, early TR250)

Fig. 10.28. Instrument illumination bulb and holder

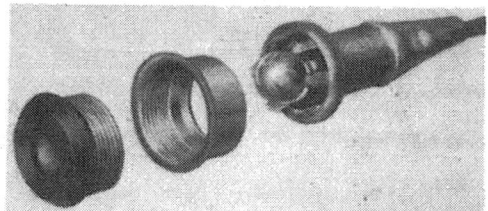

Fig. 10.30. Hazard flasher and relay location

Fig. 10.29. Warning light bulb assembly

washer is correctly fitted to prevent dirt and water ingress.

Front and rear marker lights (TR6 and later TR250)

To gain access to the bulb, undo and remove the screws that secure the lens and lift away the lens.

The bulb may now be detached from the bulb holder. Refitting the bulb and lens is the reverse sequence to removal. Make sure that the sealing washer is correctly fitted to prevent dirt and water ingress.

37 Number plate light bulb - removal and replacement

TR5 and early TR250

1 Undo and remove the two screws that secure the cowled rim. Lift away the rim.
2 Carefully remove the bulb by pressing and turning in an anti-clockwise direction to release the bayonet fitting. As the bulb is a tight fit in the bulb holder it may be necessary to use a screwdriver to partially dismantle the bulb and remove the bayonet cap.
3 Refitting the bulb is the reverse sequence to removal. Make sure that the cowled rim is fitted the right way round.

TR6 and later TR250

Access to the bulb is gained by undoing and removing the lens rim securing screws and lifting away the rim and lens. Remove the bulb and fit a new one. Make sure that the sealing washer is correctly fitted to prevent dirt and water ingress before the lens is replaced.

38 Reverse light bulb - removal and replacement

TR5 and early TR250

1 Use a small screwdriver and turn back the lip retaining the

rim. Carefully ease out the rim.
2 Remove the lens in a similar manner as for the rim.
3 Push the bulb in and turn in an anti-clockwise direction so as to release the bayonet fitting.
4 Refitting the bulb, lens and rim is the reverse sequence to removal. It is best to locate the lens and rim using a screwdriver to ease the rubber lip over the lens and rim flanges.

TR6 and later TR250

Access to the bulb is gained in a similar manner as for the stop/tail light bulbs as described in section 36.

39 Instrument illumination and warning light bulb - removal and refitting

Carefully pull the bulb holder from the rear of the instrument or housing and unscrew the bulb from the holder. Note that the tachometer and speedometer leads have two illumination bulbs. Refitting the bulb and holder is the reverse sequence to removal.

40 Hazard warning system - general description

By operating the hazard switch on the facia panel the direction indicator light circuit is isolated and battery voltage is supplied to the hazard flasher unit and hazard relay connection W1.

The relay winding positioned across the connectors W1 and W2 is energised so as to make the contacts C1, C2 and C4 common. A circuit now exists through the hazard flasher unit to both the left hand and right hand flasher lights.

A hazard warning light mounted on the facia panel also operates with the exterior lights.

Should minor crash damage occur the system can be used

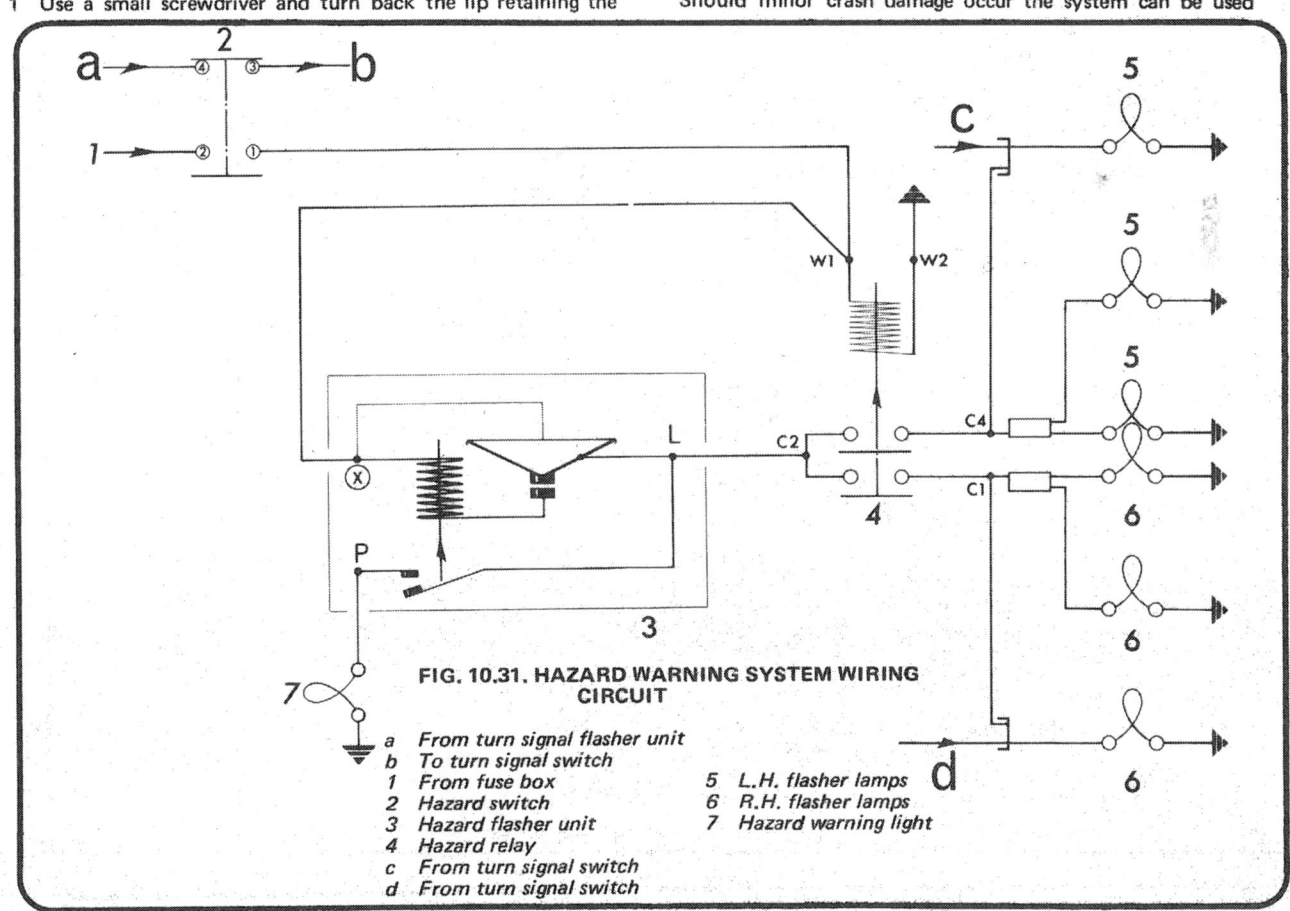

FIG. 10.31. HAZARD WARNING SYSTEM WIRING CIRCUIT

a   From turn signal flasher unit
b   To turn signal switch
1   From fuse box
2   Hazard switch
3   Hazard flasher unit
4   Hazard relay
c   From turn signal switch
d   From turn signal switch

5   L.H. flasher lamps
6   R.H. flasher lamps
7   Hazard warning light

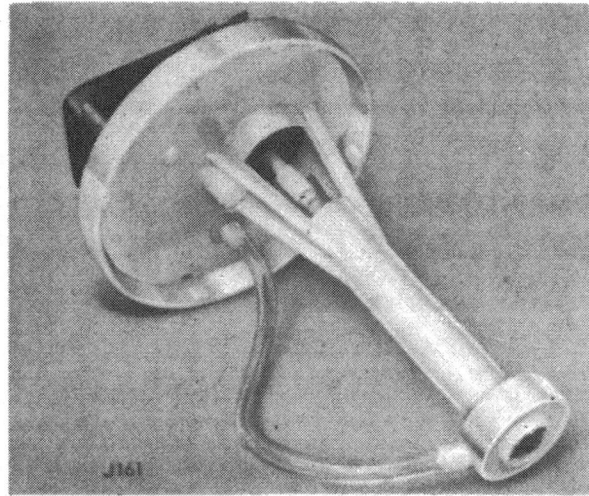

Fig. 10.32. Windscreen washer pump assembly

Fig. 10.33. Windscreen washer motor with cover removed

Fig. 10.34. Location of fuse box

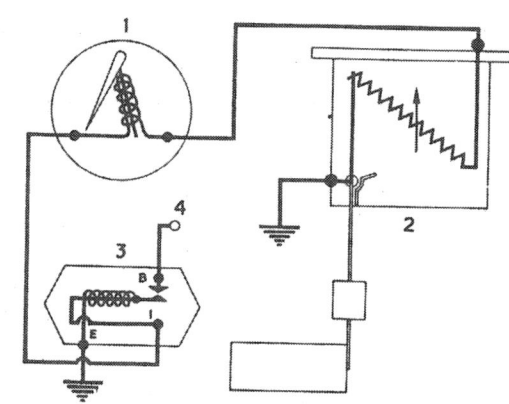

FIG. 10.35. ELECTRICAL CIRCUIT FOR FUEL GAUGE, TANK SENDER UNIT AND VOLTAGE STABILISER

1 Fuel indicator gauge
2 Tank unit
3 Voltage stabiliser
4 To 'A4' terminal on fuse unit

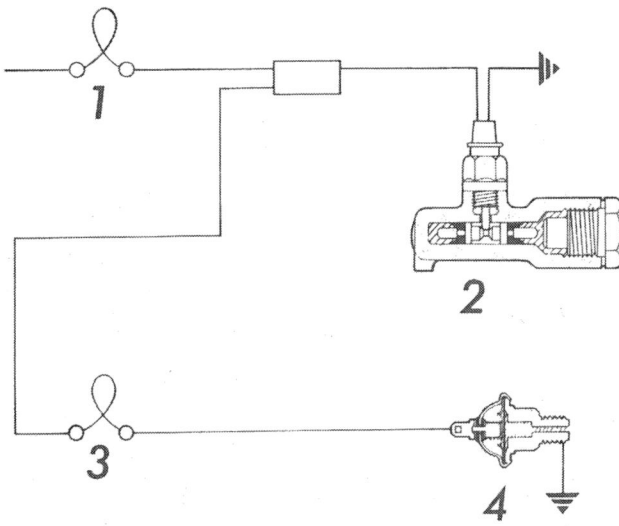

FIG. 10.36. BRAKE LINE FAILURE WIRING CIRCUIT

1 Brake line failure warning light
2 Brake line failure switch
3 Oil pressure warning light
4 Oil pressure switch
   See also Chapter 9.

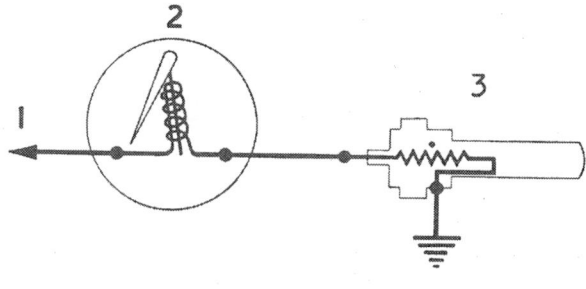

FIG. 10.37. TEMPERATURE GAUGE CIRCUIT

1 To voltage stabilizer
2 Gauge
3 Sender unit

safely. If one or more lights are inoperative the remaining good lights may continue to flash at the correct speed. If the circuit has become earthed the relevant section will blow a fuse and the system will then be inoperative which is a safeguard against fire or the harness burning out.

In event of failure of the switch, flasher unit, relay or warning light, service repair is by means of substitution.

41 Electric windscreen washers - removal, dismantling and overhaul

1   Before the screen washer unit is dismantled because of unsatisfactory fluid ejection from the jets, the other parts should be checked first. Use a voltmeter or test lamp and check that a current is being supplied to the unit. Inspect all tubing and connections for damage or blockage. Test the jets for damage or blockage.

2   To remove the unit, disconnect the external tubing from the reservoir cap.

3   Note the two electric cable connection positions and disconnect the two spade terminals.

4   Lift the cover and pump assembly from the liquid container.

5   Undo and remove the self tapping screw that secures the motor to the cover. These parts are shown in Fig.10.33. Lift the motor unit from the cover taking extreme care not to lose the little intermediate coupling which connects the pump and armature spindles.

6   Hold the armature shaft firmly with a pair of pointed pliers and remove the armature coupling with a second pair of pliers.

7   Undo and remove the two self tapping screws from the bearing plate. Lift away the plate and rubber gasket.

8   Once the plate and gasket have been removed lift away the bearing washer which is a loose fit onto the armature shaft.

9   Undo and remove the two terminal screws. Also remove the terminal nuts and then the brushes. Lift away the armature.

10   Except in extreme cases the pole assembly will not need to be disturbed.

11   Inspect the parts for wear, damage or signs of overheating. If the motor housing has been accidently damaged a replacement motor should be fitted.

12   Check the armature for damage, signs of overheating, loose windings, discoloured windings or bent shaft and if f evident a new armature should be fitted.

13   If the electrical performance of the armature is suspect, clean with a petrol moistened non-fluffy rag and polish the commutator with a fine grade glass paper. If an ohmmeter is available test the resistance of the armature which should be between 2.8 and 3.1 ohms.

14   Inspect the copper brushes for wear and if they are less than 0.0625 in (1.588 mm) they should be renewed.

15   To reassemble, if the pole assembly was removed, replace the pole assembly with the narrower pole adjacent to the terminal locations. Also ensure that the pole assembly does not rock on its seating and is firmly located on the circular spigot.

16   Refit the pole clamping member so that pressure is applied to both pole pieces.

17   Carefully insert a little molybdenum based grease into the bearing recess in the motor housing. Refit the armature into this recess.

18   Refit the brushes making sure that they bear firmly against the commutator.

19   Replace the terminal nuts, terminals and terminal screws.

20   Refit the bearing washer, rubber gasket and base plate and secure in position with the two self tapping screws.

21   Slide the armature coupling onto the shaft and push it fully home.

22   Place the motor over the cover and connect the intermediate coupling. Lower the motor and secure with the long self tapping screw.

23   Refit the two spade terminals in their original positions and reconnect the external tubing on the reservoir cap.

42 Fuse box

The fuse box is located on the left hand side of the engine compartment and contains three operational fuses and one ready for accessories. Two spare fuses are housed in the unit.

Should any fuse blow due to a short circuit or other similar trouble, trace and rectify the cause before renewing the fuse. When a spare fuse is used always replace it at the earliest opportunity.

The topmost fuse is not used on standard production models.

The fuse which is fed by a white cable from the ignition/starter switch protects the following circuits:
Temperature indicator circuit
Direction indicator circuit
Fuel gauge circuit
Stop light circuit
Windscreen washer circuit
Windscreen wiper circuit
Reverse light circuit
Heater circuit

The fuse fed by a brown cable from the battery protects the following circuits :
Horn circuit
Headlight flasher circuit
Hazard warning circuit (L H D models)

The fuse fed by a red/green cable from the steering column light switch protects the following circuits:
Instrument illumination circuit
Number plate illumination circuit
Tail light circuit
Stop light circuit
Front side light circuit

43 Fuel gauge - fault finding and rectification

A fuel gauge sender unit is fitted to the petrol tank so that a float connected to an arm and a rheostat is able to vary the resistance of the gauge circuit depending on the amount of petrol in the tank. The gauge which is mounted on the instrument panel is able to measure the resistance and indicate the tank contents.

The fuel gauge can misread in four different ways. There can be no reading at all, there can be an intermittent reading, the needle on the gauge can read too high or too low. If there is no reading at all check for loose electrical connections. Providing the wiring is in order check the components one at a time by substitution, unfortunately if one of these items proves to be faulty   it must be renewed as they are sealed and cannot be repaired.   To ensure a constant voltage supply to this circuit a voltage stabiliser is also fitted into the circuit and to test this requires specialist equipment. As a rough check if the water temperature gauge also gives suspect readings the chances are that the voltage stabiliser is not functioning correctly.

See following pages for "Fault Finding".

44 Fault finding - Electrical system

Symptom	Reason/s	Remedy
STARTER MOTOR FAILS TO TURN ENGINE		
No electricity at starter motor	Battery discharged	Charge battery.
	Battery defective internally	Fit new battery.
	Battery terminal leads loose or earth lead not securely attached to body.	Check and tighten leads.
	Loose or broken connections in starter motor circuit	Check all connections and tighten any that are loose.
	Starter motor switch or solenoid faulty	Test and replace faulty components with new.
Electricity at starter motor: faulty motor	Starter motor pinion jammed in mesh with flywheel gear ring	Disengage pinion by turning squared end of armature shaft.
	Starter brushes badly worn, sticking, or brush wires loose	Examine brushes, replace as necessary, tighten down brush wires.
	Commutator dirty, worn or burnt	Clean commutator, recut if badly burnt.
	Starter motor armature faulty.	Overhaul starter motor, fit new armature.
	Field coils earthed	Overhaul starter motor.
STARTER MOTOR TURNS ENGINE VERY SLOWLY		
Electrical defects	Battery in discharged condition	Charge battery.
	Starter brushes badly worn, sticking, or brush wires loose	Examine brushes, replace as necessary, tighten down brush wires.
	Loose wires in starter motor circuit	Check wiring and tighten as necessary.
STARTER MOTOR OPERATES WITHOUT TURNING ENGINE		
Dirt or oil on drive gear	Starter motor pinion sticking on the screwed sleeve	Remove starter motor, clean starter motor drive.
Mechanical damage	Pinion or flywheel gear teeth broken or worn	Fit new gear ring to flywheel, and new pinion to starter motor drive.
STARTER MOTOR NOISY OR EXCESSIVELY ROUGH ENGAGEMENT		
Lack of attention or mechanical damage	Pinion or flywheel gear teeth broken or worn	Fit new gear teeth to flywheel, or new pinion to starter motor drive.
	Starter drive main spring broken	Dismantle and fit new main spring.
	Starter motor retaining bolts loose	Tighten starter motor securing bolts.
BATTERY WILL NOT HOLD CHARGE FOR MORE THAN A FEW DAYS		
Wear or damage	Battery defective internally	Remove and fit new battery.
	Electrolyte level too low or electrolyte too weak due to leakage	Top up electrolyte level to just above plates.
	Plate separators no longer fully effective	Remove and fit new battery.
	Battery plates severely sulphated	Remove and fit new battery.
Insufficient current flow to keep battery charged	Alternator belt slipping	Check belt for wear, replace if necessary, and tighten.
	Battery terminal connections loose or corroded	Check terminals for tightness, and remove all corrosion.
	Alternator not charging properly	Check all connections. Seek specialist attention.
	Short in lighting circuit causing continual battery drain.	Trace and rectify.
	Regulator unit not working correctly	Check setting, clean and replace, if defective.
IGNITION LIGHT FAILS TO GO OUT, BATTERY FLAT IN A FEW DAYS		
Alternator not charging	Belt loose and slipping, or broken	Check, replace and tighten as necessary.
	Internal fault	Seek specialist attention.
FUEL GAUGE		
Fuel gauge gives no reading	Fuel tank empty!	Fill fuel tank.
	Electric cable between tank sender unit and gauge earthed or loose	Check cable for earthing and joints for tightness.
	Fuel gauge case not earthed	Ensure case is well earthed.
	Fuel gauge supply cable interrupted	Check and replace cable if necessary.
	Fuel gauge unit broken	Replace fuel gauge.
Fuel gauge registers full all the time	Electric cable between tank unit and gauge broken or disconnected	Check over cable and repair as necessary.

HORN

Symptom	Cause	Remedy
Horn operates all the time	Horn push either earthed or stuck down	Disconnect battery earth. Check and rectify source of trouble.
	Horn cable to horn push earthed	Disconnect battery earth. Check and rectify source of trouble.
Horn fails to operate	Blown fuse	Check and renew if broken. Ascertain cause.
	Cable or cable connection loose, broken or disconnected	Check all connections for tightness and cables for breaks.
	Horn has an internal fault	Remove and overhaul horn.
Horn emits intermittent or unsatisfactory noise	Cable connections loose	Check and tighten all connections.
	Horn incorrectly adjusted	Adjust horn until best note obtained.

LIGHTS

Symptom	Cause	Remedy
Lights do not come on	If engine not running, battery discharged	Push-start car, charge battery.
	Light bulb filament burnt out or bulbs broken	Test bulbs in live bulb holder.
	Wire connections loose, disconnected or broken	Check all connections for tightness and wire cable for breaks.
	Light switch shorting or otherwise faulty	By-pass light switch to ascertain if fault is in switch and fit new switch as appropriate.
Lights come on but fade out	If engine not running, battery discharged	Push-start car, and charge battery.
Lights give very poor illumination	Lamp glasses dirty	Clean glasses.
	Reflector tarnished or dirty	Fit new reflectors.
	Lamps badly out of adjustment	Adjust lamps correctly.
	Incorrect bulb with too low wattage fitted	Remove bulb and replace with correct grade.
	Existing bulbs old and badly discoloured	Renew bulb units.
	Electrical wiring too thin not allowing full current to pass	Rewire lighting system.
Lights work erratically - flashing on and off, especially over bumps	Battery terminals or earth connection loose	Tighten battery terminals and earth connection.
	Lights not earthing properly	Examine and rectify.
	Contacts in light switch faulty.	By-pass light switch to ascertain if fault is in switch and fit new switch as appropriate.

WIPERS

Symptom	Cause	Remedy
Wiper motor fails to work	Blown fuse	Check and replace fuse if necessary.
	Wire connections loose disconnected, or broken	Check wiper wiring. Tighten loose connections.
	Brushes badly worn	Remove and fit new brushes.
	Armature worn or faulty	If electricity at wiper motor remove and overhaul and fit replacement armature.
	Field coils faulty	Purchase reconditioned wiper motor.
Wiper motor works very slowly and takes excessive current	Commutator dirty, greasy, or burnt	Clean commutator thoroughly.
	Drive to wheelboxes too bent or unlubricated	Examine drive and straighten out severe curvature. Lubricate.
	Wheelbox spindle binding or damaged	Remove, overhaul, or fit replacement.
	Armature bearings dry or unaligned	Replace with new bearings correctly aligned.
	Armature badly worn or faulty	Remove, overhaul, or fit replacement armature.
Wiper motor works slowly and takes little current	Brushes badly worn	Remove and fit new brushes.
	Commutator dirty, greasy, or burnt	Clean commutator thoroughly.
	Armature badly worn or faulty	Remove and overhaul armature or fit replacement.
Wiper motor works but wiper blades remain static	Driving cable rack disengaged or faulty	Examine and if faulty, replace.
	Wheelbox gear and spindle damaged or worn	Examine and if faulty, replace.
	Wiper motor gearbox parts badly worn	Overhaul or fit new gearbox.

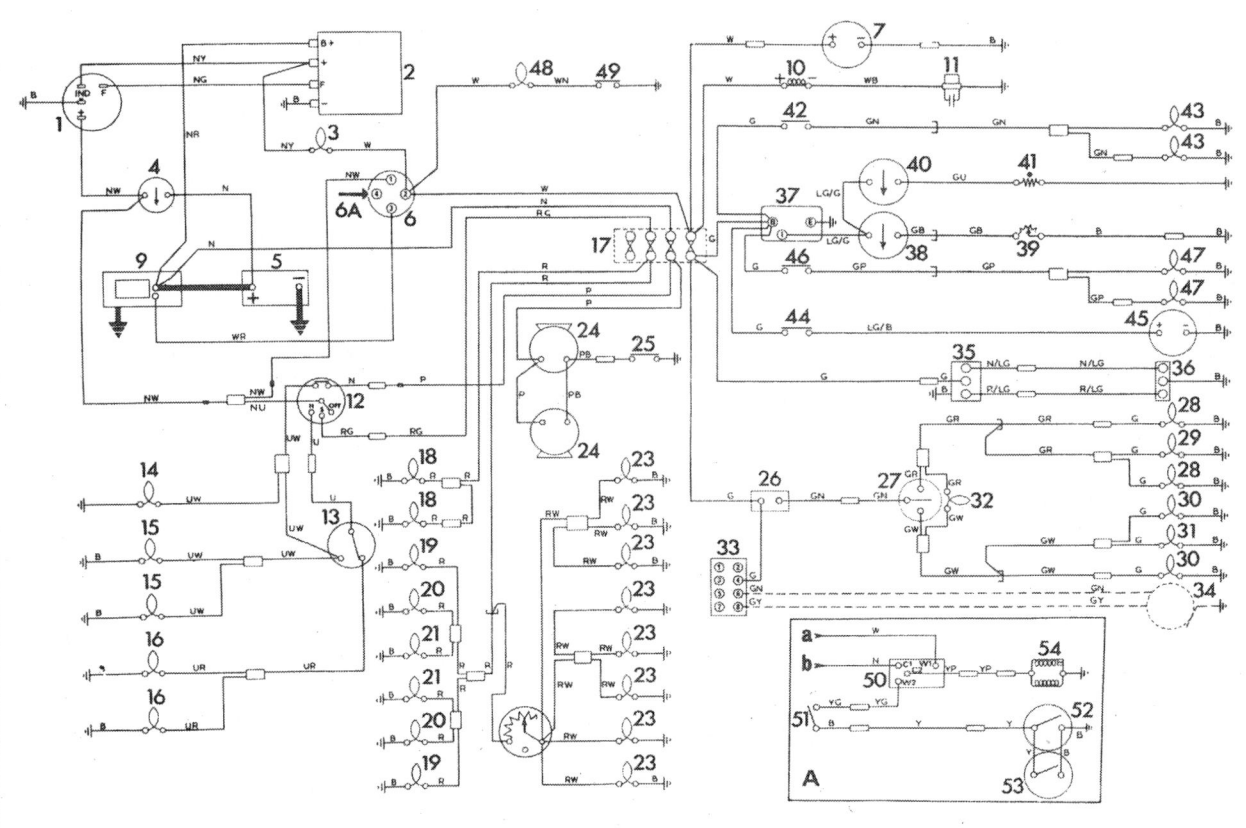

KEY TO WIRING DIAGRAM TR5 P I (RIGHT HAND STEER)

1 Alternator	15 Main beam	30 RH flasher lamp	46 Stop lamp switch
2 Alternator control unit	16 Dip beam	31 RH flasher repeater lamp	47 Stop lamp
3 Ignition warning light	17 Fuse box	32 Flasher warning light	48 Oil pressure warning light
4 Ammeter	18 Front parking lamp	33 Heater switch	49 Oil pressure switch
5 Battery	19 Rear marker lamp	34 Heater motor	
6 Ignition/starter switch	20 Tail lamp	35 Windscreen wiper motor	A Overdrive (optional extra)
6a Ignition/starter switch -	21 Plate illumination lamp	36 Windscreen wiper switch	50 Overdrive relay
radio supply connector	22 Panel theostat	37 Voltage stabilizer	51 Overdrive column switch
7 Petrol pump	23 Instrument illumination	38 Fuel indicator	52 Overdrive gearbox switch
9 Starter motor	24 Horn	39 Fuel tank unit	2nd gear ON
10 Ignition coil	25 Horn push	40 Temperature indicator	53 Overdrive gearbox switch
11 Ignition distributor	26 Turn signal flasher unit	41 Temperature transmitter	3rd and 4th gear ON
12 Column light switch	27 Turn signal flasher switch	42 Reverse lamp switch	54 Overdrive solenoid
13 Dip switch	28 LH flasher lamp	43 Reverse lamp	a From fuse box
14 Main beam warning light	29 LH flasher repeater lamp	44 Windscreen washer switch	b From fuse box
		45 Windscreen washer motor	

Colour Code

N	Brown		L/G	Light green
U	Blue		W	White
R	Red		Y	Yellow
P	Purple		S	Slate
G	Green		B	Black

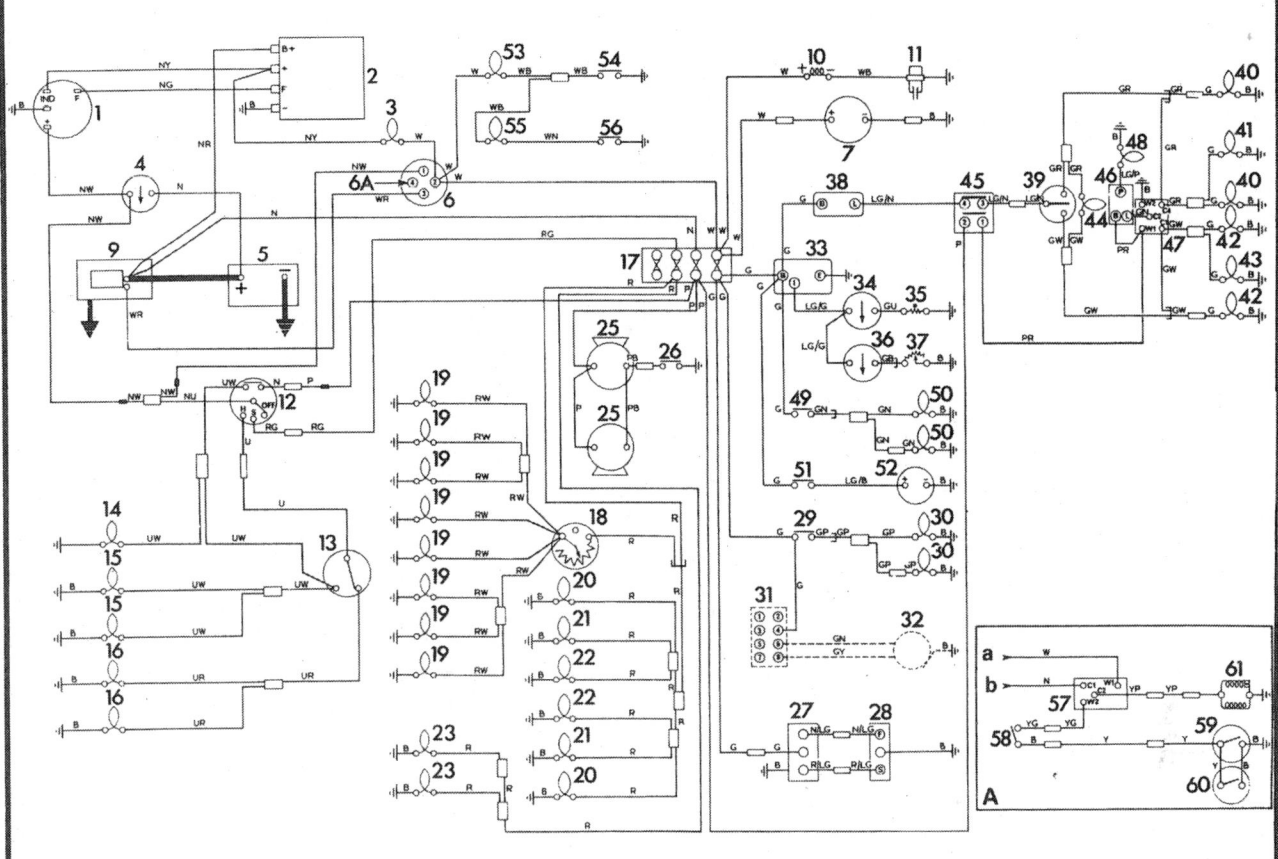

KEY TO WIRING DIAGRAM TR5 P I (LEFT HAND STEER)

1	Alternator	17	Fuse box
2	Alternator control unit	18	Panel rheostat
3	Ignition warning light	19	Instrument illumination
4	Ammeter	20	Rear marker light
5	Battery	21	Tail lamp
6	Ignition/starter switch	22	Plate illumination lamp
6a	Ignition/starter switch – radio supply connector	23	Front parking lamp
7	Petrol pump	25	Horn
9	Starter motor	26	Horn push
10	Ignition coil	27	Windscreen wiper motor
11	Ignition distributor	28	Windscreen wiper switch
12	Column light switch	29	Stop lamp switch
13	Dip switch	30	Stop lamp
14	Main beam warning light	31	Heater switch
15	Main beam	32	Heater motor
16	Dip beam	33	Voltage stabilizer
		34	Temperature indicator

35 Temperature transmitter
36 Fuel indicator
37 Fuel tank unit
38 Turn signal flasher unit
39 Turn signal flasher unit switch
40 LH flasher lamp
41 LH flasher repeater lamp
42 RH flasher lamp
43 RH flasher repeater lamp
44 Flasher warning light
45 Hazard switch
46 Hazard flasher unit
47 Hazard relay
48 Hazard warning light
49 Reverse lamp switch
50 Reverse lamp
51 Windscreen washer switch

52 Windscreen washer motor
53 Brake line failure warning light
54 Brake line failure switch
55 Oil pressure warning light
56 Oil pressure switch

A Overdrive (optional extra)
57 Overdrive relay
58 Overdrive column switch
59 Overdrive gearbox switch – 2nd gear ON
60 Overdrive gearbox switch – 3rd and 4th gear ON
61 Overdrive solenoid

a From fuse box
b From fuse box

Colour Code

N	Brown	L/G	Light green
U	Blue	W	White
R	Red	Y	Yellow
P	Purple	S	Slate
G	Green	B	Black

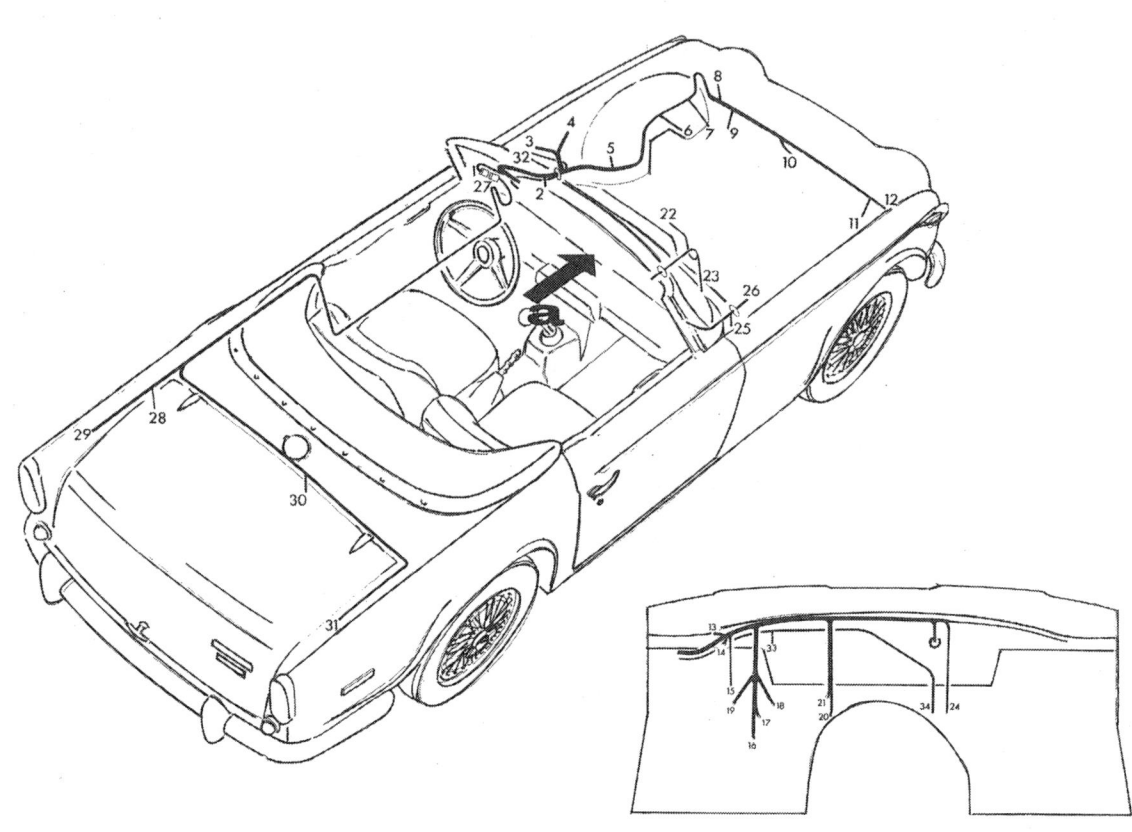

KEY TO HARNESS - TR5 P I - LEFT HAND STEER SHOWN - RIGHT HAND STEER SIMILAR

Main harness

1 Plug connection to body harness
2 Dip switch
3 Windscreen wiper motor
   Hazard relay - LH steer only
   Fuse box
4 Fuse box
   Alternator control unit
   Hazard flasher unit - LH steer only
5 Brake line failure switch - LH steer only
6 Oil pressure switch
   Ignition coil
   Alternator
   Temperature transmitter
7 Horn push - earth return wire connected to steering unit
8 Flasher repeater lamp
   Front parking lamp
   Front flasher lamp
9 Horn

10 Headlamps
11 Horn
12 Front flasher lamp
   Front parking lamp
   Flasher repeater lamp
13 Column light switch
14 Turn signal flasher switch
   Horn push
15 Stop lamp switch
16 Windscreen wiper switch
   Windscreen washer switch
17 Speedometer - flasher warning light
   Speedometer - main beam warning light
   Speedometer - instrument illumination
   Voltage stabilizer
18 Brake line failure warning light - LH steer only
   Hazard warning light - LH steer only
   Hazard switch - LH steer only

19 Tachometer - ignition warning light
   Tachometer - oil pressure warning light
   Tachometer - instrument illumination
20 Ignition/starter switch
   Heater switch
21 Ammeter
   Fuel indicator
   Panel rheostat
   Oil pressure indicator - instrument illumination
   Temperature indicator
22 Battery
23 Starter motor
24 Reverse lamp switch
25 Turn signal flasher unit
26 Windscreen washer pump

Body harness
27 Plug connection to main harness
28 Petrol pump

29 Rear marker lamp
   Rear flasher lamp
   Tail/stop lamp
   Reverse lamp
   Plate illumination lamp
30 Fuel tank unit
31 Rear marker lamp
   Rear flasher lamp
   Tail/stop lamp
   Reverse lamp
   Plate illumination lamp
Overdrive harness (optional extra)
32 Fuse box
   Overdrive relay
33 Overdrive column switch
34 Overdrive gearbox switch
   2nd gear ON
   Overdrive gearbox switch
   3rd and 4th gear ON
   Overdrive solenoid

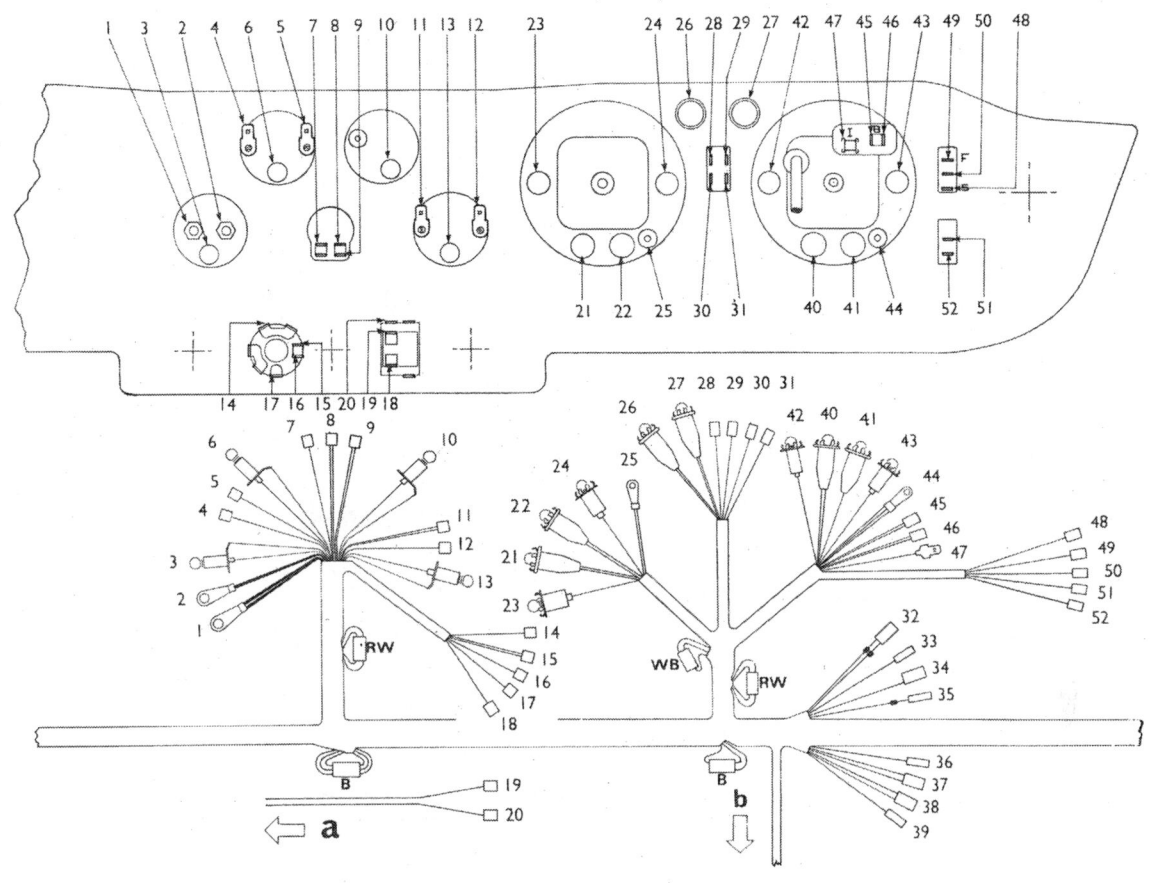

KEY TO FACIA CONNECTIONS – TR5 PI

No.	Colour	Connection	Component	No.	Colour	Connection	Connection
1	NW	Eyelet–2 wire	Ammeter	28	LG/N	Lucar	Hazard switch
2	N	Eyelet	Ammeter	29	LG/N	Lucar	Hazard switch
3	RW and B	Bulb holder	Ammeter	30	P	Lucar	Hazard switch
4	LG/G	Lucar	Fuel indicator	31	PR	Lucar	Hazard switch
5	GB	Lucar	Fuel indicator	32	NW with blue idents s	Double snap connector–2 wire	Column light switch
6	RW and B	Bulb holder	Fuel indicator	33	RG	Snap connector	Column light switch
7	R	Lucar	Panel rheostat	34	U	Double snap connector	Column light switch
8	RW	Lucar–2 wire	Panel rheostat	35	P with brown ident	Snap connector	Column light switch
9	RW	Lucar–2 wire	Panel rheostat	36	LG/N	Snap connector	Flasher switch
10	RW and B	Bulb holder	Oil pressure indicator	37	GR	Double snap connector–2 wire	Flasher switch
11	LG/G	Lucar–2 wire	Temperature indicator	38	GW	Double snap connector–2 wire	Flasher switch
12	GU	Lucar	Temperature indicator	39	PB	Snap connector	Horn push
13	RW and B	Bulb holder	Temperature indicator	40	GR and GW	Bulb holder	Speedometer warning light
14	NW	Lucar	Ignition/starter switch	41	UW	Bulb holder	Speedometer - main beam warning light
15	W	Lucar–2 wire	Ignition/starter switch	42	RW	Bulb holder	Speedometer
16	W	Lucar	Ignition/starter switch	43	RW	Bulb holder	Speedometer
17	WR	Lucar	Ignition/starter switch	44	B	Eyelet–3 wire	Speedometer
18	G	Lucar	Heater switch	45	G	Lucar–2 wire	Voltage stabilizer
19	GN	Lucar	Heater switch	46	G	Lucar–2 wire	Voltage stabilizer
20	GY	Lucar	Heater switch	47	LG/G	Lucar blade	Voltage stabilizer
21	W and NY	Bulb holder	Tachometer - ignition warning light	48	R/LG	Lucar	Windscreen wiper switch
22	WB and WN	Bulb holder	Tachometer - oil pressure warning light	49	N/LG	Lucar	Windscreen wiper switch
23	RW	Bulb holder	Tachometer	50	B	Lucar	Windscreen wiper switch
24	RW	Bulb holder	Tachometer	51	G	Lucar	Windscreen washer switch
25	B	Eyelet–2 wire	Tachometer	52	LG/B	Lucar	Windscreen washer switch
26	W and WB	Bulb holder	Brake line failure warning light				
27	LG/P and B	Bulb holder	Hazard warning light				

a. GN and GY — to heater motor.
b. G and GP — to stop lamp switch.
Left hand steer shown – right hand steer similar.

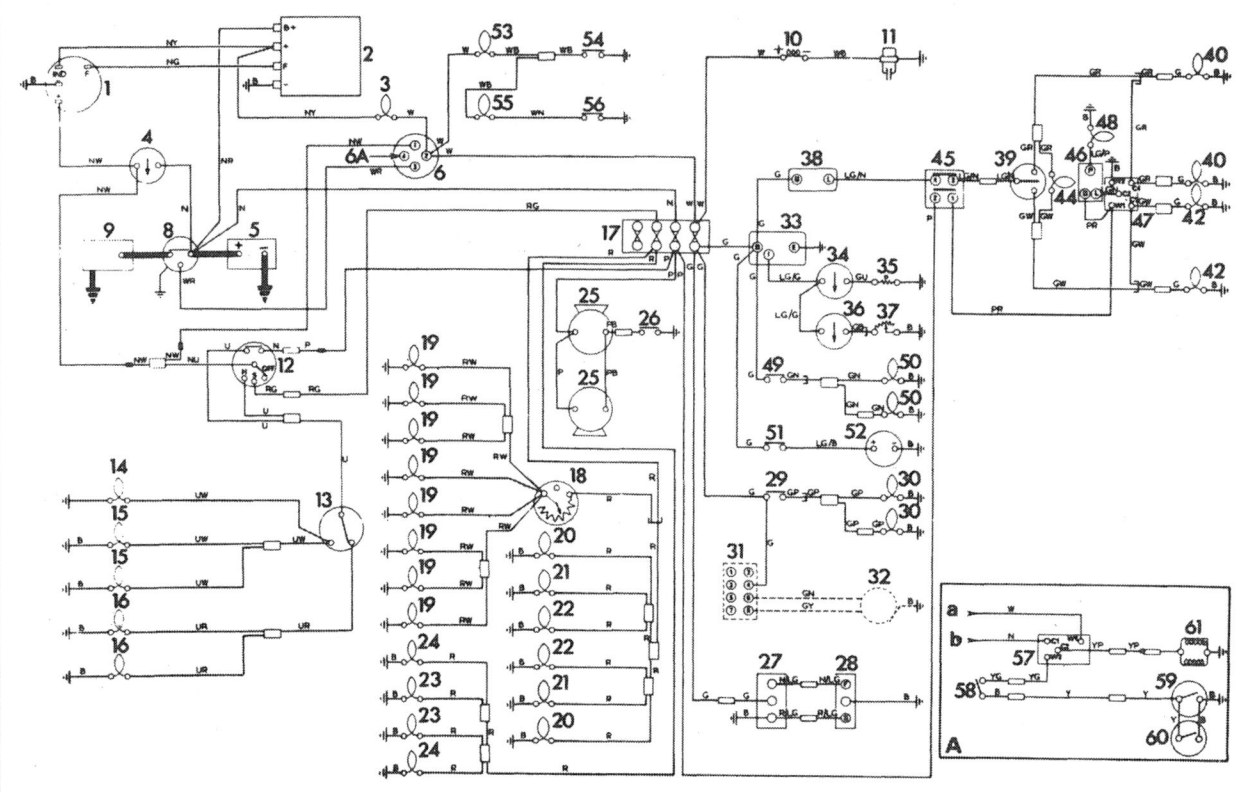

KEY TO WIRING DIAGRAM — TR250

1 Alternator
2 Alternator control unit
3 Ignition warning light
4 Ammeter
5 Battery
6 Ignition/starter switch
6a Ignition/starter switch - radio
    supply connector
8 Starter solenoid
9 Starter motor
10 Ignition coil
11 Ignition distributor
12 Column light switch
13 Dip switch
14 Main beam warning light
15 Main beam
16 Dip beam

17 Fuse box
18 Panel rheostat
19 Instrument illumination
20 Rear marker lamp
21 Tail lamp
22 Plate illumination lamp
23 Front parking lamp
24 Front marker lamp
25 Horn
26 Horn push
27 Windscreen wiper motor
28 Windscreen wiper switch
29 Stop lamp switch
30 Stop lamp
31 Heater switch
32 Heater motor
33 Voltage stabilizer

34 Temperature indicator
35 Temperature transmitter
36 Fuel indicator
37 Fuel tank unit
38 Flasher unit
39 Flasher switch
40 LH flasher lamp
42 RH flasher lamp
44 Flasher warning light
45 Hazard switch
46 Hazard flasher unit
47 Hazard relay
48 Hazard warning light
49 Reverse lamp switch
50 Reverse lamp
51 Windscreen washer switch
52 Windscreen washer motor

53 Brake pressure differential
    warning light
54 Brake pressure differential
    switch
55 Oil pressure warning light
56 Oil pressure switch

A Overdrive (optional extra)
57 Overdrive relay
58 Overdrive column switch
59 Overdrive gearbox switch
    2nd gear ON
60 Overdrive gearbox switch
    3rd and 4th gear ON
61 Overdrive solenoid
a From fuse box
b From fuse box

Colour Code

N	Brown	L/G	Light green
U	Blue	W	White
R	Red	Y	Yellow
P	Purple	S	Slate
G	Green	B	Black

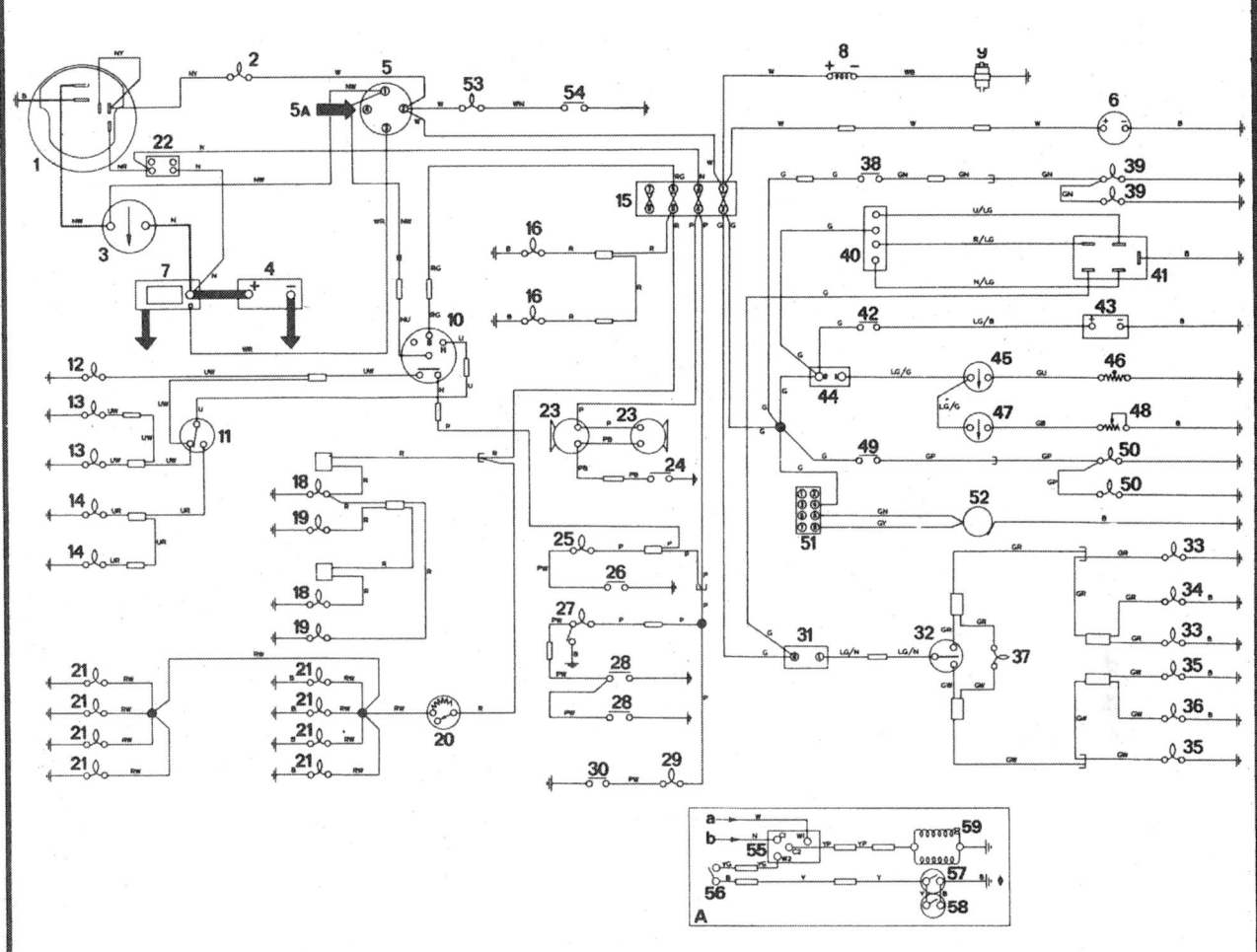

KEY TO WIRING DIAGRAM - TR6 1 (RIGHT HAND STEER)

1 Alternator
2 Ignition warning light
3 Ammeter
4 Battery
5 Ignition/starter switch
5a Ignition/starter switch-
   radio supply connector
6 Petrol pump
7 Starter motor
8 Ignition coil
9 Ignition distributor
10 Column light switch
11 Dip switch
12 Main beam warning light
13 Main beam
14 Dip beam
15 Fuse box

16 Front parking lamp
18 Tail lamp
19 Plate illumination lamp
20 Panel rheostat
21 Instrument illumination
22 Connector block
23 Horn
24 Horn push
25 Cubby box illumination
26 Cubby box illumination
   switch
27 Transmission tunnel lamp
28 Transmission tunnel lamp
   door switch
29 Luggage boot lamp
30 Luggage boot lamp switch
31 Turn signal flasher unit
32 Turn signal switch
33 LH flasher lamp

34 LH flasher repeater lamp
35 RH flasher lamp
36 RH flasher repeater lamp
37 Turn signal warning light
38 Reverse lamp switch
39 Reverse lamp
40 Windscreen wiper switch
41 Windscreen wiper motor
42 Windscreen washer switch
43 Windscreen washer pump
44 Voltage stabilizer
45 Temperature indicator
46 Temperature transmitter
47 Fuel indicator
48 Fuel tank unit
49 Stop lamp switch
50 Stop lamp

51 Heater switch
52 Heater motor
53 Oil pressure warning light
54 Oil pressure switch

A Overdrive (optional extra)
55 Overdrive relay
56 Overdrive column switch
57 Overdrive gearbox switch-
   2nd gear ON
58 Overdrive gearbox switch-
   3rd and 4th gear ON
59 Overdrive solenoid

a From fuse box
b From fuse box

Colour Code

N	Brown	LG	Light Green
U	Blue	W	White
R	Red	Y	Yellow
P	Purple	S	Slate
G	Green	B	Black

188

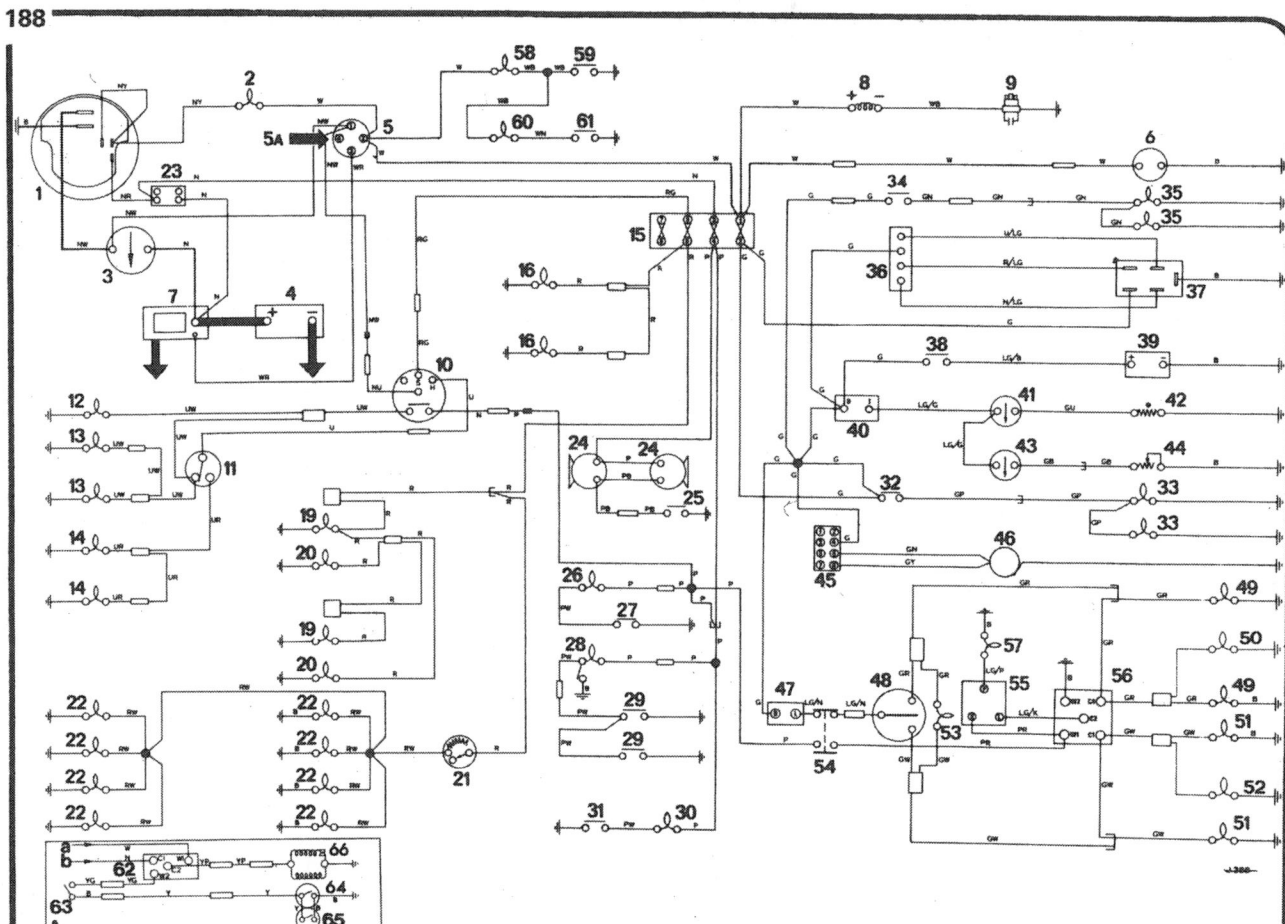

KEY TO WIRING DIAGRAM - TR6 P I (LEFT HAND STEER)

1	Alternator	19	Tail lamp
2	Ignition warning light	20	Number plate illumination lamp
3	Ammeter	21	Panel rheostat
4	Battery	22	Instrument illumination
5	Ignition/starter switch	23	Connector block
5a	Ignition/starter switch — radio supply connector	24	Horn
6	Petrol pump	25	Horn push
7	Starter motor	26	Glove box illumination
8	Coil	27	Glove box illumination switch
9	Distributor	28	Transmission tunnel lamp
10	Column light switch	29	Transmission tunnel lamp door switch
11	Dip switch	30	Luggage boot lamp
12	Main beam warning light	31	Luggage boot lamp switch
13	Main beam	32	Stop lamp switch
14	Dip beam	33	Stop lamp
15	Fuse box	34	Reverse lamp switch
16	Front parking lamp		

35 Reverse lamp
36 Windscreen wiper switch
37 Windscreen wiper motor
38 Windscreen washer switch
39 Windscreen washer pump
40 Voltage stabilizer
41 Temperature indicator
42 Temperature transmitter
43 Fuel indicator
44 Fuel tank unit
45 Heater switch
46 Heater motor
47 Turn signal flasher unit
48 Turn signal switch
49 LH flasher lamp
50 LH flasher repeater lamp
51 RH flasher lamp
52 RH flasher repeater lamp

53 Turn signal warning light
54 Hazard switch
55 Hazard flasher unit
56 Hazard relay
57 Hazard warning light
58 Brake line failure warning light
59 Brake line failure switch
60 Oil pressure warning light
61 Oil pressure switch

A Overdrive (optional extra)
62 Overdrive relay
63 Overdrive column switch
64 Overdrive gearbox switch — 2nd gear ON
65 Overdrive gearbox switch — 3rd & 4th gear ON
66 Overdrive solenoid

a From fuse box
b From fuse box

Colour Code

N	Brown	LG	Light Green
U	Blue	W	White
R	Red	Y	Yellow
P	Purple	S	Slate
G	Green	B	Black

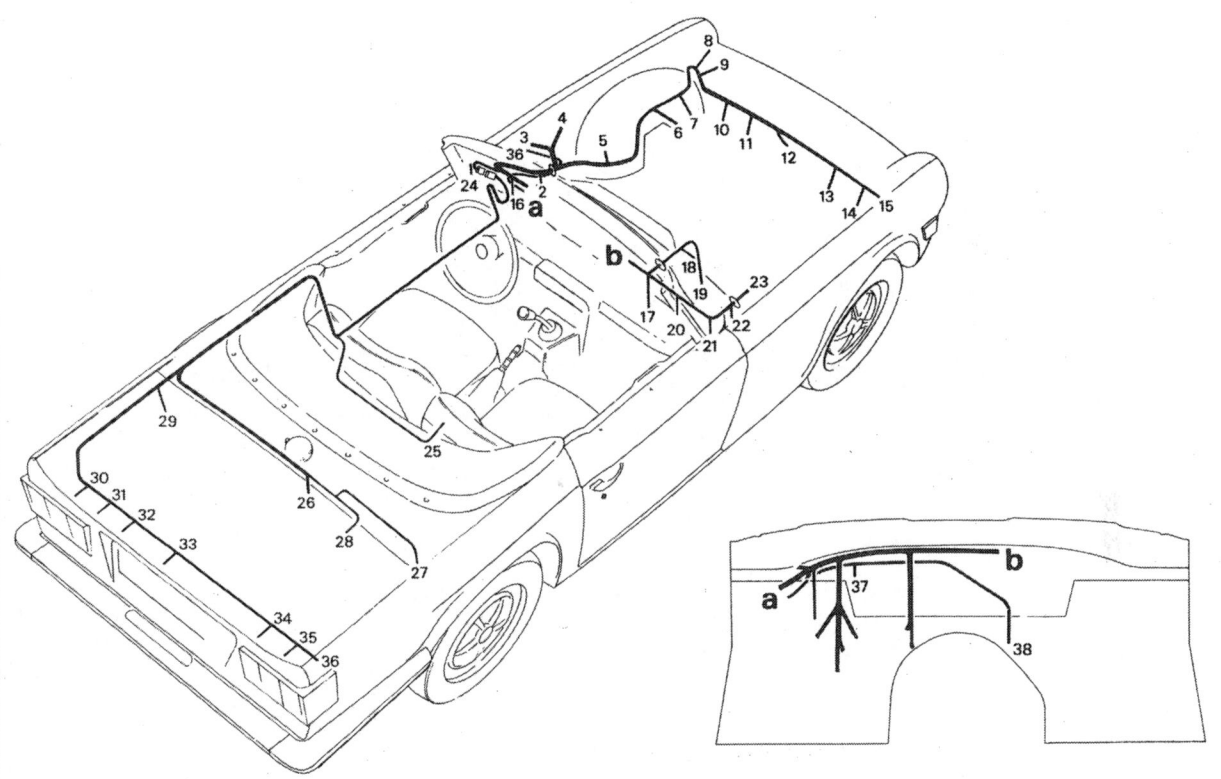

KEY TO HARNESS - TR6 PI
Left hand steer shown - right hand steer similar

Main harness
1 Plug connection to body harness
2 Dip switch
3 Windscreen wiper motor
   Hazard relay - LH steer only
   Fuse box
4 Fuse box
   Connector block
   Hazard flasher unit - LH steer only
5 Brake line failure switch - LH steer only
6 Alternator
   Ignition coil
   Temperature transmitter
   Oil pressure switch
7 Horn push - earth return wire
   Connected to steering unit
8 Harness earth

9 Front parking lamp
   Front flasher lamp
   Flasher repeater lamp
10 Headlamp
11 Horn
12 Harness earth
13 Horn
14 Headlamp
15 Front parking lamp
   Front flasher lamp
   Flasher repeater lamp
16 Transmission tunnel lamp door switch
a Refer to Facia connections for continuation
b Refer to Facia connections for continuation
17 Reverse lamp switch
18 Harness earth

19 Starter motor
20 Cubby box illumination
21 Transmission tunnel lamp door switch
22 Turn signal flasher unit
23 Windscreen washer pump

Body harness
24 Plug connection to main harness
25 Transmission tunnel lamp
26 Fuel tank unit
27 Luggage boot lamp switch
28 Luggage boot lamp
29 Petrol pump
30 Rear flasher lamp
31 Tail/stop lamp
32 Reverse lamp

33 Plate illumination lamp
34 Reverse lamp
35 Tail/stop lamp
36 Rear flasher lamp

Overdrive harness (optional extra)
36a Fuse box
   Overdrive relay
37 Overdrive column switch
38 Overdrive gearbox switch - 2nd gear ON
   Overdrive gearbox switch - 3rd and 4th gears ON
   Overdrive solenoid

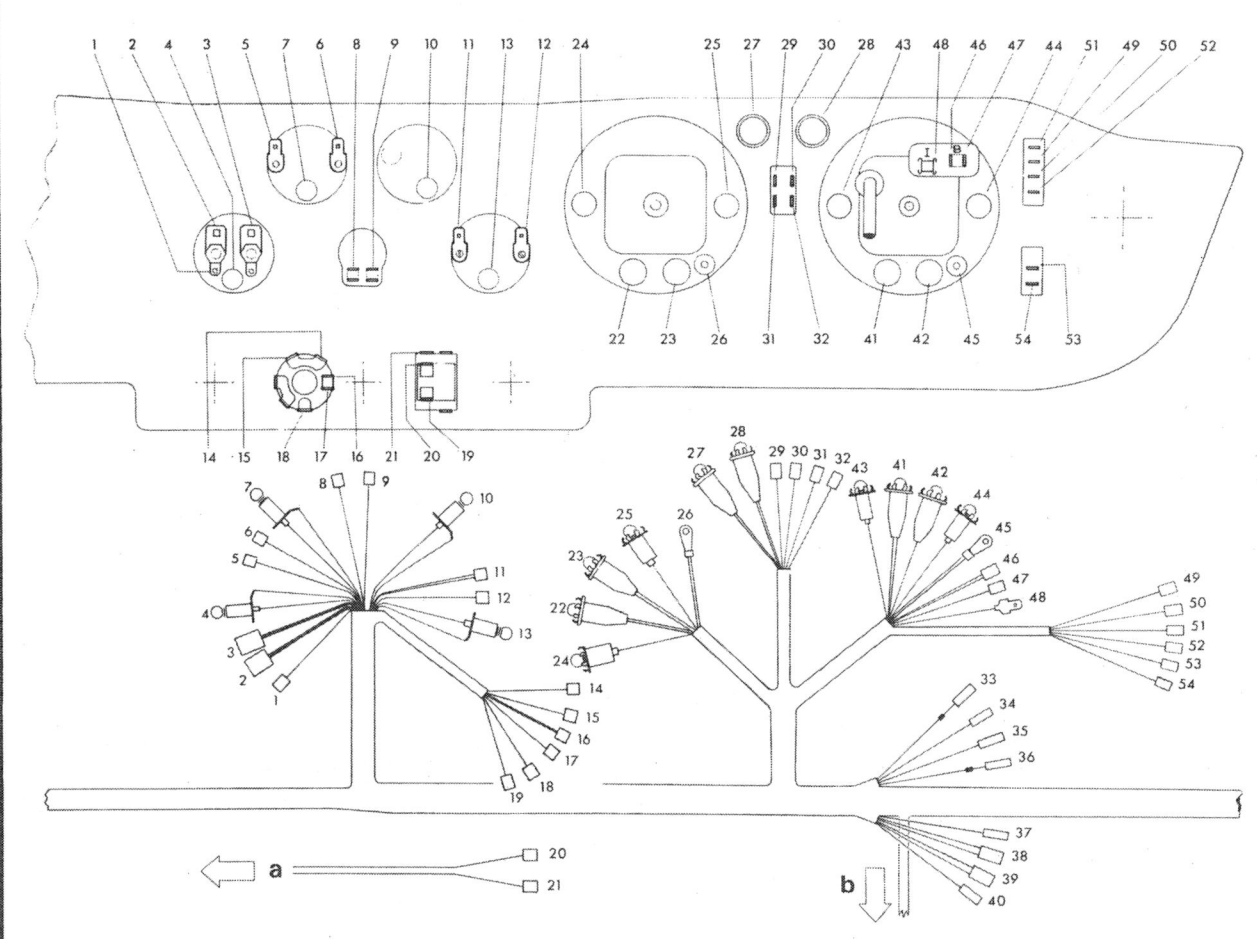

KEY TO FACIA CONNECTIONS TR6 PI
Left hand steer shown · right hand steer · similar

No.	Colour	Connection	Component	No.	Colour	Connection	Component
1	NW	Lucar	Ammeter	28	LG/P and B	Bulb holder	Hazard warning light · LH steer only
2	NW	Lucar	Ammeter	29	LG/N	Lucar	Hazard switch - LH steer only
3	N	Lucar	Ammeter	30	LG/N	Lucar	Hazard switch - LH steer only
4	RW and B	Bulb holder	Ammeter	31	P	Lucar	Hazard switch - LH steer only
5	LG/G	Lucar	Fuel indicator	32	PR	Lucar	Hazard switch - LH steer only
6	GB	Lucar	Fuel indicator	33	NW with blue ident	Snap connector	Column light switch
7	RW and B	Bulb holder	Fuel indicator	34	RG	Snap connector	Column light switch
8	R	Lucar	Panel rheostat	35	U	Snap connector	Column light switch
9	RW	Lucar	Panel rheostat	36	P with brown ident	Snap connector	Column light switch
10	RW and B	Bulb holder	Oil pressure indicator	37	LG/N	Snap connector	Turn signal switch
11	LG/G	Lucar—2 wire	Temperature indicator	38	GR	Double snap connector—2 wire	Turn signal switch
12	GU	Lucar	Temperature indicator	39	GW	Double snap connector—2	Turn signal switch
13	RW and B	Bulb holder	Temperature indicator	40	PB	Snap connector	Horn push
14	NW	Lucar	Ignition/starter switch	41	GR and GW	Bulb holder	Speedometer - turn signal warning light
15	NW	Lucar	Ignition/starter switch	42	UW	Bulb holder	Speedometer - main beam warning light
16	W	Lucar—2 wire	Ignition/starter switch	43	RW	Bulb holder	Speedometer
17	W	Lucar	Ignition/starter switch	44	RW	Bulb holder	Speedometer
18	WR	Lucar	Ignition/starter switch	45	B	Eyelet—2 wire	Speedometer
19	G	Lucar	Heater switch	46	G	Lucar—2 wire	Voltage stabilizer
20	GN	Lucar	Heater switch	47	G	Lucar	Voltage stabilizer
21	GY	Lucar	Heater switch	48	LG/G	Lucar blade	Voltage stabilizer
22	W and NY	Bulb holder	Tachometer - ignition warning light	49	G	Lucar	Windscreen wiper switch
23	WB and WN	Bulb holder	Tachometer - oil pressure warning light	50	R/LG	Lucar	Windscreen wiper switch
24	RW	Bulb holder	Tachometer	51	U/LG	Lucar	Windscreen wiper switch
25	RW	Bulb holder	Tachometer	52	N/LG	Lucar	Windscreen wiper switch
26	B	Eyelet—2 wire	Tachometer	53	G	Lucar	Windscreen washer switch
27	W and WB	Bulb holder	Brake line failure warning light - left hand steer only	54	LG/B	Lucar	Windscreen washer switch

a. GN and GY - to heater motor
b. G and GP - to stop lamp switch

Chapter 11 Suspension and steering

Contents

Specifications

Front suspension

Type	Independent
Type of spring	Coil

Spring specifications:	TR5/TR250	TR6
Number of working coils	6	5¼
Rate	312 lb/in (3.595 Kg m)	312 lb in (3.595 Kg m)
Free length (approx)	10.28 in (261.112 mm)	10.03 in (261 mm)

Fitted length	8.12 ± 3/32 in
Fitted load	925 lb
Hand of helix	Right
Static deflection (approx)	3 in
Wire diameter	0.5 ± 0.002 in
Front lock	31½°½
Back lock	30°
Front shock absorber	Telescopic sealed unit - non adjustable
Anti-roll bar rate	150 lb in (1.73 Kg m)

Rear suspension

Type	Independent

Spring specifications

Number of working coils	6¾
Free length	10.92 in (278 mm)
Rate	349 lb in (3.595 Kg m)

Rear shock absorber

Type	Two piston with filler plug
Fluid	Armstrong Shock Absorber Fluid 624
Camber angle	1° negative ± ½°
Toe in	0 - 1/16 in (0 - 1.6 mm)

Steering

Type	Rack and pinion
Angles:	
Toe in	0 - 1/16 in (0 - 1.6 mm)
Castor	2¾° ± ½°
Camber	¼° negative ± ½°

KPI		9¼° ± ¾°
Toe out on turns		20° front lock gives 19¾° back lash
Pinion end float adjustment		Shims
Rocker damper adjustment		Shims
Inner ball joint pin adjustment		Shims
Turning circle		33 feet (10.1 m)

TORQUE WRENCH SETTINGS

	description	lb ft	Kg m
Front suspension			
Brake disc attachment	3/8 in UNF bolt	32 - 35	4.42 - 4.84
Brake caliper and shield attachment	7/16 in UNF bolt	50 - 55	6.91 - 7.60
Brake caliper mounting bracket and tie rod lever			
attachment	3/8 in UNF setscrew	26 - 28	3.60 - 3.87
Brake caliper mounting bracket and tie rod lever			
attachment	3/8 in UNF bolt	26 - 28	3.60 - 3.87
Damper to spring pan mounting	7/16 in UNF x 2 3/8 in bolt	55 - 60	7.60 - 8.30
Lockstop bolts to trunnion	5/16 in UNF x 1 3/8 in setscrew	18 - 20	2.49 - 2.77
Lower wishbone mounting bracket to frame ...	3/8 in UNF x 1¼ in bolt	28 - 30	3.87 - 4.15
Lower wishbone to mounting bracket	½ in UNF x 2 5/8 in bolt	45 - 50	6.22 - 6.91
Lower wishbone to vertical link	9/16 in UNF bolt	45 - 60	6.22 - 8.30
Lower wishbone to spring pan	3/8 in UNF bolt/stud	28 - 30	3.87 - 4.15
Shock absorber mounting to spring pan	3/8 in UNF weld bolt	26 - 28	3.60 - 3.87
Stub axle to vertical link	½ in UNF on axle	55 - 60	7.60 - 8.30
Stub axle to front hub	½ in UNF on axle		
Note: Tighten above item to 5 lb ft, unscrew one flat and insert split pin to give .003 in to .005 in end float.			
Top ball joint to upper wishbone	3/8 in UNF x 2¾ in bolt	26 - 28	3.60 - 3.87
Top ball joint to vertical link	½ in UNF ball pin	55 - 65	7.60 - 8.99
Upper wishbone to fulcrum pin	7/16 in UNF on pin	26 - 40	3.60 - 5.54
Upper wishbone fulcrum to chassis frame ...	3/8 in UNF x 1 in setscrew	28 - 30	3.87 - 4.15
Anti-roll bar mounting bracket to lower wishbone	3/8 in x 2 5/8 in bolt	28 - 30	3.87 - 4.15
Anti-roll bar fixing	5/16 in UNF 'U' bolts with nyloc nuts	3 - 4	0.42 - 0.55
Wheel stud	7/16 in UNF stud	55 - 60	7.60 - 8.30
Rear suspension			
Bumper rubber attachment	3/8 in UNF on bump rubber	18 - 20	2.49 - 2.77
Damper to mounting bracket	7/16 in UNF x 1¼ in setscrew	55 - 60	7.60 - 8.30
Damper link attachment	3/8 in UNF link	18 - 20	2.49 - 2.77
Inner driven flange to outer axles	3/8 in UNF x 1.13 in bolt	28 - 30	3.87 - 4.15
Outer driven flange to axle and hub	1 3/8 in UNF on stub axle		
Note: Above item to be tightened to give .002 in to .005 in end float. End float obtained by tightening only. Not by slackening.			
Rear hub assembly	5/8 in UNF stub axle	100 - 110	13.83 - 15.21
Trailing arm to mounting bracket	7/16 in UNF x 3 5/8 in bolt	45 - 50	6.22 - 6.91
Trailing arm mounting brackets to frame ...	3/8 in UNF bolt	28 - 30	3.87 - 4.15
Trailing arm to brake back plate	5/16 in UNF x 1½ in stud	14 - 16	1.94 - 2.21
Wire wheel extension attachment	7/16 in UNF stud	65	8.99
Wheel attachment	7/16 in UNF stud	55 - 60	7.60 - 8.30
Damper arm to link	7/16 in UNF	40 - 45	5.53 - 6.22
Steering			
Adaptor to upper and lower column	¼ in UNF bolt	8 - 10	1.11 - 1.38
Adaptor to rubber coupling	5/16 in UNF bolt	14 - 16	1.94 - 2.21
Ball joint to tie rod locknut	½ in UNF locknut on tie rod	30 - 35	4.15 - 4.84
Ball joint tie rod to steering lever	7/16 in UNF ball pin	55 - 60	7.60 - 8.29
Lower clamp to outer column and body	¼ in UNF x ¾ in setscrew	8 - 10	1.11 - 1.38
Outer column tie rods to body	¼ in UNF x 5/8 in setscrew	8 - 10	1.11 - 1.38
Rack to chassis	5/16 in UNF 'U' bolt	14 - 16	1.94 - 2.21
Safety clamp to column	¼ in UNF x 1¼ in bolt	6 - 8	0.83 - 1.11
Safety clamp grub screw	7/16 in UNF grub screw	18 - 20	2.49 - 2.77
Steering wheel attachment	9/16 in UNS inner column	28 - 30	3.87 - 4.15
Top clamp to outer column	5/16 in UNF x 1 in setscrew	16 - 18	2.21 - 2.49
Top clamp to body	¼ in UNF x ¾ in setscrew	8 - 10	1.11 - 1.38
Top clamp to body	¼ in UNF x ¾ in weld bolt	6 - 8	0.83 - 1.11
Universal joint attachment	5/16 in UNF x 1½ in bolt	18 - 20	2.49 - 2.77

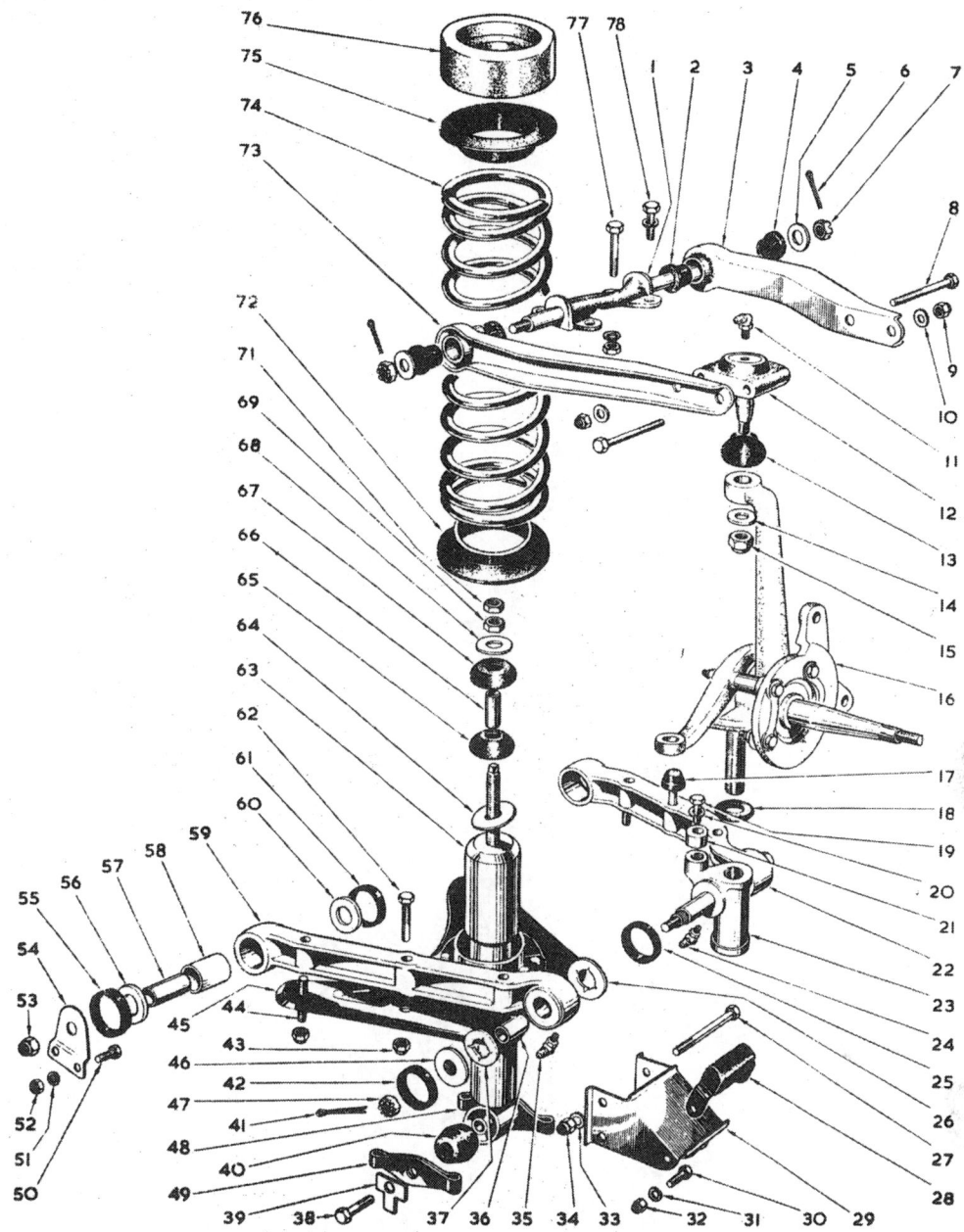

FIG. 11.1. LEFT HAND FRONT INDEPENDENT SUSPENSION COMPONENT PARTS (EARLY MODELS)

1 Upper inner fulcrum	20 Spring washer	40 Rubber bush	58 Nylon bush
2 Rubber bush	21 Lock stop collar	41 Split pin	59 Lower wishbone - front
3 Upper wishbone arm - rear	22 Lower wishbone arm - rear	42 Rubber seal	60 Thrust washer
4 Rubber bush	23 Lower trunnion bracket	43 Nyloc nut	61 Rubber seal
5 Washer	24 Grease nipple	44 Stud	62 Bolt
6 Split pin	25 Rubber seal	45 Spring pan	63 Damper
7 Slotted nut	26 Thrust washer	46 Serrated washer	64 Washer
8 Bolt	27 Bolt	47 Slotted nut	65 Rubber bush
9 Nyloc nut	28 Rebound rubber	48 Damper attachment	66 Sleeve
10 Plain washer	29 Bracket	bracket - rear	67 Rubber bush
11 Grease nipple	30 Bolt	49 Damper attachment	68 Washer
12 Upper ball joint	31 Spring washer	bracket - front	69 Nut
13 Rubber gaiter	32 Nyloc nut	50 Bolt	71 Locknut
14 Plain washer	33 Plain washer	51 Spring washer	72 Rubber collar
15 Nyloc nut	34 Nyloc nut	52 Nut	73 Upper wishbone arm - front
16 Calliper bracket and	35 Grease nipple	53 Nyloc nut	74 Spring
vertical link	36 Bush - nylon	54 Fulcrum bracket	75 Rubber collar
17 Bump rubber	37 Thrust washer	55 Rubber seal	76 Distance piece
18 Rubber seal	38 Bolt	56 Thrust washer	77 Bolt
19 Bolt	39 Tab washer	57 Steel sleeve	78 Bolt

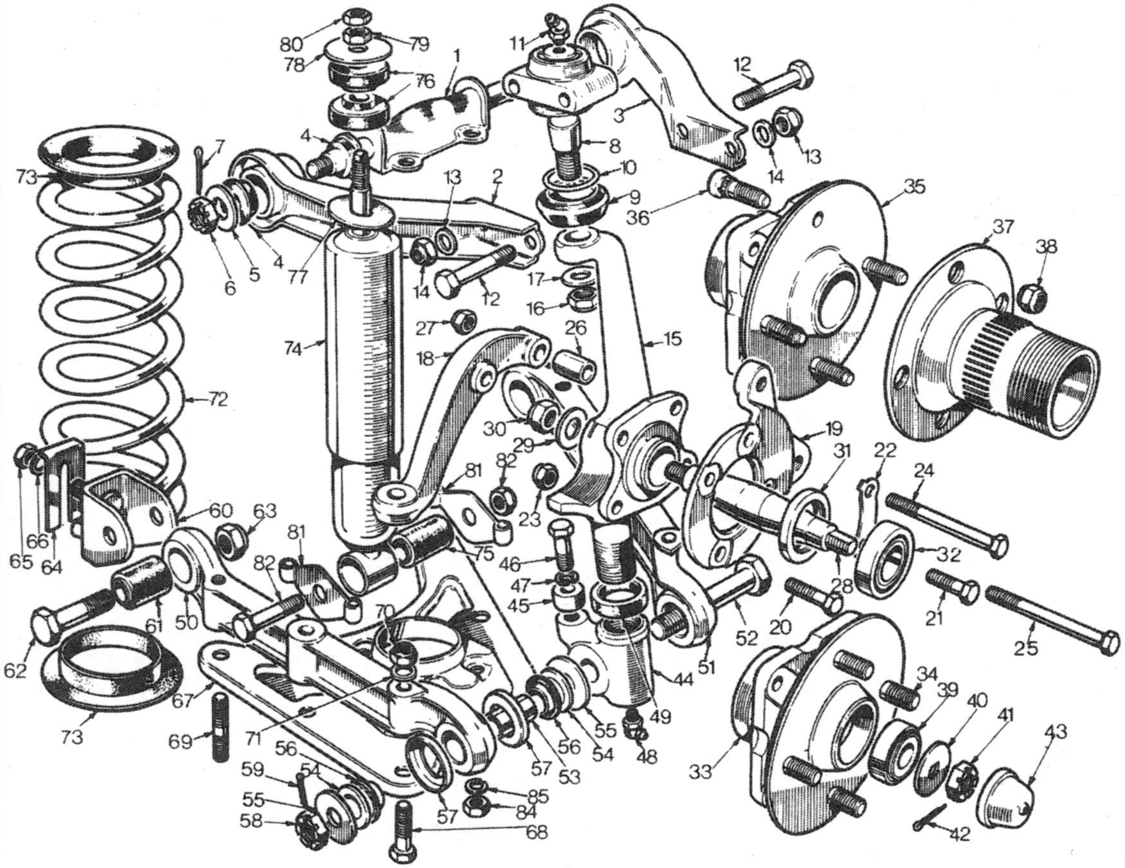

FIG. 11.1a LEFT-HAND FRONT INDEPENDENT SUSPENSION
COMPONENT PARTS (LATER MODELS)

1 Upper inner fulcrum
2 Upper wishbone arm - front
3 Upper wishbone arm - rear
4 Rubber bush
5 Washer
6 Slotted nut
7 Cotter pin
8 Upper balljoint
9 Rubber gaiter
10 Clip for rubber gaiter
11 Grease nipple
12 Bolt
13 Nyloc nut
14 Washer
15 Vertical link
16 Nyloc nut - thin
17 Washer
18 Steering arm
19 Brake caliper disc mounting plate
20 Bolt
21 Bolt
22 Tabwasher
23 Nyloc nut
24 Bolt
25 Bolt
26 Distance piece
27 Nyloc nut
28 Stub axle
29 Washer
30 Nyloc nut - thin
31 Felt oil seal and retainer assembly
32 Hub inner bearing
33 Hub assembly } Disc wheels
34 Wheel stud   only
35 Hub assembly } Wire wheels
36 Wheel stud   only
37 Hub extension LH
38 Nut
39 Hub outer bearing
40 D-washer
41 Slotted nut
42 Cotter pin
43 Grease retaining cap
44 Lower trunnion bracket
45 Steering lock strap
46 Setscrew
47 Lockwasher
48 Grease nipple
49 Oil seal
50 Lower wishbone arm - front
51 Lower wishbone arm - rear
52 Pivot bolt
53 Distance piece
54 Nylon bearing
55 Backing washer
56 Sealing ring
57 Water shield
58 Nut
59 Cotter pin
60 Bracket
61 Bush
62 Bolt
63 Nyloc nut
64 Shim
65 Nyloc nut
66 Washer
67 Lower spring pan
68 Bolt
69 Stud
70 Nyloc nut
71 Washer
72 Spring
73 Rubber washer
74 Shock absorber
75 Lower mounting rubber
76 Upper mounting rubber
77 Washer
78 Washer
79 Nut
80 Locknut
81 Shock absorber bracket
82 Bolt
83 Nyloc nut
84 Nut
85 Lockwasher

1 General description

The front suspension units are of the wishbone design and each unit is mounted independent to each other on the chassis. The inboard ends of the wishbones are mounted in special nylon bushes so that vertical movement can be accommodated. A ball joint is attached to the outer end of the top wishbones, whilst attached to the lower wishbone is a trunnion bearing. Connecting the upper and lower wishbones is the vertical link onto which is attached the stub axle.

The vertical link is controlled by tie rods connected to the rack and pinion steering. The maximum lock of the front wheels is limited by an eccentric collar which is bolted onto the upper face of the trunnion.

The bushed ends of the wishbones are fitted with white metal washers so as to provide a positive location as well as to take up any end thrust. To prevent rapid wear due to road dust and dirt rubber seals are fitted to protect the moving parts.

The suspension vertical link is so designed to act as a mounting for the disc brake dust shield. A caliper mounting bracket is also fitted.

The stub axle mounting is tapered and mates with a similar taper in the vertical link. It is pressed into position and secured with a large nut. It is onto the stub axle that the front hub is attached using taper roller bearings. Attached to the hub is the brake disc and road wheel.

Positioned between the lower wishbone and the chassis is a coil spring to absorb road shocks. Spring damping is achieved by using a non-adjustable telescopic shock absorber positioned in the centre of the coil spring.

The independent rear suspension is so designed that the final drive (differential unit) is bolted to the chassis and the rear wheels are driven by two drive shafts incorporating splined joints to accommodate vertical wheel movement. The wheels are mounted on trailing suspension arms that pivot on the chassis and a coil spring is positioned between the suspension arm and chassis. A piston type damper/shock absorber is used to control spring movement.

The steering unit is of rack and pinion design with adjustable tie rods interconnecting the rack ends with the swivel arms. The rack is fitted with a special adjustable damper and an adjustable ball joint at the inner end of each tie rod. The pinion shaft end float is controlled by shims situated at the upper pinion bush. The steering column is attached to the pinion via universal couplings.

2 Front hubs - removal, dismantling, inspection, reassembly and refitting

1 Chock the rear wheels and apply the handbrake. Jack up and support the front of the car and remove the road wheel.
2 Undo and remove the two bolts that secure the caliper to the vertical link. It is not necessary to disconnect the hydraulic flexible hose. Suspend the caliper using wire or string so not to strain the flexible hose.
3 Remove the grease cap from the hub using a wide blade screwdriver. It may be found that on some early cars produced before chassis No. TS 5358 a grease nipple may be fitted and this should be removed.
4 Extract the split pin from the castellated nut and undo this nut and washer.
5 Remove the hub assembly from the stub axle. If this is tight use a two leg puller with a thrust pad over the end of the stub axle so preventing damage to the threads.
6 With the hub removed the outer bearing will have also been removed. The inner bearing may be left on the stub axle or may be loose so be careful not to allow it to drop on the floor as the hub is being withdrawn.
7 Using a soft metal drift carefully remove the two bearing outer tracks from the hub making a note of which way round they are fitted.

8 With a universal two leg puller remove the inner track of the bearing from the stub axle.
9 Remove the four nuts, spring washers and bolts which secure the hub grease catcher to the brake backplate. Lift away the grease catcher.
10 Thoroughly wash all dismantled parts in clean petrol and dry using a non-fluffy rag. Inspect the oil seal for signs of deterioration and, if evident, the oil seals should be renewed.
11 Carefully examine both races for signs of wear or overheating. The rollers should show no signs of pitting or grooving and when each bearing is assembled in the hand and rotated between the fingers their operation should be smooth. Fit new bearings if any part is suspect.
12 If the oil seal is to be renewed, remove the old felt from the backing washer and affix a new piece using a jointing compound. When dry, soak the felt in clean engine oil and squeeze out any surplus oil.
13 Seat the grease seal on its spigot of the vertical link with the felt pad facing towards the centre of the car. Refit the inner wheel bearing.
14 Replace the hub grease catcher so that the shaped end of the pressing is below the vent hole in the brake backplate. Refit the grease catcher retaining nuts, bolts and spring washers.
15 If the bearing outer tracks have been removed from the hub, these or new ones should be refitted to the hub using a soft faced hammer and a soft metal drift. Ensure that the tracks are fitted the correct way round.
16 Repack the hub and bearings with grease working it well into the bearing and refit the hub to the stub axle. Replace the 'D' washer and the castellated nut.
17 It will now be necessary to adjust the hub bearings by first tightening the castellated nut to a torque wrench setting of 10 lb ft (1.38 kg m) and then turning back by between 1½ to 2 flats until a new split pin can be inserted into the stub axle end.
18 The grease cap should not be packed with grease but refitted dry. If a grease nipple was originally fitted this should be replaced and the hub greased with a grease gun.
19 Fit the disc brake caliper over the disc and secure the caliper to the vertical link with the two bolts.
20 Refit the road wheel and remove the axle stands.

3 Stub axle - removal and refitting

1 Refer to Section 2 of this Chapter and remove the hub assembly.
2 To remove the stub axle from the vertical link refer to Fig. 11.1 and extract the split pin. Undo the castellated nut and remove together with the plain washer.
3 The stub axle may be removed from the vertical link by placing a soft wood block on the threaded end of the stub axle and tapping the wood block so as to release the stub axle.
4 Refitting the stub axle is the reverse sequence to removal.

4 Front suspension coil spring - removal and refitting

1 Chock the rear wheel and apply the handbrake. Slacken the road wheel nuts, jack up the front of the car and place on axle stands positioned under the chassis frame. Remove the road wheels.
2 Place a small jack under the spring pan (Fig. 11.1). and partially compress the road spring. Ensure that the jack is firmly positioned on the ground and well located on the spring pan otherwise it may fly out.
3 Undo and remove the upper shock absorber retaining lock nut and nut from the stud on the end of the shock absorber. Lift away the plain washer and upper rubber mounting.
4 Undo and remove the two long bolts, nuts and spring washers that secure the suspension rebound rubber and its bracket from the side of the chassis frame. Lift away the rebound rubber and bracket.
5 Carefully lower the small jack from under the spring pan.

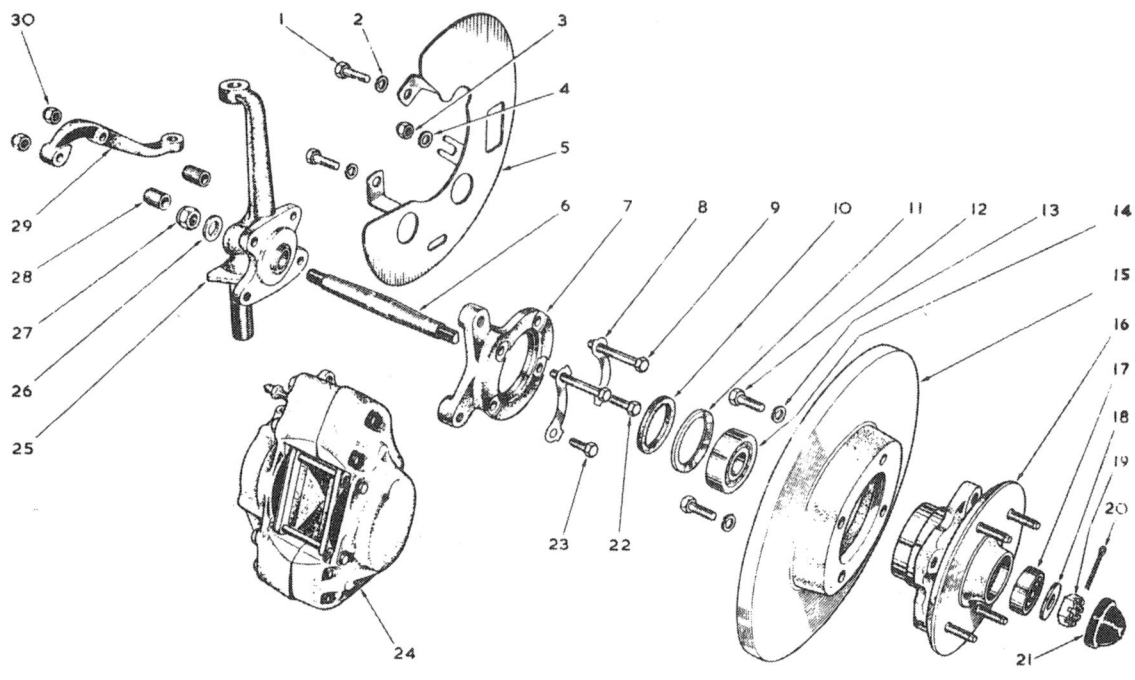

FIG. 11.2. DISC BRAKE AND HUB COMPONENTS

1	Bolt	9	Bolt	17	Outer taper race	25 Vertical link
2	Spring washer	10	Felt seal	18	Washer	26 Plain washer
3	Nyloc nut	11	Seal retainer	19	Slotted nut	27 Nyloc nut
4	Plain washer	12	Bolt	20	Split pin	28 Distance pieces
5	Dust shield	13	Spring washer	21	Hub cap	29 Steering arm
6	Stub axle	14	Inner taper race	22	Bolt	30 Nyloc nut
7	Calliper bracket	15	Disc	23	Bolt	
8	Tab plate	16	Hub	24	Calliper unit	

6 Undo and remove the four nuts and lock washers from the underside and centre of the spring pan. Lift away the rebound rubber abutment plate and the shock absorber may then be withdrawn through the spring plate.

7 Extract the six split pins (Fig. 11.1). , from the castellated nuts on the underside of the lower wishbones.

8 Remove the bump rubber from the rear wishbone and also the bolt from the front wishbone. At this stage do not remove the four remaining nuts.

9 Insert two pieces of 3/8 inch threaded metal rod six inches long into the holes left by the bolt and bump rubber to act as a guide and place the small jack under the spring pan and compress the spring again.

10 Undo and remove the four remaining nuts and very carefully lower the jack ensuring that the spring pan slides down the two previously positioned guide pins. When all tension on the spring has been released, remove the jack and lift away the spring together with rubber washers and packing piece.

11 Inspect the coil spring for signs of excessive corrosion or cracking and if evident, the coil springs must be renewed as a pair otherwise the stability of the car can be affected.

12 Check that the length of the spring is within the limits specified at the beginning of this Chapter. Examine the rubber washers for oil contamination or deterioration and obtain new ones if suspect.

13 To refit the coil spring a length of high tensile steel threaded rod will be required together with two high tensile steel nuts and a selection of thick washers.

14 Refit the spring by first assembling the rubber washers at either end and the packing piece with its spigot facing downwards onto the top of the spring.

15 Position the spring assembly up into the suspension unit with the packing piece to the top.

16 Slide the spring pan onto the guide pins which were previously placed in the centre holes of the wishbones for spring removal purposes.

17 Using the high tensile steel rod, washers and nuts with the rod positioned through the centre of the coil spring, screw up the lower nut until the spring pan is in position and secure in place with the four nuts and the two bolts at the outer ends of the wishbones. At this point the high tensile steel rod and the two guide rods may be removed.

18 Refit the bump stop onto the rear wishbone. Also refit the bolt to the front wishbone.

19 Tighten all six nuts in a diagonal manner and lock in position using new split pins.

20 The shock absorber may now be refitted by inserting it through the hole in the spring pan until the two retaining brackets locate on the studs of the spring pan assembly and, at the same time, the upper part of the shock absorber passes through the spring abutment on the chassis spring. The spring will have to be compressed slightly using a small jack to achieve the correct shock absorber fitting position.

21 Refit the second rubber mounting with its spigot facing downwards onto the metal sleeve, followed by the plain washer and nut. Tighten the nut until it just nips the plain washer and metal sleeve and lock this nut with the locknut.

22 Position the rebound rubber abutment plate onto the lower mounting studs, these being welded to the spring pan. Ensure that the apex of the wedge is pointing towards the centre of the car and retain in position using nuts and spring washer.

23 Refit the rebound rubber and its bracket into the chassis frame using the two long bolts and secure with nuts and spring washers.

24 Remove the small jack and refit the road wheel. Lift the car from the axle stands and lower to the ground.

5 Front suspension shock absorber - removal and refitting

1 Chock the rear wheels and apply the handbrake. Slacken the road wheel nuts, jack up the front of the car and place on axle stands positioned under the chassis frame. Remove the road wheels.

2 Place a small jack under the spring pan (Fig. 11.1). and partially compress the road spring. Ensure that the jack is firmly positioned on the ground and well located on the spring pan otherwise it may fly out.

3 Undo and remove the upper shock absorber retaining locknut and nut from the stud on the end of the shock absorber. Lift away the plain washer and upper rubber mounting.

4 Undo and remove the two long bolts, nuts and spring washers that secure the suspension rebound rubber and its bracket from the side of the chassis frame. Lift away the rebound rubber and bracket.

5 Carefully lever the small jack from under the spring pan.

6 Undo and remove the four nuts and lock washers from the underside and centre of the spring pan. Lift away the rebound rubber abutment plate and the shock absorber may then be withdrawn through the spring plate.

7 Once the shock absorber has been removed from the car, bend back the locking plate tabs and undo the setscrew. Lift away the setscrew followed by one of the brackets. The other bracket may be withdrawn from the shock absorber eye together with the two part rubber bush. This second bracket has the fulcrum pin attached to it.

8 Check the rubber bushes for signs of deterioration due to oil contamination. Also check that the fulcrum pin is firmly attached to its bracket.

9 Inspect the external part of the damper for signs of hydraulic fluid leaks, denting or a bent ram and, if any of these points are evident fit a new shock absorber.

10 The easiest way to test a shock absorber is to place the lower mounting eye between the soft faces of a firm bench vice and the shock absorber vertically positioned. Very slowly compress and extend the shock absorber for its full movement range twelve times and it should be observed that an equal and constant resistance is felt on the upward and downward strokes. If unequal resistance is felt on either or both strokes the shock absorber must be renewed as it is not possible to dismantle it.

11 To refit the shock absorber first press one rubber bush onto the fulcrum pin bracket and insert the bush into the eye of the shock absorber. Fit the second part of the rubber bush onto the fulcrum pin. Fit the second bracket followed by the tab washer and secure with the setscrew. Lock the setscrew head by bending over the tab washer tabs.

12 With the shock absorber held vertically slide the plain washer onto the upper mounting stud followed by the rubber mounting with its spigot uppermost and the metal sleeve.

13 The shock absorber may now be refitted by inserting it through the hole in the spring pan until the two retaining brackets located on the studs of the spring pan assembly and at the same time the upper part of the shock absorber passes through the spring abutment on the chassis spring. The spring will have to be compressed slightly using the small jack to achieve the correct shock absorber fitting position.

14 Refit the second rubber mounting with its spigot facing downwards onto the metal sleeve followed by the plain washer and nut. Tighten the nut until it just nips the plain washer and metal sleeve and lock this nut with the lock nut.

15 Position the rebound rubber abutment plate onto the lower mounting studs, these being welded to the spring pan. Ensure that the apex of the wedge is pointing towards the centre of the car and retain in position using nuts and spring washers.

16 Refit the rebound rubber and its bracket onto the chassis frame using two long bolts and secure with nuts and spring washers.

17 Remove the small jack and refit the road wheel. Lift the car from the axle stands and lower to the ground.

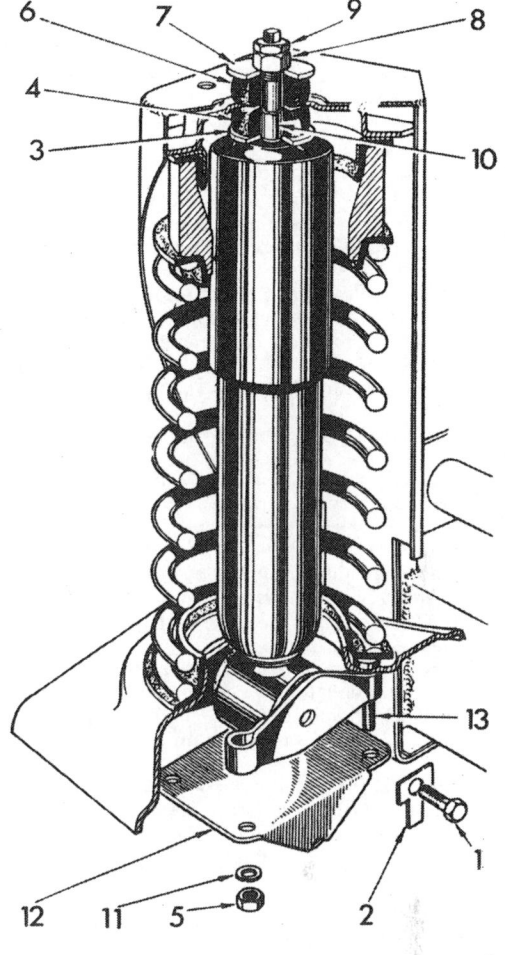

FIG. 11.3. FRONT SHOCK ABSORBER MOUNTING

1	Bolt	8	Nut
2	Lockplate	9	Locknut
3	Washer	10	Bush
4	Rubber bush	11	Spring washer
5	Nut	12	Rebound stop plate
6	Rubber bush	13	Stud
7	Plain washer		

6 Front suspension top ball joint - removal and refitting

It is difficult to test a ball joint for wear once it has been removed from the car. Better to do this by rocking the road wheel with the hands placed in the 6 and 12 o'clock positions whilst a second person watches for movement of the top ball joint.

1 Chock the rear wheels, apply the handbrake and jack up the front of the car. Place the car on axle stands placed on the main chassis members. Remove the road wheel.

2 Using a small jack support the weight of the suspension unit under the spring pan.

3 Refer to Fig. 11.1c and undo the nyloc nuts. Remove the nut followed by the plain washer.

4 Using a small ball joint separator disconnect the ball joint from the vertical link. Should a ball joint separator not be available place a metal block or large hammer on one side of the tapered eye of the vertical link. Using a second hammer tap the opposite side of the eye to the block so as to spring the tapers.

5 Undo the two nyloc nuts securing the upper ball joint retaining bolts and lift away the nuts, bolts and plain washers. Note the positioning of the two bolts. The upper ball joint may now be removed.

6 Refitting the upper ball joint is the reverse sequence to removal.

7 Front suspension top wishbones - removal and refitting

1 Chock the rear wheels, apply the handbrake and jack up the front of the car. Place the car on axle stands positioned on the main chassis member. Remove the road wheel.

2 Using a small jack support the weight of the suspension unit under the spring pan.

3 Undo the two nyloc nuts (Fig. 11.1). securing the upper ball joint retaining bolts and lift away the nuts, bolts and plain washers. Note the positioning of the two bolts.

4 Extract the split pins and undo the nuts. Lift away the nuts and plain washers.

5 Carefully pull the two upper wishbones away from the fulcrum pin together with the rubber bushes.

6 Remove the rubber bushes and inspect for signs of oil contamination or deterioration, and, if evident, new bushes should be fitted.

7 Reassembly is the reverse sequence to removal. Do not however tighten the nuts fully until the car has been lowered to the ground and with two people sitting in the car so as to allow the suspension to be set at its normal working height. Then tighten the nyloc nuts fully.

8 Front suspension vertical link and lower wishbones - removal and refitting

1 Chock the rear wheels, apply the handbrake and jack up the front of the car. Place the car on axle stands positioned on the main chassis members. Remove the road wheel.

2 Refer to Section 2 and remove the hub.

3 Refer to Section 3 and remove the coil spring and shock absorber.

4 Refer to Fig. 11.1. and bend back the tabs on the locking plate. Undo and remove the two bolts and nuts which secure the steering lever to the vertical link. Collect the distance piece.

5 Undo the two setscrews that secure the brake dust cover to the vertical link, once the tab washer tabs have been bent back. The dust cover may now be withdrawn.

6 Remove the nyloc nuts and the bolt securing the bracket and lift away the brackets. On suspensions having shims fitted between the brackets and the chassis frame (see Fig. 11.5), note the number and position of the shims so that they can be refitted in their original positions. If the shims are mixed up the castor and camber angles will have to be checked and adjusted by your local garage.

7 Withdraw the split pin and remove the nuts followed by the seal washers and bush. Carefully remove the two lower wishbones and this will leave the remainder of the suspension only attached to the two top wishbones.

8 To remove the remainder of the suspension system undo the two bolts that secure the fulcrum pin in position and then lift away the remaining suspension system.

9 If it is not required to disturb the upper wishbones or top ball joint the vertical link must be separated at the ball joint by extracting the split pin from the castellated nut. Undo and remove the nut followed by the plain washer.

10 Using a small ball joint separator disconnect the ball joint from the vertical link. Should a ball joint separator not be available place a metal block or large hammer on one side of the tapered eye of the vertical link. Using a second hammer tap the opposite side of the eye to the block so as to spring the tapers.

11 Undo the bolt and lift away the eccentric collar. This will allow the bottom trunnion to be unscrewed from the vertical link. Lift away the oil seal.

12 Thoroughly wash all parts in paraffin and wipe dry using a non fluffy rag.

13 Inspect the trunnion and the vertical link for signs of wear especially the threads in the lower trunnion and on the end of the vertical link. If these are worn a new trunnion and vertical link must be fitted as a pair and not singly.

14 Carefully examine all pivoting parts for wear. Also inspect the steel and nylon bushes and rubber sealing rings. Do not forget the white metal thrust washers.

15 Generally inspect the wishbone for signs of twisting or bending and obtain new parts if suspect. Do not attempt to straighten them.

16 With all parts ready for reassembly and new items obtained where required the method of reassembly will depend to a certain extent on how far the unit was dismantled. Instructions are given assuming that the upper wishbone members are still in position.

17 First fit the ball pin taper into the vertical link with the rubber gaiter in position. Refit the plain washer and secure with the castellated nut. Lock the castellated nut with a new split pin.

18 Check that the pin in the trunnion assembly is a tight fit as it should be a press fit being held in position by splines. Also ensure that it is centralised with the ends equidistant from the centre of the trunnion. If it is not central refit one nut and tap the end with a soft faced hammer.

19 Replace the rubber sealing ring to the lower threaded end of the vertical link and screw on the bottom trunnion. It should be screwed home, without forcing and then turned back one complete turn, and then positioned so that the shackle pin lies parallel to the body of the car, but inwards, between the base of the vertical link and the chassis frame as the shackle pin is offset.

20 Refit the locking spring washer and steering lock stop bush onto the steering stop securing bolt and replace on the bottom trunnion assembly. Do not tighten fully at this stage.

21 Fit the rubber sealing rings to the nylon washers into the ends of the lower wishbone arms. Next smear the fulcrum pin with a little grease and slide the bushes into place on the fulcrum pin. Smear the outside of the steel bushes and fit one pair of nylon washers complete with sealing rings. Also smear the lower trunnion shackle pin with a little grease and slide the lower wishbone onto the steel bushes on the fulcrum pin and the shackle pin of the trunnion at the same time. When in position place the outer pair of nylon washers, and sealing rings over the fulcrum pin and shackle pin.

22 Refit the nuts securing the lower wishbone arms in place and set the end float as detailed in the next paragraph.

23 To give the required end float, tighten the two castellated nuts equally until the assembly feels solid. Next turn back the nuts between ½ to 2 flats until the split pin holes are visible. Lock the nut with a new split pin. By these means the required end float of between 0.004 and 0.012 inch should be obtained.

24 Using a soft faced hammer carefully tap the lower wishbones outwards so as to set the lockwashers correctly.

25 Refer to Section 4 and refit the coil spring and shock absorber.

26 Refer to Section 2 and refit the front hub assembly.

27 Replace the road wheel and lower the car to the ground. By bouncing the front of the car up and down check that the front suspension unit is able to move vertically and freely without signs of binding. The steering lockstop collar should be adjusted to 31 degrees back lock and 28½ degrees front lock, and to make this adjustment correctly a specialist calibrated turntable which is used to check front wheel alignment will be required. This is therefore a job to be left to the local garage.

9 Rear spring - removal and refitting

1 Chock the front and rear of the front wheel and raise the rear end of the car as high as possible and place on axle stands positioned on the chassis member. Remove the road wheel. Place a small jack under the suspension arm.

2 Refer to Fig. 11.7. and undo the locknut. Remove the locknut followed by the nut backing plate rubber buffer and separate the shock absorber link from the suspension arm. Recover the upper rubber buffer and backing plate.

3 Thread some wire through the two universal joints to stop the two halves separating. Undo the four nyloc nuts and bolts that secure the inner universal joint coupling flange to the final drive unit.

4 Carefully lower the small jack under the suspension arm keeping a check on the flexible hose to make sure that it is not strained. The spring may now be lifted out followed by the

lower rubber insulator and upper rubber insulator.

5 Inspect the spring for signs of excessive rusting or cracking and, if evident, a new pair of springs must be fitted. If only one new spring is fitted the stability of the car can be affected. Check the height of the spring against dimensions given in the specifications at the beginning of this Chapter. Check that the rubber insulators are in good order and they should be renewed if suspect.

6 Refitting the spring is the reverse sequence to removal.

10 Rear suspension arm - removal and refitting

1 Refer to Section 9 and remove the rear spring.

2 Using a small jack raise the suspension arm so as to relieve the weight from its mountings.

3 Place a piece of plastic hose onto the rear brake bleed nipple. Insert the free end of the plastic hose into a clean glass jar and open the bleed nipple. Drain the brake hydraulic system by operating the brake pedal. Close the bleed nipple and remove the plastic hose.

4 Remove the brake drum from the hub assembly. If difficulty is experienced in withdrawing the drum slacken off the brake adjustment and tap the back flange of the drum using a soft faced hammer.

5 Thread some wire through the two universal joints to hold the two halves of the axle shaft together and, using a socket wrench passed through the holes in the driving flange (Fig. 8.1). remove the six nuts securing the hub assembly to the suspension arm.

6 Undo the four nuts and bolts which secure the inboard coupling to the flange on the final drive unit.

7 Carefully withdraw the axle shaft through the boss in the suspension.

8 Disconnect the handbrake cable from the handbrake lever at the rear of the brake backplate.

9 Refer to Chapter 9, Section 4x and disconnect the brake hydraulic flexible hose.

10 Undo the nyloc nuts and lift away followed by the plain washers. Withdraw the bolts and lift the suspension arm from the underside of the car.

11 Inspect the rubber bushes for signs of deterioration and, if evident, the bushes should be renewed. To remove the bushes they may be pressed out using a socket of suitable diameter between the jaws of a vice. When new bushes are being fitted insert a bolt into the centre bush to protect the bush against distortion and lubricate the bush with rubber grease.

12 Normally it should not be necessary to remove the two

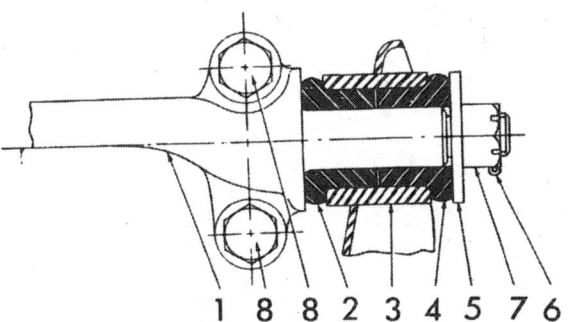

FIG. 11.4. CROSS SECTION THROUGH UPPER INNER FULCRUM

1   Upper inner fulcrum   5   Washer
2   Rubber bush   6   Split pin
3   Upper wishbone arm - rear   7   Slotted nut
4   Rubber bush   8   Securing bolts

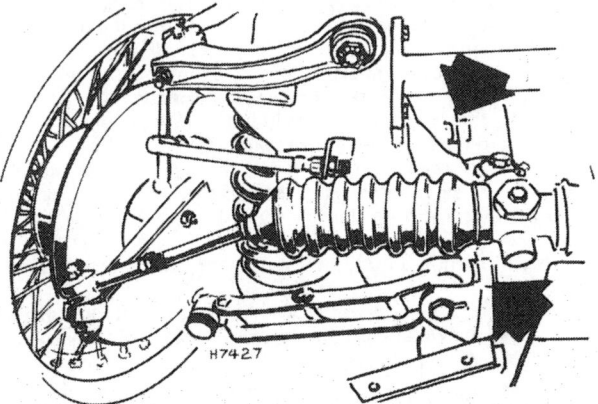

Fig. 11.5 Location of shims behind fulcrum brackets

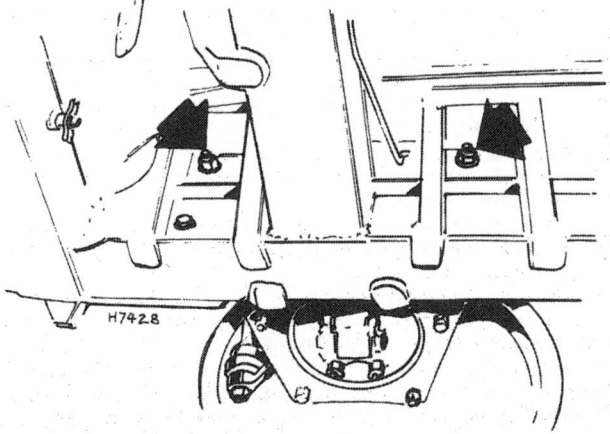

Fig. 11.6 Fulcrum bracket securing nuts

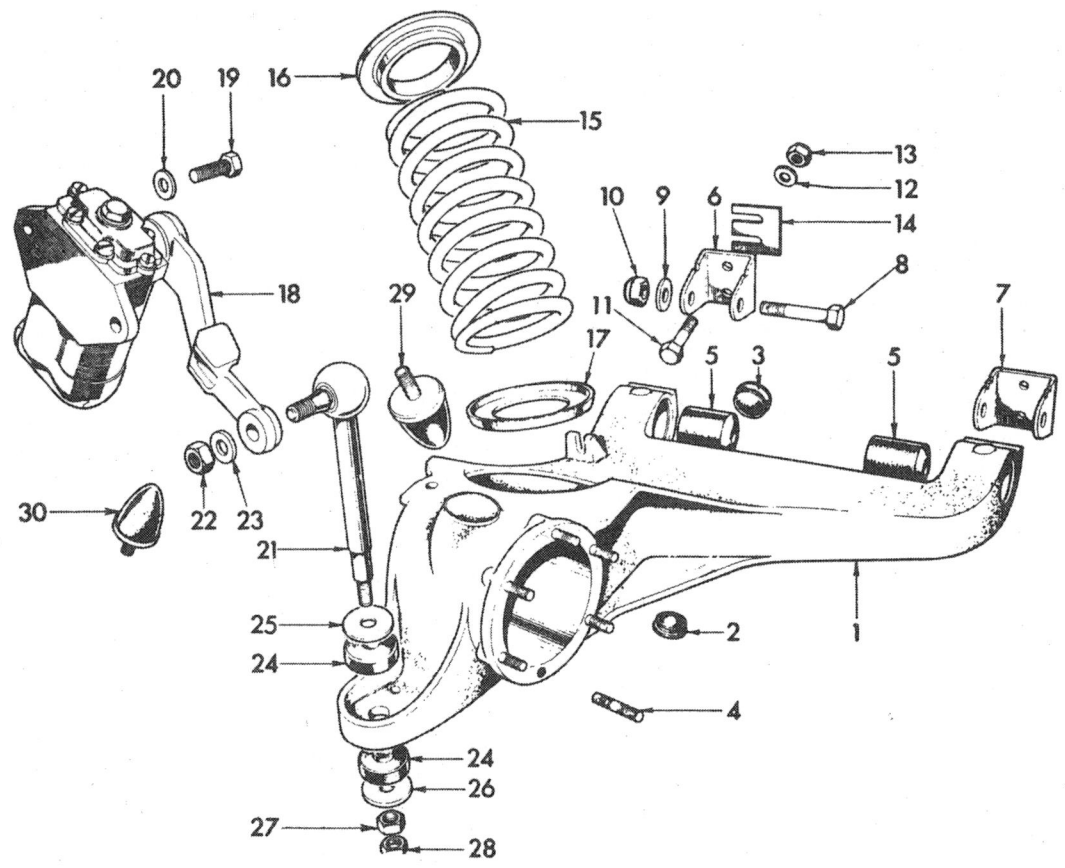

FIG. 11.7. REAR SUSPENSION UNIT COMPONENT PARTS

1	Suspension arm	9	Plain washer
2	Rubber plug	10	Nyloc nut
3	Rubber plug	11	Bolt
4	Stud	12	Plain washer
5	Metalistik bush	13	Nyloc nut
6	Fulcrum bracket, inner	14	Shim
7	Fulcrum bracket, outer	15	Road spring
8	Bolt	16	Rubber insulator

17	Rubber insulator	25	Backing plate
18	Damper arm	26	Backing plate
19	Bolt	27	Nut
20	Washer	28	Locknut
21	Damper link	29	Bump stop
22	Nut	30	Rebound rubber
23	Washer		
24	Rubber buffer		

brackets but should this be required take great care of the shims and refit them in their original position. Also ensure that the brackets are fitted in their original position and are identified with four grooves to be fitted uppermost on the outside bracket and the inside bracket has two grooves which again must be fitted uppermost.

13 Refitting the suspension arm is the reverse sequence to removal but the following additional points should be noted.

14 Do not fully tighten the nuts until all is assembled and the car is back on the ground. With two people sitting in the car to give it a normal ride condition then tighten the nuts.

15 Whenever the suspension arm is removed it is recommended that the car be taken to the local agent so that the rear wheel alignment may be checked, otherwise if it is incorrect car stability and tyre wear will be affected.

11 Outer axle shaft and hub assembly - removal and refitting

1 The drive shafts and hubs are removed from the suspension arm and this will be necessary if the universal joints or hub bearings require service attention.

2 Working on one side of the car, remove the hub cap and loosen the wheel nuts. Chock the front wheel, jack up the rear of the car and support on stands. Take off the road wheel.

3 Undo the two countersunk screws holding the brake drum to the hub drive flange (Fig. 8.1).

4 Carefully pull off the brake drum. If it is tight slacken off the brake adjustment, full details of which are given in Chapter 9, Section 9. Using a soft faced hammer tap the flange on the circumference of the brake drum to free it from the studs.

5 Upon close inspection it will be found that there is a hole in the hub flange which is sufficiently large to allow a socket to pass through. Undo and remove the six nyloc nuts which hold the bearing housing to the boss on the suspension arm boss.

6 Undo the four nuts and bolts holding the inboard universal coupling to the inner axle shaft flange.

7 Use a piece of wire threaded through the two universal joints of the axle shaft to stop the half shafts from separating.

8 Carefully withdraw the axle shaft through the suspension arm boss.

9 It will be noted that it is not necessary to disturb the braking system.

10 Refitting is the reverse procedure to removal. Do not forget to remove the wire holding the two universal joints together.

12 Stub axle shaft and hub assembly - dismantling and re-assembly

1 To dismantle this shaft three special tools numbered S.109A, S.318 and S.4221A16 are required as well as a torque wrench

capable of being set to give a reading of 90-100 lb ft (12.4 - 13.83 kg m) and a dial indicator gauge. If these can be borrowed from a local Triumph agent so well and good but if not then we would recommend that the following work be left to the local agents.

2 Place a shaft in the holder S.318 which should be mounted in a good size vice.

3 Using a socket wrench undo and remove the nut (Fig. 8.1). Lift away the washer and with tool S.109A withdraw the hub. Unfortunately there is no safe alternative method of removing the hub because of the high pressures required (Fig. 8.1).

4 Whilst the hub is being removed, the bearing housing will also come away with the hub.

5 Lift away the rectangular key and throw away the collapsible spacer as it must not be used again. Lift away the inner hub bearing cone followed by the bearing spacer and stone guard making sure to take note which way round it fits.

6 Undo the lockwasher tabs and turn the adjustment nut and locknut one complete revolution towards the universal joint.

7 Support the housing under its mounting face and, using a soft metal drift, carefully drive out the bearing outer race.

8 It will now be necessary to use tool number S.4221A16 to extract the outer hub bearing cone from the hub. A large three leg puller can do this operation provided the feet are such that they can locate at the rear of the bearing inner track.

9 Thoroughly wash all displaced components in paraffin and dry using a clean rag.

10 Inspect the bearing rollers for signs of wear, pitting or cracking and, if evident, the bearing must be renewed. Also inspect the stub shaft and the hub for wear or damage especially around the inner hub bearing seat. If any part is suspect it should be renewed.

11 To reassemble first press the outer hub bearing cone up to the shoulder on the hub. A metal tube of suitable diameter may be used to drift the bearing cone into place if a press is not available. Be careful not to tilt the cone when refitting to the hub.

12 Press the outer and inner hub bearing outer races up to the shoulder in the bearing housing. Alternatively a soft metal drift may be used. As in the previous operation be careful not to tilt the cone when refitting the hub.

13 Refit the inner and outer oil seals.

14 Replace the stone guard bearing spacer, the inner cone of the inner hub bearing and a new collapsible spacer onto the stub shaft and fit the rectangular key into the stub shaft. The inner end of the key should be in line with the two indentations on the shoulders of the keyway.

15 The bearing housing should be well packed with correct grade grease. Ensure that there is plenty of grease in the spacer between the two roller bearings.

16 Fit the bearing housing over the stub shaft until the inner hub bearing outer race engages with its mating cone. Special care must be taken not to damage the lip of the inner oil seal.

17 Refit the hub onto the stub shaft followed by the plain washer and nut. Using a torque wrench set to a reading of between 90 - 100 lb ft (12.4 - 13.83 kg m) tighten the stub shaft nut.

18 It will now be necessary to reset the bearing end float, first with the axle shaft assembled to the holding tool, tighten the nut to the stoneguard until it is finger tight.
tight.

19 Attach a dial indicator gauge onto the hub flange with the stylus touching the bearing housing flange.

20 Firmly pull the bearing housing as far as possible downwards away from the dial indicator gauge. Use a rocking motion to ensure correct contact of the bearing parts and set the dial to zero.

21 Push the bearing housing towards the dial indicator gauge once more using a rocking motion to ensure correct contact of the bearing parts and this time note the reading on the dial.

22 Slowly tighten the large nut one flat at a time. At each flat repeat operations 20 and 21 above until an end float reading of between 0.004 - 0.002 inch is obtained and lock the adjustment

nut with the nut and tab washer.

23 Should for any reason insufficient care have been taken and the end float is accidently reduced to below 0.002 inch the collapsible spacer must be renewed. It will not spring back to its original dimensions.

13 Outer axle shaft - dismantling and reassembly

1 Wash the exterior of the shaft and joints in paraffin and dry using a clean non-fluffy rag.

2 Place the assembly on a clean bench top and remove the wire that was previously threaded through the two universal joints.

3 Undo the clips holding the two ends of the rubber gaiter. (Fig. 8.1), to the inner and outer axle shafts.

4 Carefully withdraw the outer sliding axle shaft from the fixed shaft. Lift away the gaiter and clips.

5 Inspect the gaiter for signs of cracking, splitting or hardening especially the area around the two clips and obtain a new gaiter if necessary.

6 Dismantling of the universal joints is identical to that for the propeller shaft universal joint, full details of which are given in Chapter 7, Section 4.

14 Rear shock absorber - removal and refitting

1 Chock the front and rear of the front wheel and raise the rear end of the car as high as possible and place on axle stands positioned on the chassis members. Remove the road wheel.

2 Using a small jack raise the suspension arm so as to relieve the weight from its mountings.

3 Refer to Fig. 11.7. and undo the locknut. Remove the locknut followed by the nut backing plate and rubber buffer, separate the shock absorber link from the suspension arm. Recover the upper rubber buffer and backing plate.

4 Undo and remove the two nuts and bolts that secure the shock absorber to the chassis and lift away the nut, bolts, and spring washers followed by the shock absorber itself.

5 Undo and remove the nut that secures the shock absorber arm to the link.

6 It may be necessary to use a small universal ball joint separator to disconnect the arm from the link as it is a taper fit. Should a universal ball joint separator not be available place a metal block or heavy hammer against one side of the tapered eye on the steering arm. Using a second hammer, shock the taper apart by tapping on the opposite side of the eye to the metal block or hammer.

7 Thoroughly clean the exterior of the shock absorber and place in a vertical position in a vice so that the arm can be moved up and down.

8 Undo the filler plug and top up the oil level, using correct grade oil, to the base of the filler plug boss. Refit the filler plug.

9 Move the arm up and down about ten times so as to expel any air that might be in the system. It should be found that on the final strokes an equal and constant resistance should be felt on both the upwards and downwards strokes. If unequal resistance is felt on either stroke a replacement shock absorber should be obtained.

10 Refitting the shock absorber is the reverse sequence to removal.

15 Steering wheel - removal and refitting

TR5 and TR250

1 Disconnect the positive terminal from the battery for safety reasons.

2 Using a screwdriver or a knife remove the horn push from the centre of the steering wheel. (Fig. 11.8).

3 Lift out the horn push from the inside of the steering wheel hub.

4 Using a centre punch mark the inner column and the hub of

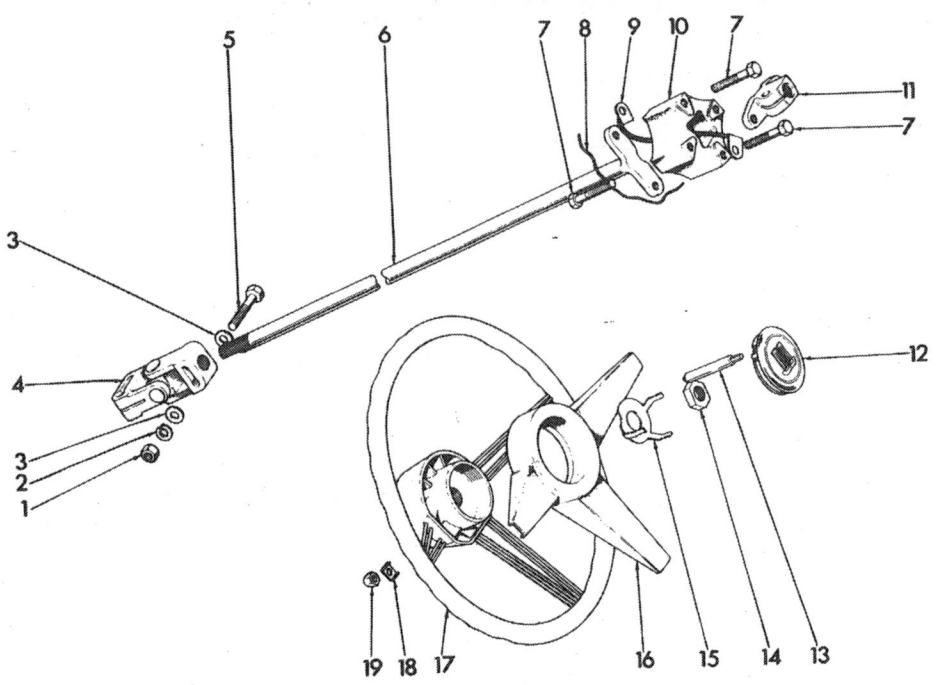

FIG. 11.8. STEERING COLUMN ASSEMBLY (TR5 AND TR250 MODELS)

1 Nut	6 Lower steering column	11 Adaptor	16 Wheel trim
2 Spring washer	7 Bolt	12 Horn push	17 Steering wheel
3 Plain washer	8 Locking wire	13 Horn brush	18 Clamp
4 Universal coupling	9 Earthing cable	14 Nut	19 'Dotloc' acorn unit
5 Pinch bolt	10 Rubber coupling	15 Clip	

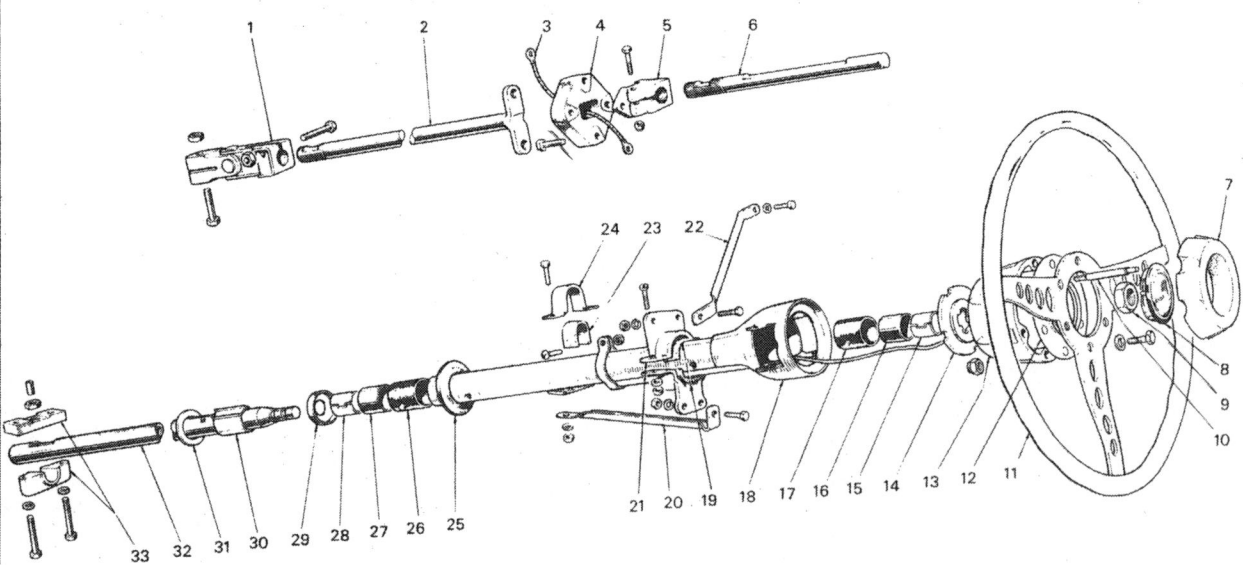

FIG. 11.9. STEERING COLUMN ASSEMBLY (TR6 MODELS)

1 Lower steering coupling	10 Horn connection brush	18 Upper steering column - outer	26 Rubber bush
2 Lower steering column	11 Steering wheel	19 Felt pads	27 Steel bush
3 Earth cable	12 Horn push retaining plate	20 Lower stay bracket	28 Nylon bush
4 Rubber coupling	13 Steering wheel support boss	21 Upper clamp bracket	29 Cap
5 Adaptor	14 Slip ring	22 Upper stay bracket	30 Trafficator canceller
6 Intermediate steering column	15 Nylon bush	23 Felt pad	31 Washer
7 Padded bezel	16 Steel bush	24 Clamp	32 Upper steering column - inner
8 Horn push	17 Rubber bush	25 Rubber grommet	33 Steering column connection clamp
9 Column nut			

the steering wheel to ensure correct reassembling. Undo the steering wheel retaining nut using a socket or box spanner.

5 Undo and remove the three domed nuts and clamps located behind the steering wheel spokes. The wheel trim and shaped clip may now be lifted away from the steering wheel.

6 To refit the steering wheel replace the wheel on the inner column carefully aligning the previously made centre punch marks. With the steering wheel in position refit the retaining nut and tighten securely. It is advisable to peen the metal of the nut to the inner column to prevent the nut working loose.

7 Insert the horn push into its hole in the steering wheel hub. Refit the wheel trim and secure with the three clips and domed nuts. Also replace the shaped clip in the centre of the wheel.

8 Replace the horn button assembly making sure the emblem is the correct way up relative to the spokes.

9 Reconnect the positive terminal of the battery.

TR6

1 Disconnect the positive terminal from the battery for safety reasons.

2 Using a screwdriver or a knife remove the horn push and padded bezel from the centre of the steering wheel. (Fig. 11.9)..

3 Undo and remove the ring of bolts that secure the steering wheel to the support boss. Lift away the steering wheel.

4 The support boss is secured to the upper inner steering column by the column nut.

5 Turn the front wheels to the straight ahead position and mark the boss so that the steering wheel may be refitted in its original position. Lift away the boss.

6 Refitting the support boss and steering wheel is the reverse sequence to removal.

16 Steering column - removal, dismantling and reassembly and refitting

1 Disconnect the positive terminal from the battery for safety reasons.

2 Wipe the electric cables free of dust at the connectors for the horn, direction indicator and overdrive unit (if fitted), to enable the colour coding to be seen. If the cables are faded mark the cables for correct refitting during reassembly. Disconnect the cables from the connectors.

3 Undo and remove the bolt that secures the lower all metal type steering coupling to the steering rack pinion.

4 Undo and remove the two bolts and spring washers and lift away the two parts of the impact clamp.

5 Push the intermediate column upwards inside the inner column so disengaging the lower coupling from the rack pinion.

6 Carefully swing the coupling to one side and withdraw the intermediate shaft complete with both the steering couplings and lower column from the inside of the upper inner steering column. Recover the nylon washer.

7 Now working inside the car, undo and remove the nuts and bolts that hold the clamp and felt. Also remove the stay and the upper clamp half with its felt and then carefully pull the steering column assembly complete with steering wheel, rearwards, through the bulkhead rubber grommet and aperture in the facia.

8 Normally it is not necessary to dismantle the two steering couplings unless of course they are worn or damaged or the rubber coupling has been contaminated with oil, or cracked.

9 To clean the bottom all metal coupling wash in petrol, shake dry and then lubricate the pivots with Castrol GTX.

10 To dismantle the steering column first undo and remove the switch cover screws and lift away the cover.

11 Undo and remove the nut and bolt that secures the cable trough clip to the outer column. Lift away the trough (Fig. 11.10). Note the cardboard sleeve fitted to the upper outer column between the end of the cable trough and the upper clamp. This is to ensure that the correct degree of collapse occurs on impact.

12 Where an overdrive unit is fitted undo the nut from the switch body.

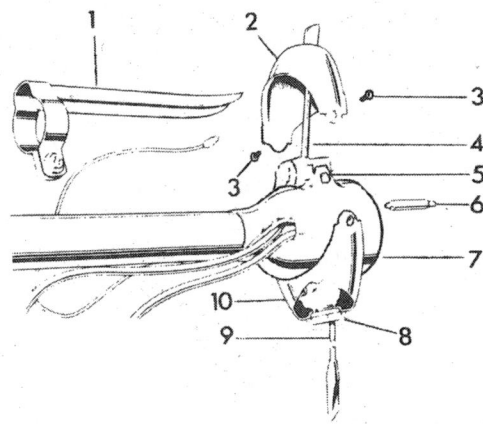

FIG. 11.10. DIRECTION INDICATOR AND OVER-DRIVE SWITCH MOUNTED TO UPPER COLUMN

1 Cable trough	securing screw
2 Direction indicator switch	6 Horn brush
cover	7 Upper outer column
3 Screw	8 Overdrive cover securing
4 Direction indicator switch	nut
5 Direction indicator switch	9 Overdrive switch
	10 Overdrive switch cover

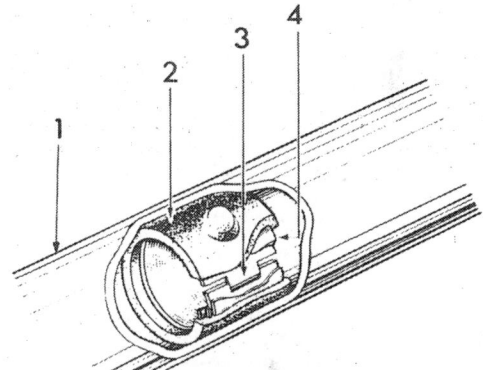

FIG. 11.11. CORRECT FITTING OF STEERING COLUMN BUSH ASSEMBLY

1 Upper steering column	3 Steel bush
(inner)	4 Nylon bush
2 Rubber bush	

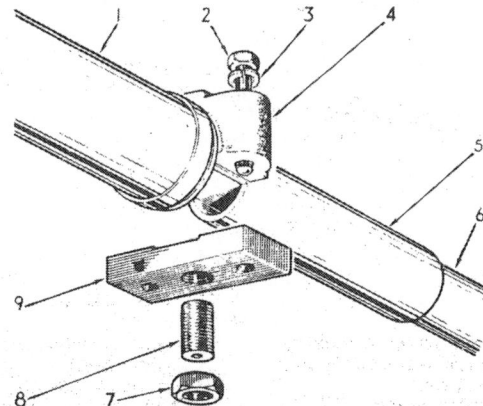

FIG. 11.12. IMPACT CLAMP ON STEERING COLUMN

1 Upper outer column	6 Lower column
2 Bolt	7 Locknut
3 Washer	8 Allen screw
4 Impact column bracket body	9 Impact bracket clamp
5 Upper inner column	plate

13 To remove the switches undo and remove the two screws which secure them to the outer column hub lugs. The switches may then be withdrawn, taking care to feed the cables through the hole in the hub.

14 The steering wheel assembly may next be removed as described in Section 15.

15 Carefully remove the outer column end cap and with two pieces of metal rod of suitable diameter press in the rubber bush ears. A second person should now push out the rubber bush using a long metal rod. (Fig. 11.11).

16 Remove the nylon bush and steel bush from the flexible end of the rubber bush.

17 Removal of the column upper bush is identical to that for the lower bush.

18 Reassembly and refitting the steering column assembly is the reverse sequence to dismantling but the following additional points should be noted:

a) When refitting the outer column top and bottom bushes make sure that the metal reinforcing rings are towards the bottom of the column.

b) When refitting the steering wheel and inner column make sure that the direction indicator cancel lugs are correctly aligned.

c) When refitting the steering column assembly leave all attachments loose so that the assembly is free to slide in the clamps.

d) To correctly refit the impact clamp slacken the locknut and unscrew the Allen screw two complete turns. Next turn the shaft so as to align the machined flat with the slot in the upper inner steering column Fit the two clamp halves and secure with the two bolts and spring washers. Do not tighten the Allen screw yet. Now push the column inside the inner column and reconnect the lower steering coupling back onto the rack pinion making sure that the front wheels and steering wheel are in the straight ahead position. Refit the pinch bolt to the steering coupling and secure it with the nut. Set the steering wheel to the required height and then fully tighten the upper and lower clamps. Finally tighten the Allen screw as firmly as possible and lock it with the nut.

---

17 Rack and pinion - removal and replacement

1 Loosen the front wheel securing nuts, jack up the front of the car, place on supports under the coil spring pans between the wishbones and remove the front wheels.

2 Undo and remove the bolt that secures the universal joint coupling to the pinion.

3 Refer to Chapter 2, and remove the engine cooling fan assembly.

4 Undo and remove the nyloc nuts securing the two tie rod ends to the steering arms and using a small universal ball joint separator disconnect the tie rod ends from the steering arms on the vertical links. Should a universal ball joint separator not be available place a metal block or heavy hammer against one side of the tapered eye on the steering arm. Using a second hammer, shock the taper apart by tapping on the opposite side of the eye to the metal block or hammer.

5 Undo and remove the nuts (Fig. 11.13)., and plain washers that secure the 'U' bolts to the locating plate.

6 Lift away the two locating plates followed by the two 'U' bolts complete with metal shrouds.

7 Carefully move the steering rack assembly forwards so as to disengage the pinion spline coupling and then withdraw through the wheel arch. Take great care not to split the rubber bellows.

8 If the unit is to be dismantled for overhaul thoroughly wash in paraffin and dry using a non-fluffy rag.

9 Refitting is the reverse procedure to removal but certain precautions must be taken to simplify the form. It is advisable to check the length of the two tie rods and adjust as necessary until they are exactly equal length. The tie rod ball joints have nylon inserts which do not require lubrication. Should the rubber boots have become damaged or perished in service a complete new

joint must be fitted. If the rubber boot has been damaged only during lifting away the steering rack assembly then the rubber boot only may be renewed. There should be no exception to this rule.

10 Before the steering rack assembly is finally fitted to the car it will facilitate installation if the rack is brought to its central position. This position is easily obtained by turning the pinion from one stop to the other and measuring the complete distance the rack has travelled at one end. The rack will be in its central position when it is moved back through half the measurement made.

11 Carefully insert the rack assembly making sure that the setting in operation 10 is not disturbed, locate and insert the pinion splines with the universal joint coupling, checking that the steering wheel spokes are correctly positioned for the straight ahead position.

12 Refit the 'U' bolts, metal rubber mounting covers, locating plate, washers, and nyloc nuts. Lightly tighten the nuts.

13 Slide one of the 'U' bolts outwards as far as possible to the ends of the elongated holes in the crossmember brackets. Ease the locating plate inwards until the edge of 'B' (Fig. 11.13). completely contacts the side of the bracket. Should this not be possible file the elongated holes further so that this position may be obtained.

14 Tighten the two 'U' bolt nyloc nuts using a torque wrench set to between 14 - 16 lb ft and compress the mounting rubbers to give a clearance of 0.125 inch (3.175 mm) between the flange plates on the rack tube 'A' and the 'U' bolts retainer flange 'A'.

15 Refit the second 'U' bolt mounting and position in the same manner.

16 Reconnect the two tie rod ends to the steering arms and tighten the nuts to a torque wrench setting of between 55 - 60 lb ft. Fit new split pins.

17 Replace the road wheel and remove the axle stands.

18 Position the front wheels so that they are in the straight ahead position. Tighten the universal coupling pinch bolt.

19 Refit the engine cooling fan.

20 Refer to Fig. 11.12. and undo the pinch bolt. With the steering wheel spokes in the horizontal position pull upwards on the spokes so as to compress the spring.

21 A second person should move the intermediate shaft towards the rear and engage the splines of the rack pinion with the universal joint. Retighten the pinch bolt.

22 Check and adjust the front wheel alignment.

---

18 Rack and pinion steering - dismantling, reassembly and adjustment

1 All numbers in brackets refer to Fig. 11.15. Undo the clips (27, 31) on the rubber gaiters (15, 29) and pull the gaiters back to expose the inner ball joint assemblies.

2 Loosen the locknuts (28) and completely unscrew both the tie rod assemblies (26) from the rack (20).

3 Pull out the coil springs (24), free the tab washer (23) unscrew the nut (22) and take off the shim (42) and cup (25).

4 Mark the positions of the locknuts (30) on the tie rods so the toe in is approximately correct on reassembly, undo the locknuts (30) and screw off the ball joints.

5 Pull off the rubber gaiters (15, 29) and undo the cup nut (28) from the tie rods, and then remove the locknuts (21).

6 Unscrew and remove the damper cap (10), spring (12), plunger (13), and shims (9).

7 The pinion can be removed after taking out the circlip (1). Take great care not to lose the small locating peg (2).

8 The rack can now be pulled from the housing tube and the thrust washer (40) and bush (41) taken from the pinion housing (19).

9 Clean all the parts thoroughly and examine the teeth of the rack and pinion for wear or damage. Also examine the pinion thrust washer and bushes, thrust pad, and inner and outer ball joints and replace as necessary.

10 Reassembly commences by sliding the rack (20) into place.

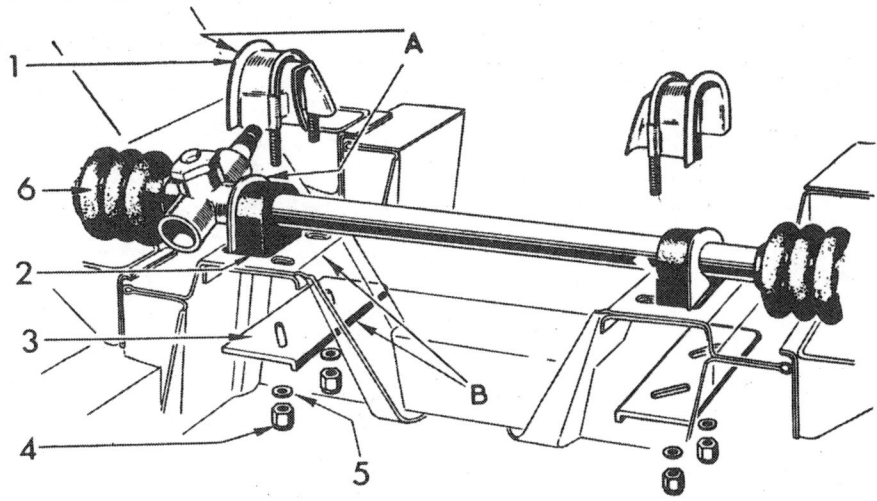

FIG. 11.13. STEERING RACK AND PINION MOUNTING

A   Distance between flanges must be 0.125 inch (3,17 mm)
B   Flange of item 3 must contact innermost flange of frame

1 'V' bolt	3 Locating plate	4 Nyloc nut	5 Plain washer
2 Rubber bush			6 Rubber gaiter

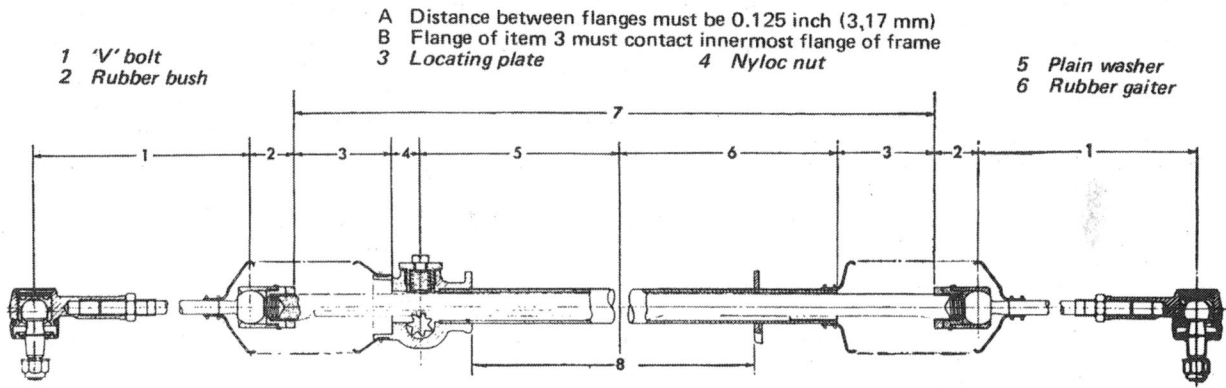

FIG. 11.14. RACK AND PINION STEERING UNIT DIMENSIONS

1	8.42 inch	(213.87 mm)
2	1.42 inch	(36.06 mm)
3	3.09 inch	(78.5 mm)
4	0.88 inch	(22.35 mm)
5	8.00 inch	(203.2 mm)
6	8.88 inch	(225.55 mm)
7	23.94 inch	(608.1 mm)
8	12.65 inch	(321.31 mm)

Then fit the bush (41) and thrust washer (40) and adjust the pinion end float after assembling the thrust washer (6) bush (5) and retaining ring (3) to the pinion, and fitting and securing the pinion to the housing with the circlip (1).

11 By trial and error fit a different number of shims (4) (available in thickness of 0.004 inch and 0.016 inch (0.1016 - 0.4064 mm)) until the minimum amount of endfloat exists when the pinion is pushed in and out commensurate with free rotation of the pinion.

12 When the correct shim thickness has been ascertained fit a new rubber 'O' ring to the retaining ring and, after the assembly has been fitted, fit the dowel (2) and circlip (1).

13 Then adjust the rack and pinion backlash as described in Section 19. Reassembly is now a straightforward reversal of the dismantling sequence. Check that the rack ball joints fit tightly but are free to move. If they are excessively loose or tight adjustment can be made by varying the number and thickness of shims (42) between the ball joint cup (25) and the ball housing.

14 After fitting the rack and pinion in place fill it with the recommended lubricant.

19 Rack and pinion backlash - adjustment

Backlash between the pinion and the rack can be taken up by means of an adjustment between the rack damper cap and the rack housing. If backlash is present adjust the rack damper in the following manner. Numerical references in brackets refer to Fig. 11.15.

1   Disconnect the outer ends of the steering tie rods, (26) by knocking out the tie rod ball joint shanks from the holes in the steering arms.

2   Unscrew the damper cap (11) and remove the spring (12) and shims (9).

3   Refit the damper cap together with the plunger (13) but without the spring and shims.

4   Tighten the damper cap until it requires about a 2lb pull at the steering wheel rim to turn the wheel.

5   Measure the gap between the underside of the damper cap and the rack housing with a feeler gauge and add to this figure a clearance figure of .002 inch to .005 inch (.05 to .127 mm). The total figure represents the thickness of the shims that must be fitted under the cap. Shims are available in thicknesses of .003 inch and .010 inch (.76 and .254 mm).

6   Remove the cap, replace the spring, fit the necessary shims and tighten the cap down firmly. Reconnect the tie rod ball joints to the steering arms and note the improvement when the car is taken on the road.

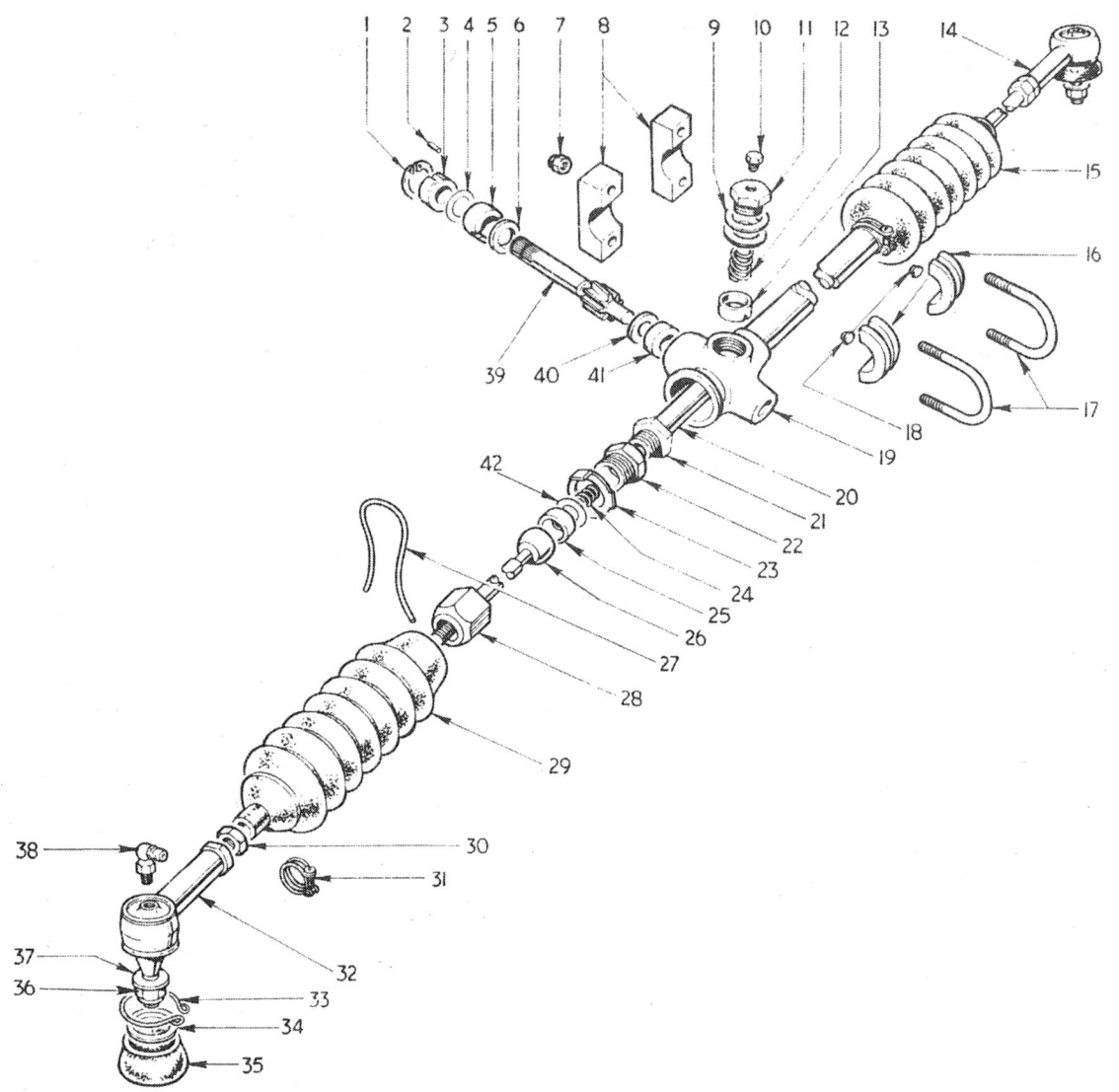

FIG. 11.15. RACK AND PINION UNIT WITH COMPONENT PARTS

1 Circlip	12 Spring	23 Lockplate	34 Washer
2 Peg	13 Thrust button	24 Spring	35 Rubber gaiter
3 Retainer	14 Tie rod ends	25 Cup	36 Nyloc nut
4 Shim	15 Rubber gaiter	26 Outer tie-rod	37 Washer
5 Bush	16 Packing pieces - front	27 Locking wire	38 Grease nipple
6 Thrust washer	17 'U' bolts	28 Cup nut	39 Pinion
7 Nyloc nut	18 Dowels	29 Rubber gaiter	40 Thrust washer
8 Packing pieces - rear	19 Rack tube	30 Locknut	41 Bush
9 Shim	20 Rack	31 Wire clip	42 Shim
10 Plug	21 Locknut	32 Outer tie rod end	
11 Cap	22 Sleeve nut	33 Clip	

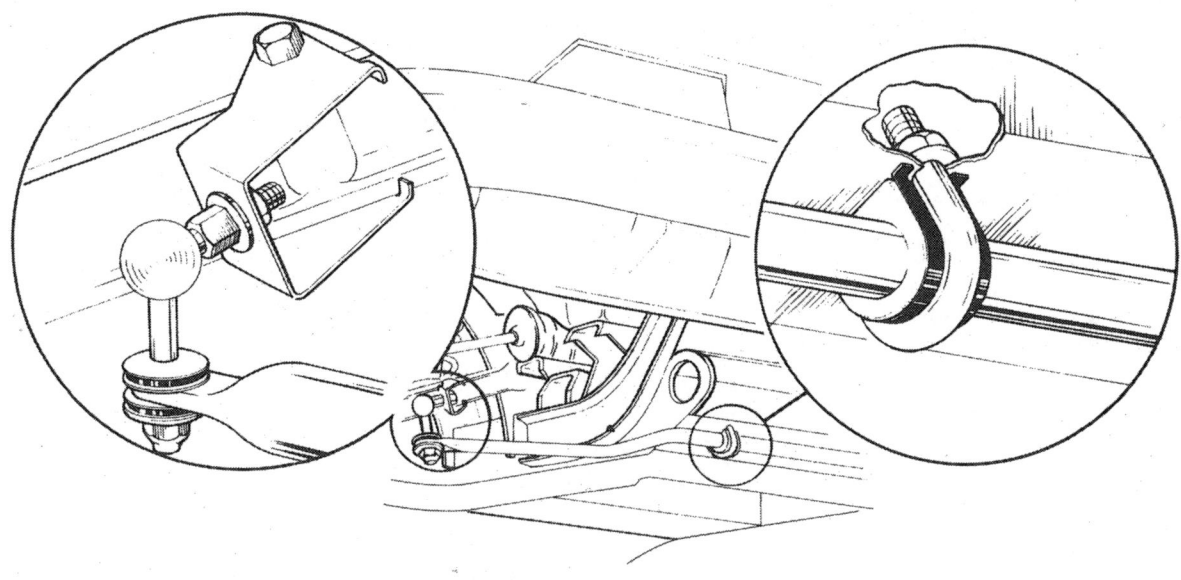

Fig. 11.16. Anti roll bar attachments

20 Outer ball joint - removal and replacement

If the tie rod outer ball joints are worn it will be necessary to renew the whole ball joint assembly as they cannot be dismantled and repaired. To remove a ball joint, free the ball joint shank from the steering arm and mark the position of the locknut on the tie rod accurately to ensure near accurate toe in on reassembly.

Slacken off the ball joint locknut and, holding the tie rod by the flat with a spanner to prevent it from turning unscrew the complete ball assembly from the rod. Replacement is a straightforward reversal of this process. Visit your local Triumph agent to ensure that toe in is correct.

21 Wheel alignment

The wheels are correctly aligned when they are turning in at the front of the wheel by 1/16 inch (1.6 mm). It is important that this measurement is taken on a centre line drawn horizontally and parallel to the ground through the centre line of the hub. The exact point should be in the centre of the sidewall of the tyre and not on the wheel rim which could be distorted and therefore give inaccurate readings.

The adjustment is effected by loosening the locknut on each tie rod balljoint and also slackening the rubber gaiter clip holding it to the tie rod, both tie rods then being turned equally until the adjustment is correct.

This is best left to a Triumph garage, as accurate alignment requires the use of special equipment. If the wheels are not in alignment, tyre wear will be heavy and uneven and the front wheel steering stiff and unresponsive.

22 Anti-roll bar

An anti roll bar is fitted to TR 250 and TR6 models and is attached as shown in Fig. 11.16. It acts as a connection between the two front wheels in a manner such that on cornering when one road wheel is being pushed up into the wheel arch by the cornering forces, the load is partially transferred through the anti roll bar and its mounting to the second front wheel.

Removal and refitting is a straightforward operation. To check for distortion lay on a flat surface and take measurements at each end. Any differences in measurements indicates distortion.

Table of tyre pressures - all models of TR5, TR250 and TR6

	Front	Rear
165HR - 15 (Nylon/rayon) Radial	22/1.54	26/1.82 psi/kg. cm
165HR - 15 (Steel braced) Radial	22/1.54	26/1.82 psi/kg. cm

For continuous high speed, over 100 mph/160 kph ADD 6/0.42 psi/kg. cm to each tyre.
For special oversize fitment base tyre pressures on figures given above but then check with tyre manufacturer for accurate figure.
NOTE' Tubed tyres must be fitted on wire wheels. Tubed or tubeless can be fitted on steel disc wheels.

23 Fault Finding - Suspension and steering

Before diagnosing faults from the following chart check the irregularities are not caused by:-
1. Binding brakes.
2. Incorrect 'mix' of radial and cross-ply tyres.
3. Incorrect tyre pressures.
4. Misalignment of the body frame.

Symptoms	Reason	Remedy
Steering wheel can be moved considerably before any sign of movement is apparent at the road wheels	Wear in steering linkage, gear and column coupling	Check all joints and gears. Renew as necessary.
Vehicle difficult to steer in a straight line - 'Wanders'	As above Wheel alignment incorrect (shown by uneven front tyre wear) Front wheel bearings loose Worn suspension unit swivel joints	As above. Check wheel alignment. Adjust or renew. Renew as necessary.
Steering stiff and heavy	Incorrect wheel alignment (uneven or excessive tyre wear) Wear or seizure in steering linkage joints Wear or seizure in suspension linkage joints Excessive wear in steering gear unit	Check and adjust. Grease or renew. Grease or renew. Adjust or renew.
Wheel wobble and vibration	Road wheels out of balance Road wheels buckled Wheel alignment incorrect Wear in steering and suspension linkages Broken front spring	Balance wheels. Check for damage. Check. Check or renew. Renew.
Excessive pitching and rolling on corners and during braking.	Defective damper and/or broken spring	Renew.

Chapter 12 Bodywork and underframe

Contents

1 General description

The all steel welded body is bolted to a separate box section chassis. It comprises two longitudinal members joined by cross-members at front and rear. In the centre of the two longitudinal members is a cruciform bracing system which gives the chassis frame the required rigidity.

Short bracket extendingfrom the two longitudinal members provide the necessary mountings for the extremities of the body.

Although a relatively straightforward operation, it is possible for the body to be removed from the chassis but in normal circumstances this is not necessary except for accident damage repair and, as this should be left to the specialist body repairer, the details of this are outside the limits of this manual.

2 Maintenance - body and chassis

1 The condition of your car's bodywork is of considerable importance as it is on this that the secondhand value of the car will mainly depend. It is much more difficult to repair neglected bodywork than to renew mechanical assemblies. The hidden portions of the body, such as the wheel arches and the underframe and the engine compartment are equally important, though obviously not requiring such frequent attention as the immediately visible paintwork.

2 Once a year or every 12,000 miles (20,000 Km) it is a sound scheme to visit your local main agent and have the underside of the body steam cleaned. This will take about 1½ hours.

All traces of dirt and oil will be removed and the underside can then be inspected carefully for rust, damaged hydraulic pipes, frayed electrical wiring and other faults.

3 At the same time the engine compartment should be cleaned in the same manner. If steam cleaning facilities are not available then brush 'Gunk' or a similar cleanser over the whole engine and engine compartment with a stiff paintbrush, working it well in where there is an accumulation of oil and dirt. Do not paint the ignition system but protect it with oily rags when the 'Gunk' is washed off. As the 'Gunk' is washed away it will take with it all traces of oil and dirt, leaving the engine looking clean and bright.

4 The wheel arches should be given particular attention as undersealing can easily come away here and stones and dirt thrown up from the road wheels can soon cause the paint to chip and flake, and so allow rust to set in. If rust is found, clean down the bare metal with wet and dry paper, paint on an anti-corrosive coating or, if preferred, red lead, and renew the paintwork and undercoating.

5 The bodywork should be washed once a week or when dirty. Thoroughly wet the car to soften the dirt and then wash the car down with a soft sponge and plenty of clean water. If the surplus dirt is not washed off very gently, in time it will wear the paint down as surely as wet and dry paper. It is best to use a hose if this is available. Give the car a final wash down and then dry using a soft chamois leather to prevent the formation of spots.

6 Spots of tar and grease thrown up from the road can be removed with a rag dampened with petrol.

7 Once every six months, or every three months, if wished, give the bodywork and chromium trim a thoroughly good wax polish. If a chromium cleaner is used to remove rust on any of the plated parts remember that the cleaner also removes part of the chromium so use sparingly.

3 Maintenance - upholstery and carpets

1 Remove the carpets or mats and thoroughly vacuum clean the interior of the car every three months or more frequently if necessary.

2 Beat out the carpets and vacuum clean them if they are very dirty. If the upholstery is soiled apply an upholstery cleaner with a damp sponge and wipe off with a clean dry cloth.

4 Maintenance - hoods and tonneau covers

Under no circumstances try to clean hoods, and tonneau covers with detergents, caustic soaps, or spirit cleaners. Plain soap and water is all that is required with a soft brush to clean dirt that may be ingrained. Wash the hood as frequently as the rest of the car.

5 Minor body repairs

There comes a time in the life of a car when rust appears on some part or other of the many exterior body panels. To the do-it-yourself motorist even the most formidable looking rust patches or panels that have corroded through can be repaired provided that their condition has not been allowed to become so bad as necessitating a new panel or section to be fitted.

Many shops stock body repair and filler kits and it was by using one of these kits that a TR, having bad rust patches, was given a new lease of life. By following the maker's instructions very satisfactory results may be obtained as will be seen once this section has been studied.

1 The offside rear wing panel had bad rust marks and in several places there were actual holes.

2 The first stage of repair is to knock the loose pieces of metal away until firm metal surrounds the hole. To enable an adequate depth of filler to be used so that the body panel curves may be reproduced the area around the hole should be hammered in by about ½ inch.

3 Any stainless steel or chrome trim near to the area being repaired should be removed otherwise it could be damaged or impair the work.

4 Using a wire brush, remove all paintwork and rust from around the area to be repaired. Care must be taken at this stage to remove as much as possible so that a good bond between the filler and the body panel will be obtained.

5 Either supplied with the repair kit, or offered as an extra, will be a piece of gauze. Cut a piece just a little bigger than the size of the hole.

6 Bend over the edges of the gauze and shape it so that it will catch on the inside of the hole. If it is found that the hole is in place where the gauze will fall out, retain it in place with bent paper clips.

7 Follow the instructions given on the filler pack and mix the filler accordingly. Mix only sufficient for immediate needs as it hardens quickly and will only be wasted.

8 Apply a little filler to each corner of the gauze to give additional support to it and then work around the outside of the hole. Allow the filler to dry (photo).

9 Using a wide spreader fill up the remainder of the hole and the surrounding, if possible keeping to the contour of the body panel so making the subsequent operations easier.

10 If necessary build up the contour in several stages.

11 Using a very coarse file, or Dreadnought milling file, carefully shape the hardened filler so that it blends in with the panel shape. Ensure that not too much is removed otherwise it will have to be built up again.

12 To stop any paint spray in subsequent operations finding its way onto the surrounding panels use newspaper and Sellotape to mask off the area under repair.

13 With a little 'wet or dry' rubbing paper, backed with a piece of wood, remove the teeth marks and scratches left from the previous operation. If it is found that the grain clogs, the rubbing paper may be thoroughly wetted.

14 The edges of existing paintwork should be feathered so that no ridges will be evident when the repaired section is finally resprayed.

15 If there are any chrome fittings such as letters or badges which are in the area of repair and may be difficult to mask from paint spray, then coat them with a little grease so that the paint spray does not adhere to the chrome work.

16 When the surface is perfectly smooth it is now time to put on the first coat of paint. This should be a primer coat and may be obtained in an aerosol tin. Before spraying for the first time read the instructions and then practice on a piece of flat metal or wood.

17 Holding the jet about six inches away from the surface spray the area taking care that runs are not allowed to form. This is usually caused by holding the jet too near to the area being painted.

18 Very carefully inspect the dry primer coat for signs of imper-

fections of the paint feathering or flatting sequences previously completed. Any imperfections should be attended to at this stage. Respray with primer.

19 When the surface is really flat and smooth lightly rub the primer to give a key for the top coat.

20 Just before the top coat is applied try a little of the paint on a less prominent part of the bodywork to ensure a good colour match. If the colours vary considerably due to weathering it will be better to have some matching paint mixed at the local garage and the affected parts sprayed otherwise results could look very patchy.

21 When the final coat is dry remove the newspaper and tape. Allow the paint to harden before refitting any chrome trim. Leave the repainted surfaces for about seven days before using any polish.

22 Where the paintwork has blistered due to rust forming behind the paint, the area affected must be rubbed down well with emery paper.

23 Do not confine the area to the paint blisters alone but increase it to about 1½ inches around the affected area.

24 When the extent of rust has been determined use a wire brush to derust any deeply rusted areas. Tap in any holes to give a key for the filler.

25 Using a wide spreader apply some prepared filler to the area under repair.

26 Allow the filler to dry and then prepare the surface as previously described in this Section.

27 This is what the finished panel should look like (photo).

6 Major chassis and body repairs

1 Major chassis and body repair work cannot successfully be undertaken by the average owner. Work of this nature should be entrusted to a competent body repair specialist who should have the necessary jigs, welding and hydraulic straightening equipment as well as skilled panel beaters to ensure that a proper job is done.

2 If the damage is severe it is vital that on completion of repair the chassis is in correct alignment. Less severe damage may also have twisted or distorted the chassis although this may not be visible immediately. It is therefore always best on completion of repair to check for twist and squareness to ensure that all is correct.

3 To check for twist, position the car on a clean level floor, place a jack under each jacking point, raise the car, and take off the wheels. Raise or lower the jacks until points C and D (Fig. 12.1). are exactly equidistant from the floor.

4 With the points C and D correctly set, should it prove impossible to obtain equal height measurements at A and G, then the chassis is twisted.

5 If the previous test proved satisfactory the next check should be for squareness by taking a series of measurements on the floor. Drop a plumb line and bob weight from the lettered points on the chassis frame (Fig. 12.1). to the floor and mark these points with a sharpened piece of chalk. Letter them to correspond with the letters in Fig. 12.1.

6 When all datum marks have been made carefully remove the car from the area.

7 Connect the letters in pairs, i.e., AA,DD,GG together by drawing a line between them using a straight edge (Fig. 12.1).

8 Draw a centre line through the previously made lines so that the floor pattern is similar to that shown in Fig. 12.1. and measure each line from the centre line to the lettered end. Obviously each corresponding line from the centre line outwards should measure the same.

9 A further check may be made by joining diagonals as shown in Fig. 12.2. The points of intersection of the diagonals should also be on the centre line of the floor pattern.

7   Maintenance - hinges and locks

Once every six months, or every 6,000 miles, the door, bonnet and boot hinges should be oiled, using a few drops of engine oil from an oil can. The door striker plates should be given a thin smear of grease to reduce wear and ensure free movement.

8   Front bumper and brackets - removal, dismantling and refitting

1   Undo and remove the two bolts that secure the overrider support stay to the inner valance.
2   Undo and remove the two bolts which secure the bumper bar support brackets to the mounting bracket.
3   Carefully lift away the bumper complete with the overriders and support stays.
4   If necessary the overrider can be separated from the bumper bar by undoing the retaining bolts and removing them together with plain and spring washers. Recover the two P.V.C. mouldings.
5   The support brackets may be removed from the bumper bar by undoing the nuts and lifting away the nuts, spring washers, plain washers and distance pieces.
6   To remove the bumper support brackets from the body loosen the securing nuts, remove the nuts, spring washers and plain washers, then withdraw the clamp plates with studs.
7   Refitting is the reverse sequence to removal. Do not tighten fully any nuts or bolts until all have been correctly positioned and loosely fitted.

9   Rear bumper and brackets - removal, dismantling and refitting

1   Disconnect the battery earth terminal for safety reasons.
2   Locate the rear number plate illumination light cable connectors within the rear luggage compartment and disconnect the cables. Withdraw the cables through the luggage compartment to the underside of the car.
3   Remove the bolts that secure the two overrider support brackets to the chassis.
4   Slacken but do not remove the nuts and remove the stud. As the inner end of the stud has a slot it is possible to remove the stud.
5   On later models it will be found that the nuts and washers shown in the dotted part of   Fig. 12.3.   are superseded by a distance piece.
6   Undo and remove the two bolts that secure the two overriders to the bumper and support brackets.
7   Remove the two nuts that secure the bumper to the support brackets.
8   Carefully lift away the bumper from the rear of the car noting the position of the two distance pieces.
9   To remove the two support brackets from the body undo and remove the four bolts and lift away the support brackets.
10 Refitting is the reverse sequence to removal but the following additional points should be noted.
11 Do not completely tighten any nuts and bolts until all have been positioned and loosely fitted.
12 There should be a clearance of 0.75 inch between the bumper and body panels which may be adjusted by positioning the support and outrigger brackets.

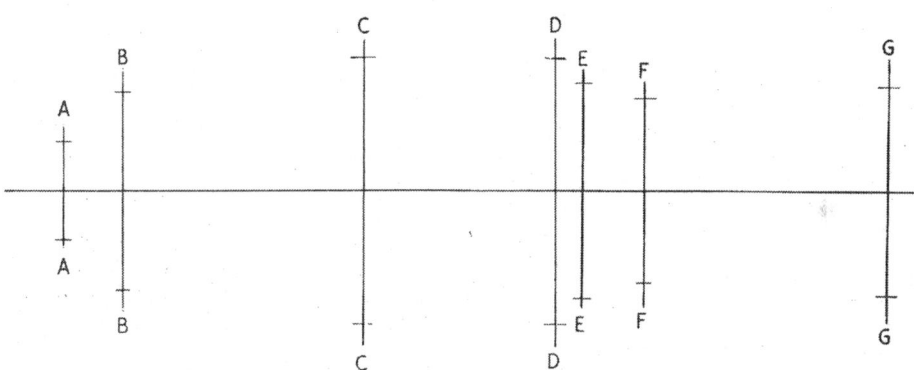

Fig. 12.1. Body mounting, spring and major checking points as transferred to floor

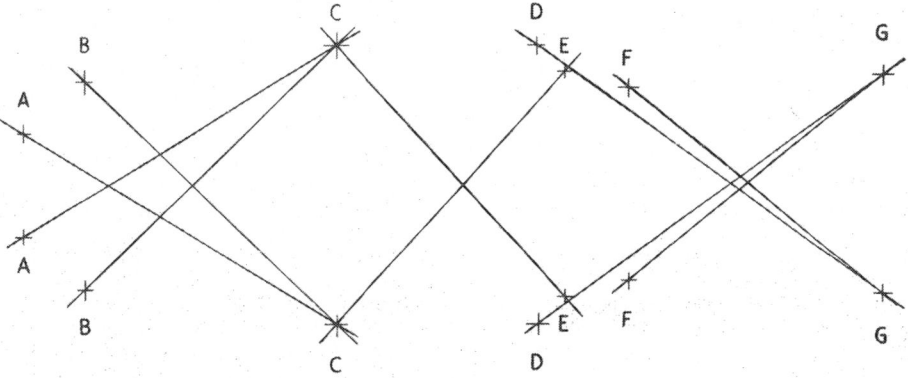

Fig. 12.2. Diagonal cross check once the points in Fig. 12.1. have been marked on the floor

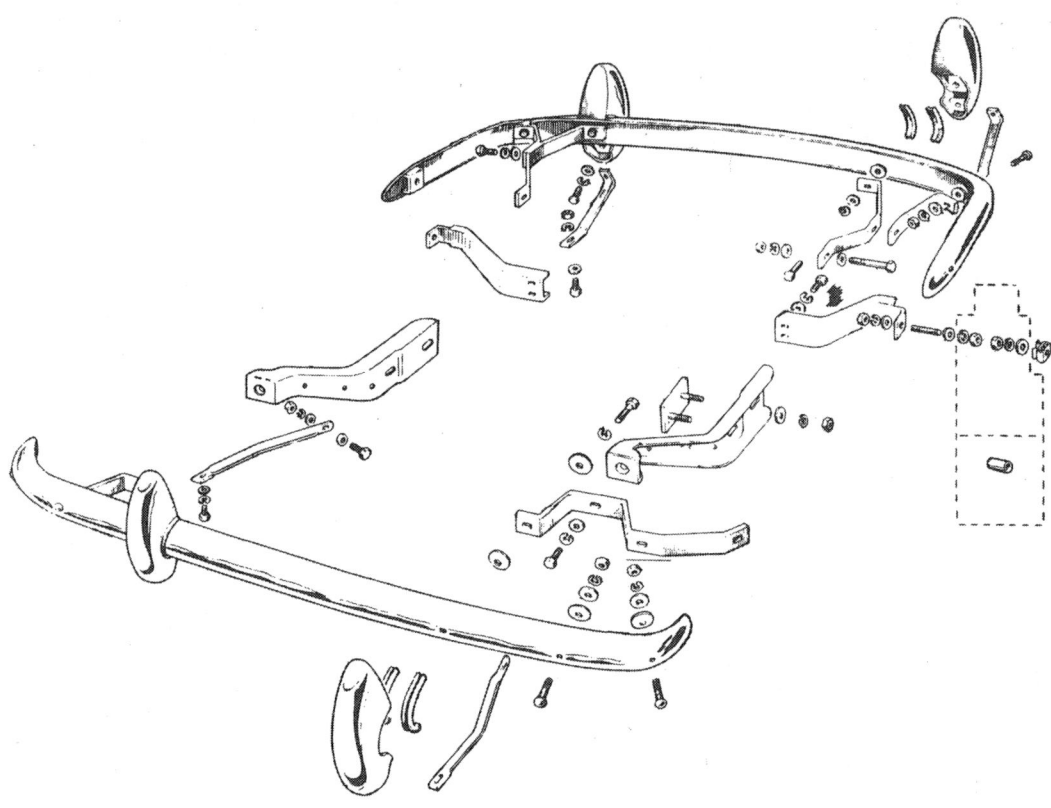

Fig. 12.3. Front and rear bumper and bracket assemblies (TR5/250)

10 Front wing - removal and refitting

1 The removal of a front wing is a very easy procedure and should present no difficulties except in extreme cases of corrosion. It is recommended that all nuts and bolts likely to be rusted be soaked in penetrating oil overnight prior to removal.

2 Remove the two bolts that secure the overrider support stay to the inner valance.

3 Undo and remove the two bolts and lift the front bumper assembly away from the front of the car.

4 The location of the front wing retaining screws is shown in Fig.12.4. and these should be undone and removed in a diagonal manner so as to provide support to the front wing.

5 When all screws have been removed the front wing may be removed. Undo the two screws securing each of the bonnet side buffer rubbers and lift away the rubbers. Also remove the chromium beading that is sandwiched between the wing and the body.

6 Refitting the wing is the reverse sequence to removal but the following additional points should be noted:

7 Carefully remove all traces of the old sealing compound before reassembly and when refitting seal the joint between the wing and the body with a non-setting sealing compound.

8 The retaining lugs on the chromium beading should be straightened before it is refitted between the wing and body. As the wing retaining screws (A) are tighened press the chromium beading down into position and once they are tight bend over the retaining tags.

11 Rear wing - removal and refitting

1 It is recommended that all nuts and bolts likely to be rusted

be soaked in penetrating oil overnight prior to removal.

2 Disconnect the battery earth terminal for safety reasons.

3 Locate the cable terminal connectors for the rear lights and check that the cable colour coding can be readily indentified. If the colouring has faded use a tape to indentify each pair of cables to assist reconnection. Also disconnect the flasher rear marker and number plate light cables from the snap connectors positioned in the upper corners of the luggage compartment.

4 From inside the luggage compartment undo and remove the rear light cluster four securing nuts and spring washers. Lift away the rear light cluster.

5 Refer to Section 9 of this Chapter and remove the rear bumper and support brackets.

6 Undo and remove the four retaining screws that secure the interior trim panel at the rear of the fuel tank.

7 Cars fitted with the soft top should have the soft top and hoodstick assembly removed.

8 Undo the six screws that secure the quarter trim panel in place, lift away the screws and the trim panel.

9 Remove the screws that hold the wing panel to the body. Lift away the wing and chrome beading from the body.

10 Refitting the wing is the reverse sequence to removal but the following additional points should be noted.

11 Carefully remove all traces of the old sealing compound before reassembly and when refitting seal the joint between the wing and the body with a non-setting sealing compound.

12 The retaining tags on the chromium beading should be straightened before it is refitted between the wing and body. As the wing retaining screws (A) are tightened press the chromium beading down into position and once they are tight bend over the retaining tags.

13 Once the rear lights and battery have been reconnected check that all the lights function correctly.

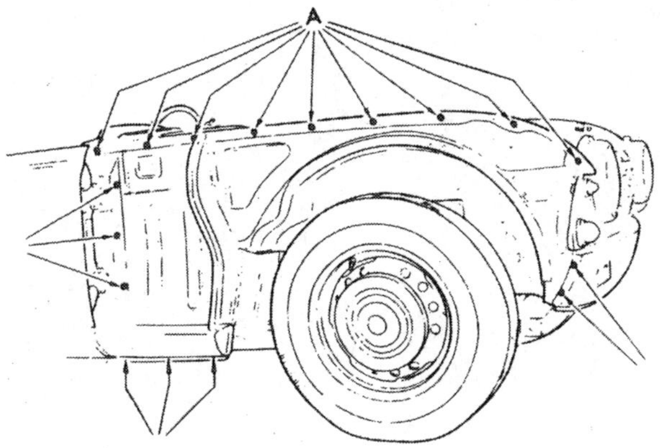

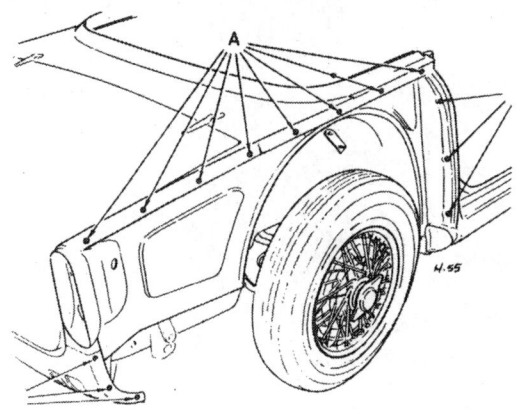

Fig. 12.4. Front wing attachment points (TR5/250)

Fig. 12.5. Rear wing attachment points (TR5/250)

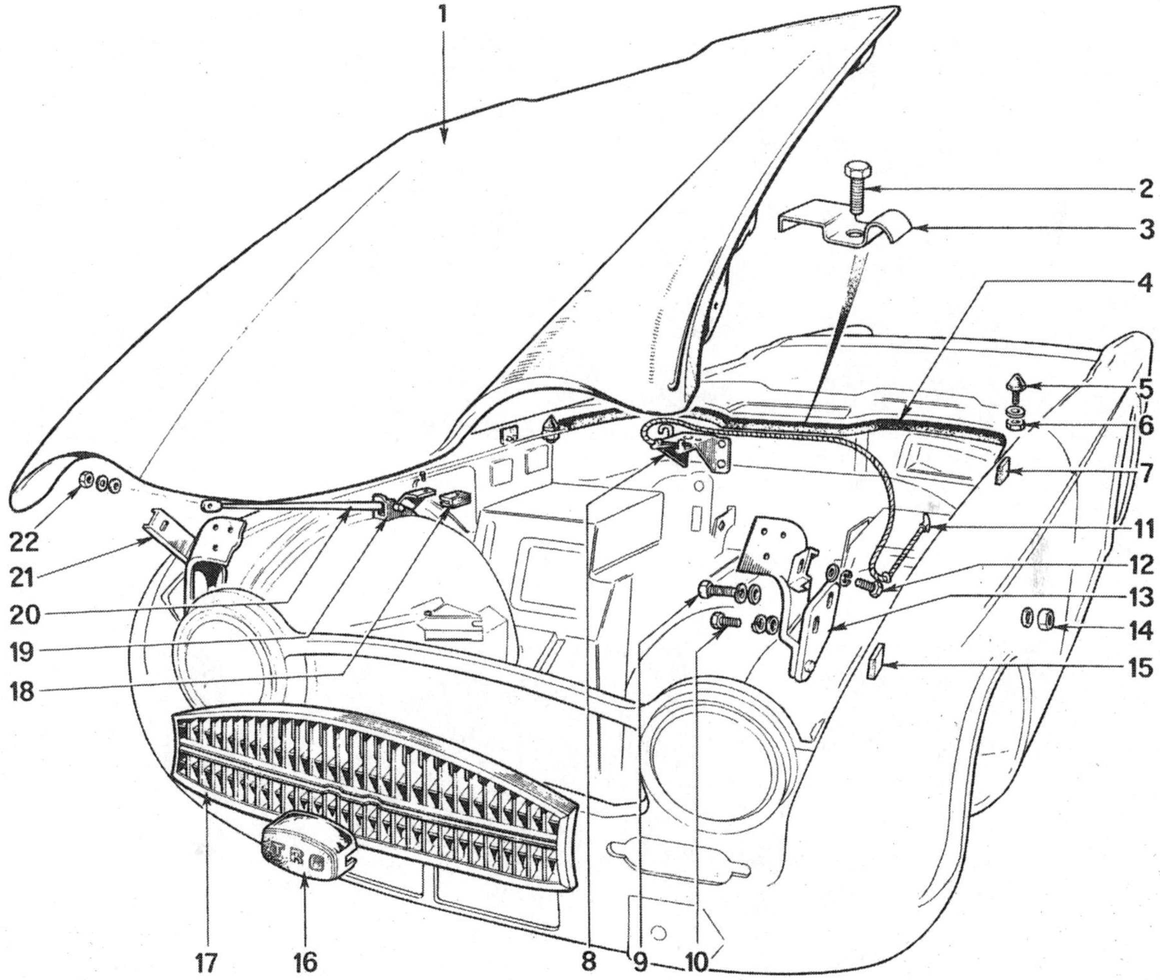

FIG. 12.6. BONNET AND GRILLE ATTACHMENTS (TR6)

1 Bonnet assembly	pin	12 Bolt - hinge to closing panel	18 Rubber buffer - bonnet stay bracket
2 Setscrew - cable clip	7 Rubber buffer	13 Hinge assembly	19 Bracket - bonnet stay rod
3 Clip - retaining cable to body	8 Lock plate assembly	14 Bolt - hinge to body	20 Bonnet stay rod
4 Bonnet sealing rubber	9 Bolt) hinge to body	15 Rubber buffer	21 Hinge assembly
5 Locating pin-bonnet	10 Bolt)	16 Nameplate medallion	22 Nyloc nut - stay rod
6 Nut - securing locating	11 Bonnet release cable assembly	17 Front grille	

This photographic sequence shows the steps taken to repair the dent and paintwork damage shown above. In general, the procedure for repairing a hole will be similar; where there are substantial differences, the procedure is clearly described and shown in a separate photograph.

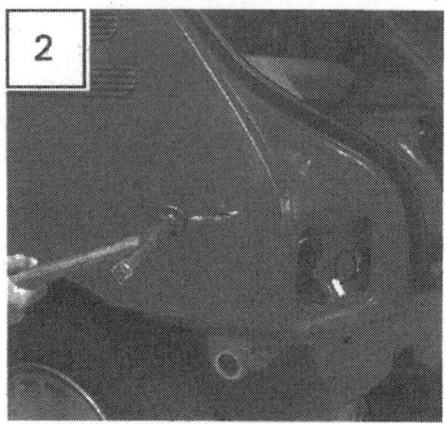

First remove any trim around the dent, then hammer out the dent where access is possible. This will minimise filling. Here, after the large dent has been hammered out, the damaged area is being made slightly concave.

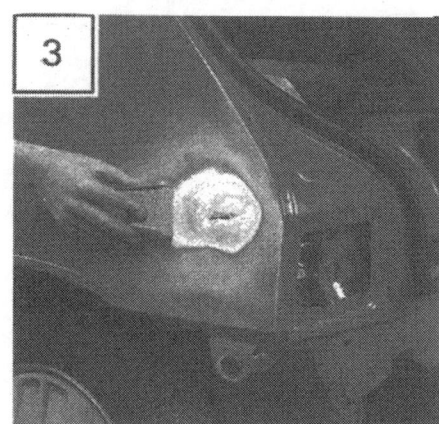

Next, remove all paint from the damaged area by rubbing with course abrasive paper or using a power drill fitted with a wire brush or abrasive pad. 'Feather' the edge of the boundary with good paintwork using a finer grade of abrasive paper.

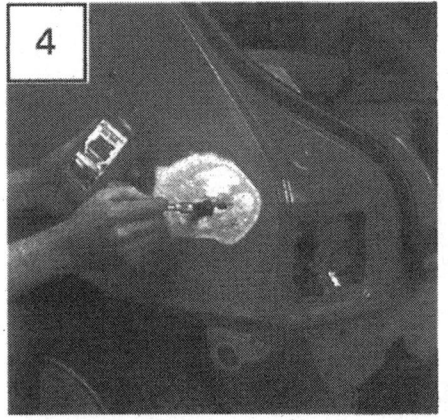

Where there are holes or other damage, the sheet metal should be cut away before proceeding further. The damaged area and any signs of rust should be treated with Turtle Wax Hi-Tech Rust Eater, which will also inhibit further rust formation.

For a large dent or hole mix Holts Body Plus Resin and Hardener according to the manufacturer's instructions and apply around the edge of the repair. Press Glass Fibre Matting over the repair area and leave for 20-30 minutes to harden. Then ...

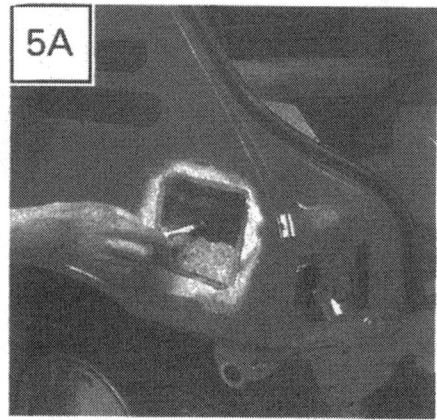

... brush more Holts Body Plus Resin and Hardener onto the matting and leave to harden. Repeat the sequence with two or three layers of matting, checking that the final layer is lower than the surrounding area. Apply Holts Body Plus Filler Paste as shown in Step 5B.

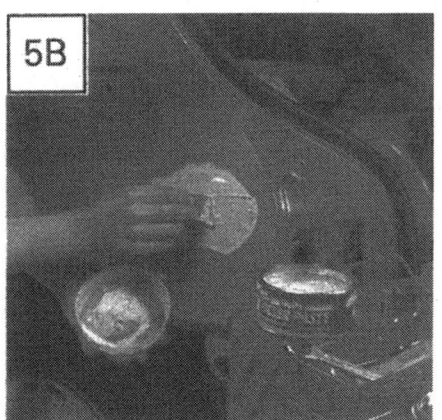

For a medium dent, mix Holts Body Plus Filler Paste and Hardener according to the manufacturer's instructions and apply it with a flexible applicator. Apply thin layers of filler at 20-minute intervals, until the filler surface is slightly proud of the surrounding bodywork.

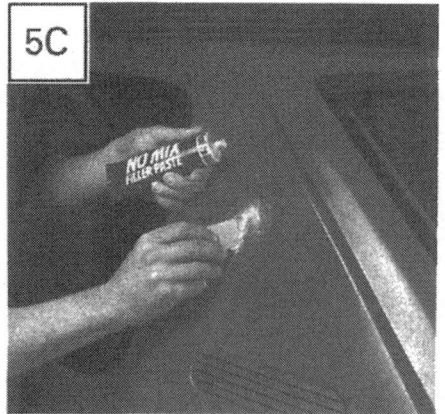

For small dents and scratches use Holts No Mix Filler Paste straight from the tube. Apply it according to the instructions in thin layers, using the spatula provided. It will harden in minutes if applied outdoors and may then be used as its own knifing putting.

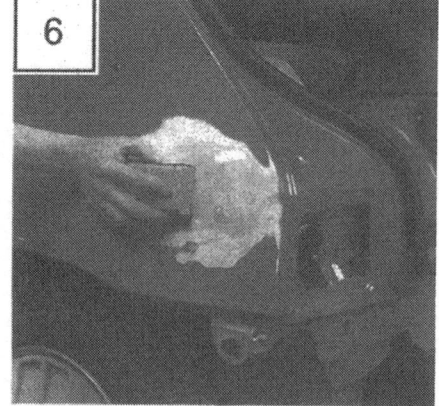

Use a plane or file for initial shaping. Then, using progressively finer grades of wet-and-dry paper, wrapped around a sanding block, and copious amounts of clean water, rub down the filler until glass smooth. 'Feather' the edges of adjoining paintwork.

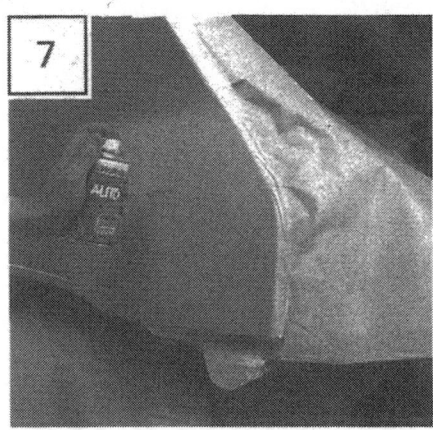

Protect adjoining areas before spraying the whole repair area and at least one inch of the surrounding sound paintwork with Holts Dupli-Color primer.

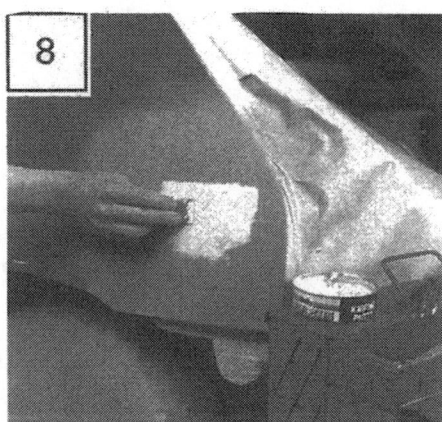

Fill any imperfections in the filler surface with a small amount of Holts Body Plus Knifing Putty. Using plenty of clean water, rub down the surface with a fine grade wet-and-dry paper - 400 grade is recommended - until it is really smooth.

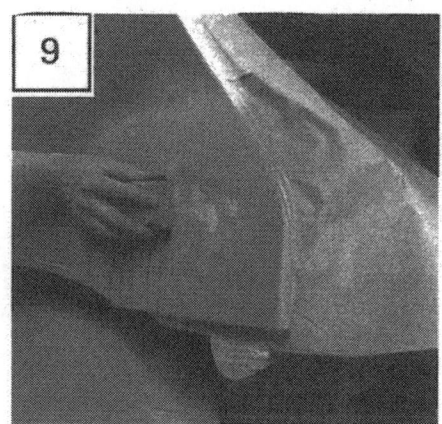

Carefully fill any remaining imperfections with knifing putty before applying the last coat of primer. Then rub down the surface with Holts Body Rubbing Compound to ensure a really smooth surface.

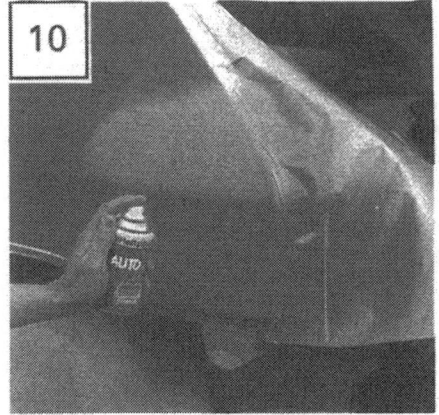

Protect surrounding areas from overspray before applying the topcoat in several thin layers. Agitate Holts Dupli-Color aerosol thoroughly. Start at the repair centre, spraying outwards with a side-to-side motion.

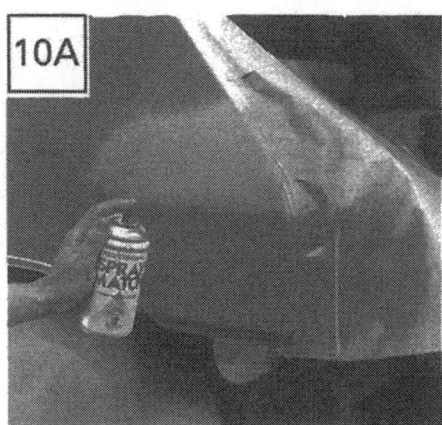

If the exact colour is not available off the shelf, local Holts Professional Spraymatch Centres will custom fill an aerosol to match perfectly.

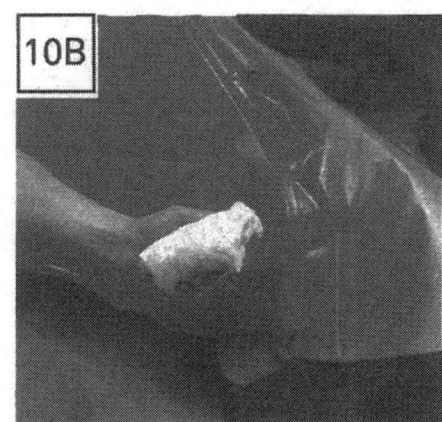

To identify whether a lacquer finish is required, rub a painted unrepaired part of the body with wax and a clean cloth.

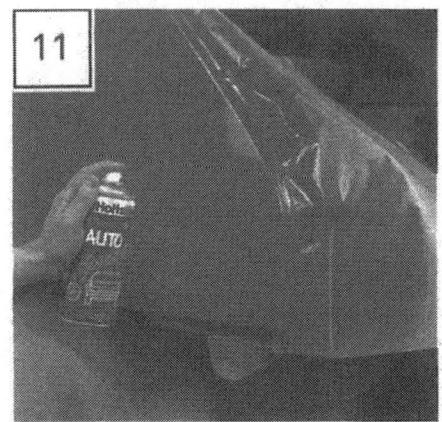

If no traces of paint appear on the cloth, spray Holts Dupli-Color clear lacquer over the repaired area to achieve the correct gloss level.

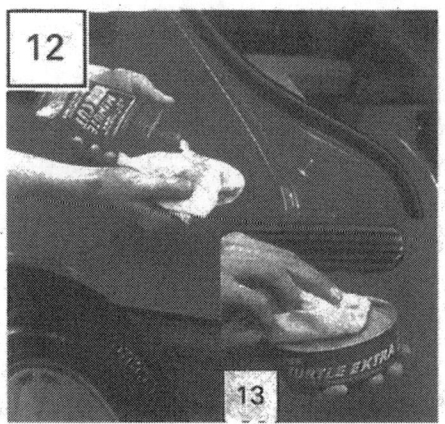

The paint will take about two weeks to harden fully. After this time it can be 'cut' with a mild cutting compound such as Turtle Wax Minute Cut prior to polishing with a final coating of Turtle Wax Extra.

When carrying out bodywork repairs, remember that the quality of the finished job is proportional to the time and effort expended.

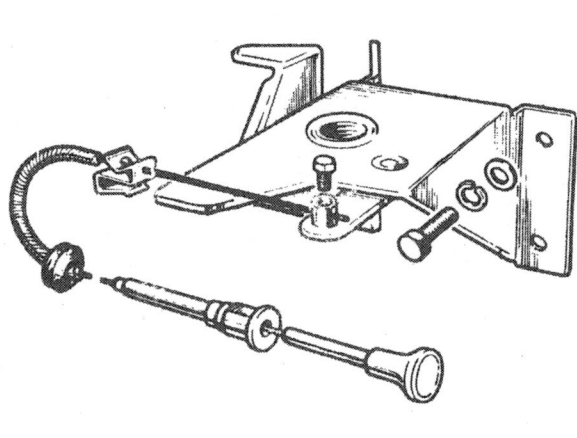

Fig 12.7. Bonnet lock assembly

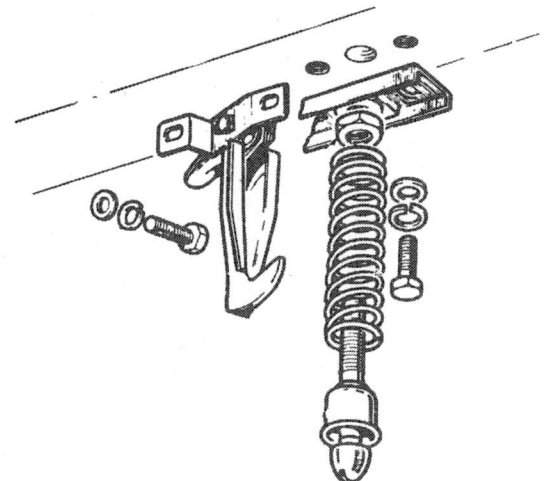

Fig. 12.8. Bonnet striker assembly

12 Bonnet lock and striker adjustment

1 If the bonnet has been removed, refitted and hinges adjusted, the lock and strikers should be checked for correct adjustment.
2 Undo but do not remove the clamping ferrule screw.
3 A second person should push and hold the bonnet lock control situated inside the car until it is within 1/8 inch of its 'fully in' position.
4 Tighten the clamping ferrule screw.
5 Lubricate the cable and lock moving plate and lever.
6 The bonnet striker mechanism may be adjusted by slackening the locknut on the fastener assembly.
7 Turn the dovetail centre bolt with a wide blade screwdriver in a clockwise direction to take up movement at the catch plate or in an anti-clockwise direction to increase movement at the catch plate. This adjustment is made by trial and error. When correct tighten the locknut.
8 Provision is made for adjusting the rubber buffer located at the rear corner of the engine compartment if excessive movement is evident with correct lock adjustment.

13 Bonnet lid - removal and refitting

1 Operate the bonnet release catch and open the bonnet fully.
2 It is recommended that the services of a second person be obtained to assist by taking the weight of the bonnet as the hinges are released.
3 To give a guide as to the location of the hinges for adjustment after refitting outline the hinges on the wing valance with a pencil before removal.
4 Undo the two bolts that secure each hinge to the wing valance. Lift away the bolts, spring and plain washers; the bonnet may now be lifted away over the front of the car.
5 Refitting is the reverse sequence to removal. If hinge adjustment from the original setting is necessary the release catch and bonnet striker mechanism may require adjustment, details of which are given in Section 12.

14 Luggage compartment lid - removal and refitting

1 Open the luggage compartment lid and undo the bolt that secures the upper end of the sliding stay to the lid. A second person will now be required to hold the lid open.
2 Undo the self tapping screws that secure the fuel tank casing board to the luggage compartment interior and draw the casing board rearwards.
3 Mark the outline of the hinges so that they may be refitted in their original positions and then undo and remove the two bolts, spring and plain washers that secure each hinge to the body.
4 Refitting the luggage compartment lid is the reverse sequence to removal. Line up the previously made pencil marks to ensure correct fitting. The bolt holes are elongated to allow for any necessary adjustments.

15 Luggage compartment lock assembly - removal and refitting

Lock

1 Open the lid and undo and remove the four cross head screws that secure the lock to the body.
2 Carefully manipulate the lock assembly from the rear valance panel.
3 Refitting is the reverse sequence to removal. Well lubricate all moving parts.

Locking device

1 To remove the locking device first detach the lock assembly as described earlier in this section.
2 Using a 0.125 in (3.17 mm) drill remove the two rivets that secure the catch portion of the lock to the push button mounting plate.
3 Undo and remove the two round head screws that secure the push button sub assembly to the mounting plate.
4 Release the locking pin and withdraw the locking device.
5 Refitting the locking device and push button sub assembly is the reverse sequence to removal.

Striker plate

1 To remove the striker plate undo and remove the two screws and washers that secure the striker plate to the lid. Lift away the striker plate.
2 Refitting the striker plate is the reverse sequence to removal.
3 Should adjustment be necessary, elongated holes are provided in the plate to ensure correct alignment between the plate and lock.
4 Slacken the locknut and then screw the bolt in or out as necessary. Retighten the locknut.

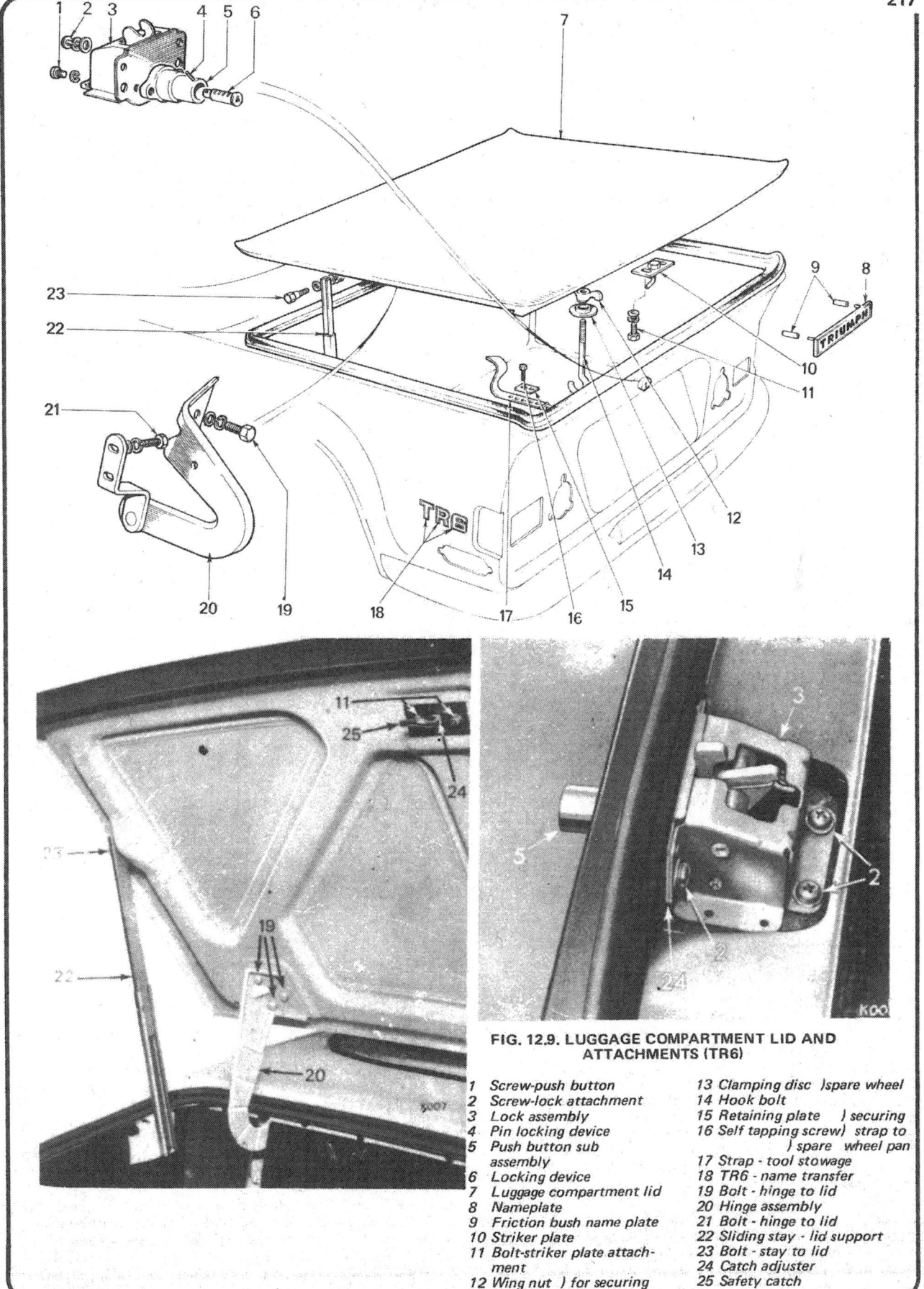

FIG. 12.9. LUGGAGE COMPARTMENT LID AND ATTACHMENTS (TR6)

1 Screw-push button
2 Screw-lock attachment
3 Lock assembly
4 Pin locking device
5 Push button sub assembly
6 Locking device
7 Luggage compartment lid
8 Nameplate
9 Friction bush name plate
10 Striker plate
11 Bolt-striker plate attachment
12 Wing nut) for securing

13 Clamping disc)spare wheel
14 Hook bolt
15 Retaining plate) securing
16 Self tapping screw) strap to
) spare wheel pan
17 Strap - tool stowage
18 TR6 - name transfer
19 Bolt - hinge to lid
20 Hinge assembly
21 Bolt - hinge to lid
22 Sliding stay - lid support
23 Bolt - stay to lid
24 Catch adjuster
25 Safety catch

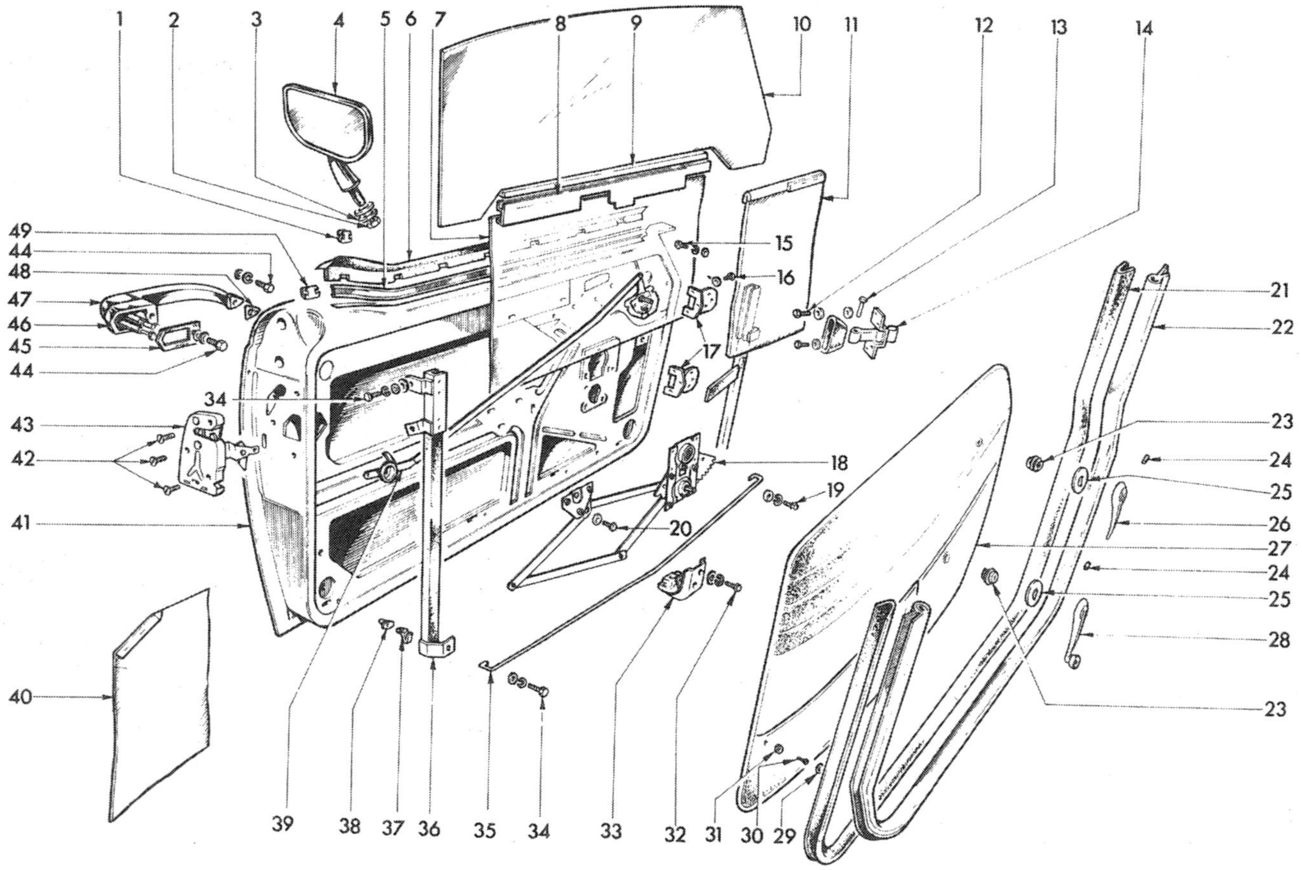

FIG. 12.10. DOOR INTERNAL AND EXTERNAL COMPONENTS

1 Trim clip
2 Nut) door mirror
3 Washer) attachment
4 Exterior door mirror
5 Inner weatherstrip
6 Outer weatherstrip
7 Water deflector curtain
8 Glass channel
9 Glazing strip
10 Glass
11 Water deflector curtain

12 Screw - check arm
13 Pin - check arm
14 Check arm
15 Bolt - hinge to 'A' post
16 Bolt - hinge to door
17 Door hinge
18 Window regulator mechanism
19 Setscrew) window regulator
20 Setscrew) attachment
21 Sealing rubber
22 Draught excluder

23 Spring
24 Retaining pin
25 Escutcheon plate
26 Remote control handle
27 Trim panel
28 Window regulator handle
29 Cover button) door pocket
30 Screw) attachment
31 Retaining washer)
32 Screw - stop bracket
33 Glass - stop bracket

34 Setscrew - glass run channel
35 Tie rod
36 Glass run channel
37 Clip
38 Snap-sac
39 Remote control unit
40 Water deflector curtain
41 Door
42 Screw - lock attachment
43 Anti-burst lock

44 Setscrew - door handle
attachment
45 Seating washer
46 Outside door handle
47 Push button - door handle
48 Seating washer
49 Trim-clip
50 Locknut
51 Adjustment screw
52 Lock contactor
53 Anti-burst strap

54 Screw - striker plate
56 Waved washer
57 Spring clip
58 Lever
59 Spring
60 Setscrew - remote
control unit
61 Lock operating lever
62 Locking lever
63 Operating fork
64 Spring collar

16 Door - removal and refitting

1 Undo the five screws that retain the kick pad to the 'A' post and remove the pad from the car.

2 Release the clip retaining the pin in the door check arm. Extract the pin noting that the head is uppermost.

3 Using a pencil outline the position of the door hinge relative to the body to assist correct refitting.

4 Undo and remove the six bolts that secure the hinges to the body and lift away the complete door. An assistant to take the weight of the door whilst the hinge securing bolts are undone would be an advantage to save any damage by one person trying to take the weight of the door while undoing the bolts.

5 If required, with the door removed, the hinges can be removed by undoing the three hinge retaining bolts.

6 Refitting the door is the reverse sequence to removal. Take care to ensure that it is hung correctly and that the lock engages smoothly. Before the hinges are finally tightened check that the hinges align with the previously made pencil marks.

7 Should it be necessary to adjust the position of the hinges, vertical movement can be adjusted by means of the bolts securing the hinges to the 'A' post. In and out movement can be adjusted by means of the bolts securing the hinge to the door. Adjustment is considered correct when the door is evenly fitted into the door aperture when closed.

17 Door lock and remote control - removal and refitting

1 Before removing the door lock first wind up the door glass and make a note of the position of the handles for correct refitting.

2 Using a small electrician's size screwdriver push in the door handle escutcheon and push out the small tapered pin. The door handle can then be removed from the remote control unit.

3 Repeat the previous operation for the window winder regulator handle and remove the handle from the regulator.

4 Undo the two screws that secure the interior handle to the door panel.

5 Undo the screw having first removed the cover button that secures the rear edge of the trim panel to the door. Lift away the screw and special cover button retaining washer. Repeat this procedure on the forward positioned screw of the trim pocket.

6 Using a wide blade screwdriver or a knife carefully ease the trim panel clips from their holes in the door panel. When they are all free lift away the trim panel.

7 Release the spring clip and wave washer and then disconnect the remote control link from the lock assembly.

8 Carefully disconnect the link connecting the exterior door handle control to the lock at the lock end of the link.

9 Undo the three screws that secure the door glass channel to the door at the rear of the lock and lift away the channel.

10 Undo and remove the four screws and spring washers that secure the lock to the door and lift away the lock assembly.

11 The remote control assembly can be removed by undoing the three screws and removing the screws and spring washers. Lift away the remote control assembly.

12 Refitting is the reverse sequence to removal. It is recommended that all moving parts be well greased before refitting to ensure long and reliable service.

13 The lock is not adjustable in any way but if difficulty is experienced in closing or opening the door the cause could well be the striker dovetail and door restraint device. The position is easily adjusted by slackening the mounting screws and adjusting the position accordingly until the correct setting is found by trial and error. Do not slam the door when adjusting the lock assembly.

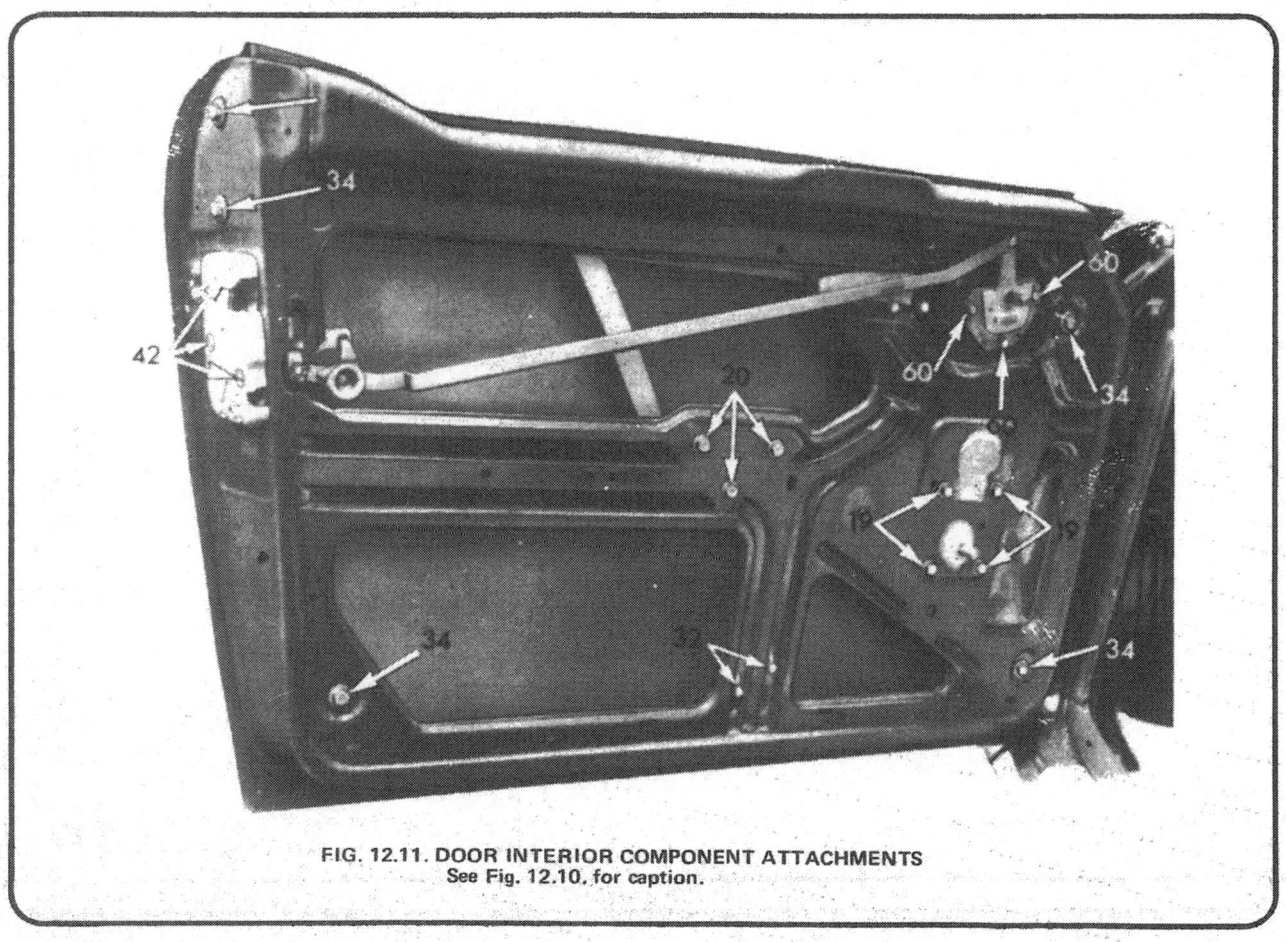

FIG. 12.11. DOOR INTERIOR COMPONENT ATTACHMENTS
See Fig. 12.10. for caption.

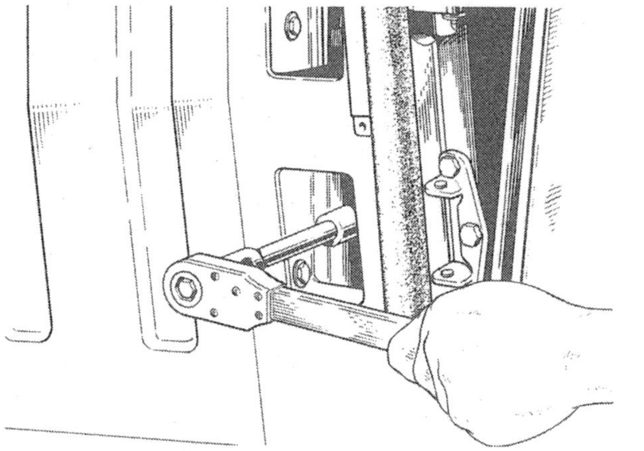

220

Fig.12.12   Removal of door securing bolts.

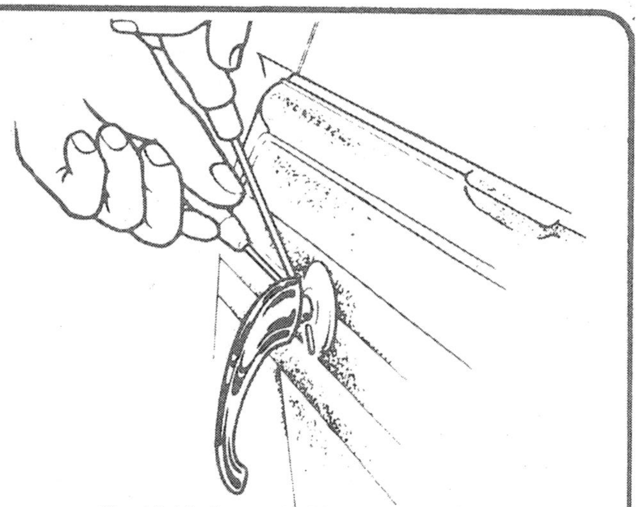

Fig. 12.13. Removal of interior handle

Fig. 12.14. Door lock anti-burst striker plate
Arrows show securing screws.

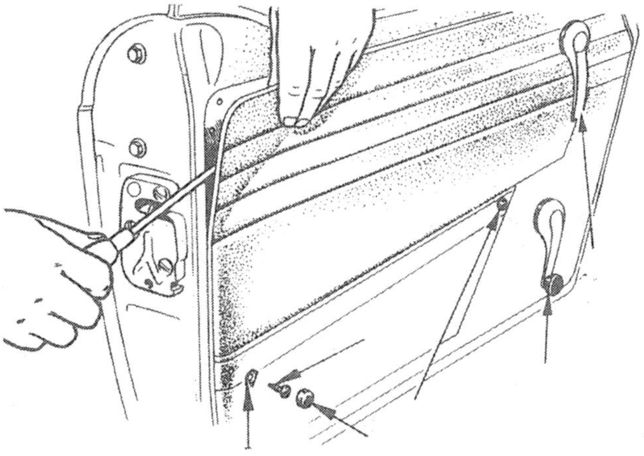

Fig. 12.15. Removal of trim panel
Items to be removed arrowed.

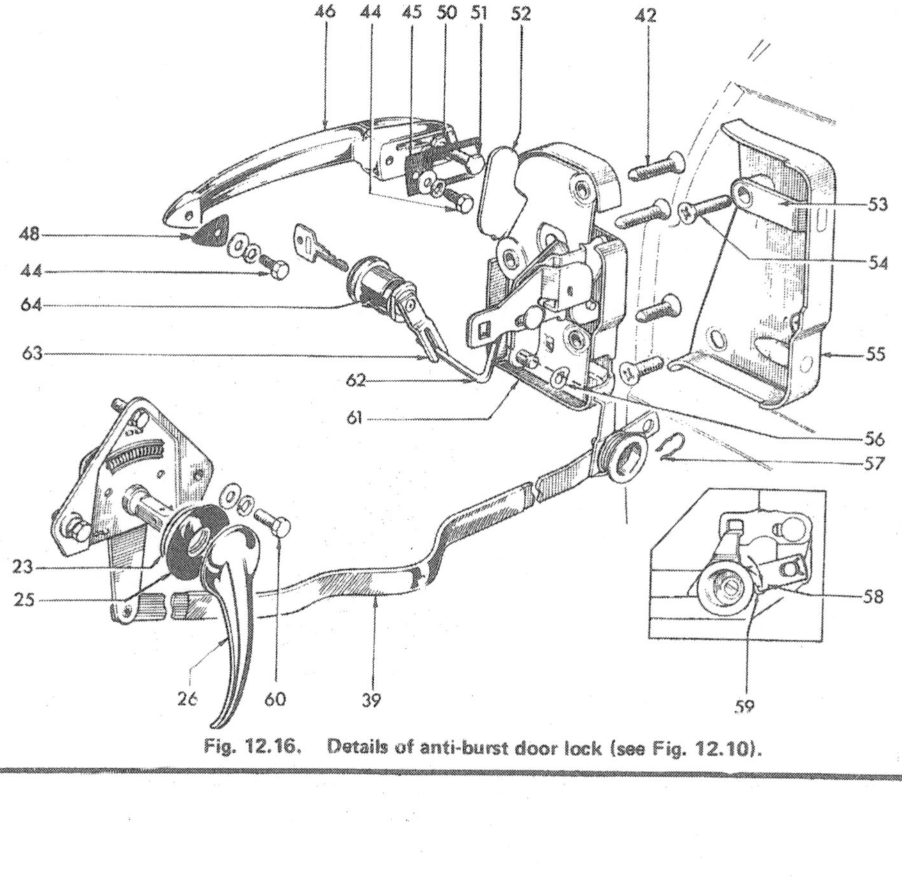

Fig. 12.16.   Details of anti-burst door lock (see Fig. 12.10).

18 Door glass and regulator - removal and refitting

1 To remove the door glass and regulator first wind up the door glass and make a note of the position of the handles for correct refitting.

2 Using a small electrician's size screwdriver push in the door handle escutcheon and push out the small tapered pin. The door handle can then be removed from the remote control unit.

3 Repeat the previous operation for the window winder regulator handle and remove the handle from the regulator.

4 Undo the two screws that secure the interior handle to the door panel.

5 Undo the screw having first removed the cover button that secures the rear edge of the trim panel to the door. Lift away the screw and special cover button retaining washer. Repeat this procedure on the forward positioned screw of the trim pocket.

6 Using a wide blade screwdriver or a knife carefully ease the trim panel clips from their holes in the door panel. When they are all free lift away the trim panel.

7 Lower the glass until it is in its midway position.

8 Disconnect the arms from the channel located at the base of the door glass by removing the spring clips with leather washers and then springing the arms clear of the channel.

9 Raise the glass to give better access and support with a piece of wood.

10 Undo the nut and remove together with the spring washer securing the pivot to the door inner panel.

11 Remove the pivot and the double coil spring washer placed between the regulator and the inner panel of the door.

12 Undo and remove the four screws that secure the regulator mechanism to the door inner panel and lift away the assembly through the largest cut out in the rear of the inner door panel.

13 Next remove the inner weatherstrip by pushing its lower edge upwards from inside the door panels using a screwdriver. It will be observed that the weatherstrip is held in position by seven small spring clips.

14 The glass may now be removed from the door but take care that the water deflector panel is not damaged.

15 Refitting the glass and regulator assembly is the reverse sequence to removal but care must be taken when replacing the weatherstrip. For this a special tool should be used so that when pushing in the weatherstrip the clips do not fall out. The inset in Fig. 12.17 shows the tool in use.

19 Door exterior handle - removal, refitting and adjusting

1 To remove the door exterior handle first wind up the door glass and make a note of the position of the handles for correct refitting.

2 Using a small electrician's size screwdriver push in the door handle escutcheon and push out the small tapered pin. The door handle can then be removed from the remote control unit.

3 Repeat the previous operation for the window winder regulator handle and remove the handle from the regulator.

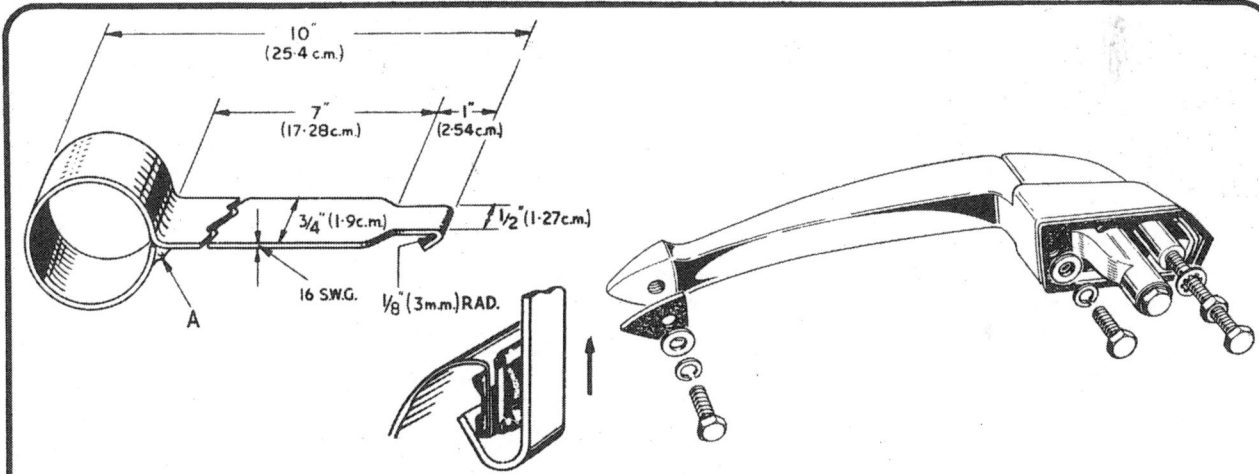

Fig. 12.17. Details of hooked tool for fitting spring clips

Fig. 12.18. Exterior door handle attachments

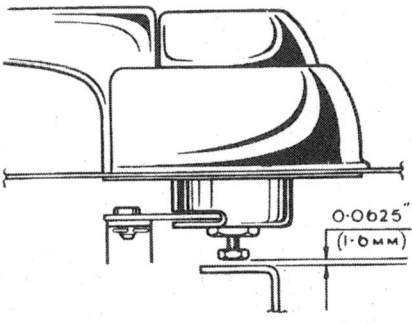

Fig. 12.19. Correct adjustment of exterior door handle

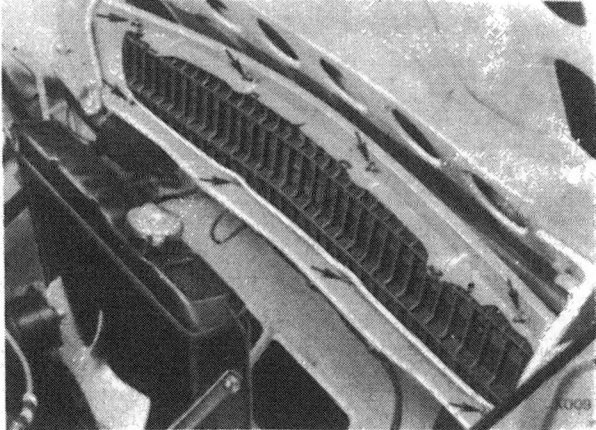

Fig. 12.20. Front grille attachment points (TR6) (arrowed)

4 Undo the two screws that secure the interior handle to the door panel.

5 Undo the screw having first removed the cover button that secures the rear edge of the trim panel to the door. Lift away the screw and special cover button retaining washer. Repeat this procedure on the forward positioned screw of the trim pocket.

6 Using a wide blade screwdriver or a knife carefully ease the trim panel clips from their holes in the door panel and when all are free lift away the trim panel.

7 Disconnect the interconnecting link placed between the lock and the exterior handle at the lock end.

8 Undo and remove the two screws and take off the handle and seating washers.

9 To refit the handle, and adjust it, hold the handle, with its seating washers in position, firmly in position on the door panel. Check the clearance between the push button plunger and the lock contactor through the hole in the inner door panel. It is recommended that the clearance is not checked by simply depressing the push button as by this method it can be deceptive. The correct clearance should be 0.0625 inch and should be checked with feeler gauges.

10 Rotate the plunger operating lever to the unlocked position so that when the push button is depressed the plunger moves through the housing.

11 Release the locknut and screw the plunger bolt in or out until the required setting is obtained, then tighten the locknut before releasing the push button.

12 Refit the connecting link to the plunger operating lever and secure with a circlip. The link should be fitted so that the bent section at the top is inclined away from the handle.

13 Rotate the plunger operating lever to the locked position so that the location holes in the operating lever and plunger housing are lined up. Insert a short length of 1/8 in diameter rod cranked to a right angle and carefully manipulate the connecting rod through the handle aperture so that they hang downwards in the door when the handle and seating washers are finally secured to the door with the two screws.

14 Refitting the remaining parts is the reverse sequence to removal.

20 Front grille - removal and refitting

1 Undo and remove the two screws that secure the valance stay rod to the grille surround.

2 Slacken the nut that secures the rod to the wheelarch and carefully move the rod away from the grille.

3 Undo and remove the two screws that secure the radiator millboard cowl to the grille surround.

4 Detach the overflow pipe from the radiator filler cap neck.

5 Carefully manipulate the cowl from the engine bay.

6 Undo and remove the eight nuts and washers that secure the grille to the body front panel.

7 The front grille may now be lifted forwards from the front of the car.

8 Refitting the front grille is the reverse sequence to removal.

21 Windscreen - removal and refitting

1 To remove the complete windscreen assembly first slacken the mounting bracket securing bolts. It is not necessary to remove the bolts completely.

2 Undo the two nuts and remove together with their spring washers. These will be found under the facia panel.

3 Using an open ended spanner undo and remove the three bolts which secure plates at the lower part of the windscreen frame.

4 With the assistance of a second person the windscreen may be lifted away from the car.

5 Refitting is the reverse sequence to removal. Grease the nuts to ensure that they can be easily undone in the future.

6 Ensure that the rubber seal is fitted correctly and is a water-tight joint in adverse weather conditions.

22 Windscreen glass -refitting

1 It is more simple to fit the glass with the windscreen frame in position on the car. As it is not normally necessary to remove the windscreen glass instructions for refitting are given only to replace a broken glass screen. Should removal of an unbroken screen be necessary simply reverse the refitting sequence. On cars fitted with a hard top the rear glass may be refitted or removed in a similar manner to the windscreen.

2 Taking care not to damage the frame remove the old rubber weatherstrip. Discard the old rubber weather strip as a new one should be fitted.

3 Using a vacuum cleaner remove any traces of the shattered glass from the interior. Lift up the carpeting as particles often find their way underneath it.

4 Turn the heater controls to demist and switch on the boost motor to blow out any glass lodged in the ducting. If rattling noises are heard disconnect the flexible hoses to the heater unit and collect any glass that may be in the hose or ducting not blown out by the booster motor.

5 Fit the rubber weatherstrip onto the glass and insert the mouldings in position in the weatherstrip. If difficulty is experienced in this operation use a little concentrated soap solution as a lubricant.

6 Obtain a length of cord longer than the circumference of the weatherstrip and position it in the outer channel of the weatherstrip. The two ends should overlap about twelve inches and be located at the top of the weatherstrip.

7 Position the glass and weatherstrip in the frame and get a second person to push hard on the glass to assist it seating.

8 From the inside of the car hold one end of the cord firmly and pull on the other end so that the inner lip is pulled over the metal edge of the frame.

9 When the lip has been pulled into position seat the weatherstrip correctly in the frame using the palm of your hand.

10 Use a non-setting sealant such as Seelastick to seal the joints between the rubber, glass and frame.

23 Instrument - removal and refitting

1 Each instrument is mounted to the back of the dashboard using a 'U' shaped bridge piece and knurled nuts screwed down onto threaded studs fixed to the rear of each instrument.

2 When an instrument is to be removed the battery earth terminal should be disconnected for safety reasons.

3 To give better access to the back of the dashboard undo and remove the four self tapping screws holding the lining casing of the glove compartment in place and lift out the casing.

4 The tachometer (revolution counter) and speedometer have internal lights. These should be removed by pulling out the light sockets in each instrument before the instrument is removed.

5 To remove the oil pressure gauge first undo the union at the rear of the oil pressure gauge taking care to retain the leather washer which acts as a seal in the union. This can be easily misplaced.

24 Facia panel - removal and refitting

1 Disconnect the battery earth terminal for safety reasons.

2 Undo and disconnect the drive cables at the rear of the speedometer and tachometer heads.

3 Disconnect the choke inner and outer control cable from the carburettor installation.

4 Refer to Chapter 11, Section 16 and remove the steering column complete with its cowling.

5 Undo the two screws and remove them with the plain washers and spring washers positioned in line with the centre of the glove box casing.

6 Carefully move the reinforcement stay outwards.

7 Undo and remove the six self tapping screws securing the glove box casing to the facia panel.

8 With the glove box compartment removed it is easier to remove the speedometer and tachometer and tachometer heads. Release the instrument illumination bulb sockets and undo the 'U' shaped bracket retaining knurled nuts. Lift away the nuts, spring washers and 'U' shaped brackets and withdraw the two instrument heads from the facia panel.

9 Undo and remove the four nuts, bolts and spring washers that secure the facia board. Lift away the facia board.

10 The next part to be removed is the control panel. First undo and remove the screw, washer and nut that secures the choke control side of the control panel to the facia panel.

11 Remove the two screws and remove the panel complete with switch plate switch plinth and switch reinforcement from the facia panel until it is possible to gain access to the rear of the switches.

12 Make a note of the colour coding of the cables to the rear of the switches and then disconnect the cables. Lift away the complete control panel easing the choke control cable through

its grommet in the bulkhead.

13 Undo the trunnion screw that secures the scuttle ventilator rod to the control lever.

14 Undo and remove the instrument panel retaining screws and ease the panel forwards . Note the electric cable colour coding to the rear of the instruments and disconnect the cables and oil pressure gauge pipe. Lift away the instrument panel.

15 Undo and remove the five bolts and spring washer that secure the upper edge of the facia panel to the top of the scuttle. If difficulty is experienced in locating the bolts it will be found that one is in each upper corner of the glove compartment aperture, one is in the centre of the facia panel, and one in each of the apertures for the speedometer and tachometer heads.

16 Remove the two bolts and spring washers on each end of the facia panel.

17 The facia panel may now be carefully withdrawn from its location in the car.

18 Refitting the facia panel is the reverse sequence to removal. Take care that all electrical connections are made correctly bearing in mind the colour coding of the cables previously noted.

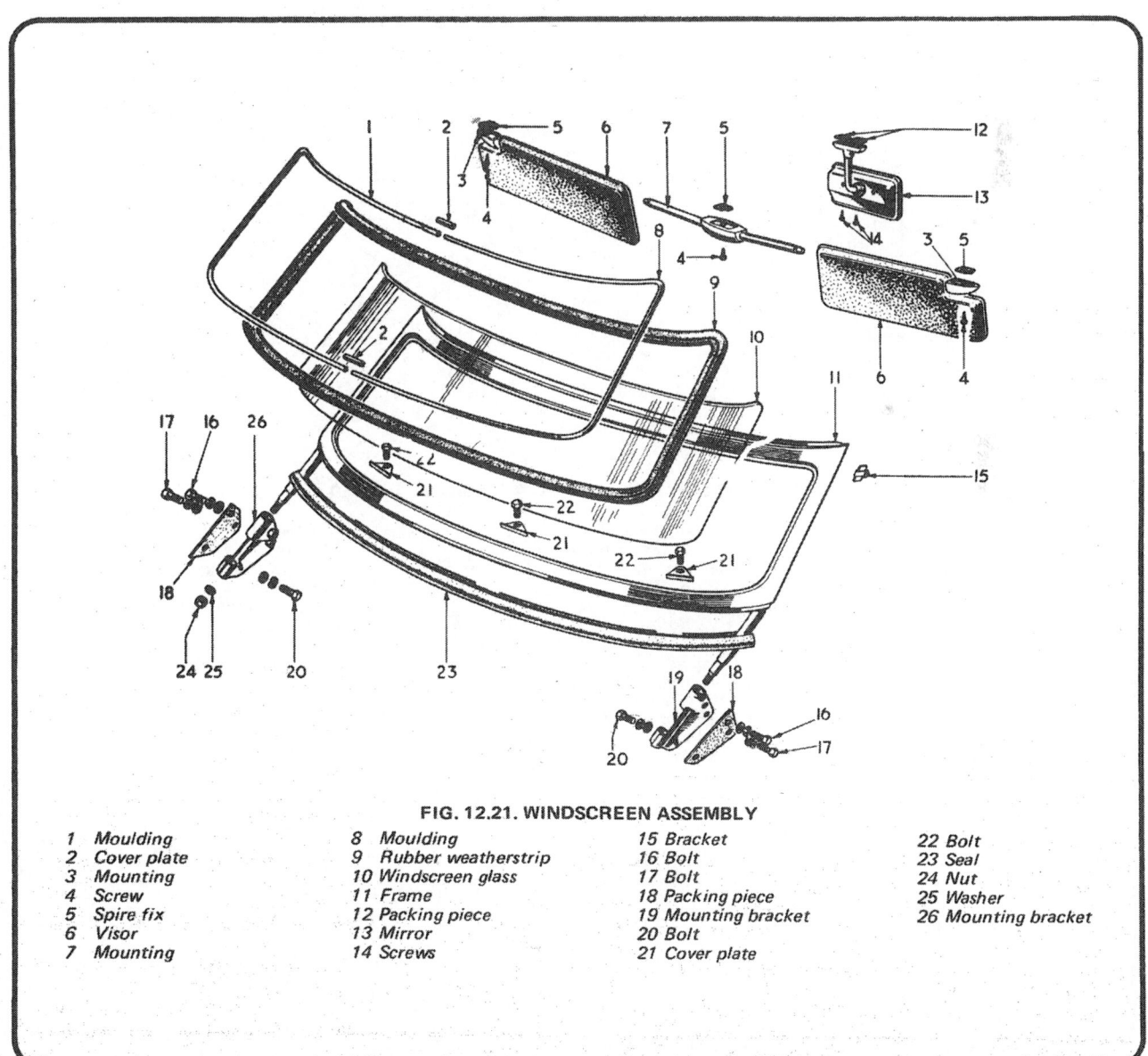

FIG. 12.21. WINDSCREEN ASSEMBLY

1 Moulding	8 Moulding	15 Bracket	22 Bolt
2 Cover plate	9 Rubber weatherstrip	16 Bolt	23 Seal
3 Mounting	10 Windscreen glass	17 Bolt	24 Nut
4 Screw	11 Frame	18 Packing piece	25 Washer
5 Spire fix	12 Packing piece	19 Mounting bracket	26 Mounting bracket
6 Visor	13 Mirror	20 Bolt	
7 Mounting	14 Screws	21 Cover plate	

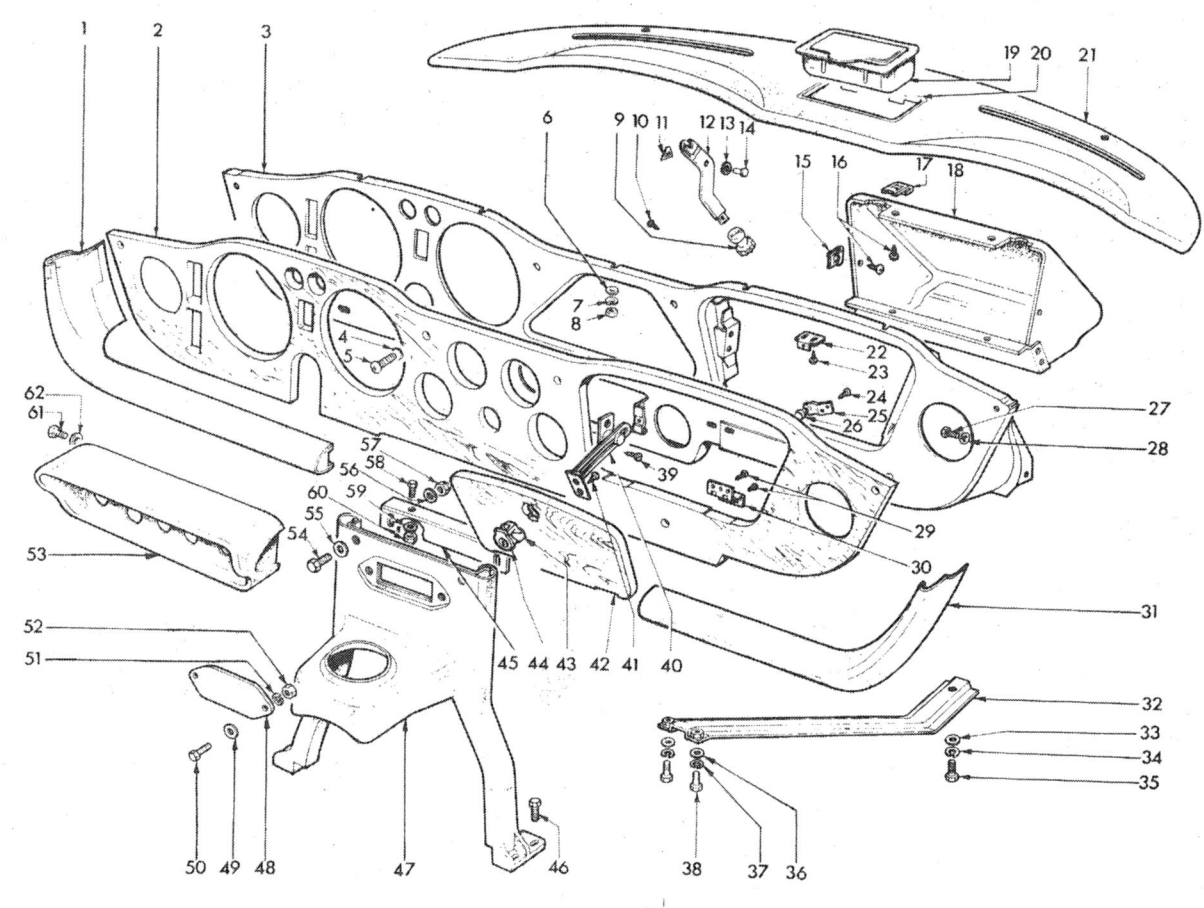

FIG. 12.22. FACIA PANEL ATTACHMENTS (LHD)

1   Crash pad
2   Veneered facia panel
3   Metal facia panel
4   Cup washer   ) veneered facia
5   Screw   ) to metal facia
6   Washer   ) complete facia
7   Lock washer   ) to scuttle top
8   Nut   ) panel
9   Vent lever-knob
10 Screw
11 Retainer
12 Vent lever
13 Lock washer
14 Rivet
15 Spire nut) glove box
16 Screw   ) to
17 Spire nut) facia
18 Glove box
19 Ash tray
20 Ash tray retainer
21 Scuttle top-crash pad

22 Striker bracket
23 Striker screw
24 Screw - buffer bracket
25 Buffer bracket
26 Buffer
27 Bolt   ) complete facia
28 Lock washer) to 'A' post
29 Screw - hinge
30 Hinge - glove box
31 Crash pad
32 Support channel - facia to dash
33 Washer   ) support channel
34 Lock washer) to
35 Setscrew   ) dash
36 Washer   ) support channel
37 Lock washer) to
38 Setscrew   ) facia panel
39 Screw - check link
40 Check link - glove box lid
41 Screw - check link

42 Glove box-lid
43 Clamp - glove box lock
44 Glove box lock
45 Bracket
46 Bolt - support bracket to floor
47 Support bracket - facia to floor
48 Cover plate - radio mounting
49 Washer   ) cover plate to
50 Setscrew   ) support bracket
51 Lock washer
52 Nut
53 Switch plinth
54 Bolt   )
55 Washer   ) support bracket
56 Washer   ) to fixing bracket
57 Nyloc nut   )
58 Setscrew) fixing bracket
59 Washer   ) to facia
60 Nut
61 Setscrew) switch plinth
62 Washer   )   to facia panel

Fig. 12.23. Underside view of facia (TR6)
(Support bracket attachments arrowed)

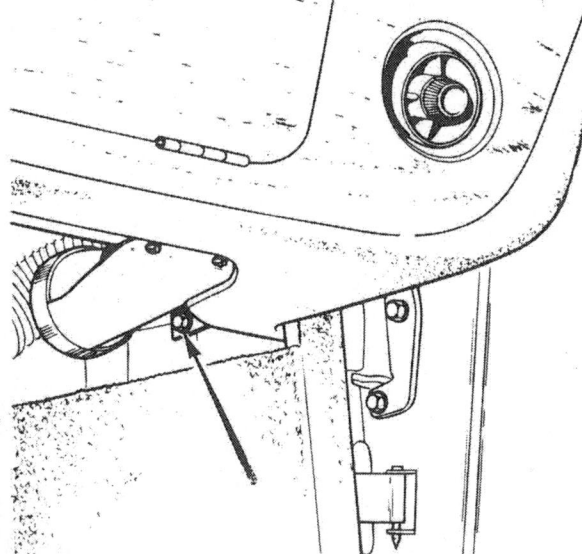

Fig. 12.24. 'A' post attachment to facia (TR6) (arrowed)

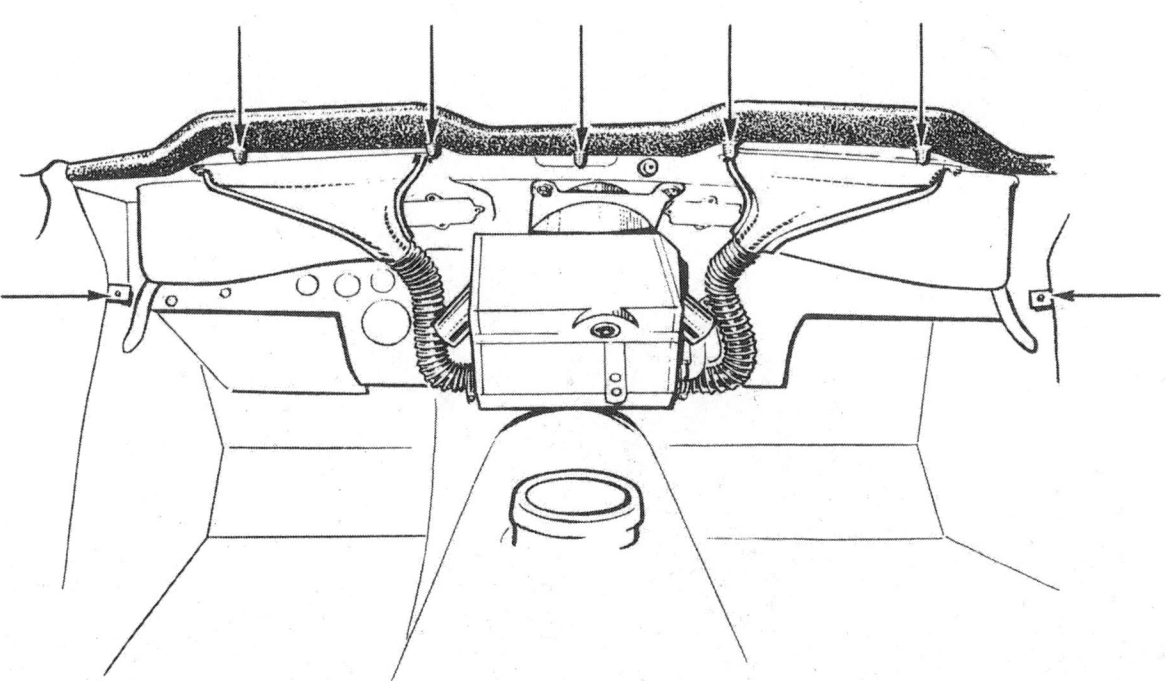

Fig. 12.25. Facia panel mounting to body. (Arrows show mounting points)

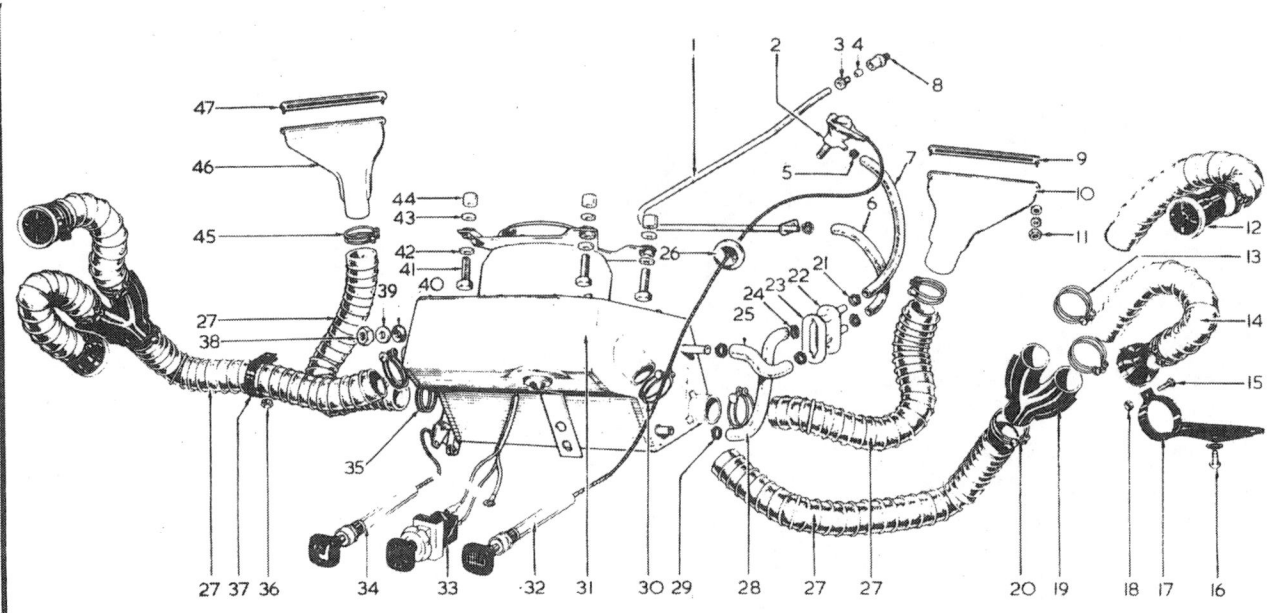

FIG. 12.26. HEATER, DEMISTER AND FRESH AIR UNIT COMPONENTS

1 Water return pipe	17 Hose bracket	32 Heat control
2 Water control valve	18 Nut - bracket attachment	33 Blower switch
3 Nut	19 Tube 'Y' piece	34 Air distribution control
4 Olive	20 Hose clip	35 Hose clip
5 Clip	21 Hose clip	36 Nut - hose
6 Hose	22 Bulkhead adaptor	37 Hose support clip
7 Hose	23 Seal - adaptor	38 Nut) heater unit to
8 Adaptor	24 Hose clip	39 Washer) dash panel
9 Finisher	25 Water hose	40 Washer)
10 Air duct	26 Control cable grommet	41 Bolt)
11 Nut - duct attachment	27 Ventilation hose	42 Washer) heater unit to
12 Air vent	28 Water hose	43 Washer) scuttle top panel
13 Hose clip	29 Hose clip	44 Spacer)
14 Ventilation hose	30 Hose clip	45 Hose clip
15 Setscrew - hose attachment	31 Heater unit	46 Air duct
16 Screw - bracket attachment		47 Finisher

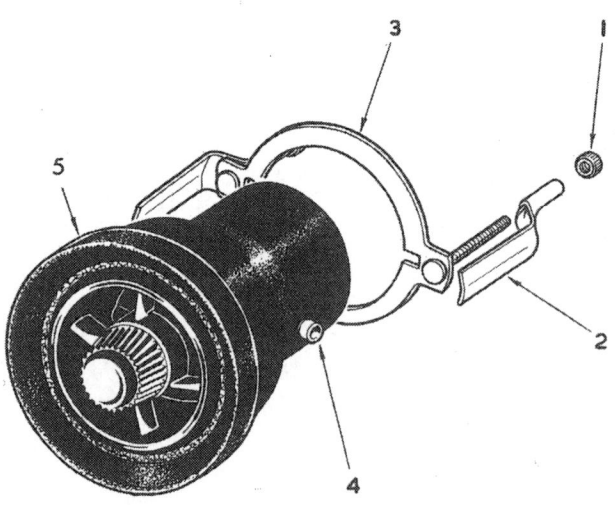

FIG. 12.27. ARRANGEMENT OF FRESH AIR VENT

1 Knurled nuts	4 Retaining pin
2 Clamp supports	5 Fresh air vent
3 Retaining clamp	

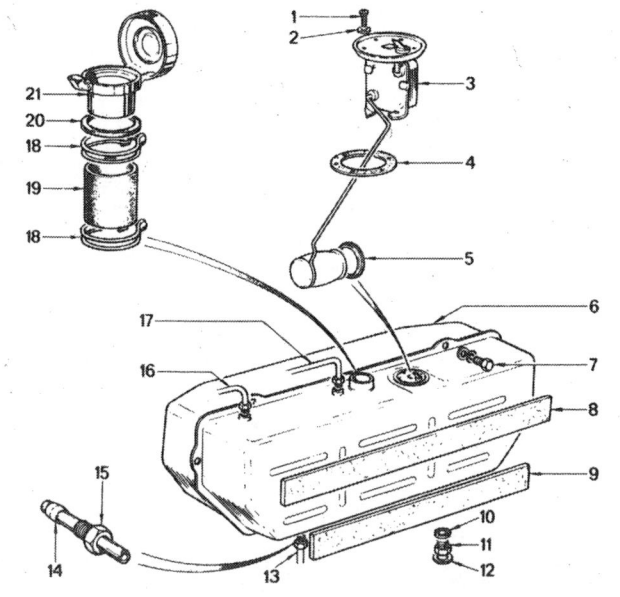

FIG. 12.28. FUEL TANK ATTACHMENTS

1 Screw) gauge unit to	12 Seal-drain plug
2 Fibre-washer) tank	13 Pipe assembly-tank outlet
3 Fuel tank-gauge unit	14 Tubing sleeve) pipe to
4 Cork sealing washer	15 Tubing nut) tank
5 Anti-rattle - washer	16 Pipe-pressure relief
6 Fuel tank assembly	valve to tank
7 Setscrew-fuel tank	17 Filter vent pipe
attachment	18 Hose clip
8 Felt pad-tank mounting	19 Filter hose
9 Felt pad-tank mounting	20 Sealing grommet-fuel
10 Fibre washer) fitted in	filler
11 Drain plug) fuel tank	21 Fuel filler cap

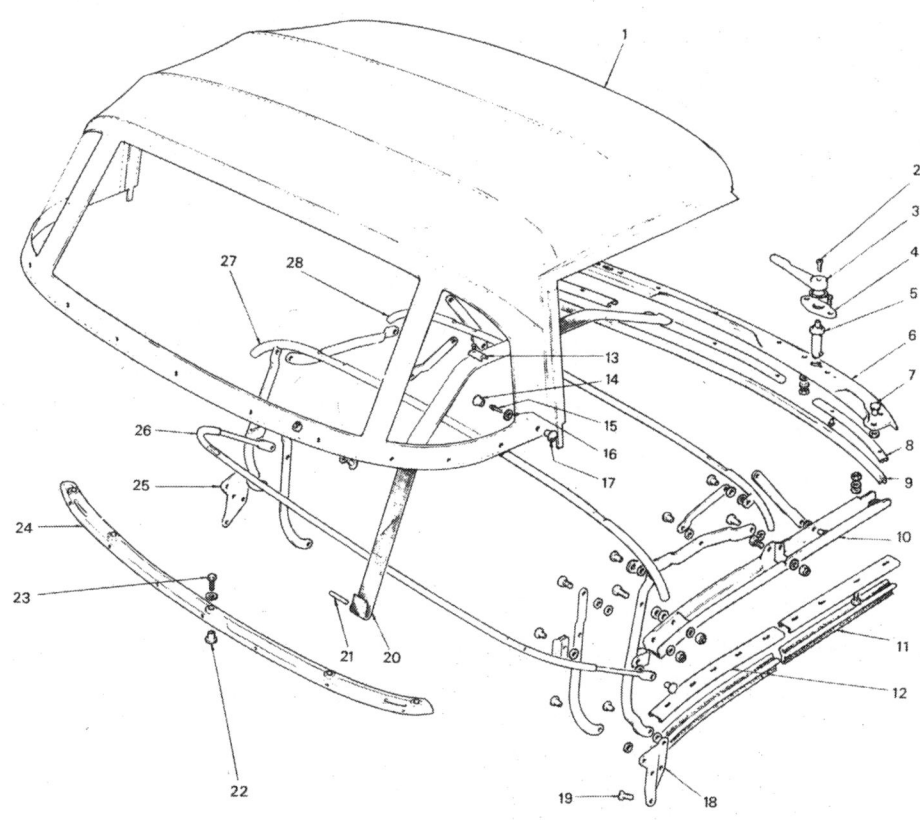

FIG. 12.29. SOFT TOP ATTACHMENTS

1 Soft top assembly	15 Imex-rivet
2 Screw - securing handle	16 Socket) hood attachment
3 Closing handle	17 Button)
4 Escutcheon - handle	18 Mounting bracket assembly - RH
5 Locking pin	19 Counter/sunk screw - soft top to body
6 Header rail	20 Webbing - soft top
7 Rivet - header rail	21 Wire - retainer
8 Retainer - headed rail seal	22 Rivet nut
9 Sealing rubber - head rail	23 Setscrew
10 Link assembly	24 Angle bracket
11 Sealing rubber	25 Mounting bracket assembly - L.H
12 Retainer - sealing rubber	26 Rear hoodstick assembly
13 Securing plate - soft top webbing	27 Main hoodstick assembly
14 Plastic stud	28 Front hoodstick assembly

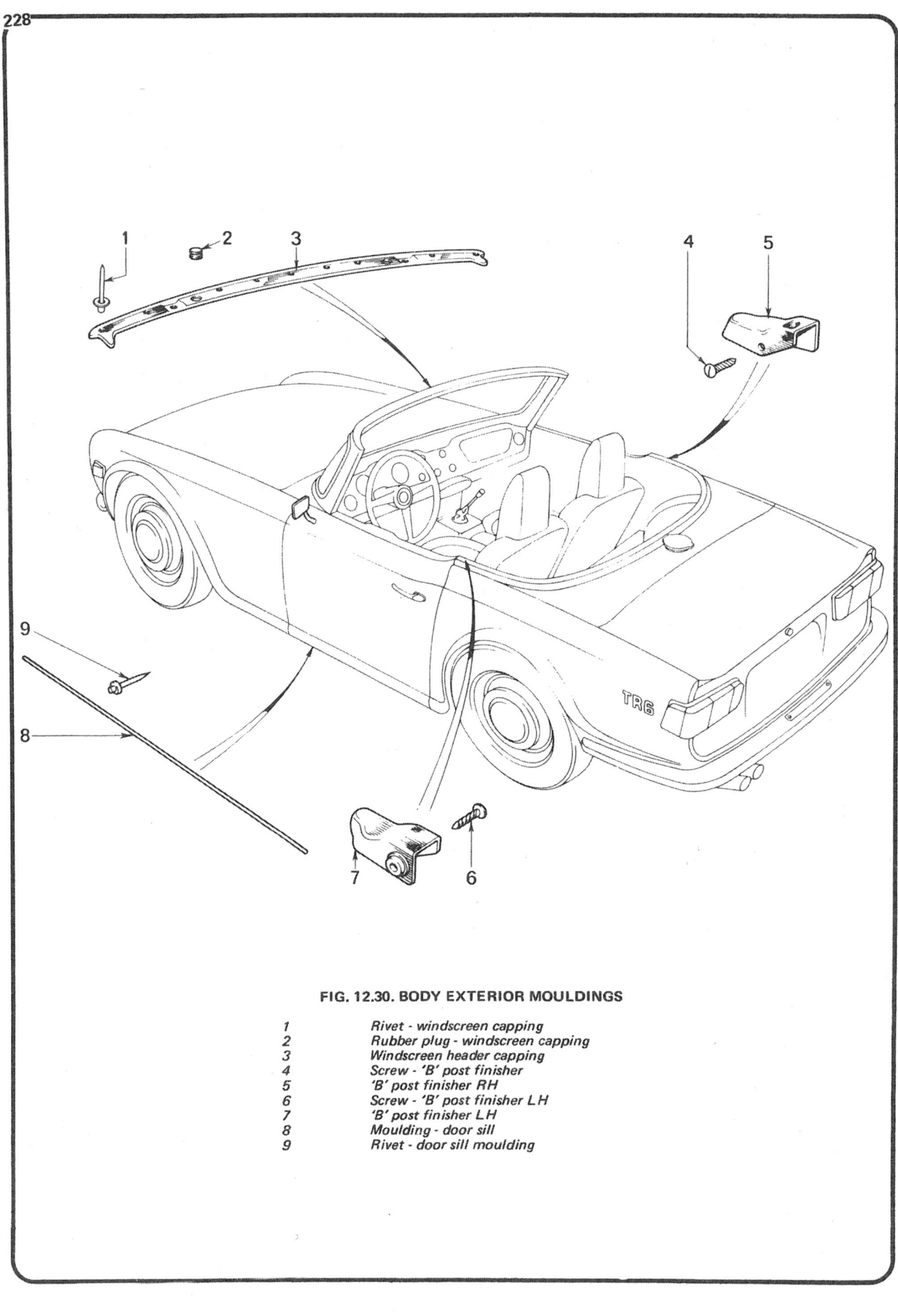

FIG. 12.30. BODY EXTERIOR MOULDINGS

1	Rivet - windscreen capping
2	Rubber plug - windscreen capping
3	Windscreen header capping
4	Screw - 'B' post finisher
5	'B' post finisher RH
6	Screw - 'B' post finisher LH
7	'B' post finisher LH
8	Moulding - door sill
9	Rivet - door sill moulding

Chapter 13   Supplement

Contents

1   Introduction

1   All Triumph models destined for North America are equipped with emission control systems. These systems enable the vehicles to conform with the current Federal legislation governing the emission of hydrocarbons, carbon monoxide, nitric oxide and the emission of fuel vapour by evaporation from the fuel system.

2   Fuel system – emission control

Routine maintenance

In addition to the tasks listed on pages 10, 13 and 14, the following should be carried out at the specified intervals:

12 000 miles (19 300 km)

1   Check the security and condition of the EGR system hoses. Renew as necessary.

Clean the EGR valve (Section 15).

Check the hoses/pipes of the crankcase and evaporative emission control systems for blockage, deterioration and security. Renew or tighten as necessary.

Check the air pump drivebelt tension (Section 9).

50 000 miles (80 500 km)

2   Renew the evaporative emission system absorption canister (Section 7).

Crankcase emission control system – description

3   The engine breather outlet from the rocker cover is connected by pipes to the ports on the side of the carburettors which lead to the depression area between the throttle disc and piston.

4   When the engine is running the depression created draws the engine fumes and blow-by gases from the crankcase into the combustion chamber. The charcoal canister air purge for the evaporative emissions is also connected into this circuit (Fig. 13.1).

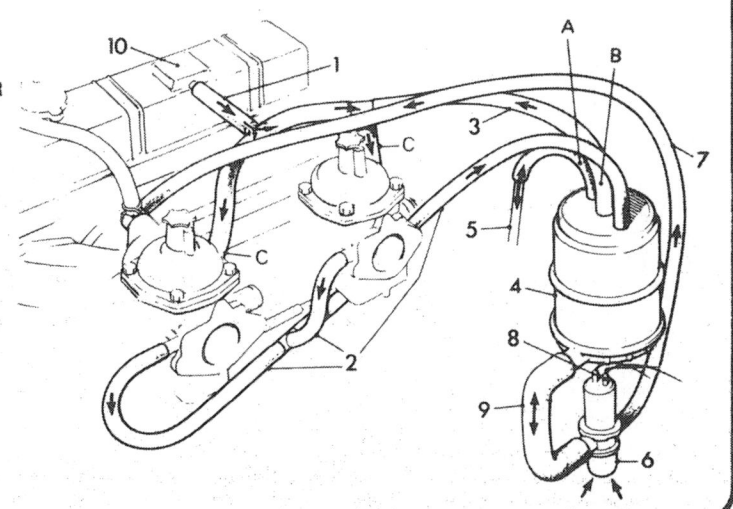

FIG. 13.1 TR6 CRANKCASE AND CANISTER PURGE SYSTEM

1   *Crankcase purge line*
2   *Carb. float chamber vent pipe*
3   *Canister purge line*
4   *Charcoal canister*
5   *Fuel tank vent pipe*
6   *Anti-run-on valve*
7   *Manifold vacuum line*
8   *Electrical connections for anti-run-on valve*
9   *Purge air to canister*
10   *Flame arrestor*
A   *1/32 in restrictor*
B   *3/32 in restrictor*
C   *5/16 in restrictor*

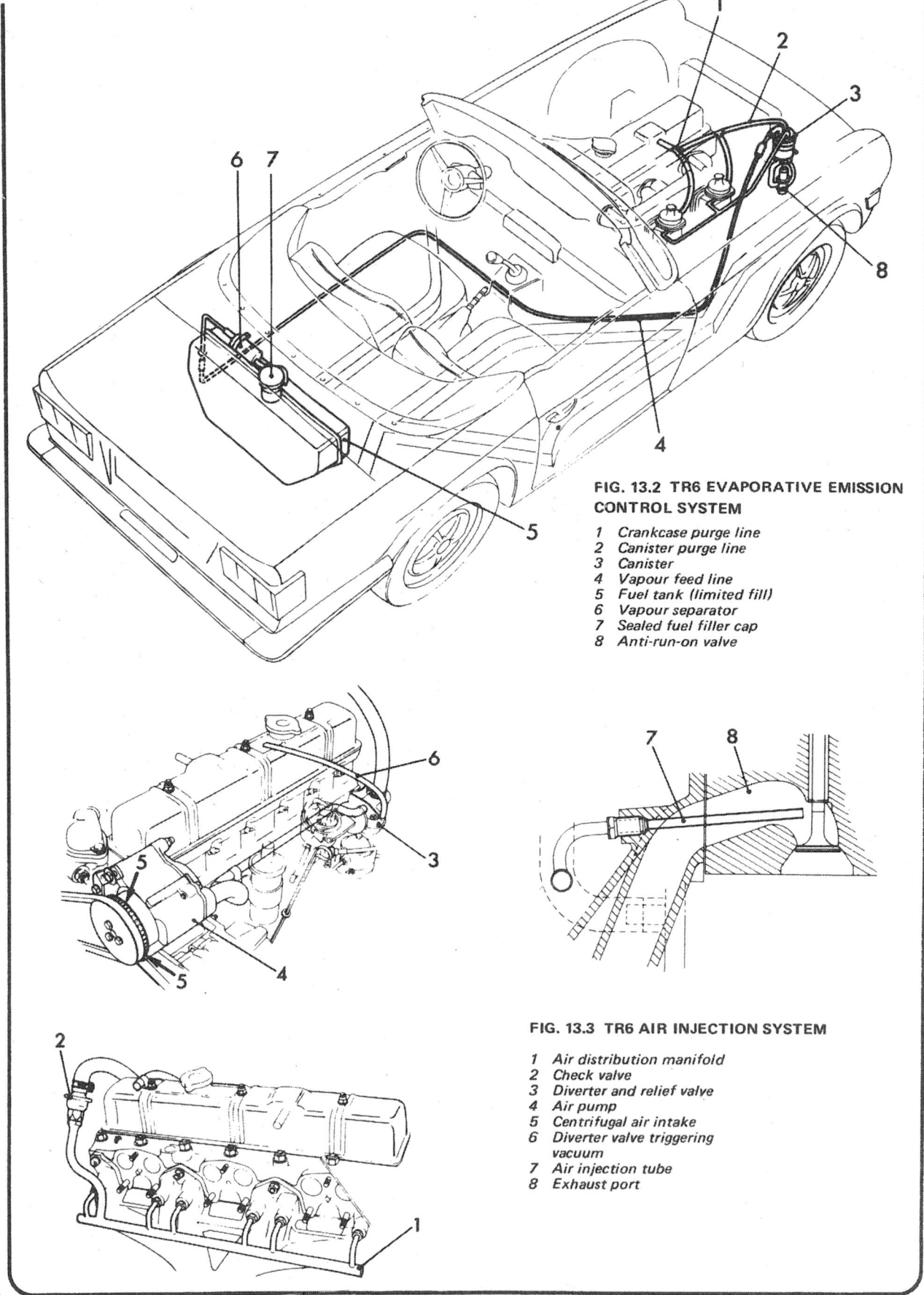

FIG. 13.2 TR6 EVAPORATIVE EMISSION CONTROL SYSTEM

1 Crankcase purge line
2 Canister purge line
3 Canister
4 Vapour feed line
5 Fuel tank (limited fill)
6 Vapour separator
7 Sealed fuel filler cap
8 Anti-run-on valve

FIG. 13.3 TR6 AIR INJECTION SYSTEM

1 Air distribution manifold
2 Check valve
3 Diverter and relief valve
4 Air pump
5 Centrifugal air intake
6 Diverter valve triggering vacuum
7 Air injection tube
8 Exhaust port

Evaporative emission control system – description

5   The evaporative emission control system is designed to prevent the fuel vapour from escaping into the atmosphere.

6   The fuel vapour, which is collected from the fuel tank and the carburettors, is stored in an absorption canister while the engine is not running. When the engine is running, the vapour is drawn from the canister and passes to the combustion chamber via the crankcase emission control system (Fig. 13.2).

7   The fuel filter cap seals the system and venting of the tank can only take place via a vapour separator to the absorption canister.

8   As the fuel tank cap seals the system the fuel tank is designed so that it cannot be completely filled, therefore leaving room for the fuel to expand in high ambient temperatures.

9   The absorption canister provides a means of storing fuel vapour when the engine is not running. The canister, which is of the disposable type, contains active charcoal granules. Fuel vapour entering the canister through the vapour hoses is absorbed by the charcoal granules. When the engine is started air is drawn by the crankcase ventilation system through the purge tube at the bottom of the canister. The resulting purge action of the air passing over the granules carries the vapours through the crankcase ventilation system to the combustion chambers.

10   Vapour hoses from the fuel tank, carburettor float chambers and the purge pipe from the crankcase ventilation system are connected to the anti-run-on valve which is at the base of the absorption canister. The purpose of the solenoid-operated anti-run-on valve is to prevent the engine 'running on' after the ignition has been switched off.

11   The solenoid is connected electrically by two leads, one to the oil pressure switch and the other to the ignition switch. When the ignition is switched off a contact in the switch closes and energises the solenoid, thus opening the valve to the manifold vacuum. At the same instant the purge vent to the atmosphere closes. Since the throttle is now closed, the carburettor vent valve has opened the passage to the float chamber. Partial vacuum has now been transferred from the base of the absorption canister via the float chamber vent pipe to the float chamber thus preventing fuel from entering the carburettor jet.

12   When the engine stops revolving the drop in oil pressure activates the oil pressure switch, opens the circuit and de-energises the solenoid valve.

Exhaust emission control system – description

13   Two exhaust emission control systems are employed to reduce the exhaust pollution to a minimum. They are an air injection system (AIS) and an exhaust gas recirculation (EGR) system.

14   The air injection system injects clean air, under pressure, into each of the six exhaust ports to combine with the combustion gases and reduce the hydrocarbon and carbon monoxide content of the exhaust gases emitted to the atmosphere (Fig. 13.3).

15   The EGR system is a method of re-cycling the engine exhaust gases by returning them to the combustion chambers where they lower the combustion temperatures and reduce the amount of noxious gases produced (Fig. 13.4).

16   The air injection system consists of the following components:

a)   **Air pump** – *The rotary vane type air pump is fitted at the front of the engine and is belt driven from a pulley on the crankshaft. The pump delivers air, under pressure, to the exhaust ports via a diverter and relief valve, check valve and an air inlet manifold.*

b)   **Diverter and relief valve** – *The combined diverter and relief valve is incorporated to divert the air from the pump during deceleration to prevent backfiring. The relief valve allows excessive air pressure at high engine speeds to discharge into the atmosphere (Fig. 13.5).*

c)   **Check valve** – *The check valve is a non-return valve positioned between the diverter/relief valve and the air*

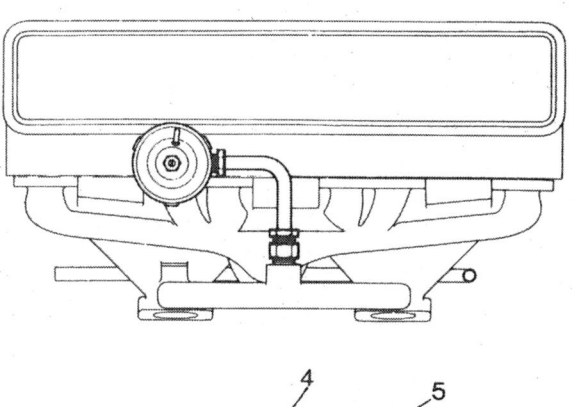

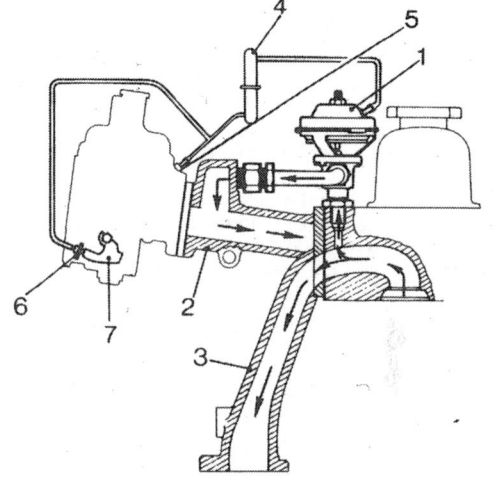

FIG. 13.4 TR6 EXHAUST GAS RECIRCULATION SYSTEM

1 EGR Valve	*5 Vacuum source*
2 Inlet manifold	*throttle edge tapping*
3 Exhaust manifold	*6 EGR Cut out valve*
4 Petrol trap	*7 Choke fast idle cam*

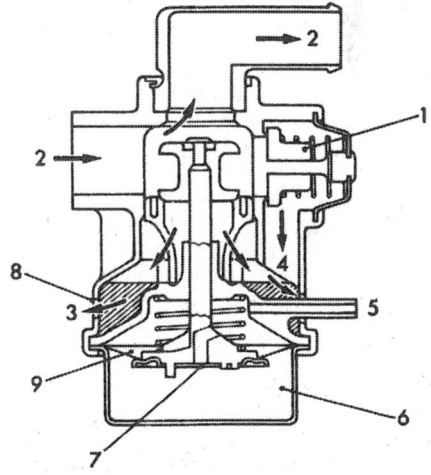

FIG. 13.5 DIVERTER AND RELIEF VALVE

1 Relief valve	*6 Timed vacuum*
2 Normal flow from	*7 Timing feature*
air pump	*8 Diverter and relief*
3 Diverted air	*valve ports*
4 Relief valve air	*9 Diaphragm*
5 Manifold vacuum	

manifold and prevents the reverse flow of gases.

d) *The air manifold – The air manifold delivers the pumped air directly into the exhaust ports through six small branch pipes.*

17 The exhaust gas recirculation system consists of a valve, mounted on the cylinder head, which controls the flow of the exhaust gases into the inlet manifold from the exhaust ports, in response to driving conditions. The control signal is taken from a throttle edge tapping which prevents recirculation of the exhaust gases at idling speed or full load, but gives a controlled amount of recirculation depending on the vacuum signal and metering profile of the valve pintle. Due to the EGR system the combustion temperature is lowered and the emission of noxious gases is reduced (Fig. 13.6).

Evaporative emission control system – checking

18 Periodic maintenance of the system should be carried out. Inspect all hoses and the fuel filler cap for damage or deterioration.
19 To test the system for leakage, disconnect the separator tank to the carbon canister hose at the canister end and fit a three-way connector, cock and water manometer. A U-shaped glass tube will do.
20 Connect an air supply to the three-way cock and apply 20 in (508 mm) of water pressure to the system, and then close the cock. Do not exceed 25 in (635 mm) of water pressure.
Caution: During this test, the pressure, though very low, may displace hose connections or cause an emission of fuel vapour. Ensure, therefore, to avoid naked lights or actions likely to cause sparks during the test. It is dangerous to exceed the maximum pressure quoted.
21 After 2 minutes, check the pressure in the system. If the pressure has fallen by more than 2 in (50 mm) of water, the leak must be traced and rectified.

Absorption canister – removal and refitting

22 Disconnect the absorption canister to anti-run-on valve hose.
23 Disconnect from the canister the following hoses:

a) *The canister to fuel tank hose.*
b) *The canister purge hose.*
c) *The carburettor vent hose.*

Note: On pre-1973 models there are only two hoses to the canister.
24 Slacken the clamp and screw nut.
25 Remove the absorption canister.
26 Refitting is the reverse of the removal procedure.

Expansion tank/vapour separator – removal and refitting

27 Disconnect the earth lead from the battery negative (–) terminal. Remove the spare wheel and cover.
28 Place a container under the fuel tank, ensure it has a suitable capacity to hold the amount of fuel in the tank. Remove the drain plug, if fitted or disconnect the rubber connection hose from the main line pipe.
Note: If the fuel is to be put back into the tank, ensure that absolute cleanliness is observed during draining and storage as foreign matter or fluids in the fuel may cause damage or faults in the fuel system.
29 Remove the screws and disconnect the two clamp connectors, then lift out the rear-trim cover from the luggage compartment.
30 Slacken the filler pipe to tank hose clip.
31 Disconnect the two connectors from the fuel gauge transmitter.
32 Remove the bolts securing the fuel tank to the body and lower the fuel tank. Disconnect the two pipes from the fuel tank.
33 Slacken the clips securing the expansion tank/vapour separator to the fuel tank.
34 Remove the expansion tank/vapour separator.

35 Refitting is the reverse of the removal procedure.

Air pump – removal and refitting

36 Disconnect the hose from the pump.
37 Remove the adjusting bolt, nut and washers (Fig. 13.7).
38 Slacken the pivot bolt nut.
39 Remove the drivebelt from the pump pulley.
40 Remove the pivot bolt and lift the air pump out of the engine compartment.
41 Refitting is the reverse of the removal procedure. The drivebelt should be tensioned so that it can be depressed by $\frac{3}{8}$ in (9·5 mm) with firm thumb pressure at the mid-point between the two pulleys.

Air distribution manifold – removal and refitting

42 Disconnect the diverter and relief valve hose from the check valve.
43 Unscrew the six union nuts securing the air injection tubes into the exhaust manifold.
44 Withdraw the air distribution manifold complete with the check valve.
45 Refitting is the reverse of the removal procedure.

Check valve – removal, testing and refitting

46 Disconnect the diverter and relief valve air hose from the check valve.
47 Use two open-ended spanners, one on the air distribution manifold hexagon to support the manifold and the other to unscrew and remove the check valve (Fig. 13.8).
Note: Take care not to impose any strain on the air manifold.
48 Blow through the valve with the mouth in both directions in turn (Do not use an air line for this test). Air should only pass through the valve when blown from the hose connection end. Should air pass through the valve when blown from the air manifold end, the valve must be renewed.
49 Refitting the valve is the reverse of the removal procedure.

Diverter and relief valve – removal and refitting

50 Disconnect the two air hoses and the vacuum hose from the diverter valve (Fig. 13.9).
51 Remove the two nuts, bolts and washers securing the diverter valve to the bracket.
52 Remove the valve and gasket.
53 Refitting is the reverse of the removal procedure. Always fit a new gasket.

Anti-run-on valve – removal and refitting

54 Remove the carbon absorption canister as described in Section 7.
55 Disconnect the two electrical leads to the solenoid at the top of the valve.
56 Disconnect the vacuum signal pipe (Fig. 13.10).
57 Remove the mounting bracket.
58 Refitting is the reverse of the removal procedure.

EGR control valve – removal and refitting

59 Disconnect the throttle control cable.
60 Disconnect the vacuum control hose.
61 Unscrew the cam retaining nut.
62 Lift off the cam complete with valve.
63 Refitting is the reverse of the removal procedure. Make sure the vacuum hose connections are secure and that the throttle cable setting is correct, ie, no tightness, no free play.

EGR valve – removal, cleaning and refitting

64 At intervals of 12 000 miles (19 300 km) a service indicator light, located on the facia will indicate that the EGR valve and operating lines require checking and cleaning.
65 Disconnect the vacuum control pipe from the top of the valve.
66 Unscrew the union nuts securing the steel pipe to the inlet manifold and the valve. As the steel pipe is longer on one side of the bend than the other, it should be marked to ensure correct

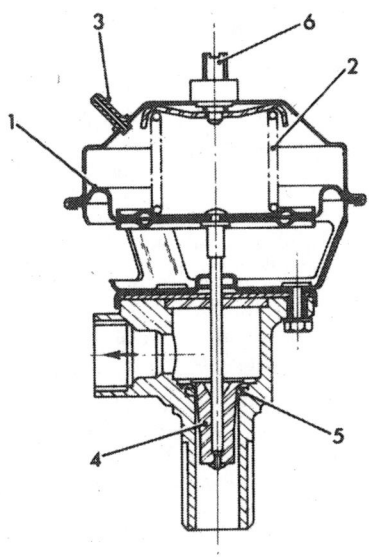

FIG. 13.6 SECTIONAL VIEW OF THE EGR VALVE

1 Diaphragm
2 Spring
3 To vacuum source
4 Metering pintle
5 Valve seat
6 Production adjustment -
    sealed after setting

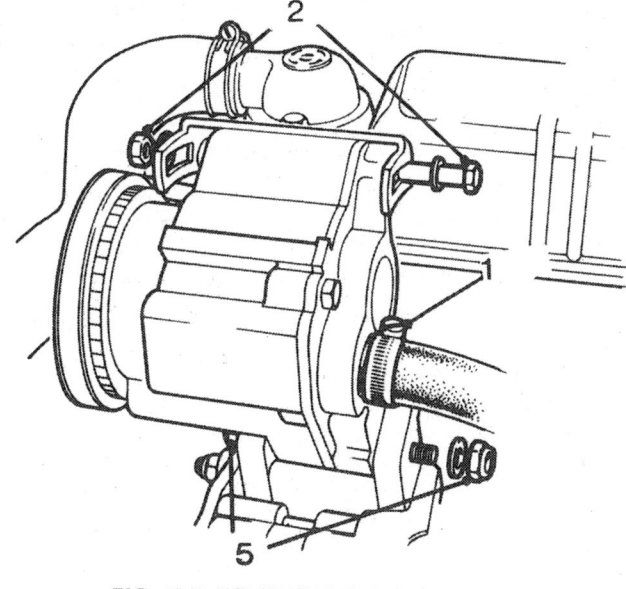

FIG. 13.7 REMOVING THE AIR PUMP

1 Hose securing clip
2 Adjusting bolt
5 Pivot bolt

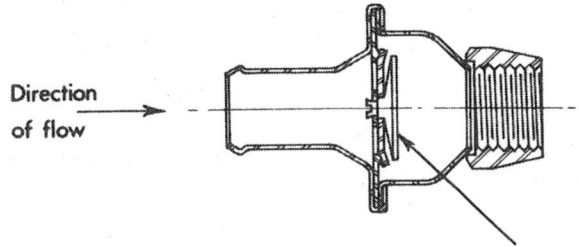

Direction
of flow

VALVE ASSY.

Fig. 13.8 Cross-section of check valve

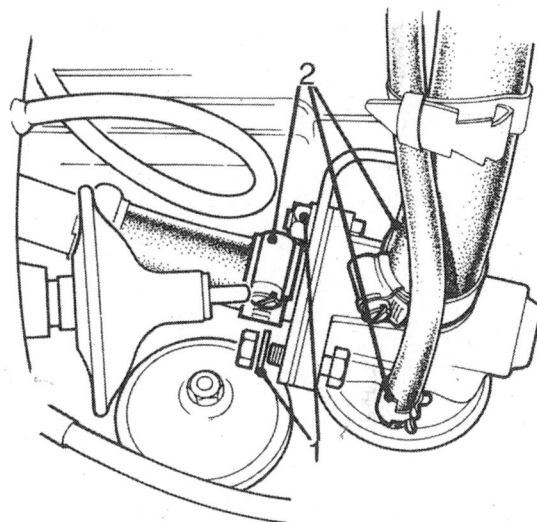

**FIG. 13.9 REMOVING THE DIVERTER AND RELIEF
VALVE**

1 Attaching nuts and bolts   2 Air and vacuum hoses

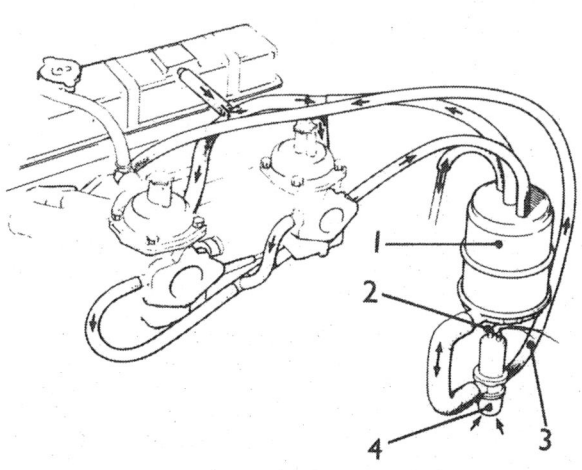

**FIG. 13.10 CARBON CANISTER AND ANTI-RUN-ON
VALVE**

1 Carbon canister
2 Electrical leads to solenoid
3 Vacuum signal pipe
4 Anti-run-on valve

refitting. Remove the steel pipe (Fig. 13.11).

67 Slacken the locknut at the base of the valve, then unscrew the valve and remove it.

68 Clean the assembly area of the valve with a wire brush. To clean the valve and its seat effectively, insert the valve opening into a standard spark plug cleaning machine and lift the diaphragm evenly with two fingers, one each side of the support strut. Blast the valve for approximately 30 seconds, remove and inspect. If necessary repeat until all carbon deposits have been removed. Blow all traces of carbon grit from the valve with an air line. Use a flexible wire brush to clean the steel pipe and then blow clear of carbon grit.

69 Refitting the valve is the reverse of the removal procedure. Ensure this steel pipe is positioned correctly before attempting to tighten it.

EGR system – checking

70 A system check of the valve can be carried out with the unit in-situ by 'blipping' the throttle and observing the valve unit. The valve must be actuated by the sudden change of engine speed. With this check the valve will settle back and it is not possible to perform a total check to find small leaks by this method.

71 For a complete check on the operation of the valve a vacuum test unit is required and this should be carried out by your Leyland dealer.

72 To check the control valve, apply a vacuum to the hose from the three-way connector to the valve. If the valve is not sealing completely this will be easily detected. Renew a defective control valve.

---

3   Suspension and steering

Steering column (later type) – removal and refitting

1 Disconnect the battery for safety reasons.

2 Wipe the electrical cables free from dust to enable the colour coding to be seen. Disconnect the cables from the connectors.

3 Remove the steering wheel (Chapter 11).

4 Remove the speedometer and the tachometer.

5 Remove the pinch bolts securing the lower steering column to the flexible coupling.

6 Remove the two set screws securing the steering column

safety clamp, and withdraw the clamp.

7 Remove the two bolts and nuts securing the forward end of the anti-torque strap to the scuttle.

8 Remove the protective covers from the steering column bracket bolts. Remove the two bolts, nuts and washers which secure the bracket halves. Withdraw the harness cover.

9 Remove the anti-torque strap and the upper half of the column bracket.

10 Rotate the steering column to bring the shearbolts of the steering lock into an accessible position.

11 Remove the two shearbolts. If they cannot be unscrewed using a small chisel, they will have to be drilled out. Remove the steering lock and withdraw the column.

12 Refitting is a reversal of the removal procedure but the following additional points should be noted:

    a) *When fitting the steering lock ensure that the spacer ring is above the steering lock. Always fit new shearbolts and tighten them evenly until the heads shear.*

    b) *When fitting the steering column bracket note that the left-hand bolt is entered from below the bracket and the right-hand bolt is entered from above the bracket.*

Steering lock/ignition switch – removal and refitting

13 Disconnect the battery for safety reasons.

14 Remove the speedometer and tachometer from the facia.

15 Disconnect the wiring harness socket from the steering lock.

16 Remove the protective covers, nuts, washers and bolts from the steering column upper bracket, and withdraw the top half of the bracket.

17 Remove the anti-torque strap from the scuttle.

18 Remove the cable harness cover from the underside of the column.

19 Withdraw the anti-torque strap from the steering lock.

20 Rotate the steering column to bring the shearbolts of the steering lock into an accessible position.

21 Remove the two shearbolts. If they cannot be removed using a small chisel, they will have to be drilled out. Remove the steering lock.

22 Refitting is the reverse of the removal procedure but the following additional points should be noted:

    Always use new shearbolts and tighten them evenly until the heads shear.

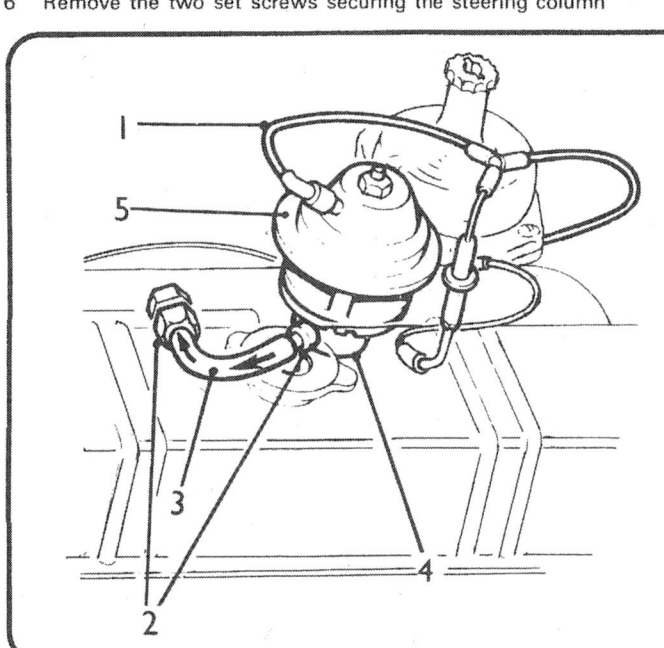

FIG. 13.11 REMOVING THE EGR VALVE

1   *Vacuum control pipe*
2   *Steel pipe union nuts*
3   *Steel pipe*
4   *Locknut*
5   *EGR valve*

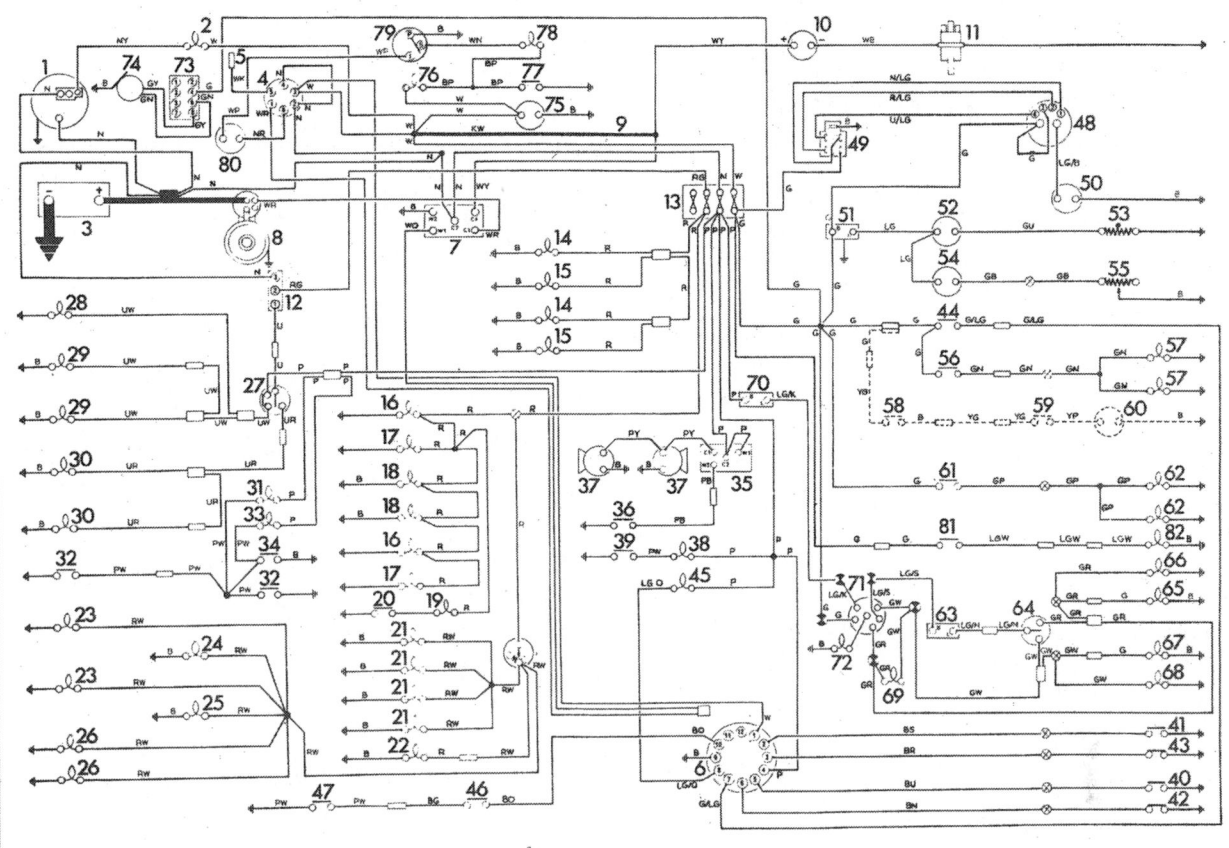

Wiring diagram for North American TR6 models

1	Alternator
2	Ignition warning light
3	Battery
4	Ignition/starter switch
5	Radio supply
6	Seat belt interlock module
7	Starter motor relay
8	Starter motor
9	Ballast resistor wire
10	Ignition coil
11	Ignition distributor
12	Master light switch
13	Fuse
14	Front parking lamp
15	Front marker lamp
16	Rear marker lamp
17	Tail lamp
18	Plate illumination lamp
19	Luggage boot lamp
20	Luggage boot lamp switch
21	Instrument illumination
22	Heater control identification light
23	Speedometer illumination
24	Wipe/wash switch identification light
25	Hazard switch identification light
26	Tachometer illumination
27	Panel rheostat
28	Main beam warning light
29	Main beam
30	Dip beam
31	Key light
32	Door switch
33	Passenger light
34	Passenger light switch
35	Horn relay
36	Horn push
37	Horn
38	Cubby box illumination
39	Cubby box illumination switch
40	Drivers seat switch
41	Passengers seat switch
42	Drivers belt switch
43	Passengers belt switch
44	Seat belt interlock gearbox switch
45	Fasten belts warning light
46	Door switch
47	Key switch
48	Windscreen washer/wiper switch
49	Windscreen wiper motor
50	Windscreen washer pump
51	Voltage stabilizer
52	Temperature indicator
53	Temperature transmitter
54	Fuel indicator
55	Fuel tank unit
56	Reverse lamp switch
57	Reverse lamp
58	Overdrive gear lever switch
59	Overdrive gearbox switch
60	Overdrive solenoid
61	Stop lamp switch
62	Stop lamp
63	Turn signal flasher unit
64	Turn signal switch
65	LH front flasher lamp
66	LH rear flasher lamp
67	RH front flasher lamp
68	RH rear flasher lamp
69	Turn signal warning light
70	Hazard flasher unit
71	Hazard switch
72	Hazard warning light
73	Heater switch
74	Heater motor
75	Battery condition indicator
76	Brake warning light
77	Brake line failure switch
78	Oil pressure warning light
79	Oil pressure switch
80	Anti run on valve
81	EGR service interval counter
82	EGR service warning light

Colour code

N	Brown	G	Green	Y	Yellow
U	Blue	K	Pink	S	Slate
R	Red	LG	Light green	B	Black
P	Purple	W	White	O	Orange

Conversion factors

Length (distance)

Inches (in)	X	25.4	= Millimetres (mm)	X 0.0394	= Inches (in)
Feet (ft)	X	0.305	= Metres (m)	X 3.281	= Feet (ft)
Miles	X	1.609	= Kilometres (km)	X 0.621	= Miles

Volume (capacity)

Cubic inches (cu in; in^3)	X	16.387	= Cubic centimetres (cc; cm^3)	X 0.061	= Cubic inches (cu in; in^3)
Imperial pints (Imp pt)	X	0.568	= Litres (l)	X 1.76	= Imperial pints (Imp pt)
Imperial quarts (Imp qt)	X	1.137	= Litres (l)	X 0.88	= Imperial quarts (Imp qt)
Imperial quarts (Imp qt)	X	1.201	= US quarts (US qt)	X 0.833	= Imperial quarts (Imp qt)
US quarts (US qt)	X	0.946	= Litres (l)	X 1.057	= US quarts (US qt)
Imperial gallons (Imp gal)	X	4.546	= Litres (l)	X 0.22	= Imperial gallons (Imp gal)
Imperial gallons (Imp gal)	X	1.201	= US gallons (US gal)	X 0.833	= Imperial gallons (Imp gal)
US gallons (US gal)	X	3.785	= Litres (l)	X 0.264	= US gallons (US gal)

Mass (weight)

Ounces (oz)	X	28.35	= Grams (g)	X 0.035	= Ounces (oz)
Pounds (lb)	X	0.454	= Kilograms (kg)	X 2.205	= Pounds (lb)

Force

Ounces-force (ozf; oz)	X	0.278	= Newtons (N)	X 3.6	= Ounces-force (ozf; oz)
Pounds-force (lbf; lb)	X	4.448	= Newtons (N)	X 0.225	= Pounds-force (lbf; lb)
Newtons (N)	X	0.1	= Kilograms-force (kgf; kg)	X 9.81	= Newtons (N)

Pressure

Pounds-force per square inch (psi; lbf/in^2; lb/in^2)	X	0.070	= Kilograms-force per square centimetre (kgf/cm^2; kg/cm^2)	X 14.223	= Pounds-force per square inch (psi; lbf/in^2; lb/in^2)
Pounds-force per square inch (psi; lbf/in^2; lb/in^2)	X	0.068	= Atmospheres (atm)	X 14.696	= Pounds-force per square inch (psi; lbf/in^2; lb/in^2)
Pounds-force per square inch (psi; lbf/in^2; lb/in^2)	X	0.069	= Bars	X 14.5	= Pounds-force per square inch (psi; lbf/in^2; lb/in^2)
Pounds-force per square inch (psi; lbf/in^2; lb/in^2)	X	6.895	= Kilopascals (kPa)	X 0.145	= Pounds-force per square inch (psi; lbf/in^2; lb/in^2)
Kilopascals (kPa)	X	0.01	= Kilograms-force per square centimetre (kgf/cm^2; kg/cm^2)	X 98.1	= Kilopascals (kPa)

Torque (moment of force)

Pounds-force inches (lbf in; lb in)	X	1.152	= Kilograms-force centimetre (kgf cm; kg cm)	X 0.868	= Pounds-force inches (lbf in; lb in)
Pounds-force inches (lbf in; lb in)	X	0.113	= Newton metres (Nm)	X 8.85	= Pounds-force inches (lbf in; lb in)
Pounds-force inches (lbf in; lb in)	X	0.083	= Pounds-force feet (lbf ft; lb ft)	X 12	= Pounds-force inches (lbf in; lb in)
Pounds-force feet (lbf ft; lb ft)	X	0.138	= Kilograms-force metres (kgf m; kg m)	X 7.233	= Pounds-force feet (lbf ft; lb ft)
Pounds-force feet (lbf ft; lb ft)	X	1.356	= Newton metres (Nm)	X 0.738	= Pounds-force feet (lbf ft; lb ft)
Newton metres (Nm)	X	0.102	= Kilograms-force metres (kgf m; kg m)	X 9.804	= Newton metres (Nm)

Power

Horsepower (hp)	X	745.7	= Watts (W)	X 0.0013	= Horsepower (hp)

Velocity (speed)

Miles per hour (miles/hr; mph)	X	1.609	= Kilometres per hour (km/hr; kph)	X 0.621	= Miles per hour (miles/hr; mph)

Fuel consumption*

Miles per gallon, Imperial (mpg)	X	0.354	= Kilometres per litre (km/l)	X 2.825	= Miles per gallon, Imperial (mpg)
Miles per gallon, US (mpg)	X	0.425	= Kilometres per litre (km/l)	X 2.352	= Miles per gallon, US (mpg)

Temperature

Degrees Fahrenheit = (°C x 1.8) + 32

Degrees Celsius (Degrees Centigrade; °C) = (°F - 32) x 0.56

*It is common practice to convert from miles per gallon (mpg) to litres/100 kilometres (l/100km), where mpg (Imperial) x l/100 km = 282 and mpg (US) x l/100 km = 235

Index

Zeitfracht Medien GmbH
Ferdinand-Jühlke-Straße 7
99095 Erfurt, Deutschland
produktsicherheit@kolibri360.de